ALWAYS UNRELIABLE

Clive James is the author of more than thirty books. As well as the four volumes of autobiography collected here, and the most recent, *The Blaze of Obscurity*, he has published collections of literary and television criticism, essays, travel writing, verse and novels. As a television performer he has appeared regularly for both the BBC and ITV, most notably as writer and presenter of the 'Postcard' series of travel documentaries. He helped to found the independent television production company 'Watchmaker' and the Internet enterprise 'Welcome Stranger', one of whose offshoots is a multimedia personal website, www.clivejames.com. In 1992 he was made a Member of the Order of Australia and in 2003 he was awarded the Philip Hodgins memorial medal for literature.

AUTOBIOGRAPHY

The Blaze of Obscurity

FICTION

Brilliant Creatures

The Remake

Brrm! Brrm!

The Silver Castle

VERSE

Peregrine Prykke's Pilgrimage Through the London Literary World

Poem of the Year

The Book of My Enemy: Collected Verse 1958–2003

Angels Over Elsinore: Collected Verse 2003–2008

Opal Sunset: Selected Poems 1958–2008

CRITICISM

The Metropolitan Critic
(new edition, 1994)

Visions Before Midnight

At the Pillars of Hercules

First Reactions

From the Land of Shadows

Glued to the Box

Snakecharmers in Texas

The Dreaming Swimmer

Fame in the Twentieth Century

On Television

Even As We Speak

Reliable Essays

As of This Writing

The Meaning of Recognition

Cultural Amnesia: Notes in the Margin of My Time

The Revolt of the Pendulum

TRAVEL

Flying Visits

CLIVE JAMES
ALWAYS UNRELIABLE

THE MEMOIRS

PICADOR

Unreliable Memoirs first published 1980 by Jonathan Cape Ltd
and first published by Picador 1981
Falling Towards England first published 1985 by Jonathan Cape Ltd
and first published by Picador 1986
May Week Was in June first published 1990 by Jonathan Cape Ltd
and first published by Picador 1991

This omnibus edition first published 2001 by Picador

This edition published 2004 by Picador
an imprint of Pan Macmillan, a division of Macmillan Publishers Limited
Pan Macmillan, 20 New Wharf Road, London N1 9RR
Basingstoke and Oxford
Associated companies throughout the world
www.panmacmillan.com

ISBN 978-0-330-41881-2

11 13 15 17 19 18 16 14 12

A CIP catalogue record for this book is available from
the British Library.

Typeset by Intype London Ltd
Printed and bound in the UK by
CPI Mackays, Chatham ME5 8TD

Visit **www.picador.com** to read more about all our books and to buy
them. You will also find features, author interviews and news of any author
events, and you can sign up for e-newsletters so that you're always first to hear
about our new releases.

Contents

MAY WEEK WAS IN JUNE

321

Introduction to *Always Unreliable*

After *Unreliable Memoirs* was irretrievably launched on its first printing back there in 1979, I started remembering things that I had forgotten to put into it. Since the texture of the book depended on the vividness of recalled experience from my infancy and adolescence, it was unsettling to discover that some of the most resonant sensory impressions of my early years had slipped my mind at the very moment when I was searching its subconscious with an echo-sounder. I had forgotten Freddo the Frog, and I had forgotten the Eightsome Reel. How could it happen?

A staple item in the sugar-heavy supplementary nutrition of all Australian children growing up post-war, Freddo the Frog was a chocolate frog. He was flattened as if by a truck and the outlines of his plump limbs were merely incised, as with an obsidian scarab or a soapstone cicada. Bought in a cool shop, he could be unwrapped easily from his silver paper and consumed in a few crisp bites. Bought warm, he separated from his wrappings less easily and it took time to ingest him, leaving extensive stains to be cleared up afterwards with a handkerchief that had already had a hard day.

Freddo is still going: an Australian talisman, or talisfrog, he is often part of a larger symbolic construction, the Frog in a Pond. A treat delivered at any party from a child's birthday celebration to a bonding exercise at boardroom level, the Frog in a Pond is a squadron of Freddos gathered nose-first around an expanse of green jelly on a large serving plate. The last Frog in a Pond I saw was at a welcoming party that the Australian Broadcasting Commission in Sydney threw for me and my executive producer when we came out from England to make a talk-show series. Grown men and women manoeuvred to extract their Freddo from the edge of the agitated pond. On one of my diets at the time, I settled for a few spoonfuls of quivering green, but the mere spectacle was enough to haul me back to the first proper birthday party I was ever invited to, and all its attendant emotions of love, hatred, anxiety and remorse. When reproved for detaching more than my share of frogs from the pond, I should never have thrown that tantrum. There was no necessity, and little Janice Breen was not impressed. Just following her around as usual would have been better.

Where there is a memory, there is always an emotion, and often a retrospective desire for early death. The Eightsome Reel was danced at the Kogarah Presbyterian Church Social on Saturday nights. In the book I recorded the fearful sweat of those occasions for a young man already convinced that if he could not be amusing nobody would put up with him, yet also aware that nobody puts up for long with the continually amusing. Already on the rack, I was broken on the wheel by the formation dances. The one called Strip the Willow was bad enough, but at least there was some chance of being left out. The Eightsome Reel was for everybody. We were all compelled to participate, but I couldn't get it right. The boy with the built-up shoe did it better than I did. The Eightsome Reel, of course, had come from Scotland, the same source that had provided our church's austere decoration (mainly white plaster, punctuated with dark-wood honour rolls perpetuating the names of past Eightsome Reel champions in gold letters) and the oratorical style of the minister, who could lay down a moral precept like a council road-works team pouring a concrete footpath, but without the frivolity. The Eightsome Reel was down there in my brain's frog-pond like a bunyip, a nodal point of life-forming early inadequacies. In the Eightsome Reel I had sent my beloved Shirley Hill hurtling out of the circle to bark her exquisite shin on the seat of one of the pews ranged against the wall, and I had inadvertently seized the left breast of the minister's buxom daughter, Flora. That was something I would have quite liked to do advertently, in the dark passage between the church and the church hall, but in front of everybody else it was a catastrophe. Decades later, while studying the tango in Buenos Aires, I remembered the Eightsome Reel when I climaxed an otherwise immaculate _media luna_ by kicking the great dancer Aurora Firpo excruciatingly in the ankle. I sobbed louder than she did. The Eightsome Reel was a trauma. Was that the reason why the bunyip had not risen from the pond at the right moment to get into my book?

Similarly, the second volume of my memoirs, _Falling Towards_

England, was well embarked on its career before I remembered an afternoon in Soho with the writer Colin MacInnes and the character I called Huggins. As readers of the book will readily detect now that he is world famous, Huggins was based on Robert Hughes. In Sydney, though we had been close friends, our lives had been very different, because he came from a grand family where the arts were part of the furniture, whereas I was unsystematically discovering the whole thing, and feeling awkward about doing so. Bob's glamour, cultivation and protean fluency had thrown this awkwardness into sharp contrast in my own mind. I doubt if they did the same in his, because his soul was generous, and in the position of mentor he played Maecenas, not Pygmalion; but I had seen myself as a subaltern, and characteristically looked forward to a change of circumstances that might lead to equal rank.

In London, however, our lives proved more different than ever. I had been there longer than he, but I was getting nowhere. When Hughes blew in, he was already halfway to everywhere. While I was inhaling the rising damp of a stygian basement in Tufnell Park, he was installed in a suite of rooms in Albany, just off Piccadilly. Albany, or The Albany as it was sometimes less confusingly called, was an enclave for illustrious gentlemen: men with more than one pair of shoes. I had never even seen it before Bob asked me to call, and I passed Graham Greene on the way in. Bob had probably met him. Bob seemed to know everybody. Colin MacInnes was his catch, not mine.

MacInnes was a very big deal at the time. His books have rather faded by now, but several of them are bound to revive eventually, because he was a truly adventurous cultural reporter. His homosexuality helped there: it was a passport to some out-of-the-way social strata, including the black underclass that nobody then knew very much about, even in the allegedly swinging sixties when everything was supposed to be up front. MacInnes had made a date with Bob for an afternoon's drinking at the Colony Room, still run at the time by the notorious Muriel Belcher, a flinty amalgam of Marguerite Dumont, Margarita Pracatan and the Australian wrestler Big Chief Little Wolf. Again, I had never seen the place before, and tried hard to look indifferent when I noticed Francis Bacon propping up the bar. MacInnes was trying to look indifferent too, but no more successfully. Clearly he had expected Bob to be unaccompanied. Instead, he had this clueless scruff with him. MacInnes did not exactly demand that I leave, but he waxed very hostile, greeting my unsolicited contentions on the subject of Literature with patronizing scorn. That he prefaced his every put-down with a swooping 'Look, darling' made it no more friendly. Literature, he made it clear, was *his* concern. (Actually he had a perfect right to think that: his name was already on a row of books, whereas mine was nowhere except on the self-addressed envelope that kept coming back from the *London Magazine* and *Encounter*.) He spoke *de haut en bas*, an exercise made easier by his physical stature: he was so tall that he was tall sitting down.

Inside my winkle-pickers, the crusty texture of socks that had been on for three days became detectable to my curling toes, but nothing could stop my mouth. I went on spoiling the party until deep into the afternoon, with MacInnes escalating from suave contempt to outright vituperation. To Bob he was all charm, of course, and it was only much later that I rumbled the caper. Bob was very good-looking, and MacInnes must have thought he was a hot prospect. In reality MacInnes had no chance, because Bob was as straight as a road, a fact to which a flotilla of beautiful women might well have attested. Bob would have been the Warren Beatty of the arts world if not hampered by a capacity for genuine passion which in later years several times brought him close to ending it all for the sake of love. Women spot that, and it only drives them crazier. The besotted MacInnes was on a hiding to nothing, but he made sure that the hiding was transferred to me. When I finally staggered out of the place and left them to it, my morale was in shreds. 'Look, darling' haunted me for months. But then it submerged to join the bunyips, and like the Eightsome Reel disaster it failed to come up again at the appointed time. This, I think, was probably because I was writing a story about being out of the swim, and the Colony Room episode would have seemed too in. But there is also the possibility that the faculty of recollection is disinclined to work by numbers. It will not serve. Anyway, as far as I remember – and here I am trying to remember when I remembered, which puts in yet another layer of unreliability – I didn't recall the incident in its full horror until many years later, when I was watching the hugely unsuccessful film made from MacInnes's *Absolute Beginners*. Patsy Kensit I thought wonderfully pretty but too well brushed and untroubled to fit the time. Then I remembered the time – the time when I, too, had been an absolute beginner, carved up and left for dead by the man who wrote the book.

When I read through my pre-publication copy of the third volume, *May Week Was in June*, I thought that it had caught most of the key points and that what had been left out had been left out deliberately. I was beset with doubts about the commercial wisdom of having called Germaine Greer Romaine Rand – she hated that, it turned out – but I had no doubts about the morality of it: one could not attribute bad language to a living woman. Though chivalry might be just another form of condescension, I had been brought up to give my seat to ladies in trains. But that was just a change of name. The editing of events I thought finely judged. I left out the story of how Eric Idle and I had quarrelled over a croquet match, but that was because it might have reflected badly on him as well as on me, and I had too many reasons to be grateful to him. At Cambridge we had collaborated for a while on scripts, and in the long run it had not worked out, leaving a *froideur* between us that went on for years, and which we could not have crossed with skates. (The phenomenon is quite usual, incidentally: creative collaboration is a relationship more intimate than marriage and seldom ends without rancour, even when you have settled the terms of the divorce on the way in.) But my time in Footlights was a liberating period in my life and he had generously paved the way for it, so my debt was eternal: hence the omission of the croquet match, although I still think he had no warrant for hitting my ball into the rhododendrons. There were all kinds of decisions involved in choosing what to put in and what to leave out, but they were all *decisions* – or so I thought, until I remembered something I had plain forgotten: my bad day in Nottinghamshire. Roughly comparable in its effects to King Harold's bad day at Hastings, it had been one in the eye that should have stayed with me.

Under my direction, a Footlights revue was on tour at the little Robin Hood Theatre, Averham. The show had not gone down very well and the cast, with myself providing a vocal back-up, was making the classic mistake of blaming the audience, the theatre, the time of year and the inflation rate of the currency. While we were helping ourselves to breakfast in her kitchen, the proprietress of the theatre overheard some of this whingeing rigmarole and was later seen weeping. Luckily I guessed the reason. For once summoning the appropriate moral courage at the time instead of too late, I nerved myself to apologize. But the shameful episode could not be undone, and I am afraid its residue might have never left her mind. More shameful still is that it did leave mine. As a step in my indecently protracted graduation to presentability, it should have been uppermost in my thoughts when I was trying to give written shape to that period. Instead, it was lowermost. The mind, or my mind at any rate, protects itself even when attempting an honest audit of its interior accounts. *Mon coeur mis a nu* is a delusion. From which consideration, there is only one conclusion to draw.

The conclusion must be that the three books collected in this volume were written to my own glory. Nobody except an egomaniac expects other people to find his life interesting. Luckily there are degrees of egomania. Sometimes it can look so much like modesty that it might almost be the real thing. Not all military memoirs, for example, are as demented as Montgomery's. Men retired from high command have written self-effacing books. But if those same men had been truly self-effacing, they would not have written their books at all. So even at the low end of the scale, the self is being asserted. At the high end, there are no limits. From the turgid cauldron of solipsism called *Seven Pillars of Wisdom* it can be deduced that T. E. Lawrence, given the means, would have died on Golgotha to be buried in the Valley of the Kings. He was so convinced of his right to public acclaim that when he sought mortification for his sins the only fitting path was to obscurity. Just as his earlier understatement had been all bombast, his later reticence was all guile. Beside him, a self-proclaimed genius like Frank Harris was a shrinking violet.

But Lawrence of Arabia did great things. They were never quite as great as he made out, but they were deeds. Beyond the top of the scale occupied by the men of action who are writing their lives up the better to face eternity, there is the stratosphere occupied by the writers *tout court*. This is where the power of the ego goes off the clock. It can safely be assumed that any writer who gives you a record of his own life is nuts about himself. After a lifetime of considering the subject I can only conclude that it would be strange if it were otherwise. Writers would not go on writing unless they thought they were unique. Their humility consists in, and is exhausted by, their recognition that other writers are more gifted. (There are some writers who can't even manage that: a famous female novelist of the last generation would leave the room if Tolstoy was mentioned, and I personally knew a male novelist who thought Shakespeare wasn't up to it.) But to think themselves unique, they need their conceit. If they recognize this fact, they can write memoirs that evince a delightful and seemingly genuine self-deprecation, as they balance their necessary self-esteem with an awareness of their own failings, although usually on the understanding that the failings are rendered nugatory by talent and might even have contributed to its formation. But it is remarkable how few writers can do even that much, and somehow those who can't are the very ones most concerned to write memoirs.

The results almost invariably make fascinating reading. The more humble the pose, the more the *amour propre* comes shining through. It is almost better to boast. Casanova boasted of his seductive prowess. Correctly placing his awesome track record as a lounge lizard far above the mere finagling of worldly business, he was ready to admit his fiascos as a wheeler-dealer. The funds that he had half-inched always dried up, the bailiffs always moved in, he always had to leave town on the dawn coach, and you can hear him grappling with the dreadful possibility that it might have all been his fault. But with Rousseau it was never his fault; and he, unlike Casanova, was hurting a lot of innocent people beside himself. Rousseau was more the writer; Casanova was more the man of action; and the distinction seems always to apply. The writer brings more resources to the cover-up, but the cover-up is the very thing that reveals where the bodies are buried: a tumulus of subterfuge. In modern times, perhaps the most flagrant example is provided by Ernest Hemingway. His book of memoirs *A Moveable Feast* is an unputdownable masterpiece, but one of the things it is masterly at is self-deception, which as always brings self-revelation prancing in its train. Though the book purports to show the young writer in his years of struggle, its narrative tone suggests that he was already a man of destiny, around whom the whole of existence revolved like a wheel on a jewelled pivot. He evokes post-First World War Paris enchantingly, but as his personal fiefdom. Its other inhabitants, no matter how distinguished, are important only in relation to him, and it soon transpires that he is adjusting the record to suit his self-esteem. Gertrude Stein emerges as a monster of selfishness. In fact she selflessly helped him to get started. Ford Madox Ford is drawn as a buffoon. In fact he was appreciative of Hemingway's talent and did everything he could to help.

It has been said of Hemingway that he was the type of man who could never forgive a favour, and you would guess that to be true even if you had no documentary evidence to go on except *A Moveable Feast*. Hemingway's eminence has decreed that the documentary evidence is abundant. All of his biographers, without exception, have come reeling back from the archives with the awful knowledge that he never spoke the truth about anything, but really you don't need them to tell you. His memoirs do the job. The account of his Paris adventures with Scott Fitzgerald leaves the indelible impression that Fitzgerald was the more honest man. Fitzgerald, indeed, was incurably honest: his articles about his breakdown (collected by Edmund Wilson in *The Crack-Up*, a book every would-be writer should keep nearby as a touchstone and a warning) are sufficient proof of that. In *A Moveable Feast* Hemingway tells the story of his impromptu boxing match with the Canadian writer Morley Callaghan, with Fitzgerald as the referee. According to Hemingway, Callaghan's victory was due to Fitzgerald's incompetence, perhaps even his malice. Callaghan, in his own memoirs of the period, *That Summer in Paris*, makes it clear that he thrashed Hemingway fair and square. No other result was ever likely, because Callaghan actually knew how to box. But really we don't need Callaghan to tell us. Hemingway's remarks on the subject have the giveaway shapeliness of self-serving fabrication. *That Summer in Paris* is an excellent book, a little classic of modest veracity. But *A Moveable Feast* is a big classic, in which a flawed man makes perfect art by the same impulse that made all his other perfect art – to get away from himself. When Hemingway's true nature finally got him cornered, there was only one thing left to do. He shot himself for the same reason he wrote the books.

On the quiet, William Faulkner had the same problem as Hemingway with telling the truth. Hemingway exaggerated his war service, even going to the extent of wearing medals to which he was not entitled. (Compare Fitzgerald's rueful acknowledgment of 'the overseas cap never worn overseas'.) Faulkner saw no war service at all, but allowed people to think he did. By maintaining a tactical silence at the right time, he gave the impression that he had flown in combat. That he never did makes *Pylon* no lesser a book about flying. Faulkner knew enough about the trickiness of his personality not to make the mistake of writing a memoir. He found his refuge in the bottle, as so many writers have. Almost always it is a case of a self that can't live with itself. Why an ordinary ego should judge itself by standards appropriate only to Jesus Christ is a continuing mystery, but it probably has something to do with the unnatural concentration of will that it takes to function as any kind of artist at all.

In other words, when it comes to writers the ordinary ego is extraordinary. The Nobel laureate and international man of mystery Elias Canetti published three volumes of memoirs in which he is always acute on the subject of writers and their self-regard. In his years in Vienna before the _Anschluss_, the young Canetti was in awe of the great Robert Musil, author of _The Man Without Qualities_. One of Musil's qualities was a daunting capacity to keep himself to himself, even in the smoky propinquity of the literary café in which all the artists of the period set up their second home. Canetti fretted that he could not get Musil's attention. Then Canetti published his own novel, _Die Blendung_ (called _Auto da Fé_ in English, which makes you wonder what it is called in Spanish) to some acclaim, including an enthusiastic letter from Thomas Mann, whom Canetti admired almost as much as he admired Musil. Flushed with his favourable reviews and the warm glow of Thomas Mann's letter in his pocket, Canetti entered the café and found to his delight that Musil was rising to his feet to congratulate him on a brilliant success. Canetti momentarily interrupted Musil's encomium to say, Yes, and I have just received a letter from Thomas Mann saying the same thing, can you imagine? Musil retreated instantly into his usual hauteur and hardly acknowledged Canetti's existence ever again. The anecdote is a nice study in Musil's high estimation of himself: embittered by a lack of international recognition, Musil had Thomas Mann's towering prestige on the brain, and Canetti made an irreparable mistake in forgetting that fact even for an instant. But what makes it an even nicer study is that Canetti's memoirs, from beginning to end, are an unrestrained hosanna to his own importance. Reading them in a mixture of boredom and astonishment, you would think that nothing in the history of the time mattered a damn except Canetti's literary career: Hitler barely gets a mention.

Canetti overdid it, to the point where his writings, though much lauded, are doomed to remain little read. But very few writers underdo it. Thomas Mann himself took fanatical pains to guard his status: he never turned down an honorary degree, and by the end of his life his accumulated gowns, hoods and velvet caps could have outfitted an entire academic procession. Along with his priestly dedication to his art there was a monumental effort expended on putting up a front. Sensibly he never wrote a memoir as such, confining most of his personal writings to a diary, in which we find, during the later years of his exile in California, that while whole armies were tearing each other to pieces in Europe he was concerned with a new manicure for himself, and a shampoo for the family poodle. His world view was of an unmatched scope and depth, but at the centre of it was an unrelenting self-regard, and it is hard to see how he could ever have reconciled the two things in an account of his life, even though the two things were the one thing in their essence. The same applied to Proust, justifiably seen by Mann as his worthy predecessor. *In Search of Time Past* is a divine act of self-sacrifice, but the human being who wrote it was perfectly capable of rigging a prize committee to vote his way. Nowadays there is a whole biographical industry devoted to proving our artistic heroes fallible, but really it is money for jam, because fallibility is what they are made of. It's what they make of it that counts.

That any writer, of any magnitude, serves himself in the first instance is what Montesquieu would have called a *loi*: one of those general principles that apply in any society at all times. Down here at my end of the scale, I can only say that I never doubted its truth. My own memoirs were written to give containment and a measure of tranquillity to psychic turmoil, and in the certainty that any of my troubles which I tried to conceal would come percolating through in accordance with the further *loi* formulated above. All I can claim beyond that is a hope – the hope that what has always been a burden to me will lighten the spirits of someone else if only by demonstrating that a public performance, though it might assuage private regrets, can't always blot them out. But leaving these protestations of humility aside (the best thing to do with them, now that we know what they are worth) I don't delude myself that the original books achieved their measure of welcome solely on the grounds of their validity as self-administered psychotherapy. They have a story to tell, and stories within the story. Here is the narrative of a young man who went in search of something. He knew it wasn't a white whale, or El Dorado, or King Solomon's mines. But what was it?

Whatever it was, it seemed to him that it could not be had in the land of his birth: not at that time, anyway. Later on, in the Whitlam years, Australia boomed for all to see. Actually it had already started to boom when I was there: the migrants from ravaged Europe were enriching our culture from the bottom up. But that early stage of expansion I was too dull to spot, and the later stage I wasn't around to witness. While I was slowly struggling to my feet in London, Australia went on exfoliating, so that by the time I made my first trip back I could scarcely find my way through the blooms of its achievements, and ever since, no matter how often I return, I have always been overwhelmed by the sense that the whole thing got away from me after I took my eyes off it.

In Australia it is now sometimes said that we, the last expatriates, no longer have any right to our superior attitude to the country we renounced. For my own part, I can only protest that if I ever seemed to express such an attitude, it was all bluster. In some of my articles and broadcasts, when I finally got going in the British media, I tended to belittle developments in Australia, which was very foolish of me: but I had burned my boats, was by no means certain of being able to live off the land, and might have been whistling to keep my courage up. Any superior attitude I really had was towards Britain: I thought that we Aussies, less hampered by the weight of tradition and therefore closer to the bubbling well-spring of the English language, could write rings around the locals if given the chance. I got my chance writing about television for the *Observer*; but when, in the middle of that, I wrote a book that clicked, it was a book that unreservedly celebrated Australia – *Unreliable Memoirs*. Its two sequels were about an Australian in Britain, and if there are ever any further volumes, they, too, will be about someone who has never forgotten where he came from. To the eternal journalistic question about an Australian expatriate's relationship with the National Identity, that is still the only answer I can summon: if this famous national identity means anything, it means something that comes with you wherever you go, and stays with you no matter how long you stay away. But the Australian journalists, as always, have yet another awkward question up their sleeves: why *do* you stay away?

It's hard to answer. In Sydney to cover the Olympic Games, I found the Australia of my dreams, and all the world's dreams too: the good place, full of confidence and generosity, a hot-house for the talents. The contrast with present-day Britain was almost pitiful: at the very moment when Britain's entire, time-honoured creative effort seemed to be disappearing forgetfully into a dome-shaped black hole, Sydney Harbour Bridge was a light-storm, a flame fountain, a *feu de joie*. How could I go back to the cold, the crumbling transport system, the rampant yobbery, the suicidal repudiation of history, the hopelessly misbegotten public projects, and the witless re-branding of perennial humanist institutions as a prelude to their going bankrupt? One answer is that there is an adventure in Britain too, and perhaps it is still a more interesting one. There is no hardship allowance for describing Australia's rise to glory – you could take half your pay in sheer euphoria – but to make sense of Britain in its flailing post-imperial transformations takes everything you've got. Another answer is more personal, and thus more likely to be true.

In twenty years or so, *Unreliable Memoirs*, while presenting no threat to Jeffrey Archer, has clocked up sales figures that I would be a fool to quarrel with, because they have provided the basis for a financial independence without which my two decades in television would have seemed like a century in a salt mine. But in Australia the book has had something better than a success. For two generations of the reading public, it has become their picture of a lost childhood – of what it was like to grow up when Australian life still had a dependable structure, before the pressures of global competition broke up the old certainties. As a result, its author has become part of the mental landscape: he is included in the conversation of an enormous family. When I sit to read and write at Rossini's café on Circular Quay – my hangout for a long breakfast whenever I am in Sydney – every few minutes a different passer-by asks the same question: 'When are you coming home?' The answer that I *am* home cuts no ice. Nor should it. I know what they mean. It is a great privilege to be surrounded by so much intimacy, but the affection is more than I am equipped to answer except through writing, where affection comes easily, out of my better nature. My deeper nature, however, is to keep my distance from all ties, and London is still the place for that. Even in its latterday form as a behavioural sink, a den of thieves and a bedlam of managerial fatuity, the *magna civitas* is still a *magna solitudo*, and a great solitude is what I need, while I work on the long task of forgiving myself for having been born blessed, and for a consuming melancholy that I never earned.

No doubt this is a distortion of personality: un-Australian, to use the word that came briefly into vogue when a referendum to favour a republic was put to the judgment of the Australian people. I suspect many of them declined the offer because they could hear the sinister note of compulsory patriotism. Freedom and diversity guard each other, and if a country could form the whole of one's character, Napoleon III and Victor Hugo would have been the same person. There will always be some people who, loving the land where they were born, nevertheless pack up their kit, set out in a strange direction, and go so far that they can't get back. The direction is set by an internal compass, and the distance by an unfathomable desire. Nor is it certain that there is no longer any role for the absentee. If Australia, on a necessarily small scale but with a certain laconic zest, has now entered its own imperial phase, and one which could be all the more dazzling because it depends on art and not on armies, a sentinel at the northern ramparts will always have a message to send home. One part of the message would be that artists and intellectuals, in the hot flush of national enterprise, should beware of being drawn by barons into a conspiracy against the people. The urge of the barons is to arrogate to themselves a preponderance of political influence, and so protect their windfall gains. But talent, too, is a windfall gain. Creative achievement earns its merit, but the capacity for such achievement can be handed out to anyone, and is often given to those who could hardly hold down an ordinary job. In that respect, the author of this tripartite divertissement is without illusions. In every other respect he has always been prey to every illusion possible, wherein lies the comedy. When Janice Breen hit me with her stuffed cloth rabbit, I thought she liked me.

London, 2001

UNRELIABLE MEMOIRS

To

Rhoisin and Bruce Beresford

and the getting of wisdom

Andromache led the lamentation of the women, while she held in her hands the head of Hector, her great warrior:

'Husband, you are gone so young from life, and leave me in your home a widow. Our child is still but a little fellow, child of ill-fated parents, you and me. How can he grow up to manhood? Before that, this city shall be overthrown. For you are gone, you who kept watch over it, and kept safe its wives and their little ones ...

'And you have left woe unutterable and mourning to your parents, Hector; but in my heart above all others bitter anguish shall abide. Your hands were not stretched out to me as you lay dying. You spoke to me no living word that I might have pondered as my tears fell night and day.'

Iliad, xxiv, translated by S. E. Winbolt,
from *The Iliad Pocket Book*, Constable 1911

Preface

Most first novels are disguised autobiographies. This autobiography is a disguised novel. On the periphery, names and attributes of real people have been changed and shuffled so as to render identification impossible. Nearer the centre, important characters have been run through the scrambler or else left out completely. So really the whole affair is a figment got up to sound like truth. All you can be sure of is one thing: careful as I have been to spare other people's feelings, I have been even more careful not to spare my own. Up, that is, of course, to a point.

Sick of being a prisoner of my childhood, I want to put it behind me. To do that, I have to remember what it was like. I hope I can dredge it all up again without sounding too pompous. Solemnity, I am well aware, is not my best vein. Yet it can't be denied that books like this are written to satisfy a confessional urge; that the mainspring of a confessional urge is guilt; and that somewhere underneath the guilt there must be a crime. In my case I suspect there are a thousand crimes, which until now I have mainly been successful in not recollecting. Rilke used to say that no poet would mind going to gaol, since he would at least have time to explore the treasure house of his memory. In many respects Rilke was a prick.

Premature memoirs can only be conceited. I have no excuses against this charge, except to say that self-regard is itself a subject, and that to wait until reminiscence is justified by achievement might mean to wait for ever. I am also well aware that all attempts to put oneself in a bad light are doomed to be frustrated. The ego arranges the bad light to its own satisfaction. But on that point it is only necessary to remember Santayana's devastating comment on Rousseau's *Confessions*, which he said demonstrated, in equal measure, candour and ignorance of self. However adroitly I have calculated my intentional revelations, I can be sure that there are enough unintentional ones to give the reader an accurate impression. I had an absurdly carefree upbringing. If my account of it inspires disapproval, that can only serve to help redress the balance. One doesn't expect to get away with it for ever.

C. J.

1. THE KID FROM KOGARAH

I was born in 1939. The other big event of that year was the outbreak of the Second World War, but for the moment that did not affect me. Sydney in those days had all of its present attractions and few of the drawbacks. You can see it glittering in the background of the few photographs in which my father and I are together. Stocky was the word for me. Handsome was the word for him. Without firing a shot, the Japanese succeeded in extricating him from my clutches. Although a man of humble birth and restricted education, he was smart enough to see that there would be war in the Pacific. Believing that Australia should be ready, he joined up. That was how he came to be in Malaya at the crucial moment. He was at Parit Sulong bridge on the day when a lot of senior officers at last found out what their troops had guessed long before – that the Japanese army was better led and better equipped than anything we had to pit against it. After the battle my father walked all the way south to Singapore and arrived just in time for the surrender. If he had waited to be conscripted, he might have been sent to the Western Desert and spent a relatively happy few months fighting the kind of Germans whose essential decency was later to be portrayed on the screen by James Mason and Marlon Brando. As it was, he drew the short straw.

This isn't the place to tell the story of my mother and father – a story which was by no means over, even though they never saw one another again. I could get a lot of mileage out of describing how the good-looking young mechanic wooed and won the pretty girl who left school at fourteen and worked as an upholsterer at General Motors Holden. How the Depression kept them so poor that they had to wait years to get married and have me. How fate was cruel to both of them beyond measure. But it would be untrue to them. It was thirty years or more before I even began to consider what my parents must have meant to each other. Before that I hardly gave them a thought, except as vague occurrences on the outskirts of a solipsistic universe. I can't remember my father at all. I can remember my mother only through a child's eyes. I don't know which fact is the sadder.

Anyway, my mother let our little house in Kogarah and we went to stay with my Aunt Dot in Jannali, another half hour down the Illawarra line. This move was made on the advice of my father, who assumed that the centre of Sydney would be flattened by Japanese bombs about two hours after the whistle blew. The assumption proved to be ill-founded, but the side effects were beneficial, since Jannali was a perfect spot to grow up in. There were only a dozen or so streets in the whole area. Only one of them was paved. The railway line ran through a cutting somewhere in the middle. Everything else was bush.

The houses were made of either weatherboard or fibro. Ours was weatherboard. Like all the others, it was surrounded by an area of land which could be distinguished from the bush only because of its even more lavish concentrations of colour. Nasturtiums and honeysuckle proliferated, their strident perfumes locked in perpetual contention. Hydrangeas grew in reefs, like coral in a sea of warm air. At the bottom of the back yard lay an air-raid trench full of rainwater. I fell into it within minutes of arriving. Hearing a distant splash, Aunt Dot, who was no sylph, came through the back door like a train out of a tunnel and hit the lawn running. The door, a fly-screen frame with a return spring, made exactly the same sound as one of those punching-bags you try your strength on. Aunt Dot was attired in a pink corset but it didn't slow her down. She covered the ground like Marjorie Jackson, the girl who later became famous as the Lithgow Flash. The earth shook. I was going down for the third time but I can distinctly remember the moment she launched herself into the air, describing a parabolic trajectory which involved, at one point, a total eclipse of the sun. She landed in the trench beside me. Suddenly we were sitting together in the mud. All the water was outside on the lawn.

Usually my mother was first to the rescue. This time she was second. She had to resuscitate both of us. She must have been in the front of the house looking after my grandfather. He needed a lot of looking after. Later on my mother told me that he had always been a selfish man. She and Aunt Dot had given a good part of their lives to waiting on him. Mentally, he had never left England. I remember him as a tall, barely articulate source of smells. The principal smells were of mouldy cloth, mothballs, seaweed, powerful tobacco and the tars that collect in the stem of a very old pipe. When he was smoking he was invisible. When he wasn't smoking he was merely hard to pick out in the gloom. You could track him down by listening for his constant, low-pitched, incoherent mumble. From his carpet slippers to his moustache was twice as high as I could reach. The moustache was saffron with nicotine. Everywhere else he was either grey or tortoise-shell mottle. His teeth were both.

I remember he bared them at me one Christmas dinner. It was because he was choking on a coin in a mouthful of plum pudding. It was the usual Australian Christmas dinner, taking place in the middle of the day. Despite the temperature being 100°F in the shade, there had been the full panoply of ragingly hot food, topped off with a volcanic plum pudding smothered in scalding custard. My mother had naturally spiced the pudding with sixpences and threepenny bits, called zacs and trays respectively. Grandpa had collected one of these in the oesophagus. He gave a protracted, strangled gurgle which for a long time we all took to be the beginning of some anecdote. Then Aunt Dot bounded out of her chair and hit him in the back. By some miracle she did not snap his calcified spine. Coated with black crumbs and custard, the zac streaked out of his mouth like a dum-dum and ricocheted off a tureen.

Grandpa used to take me on his knee and read me stories, of which I could understand scarcely a word, not because the stories were over my head but because his speech by that stage consisted entirely of impediments. 'Once upon a mpf,' he would intone, 'there wah ngung mawg blf . . .' My mother got angry with me if I was not suitably grateful to Grandpa for telling me stories. I was supposed to dance up and down at the very prospect. To dodge this obligation, I would build cubbyholes. Collecting chairs, cushions, breadboards and blankets from all over the house, I would assemble them into a pillbox and crawl in, plugging the hole behind me. Safe inside, I could fart discreetly while staring through various eye-slits to keep track of what was going on. From the outside I was just a pair of marsupial eyeballs in a heap of household junk, topped off with a rising pall of sulphuretted hydrogen. It was widely conjectured that I was hiding from ghosts. I was, too, but not as hard as I was hiding

from Grandpa. When he shuffled off to bed, I would unplug my
igloo and emerge. Since my own bedtime was not long after dark, I
suppose he must have been going to bed in the late afternoon. Finally
he went to bed altogether.

With Grandpa laid up, I was the man of the house, except when
Uncle Vic or Ray came home on leave. Uncle Vic was Aunt Dot's
husband and Ray was her son, therefore my cousin. Uncle Vic was
an infantry corporal stationed in New Guinea. Sometimes when he
got leave he would bring his Owen gun home, minus the bolt. I was
allowed to play with the gun. It was huge. I stumbled around pointing
it at bull-ants' nests. The bull-ants, however, didn't bluff so easily.
The only argument they understood was a few gallons of boiling
water poured down their central stairwell. I once saw Uncle Vic
administer this treatment, in revenge after half a dozen bull-ants
stung me on the right foot. They were the big red kind with the
black bag at the back. When that size bull-ant stings you, you stay
stung. My foot came up like a loaf of bread. I just lay in the road
and screamed. The same foot got into even worse trouble later on,
as I shall relate.

While I staggered around blasting the nasturtiums, Uncle Vic did
a lot of enigmatic smiling. One day I struggled all the way down to
the railway cutting so that I could show the gun to some local
children I hoped to impress. They hadn't waited. I could see them
climbing the hill on the other side of the railway line. I shouted to
them, holding the gun up as high as I could, which I suppose was
no height at all. They couldn't hear me. I think it was the first big
disappointment of my life. When I came back dragging the gun
through the dirt, Uncle Vic did a bit more of his enigmatic smiling.
Talking to him years later, I realized why he was so quiet at the time.
It was because he wasn't too thrilled about what he had seen in New
Guinea. Japanese scouts used to sneak up on our sentries through
the thick white morning jungle mist and punch meat-skewers
through their heads from ear to ear.

Ray was more forthcoming, until he got sick. He was a fitter with
the RAAF somewhere up there but after his first leave he never went
back. He just stayed around the house in his dressing gown, getting
thinner. He used to let me stand on his feet while he walked me
around. The game was called Giant Steps. I loved it. Then the day
came when he didn't want to play it any more. My mother told me

he wasn't strong enough. I got into trouble at the dinner table when I asked him why he was holding his fork with both hands.

So really my mother was the only pillar of strength available. One parent is enough to spoil you but discipline takes two. I got too much of what I wanted and not enough of what I needed. I was a child who was picked up. The effects have stayed with me to this day, although in the last few years I have gradually learned to blame myself instead of circumstances. My mother had a strong will but she would have had to be Fabius Cunctator to cope with my tantrums when I didn't feel like going to school. Every second day I played sick and stayed home. Her only alternative was to see how far she could drag me. She would have had a better chance dragging a dead horse through soft sand. The school was a single-room wooden hut with twelve desks. Painted cream, it sat in half an acre of dirt playground about a mile from our house. Bushfires burned it down every couple of years but unfortunately it was easy to replace. The first year of school wasn't so bad. I liked Miss Dear. Usually I got more questions right than anybody else and was awarded first choice of blocks. I chose the set with the arches and the columns. I would go off on my own into a corner of the playground and build structures akin to the Alhambra or the Escorial, throwing a fit if any other child tried to interfere.

Even the best set of school blocks wasn't as good as the set I had at home. Passed on to me by Grandpa, they were satin-smooth Victorian creations of inch-by-inch oak, every length from one to twelve inches, plus arches, Doric columns, metopes, triglyphs and sundry other bits and pieces. With them I could build a tower much taller than myself. The usual site was the middle of the lounge room. A length of cotton could be tied to one of the lower columns, so that I could retire into hiding and collapse the tower by remote control at the precise moment when Aunt Dot lumbered into range. It made a noise like Valhalla falling. She would have one of her turns – these needed plenty of space – and demand that I be sent to school next day.

Toys were scarce. A few crude lead soldiers were still produced so that children could go on poisoning themselves but otherwise there was almost nothing. It was a big event when my mother bought me a little painted red cow. Presumably it was English. I took it to school and lost it. Next day she came with me to school, wanting to find out what had happened to it. My carelessness with everything she bought me went on hurting her for years. She construed it, accurately, as ingratitude. From the sensitivity angle I was about as obtuse as a child can be. I was sensitive enough about myself, but that's a different thing.

School, passable for the first year, became unbearable in the second, when the kind Miss Dear was supplanted by a hard case called Miss Turnbull. Dark, cold and impatient, Miss Turnbull might have been the firm hand I needed, but already I was unable to cope with authority. I still can't today, tending to oscillate between nervous flippancy and overly solicitous respect. In those days, when I was about a third of my present height and a quarter of the weight, there was nothing to do except duck. I did everything to get out of facing up to Miss Turnbull. I had Mondayitis every day of the week. As my mother dragged me down the front path, I would clutch my stomach, cross my eyes, stick out my tongue, cough, choke, scream and vomit simultaneously.

But there were some occasions when I ended up at school no matter what I did. It was then revealed that I had Dropped Behind the Class. Words I could not recognize would come up on the spelling wheel. The spelling wheel was a thick card with a window in it and a cardboard disc behind. As you turned the disc, words appeared one at a time in the window. I remember not being able to pronounce the word 'the'. I pronounced it 'ter-*her*'. The class had collective hysterics. They were rolling around on the floor with their knees up. I suppose one of the reasons why I grew up feeling the need to cause laughter was perpetual fear of being its unwitting object.

From the start of Miss Turnbull's reign until the day we left Jannali, every morning I would shout the house down. For my mother, the path leading from the front porch to the front gate became a Via Dolorosa. My act reached ever new heights of extravagance. Either it worked or it didn't. If it didn't I would sit in school praying for the bushfires to come early and incinerate the place. If it did I would either hang around the house or go and play with Ron, a truant of my own age who lived next to Hally the butcher down near the station. Ron was a grub. I was always being warned off him because he was so filthy. He and I used to squat under his house tweaking each other's ding, watching each other pee, and so on. I can't remember it all now. I suppose I have repressed it. If there was any sexual excitement, it took the form of intense curiosity, just as I was curious about my mother when we were in the bath together. I remember the shock of seeing Ray undressed. He looked as if he had a squirrel hanging there. I had an acorn.

Ron's wreck of a mother used to give us buttered bread with hundreds and thousands on it. It was like being handed a slice of powdered rainbow. They must have been a poor family but I remember my visits to them as luxuries. As well as the technicolor bread and butter, there were vivid, viscid green drinks made from some kind of cordial. Ron's place would have been Beulah Land except for one drawback. They had a cattle dog called Bluey. A known psychopath, Bluey would attack himself if nothing else was available. He used to chase himself in circles trying to bite his own balls off. To avert instant death, I was supposed to call out from the front gate when I arrived and not open it until I was told that Bluey had been chained up. One day I opened it too early and Bluey met me on the front path. I don't know where he had come from – probably around the side of the house – but it was as if he had come up out of the ground on a lift. He was nasty enough when chained up but on the loose he was a bad dream. Barking from the stomach, he opened a mouth like a great, wet tropical flower. When he snapped it shut, my right foot was inside it.

If Bluey hadn't been as old as the hills, my foot would have come right off. Luckily his teeth were in ruins, but even so I was only a few tendons short of becoming an amputee. Since Bluey's spittle obviously contained every bacterium known to science, my frantic mother concluded that the local doctor would not be enough. I think I went to some kind of hospital in Sutherland. Needles were stuck into me while she had yet another case of heart failure. Bluey was taken away to be destroyed. Looking back on it, I can see that this was tough on Bluey, who had grown old in the belief that biting ankles was the thing to do. At the time I was traumatized. I loathed dogs from that day forward. They could sense my terror from miles away. Any dog could back me against a wall for hours. Eventually I learned not to show fear. The breakthrough came when I managed to walk away from a dog who had me bailed up against the door of a garage. Admittedly he was only a Pekinese about eight inches long, but it was still a triumph. That was more than a year ago.

2. VALLEY OF THE KILLER SNAKES

Such incidents must have been hell on my mother's nerves. I would have been enough of a handful even in normal circumstances but the sweat of looking after me was made worse by her uncertainty about what was happening to my father. She got some news of him when he was in Changi but after he was moved to Japan there was not much to go on. The mail from Kobe, when there was any, was so censored it looked like shredded lettuce. During the last part of the war she wasn't even certain that he was alive. In those circumstances it couldn't have been much help to her, having the kind of son who goes off and gets half-eaten by a dog.

Lesser catastrophes were no doubt just as wearing, since they happened all the time. My collection of marbles consisted mainly of priceless connie agates handed down by Grandpa. Ocean crystals, iced roses and butterflies in amber, they tumbled from their draw-string bag like a Byzantine avalanche. I took them out and lost the lot to a local thug called Mick Roach. Years older than I, Mick dated up clay-dabs against my connies. A clay-dab, as its name suggests, could be dissolved in water or squeezed flat with a thumb. Mick used steelies for taws. Steelies were ball bearings an inch in diameter. They blasted my defenceless cannon-fodder from the ring. On top of his superior artillery, Mick could actually play marbles, whereas I had no idea of what I was doing, otherwise I would not have allowed him to readjust the size of the ring for each go. When it was his turn, the ring was about four inches in diameter. When it was my turn, the Arunta tribe could have held a corroboree around its circumference.

I lurched home in tears, trailing an empty bag. My mother went berserk. She tried to shame Mick's parents into giving my marbles back, but Mick's father talked some confident nonsense about a fair fight. 'If your father was here,' said my mother with a strangely shaking voice, 'there'd be a fair fight.' I wish I could say that I shared her anger, but I think I was just embarrassed about the fuss. I wanted my mistakes forgotten, not faced up to – the foundations of a bad habit.

Quite apart from moral disasters, there was the question of my physical safety. Even after Bluey's demise, there was still good reason to believe that I would do myself an injury if left unsupervised. I had a terrifying gift for carving myself up. Running around barefoot, I would go out of my way to jump on a broken bottle. Gashes caused by rusty corrugated iron were treated with Acriflavine, an antiseptic that turned the surrounding skin variously blue and yellow, so that I looked half ancient Briton, half Inca. The only asphalt road in the area led down to the railway line at about the same angle as a door-wedge. It might not sound a very perilous incline, but I was able to prove empirically that it was more than steep enough for a small boy on a tricycle to attain terminal velocity. The pedals became a vicious blur. There was no hope of getting my feet back on them. It was apparent that I would arrive at the bottom of the hill just in time to be flung on to the line in the path of a train even then looming out of the cutting. Hearing my screams, my mother came after me like the back half of Zeno's paradox about Achilles and the tortoise, if you can imagine Achilles in drag and the tortoise screaming its head off while balanced on a shaking bicycle seat with its legs stuck out. She caught up with me at the last moment. It was part of the pattern. I always survived, but only after scaring her to death.

And then there were Australia's natural wonders. Jannali was not quite the bush proper, but it was certainly an outer suburb. You could walk over the next hill and be back in the sort of country that the convicts used to die in when they ran away. Not that they would necessarily have died of hunger. There is plenty for you to eat. Unfortunately there is also plenty that wants to eat you.

By now I have grown used to the benevolence of the English countryside, where there are no natural hazards beyond the odd clump of poison ivy, a few varieties of inimical mushroom, and half a dozen adders all of which wear number plates and have exclusive contracts with BBC television. Walking at ease in such an Augustan context, it is sometimes difficult to remember what it was like to inhabit a land crawling with danger. I have already mentioned the bull-ants. There were also snakes. Walking to school bare-footed along dirt paths lined with banksias and waratahs, I was always expecting to meet one of the snakes portrayed in the gaudily detailed charts which were hung up in the railway station and the post office. Luckily the only snakes I ever encountered were harmless civilians: the filing clerks and secretaries of the serpentine world. But Uncle Vic caught a full-sized fighting snake right outside our front gate. It was a black snake – one step worse than a brown snake. A black snake can kill an adult if it is big enough. This one was big enough. Uncle Vic pinned it to the ground in the middle but both ends of it went on trying to get at him.

The next step up from the black snake is the tiger snake. It was statistically likely that at least a few tiger snakes were in our district, probably holed up in some shack and sending their girlfriends out to buy liquor. Over and above the tiger snake, so to speak, is the taipan. Luckily ours was not taipan country. Indeed at that time the taipan was not yet famous anywhere. Up in Queensland, in the sugar cane belt, the taipan was soon to begin making headlines and getting its photograph in *Pix*. Tiger snakes and black snakes can't compete with taipans, but they are bad enough. Brown snakes are pretty bad. Allegedly harmless snakes don't look very benevolent either. I used to think about all this a lot on the way to or from school. Whether to run fast or tip-toe silently was a constant dilemma, which I tried to solve by doing both at once.

I also thought about spiders. Two of the worst Australian spiders are the funnel-web and the trap-door. One is even more lethal than the other but I can't remember which. It doesn't matter, because either can put a child in peril of its life. The funnel-web is a ping-pong ball in a fox fur. It inhabits a miniature missile silo in the ground, from which it emerges in a savage arc, ready to sink its mandibles into anything that breathes. The trap-door spider is really a funnel-web plus cunning, since it conceals the mouth of its silo with a tiny coal-hole door. Both kinds of spider can leap an incredible distance. A wood pile might contain hundreds of each kind. If you even suspected the presence of either species in your garden you were supposed to report immediately to the responsible authorities. After the war an English immigrant lady became famous when she was discovered gaily swatting funnel-webs with a broom as they came flying at her in squadrons. Any one of them, if it had got close enough even to spit at her, would have put her in bed for a year.

I somehow managed to avoid meeting trap-door spiders or funnel-webs. Quite often I came face to face with a harmless relative, which Aunt Dot called a tarantula and I called a triantelope. Actually it was just a common or garden spider called the huntsman, whose idea of a big thrill was to suck a wasp. The huntsman wove big vertical webs which I used regularly to walk into when heading tentatively down the back path to the lavatory after dark. Getting mixed up in the web, to which I knew the triantelope must be at some point attached, was a frightening sensation which I attempted to forestall by inching forward very slowly, with one hand held out. It didn't help.

But the real horror among spiders was more likely to be encountered in the lavatory itself. This was the red-back. The red-back is mainly black, with a scarlet stripe down where its spine would be if it were a vertebrate. Looking like a neatly rigged and painted single-seater that might once have been flown by von Richthofen, the red-back had enough poison in it to immobilize a horse. It had the awkward habit, in unsewered areas like ours, of lurking under the lavatory seat. If a red-back bit you on the behind you were left with the problem of where to put the tourniquet and not long to think about it. Nor could you ask anyone to suck out the poison, unless you knew them very well indeed. I saw plenty of red-backs and actually got bitten by one, luckily not on the behind. I think it was a red-back. Certainly I told my mother it was. Once again the site of the wound was my right foot, which by this time must have been looking as if it belonged to Philoctetes. My mother knelt, sucked and spat. We were both frightened but she was not too frightened to act. She must have been getting tired, however, of being both father and mother.

After the first atomic bomb there was a general feeling that Japan had surrendered. The street was decorated with bunting. Strings of all the Allied flags were hung up between the flame trees. The Japanese missed their cue and all the bunting had to be taken in. Finally the Japanese saw the point and all the bunting was taken out again. Everybody was in ecstasies except my mother, who still had no news. Then an official telegram came to say that he was all right. Letters from my father arrived. They were in touch with each other and must have been very happy. The Americans, with typical generosity, arranged that all the Australian POWs in Japan should be flown home instead of having to wait for ships. My mother started counting the days. Then a telegram arrived saying that my father's plane had been caught in a typhoon and had crashed in Manila Bay with the loss of everyone aboard.

Up until that day, all the grief and worry that I had ever seen my mother give way to had been tempered for my ears. But now she could not help herself. At the age of five I was seeing the full force of human despair. There were no sedatives to be had. It was several days before she could control herself. I understood nothing beyond the fact that I could not help. I think that I was marked for life. I know now that until very recent years I was never quite all there – that I was play-acting instead of living and that nothing except my own unrelenting fever of self-consciousness seemed quite real. Eventually, in my middle thirties, I got a grip on myself. But there can be no doubt that I had a tiresomely protracted adolescence, wasting a lot of other people's time, patience and love. I suppose it is just another sign of weakness to blame everything on that one moment, but it would be equally dishonest if I failed to record its piercing vividness.

As for my mother, I don't presume even to guess at what she felt. The best I can say is that at least they got the chance of writing a few words to one another before the end. In one respect they were like Osip and Nadezhda Mandelstam in the last chapters of *Hope Against Hope* – torn apart in mid-word without even the chance to say goodbye. But in another way they were not. My father had taken up arms out of his own free will. In Europe, millions of women and children had been killed for no better reason than some ideological fantasy. My father was a free human being. So was my mother. What happened to them, terrible though it was, belongs in the category of what Nadezhda Mandelstam, elsewhere in that same great book, calls the privilege of ordinary heartbreaks. Slowly, in those years, the world was becoming aware that things had been happening which threw the whole value of human existence into doubt. But my father's death was not one of them. It was just bad luck. I have disliked luck ever since – an aversion only increased by the fact that I have always been inordinately lucky.

Grandpa's death was easier for me to deal with. Everybody was ready for it. Grief was kept in bounds. There was no way of pin-pointing the moment when he passed to the beyond. In his dark bedroom he merely turned into a slightly more immobile version of what he had already been for years. It was time to open the windows and let in the light. I was encouraged to take a look at the corpse – a wise decision, since it immediately became clear to me that there are more terrible things than dying a natural death. The old man merely looked as if he had been bored out of existence. Perhaps I got it all wrong then and have still got it all wrong now. Perhaps he died in a redemptive ecstasy after being vouchsafed a revelation of the ineffable. But I doubt it. I think he just croaked.

Ray was harder to be blasé about. We hadn't played Giant Steps for a long time. Eventually he was too weak to stand. He was taken away to the military hospital at Yaralla, where over the next few years he gradually wasted to nothing. He used to smile at me through the mirror mounted over his face as he lay in the iron lung. The smile took an age to arrive and another age to go away. It was like watching sand dry in the sun. I can remember being scolded for not caring enough. I think it was Aunt Dot who did the scolding. The unremitting gradualness of it all must have been hard for her to take. People's emotions are no less real just because they carry on a lot. Aunt Dot could do the mad scene from *Lucia* when her lemon meringue pie collapsed. But there is no reason to believe that she felt her bereavement any the less for feeling little things too much. She was, and is, a good woman who would have mothered me if she had been called upon. Mothering, however, wasn't what I was short of.

My mother decided it was time to go back to our house at No. 6, Margaret Street, Kogarah, a place I couldn't remember having seen. There was nothing to keep us in Jannali, where losses appeared to be accumulating steadily. Changing schools was certainly no great wrench. There were no playmates I would particularly miss, except perhaps the unspeakable Ron. I was taken to a party that year where there was a present for every child except me. It turned out that my present, a box of soldiers, had been mislaid. The mistake was quickly rectified. But it took all afternoon and half the night to coax me down from my tree. Definitely time for a change of scene.

Besides, Kogarah was more of a built-up area, and therefore, my mother reasoned, safer. It would even have the sewer on soon – an unheard-of luxury. The only problem was to get the tenants out. They had promised to move when asked, but by now there was a housing shortage and they didn't want to go. My mother, however, had lost too much. She wouldn't stand for losing her house as well. It had cost her and my father everything they had ever earned. She was firm about not letting the tenants break their agreement. Out they went and in we moved.

Even in my memory the house is small. Early on there were a lounge, two bedrooms, a kitchen-dining room, a bathroom and a back veranda, with laundry and lavatory built into the back wall. Later we had the back veranda enclosed with fibro and Cooper louvres so that it could count as a room too. Between the front fence and the paved street there was a concrete footpath and a piece of lawn, known as the front strip, which included a box gum tree big enough for a child to swing upside down from and drop on its head. Every household mowed its own front strip. It was to be a constant source of shame to my mother that our piece of front strip was never as finely mown or sharply edged as the front strips of the next-door neighbours.

From the front fence to the house was the front lawn. There was a car's-width of lawn down the right side of the house, leading in almost every case but ours to a garage. This was called the driveway whether you had a car or not. On the other side of the house was a much narrower passage between house and fence, just wide enough to walk through. Behind the house was a back yard. Most of this, in our case, was lawn: a mixture of buffalo grass, couch and tenacious crops of paspalum. There were passion-fruit vines growing on the fence where the garage should have been. In the opposite back corner was a peach tree, in which over the years I made various attempts, all unsuccessful, to build a tree house. There were patches of vegetable garden along all three edges of the back yard. These were devoted to the growing of the kind of vegetables I always refused to eat – chocos, beetroot, rhubarb and so on. Or is rhubarb a fruit? Despite my mother's imprecations, I could never see the point of the choco. Whatever you do with it, it's still nothing. It looks like an albino avocado and tastes like cellophane. Its only advantage lies in its cheapness. You can't stop chocos growing. It takes a flame-thrower to keep them down.

The widest of these vegetable patches lay parallel to the back fence, beyond which was a poultry farm inhabited by thousands of chooks all synchronized to wake you up at dawn. Later on the farm became a housing estate. Whatever lay beyond the back fence, I was always tunnelling towards it. The back patch was the site of my unflagging efforts to get back to the womb by digging into the earth. I started this at quite an early age, attaining more proficiency as time went on. My early burrows were simple dugouts roofed over with box tops, after which the earth was heaped back on. There was just room for me. I would persuade my mother to cover up the entrance and leave me down there all afternoon. It didn't matter if the thing collapsed – it was only a few inches of dirt. Older children had been known to try the same trick in sand dunes, with fatal results. She probably reasoned that it was better to let me indulge these fantasies where she could keep an eye on me.

Over the next few years, the back patch started looking like the Ypres Salient. I would dig complicated networks of trenches, roof them over, and continue tunnelling from inside, honey-combing the clay all the way down to the water table. Other boys in the street were fascinated. It became known that I was taking my Donald Duck comics down there and reading them by torch-light. They, too, turned up with armfuls of comics. Suddenly I had friends. I had stumbled on one of the secrets of leadership – start something, then let people know you are doing them a favour by bringing them in on it. Candidates for my tunnel club had to go through a probationary period of hovering on the outskirts. It was like being put up for the Garrick. Finally half the small boys in the district were spending the whole weekend somewhere under our back yard. Similar scenes must have occurred on the night of the Great Escape from Stalag Luft III. I overdid it when I started letting the little kids down there. Little kids, I should have known, ruin things. Geoffrey Teichmann was only about four years old, Crawling somewhere down around Level 7 leading off Shaft 4, he brushed against one of the fruit-case slats I used for pit props. The whole system fell on him. Parents arrived from everywhere to dig the little twerp out. The was the end of that.

But my new-found acceptability was strictly a local phenomenon. School was still a nightmare. I went to Kogarah Infants' School and then to Kogarah Primary. They were both in the same place, near Kogarah station, more than a mile away on the trolley bus. The fare was a penny. The trolley bus went down Rocky Point Road, through a shopping centre called the Bundy, then turned left to cut across

Prince's Highway and climb over the hill to the station, where it either turned around at the Loop or went on to Rockdale. There were shops at the Loop, including Parry's Milk Bar, the centre of local night life for years to come. Being bought a fruit sundae in Parry's late at night was pretty well the most luxurious thing that could happen to you.

Two minutes' walk up the hill from the Loop was the school. I could make that two minutes last an hour – sometimes a whole day. If it had not been for another boy called McGowan, I would have been cast as the school's problem child. Luckily McGowan was so disturbed that I seemed unobtrusive by comparison. A ginger shambles, McGowan wore glasses with one lens covered up by brown sticky paper, presumably to correct a fault of vision. He screamed without provocation, frothed at the mouth, bit pieces out of other children and kicked teachers in the stomach. In the playground he would run at the supervising teacher while her back was turned, so that he would be going at full speed when she wheeled at the sound of his running footsteps. He was thus able to get plenty of force behind the kick. The teacher would be taken away on a stretcher. Eventually there were no longer any members of the staff willing to take on the job of supervising any classroom or playground with McGowan in it, so he was removed. That left me looking more conspicuous.

The only thing I liked about school was skipping around in circles until the music stopped, then lying down on the floor for Quiet Time. I was very good at Quiet Time. Otherwise it was all a bit hopeless. I piddled on the floor when it was my turn to sing. Conversely, I got caught drinking my daily bottle of milk in the lavatory. For some reason this was regarded as a fearful crime. My mother used to pick me up after school. One day we missed each other and I went home alone on the bus. Meanwhile my mother was going frantic at the school. There were mutual tears that night. Next day when I answered my name at the morning assembly roll-call, the headmistress said, 'Ah yes, that's the little boy who ran away from his mother.' Thanks a lot, witch. I kacked my pants on the spot.

The whole secret of kacking your pants, incidentally, is to produce a rock-solid blob which will slide down your leg in one piece and can be rolled away into hiding at the point of the toe. That way, your moment of shame can be kept to the proportions of a strictly local disaster. But if you let go with anything soft, it takes two teachers to clean you up and the whole affair attracts nationwide publicity. You get people interviewing you.

3. BILLYCART HILL

The name I answered to in my early years was Vivian James. Later on my mother gave me my choice of new first names and I picked Clive out of a Tyrone Power movie. She sympathized with the fix she and my father had got me into by naming me after Vivian McGrath, star of the 1938 Davis Cup squad. After Vivien Leigh played Scarlett O'Hara the name became irrevocably a girl's name no matter how you spelled it, so those few little boys who had been saddled with it went through hell. I just got sick of ending up on the wrong lists, being sent to sewing classes, etc. Children in Australia are still named after movies and sporting events. You can tell roughly the year the swimming star Shane Gould was born. It was about the time *Shane* was released. There was a famous case of a returned serviceman who named his son after all the campaigns he had been through in the Western Desert. The kid was called William Bardia Escarpment Qattara Depression Mersa Matruh Tobruk El Alamein Benghazi Tripoli Harris.

Things marginally improved when I was promoted, a year early, from the Infants' School to the Primary School. The embarrassments of co-education were at last left behind. No longer were we obliged to pair off and hold hands tweely when marching into the classroom – a huge advance on previous conditions. I achieved early promotion solely through being good at reading. The reason I was good at reading had nothing to do with school. In our last year at Jannali I had started to pick my way through Grandpa's musty old bound sets of *Wide World* magazine. Also there were bright yellow heaps of the *National Geographic*. In our first years at Kogarah, while searching my mother's room, I found the wardrobe half full of magazines. These were mainly *Picture Post*, *Lilliput*, *Collier's*, the *Saturday Evening Post*, *Life* and *Reader's Digest*. I started off by looking at the pictures but gradually progressed to being able to read the text.

I can't remember what it was like not to be able to read English fluently. Nowadays, if I am learning to read a new language, I try to savour the moment that separates not knowing how to from not knowing how not to. At the time, I simply found myself able to read. Over the next few years I absorbed everything in those few hundred magazines. I read them until there was nothing left to read and then read them again until the covers pulled away from the staples. The *Saturday Evening Posts* with the Norman Rockwell covers satisfied every demand of my aesthetic sense, the gustatory requirements included. I used to read them instead of eating. I felt about them the way Turgenev felt about the emblem book he wrote of to Bakunin, and made a part of Laretsky's childhood in *A Nest of Gentlefolk.*

I suppose if I had been John Stuart Mill I would have sought out a better class of reading matter. Indeed my father and mother had done a lot of fairly solid reading together: stacked away at the top of the cupboard in the hall were cheap sets of Dickens, Thackeray and the Brontës. For some reason I was never to seek them out, even in my teens. I always had an automatic aversion to the set books. Reading off the course was in my nature. My style was to read everything except what mattered, just as I ate everything except what was good for me.

In Primary School I ceased being the class halfwit and became class smart alec instead. This presented a whole new set of difficulties. Coming out first in the term tests attracted accusations of being teacher's pet. It was true, alas: Mr Slavin, although a fair-minded man, couldn't help smiling upon anyone who knew how to answer the questions. Too many boys in the class had trouble remembering their own names. Most of the heat was focused on an unfortunate called Thommo, who was caned regularly. For ordinary offences Thommo was caned by Mr Slavin and for more serious transgressions he was caned by the Deputy Headmaster. Mr Slavin was authorized to impart up to four strokes. Thommo usually required six even to slow him down. We used to sit silent while the Deputy Head gave Thommo the treatment outside is the corridor. The six strokes took some time to deliver, because Thommo had to be recaptured after each stroke, and to be recaptured he had first to be found. His screams and sobs usually gave away his location, but not always. One day the police came to the classroom and made Thommo open his Globite school case. It was full of stolen treasures from Coles and

Woolworths: balloons, bulldog paper clips, funny hats, a cut-glass vase. Thommo was led howling away and never seen again.

Despite Thommo's fate, on the whole I would rather have been him than me. His manly activities merited respect. As teacher's pet, I was regarded with envy, suspicion and hatred. I had not yet learned to joke my way out of trouble and into favour. Instead I tried to prove that I, too, could be rebellious, untrammelled, dangerous and tough. To register, any demonstration of these qualities would have to be made in view of the whole class. This would not be easy, since my desk was at the back of the room. There were five columns of desks with seven desks in each column. The five most academically able boys sat in the back five desks and so on down the line, with the desks at the front containing the dullards, psychopaths, Thommo, etc. The problem was to become the cynosure of all eyes in some way more acceptable than my usual method of throwing my hand in the air, crying 'Sir! Sir! Sir!', and supplying the correct answer.

The solution lay in the network of railway tracks carved into the top of each desk by successive generations of occupants. Along these tracks fragments of pencil, pen holders or bits of chalk could be pushed with chuffing noises. I also found out that the exposed wood was susceptible to friction. At home I was already an established fire-bug, running around with a magnifying glass frying sugar-ants. I had learned something of what pieces of wood could do to each other. This knowledge I now applied, rubbing the end of my box-wood ruler against the edge of one of the tracks. A wisp of smoke came up. Eyes turned towards me. The wisp became a billow. More eyes turned towards me. The billow was fretted with fire. Mr Slavin's eyes turned towards me.

He gave me his full four strokes. The pain was considerable, but the glory was greater. 'What's sauce for the goose,' he said as I tucked my smarting hands under my armpits, 'is sauce for the gander.' Mr Slavin's epigrams were distinctly sub-Wildean but he had a knack for trotting them out at precisely the appropriate moment. He might even have had an inkling of how much I wanted to be a goose.

This small triumph spurred me fatally towards bigger things. There was a craze on for dongers. Crazes came one after the other. There was a craze for a game of marbles called followings. There was a craze for cigarette cards: not the cards that used to come in packets of English cigarettes, but cards made elaborately out of the cigarette packets themselves. The cards had different values according to brands, with English Gold Flake scoring highest and Australian Craven 'A' scoring lowest. You flicked your cards at a wall. The one who finished nearest the wall got a chance to toss all the cards in the air at once. The ones that fell face up were his. Bottletops worked roughly the same way, except that the one who got closest to the wall stacked all the bottletops on his upturned elbow and then swiped downwards with his hand, getting to keep as many of the bottletops as he could catch between hand and wrist. It is difficult to describe and even more difficult to do. I always lost. I wasn't bad at cock-a-lorum, but falling over on the asphalt playground added painfully to my usual array of sores and scabs. The craze I hoped to be good at was dongers.

A donger was an ordinary handkerchief folded into a triangle. You held each end of the hypotenuse and twirled until the handkerchief had rolled itself tight. Then you held the two ends together in one hand while you rolled the fat centre part even tighter with the other. The result was then soaked in water to give it weight. The more reckless boys sometimes inserted a lead washer or a small rock. The completed donger was, in effect, a blackjack. Every playtime, with me hovering cravenly on the outskirts, donger gangs would do battle against each other. The brawls looked like the battle of Thermopylae. Finally the teacher on playground duty would plunge into the mêlée and send everyone in possession of a donger up to the Deputy Headmaster to get six. With me hovering elsewhere, solo desperadoes would then creep up on their victims behind the teacher's back. The idea was to clobber the target and be walking in the opposite direction with the donger in your pocket before the teacher turned around. He always turned around because the sound of the donger hitting someone's head was unmistakable. It sounded like an apple hitting concrete.

I was very keen not to be among those victimized. It followed that I should become one of those doing the victimizing. To this end I built a donger and chose the target likely to win me the most fame. At one point in the circumference of the playground there was a low picket fence separting the Boys' Primary School from the Girls' Primary School. It was forbidden to linger at this fence. I noticed a girl using the fence as a whippy. She was leaning against it with her face buried in her folded arms while other girls hid. If some other girl got to the whippy while she was away searching, there would be a cry of 'All in, the whippy's taken.' But at the moment she was still busy counting to a hundred. I came at her in a long curving run, swinging the donger like a sling. Contact was perfect. She dropped as though pole-axed – which, to all intents and purposes, she had been. I ran right into the teacher's arms.

And so I kept my feared but wished-for appointment with the Deputy Headmaster. He was a tall, slim man in a grey dustcoat. I can't remember his name, but I can well remember his quietly sardonic manner. He pointed out to me that in hitting the little girl I had caused her pain, and that he was now about to show me what pain was like. The instrument I had employed on the little girl had been strictly banned. The same embargo, he explained, did not apply to the instrument he would now employ on me. I was inspecting this while he spoke. It was a long, thick cane with a leather-bound tip. Unlike other canes I had seen, it did not seem to be flexible. Instead of swishing when it came down, it hummed. The impact was like a door slamming on my hand. I was too stunned even to pee my pants. The same thing happened to the other hand. Then the same thing again happened to each hand twice more in succession. That would teach me, he informed me, to hit little girls with dongers.

If he meant that it would teach me *not* to hit little girls with dongers, he was right. For one thing, I couldn't have lifted a donger, let alone swung one. When I tried to feed myself my play-lunch sandwiches, I kept missing my mouth. But at least the fame accruing to the maximum penalty had raised my status somewhat. I was never admitted to the inner circle of Kenny Mears, the school's most impressive bully. But for a while I was not so often among those bullied. Probably I was lucky not to be included among the oppressors. I admired Mears, but for his self-possession more than for his capacity to inflict suffering. He was completely without fear. Like Napoleon or Hitler, he seemed imaginative through having no idea of natural limits to his actions. He was a sawn-off Siegfried, a Nietzschean superman in short pants. He embodied Gibbon's definition of the barbarian, since his liberty was to indulge the whim of the moment, and his courage was to ignore the consequences. He was a frightful little shit.

But he had the kind of poise that I have always envied. He swore at the teachers man-to-man and could absorb an infinite amount of punishment without batting an eye. Indeed he never even blinked. Playing marbles, he made Mick Roach look like the Marquis of Queensberry. Mears fudged unblushingly. Wittgenstein defined a game as consisting of the rules by which it is played. If he had seen Mears in action, he would have realized that a game is further defined by what the dominant player can get away with. The basic rule of marbles is that the taw must be fired from outside the ring. If the firing hand creeps inside the ring before the moment of release, it's a fudge. Mears fudged more blatantly than his helpless opponents would have believed possible. Standing up instead of crouching down, he fell forward until his firing hand was almost touching the dates. Then he released his taw. The dates sang out of the ring and into his keeping. If anybody protested, violence would ensue. Nor was anyone allowed not to play. Years later I saw the film of *Guys and Dolls*. There is a famous scene where Nathan Detroit's floating crap game moves to the sewers, and Big Julie from Chicago proposes to roll his own dice, which have no spots. When challenged, he produces a .45 automatic. I thought immediately: 'Mears'.

Mears's favourite means of persuasion was the Chinese Burn. Grasping your hand in one of his, he would twist your wrist with the other. After having this done to me by boys older and bigger, I sought revenge by doing it to boys younger and smaller. But I quickly found out that I was naturally averse to being cruel. Reading the *Wide World* magazines, I had been excited by a chapter dealing with torture chambers. I still find it disturbing that sex and cruelty should be connected somewhere in my instincts. But the human personality is a drama, not a monologue; sad tricks of the mind can be offset by sound feelings in the heart; and the facts say that I have always been revolted by the very idea of deliberately causing pain. Considering the amount of pain I have been able to cause without meaning to, I suppose this is not much of a defence, but to me it has always seemed an important point. I burned a lot of sugar-ants with my magnifying glass, but if the sugar-ants had spoken to me as they might have spoken to St Francis, I would have desisted soon enough. Having a character that consists mainly of defects, I try to correct them one by one, but there are limits to the altitude that can be attained by hauling on one's own bootstraps. One is what one is, and if one isn't very nice or good, then it brings some solace to remember that other men have been worse. At various times in my life I have tried to pose as a thug, but the imposture has always collapsed of its own accord. I could be coerced into hurting other people. I have done it by chance often enough. But I could never enjoy it.

At home things were a bit easier than at school. Once or twice I announced my intention of running away, but my mother defused the threat by packing me a bag containing peanut butter sandwiches and pyjamas. The first time I got no further than the top of our street and was back home within the hour. The second time I got all the way to Rocky Point Road, more than two hundred yards from home. I was not allowed to cross Rocky Point Road. But I sat there until sunset. Otherwise I did my escaping symbolically, tunnelling into the poultry farm and surfacing among the chooks with a crumbling cap of birdshit on my head.

The teacher's pet image would have followed me home if my mother had had her way. She had a deadly habit of inviting the neighbours in for tea so that she could casually refer to my school reports a couple of hundred times. The most favoured recipient of these proud tirades was Nola Huthnance, who lived four doors down. Nola Huthnance was no mean talker herself, being joint holder, with her next-door neighbour Gail Thorpe, of the local record for yapping across the back fence – an unbeatable lunch-to-sunset epic during which there was no point at which one or the other was not talking and very few moments when both were not talking simultaneously. But not even Nola Huthnance could hold her own when my mother got going on the subject of her wonderful son and his outstanding intelligence. Long after I had been sent to bed, I would lurk in the hall listening to my mother extolling my virtues in the lounge room. Apparently Gogol's mother was under the impression that her son had invented the printing press and the steam engine. My own mother thought along roughly the same lines. I lapped it all up, but could see even at the time that such talk would do me no good with the locals, unless I cultivated a contrary reputation on my own account.

Luckily, whether by being just the right age or by having more than my fair share of productive neuroses, I continued to think up the kind of games that most of the other children in Margaret Street were keen to get in on. Wet weather put an end to the tunnelling season, but it produced flooded gutters. In those days proper concrete kerbing had not yet been laid down. Water flowed down erratic gutters through the width of bare earth and clay between the front strip and the ragged-edged asphalt road. Swollen with rain, these gutters were ripe for having sticks and plastic boats raced down them. At the top of Margaret Street, beyond the T-junction with Irene Street, was a block of waste ground known as the quarry. Probably the convicts had once hacked stone there – Botany Bay was only about a mile to the east. The fall of ground from the back to the front of the block was only fifteen feet or so but to us it looked like Annapurna. In wet weather the water poured down the exposed rock face of the quarry and formed streamlets begging to be dammed. I used to build whole networks of mud dams, fanatically smoothing them off and facing them with pieces of fibro, so that they resembled the photographs of the Boulder and Grand Coulee dams in my *Modern Marvels Encyclopedia*. In the lakes formed by the dams I built harbours for plastic boats. Liberated from the confines of the bath, they could be pushed around in a more interesting seascape than that bounded by my soapy knees. There were secret bases under tufts of overhanging grass. Holding my face close to a boat as I pushed it, I could study the bow waves and the wake. The boats were only a few inches long but they looked like the *Bismarck* if you got near enough. I built roads along the docks and up through the foothills. Plastic, lead and tin toy cars could be pushed along them. Dinky Toys were rare at that time. A Triang Minic jeep – later lost, to my mother's anguished disgust – was the star turn. Wound up, it could make progress even through mud. Other vehicles had to be pushed. With them it was all pretend.

But it was pretend in ideal surroundings. Other children brought their boats and cars, blundering into my ashlared revetments, gouging crude paths, botching together laughable garages and ludicrous U-boat pens. At first I told them to go and build their own dams. Then I resigned myself to having my work ruined. At the small price of an offence to my aesthetic instincts, I was able to rule the roost. Besides, with cheap labour available my schemes could be allowed to wax ever grander. Like Themistocles linking Athens with Piraeus, I walled in the whole area. My designs assumed the proportions of Karnak or Speer's Berlin. I was the overseer, the construction boss, the superintendent of works. But even when my loyal slaves were toiling away in every direction, I would sometimes relapse into a detailed concern for a certain stretch of road or dockside, smoothing it endlessly with the edge of my hand into an ever sweeter curve or sharper edge.

None of this meant that I was a good practical hand. For example, I could not build billycarts very well. Other children, most of them admittedly older than I, but some of them infuriatingly not, constructed billycarts of advanced design, with skeletal hard-wood frames and steel-jacketed ball-race wheels that screamed on the concrete footpaths like a diving Stuka. The best I could manage was a sawn-off fruit box mounted on a fence-paling spine frame, with drearily silent rubber wheels taken off an old pram. In such a creation I could go at a reasonable clip down our street and twice as fast down Sunbeam Avenue, which was much steeper at the top. But even going down Sunbeam my billycart was no great thrill compared with the ball-race models, which having a ground-clearance of about half an inch and being almost frictionless were able to attain tremendous velocities at low profile, so that to the onlooker their riders seemed to be travelling downhill sitting magically just above the ground, while to the riders themselves the sense of speed was breathtaking.

After school and at weekends boys came from all over the district to race on the Sunbeam Avenue footpaths. There would be twenty or thirty carts, two-thirds of them with ball-races. The noise was indescribable. It sounded like the Battle of Britain going on in somebody's bathroom. There would be about half an hour's racing before the police came. Residents often took the law into their own hands, hosing the grim-faced riders as they went shrieking by. Sunbeam Avenue ran parallel to Margaret Street but it started higher and lasted longer. Carts racing down the footpath on the far side had a straight run of about a quarter of a mile all the way to the park. Emitting shock-waves of sound, the ball-race carts would attain such speeds that it was impossible for the rider to get off. All he could do was to crash reasonably gently when he got to the end. Carts racing down the footpath on the near side could go only half as far, although very nearly as fast, before being faced with a right-angle turn into Irene Street. Here a pram-wheeled cart like mine could demonstrate its sole advantage. The traction of the rubber tyres made it possible to negotiate the corner in some style. I developed a histrionic lean-over of the body and slide of the back wheels which got me around the corner unscathed, leaving black smoking trails of burnt rubber.

Mastery of this trick saved me from being relegated to the ranks of the little kids, than which there was no worse fate. I had come to depend on being thought of as a big kid. Luckily only the outstanding ball-race drivers could match my fancy turn into Irene Street. Others slid straight on with a yelp of metal and a shower of sparks, braining themselves on the aphalt road. One driver scalped himself under a bread van.

The Irene Street corner was made doubly perilous by Mrs Branthwaite's poppies. Mrs Branthwaite inhabited the house on the corner. She was a known witch whom we often persecuted after dark by throwing gravel on her roof. It was widely believed she poisoned cats. Certainly she was a great ringer-up of the police. In retrospect I can see that she could hardly be blamed for this, but her behaviour seemed at the time like irrational hatred of children. She was a renowned gardener. Her front yard was like the cover of a seed catalogue. Extending her empire, she had flower beds even on her two front strips, one on the Sunbeam Avenue side and the other on the Irene Street side – i.e., on both outside edges of the famous corner. The flower beds held the area's best collection of poppies. She had been known to phone the police if even one of these was illicitly picked.

At the time I am talking about, Mrs Branthwaite's poppies were all in bloom. It was essential to make the turn without hurting a single hair of a poppy's head, otherwise the old lady would probably drop the telephone and come out shooting. Usually, when the poppies were in bloom, nobody dared make the turn. I did – not out of courage, but because in my ponderous cart there was no real danger of going wrong. The daredevil leanings-over and the dramatic skids were just icing on the cake.

I should have left it at that, but got ambitious. One Saturday afternoon when there was a particularly large turn out, I got sick of watching the ball-race carts howling to glory down the far side. I organized the slower carts like my own into a train. Every cart except mine was deprived of its front axle and loosely bolted to the cart in front. The whole assembly was about a dozen carts long, with a big box cart at the back. This back cart I dubbed the chuck wagon, using terminology I had picked up from the Hopalong Cassidy serial at the pictures. I was the only one alone on his cart. Behind me there were two or even three to every cart until you got to the chuck wagon,

which was crammed full of little kids, some of them so small that
they were holding toy koalas and sucking dummies.

From its very first run down the far side, my super-cart was a
triumph. Even the adults who had been hosing us called their families
out to marvel as we went steaming by. On the super-cart's next run
there was still more to admire, since even the top-flight ball-race
riders had demanded to have their vehicles built into it, thereby
heightening its tone, swelling its passenger list, and multiplying its
already impressive output of decibels. Once again I should have left
well alone. The thing was already famous. It had everything but a
dining car. Why did I ever suggest that we should transfer it to the
near side and try the Irene Street turn?

With so much inertia the super-cart started slowly, but it accelerated like a piano falling out of a window. Long before we reached
the turn I realized that there had been a serious miscalculation. The
miscalculation was all mine, of course. Sir Isaac Newton would have
got it right. It was too late to do anything except pray. Leaning into
the turn, I skidded my own cart safely around in the usual way. The
next few segments followed me, but with each segment describing
an arc of slightly larger radius than the one in front. First gradually,
then with stunning finality, the monster lashed its enormous tail.

The air was full of flying ball-bearings, bits of wood, big kids,
little kids, koalas and dummies. Most disastrously of all, it was also
full of poppy petals. Not a bloom escaped the scythe. Those of us
who could still run scattered to the winds, dragging our wounded
with us. The police spent hours visiting all the parents in the district,
warning them that the billycart era was definitely over. It was a police
car that took Mrs Branthwaite away. There was no point waiting for
the ambulance. She could walk all right. It was just that she couldn't
talk. She stared straight ahead, her mouth slightly open.

4. THE FORCE OF DESTRUCTION

Such catastrophes distressed my mother but she wrote them off as growing pains. Other exploits broke her heart. Once when she was out shopping I was riding my second-hand Malvern Star 26-inch frame bicycle around the house on a complicated circuit which led from the back yard along the driveway, once around a small fir tree that stood in the front yard, and back along the narrow side passage. Passing boys noticed what I was up to and came riding in. In a while there were a dozen or so of us circulating endlessly against the clock. Once again I could not leave well alone. I organized a spectacular finish in which the riders had to plunge into my mother's prize privet hedge. The idea was for the bike's front wheel to lodge in the thick privet and the rider to fall dramatically into the bush and disappear. It became harder and harder to disappear as the privet became more and more reduced to ruins.

Giddy with success, I started doing the same thing to the hydrangeas. Finally I did it to the fir tree, ramming it with the bike and falling through it, thereby splitting its trunk. When my mother came wearily down the street with the shopping she must have thought the house had been strafed. I was hiding under it – a sure sign of advanced guilt and fear, since it was dark under there and red-backs were plentiful. She chased me up the peach tree and hit me around the ankles with a willow wand. It didn't hurt me as much as her tears did. Not for the only time, I heard her tell me that I was more than she could cope with. I suppose there was a possibility that I somehow felt compelled to go on reminding her of that fact.

Bombing my bed didn't make me very popular either. It was a trick I learned while recovering from mumps. Climbing on to the top of the wardrobe in my room, I would jump off and land on my bed, which seemed an immense distance below. Actually it was only a few feet, but the bed groaned satisfactorily. Eventually there were half a dozen of us climbing up and jumping off in rapid succession. It was a mistake to let Graham Truscott play. He had a double chin even at that age and a behind like a large bag of soil. But it took him so long to climb the wardrobe that it seemed unreasonable not to let him jump off it. The frame of the bed snapped off its supports with the noise of a firing squad and crashed to the floor with the roar of cannon. I sent everyone home and tried to restore the bed to its right height by putting suitcases under it, but all that did was cave in the suitcases. Once again it was very dark under the house.

And once again there was an element of panic in my mother's fury. It sprang, of course, from the fact that what we owned was all we had. My mother had a War Widow's pension to bring me up on. It wasn't much. The Returned Servicemen's League, always known as the RSL, was a formidable pressure group in the post-war years but those servicemen who had not returned exerted no pressure at all. The Legacy Club threw a Christmas party every year. Otherwise the bereaved wives were paid off mainly in rhetoric, most of it emanating from the silver tongue of Robert Gordon Menzies, alias Ming, who went on being Prime Minister for what seemed like eternity. My mother never failed to vote for him. She had quite a lot of political nous, but Ming's patrician style numbed her judgment. Thus she went on remaining loyal to the Liberal Party, while the Liberal Party went on ensuring that her pension would never be so lavish as to encourage idleness.

She eked out her pittance by smocking babies' dresses. The smocking was done on a brick wrapped in cloth. The panel to be smocked was threaded on a long pin and the pin was in turn pushed through the cloth along the top edge of the brick. Then with a needle and thread she produced row after row of tiny stitches, the stitches forming exquisite patterns on the pink or blue cloth. She was paid piece rates. They were not high. She worked pretty well all day and often far into the evening while we listened to the radio. She would stop only for Jack Davey, who we were agreed was a great wit. Bob Dyer she found ridiculous, but listened to him just so that she could loathe him. After I went to bed she often went on working. Once a week she took the finished pieces up to the woman in Oatley who assembled the dresses. The round trip took the whole day. It was often during these absences that I perpetrated my worst crimes, such as the bed-wrecking incident. Right back at the very start, almost the first week we were in Kogarah, I distinguished myself by helping to restore the colour in a faded patch of the lounge-room carpet. I did this by rubbing a whole tin of Nugget dark tan boot polish into the deprived area. By the time she got back from Oatley I was already in pre-emptive tears, having divined that the results did not look quite right. On such occasions she looked beyond anger, manifesting a sort of resigned desperation.

Gradually I learned that damaging anything around the house produced more emotional wear and tear than I could deal with. So I started damaging things away from the house. I became adept at knocking out street lights. There was plenty of gravel lying around at the edge of the road. After dusk I could bend down, pick up a stone, flick it up at the light, and be halfway home before the pieces of shattered bulb hit the ground. These were small-time depredations but they led on to bigger things.

Every Saturday afternoon at the pictures there was a feature film, sixteen cartoons and an episode each from four different serials. The programme just went on and on like Bayreuth. The Margaret Street children would join up with the Irene Street children and the combined mass would add themselves unto the Sunbeam Avenue children and the aggregate would join the swarm of children from all the other areas all moving north along Rocky Point Road towards Rockdale, where the Odeon stood. In summer the concrete footpaths were hot. The asphalt footpaths were even hotter: bubbles of tar formed, to be squashed flat by our leathery bare feet. Running around on macadamized playgrounds throughout the spring, by summer we had feet that could tread on a drawing pin and hardly feel it.

When you got to the Odeon the first thing you did was stock up with lollies. Lollies was the word for what the English call sweets and the Americans call candy. Some of the more privileged children had upwards of five shillings each to dispose of, but in fact two bob was enough to buy you as much as you could eat. Everyone, without exception, bought at least one Hoadley's Violet Crumble Bar. It was a slab of dense, dry honeycomb coated with chocolate. So frangible was the honeycomb that it would shatter when bitten, scattering bright yellow shrapnel. It was like trying to eat a Ming vase. The honeycomb would go soft only after a day's exposure to direct sunlight. The chocolate surrounding it, however, would liquefy after only ten minutes in a dark cinema.

Fantails came in a weird, blue, rhomboidal packet shaped like an isosceles triangle with one corner missing. Each individual Fantail was wrapped in a piece of paper detailing a film star's biography – hence the pun, fan tales. The Fantail itself was a chocolate-coated toffee so glutinous that it could induce lockjaw in a mule. People had to have their mouths chipped open with a cold chisel. One packet of Fantails would last an average human being for ever. A group of six small boys could go through a packet during the course of a single afternoon at the pictures, but it took hard work and involved a lot of strangled crying in the dark. Any fillings you had in your second teeth would be removed instantly, while children who still had any first teeth left didn't keep them long.

The star lolly, outstripping even the Violet Crumble Bar and the Fantail in popularity, was undoubtedly the Jaffa. A packet of Jaffas was loaded like a cluster bomb with about fifty globular lollies the size of ordinary marbles. The Jaffa had a dark chocolate core and a brittle orange candy coat: in cross section it looked rather like the planet Earth. It presented two alternative ways of being eaten, each with its allure. You could fondle the Jaffa on the tongue until your saliva ate its way through the casing, whereupon the taste of chocolate would invade your mouth with a sublime, majestic inevitability. Or you could bite straight through and submit the interior of your head to a stunning explosion of flavour. Sucking and biting your way through forty or so Jaffas while Jungle Jim wrestled with the croco-diles, you nearly always had a few left over after the stomach could take no more. The spare Jaffas made ideal ammunition. Flying through the dark, they would bounce off an infantile skull with the noise of bullets hitting a bell. They showered on the stage when the manager came out to announce the lucky ticket. The Jaffa is a part of Australia's theatrical heritage. There was a famous occasion, during the Borovansky Ballet production of *Giselle* at the Tivoli in Sydney, when Albrecht was forced to abandon the performance. It was a special afternoon presentation of the ballet before an audience of schoolchildren. Lying in a swoon while awaiting the reappear-ance of Giselle, Albrecht aroused much comment because of his protuberant codpiece. After being hit square on the power-bulge by a speeding Jaffa, he woke up with a rush and hopped off the stage in the stork position.

Everyone either ate steadily or raced up and down the aisles to and from the toilet, or all three. The uproar was continuous, like Niagara. Meanwhile the programme was unreeling in front of us. The feature film was usually a Tarzan, a Western, or the kind of Eastern Western in which George Macready played the grand vizier. At an even earlier stage I had been to the pictures with my mother and been continuously frightened without understanding what was going on – the mere use of music to reinforce tension, for example, was enough to drive me under the seat for the rest of the evening. At a later stage I accompanied my mother to every change of evening double bill both at Ramsgate and Rockdale – a total of four films a week, every week for at least a decade. But nothing before or since had the impact of those feature films at the Rockdale Saturday matinees.

In those days Johnny Weissmuller was making his difficult transition from Tarzan to Jungle Jim. As Tarzan he got fatter and fatter until finally he was too fat to be plausible, whereupon he was obliged to put on a safari suit and become Jungle Jim. I was glad to learn subsequently that as Jungle Jim he had a piece of the action and was at last able to bank some money. At the time, his transmogrification looked to me like an unmitigated tragedy. His old Tarzan movies were screened again and again. Many times I dived with Tarz off Brooklyn Bridge during the climactic scene of *Tarzan's New York Adventure*. In my mind I duplicated the back somersaults executed by Johnny's double as he swung from vine to vine on his way to rescue the endangered Jane and Boy from the invading ivory hunters. In one of the Tarzan movies there is a terrible sequence where one lot of natives gives another lot an extremely thin time by arranging pairs of tree trunks so that they will fly apart and pull the victim to pieces. This scene stayed with me as a paradigm of evil. No doubt if I saw the same film today I would find the sequence as crudely done as everything else ever filmed on Poverty Row. But at the time it seemed a vision of cruelty too horrible even to think about.

I can remember having strong ideas about which cartoons were funny and which were not. Mr Magoo and Gerald McBoing-Boing, with their stylised backgrounds and elliptical animation, had not yet arrived on the scene. Cartoons were still in that hyper-realist phase which turns out in retrospect to have been their golden age. The standards of animation set by Walt Disney and MGM cost a lot of time, effort and money, but as so often happens the art reached its height at the moment of maximum resistance from the medium. Knowing nothing of these theoretical matters, I simply consumed the product. I knew straight away that the Tom and Jerry cartoons were the best. In fact I even knew straight away that some Tom and Jerry cartoons were better than others. There was an early period when Tom's features were puffy and he ran with a lope, motion being indicated by the streaks that animators call speed lines. In the later period Tom's features had an acute precision and his every move was made fully actual, with no stylisation at all. Meanwhile Jerry slimmed down and acquired more expressiveness. The two periods were clearly separated in my mind, where they were dubbed 'old drawings' and 'new drawings'. I remember being able to tell which category a given Tom and Jerry cartoon fell into from seeing the first few frames. Eventually I could tell just from the logo. I remember clearly the feeling of disappointment if it was going to be old drawings and the feeling of elation if it was going to be new drawings.

But the serials were what caught my imagination most, especially the ones in which the hero was masked. It didn't occur to me until much later that the producers, among whom Sam Katzman was the doyen, kept the heroes masked so that the leading actors could not ask for more money. At the time it just seemed logical to me that a hero should wear a mask. It didn't have to be as elaborate as Batman's mask. I admired Batman, despite the worrying wrinkles in the arms and legs of his costume, which attained a satisfactory tautness only in the region of his stomach. But Robin's mask was easier to copy. So was the Black Commando's. My favourite serials were those in which masked men went out at night and melted mysteriously into the urban landscape. Science-fiction serials were less appealing at that stage, while white-hunter epics like *The Lost City of the Jungle* merely seemed endless. I saw all fourteen episodes of *The Lost City of the Jungle* except the last. It would have made no difference if I had seen only the last episode and missed the thirteen leading up to it. The same things happened every week. Either two parties of white hunters in solar topees searched for each other in one part of the jungle, or else the same two parties of white hunters in solar topees sought to avoid each other in another part of the jungle. Meanwhile tribesmen from the Lost City either captured representatives of both parties and took them to the High Priestess for sacrifice, or else ran after them when they escaped. Sometimes white hunters escaping ran into other white hunters being captured, and were either recaptured or helped the others escape. It was obvious even to my unschooled eye that there was only about half an acre of jungle, all of it composed of papier mâché. By the end of each episode it was beaten flat. The screen would do a spiral wipe around an image of the enthroned High Priestess, clad in a variety of teatowels and gesturing oburately with a collection of prop sceptres while one of the good white hunters – you could tell a good one from a bad one by the fact that a bad one always sported a very narrow moustache – was lowered upside down into a pit of limp scorpions.

Exotic locations left me cold. What I liked was the idea of possessing unlimited powers and yet blending undetectably into everyday life, although not so undetectably that ordinary people would not be able to tell at a glance who I was. The trouble with Superman, Captain Marvel, Captain Marvel Jr, Batman and the rest of the dual-identity squad was that no one thought much of them when they were in mufti. Lois Lane practically wore her lip out sneering at Clark Kent while the poor drongo stood there and took it. Billy Batson was always getting his crutch kicked. Bruce Wayne was derided as a playboy. None of that happened to me. Discreetly informing people one by one, I made sure everybody in the district knew that when dusk descended it was I, and nobody else, who became the Flash of Lightning.

5. ENTER THE FLASH OF LIGHTNING

Thus there was no fruitless speculation about my real identity as I streaked past in my green felt mask and black cape. Like Dracula, the Flash of Lightning made his appearance only after nightfall. In the hours between sunset and bedtime an imposing figure could be seen outlined against the stars. In less time than it took to pronounce his name in an awed whisper, he was gone, running down one side of the street and up the other, darting along driveways, clambering over back fences and making his inexorable progress from back yard to back yard. You would not have known, when this sinister avatar caught and slipped your startled gaze, that his mask and cape had been made by his mother.

Actually the Flash of Lightning's cape was almost his undoing. It was fastened at his neck by two short lengths of rope tied in a bow. Flitting awkwardly homeward over our back-yard fence one night, I got the rope tangled around the top of a paling. The result should have been death by strangulation. There was a frantic, wordless struggle in which the Flash of Lightning's proverbial dignity was overwhelmed by a mortal urge to breathe. Just when it looked like curtains for the Flash of Lightning, the cape popped a seam and I dropped vertically into the choco patch.

But such failures were few. Generally the Flash of Lightning was a success. Other boys started appearing in masks and capes. Moments after the sun dropped they would come swooping towards me like fruit bats. Obviously everything was up to me. Standing around in mysterious attire, surrogates of the Flash of Lightning awaited their instructions. Meanwhile they announced their names. There was a Green Flash, a Black Flash and a Red Flash. Graham Truscott wanted to call himself the Flash of Thunder. I took pity on them all and gave them their assignments. These started off as harmless games of doorbell-ringing but became less cute with time. Throwing gravel on

Mrs Branthwaite's roof must have been agony for her, even though it was endlessly amusing to us. Films of *Kristallnacht* never fail to make me think of those brilliantly staged raids by the Flash of Lightning, in which a dozen handfuls of gravel would all land on Mrs Branthwaite's tiles only seconds before the perpetrators, magically divested of capes and masks, were back at home sitting around the Kosi stove and helping their parents listen to *Pick a Box*. The difference between mischief and murder is no greater than what the law will allow. All we were allowed, thank God, was mischief – and in retrospect that looks bad enough.

What I had going, of course, was a gang. Only lack of opportunity saved us from outright deliquency. There was a limit to what destruction we could cause, but everything within that limit sooner or later got done. Overwhelming temptation was provided by a sudden increase in the number of building sites. The bottom half of the street, towards the park, had previously been vacant blocks. These were suddenly all built on at once by the Housing Commission. The plan was to provide a lot of new houses in a tearing hurry. People at the top of the street started sneering at the people at the bottom of the street before the people at the bottom of the street had even moved in. Adults were agreed that this sudden influx would lower the tone. By night, and even by day if conditions were favourable, the Flash of Lightning and his gang made sure that work on the building sites proceeded as slowly as possible.

It is remarkable how much damage a group of small boys can do to a building site if it is left unguarded. In loose moments I might pride myself on possessing a creative impulse but I don't have to do too much introspection before being forced to admit that a destructive impulse is in there somewhere as well. Under my supervision, dumps of mixed lime were well seeded with bricks. A brick dropped from high up into soft lime makes a very satisfactory glurp. Studded with bricks like ice-cream full of chipped chocolate, the lime quickly became unusable. We smashed tiles by the hundred. Porcelain lavatory bowls were reduced to their constituent molecules. Timber frames stood upright, waiting for brick walls to be formed around them. Using an umbrella as a parachute, the Flash of Lightning could jump from the top of one of these frames and land in a sandpit. Or the Flash of Lightning thought he could. The Flash of Lightning was lucky to land perfectly flat, so that he was merely winded instead of crippled for life.

That put a temporary end to my share in the marauding. But if we had all gone out every night and worked until dawn taking apart everything that had been put together, transformation would still have been inevitable. The district was changing. The poultry farm was sold up and subdivided into blocks of building land. Irene Street was extended through it, to join up with a new road called Madrers Avenue, so that there were now two ways up to Rocky Point Road. This must have happened in fits and starts over the course of years, but I remember it as a surge of innovation. Concrete kerbing was laid down, so that everybody's front strip had two edges to be kept sharply defined instead of one. Most sensational change of all, the sewer came. Vast trenches were dug in which pipes were laid. My mother boldly proposed that one of the miraculous new devices should be installed not only in the outside lavatory but in the bathroom itself. The very notion spelled doom for the dunny man.

Ever since I could remember, the dunny man had come running down the driveway once a week. From inside the house, we could hear his running footsteps. Then we could hear the rattle and thump as he lifted the lavatory, took out the full pan, clipped on a special lid, and set down an empty pan in its place. After more rattling and banging, there was an audible intake of breath as he hefted the full pan on to his shoulder. Then the footsteps went back along the driveway, slower this time but still running. From outside in the street there was rattling, banging and shouting as the full pan was loaded on to the dunny cart along with all the other full pans. I often watched the dunny cart from the front window. As it slowly made its noisome way down the street, the dunny men ran to and from it with awesome expertise. They wore shorts, sand-shoes, and nothing else except a suntan suspiciously deep on the forearms. Such occasional glimpses were all one was allowed by one's parents and all that was encouraged even by the dunny men themselves. They preferred to work in nobody's company except their own. They were a band apart.

Years went by without those running footsteps being acknowledged by any other means except a bottle of beer left standing in the lavatory on the closest visiting day to Christmas Day. Otherwise it seemed generally agreed that the lavatory pan was changed by magic.

From day to day it got fuller and fuller, generating maggots by about the third day. To combat the smell, honeysuckle was grown on a trellis outside the lavatory door, in the same way that the European nobility had recourse to perfume when they travelled by galley. The maggots came from blowflies and more blowflies came from the maggots. Blowflies were called blowies. The Australian climate, especially on the Eastern seaboard in the latitude of Sydney, was specifically designed to accommodate them. The blowies' idea of a good time was to hang around the dunny waiting for the seat to be lifted. They were then faced with the challenge of getting through the hole before it was blocked by the descending behind of the prospective occupant. There was no time for any fancy flying. Whether parked on the wall or stacking around in a holding pattern near the ceiling, every blowie was geared up to make either a vertical dive from high altitude or a death-defying low-level run through the rapidly decreasing air-space between the seat and your descending arse. The moment the seat came up, suddenly it was Pearl Harbor.

Once inside, enclosed under a dark sky, the blowies set about dumping their eggs. The memory of the results has always, in my mind, given extra vividness to Shakespeare's line about life in excrements. God knows what would have happened if ever the dunny men had gone on strike. Even as things were, by the end of the week the contents of the pan would be getting too close for comfort. Luckily the dunny man was a model of probity. Never putting a foot wrong, he carried out his Sisyphean task in loyal silence. Only when he was about to leave our lives for ever did his concentration slip. Perhaps he foresaw that one day the sewer would come to everywhere in the world. Perhaps, in order to ward off these grim thoughts, he partook of his Christmas beer while still engaged in the task. Because it was on that day – the day before Christmas Eve – that the dunny man made his solitary mistake.

My mother and I were having breakfast. I heard the dunny man's footsteps thumping along the driveway, with a silent pause as he hurdled my bicycle, which in my habitual carelessness I had left lying there. I heard the usual thumps, bangs and heaves. I could picture the brimming pan, secured with the special clipped lid, hoisted high on his shoulder while he held my mother's gift bottle of beer in his other, appreciative hand. Then the footsteps started running back the other way. Whether he forgot about my bicycle, or simply

mistimed his jump, there was no way of telling. Suddenly there was
the noise of . . . well, it was mainly the noise of a dunny man running
full tilt into a bicycle. The uproar was made especially ominous by
the additional noise – tiny but significant in context – of a clipped
lid springing off.

While my mother sat there with her hands over her eyes I raced
out through the fly-screen door and took a look down the driveway.
The dunny man, overwhelmed by the magnitude of his tragedy, had
not yet risen to his feet. Needless to say, the contents of the pan
had been fully divulged. All the stuff had come out. But what was
really remarkable was the way none of it had missed him. Already
you could hear a gravid hum in the air. Millions of flies were on
their way towards us. They were coming from all over Australia. For
them, it was a Durbar, a moot, a gathering of the clans. For us, it
was the end of an era.

Once the new lavatories were installed, the bathroom became the
centre of all ablutions. I no longer took a book to the outside lavatory
and sat absorbed, the door thrown open to admit light. Just as well,
because towards the end of the unsewered epoch I was caught in that
position by Valma Chappelow, the girl from across the road. She was
older than I was too, which made it worse. She came pounding
around the corner of the house on her way to borrow something that
her scatter-brained mother had forgotten to buy when out shopping –
bread, butter, milk, meat or some other frippery like that. Valma got
a good look at me sitting there with my pants around my ankles.
She made sure everybody in the district got to hear about it. She
told her pen-pals. Years later at a party in Caringbah, more than
twenty miles away by train, I met a stranger who knew all about it.
If I went to live in the Outer Hebrides I would probably find the
inhabitants all giggling behind their hands.

But the district didn't change as much as it stayed the same. As I
grew older, my picture of where I lived grew wider and more complicated. The expanding of one's vision is usually enough in itself to
generate a feeling that everything is falling apart. Nevertheless one
had a sense of constancy even at the time, and looking back on it I
can see that my whole childhood was remarkable for the amount of
entertainment permanently on flow. All you had to do was turn the
tap and bend your pursed lips to the bubbler.

Admittedly some of the local adults were terrifying. Gail Thorpe's husband Wally was a pastry cook whose business had failed. His principal means of revenge was to brow-beat his wife, who went away for electric convulsion therapy every year or so. The only result of the treatment was to alter the position of her nervous smile, so that instead of being on the front of her face it ended up under one ear. By the time it drifted around to the front again she was ready for another course of treatment. Wally also tormented his children in various ways. He would go on tickling his younger daughter, Carmel, long after the desperately sobbing child had begged him to stop. Watching these performances, I woke up early to the reality of human evil. News of mass political atrocity has always saddened me but never come as a surprise. The only time I tried to interfere with one of Wally Thorpe's divertissements, he swore at me for ten minutes on end at the top of his voice. I went home stunned. My mother did her best to tell him off but it was clear that at such moments she sorely felt her loneliness. That night was one of the few times I ever heard her say, 'I wish your father had come home.'

The Goodhews were likewise a bit of a pain. They were so protective about their sons, Darryl and Des, that they would trail them about, checking up on what was going on. This could be awkward when what was going on was a full-scale battle involving the throwing of stones and bits of fibro. These battles usually took place up in the quarry, with the defenders occupying fox-holes in the heights and the attackers moving up through the lowlands from one clump of lantana to another. Very properly concerned about their children losing an eye, the Goodhew parents would invariably show up just in time to see one of their little darlings sconed by a rock or sliced open by a whizzing piece of fibro. The fuss would take weeks to die down. According to Mr and Mrs Goodhew, their children were being led astray by the local toughs. In fact their own progeny were the worst of the lot. Darryl Goodhew could look wonderfully innocent when his parents were around, but he was a dead shot when they weren't looking. He once knocked Beverley Hindmarsh off her dinkey at an incredible range. The missile was a lump of sandstone. He was sharing a fox-hole with me at the top of the quarry. It was the best fox-hole: you had to crawl through a lantana tunnel to get to it. Halfway down Margaret Street, Beverley was a dot on the horizon when Darryl launched the rock. It was a long time on its way. I had lost sight of it long before she abruptly stopped pedalling and crashed

sideways with awful finality. Darryl immediately ran towards the
scene of the crime with a look of concern. His air of innocence was
so persuasive that Beverley's parents never thought of blaming him.
They would have blamed me if I had been stupid enough to emerge
from the lantanas. I was already established as Beverley's persecutor,
having pinched her bottom one day with a metal reinforcing clip
stolen from a building site. It was meant to be a joke, but it took a
piece out of her pointed behind. I got belted for that, and if I surfaced
now I would get belted again. Besides, Darryl would undoubtedly
have pointed the finger at me. So I stayed up there until the stars
came out. Beverley suffered nothing more severe than shock and a
badly bruised infantile bud. When you consider that the stone might
just as easily have removed an eyeball, you can see that we must have
had a guardian angel.

Otherwise the adults left us pretty much alone. On the weekends
we made our big expeditions to the pictures, the swamp or the dump.
In the afternoons and evenings after school we played in the street.
We played cock-a-lorum from one side of the street to the other. We
played a game with half a dozen sticks spaced out along the front
strip and you were allowed to take only one step between every two
sticks. You kept moving the sticks further and further apart until
nobody was left in except some visiting kid built like a praying
mantis. You had to do as many chin-ups as you could on the box
tree. There were complicated bike races around the block. The older
boys did a lot of elaborate riding up and down in front of the girls,
who used to sit in line on the Chappelows' front fence. Warren
Hartigan could sit on his bicycle backwards and ride past very slowly.
They stopped giggling when he did that. Graham Truscott should
never have tried it. A spoke from one of the wheels went right
through his calf.

We played hidings and countries. In countries you threw a tennis
ball in the air and ran, calling out the name of a country. Each player
had the name of a country. If your country was called, you tried to
catch the ball before it bounced, whereupon you could throw it up
again and call out somebody else's country. If you only caught it on
the bounce, you had to . . . Forget it. The rules went on and on. All
that mattered was to throw the ball high. Greg Brennan could put it
into orbit. He lived next door but one. Nobody lived very far away.
We played on and on through the hot afternoon into the brief dusk

and the sudden nightfall. Towards sunset the adults would appear on the front porches and start watering the lawn. They would tune the nozzles to a fine spray, which would drift in the air at the first breath of the summer wind that came every night. Usually it was a nor'easter. Sometimes it was the Southerly Buster. The Christmas beetles and cowboy beetles held jamborees around the street lights, battering themselves against the white enamel reflectors and falling into the street. They lay on their backs with their legs struggling. When you picked them up they pulsed with the frustrated strength of their clenched wing muscles.

Before there was the refrigerator there was the ice-chest. A block of ice was loaded into it every couple of days. If you left a bottle of lemonade on top of the block of ice the bottle would sink in and get deliciously cold. We weren't rich but we had meat three times a day, even if it had to be rabbit. Before myxomatosis was introduced, the Australian rabbit was a lightly built racing model that made excellent food. Only in a protein-rich country like Australia could such a marvellous beast be looked down on. Left-over rabbit legs could be put in the ice-chest after dinner and eaten for breakfast next day. Surrounded with cold white fat, they looked like maps of Greenland and tasted like a dryad's inner thigh.

When the watermelon man came there was more melon than anyone could eat. You scooped the lines of black seeds out with your crooked finger and bit a face-sized piece out of the cool, crisp, red, sweet slice. Chomping away until your ears were full of sugar. Slurping and snarling until there was hardly a trace of pink left on the white lining of the rind. There was a kind of drink-on-a-stick called the Skybomber – a tetrahedron of deep green, lime-flavoured water frozen so hard that its surface had no grain. You had to suck it for half an hour before it gave in and became friable. Then whole layers of it would come away sweetly and easily in your numb mouth, as if the molecules had been arranged in strata, like graphite. Every time I see that shade of green I think immediately of Skybombers.

I'm sure it was aesthetically justifiable for Proust to concentrate on his piece of cake, but in fact almost anything can take you back. There is a rhapsodic stretch about ice-cream in *La Prisonnière* that proves the point exactly. He imagines his tongue shaping the ice-creams of long ago, and suddenly all the past comes rushing back with authentically uncontrolled force. Elsewhere in the novel he keeps his memory on a tight rein. Herzen was closer to the truth when he said that every memory calls up a dozen others. The real miracle of Proust is the discipline with which he stemmed the flow. Everything is a Madeleine.

6. DIB, DIB, DIB, DIB

Somewhere about this time I was in the Cubs. When the time came for graduation to the Scouts, I was not accepted, and thus became, for the brief time before I tossed the whole thing in, the oldest Cub in the First Kogarah Wolf Cub Pack and probably the world. Lacking the precious gift of taciturnity, I could never achieve the grim face essential to success in paramilitary organizations. Considering this fatal flaw, it is remarkable how many of them I tried to get into. The Cubs were merely the first in a long line. My mother made my scarf. It had to be in First Kogarah colours – maroon with yellow piping. She made me a woggle out of leather. Every Cub had to have a woggle. It held your scarf on. As well as the woggle, there were special sock-tops – called something like fuggles – which always fell down. After you passed your Tenderfoot you got a wolf's head, or diggle, to wear on your cap. Also on the cap went a scraggle for each year of service. In addition to woggles, fuggles, diggles and scraggles, successful Cubs had the right, indeed obligation, to wear a whole collection of insignia and badges. The second in command of a sub-pack of six Cubs was called a Seconder and wore a yellow stripe on his sleeve. The commander of a sub-pack was called a Sixer and wore two stripes. A sixer in his final year would be so covered in decorations that promotion to the Scouts became a physical necessity, lest he expire under the weight.

Ruling over the whole pack was Akela. Her name was taken from *The Jungle Book*. She wore a brown uniform with a Scout hat. Otherwise she, too, was burdened down with woggles and fuggles. At the beginning of our weekly meetings, we Cubs would squat in a circle and worship her. While squatting, we made wolf-head signs with our fingers and pointed them at the floor. Then we chanted, 'Akela, we'll do our best. We'll dib dib dib dib. We'll dob dob dob dob . . .' This routine was climaxed by a mass throwing back of heads and emitting of supposedly lupine howls. I used to get through the dibbing and dobbing all right but during the howling I usually rolled over backwards.

My lack of poise could possibly have stemmed from a never-to-be-satisfied wonderment about what dibbing and dobbing might actually consist of, but more probably it was just the result of an overwhelming love for Akela. I adored her. A school teacher in real life, she was a mother figure with none of the drawbacks. For her own part, she must have found me a problem, since I trailed her around everywhere. The theory of Scouting, or in this case Cubbing, was that boys should become independent through the acquisition of woodcraft and related skills. All I ever learned was how to attach myself to Akela's skirt. This made it hard for Akela and Baloo to be alone. Baloo the Bear was a young adult King's Scout who visited the pack once a month. Decorated like a combination of Boris Godunov and General MacArthur, a King's Scout in full regalia could be looked at only through smoked glass.

Baloo also accompanied us on camps. We went on a camp to Heathcote, in the National Park. My mother came along to help. I had talked her into coming by telling her that every other mother would be there and that the camp site was yards from the station. It was seven thousand yards from the station. Mine was the only mother large-hearted enough to contribute her services. The trek to the camp site was along bush tracks and down cliffs. Swinging white-lipped from vines, my mother vowed to pick a bone with me later. By the time we got to the camp site she was too far gone to expend any of her remaining energy remonstrating with me. She cooked the sausages while Akela and Baloo put up the tents. It took Akela and Baloo about an hour's walk in the bush to find each tent pole. Meanwhile my mother doled out the exploding sausages and bandaged the hands of those Cubs – all of them heavily decorated with badges denoting proficiency in woodcraft – who had burned themselves picking up aluminium mugs of hot tea.

That night it rained like the Great Flood. The river rose. Tents collapsed. All the Cubs ended up in one big tent with my mother. Akela ended up in a pup tent with Baloo. Shortly afterwards they were married. Presumably Akela gave birth to either a bear or a wolf. By that time I had left the Cubs. You couldn't get into the Scouts without a certain number of badges. My own score was zero. Besides, I couldn't face a change of Akelas.

The big change I couldn't get out of was being sent to a special school. In fourth class at Kogarah, when we were all about ten years old, we took an IQ test. It was the Stanford Binet, on which I score about 140. On the more searching Wechsler-Bellevue I get about 135. Such results are enough to put me into the 98th percentile, meaning that 97 per cent of any given population is likely to be less good at doing these tests than I am. This is nothing to boast about. Intelligence starts being original only in the next percentile up from mine, where the scores go zooming off the scale. Time has taught me, too slowly alas, that there is nothing extraordinary about my mental capacities. In my romantic phase, which lasted for too long, I was fond of blaming my sense of loneliness on superior intellect. In fact the causes were, and are, psychological.

At the time, of course, none of these questions came up. My mother was simply informed that her son had revealed himself as belonging to a category which demanded two years of special education in the Opportunity 'C' school at Hurstville. Opportunity 'A' schools were for the handicapped and Opportunity 'C' schools were for the gifted. At either end of the scale special schooling was a dubious privilege, since it involved travel by electric train. Hurstville was only three stops down the Illawarra line but even such a short voyage offered plenty of opportunities for sudden death. Mothers very understandably worried themselves sick about what their precious little sons might be getting up to on trains that conveyed whole generations of school children at dizzy speeds without benefit of automatic doors. For boys of any age it was considered mandatory to stand near doorways. For older boys it was compulsory to stand at the very edge of the doorway, holding the door open with their shoulders, draping their arms negligently behind their backs with their hands loosely grasping the door handle, and keeping balance with their feet and legs as the swaying train hurtled through cuttings and over viaducts. Stanchions had been provided every hundred yards. They were meant to hold up the power lines, but had the additional function of braining anybody who stuck his head out of the window. Everybody stuck his head out of the window, drawing it back again as a stanchion loomed.

Every second train was a through, meaning it did not stop at

Carlton and Allawah but attempted to break the world land-speed record on an uninterrupted run from Kogarah to Hurstville or vice versa. At either end it was considered *de rigueur* to alight as early as possible. Anyone waiting for the train to stop was considered a cissy. The more athletic boys could languidly step off and hit the platform running flat out. If they mistimed it they ended up with a gravel rash starting at the forehead and extending all the way to the toes. The sport came to an end when the champion, a boy named Newell, got his stations mixed up and stepped off at Allawah from the through train to Hurstville. When we got the news about his injuries – his left femur, apparently, was the only bone that remained intact – we became somewhat meeker about leaving the train early. Nevertheless the deaths continued to run at the rate of one a year. It was another ten years before automatic doors were tried out even experimentally. Perhaps someone was afraid that the Australian national character would be weakened.

At Hurstville there was an Opportunity 'C' fifth and sixth class with about thirty of us freaks in each class. Otherwise the school was normal. The freaks strove to be even more normal than everybody else – an instructive example of the Australian reluctance to stand out from the pack for any reason other than athletic skill. Some of our number, however, ranked as exotica no matter how hard they tried to blend into the scenery. There was a boy called Nelson, for example, who made Graham Truscott look emaciated. Nelson needed two desks. But he could play chess at an exalted level. So could almost everybody else in the class except me. I didn't even know the moves. A lot of the boys in the class wore glasses and had notes from their parents excusing them from soccer, swimming, running, jumping or even crossing the playground unattended. They were all drafted into the school's fife band. On sports day they spent the afternoon marching awkwardly backwards and forwards while playing 'Colonel Bogey' on their black wooden fifes. The total effect was pathetic in the extreme.

The fife players also tended to wear those cissy sandals that looked like ordinary shoes with bits cut out of them. Whenever I could get away with it I defiantly stuck to bare feet. This was not, I think, any kind of class-conscious social gesture. I had no inkling of class differences. In Australia there is a widespread illusion that there are no class barriers. In fact they exist, but it is possible to remain unaware of them. There are social strata whose occupants feel superior but there is almost nobody who feels inferior, probably because the poor are as well nourished as the rich. It never occurred to me that most of the boys in the class came from more privileged homes than mine. If I had been smarter it might have done. The evidence was abundant. Graham Slender brought expensive toys to school. His father had bought them for him in America. One of the toys was a machine gun that fired ping-pong balls. For a few delirious seconds he showered the astonished class with bouncing celluloid spheres before the gun was impounded. Robert Lunn, David Carnaby, John Elstub and I usually occupied the back four desks in the class. Lunn seemed inordinately well supplied with funds. Sometimes after school he would shout half a dozen of us to a cream-cake blow-out in one of the Hurstville teashops. He and I both knew what a blow-out was, since we had both been reading English comics and boys' weeklies. Most Australian boys at that time read American comics but a few read English ones as well. With Lunn it was all in the family: his parents brought him up in the English manner and eventually he went to Sydney Grammar and after that to Duntroon. With me it was an accident. When I had a suspected case of diphtheria just after the war I was taken by screaming ambulance to South Coast Hospital near Bunnerong power-house for three unforgettable weeks of ice cream and lemonade. There were papers like *Tip-Top* and *Radio Fun* lying around in the playroom. I made my mother buy more of them. On visiting days my mother would arrive looking like a news-vendor. It took the edge off having to pee in a jar.

From then on I read *Tip-Top* every week and later graduated to the *Wizard, Rover, Hotspur* and *Champion*. By the time I got to Hurstville school I was an expert on these papers and could discuss their contents endlessly. I certainly identified with characters like Braddock VC and Alf Tupper, the Tough of the Track. Braddock was a non-commissioned pilot who defeated the Luftwaffe single-handed but contemptuously refused all promotions and decorations except the VC, whose ribbon he wore half hanging off. Stuffed shirts were always objecting to his behaviour in railway carriages and then having to apologize when they found out he was the RAF's greatest hero. Alf Tupper trained on fish and chips and ran the first four-minute mile. While admiring the prowess of these demigods, I completely failed to realize that they were fantasy figures specifically aimed at

Britain's lower orders. Perhaps Lunn had a better understanding but I suspect that he, too, was largely in the dark. There was a serial in the *Wizard* about a poor lad who with the aid of his tremendously self-sacrificing mother was able to attend a Public School. He wore patched trousers and had to endure much scorn from the toffs but ended up Captain of Swimming, Cricket, Football, Debates and finally of the School itself. I don't think I really understood what this story was all about. After all, in Australia all the schools were public – or so it seemed. It never occurred to me that in an English context 'public' meant 'private'. Possibly because I was clueless, but more likely because the provocation simply wasn't there, I didn't develop any kind of chip on my shoulder until much later, so the social content of almost everything I was reading failed to register, even when social content was the only kind of content it had.

By this time I was starting to devour books as well as magazines and comics. I went Biggles-crazy and generally became an expert on aeroplanes. While the chess players were getting on with their chess I would be busy reading *Worrals Wipes It Off* or memorizing air-recognition charts. At the age of eleven I could recognize a photograph of any aircraft that had been built at any time in any country in the world. The Opportunity system gave its pupils plenty of time to develop such interests. The normal curriculum was dealt with in the morning and the afternoon was left free for the development of potentialities. Unfortunately like most educational concepts this idea yielded pretty thin results. No reflection on our teacher, Mr Davis – who had been a navigator in a Lancaster during the war and could turn a back somersault off the one-metre board – but learning to recognize aeroplanes is not the same as acquiring knowledge. The inevitable result was that those boys who were receiving some guidance from home flourished while those whose sole stimulus was the school did little more than fool around with 'projects'. Since the choice of project was left to us, the results were hopelessly variable as to quality. One boy with bifocals would be turning an old washing-machine into a particle accelerator while the boy at the next desk would be cutting out pictures of giraffes. I've just remembered the name of the boy at the next desk. His name was Tommy Pillans. He was unhappy at home and committed suicide in his first year with us – the first premature death in my generation. His desk was empty for only a few days. Then there was a reshuffle. Perhaps part of

Nelson moved into it. Anyway, that was Tommy Pillans. Gone without a ripple. Not for the last time, I accommodated myself with ease to the idea of someone vanishing.

As well as glasses, John Elstub had all the other attributes of dampness – shoe-like sandals, knee-length khaki shorts, fife, and a purse full of notes from his mother saying that he was not to be exposed to direct sunlight. The only day he ever appeared on the soccer field he ran away from the ball. He was the son of an academic of some kind and spent his time at home absorbing the contents of the *Encyclopedia Britannica*. He always knew the answers but had a way of calling out 'Sir! Sir!' that not even Sir could stand. Elstub was a standing joke. Yet he was reading *Ulysses* while I was learning to tell a Messerschmitt Bf 109E from a Bf 109F. (The Bf 109E had struts supporting the tail-plane and the Bf 109F didn't.) I was invited to Elstub's house once. There were a lot of pre-war American aviation magazines lying around. I asked if I could borrow them and when I got home I cut them up and pasted the best pictures in my scrapbooks. Next day at school I presented Elstub with the *fait accompli* and he said it was all right. It never occurred to me at the time that he had behaved well and I badly, or that what I had done would have been considered thoughtless in someone half my age. I was simply convinced that aircraft were my department and that those magazines had no business being in Elstub's possession.

During the afternoons at school I spent a lot of time constructing sand-pit battlefields full of lead soldiers. Later on, copying the school newspaper in *The Fifth Form at St Dominic's*, I started a wall magazine to which everyone was invited to contribute. I usually decided that hardly anybody's contributions were up to standard except mine. At the annual exhibition day, held in the school library, my sand-pit battlefield made a huge impact. While all the parents stood devoutly around, I explained the strategic picture and announced that token detonations had been arranged in order to represent the effect of artillery fire and tactical bombing. Actually Slender, a dab hand at such matters, had sown the sand with bungers which could be set off in sequence by touching a wire to a battery. Slender was under the sand-tray with the battery. At the rehearsal we used Kwong Man Lung penny bungers and everything went all right. But for the performance proper Slender had planted something more ambitious – fourpenny bungers the size of a stick of dynamite. On top of this he got nervous and touched the whole lot off at once. The Korean War was in progress at the time and the parents must have thought that the Chinese communists had arrived in Hurstville. One man jumped into his wife's arms – an extraordinary role-reversal which I would have laughed at if I had not had a mouth full of sand. It was cowardly of Slender not to come out.

The wall magazine was rather better received. Verbally it was derivative in every respect, with stories about heroic wartime fliers, athletes training on fish and chips, and stoic young schoolboys rising above their patched trousers to become Captain of the School. Nearly all of it was written by me. But I shared responsibility for graphic design with David Carnaby. In the wall magazine as in his notebooks, Carnaby had a subtle touch with lettering and a ravishing sense of colour. We usually shared the awards for the best set-out and decorated exercise books. I still like to think that my own lettering had a firmness of outline that his lacked. The grand designs were all mine. But he was unbeatable on tone and detail. Everything he did breathed a pastel elegance. It often happens that we are most touched by what we are least capable of. Evanescent delicacy is not the quality in the arts that I admire most, but it is often the characteristic by which I am most reduced to envy. Nowadays I know exactly what enchantment is being worked on me by Alain-Fournier's hedgerows or Monet's waterlilies. I can put 'Miroirs' on the turntable and willingly succumb. I know that I can't do it myself but nowadays I can live with the knowledge. In those days I would look over Carnaby's shoulder and wonder if it was worth going on at all.

But go on I did, finding success easy. I was made class captain – a clear endorsement of my personality and attainments. There was thus no pressure on me to change my ways, which remained selfish, noisy and maladroit. At that time I was as big as, or bigger than, the boys around me, so it was not entirely absurd when I presumed to dominate them. As the teacher's representative I could usually make them toe the line, confident in the knowledge that it was less trouble for them to obey than to resist. My biggest coup was to maintain discipline through the long rehearsals for the Queen's visit. This involved months of drill for every school in Sydney, so that finally when everything was put together in the Showground the Queen and Prince Philip would be stunned by a co-ordinated display of calisthenics and flag-waving. For two days before the actual event we shone our shoes, polished our belts, had our teeth filled, etc. On the day itself the school transferred *en masse* to the Showground, where our display team, with me as front right marker, lined up with hundreds of other such teams to await inspection by the Royal Party.

We stood for hours in the boiling sun. The Royal Party was running late. Children were fainting left and right, as if their serried ranks were subject to sniper fire. Suddenly there was a screech of tyres in the distance. The Queen and her consort screamed past us in a Land Rover. I remember that they were standing up. Each held on to the top of the windshield with one hand while giving the famous mechanical wave with the other. How their hats stayed on was a mystery, since they were travelling only slightly slower than a Formula One Grand Prix racing car. There were not too many details to remember, but it was evident that the Queen's complexion really was as advertised – peaches and cream. We then got on with our display. It was a measure of my almost psychopathic self-consciousness that I felt the Queen's eyes on me as I waved my flag. But I performed creditably, as did my team. Not counting Nelson, who had fainted long ago and been carried away on a couple of stretchers.

Generally it is our failures that civilize us. Triumph confirms us in our habits. I would probably have abused my power had I been given any. Fortunately my role as class captain was all responsibilities and no privileges. The most onerous duty was to keep order when Mr Davis was out of the room. I tried to do this by shouting 'Shut up!' at the top of my voice. Eventually I could stun the whole school by sheer lung-power. Otherwise, until the end of my stay there, Hurstville Opportunity 'C' hardly changed me at all, probably because what was going on at home was so intense.

I had enrolled myself in a family. The family were called the Meldrums and lived in Sunbeam Avenue. Mr Meldrum was a plumber. He and Mrs Meldrum had produced three children, all boys: in descending order of age they were Gary, Neil and Craig. There was also an Alsatian dog called Ruth, whom I will get to in a minute. All six of them lived in a house not much bigger than ours. Mr Meldrum wore a blue working singlet at all times. He was regarded in the district as something of a gypsy. In fact he was simply the most original man for miles. He made hardly any money but there was more going on in his house than in anybody else's. He had turned all the boys into good swimmers. Gary was exceptionally good and got his picture in the papers for swimming a mile at the age of ten. Neil was a bit of a black sheep and Craig was simply dense, but even they were encouraged in their interests. Neil was mad about stamps and Craig was held by Mr Meldrum to be a promising biologist. In fact Craig's biological studies consisted mainly of picking up privet grubs and eating them. He would also tuck into the occasional centipede. Mrs Meldrum's understandable hysteria at such moments would be overwhelmed by Mr Meldrum's gusto. He was the first man I ever met who had that. In short, he was a ready-made father figure.

The Meldrums taught me to swim. Mr Meldrum, Gary and Neil took me down to the creek in the park. Reeds lined the banks and willows kissed the surface. The water was as brown as oxtail soup but Mr Meldrum said that any water was clean if you could catch healthy fish in it. All the Meldrums could swim across the creek underwater. To me it seemed a fabulous distance. Gary showed me how to hold my breath and keep my eyes open underwater. I could see his hair floating. Inside an hour I was dog-paddling. Mr Meldrum threw his own boys up in the air to turn back somersaults. Then I rode on Gary's shoulders, Neil rode on his father's, and we had battles in the shallow water.

That was just the start. I think I was eight years old, or perhaps nine. Over the next few years I spent more and more time at the Meldrums'. I would bolt my dinner and scoot around to their place in time to join them for a second dessert. Thus I laid the foundation of my uncanny ability to inhale a meal instead of eating it. Another bad aspect was the inevitable encounter with Ruth. Like all dog-owning families, the Meldrums regarded their four-footed friend as some kind of genius. Ruth was Mr Meldrum's blind spot. He seemed to think that his house would not be safe without Ruth to guard it. Apart from an abundance of life there was nothing in the house worth stealing. Nor, had there been, would Ruth have ranked as an early choice to stand sentinel. She was undoubtedly ferocious enough, but was no brighter than any other dog. She vented most of her fury on the family and its close acquaintances. If any burglars had turned up she would probably have ignored them, or else let them in and minded their tools. For me, on the other hand, she never failed to go through her entire repertoire of savagery. While I waited, yelling weakly, on the outside of the trellis gate in the side passage, Ruth would hurl herself against the inside of it like a pile-driver and try to bite a piece out of it big enough to get at me through. I would stand petrified until a few of the Meldrums turned up, clubbed their pet into submission and dragged it back out of sight. Upon receipt of a written, signed guarantee that Ruth had been stapled to the ground with croquet hoops, I would advance trembling and join the family for dessert, tea and games.

There were scraps of dog-meat on the floor of the back veranda but Mr Meldrum's Rabelaisian spirit turned the chaos and squalor into luxury. He was a great one for word games after dinner. As a natural diplomat he was able to cope with the fact that I often turned out to be better at these than his own sons. Seeking his favour, I was too keen ever to try less hard. When the word games were over Mr and Mrs Meldrum would listen to the wireless in the lounge while the rest of us would try to cross the spare room in the dark without getting caught by the guard. You took turns being guard. The spare room lay at the end of the corridor and I remember it as being the size of the Grand Salon in the Louvre, although I suppose it could have been no bigger than a box room. Old cupboards and other articles of furniture were stored in it. It could be blacked out perfectly, so crossing it undetected was a test of the ability to move silently while consumed with fear. Neil had a scary trick, when he was guard, of dressing up in some frightening costume and suddenly switching the light on. The mere possibility of his doing this was enough to make the hair rise on my neck the way it did at the pictures when the music indicated tension or impending doom.

On Saturday afternoons Mr Meldrum led expeditions to the Domain. The Domain, or Dom, was an old swimming baths opposite Woolloomooloo on the south side of Sydney Harbour. We got off the train at St James and walked to the baths through long lanes of Moreton Bay fig trees. At the Dom we changed into blue vees and swam. The benches on the bleached wooden catwalks of the Dom were weighed down with ancient wrecks soaking up the sun. Men older than John D. Rockefeller or Pope Pius XIII shuffled dazedly around, their vees draped approximately across their shrivelled loins, their skins burned so brown that their sprinklings of black skin cancers looked like currants in a fruitcake. But the main point was that they had lived a long time. Mr Meldrum was obviously right about the preservative effects of sea water.

Mr Meldrum, Gary, Neil and Craig always did well in the swimming races. To me it seemed too much like hard work. I had some of the knack for swimming but I lacked the will. My main reason for going to the Dom with the Meldrums was to be able to go home with them afterwards. On the way back through the trees to St James station Mr Meldrum bought huge paper bags full of fruit. We gorged ourselves on grapes and plums and had battles with the Moreton Bay figs lying around in thousands on the grass. On the train there were more word games. Laved and cured by salt water, fed to repletion with unadulterated fruit, we were in a state of grace.

For the rest of the weekend Gary was the ringleader. While Mr Meldrum was off doing the extra jobs which were obviously all that kept the bailiffs from the door, Gary was the one who led the great treks to Botany Bay or the dump at Tempe. Down at the bay in the early winter mornings we used to watch the fishermen pull in the nets and were usually given a few yellowtail or bream to take home. Before they built the refinery at Kurnell the bay used to be as full of fish as when Banks and Solander first stepped ashore. At Tempe dump I uncovered choice items for what was to become one of the world's leading collections of old piston rings, rusty egg-beaters, quondam bed-springs and discarded transmission components for Sherman tanks. I shall not attempt to describe my mother's joy when I lugged this stuff home, staggering out of the sunset long after she had called the police. A dump in those days, before plastics had conquered the world, was a treasury of precious metals.

It was Gary who led the first, historic expedition to Kingsford Smith aerodrome, always known to us by the name of the suburb near where it was situated, Mascot. The aerodrome was only a few miles distant – in fact our house was quite near the first set of approach lights to the main runway – but walking all the way there and back seemed a feat comparable in daring to anything contemplated by Burke and Wills. As for Mascot itself, it was simply fairyland. Until well along in my teens I went there almost every weekend, just to watch the aircraft land and take off. ANA and TAA were flying mainly DC-3s and DC-4s. The arrival of the first DC-6 was a big event. The first Stratocruiser flight to arrive from America was greeted with national rejoicing. The TAA ground staff let us take a look inside a Convair 240. Gary found the *Southern Cross* standing in a hangar with its tyres down. I suppose after

Smithy's last flight they just wheeled it in there and left it. Standing with her nose tilted snootily upward in the gloom, the old blue Fokker tri-motor looked romantic past belief. There was no one in there with her except us. Gary couldn't get the cabin door open. But on a nearby stretch of waste ground there was the wingless hull of an amphibian Catalina. The guns had been taken out but the turrets and blisters were still in her. We used to climb inside and play wars for hours. Gary and I were pilot and navigator. Neil had the nose turret and Craig was the waist gunner – a good position for him, since among the ribs and stringers there were plenty of spiders to be caught and eaten. Defending Mascot from Japanese and German attack, we shot down hundreds of Zeros and FW 190s.

The Meldrums' back veranda was a combination of dormitory, playroom and workshop. All three of the boys had their beds there. Each bed had its own set of shelves for a headboard. Neil's shelves held his stamp albums and catalogues. Craig's were a teeming, pulsing nightmare of chicken embryos and legless frogs. Gary's shelves were full of balsa model aircraft made from kits. Solid balsa kits are unheard-of nowadays, when all the skill required to make a model aircraft is a light touch with the plastic parts and a steady hand with the glue. In those days you matched a block of balsa against a rudimentary diagram and got going with a razor blade, which sliced your thumb as readily as it carved the balsa. If the result was recognizable as an aeroplane, you were an expert. If your thumb was recognizable as a thumb, you were a genius. Gary worked fast and accurately. He built a Ju 88, a Hawker Sea Fury, a Heinkel He III, a Kittyhawk, a Chance-Vought Corsair . . . I can remember them all. He would have had an air force if he had looked after them. But when he got tired of having them around he soaked them with dope and set fire to them. The glue came in a tube and was called Tarzan's Grip. If I close my eyes I can remember how it felt to squeeze the last tiny transparent blob from the malleable lead tube.

7. EROS AND THE ANGEL

It was love, of course. Gary was older than I was, sure of himself, capable at everything he tackled. I suppose my sexuality would have awoken by itself but he was certainly in on the beginning of it, although by the time I was getting passionate about him he was getting passionate about girls. Having already started masturbating without knowing even vaguely what I was at, I was delighted to discover that someone else did it and even got visible results. While I was still coming nothing but air Gary was able to conjure a whole vichyssoise into being. It probably never occurred to him that our mutual masturbation sessions were looked forward to by me, and looked back on afterwards with a romantic, jealous fervour that could keep me awake for hours. Neil did his best to keep us apart out of what seemed to me sheer spite. I grew to hate Neil.

I don't think Gary was in any way homosexual or even bisexual. He was just bung full of juice, and attracted by the idea of initiating me in the ways of sex, which he was able to find out about at a precocious rate, since girls found him very attractive. After a day of battles with willow bows and reed arrows in the bush and swamp on the far side of the park, Gary would be the one who spotted the pairs of lovers parking their cars and heading for the ferns, wherein they would disappear by the simple expedient of lying down. Gary was the one who had a name for what they were up to. Neil was the one who made the mistake of firing an arrow. Reed arrows were dry, brittle and weightless until we tipped them with a piece of copper wire driven into the capillary left by the missing pith. Having no tail, the arrows lacked accuracy, but they could go a surprisingly long way if the bow was any good. Neil had spent a long time selecting his bow. It was strung so taut that it played a note when he plucked it. We were observing a distant area of ferns into which a courting couple had vanished some time before. In a low voice, Gary was imparting the unbelievable information that they were playing with each other in order to have babies. It was a fascinating speech until interrupted by a soft twang.

It would have been bad enough if the man had stood up with one hand holding the arrow and the other holding his behind. Unfortunately it was the woman. The man was running towards us, buckling his belt. We lost him by ducking into the swamp. Even then Neil's insane giggle might well have given us away. Apart from Kenny Mears, Neil was the first example I ever encountered of someone who lacked any idea of a given action having necessary consequences. If he felt like hitting you with an axe, he hit you with an axe. Once Gary and I built a tepee in the back yard. Craig sat inside it pretending to be an Indian, an impression he reinforced by preparing himself a light snack of worms and woodlice. The rest of us danced around the tent pretending to be other Indians attacking. Neil had a garden stake for a spear. He hurled it full force at the tent. Craig came screaming out of the tent with the garden stake sticking straight out of his kidneys. It often happened that way. Neil would have a brain-wave and shortly afterwards you would hear the sirens.

My erection-consciousness was exacerbated by Gary, who harped on the words 'big' and 'fat' until they became automatically funny. Whenever anybody used either of these words in conversation, Gary would smile at me and I would snicker uncontrollably. Similarly uncontrollable was my virile organ, which chose the most incon-venient moments to expand. For some reason riding on the top deck of the trolley bus led to a spontaneous show of strength. On the lower deck it didn't happen. I rode on the lower deck whenever possible, but sometimes I was forced upstairs, where my short trousers had a lot to cope with from the moment I sat down. Placed casually across my lap and held down with one negligent arm, my Globite school case kept things covered until we got to Kogarah station, but getting off the bus was a problem. If the bus terminated at Kogarah I could wait until everybody else had alighted, but if it was going on to Rockdale then I had to disembark come what might. There was a choice of carrying my school case unnaturally in front of me or else hopping along doubled over. At school there was the desk to hide under. As far as I could tell, nobody else at Hurstville had the same problem. It wasn't until I got to high school that cock-consciousness spread to fill the whole day.

At school there were friendships and crushes, but nothing physical except the usual business of walking around arm in arm. At home there was rampant sexuality, most of it centred on Gary. But if I was queer for him, it was the outward expression of an inward yearning for the feminine. My dreams were all of girls, even if I didn't, at that stage, connect what I dreamed of doing to them – I remember fantasies of being pressed against them very tightly – with what I actually did in Gary's company. Not long after the war, when I was just starting at Kogarah Primary, my mother took me for a week's holiday at Katoomba. The hotel was called the Sans Souci – the same name, confusingly, as a suburb just near Kogarah, on the George's river. But Katoomba was a long way away, in the Blue Mountains, surrounded by famous tourist attractions like the Scenic Railway, the Three Sisters, the Everglades gardens at Leura, and the Jenolan caves. Another husbandless mother staying at the hotel had a daughter my age who wore lace dresses. I christened her Lacy Skirts, after Gary's best guinea-pig.

Lacy Skirts was my first case of the *visione amorosa*. I lurked for hours near her staircase just to get a glimpse of her. Somehow I managed to get to know her and we played chasings around the hotel. Rarely touching her, I had such an awareness of her physical existence that my chest hurt every time I looked at her. I never spoke of my feelings and so never found out what she felt for me, but I can remember clearly (probably because the vision was to keep recurring, each time with a different object, for many years to come) that my obsession was as transforming and exalting as whatever passed through the heart of Augustine Meaulnes in the brief time he spent with Yvonne de Galais. A picture of Lacy Skirts is no longer in my head, but my adoration for her is still the central memory of that holiday – a fair measure of intensity, since a lot else happened. I got ear-ache on the bus to Jenolan as it wound around the mountains. Touring the limestone caves, I was in frightful pain, and was already crying when I ran off into the bush to pee. Running back to the bus again, I tripped over in full sight of everybody and fell into a patch of giant stinging nettles. Pelion was piled on Ossa. Happening one on top of the other, the ear-ache and the nettles constituted an almost biblical attack on one's equilibrium. Job wouldn't have stood for it. But concentrate as I might, I can't recall the pain, whereas when I think of Lacy Skirts, even though I can't bring back her face, I can recall exactly the sensation of beatitude. We forget the shape of the light but remain dazzled for ever.

My next amorous vision was the Pocket Venus. Again we were on holiday, this time at a resort on the Hawkesbury River called Una Voce, which was pronounced Ewna Vose even by its proprietors. Being by then almost eleven years old, I was better able to stay out of my mother's hair. If there were any patches of giant nettles, I managed to walk around them, instead of falling in. It was my mother who gave my vision its name. We were having lunch in the dining room on our first day in residence when a small adolescent girl walked in. She had on a soft pale-pink blouse, white shorts and gold sandals laced up the calf, in the manner of a miniaturized, tennis-playing Greek goddess. Sitting there in my short trousers with my feet nowhere near touching the floor, I instantly realized that my lack of years was an irreversible tragedy. There seemed no hope of making her aware that I was alive. I lurked in the corridors waiting for an opportunity to walk suddenly past her. There was, of course, no question of actually addressing her in words. As I remember it, my plan was to attract her attention by the intensity of my walk. The idea was to look so lost in thought that she would be unable to resist asking what the thought was. Alas, she resisted successfully for days on end, despite the fact that she was unable to travel far in any direction without having her path abruptly crossed by a short, swiftly moving philosopher.

When I wasn't hanging around the corridors I was immersed in the swimming pool, waiting for her to appear so that she could be impressed by my ability to swim across and back underwater. Since the pool was no bigger than a sheep-dip this was scarcely a great feat, but with the exception of the Pocket Venus everyone sitting around the pool was ready to agree, when prompted, that I had the amphibian properties of a platypus. The Pocket Venus was never there to agree about anything. On the day she finally showed up, she was wearing a light blue satin one-piece costume and looked more beautiful than the mind could bear. Desperate for recognition, I took a deep breath and went into my act. The stress of the moment, however, caused me to take this deep breath under the surface instead of above it. Having travelled about a yard, I emerged with my hair in my eyes and my lungs full of water. Exercising heroic self-control, I did not cough or splutter, but managed a terrible half smile which was meant to indicate that I had just thought of something important enough to warrant interrupting an otherwise inevitably successful assault on the world underwater-swimming record. When my vision cleared, the pocket Venus was no longer there. She had changed her mind and gone back up to the guest house. Such moments should have been educational but unfortunately there is nothing to indicate that self-consciousness can be lessened by proof of the world's indifference.

Every night there was a social in the ballroom. Wallflower was an insufficient word to describe me. I was a wallshadow, a wallstain. In order to conceal my short trousers I stood behind things. Boys only a few years older than I were dancing with her – actually *touching* her. But those few years were an unbridgeable chasm. On the far side of the abyss lay long trousers, an Adam's apple, depth of voice and tallness of stature. On the near side lay bare knees, a piping treble, sweaty hands and a head that stuck out at the back. For months that grew into years I was to spend a good part of every day checking my profile with two mirrors, hoping to find my chin sticking out more and the back of my head sticking out less. I envied boys with no backs to their heads. Even today I envy James Garner. At all costs I had to minimize the number of occasions on which the Pocket Venus could see my head from the side. I modified my approach in the corridors so that my head was always pointing straight at her even when my body was in profile. I was lucky not to walk out of a window, instead of merely into a waiter carrying a tray of custards and junkets. Even then she didn't notice me.

She finally noticed me on the second last day of the holiday. It was in the ping-pong room – a context in which noticing me was hard to avoid, since I had developed a style of play so elaborately baroque that I must have looked like one of those Russian girl gymnasts who dance with a ribbon. Every stroke of the bat was counter-balanced with an upflung pose from the other hand. The general effect, I later realized, must have been more comic than impressive: mere virtuosity, however precocious, could not have attracted such crowds. On the other hand it was impossible to imagine the Pocket Venus being cruel. It must have been kindness that led her to pick up a bat and ask if she could play. She was bad enough at it to make us an even match. We played half that day and all the next morning. I talked endlessly, trying to fascinate her. At least twenty years were to go by before I began realizing that there is no point in such efforts – what women like about us is seldom something we are conscious of and anyway people don't want to be charmed, they want to charm. I probably couldn't have managed things worse, but for a wonder she seemed to like my company, despite my never falling silent except when we touched (it was permissible to brush against her slightly when changing ends) or when she bent over to pick up the ball. When she did that I caught such glimpses of the lace edges of her panties under her shorts that I was drained of all motion. Suddenly I was a dead mackerel. She would straighten up with the ball in her hand and find herself confronted with someone who looked as if he had been zapped with a death ray or injected with cement.

Reality dispelled the dream only to the extent of revealing my light of love to be a nice, ordinary girl. I fell more in love than ever and could hardly breathe for grief when the boat took me and my mother away and left the Pocket Venus behind. The Hawkesbury had flooded during our stay and was by then almost up to the front porch of the guest house, so she was only a few feet away from me as we waved goodbye. Dropping away on the fast-flowing muddy current – the whole flux dotted thickly for miles with countless oranges from the ruined orchards – I looked back on her as she grew smaller, already embarked on the rearward voyage that would take the details of her inexpressibly sweet face beyond the reach of my memory.

No, there was never any real question about which sex I would love when the time came. But not for years would the time come, and in the meanwhile I was as queer as a coot. For most of my two-year stretch at Hurstville I led a double life. At home there were vividly physical encounters with Gary, involving a good deal of mutual masturbation, which must have been a lot more interesting for me than for him, since he had something you could get a grip on, and which produced tangible results. At school I formed crushes on the other boys. In an English public school such passionate attachments would presumably have led to buggery, rape, torture and perhaps death, but in a Sydney day school there was not much that could happen. Nevertheless the emotions were real, although it was often embarrassing to discover that they were not reciprocated in equal strength, or indeed at all. I was far keener on walking with my arm around Carnaby, for example, than he was on walking with his arm around me. But at least he took me home to show me his Dinky Toys, of which he had an amazing collection. There were avowals of inseparable companionship. I did the avowing and he nodded, or at any rate didn't shake his head.

Other boys in the class might have been more forthcoming but I was interested only in the optimates. In my fancy, we were a band of brothers – the Boys in the Back Desks. On the last day of school our class, 6A1, had to provide two teams for a softball tournament against the regular sixth class, called 6A. There was a first team and a second team. Despite my position as class captain, I somehow ended up in the second team along with all the duds in weird sandals, while the optimates headed off together over the horizon, never to be seen again as a group. I was so disappointed I couldn't even cry. For days afterwards I turned the disaster over and over in my mind, trying to think of how I might have managed things differently. I even told my mother about it. Her advice was to forget it, since they day would come when I would look back on it and laugh. She was only half right. The day eventually came when I could look back on it without howling in anguish, but closer to equanimity than that I never came. Far bigger things have gone wrong for me since, but nothing has ever seemed so unfair. I can see why it hurt then. What is hard to see is why it should still hurt now.

Behind this apparent disaster lay a real disaster, unappreciated by me at the time. My marks had won me a bursary to Sydney Boys' High School. If I had gone there I might have been educated in some of the ways of a gentleman. I suppose that was not much of a loss. More to be regretted was that I might have been educated in some of the ways of Latin, Greek, English literature, or indeed anything. That Sydney High School counted as one of the so-called Great Public Schools was a side issue. The central point to notice was that its academic standards were unquestionable. The same could not be said of Sydney Technical High School. Unlike Sydney High, which was well situated near Moore Park, Sydney Tech was a tumbledown collection of old buildings in Paddington, a district which was still fifteen years from being rediscovered by the conservationists, and which was at that time still largely inhabited by prostitutes too jaded for the brighter lights around the docks. Nor was it GPS. Instead it was CHS, or Combined High Schools – a difference its representatives spent a lot of time saying didn't matter. Nor would it have mattered, if Sydney Tech had truly been able to claim any special distinction. As it was, however, those parents who sent their boys there under the impression that they would receive outstanding instruction in mathematics and the sciences were being hoodwinked. Sydney Tech might have been a good school before my time there. For all I know it has been a good school again since I left. But while I was in attendance it was mediocre at best.

But my wanting to go there wasn't the place's fault – apart, that is, from the fact that Carnaby was on the way there too. Elstub was bound for Sydney High, naturally enough: he knew what he wanted and his father knew that that was the best place to get it. Lunn was bound for Sydney Grammar – another suitable choice. Carnaby had a marked gift for mathematics, so Sydney Tech made some kind of sense for him. But it made no sense for me to choose Sydney Tech just because Carnaby was going there. As so often happens, however, the irrational motives were the decisive ones. The rational motive – that I thought I wanted to be an aeronautical engineer – I could have been talked out of if it had been properly explained to me that Sydney High produced more of those than Sydney Tech did. But the urge to follow Carnaby was proof even against my mother's distress, which was understandably torrential. The news that Sydney Tech had a squadron of air cadets put the matter beyond question, as far as I was concerned. I imagined myself at the controls of a Mustang taking off from the school playground.

My mother wanted me to have all the prestige that Sydney High would undoubtedly bring. She didn't want to have to go around hoarsely insisting that Sydney Tech was really something rather marvellous. With Sydney High there was nothing to insist about. Everyone knew that Sydney High was as good as you could get. And Sydney High, which people fought to get their sons into, had asked me to enrol! How could I not? She didn't get it. For months she kept on and for months I fought back. She was right, of course, but it didn't help. I owed it to her as a reward for all her work. It would have been better if I had given in. It would have been better still if the means had existed to make me do the right thing no matter how determined I was on doing the wrong. But on her own she was no match for me. I just wore her down.

8. THE IMITATION OF CHRIST

Thus, by a long battle of attrition, the matter was decided. But the beginning of my first year at Sydney Tech was still a long way away, at the far end of the school holidays. By this time the Meldrum boys had become regular attendants at Kogarah Presbyterian Church, which was situated about halfway between Prince's Highway and the station. Mr Meldrum, a rationalist, would have disapproved of this development. Unfortunately Mr Meldrum was no longer around. A load of pipes had slid off his flat-bed truck and pinned him to a wall. He was brought home to die. The process took several weeks. By now a seasoned campaigner, I had prudently withheld from him the vital last tenth of my affection, so I was well able to survive the shock: indeed I hardly noticed it, since by some inexplicable coincidence I took to calling at the Meldrum house with steadily decreasing frequency. Others, notably Mrs Meldrum, were less well armoured against fortune. She was prostrated. Not just to get some relief from their presence, but also to prepare them against an uncertain world, she started sending her boys to church. After a decent interval I followed.

Kogarah Presbyterian Church was a solid purple brick and red tile affair with plaster interiors. Standing opposite the St George District Hospital, it was handily placed to entertain the polio patients with massed singing of 'Onward Christian Soldiers'. Many a surgeon must have paused gratefully during a tricky operation to relish the top notes of our resident coloratura, Mrs Pike, as she howled above the choir like a dingo with its paw caught in a trap. Scalpels must have frozen in mid-slice as the Boys' Brigade bugle band came marching by, emitting a rich collection of wrong notes and raspberries. One way and another the whole of Sunday and half the rest of the week saw the wee kirk teeming with activity. It was a whole way of life. I plunged into it gladly, egged on by my mother. I was supposed to be

Church of England, but she wouldn't have minded if I had been going to a mosque, as long as I went.

My previous Christian experience had been confined to an inter-denominational Sunday School run by the Purvis family at their house halfway down Sunbeam Avenue. Mrs Purvis played the piano and Mr Purvis showed 16mm films of aborigines being converted. In the early part of the film the aborigines were shown standing around naked with a crotch full of shadows and looking glum while flies camped on their faces. In the later part of the film they were wearing trousers and smiling like Loretta Young. It was Christ who had made the difference. They had taken Him into their hearts, whereupon the flies had upped stakes and moved on. When the lights went up Mr Purvis would launch into an attack on beer and Catholicism. He pronounced beer bee-ar. The legionaries who pee-arsed Christ's side with a spee-ar had undoubtedly been enslaved to bee-ar. A sure sign of Catholicism's fundamental evil was that it required the drinking of wine even in church, wine being mee-arly another form of bee-ar. Mr Purvis would then get us to sign the pledge all over again and send us home with a warning not to be kidnapped by nuns.

But the Purvises' Sunday School was strictly short pants, striped T-shirt and bare feet. We would have grown out of it anyway, even if Mrs Purvis hadn't died of cancer. The piano having fallen silent, there was nothing for Mr Purvis to do except remarry, move to Melbourne and start again. He became famous years later as an anti-Catholic campaigner, warning of attempts by the Vatican to invade Canberra. Once again he had films to prove it. Nuns were shown scurrying darkly down side streets, while a familiar voice on the sound track talked of how the Roman menace loomed ever more nee-ar, and of the growing fee-ar that it would soon be hee-ar.

Kogarah Presbyterian Church was the big time. On Sunday morning there was Sunday School, followed by church, at which the Boys' Brigade would frequently put in an appearance with snare-drums rattling in approximate unison and dented bugles giving out random fragments of late Schönberg. In the early evening there would be church. Then there was a Fellowship meeting for older adolescents and young adults. This would be followed by church again, featuring a sermon from the Reverend C. Cummings Campbell, whose name was the inspiration of many a leaden joke ('The Campbells are Cummingses, yes they are,' etc.), and whose oratory bored the pigeons out of the roof. If you threw in and averaged out all the Harvest Festivals, preparations for Harvest Festivals, special study sessions for Sunday School teachers, special missionary group studies for Fellowship Study Circle leaders, and so on, it would be possible to say that the devout young communicant could count on spending most of each week in constant attendance, with the odd break for meals. On Saturday night there was usually a Fellowship social. On Thursday night the Boys' Brigade drilled in the church hall. At one time or another, as I grew older, I took part in all these activities, starting with Sunday School and the Boys' Brigade.

Sunday School was a waste of time from the religious angle, but had conspicuous social value. A hundred children broken up into ten groups of ten, we learned the fundamental discipline of sitting still for an hour while an older person told boring stories. Apart from the chance to take home a deckle-edged sticker, stick it in a book and bring the book back to be marked, there was no action. The stickers had luridly coloured biblical illustrations on them. There was also a catechism to be learned. Prizes were to be won for learning it. Thus the memory was tested, if not the religious sense. Over the next five or six years I won every possible prize, up to and including the rarely awarded Cummings Campbell Bible, without experiencing, or even needing to pretend I had experienced, a moment of religious belief. Among the teachers, the few genuine believers were manifestly as crazy as Mr Purvis. Any sign of true devotion among the pupils was regarded as bad taste. Eventually I was to become a teacher myself and make a practice of getting the holy stuff over as soon as possible so that I could get on with telling stories about Pearl Harbor or the campaign in the Western Desert. No pupil ever complained.

But that's to jump the gun. As a new Sunday School pupil I learned how to sit still with girls present. As a probationary recruit in the Boys' Brigade I learned how to march up and down. The Boys' Brigade was a paramilitary organization emanating, like the Scouts, from England, but with the emphasis on parade-ground drill rather than on woodsy lore. The uniform had to be imported from England. It consisted of forage cap, white cartridge pouch and brass-buckled belt, the whole thing worn over khaki shorts and navy-blue shirts, although in winter we were expected to wear dark suits. One of the main attractions of belonging was that the merit badges, worn on the right sleeve, were made of what looked like solid silver. In practice

these tended not to arrive from England even after repeated notifi-
cations that they had been won, but you could always live in hope.
Another main attraction was that you got the chance to blow a bugle
or bang a drum. It was with high expectations, therefore, that I set
off for my first evening on parade.

My manner of dress perhaps showed questionable judgment. As
a new recruit I was not entitled to wear Boys' Brigade uniform even
if it had been available. To compensate, I eked out my shorts, shirt
and sandshoes with a few extras. On my head I put one of Ray's old
RAAF forage caps with its flaps down. The cap was covered with
about a hundred badges of various kinds, many of them celebrating
our recent alliance with the Soviet Union. There were several portraits
of Stalin. On my chest I wore my father's campaign medals – not
just the ribbons, but the medals entire. Usually I was allowed to wear
these only on Anzac Day when we went into town to watch the
march, but my mother had given me a special dispensation. On my
belt was a holster containing a Ned Kelly cap pistol fully loaded. A
multi-purpose jack-knife completed the ensemble. Since I was still
quite small the jack-knife weighed me down on one side. I thought
better of it and took it off. My mother persuaded me that the medals
were perhaps gilding the lily, so I took those off too. The rest I kept.

Kindly Captain Andrews, the senior officer, forbore from
comment on my appearance. There wasn't much he noticed by that
stage. Having grown old in the task, he tended to daydream. I fell in
at the low end of a long line, which then divided itself into four
sections of half a dozen boys each. Everyone started off as a private.
The mere ability to turn up once a week ensured one's eventual
promotion to lance corporal. If your voice broke it was enough to
make you a full corporal. To become a sergeant you had to pass
a few exams. Beyond that lay the dizzy privilege of officer status,
featuring long trousers and a cap with ribbons hanging down at the
back. Down at my end of the scale it all looked very impressive, but
even while occupying a rank more lowly than private I could see that
Captain Andrews wasn't too hot at drill. When he said 'About turn!'
we about-turned. When he said 'About turn!' again we about-turned
again. He then showed us how we should have done it. Facing towards
us, he ordered himself to about-turn. By rights, upon completion of
this manoeuvre, he should have been facing away from us, so that
we could see his back. Instead he would end up facing sideways, so

that we could see him in profile. Quickly he would add a few shuffles to take him round the rest of the way. Gary was the corporal at the head of my section. I could see his shoulders quaking every time Captain Andrews got it wrong. That got me started. Thus a sense of the ridiculous was inculcated, at an early age. For years to come I found almost everyone ludicrous except myself.

In fact the Kogarah Presbyterian Church Company of the Boys' Brigade was a shambles. Annually we came last in the District drill competition, even when it was held in our own hall. Our bugle band terrorized not just the hospital but the whole area, with bitches whelping at its strident dissonance. Not long after I joined there was a Display Night, held in conjunction with Girls' Brigade. My mother was horrified to discover that her tiny son was last in a line of crouching small boys over which, or whom, large girls awkwardly dived before turning a forward roll on a mat. Her fears were justified. Graham Truscott's older sister Maureen was built like Fatty Arbuckle and looked no lovelier for being clad in black sandshoes, blue shorts and a singlet like a two-car garage. As proud parents sat open-mouthed on the surrounding benches, she came hurtling out of the back annexe, along the corridor, through the connecting door, into the hall, up to the spring-board and into space. She drove me into the floor like a tack. Artificial respiration got my breathing started while Captain Andrews and the Rev. C. Cummings Campbell attempted to calm my mother with a few ill-chosen words.

Such incidents were too common to be thought remarkable. At the District Athletics Carnival held at Trumper Park our company got no points. Count them: none. In the swimming carnivals Gary was our only swimmer ever to reach the finals of anything. As part compensation there was a great deal of rod-walloping. Masturbation, whether solo, mutual, or of competition standard, was rife. So was petty theft. After a hard evening of copying Captain Andrews's about-turns we would all race down to Parry's milk bar, there to ingest the milkshake of our choice and rob the lolly counter when Mr Parry wasn't looking. The only time Mr Parry ever caught one of us he contented himself with delivering a white-lipped lecture. It was a wonder he didn't call the police. Anywhere in the world, immigrant shopkeepers have a particular horror of being robbed by the locals. It hurts to work so hard and suddenly discover that some of your customers subscribe to Proudhon's idea about property being theft.

If Proudhon had been running the milk bar he would probably have reacted far worse than Mr Parry. Luckily for us, Proudhon had been dead since 1865.

The other half of my double life had more hesitant beginnings. It wasn't that I hated Sydney Tech. I just didn't connect with it. On weekday mornings I put on my school uniform. It consisted, reading from bottom to top, of black shoes, grey socks, grey worsted short-pants suit with school pocket-badge, blue shirt, tie in the school colours of maroon and sky blue, and grey felt hat with hat band in school colours. Add in the enamel school lapel badge and you had an awful lot of maroon and sky blue. Exercise books, pencil case, pens, technical drawing set and Vegemite sandwiches went into the inevitable Globite school case. Lugging this, I rode the trolley bus to Kogarah station and caught the train to Central. Other Sydney Tech boys were already on the train from stations further down the line. As we got closer to town, more joined. Boys from Sydney High also got on. Their colours were chocolate and sky blue. Age for age, they seemed slightly taller than our lot, with clearer skins. They were quieter and read a great deal. At Central they caught one tram while we caught another. They went to Moore Park and we went to Paddington. Nobody except a few aesthetes had any idea at the time that Paddington's terrace houses were desirable residences. Gentrification lay far in the future. The only paint on show was kack brown and the cast iron balconies looked like scrap metal waiting to be taken away. It wasn't a slum area like Redfern – which during the Queen's visit had been masked off with hessian so that she would be unable to see it from the Royal train – but it was pretty grim. Sydney Tech was in the grimmest part and looked even grimmer than its surroundings. The playgrounds were entirely asphalt: not a blade of grass. A solitary Moreton Bay fig tree in the lower playground was the only touch of green. Jammed between the dilapidated two-storey buildings, even less prepossessing 'temporary' single-storey buildings cut the playground space down to nearly nothing. In the open air there wasn't enough bench-space for the whole school to sit down at once. We had to have lunch in two shifts.

Disaster struck on the first day, when Carnaby was assigned to a different class. In quiet desperation I sought out his company in the playground, but often he lunched in the other shift and always he was surrounded by new friends. So it had all been for nothing.

I didn't even get accepted for the Air Cadets. The fact that I knew more about air recognition than anyone else in the world counted as nothing beside the further fact that I had an unacceptable level of albumen in my blood. An independent pathologist wrote a note saying that my level of albumen was all right for me but the RAAF doctor wouldn't listen. If such an injustice had happened to me earlier it might have helped arm me against capricious Fate, but I was too spoiled to profit from the disappointment. Many, many years were to go by before I learned the truth of Noël Coward's comment about the secret of success being the capacity to survive failure.

Soon enough I made new friends in my own class, but not in the same way as Carnaby did. His natural authority was reinforced by early maturity. Either that year or the year after, his voice broke. He had acne for about two days and simultaneously grew a foot taller. During this period almost everyone except me did something similar. I obstinately stayed small. Nobody looked up to me any longer. In that first year the only thing that made me worth knowing was my good marks. The teachers weren't brilliant but they were conscientious. Besides, there was a certain flywheel effect carrying over from Hurstville, where we had been ahead of the curriculum. At the half-yearly examinations I averaged in the high nineties, coming third in the class. Things might have gone on like that for a good while longer if it had not been for Mary Luke.

I was coping with physics and chemistry well enough while Mr Ryan was still teaching them. But Mr Ryan was due for retirement, an event which was hastened by an accident in the laboratory. He was showing us how careful you had to be when handling potassium in the presence of water. Certainly you had to be more careful than he was. The school's entire supply of potassium ignited at once. Wreathed by dense smoke and lit by garish flames, the stunned Mr Ryan looked like a superannuated Greek god in receipt of bad news. The smoke enveloped us all. Windows being thrown open, it jetted into what passed for a playground, where it hung around like some sinister leftover from a battle on the Somme. Shocked, scorched and gassed, Mr Ryan was carried away, never to return.

Back from his third retirement came Mary Luke. A chronic shortage of teachers led to Mary Luke being magically resurrected after each burial. Why he should have been called Mary was a datum lost in antiquity. The school presented him with a pocket watch every time he retired. Perhaps that was a mistake. It might have been the massed ticking that kept him alive. Anyway, Mary Luke, having already ruined science for a whole generation of schoolboys, came back from the shadows to ruin science for me.

Mary was keen but incomprehensible. The first thing he said at the start of every lesson, whether of physics or chemistry, was, 'Make a Bunsen burner.' He was apparently convinced that given the right encouragement we would continue our science studies in makeshift laboratories at home. So we might have done, if we could have understood anything else he said. Unfortunately 'Make a Bunsen burner' was his one remaining fathomable sentence. In all other respects his elocution made my late grandfather sound like Leslie Howard. The same comparison applied to his physical appearance. How could anyone be that old without being dead? But there were definite signs of life. The mouth moved constantly. 'Combustioff off magnesioff,' Mary would announce keenly. 'Magnesioff off oxidoff off hydrogoff off givoff off.' Worriedly I slid the cap off the inverted jar and ignited the gaseous contents to prove that hydrogoff had been givoff off. Carefully I drew the apparatus in my book, already aware that these preliminary experiments would be the last I would ever understand.

Perhaps I was never cut out for chemistry. But I had a right to think that physics might have lain within my scope. I impressed Mary with my precocious knowledge of the planets, which I could name in their order outwards from the sun. Mary looked momentarily blank at the mention of Pluto, but otherwise he seemed well pleased. A novel rearrangement of his lips took place which I guessed to be a smile. The teeth thereby revealed featured eye-catching areas of green amongst the standard amber and ochre. If only we could have stuck to astronomy. Instead, Mary sprang optics on us. 'Thoff angloff off incidoff,' he informed us, 'equoff thoff angloff off reflectioff.' We fiddled dutifully with pins and mirrors. I had the sinking feeling of being unable to understand. The moment of breakdown came when Mary started exploring the different properties of concave and convex mirrors. I couldn't see which was which when he held them up. More importantly, I couldn't tell the difference when he said their names. 'Thoff miroff off concoff,' he explained carefully, 'off thoff miroff off convoff.' Proud of having made things clear, he smiled fixedly, giving

us a long look at his wrecked teeth. What was going *on* in that mouth
of his? I could see things moving.

But some of the other boys seemed to understand Mary even if I
couldn't, and anyway in the straight mathematical subjects I had no
excuse. The teaching might have been uninspired but it was sound
enough. Besides, if I had had any mathematical talent I probably
wouldn't even have needed teaching. As things were, I remained good
at mathematics as long as mathematics remained arithmetic and
algebra. I was passable at trigonometry. But when calculus came in,
the lights went out. My average marks gradually started to shelve
downwards. Things weren't helped by the weekly classes in woodwork
and metalwork. I could handle technical drawing well enough, helped
by my skill at lettering, but when I entered the workshop I was a
gone goose. Metalwork was bad: anything I put in the lathe refused
to come out true. It would start off as a cylinder and end up as a
blob. So much for my dream of building new jet engines to outclass
the Rolls-Royce Avon and the Armstrong Siddeley Sapphire, of
designing aircraft whose power and beauty would enrol them among
the masterpieces of Sydney Camm, Kurt Tank and Willy Messerschmitt. Woodwork was even worse. Nobody whose hands are not
naturally dry can ever be a good carpenter, and I suffered badly from
sweaty hands. My hands started to sweat with fear from the moment
I put on my calico apron. By the time the woodwork teacher had
finished explaining what we had to do my hands would be dripping
like taps. Wet hands leave a film on wood that renders it hard to
plane. Our first job was to make a breadboard. The breadboard had
to be made from half a dozen lengths of wood glued together edge to
edge. For this to succeed the edges had to be planed true. I kept on
and on from week to week, planing away at my half dozen pieces. It
took me an entire term of classes before I got them true. By that
time they were like chopsticks. When I glued my breadboard together
it was the right length but only two inches wide. You couldn't have
cut a French loaf on it.

At the end of second year my average mark was down into the
eighties. Suddenly I had lost my role. Being bright could have saved
me from the ignominy of not growing tall. Growing tall could have
saved me from the ignominy of not being bright. As things were, I
was losing on all counts. In every subject except English and German
I was obviously going nowhere. German was all right for a while. At

Sydney Tech there were only German and French to choose from. Typically I chose the less beneficial. It was taught by a huge, shambling teacher we called Lothar, after Mandrake the Magician's assistant. He was a nice man but charmless. I found it easy to keep level with Hans Kuckhoff, an immigrant from some unheard-of country whose family spoke German at home. Kuckhoff and I shared a desk and compared erections while Lothar concentrated on battering declensions into the heads of the slower boys. *Der den des dem. Die die der der.* It was back to the Cubs.

In English I shone – fitfully, but sufficiently to keep my morale from collapsing altogether. Our teacher in the early years was 'Jazz' Aked. He also doubled as our music teacher: hence the nickname. 'Jazz' taught English according to the curriculum. The curriculum was prescriptive. There were grammar, parsing and Latin roots to be learned. Without resorting to violence, 'Jazz' had a way of getting results. Eventually I learned to parse any sentence I was given. I couldn't do it now, but the knowledge is still there somewhere at an unconscious level. It was invaluable training. On top of that, he set good essay subjects. My essays were sometimes read out to the class. I was thereby established all over again as teacher's pet, but at least it was *something*, in those dreadful days when everyone else seemed to be doubling in size overnight, while simultaneously acquiring an Adam's apple like a half-swallowed rock, a voice like Wallace Beery, and a case of acne like the boiling surface of the sun. Such are the pangs of being left behind – that you can die of envy for cratered faces weeping with yellow pus.

9. MILO THE MAGNIFICENT

My mother kept on assuring me that I would 'shoot up.' She was not to know I was one of the kind that acquires altitude gradually, with no sudden alteration of the hormonal levels. My testosterone was on a drip feed. In the long run this saved me from anything more revolting than the odd pimple and left me slightly taller than average, but at the time it seemed like a disaster, especially considering that my self-consciousness about girls had abruptly attained new heights, mainly due to the influence of Milo Stefanos. Half the quarry had been sold off as a building block. A house had been built: palatial by our standards, since the garage was underneath, which effectively gave the place two storeys. The Stefanos family had moved in. Hard-working New Australians, they ran a milk bar down at Brighton, on Botany Bay. Their eldest son, Philip, was already a young man and had attained some renown as a tennis player. Even older than Gary, he was beyond my reach. But their second son, Milo, was my age. He was still in short pants like the rest of us, except that in his case the short pants bulged and pulsed as if he had a live rat stuffed down them. Milo was precocious in every sense.

By now Gary was giving most of his spare time to rebuilding the rusted wreck of a War Department 500cc side-valve BSA that was eventually to become his first motorbike. He had left Kogarah Inter-mediate High School after the Intermediate Certificate and become an apprentice fitter and turner. The balsa aeroplane days were over. He even left Boys' Brigade. I still visited him a lot and expanded my interest in aeroplanes to an interest in cars and motorbikes. I was buying and memorizing *Flight*, the *Autocar* and the *Motorcycle* every week. At that time they were still substantial publications. I acquired an immense theoretical knowledge. But it was gradually becoming clear to me that theoretical knowledge was not the same as practical capacity. Gary could strip and reassemble a gear box. All I could do was hand him the spanners. His hands were covered with grease. Cutting oil, I noticed, looked rather like sperm, but opportunities for checking this comparison were growing fewer all the time. Finally it became clear that Gary nowadays preferred doing that sort of thing with girls. Sensitive to my jealousy, he was slow to tell me, but finally the news was too big to hold in. In part recompense for my loss, I was told details. But the girls were Gary's age or older and it all happened somewhere else. There was no hope of joining in.

With Milo it was different. You could get in on all of his adventures, even the supreme one. Milo not only had access to everything, he enjoyed proving it. He had a lot in common with his compatriot Alcibiades. At the back of his garage were stacked hundreds of cartons of cigarettes – stock for the shop. Milo would appropriate the odd carton of Ardath or Craven 'A' to his own use. I thus started smoking at an early age, although it was some years before I dared do it in public. Milo smoked in public while he was still in those challenging short pants. Towards sunset he would appear at the front of the house, his crotch bulging softly in the twilight, and airily smoke a cigarette while combing his hair. Milo combed his hair constantly. Since he smoked constantly too, he spent a lot of time coughing quietly with his eyes screwed up. He looked like a small cloud preening itself. Gathering rapidly like the fast-falling Pacific night, Milo's follower's grouped around him. Some of us sat on the front fence. Others did handstands and standing long-jumps on the front strip. Still others rode their bicycles along a complicated route down one of the Margaret Street footpaths and up the other. The route just happened to pass the front of the Chappelows' house, where the girls were gathered. It was rare for the girls actually to join us at that hour. Instead they pretended not to notice the riders pretending not to notice them. Meanwhile Milo loaned out examples from his unparalleled collection of Carter Brown detective magazines. Carter Browns were famous for containing sex scenes. Pale by later standards, this was nevertheless unmistakably some kind of pornography. Erections were to be had while reading it.

Most sensationally of all, Milo had access to Laurel Smithers. Laurel lived in what used to be the house inhabited by the poultry farmers. Now that the poultry farm was gone and all the land built over, the old farmhouse on the hill was the only truly ramshackle house in the district. In effect that meant that it was the only building for miles which had any aesthetic interest at all, but since there was nobody within the same radius who had any notion of what aesthetic interest might happen to be, the house was universally regarded as a blot on the landscape. It had weatherboard walls and a corrugated iron roof, upon which, after dark, the missiles of the Flash of Lightning and his masked companions would often rain. Quailing under this bombardment, the poultry farmers, their occupation gone, either died off or moved out, or a mixture of both. The Smithers family moved in. Mr Smithers spent most of the day husbanding his energy, while Mrs Smithers pottered about busying herself with light household tasks, such as breaking stones with a sledgehammer or forging new springs for the Model 'A' Ford museum piece they called a car. Laurel was their daughter. She was Allowed to Run Wild. Yacking over the back fence, our mothers were agreed, and went on agreeing, that Laurel would surely Get Into Trouble. They had the right idea, but were using the wrong tense. Laurel was already seizing every opportunity to be sexually interfered with by Milo. Indeed interference could go no further. They were at it continually. The only reason the adults didn't tumble straight away was that Laurel was already well embarked on her teens, whereas Milo was only just turning twelve. They comforted themselves with the thought that Milo would not know how. They couldn't have been more wrong. Not only did Milo know how, he was giving lessons.

The word in use was 'root'. Milo used to root Laurel standing up in the back of the garage. He also used to root her lying down in the back of the garage. On special occasions we were all invited to watch. One by one and two by two, half the boys in the district would make their way to Milo's garage on a Saturday afternoon. Inside the garage the atmosphere was tense, mainly because about fifty pairs of lungs were breathing it. Lost in admiration, envy and cigarette smoke, we all watched Milo perform. It was hard to say what Laurel was getting out of it. If she was standing up she looked at us over Milo's heaving shoulders as if we were strangers she was encountering in the street. If she was lying down she looked at the ceiling as if engaged in a long-term entomological study of the spiders inhabiting the rafters. The only evidence that she was not indifferent to the whole process was the way she kept coming back for more.

On very special occasions the rest of us were invited to join in. This only happened when Laurel was 'in the right mood'. If it turned out, after an hour or two of being pounded by Milo, that Laurel was in the right mood, everyone queued up and took a turn. The queue shuffled forward quite rapidly since Laurel would allow even the most fervent admirer only a few seconds inside the sanctum which she had otherwise dedicated to Milo in perpetuity. Only once did I dare join the queue. It was a complete fiasco. The erection which in other circumstances I had so much trouble getting rid of failed to materialize. It was an early instance of First Night Failure, made worse by the fact that it was happening in the early afternoon, when everyone could see – or would have seen, if I had not been so careful to unveil the timorous article only during my last step forward and to rehouse it as soon as I stepped back. Nor was my recalcitrant organ content with merely not inflating. It shrivelled up the way it did after I had been in swimming. Laurel was too aphasic to be openly contemptuous. Standing on tiptoe, I pretended to push myself inside her, copying the grunting noises I had heard from Milo and some of the others. It is even possible that Laurel was fooled. I, however, was not.

The incident was just one more piece of evidence bolstering the case for my physical abnormality. When in a state of excitement I could just about convince myself that I was sufficiently well endowed. But to detumesce was the same as to disappear. Other boys seemed to be the same length 'on the slack' as they were when erect, the only difference being that the thing hung down like a length of hose instead of climbing like an extension ladder. Milo, needless to say, was a case in point. On the rare occasions when his uncircumcised tonk was hanging limp, it was still as thick as a third thigh. At full stretch, it was the size of a Japanese midget submarine.

As bad luck would have it, Laurel from then on confined her favours to Milo exclusively, so I never got a second chance. But I still had good reason to be grateful to Milo, since it was in his company that I first came up with something more substantial than a sharp pain and a puff of air. As a masturbator Milo was if anything even more impressive than as a lover. Smoking casually with one hand, he employed the other to stimulate himself, his only problem being how to choose the most satisfactory grip. If he held the near end there was apparently a certain loss of sensitivity, so that the process might occupy a minute or even more. If he held the far end he could get results in a matter of seconds, but his arm would be at full stretch.

There was no mistaking the moment when Milo was on the point of unburdening himself. You could practically hear the stuff coming. He could have put out a fire with it. With due allowance for scale, I was matching him stroke for stroke one day when suddenly I produced something. It was the only clear-cut sign of puberty I was ever to be vouchsafed. My pride knew no bounds. Even Milo was impressed – a generous reaction, since the stuff was all over one of his best Carter Browns. But the change of status might as well have been metaphysical for all the difference it made to the size of my dick when dormant. At school this problem aggravated all my other problems. After our PT sessions I lingered elaborately in the changing room so that I could duck into the communal shower after everybody else had come out. If I could manage a semi-erection everything was all right. I didn't mind joining in the towel-flicking if I had something to show. Unfortunately a semi-erection is no more easily achieved by will than a full-sized version. So I had to do a great deal of loitering.

It was an eternal anxiety. In a class full of cock-watchers, I had to keep something between my shrinking twig and a hundred prying eyes, all the while contriving the deception so that it never seemed deliberate. Emerging from the shower with a towel draped casually around me, I had to put on my underpants before I took off the towel, but make it look as if I was taking off the towel before I put on my underpants. The result was a Gypsy Rose Lee routine of extraordinary subtlety. I calculated the sight-lines and the lighting like Max Reinhardt or the Black Theatre of Prague. Either I was never spotted, or what I had down there looked less underprivileged than I thought. According to Hemingway, when Scott Fitzgerald proclaimed himself worried about the size of his tool (and we have only Hemingway's hopelessly unreliable word that this ever happened) the tall writer told the short writer that anybody's prong looks small when the owner looks down on it. On behalf of my younger self I would like to agree, but at the time I spent many an anxious hour in front of my bedroom mirror and and there could be no doubt that my tossle looked the same from the side as it did from on top – i.e., like a shy silkworm.

As self-consciousness approached its dizzy peak, I spent so much of my spare time checking up on myself in mirrors that there was hardly any left over for little matters like homework. A dressing table, strangely enough, was among the few pieces of furniture in my room, which by now was a small library of books about aircraft, cars, motorcycles and war. The table beside my bed, which had previously housed my laboratory – which is to say, the collection of malodorous junk I had brought back from the dump – was now stacked with carefully filed and cross-referenced technical magazines. The cupboard off which we had all once dived on to the bed was now mainly a bookcase, in which such titles as *The Dam Busters* and *Reach for the Sky* took pride of place. On the walls, which my mother had tolerantly always allowed me to decorate as I pleased, coloured tracings of Disney characters had been joined by elaborate cut-away drawings of aircraft, so that you had a Dornier Do 17 unloading its bombs on Donald Duck. The room was like the cell of a machine-mad monk. The only human touch was the half-length portrait on one wall, which turned out on closer examination to be the dressing-table mirror containing my reflection. Almost always the reflection was in profile, as I held up a hand mirror at an angle in front of me in order to see what I looked like from the side. Why did the back of my head stick out so far? Why did my jaw stick out so little? As all the boys around me started turning into men, I began to wonder if perhaps I was not doomed to look boyish for ever.

Even at its best, Sydney Tech was simply a waste of time. But even at its worst, it mainly just got me down, rather than driving me to despair. Had it been a boarding school I would probably have been in real trouble. As things were, most of my agonies were self-inflicted through an excess of inward-turned imagination. Unfortunately misery is not relative. For some reason the school prided itself on its achievements in rugby union. It always finished high in the CHS competitions and occasionally fielded a team which could lick the best of the GPS teams, although Sydney High always remained the unbeatable enemy. For most of my school career I was obliged to play House football, which was a joke. The very idea of dividing the school into houses was another joke. I was a member of Williams House. Nobody seemed to be bothered by the fact that no building existed which could be described as Williams House or even Williams Hut. In fact Williams House consisted exclusively of the yellow singlets its members wore during athletics competitions. Dyed at home by mothers commanding various techniques and materials, the singlets covered the range of all possible yellows from fresh butter to old urine. Wearing mine, I came third in the heats and second last in the finals. Once I had been a fast runner, but that was before I started to shrink.

House football took place in a park only a few miles' brisk march from the school. As a cold wind whipped across the grass, the two teams would position themselves in expectation of the opening whistle. The start of each half was the only time when the eye could detect even an approximation of positional sense. The moment the whistle blew, thirty small boys would gather around the ball, forming a compact, writhing, many-legged mound which during the course of what seemed like hours would transfer itself at random to different parts of the field. I was somewhere in the middle, praying it would end.

But there was worse to come. On days when a Grade football team had a bye, its members would be brought to our park so that they could practise dodging tackles. They ran down the field while we tried to tackle them. It went without saying that they were bigger, faster and more skilful than we were. The real nightmare was when the First Grade side turned up. The star of First Grade was Reg Gasnier, already tipped as the brightest schoolboy rugby prospect in years. Indeed he toured England the following year with the Australian Rugby League side. Merely to watch Gasnier run was to die a little. He was all knees and elbows. His feet scythed outwards as he ran, like Boadicea's hub-caps. There seemed no way of tackling him without sustaining a compound fracture. Up and down the field he steamed while we ran at him from different angles, only to bounce off, fall stunned, or miss completely as he side-stepped. He was beautiful to watch if you weren't among the prospective victims. The way he shifted his weight in one direction while swerving in the other was a kind of poetry. Regrettably it was also very painful if experienced at close quarters.

I can well remember the first time I was deputed to tackle Gasnier. He was three times as heavy as I was, although, density having the relationship it does to dimensions, he was of course only twice as high. There were only a couple of hundred people watching. Gasnier appeared out of the distance like an express train moving unhampered by rails. I ran at him on a despairing collision course. Casually he put his hand in my face. My head stopped while the rest of me kept going, so that I spent a certain amount of time supine in mid-air before falling deftly on my back. While I was being resuscitated on the sidelines, Gasnier kindly materialized in my blurred vision and explained that the thing to do was keep my head low so that he could not palm me off. The next time I tackled him I kept my head low. Side-stepping with uncanny ease, he put his hand on back of my head and pushed my face into the ground. So much for the friendly advice. When they picked me up, or rather pulled me out, there was an impression of my face in the turf that you could have made a plaster cast from. It would have looked disappointed but resigned.

None of this would have mattered if I could have kept up with the swimmers. Swimming had, after all, always been my best thing. The hours and days spent in the creek and the Dom with the Meldrums had paid off in a certain fluency of style. When I was twelve years old I used to hold my own in races across the creek against a local boy who subsequently was to take the silver medal for 100 metres freestyle at the Melbourne Olympics. At the time when I could keep up with him we were the same size. By the time of the Olympics he was 6 feet 3 inches tall and could close his hand around the grips of two tennis rackets. But it wasn't just a matter of height. There was the question of attitude. I simply found excuses never to start training. After Mr Meldrum's death, and with Gary playing a less important part in my life, I felt able to attend Ramsgate Baths on the weekends. Ramsgate Baths was a set of tiled pools fed by seawater from Botany Bay. Since the water was confined and remained unchanged for days on end, Mr Meldrum had frowned on Ramsgate Baths as unhealthy. He was, of course, absolutely right. The water in each pool would be green on the first day, orange on the second day and saffron the third. The whole place was one vast urinal. But there were diving boards, sands pits and giggling swarms of girls wearing Speedo swimming costumes. The Speedo was a thin, dark-blue cotton one-piece affair whose shoulder straps some of the girls tied together behind with a ribbon so as to tauten the fabric over their pretty bosoms. On a correctly formed pubescent girl a Speedo looked wonderful, even when it was dry. When it was wet, it was an incitement to riot.

At Ramsgate Baths, weekend after weekend, year after year, I would show off with the clown diving troupe, dive-bomb near the edge of the pool to drench the girls, do mildly difficult acrobatic tricks, smoke and comb my hair. There were a whole bunch of us who wasted all our time in this fashion. We were masters of the flat racing dive and the quick, flashy 55 yards. Any one of us would have sunk like a rock had he attempted a second lap, but we could all do an impressive tumble turn. When the whistle blew for races and the real swimmers appeared in their tracksuits, we repaired to the sand-pit, there to tell what we imagined were dirty jokes and share a fanatically casual cigarette with the more daring girls. Erections were either hidden or flaunted, depending on one's reputation for effrontery. I hid mine, either by draping a towel over my trunks as additional camouflage or just lying prone in the sand until the embarrassing acquisition went away. Sometimes this took a whole afternoon, but there was certainly nothing better to do. Falling for – not just perving on, but actually and rackingly falling for – a pretty girl in a Speedo certainly beat any thrills that were being experienced by the poor bastards who were swimming themselves to jelly in the heats and semi-finals. So, at any rate, I supposed. Every few minutes you could hear the spectators roar as they goaded some half-wit onward to evanescent glory. Meanwhile I concentrated on the eternal values of the way a girl's nipples hardened against her will behind their veils of blue cotton, or the way the sweet skin of her thigh near the groin might be the vellum mounting for a single black hair like the escaped mainspring of a pygmy timepiece.

The same sort of dichotomy prevailed at school. The school swimming team trained hard at North Sydney Olympic Pool. The rest of us went by toast-rack tram to Rushcutter's Bay, Redleaf Pool, Bronte or Coogee. The first two were small net enclosures in Sydney Harbour: they offered little except weeds around your legs and the constant challenge of dodging jelly-blubbers. But Bronte and Coogee pools were both beside ocean beaches, so that after the regulation hour of splashing around to no purpose and/or practising for the Bronze Medallion you could change back into uniform, have your name ticked off the roll, rush down to the dressing rooms on the beach, change back into trunks, and head for the surf. The first pairs of flippers made their appearance in those years. I had a big pair of green adjustables with straps that hurt – a characteristically bad buy – but I could catch waves with them well enough. Afraid of sharks but pleased to be at one with the elements, I surfed until I was exhausted. There were half a dozen of us, wastrels all, who thus used to consume the spare hours of every Wednesday afternoon after compulsory swimming – the beauty of our activities being, needless to say, that they were not compulsory. Frank Griffiths was our master spirit. Like Milo he was something of a lurk-man, but he had the additional quality of humour. In class he used to charm his way out of trouble. I began to see that there were advantages to playing the fool. In the surf he was completely at home. His skin was as slick as a duck's feathers. Broad-shouldered and long-legged, he could have been a competition swimmer if he had wanted to. But he didn't want to, any more than the rest of us.

For one thing, it was too much like work. For another, even if you did the work there was no guarantee of success. The best swimmer in our school was Peter Case. He trained about a hundred miles a day. He had gills. Every year from first year through to fifth he was champion. But he never finished higher than fourth in the CHS carnival. One year I watched him at North Sydney Olympic pool. He was in the same 440 race as Jon Henricks, who was then at Fort Street, and already well on the way to his Olympic gold. Henricks won by almost a length of the pool. Case was impressive to watch but you could see the strain. Henricks seemed to expend no effort whatsoever. He glided frictionless, as if salt water were interstellar space. Each arm was perfectly relaxed as it reached forward over the water, stiffening only when it became immersed. Each of his lazily waving feet seemed a third long section of the leg to which it was so loosely attached. The bow wave in front of his nose curved downwards on its way back, leaving a trough of air in which he occasionally breathed. He annihilated distance at a rate of about twenty strokes to the lap and tumble-turned like a porpoise running between wickets. He swam as if dreaming. It was clear that he had been born to swim. There was no point in even trying to compete. Contrary to the pious belief, where sports are concerned the important thing is not to have taken part, but to have won.

Nevertheless Case and his fellow swimmers, together with all the other star athletes, formed an elite within the school no matter how mediocre their performances outside it. If Case was worshipped, you can imagine what happened when John Konrads arrived. Even in his first year he was already nearly six feet tall. Still only eleven years old, he broke the school senior 880 record at his first carnival. He would have won every other senior event if he had been allowed to compete, but the 880 was the only one he was allowed to enter, and then only because there was no race at that distance in his age group. Upon being lapped for the second time, Case – then in his fifth and final year – retired with a broken heart and headed for the showers, the only healthy man I have ever seen limping with both legs. Not long afterwards Konrads went on to capture a sheaf of world records and become recognized as the greatest male swimmer on Earth. I am pleased to report, however, jumping ahead a bit, that in my last year at Sydney Tech I was privileged, in my capacity as prefect, to book him for running in the playground.

10. THE SOUND OF MUCUS

Even if I had possessed the will and the weight to be an athlete, an essential part of the wherewithal would still have been missing. Although I looked in the bloom of health, I was racked by colds throughout my adolescence. Indeed it was just one long cold that never went away. I produced mucus in thick streams. I carried half a dozen handkerchiefs and they were all full by the end of the day. Kleenex had already been invented but had not yet penetrated to Kogarah, where people still put a cold in their pockets. I was putting an epidemic in mine. Finally the floods of green slime and the interminable sniffle drove my mother to consult the local GP, Dr Bolton, who prescribed a course of penicillin injections. Over the next few years I was shot full of millions of units of penicillin. I built up a tremendous resistance to penicillin and an unquenchable fear of the hypodermic syringe – the latter phobia being destined to become a key factor, later on, in my long truancy from the dentist. I shook at the mere idea of being stuck. The actuality should have been just a dull thud in the upper arm, but I tensed up so much that the needle bounced off. Dr Bolton had to screw it in like a bradawl.

This went on for a couple of years with no diminution in the snot supply. Quite the contrary. No matter how hard I blew there was always more up there. This unabated deliquescence was gradually joined by such additional features as sharp pains above and behind the eyes. At the baths I couldn't submerge more than a few feet without feeling the extra pressure. Rather fancying myself as a diver, I was disappointed to find myself confined to the one-metre board. Not that I would ever have accomplished much from the three-metre board – an innate lack of daring guaranteed that – but one of my chief pleasures in life was to descend from a great height and somersault while making contact with the water at the very lip of the pool.

This activity was known as dive-bombing. An expert could make an impact like a 500-pounder, saturating the spectators over a range of many yards. There came a day when I surfaced in the puddle of spume produced by a particularly effective dive-bomb, and found my face hurting so much I could hardly get out of the water. For a while I thought that I had hit the tiled edge of the pool with my head.

Dr Bolton finally decided that my sinuses needed a wash. First he probed them extensively, using a stick wrapped in cotton wool soaked with local anaesthetic. This was the least funny thing that had ever happened to me, not excluding the time when I had had an abscessed tooth extracted and been sneered at by the dentist merely because a spout of pus had hit him in the eye. Dr Bolton's immortal line, 'You may feel a bit of discomfort,' still strikes me today as ranking among the understatements of the century. In a way he was right. What I felt wasn't pain so much as pressure. It was as if a wardrobe were being crammed up my nose. When he yanked out the stick and started to sluice the violated interior, I began a sobbing fit that lasted for some time. I went home traumatized. After visits to the dentist I usually tucked into a packet of Minties and a few bars of Cherry Ripe, secure in the knowledge that it would be a year before I had to go again. But with the sinuses I was on constant call. I had to keep up the treatment. Dr Bolton went on probing and sluicing for what seemed to me like years, until one day, on his way up my nose, he met a polyp coming down.

Polyps, or proud flesh, apparently favour the sinuses as a growth area. If I stuck my finger up my left nostril I could feel it entirely blocked by a convex meniscus the texture of Bakelite. This was the vanwall of what Dr Bolton assured my mother could be anything between a platoon and a battalion of polyps. Dr Bolton also assured her that a simple operation under local anaesthetic would be enough to clear the matter up. My mother, strongly supported by a silent tantrum I was staging in the background, suggested that I might be spared some suffering if the operation was done under general anaesthetic. 'No need for that,' Dr Bolton assured her. 'He'll only feel a bit of discomfort.'

After only a few weeks of sleepless waiting I found myself seated in Dr Bolton's surgery. Dressed in a white coat, he was on another chair facing me. First he did the familiar number with the dope-soaked stick of fairy floss. I found this as hilarious as always. Then he got up there with a pair of long-nosed forceps. They were slim to look at but by the time they were in my head they felt like heavy wire-cutters. It all lasted for centuries and I did a lot of crying. When I glanced into the kidney-shaped enamel basin on the table, it was heaped high with what would have looked like freshly cooked tripe if it had not been streaked with blood. My mother was waiting in the reception room when I came out. She had an awful look on her face. I have learned to recognize that look since. It is the way we look when someone we love is suffering and we can't help.

The operation was so traumatic that I spent the next year doing my best to conceal the fact that it had not worked. But there was too much mucus to hide and the pain both above and below my eyes formed a pair of invisible, hot iron spectacles that kept me awake. Dr Bolton at last referred me to a specialist. He, too, was fond of a preliminary probe or two with the fairy floss, but at least this time there was not a suggestion that the operation should be a sit-down. He wanted me down and out. I have never minded general anaesthetic. I rather relish the dreams. When I woke up, my head felt clear for the first time in years – perhaps the first time ever, since I could not remember when I had ever breathed so easily. There was some heavy bleeding, which the specialist staunched by stuffing my facial cavities full of gauze. This was only mildly amusing and the removal of the blood-caked gauze a few days later was even less so, but my new-found happiness was unimpaired. I went on suffering more than my share of colds, but the bad days ended with that operation. I can still remember the specialist's kindly look. Dr Bolton, who assisted at the operation, told me later that he had never seen such instruments: some of them had had little lights on them.

That has been the sum total of my ill-health to date: one adolescent brush with sinusitis. I didn't even have a severe case. To cure Joan Sutherland of the same thing, they had to slice her open along the top gum and cut through the bone behind her face. So I got off lightly. But the feeling of being helplessly dependent on medical skills is one I have never forgotten. Only in thoughtless moments do I take my strong constitution for granted. When I see sick, crippled or deformed people in the street, I always feel that the reason why they have too little luck is that someone gave me too much.

My hopes of heroism fading, I was obliged to find a new role, especially, when I started ceasing to be a star even at English. 'Jazz' moved on, a martinet came in, and I froze up. I was still near the top of the class, owing to my unusual powers of parsing, but I hardly stood out. Luckily a certain gift of the gab opened the way to a new career as a joker. The small boy is usually obliged to be amusing just as the fat boy is usually obliged to be amiable. I cultivated a knack of exaggeration. Lying outrageously, I inflated rumour and hearsay into saga and legend. The price of fame was small but decisive. I had to incur the accusation of being a bull artist – a charge that any Australian male of any age wants to avoid. But I wanted notoriety more. Rapidly I acquired it. From a small circle of listeners in class, I progressed to a large circle of listeners in the playground. Bigger boys came to mock and stayed to listen. Adapted from a recently seen film, my story of the Okinawa kamikazes lasted an entire lunch-time and drew an audience which, if it had not come equipped with its own sandwiches, would have had to be fed with loaves and fishes.

My new line in yarn-spinning was an expansion of the same trick that I had been working in Sunday School. All I had done was throw caution to the winds. I had also mastered the art of laughing at myself a fraction of a second before anybody else did. Climaxing a story of my close personal acquaintance with Rommel, I produced a pair of old sand-goggles from my pocket. This convinced the smaller boys, but the older boys were not fooled. Before they could laugh, I beat them to it. I ran with the hares, hunted with the hounds, and never left a swing except to step on to a roundabout. Gradually even the most scornful among my listeners came to accept that what Jamesie said wasn't *meant* to be true – only entertaining. If it wasn't that, key figures drifted away, and soon everyone else was gone along with them, leaving me alone with my uneaten sandwiches. It was my first experience of the difference between clicking and flopping.

Riding the crest, I diversified, exploiting a highly marketable capacity to fart at will. Thus I became an all-round entertainer. Somehow, perhaps by osmosis, I had learned this invaluable knack from Milo, who could fart the opening bars of 'Blue Moon'. The first time he performed this feat to a select audience in the back of his garage, the effect was shattering. Suddenly we were all outside in the sunlight, staggering around gasping with combined suffocation and astonishment. Using the Zippo cigarette lighter he had stolen from his father, Milo would set a light to his farts, producing a jet of flame rivalling that emitted by the oil refinery at Kurnell, across the bay.

I was never able to match Milo for sonority and melodic content, but I did manage to acquire the knack of letting one off whenever I wanted to. By mastering this skill I set myself on a par with those court jesters of old who could wow the monarch and all his retinue by unleashing, as a grandstand finale, a simultaneous leap, whistle and fart. Unable to extend my neo-Homeric story-telling activities from the playground to the classroom, I could nevertheless continue to hog the limelight by interpolating a gaseous running commentary while the teacher addressed himself to the blackboard. The essential factor here was volume control. My contributions had to be loud enough to amuse the class but not so strident that they caught the teacher's ear. They were bound to catch his nose eventually, but by that time they were untraceable, since I never made the mistake of either looking proud or overdoing the angelic innocence. While the teacher stood there with his nostrils twitching and scanned the room for malefactors, I stared inscrutably into the middle distance, as if lost in the middle of a quadratic equation.

Two bacon rolls and a custard pie were my undoing. Tuck shop lunches were a dangerous substitute for home-cut sandwiches, since they generated a less controllable supply of wind. Fred Pickett, the best of our maths teachers, was filling the board with some incomprehensible account of what happened to a locus on its way up the abscissa. I was waiting for a suitable cue. The whole secret of raising a laugh with a fart in class is to make it sound as if it is punctuating, or commenting upon, what the teacher is saying. Timing, not ripeness, is all. 'And since x tends to y as c tends to d,' Fred expounded, 'then the differential of the increment of x squared must be . . . must be . . . come on, come *on*! What must it flaming *be*?' Here was a chance to give my version of what it must be. I armed one, opened the bomb bay, and let it go. Unfortunately the results far exceeded the discreet limits I had intended. It sounded like a moose coughing. The shock wave and gamma radiation left people in nearby desks leaning sideways with both hands over their noses. Picking up a blackboard duster, Fred spun round, took aim and hurled it with one flowing movement. There was no question about his choice of target. Concentric circles of outward-leaning victims pointed back to me as surely as all those felled trees in Siberia pointed back to the meteor's point of impact. The duster impinged tangentially on my cranium and clattered to the floor. Within seconds I was on my way to the Deputy

Headmaster. I was carrying a note inscribed with the numeral 6, meaning that I was to be given six of the best.

The Deputy Head, Mr Dock, inevitably known as Hickory, lacked inches but made up for them with agility. A short, round man, he had a long, thin, whippy cane and would have looked like Bobby Riggs serving an ace if he had not prefaced his windup and delivery with a short swerving run starting in the far corner of the room. He didn't waste time talking. He just opened the note, glanced at it, and reached for the cane. Suddenly I wanted desperately to urinate. 'C-c-c-c-can I go to the t-t-t-t-toi-toi-toilet?' I asked bravely. To his great credit Hickory let me go. Perhaps he was not the psychopath he was cracked up to be. Perhaps he just didn't want a puddle on his floor. I raced downstairs and made it to the urinal approximately in time. My return up the same stairs was glacial, nay asymptotic, but Hickory kindly appeared on the landing to encourage me over the final stages. Since the rules stipulated that the hands be hit alternately, for each stroke Hickory had to change corners of the room before running up to serve. He covered a lot of ground. I found the shock of each impact nothing like as bad as the anticipation. Unfortunately the aftermath was worse than anything that could be imagined. I zigzagged back to class with my hands buried between my thighs. But even in the midst of my agony, I was already secure in the knowledge that fame was assured.

11. A PRONG IN PERIL

Thus I served out my remaining years at school – as a clown. It never made me especially popular, but at least I avoided unpopularity. At the end of each school year it was a bespectacled owl called Schratah who got tied to the flagpole and pelted with cream cakes. The most I can say for myself is that I didn't throw any of the cakes. But I can't pretend that I wasn't glad somebody else was being picked on instead of me. I would have found victimization hard to bear. Why Schratah didn't commit suicide was a constant mystery to me. It wasn't, after all, that they hated him for being Jewish and a foreigner. They hated him for himself.

Never shooting up with the suddenness I had been promised, I never stopped gradually growing either, until eventually it dawned on me that I was as tall as everyone else, with the necessary exception of the athletic heroes. Still checking up in the mirror, I came to realize that my neck was now if anything thicker than my head, although the back of my skull still protruded instead of sloping forward like Superman's. There had also been a mildly encouraging improvement in the behaviour of my tool. After prolonged immersion it still shrivelled up to the size of a jelly-bean, but otherwise – although I was in no danger of standing on the end of it – it was at least visible. Indeed nowadays it seemed always to be in one of two conditions: erect and semi-erect. The Smithers family had moved hurriedly away, amid rumours that Milo had finally and irrevocably Got Laurel Into Trouble. It didn't occur to me, or probably even to Milo, that such things could be attempted with any other girl except her. Ordinary girls could be kissed and fiddled with but there was no question of Going All The Way. Australia was still one of the most strictly moralistic societies in the Western world. As a natural corollary, rape was endemic. Every day and ten times on Sundays, the tabloid newspapers carried stories of young men being sentenced to life imprisonment for rape. Most of them seemed to deserve it, but sometimes you wondered. I was especially impressed by the front page stories about a young photographer who had taken twelve models down into the National Park near Heathcote and raped them all. Apparently he rendered them helpless with a roll of Elastoplast, releasing them one at a time from bondage in order to slake his fell desires. It occurred to me that either the young man or the Elastoplast must have had magic properties. But if the same thing ever occurred to the judge and jury, there was no hint of it. The rapist was taken to Goulbourn gaol and locked up to begin paying the slow price of his depravity. He's probably still there now.

Margaret, in the next street, would let me kiss her. Her mouth seemed to be always full of water and she had a way of bumping your teeth with hers, so that you were spitting chips of enamel afterwards, but she felt round and warm to hold, if you didn't mind the dribble. Jan, across the street, was pointedly eager to be kissed and even mildly interfered with, but her eyes crossed so badly that you kept wondering if she had seen something in the distance – a police car, for example. Shirley, down the street, was the most exciting of the local girls. At spin-the-bottle parties she was the number-one target. She had a fully developed figure and a marvellous hot, yielding mouth. I spent half an hour kissing her one night, pinning her against the wall in the driveway of her house. I had to go home in a running crouch, like a black-tracker. Shirley was so passionate that she might have co-operated if one of us had seriously tried to seduce her. But nobody our age had the nerve. It was an older boy from another district who had the privilege of taking Shirley's virginity, which must have felt as clean and crisp as the first bite of a sweet apple. His name was Barry Tate. Sensationally in command of his own car – a black Hillman Minx – he came booming down the street each evening after another easy day's work doing whatever it was he did. He had a concave chest and a rich, multi-coloured collection of pimples, but there was no getting past the fact that he also had his own car. He would take Shirley away in it to park down among the dunes at Doll's Point or Ramsgate. Somewhere out there, a long way beyond our envious reach, she must have yielded him her all.

Apart from Boys' Brigade, in which I became a less and less prominent participant, my church activities took up a steadily greater proportion of my spare time, principally because there were girls involved. I had one case of the amorous vision after another. Once I had graduated into long trousers, I even felt it possible to translate such adoration into real acquaintanceship. Christine Ballantine, alas, was beyond my hopes. She was almost beyond even my dreams. Short in the leg but unbelievably lovely in the face, she looked like the top half of a Botticelli angel. I burned tunnels in the air adoring her from afar. I even slogged through church twice in an evening, just to look at her as she sat in the choir. This was no mean tribute to her beauty, since the second sitting of church included a full-scale sermon from the Rev. C. Cummings Campbell. Quoting liberally from *A Man Called Peter* and various religious savants with three names each, the Rev. Campbell would unload from the pulpit a seemingly fathomless cargo of clichés. Meanwhile I drank in Christine's beauty, its every movement of lip and eyelid more pleasing to God than anything the Rev. Campbell would ever say.

Little Sandra McDougall I actually managed to touch. She was a tiny, sweet-looking blonde with a deep, grating voice like Mr Chifley, the late lamented leader of the Labor Party. The standard heavy teasing informed her of my love. With shyness on my side and understandable reluctance on hers, we got to the hand-holding stage. Unfortunately my sinuses, not yet cured at that time, ruined everything. No sooner had I picked up her white-gloved hand than I had to put it down again in order to blow my nose in whatever section of my sodden handkerchief had been used least. Behind the veil depending from her frangipani-bedecked hat, her large blue eyes would shut in what I hoped was modest sympathy, but suspected to be disgust. Eventually she took to tapping her foot while I honked and hooted. Finally she turned away.

But later on, with my health improved, the end of school approaching and some recognizable version of late adolescence approaching along with it, I began to find some of the older girls not entirely averse to being fumbled with. This was a revelation. That a mad girl like Laurel might do everything made it seem more likely, not less, that ordinary well-brought-up girls would do nothing. And yet here they were, letting you put your hand on their breasts or even – in advanced cases – between their thighs. It was a kind of warfare, with no-go areas and free fire zones. Breast fondling could go on for some time, but when it noticeably led to a deeper stage of heavy breathing then it had to stop. Thigh stroking could go on for only a short time at one go, although the hand was allowed back again at a decent interval after removal. A really determined assault might have burst through all these conventions but I would probably have been scared to death if they had suddenly ceased to be operative. Carol Pascoe, for example, didn't seem to know the rules. There was always a race to take her home after Fellowship meetings or socials. A few times I won it, usually by booking her up a week in advance. She had no inclination to remove the exploratory hand or even, as I was stunned to discover, the exploratory finger, which could work its will unchecked until numbness set in, leaving you with the disturbing sensation of having only nine fingers left. Meanwhile Carol would be bumping and grinding with her mouth open and her eyes closed. It was vaguely frightening, although one of course pretended otherwise. A dozen of us, comparing notes, loudly agreed that Carol was the Best to Take Home. Reg Hook showed us the condom that he planned to use on her. He had a detailed plan to dispel what was left of her innocence. As Reg later recounted it, the plan – involving himself, Carol, a blanket, and a Doll's Point sand dune at midnight – unfolded with ridiculous ease. In a trice Carol was lying there, sobbing with need. Unfortunately Reg was under the impression that you had to unroll the condom before putting it on. Since the rest of us would have done the same in his place, we were hardly in a position to point out his mistake.

Eventually a Scottish immigrant boy called Dorber gave Carol what she wanted. Thick of accent, repellent of epidermis and wise in the ways of the Glasgow slums, Dorber was an unlikely member of Fellowship or indeed of any organization more benign than the Parachute Regiment. But then he was not in search of religious instruction. He was out to use what we had been wasting. Our idea of the successful climax to an exciting evening was to limp home with a throbbing crotch and a finger smelling like a fishing smack. Dorber's ambitions were less oblique. He wanted everything, and in several cases, to our flabbergasted disapproval, got it.

Still, at least I had some tangible evidence that I was normally endowed. The only problem was to find the opportunity, courage and purpose which would allow of the endowment being put to use. The problem was almost solved for ever during a fortnight away at a National Fitness camp somewhere up in the bush. I attended this camp as part of a Sydney Tech contingent which included Griffiths

and others among the freaks and wastrels. I never bothered to find
out at the time precisely what National Fitness was or what aims it
was supposed to pursue, but in retrospect I can see that it was a
reasonably benevolent outfit promoting the concept of *mens sana in
corpore sano* on what it imagined to be an international scale. The
camp, constructed along military lines, consisted of weatherboard
huts scattered through the bush and linked up with winding paths.
There were several hundred boys present, including a hefty represen-
tation from Nauru Island. So black they looked blue, these were some
of the best-looking boys in creation. The one to whom all the others
deferred, although never with servility, was Detudame, son of the
Chief of Nauru.

Nowadays, Detudame is chief himself. I saw him on television
recently and was pleased to note that he had acquired a weight
problem closely resembling my own. At the time I am talking about
he was already pretty bulky, but it was all dark muscle, subtly catching
tangential light like polished hardwood. His retinue called him Det
for short. Within minutes we all did. He had Napoleonic charisma
combined with infinite charm. Through the black and white crowd
that surrounded him at all times I snatched glimpses from a distance,
awed by the amusement that spontaneously came into being around
him and which he could silence with a frown. He and the Nauruans
played a striptease game in which the object was to keep your clothes
while all around you were losing theirs. While he was doing the same
to you, you whipped your hands suddenly from behind your back
and confronted your opponent with any one of three symbols: scissors, paper, rock. Scissors cut paper but broke on rock. Paper covered
rock but was cut by scissors. If you lost, you had to remove an article
of clothing, even if it was the last thing you had on. When Det lost
– which he seldom did, being a mind reader – he stripped just as
willingly as his subjects. But on the one occasion when he was forced
down as far as his underpants, he insisted on going behind a bush.
While his entourage rolled around in hysterics, all we saw was the
royal Y-fronts being waved in the air. Thus the future monarch's
dignity was preserved. It will be apparent that I am talking about the
kind of brother I would have liked to have, and I suppose miss even
now.

This is a generous appreciation on my part, considering that Det
and his friends brought me to the edge of catastrophe. One night we

were playing Hunt the Lantern. I forget the rules. Probably I have repressed them. The relevant facts are simple. I was fleeing at full tilt through the pitch dark on a zigzag path between the gum trees. Det and a couple of his more carnivorous-looking pals were after me. Equipped with excellent night vision and the ability to run silently even over dead leaves, they were bad dreams straight out of James Fenimore Cooper. Suddenly I heard Det's voice shouting at me to look out. I thought it was a ruse and crammed on more speed. With stunning abruptness some kind of silent land-mine blew me straight up in the air. The stars raced past my eyes in parallel streaks, like the tips of porcupine quills. I landed sitting down, having performed the best part of a double forward somersault in the piked, or wrecked, position. Det and his friends arrived, vaulting unerringly over the barbed-wire fence that I had just tried to run through.

The fence had had three strands. The top strand had caused a certain amount of damage across my lower chest. The bottom strand had torn a few holes in my upper shins and knees. The middle strand had apparently done nothing more than tear my khaki shorts across the crotch. When they got me to the first-aid centre it was soon agreed that the shock was a worse threat than the cuts. The cuts were treated with the mandatory daubing of Acriflavine, tufts of cotton wool being left on the wounds so that scabs would form neatly under the gauze bandages. The shock was treated by wrapping me in a blanket and leaving me there to spend the night. When everyone was gone I reached up, switched the light back on, and snuck a look under my shorts. I had discouraged all attempts to remove them, but it couldn't be denied that a dull ache was emanating from that area. What I had felt, however, paled beside what I now saw. My tonk was sliced open on one side to what looked like a mortal depth. It was as if the captain of the *Titanic*, a few minutes after the encounter with the iceberg, had been lowered by the heels and given a sudden underwater close-up of the trouble he was in. The wound wasn't bleeding. It was just gaping. Hurriedly I covered it up again and stared at the ceiling, simultaneously pretending I hadn't seen what I had seen and wondering desperately what to do.

I chose to do nothing. In the event this proved to be the right decision, but it was prompted by nothing except cowardice. The mere thought of a doctor putting stitches in my tossle made me cross and uncross my legs very rapidly – or would have done, had I dared move them. So for days on end I kept my secret, snatching a look at the disaster area as often as I could. It was inspiring to see how quickly the antibodies rallied to the task. It was like a speeded-up film. Rapidly the whole area turned bright white, then pink. The gash itself, after first filling up with dark blood, tightened into a crisp scab that clicked satisfactorily when I tapped it with a fingernail. Before the remaining week of camp was over, it was obvious that my much-abused saveloy was out of danger. Even at this time, this was a relief. Looking back, I almost faint at the sheer range of implication. Another quarter of an inch on those barbs and my subsequent love-life would have consisted entirely of bad scenes from *The Sun Also Rises*.

12. ALL DRESSED UP

As the final years of school flowed turgidly under the bridge I became increasingly lost. Now that I had at last grown up, my comic persona no longer quite fitted. For many years I was to remain a prisoner of my own act, like a ventriloquist taken over by his dummy. Even today, unless I watch myself carefully, I take refuge in levity. Only self-discipline keeps my face straight. In *War and Peace*, if I were not allowed to identify with Andrey or even Nikolai than I suppose I would settle for Dolokhov. I would even try to be pleased if it were pointed out that I was in fact Pierre. But the man I can't help recognizing myself in is the unfortunate Zherkovim, who makes an untimely joke about the defeated General Mack and receives the full blast of Andrey's wrath.

Anyway, there is no point in carping now. My clever lip won me whatever popularity was coming to me at the time, so that I was able to go on finding myself welcome, or not unwelcome, among Griffiths' surfing parties and the school YMCA team that competed annually for the Pepsi-Cola Shield. Indeed among the latter crew I at last found myself a measure of sporting stardom, since the vaulting I had so painfully learned at Boys' Brigade was something of an advance on anything the other Centurions (that was the name of our team) could improvise uninstructed. My feet-through and flying angel-roll on the long box were instrumental in bringing the Pepsi-Cola Shield home to Sydney Technical High – a fact duly announced at school assembly. It didn't sound much of an achievement (and in fact was even less of an achievement than it sounded, since the teams we had defeated looked like pages from a Unesco pamphlet about the ravages of vitamin deficiency) but it was something. I also managed, at the eleventh hour, to be chosen for Grade football. It was only Third Grade, which consisted mainly of rejects from Second Grade, but you were given a fifth-hand jersey to wear and travelled about, meeting similarly decrepit sides from other schools. My position was five-eighth: what in Britain would be called a stand-off half. I had just enough speed and agility to tempt myself into trouble, but not enough of either to get out of it. My short career was effectively finished in a game against Manly, whose two enormous breakaways, like the clashing rocks of mythology, hit me from different directions while I was wondering what to do with the ball. Semi-conscious and feeling like an old car after it has been compressed into a block of scrap metal, I scored against my own side on the subsequent move and thus acquired the tag 'Wrong Way' James.

But at least I was able to have 'Third Grade Football 1956' embroidered in blue silk under the school badge on the breast pocket of my maroon blazer. Senior boys were encouraged thus to emblazon their achievements. My paltry single line of glory looked insignificant enough on its own and ludicrous beside the listed battle honours of the true sporting stars, which extended below their pockets on to the blazer itself. 'First Grade Football 1954. First Grade Football 1955. First Grade Football 1956. CHS Swimming 1952. CHS Swimming 1953 . . .' My lost companion Carnaby had a block of blue print on his blazer that looked, from a distance, like a page of heroic couplets. As for the Captain of the School, Leslie Halyard, it was lucky he was seven feet tall, since his credits went on and on like the titles of an epic movie.

The blazer was an important item of equipment. I bought mine after I was elected one of the school's eighteen prefects. I came in at number seventeen on the poll, one ahead of the school bell-ringer. Without the Third Grade football credit I never would have made it, and would thus never have enjoyed the heady privilege of supervising detention or of booking other boys for running in the playground. Admission to the rank of prefect was my sole latter-day school success. In other respects I might as well not have come to school at all. Indeed most of my clothes looked as if they had already left. By this time young men's fashions were reflecting the influence of *Rock Around the Clock* and *Don't Knock the Rock*. Another influence was the lingering impact of the bodgie era which had occupied the immediately preceding years. The bodgies had favoured a drape-shape rather like the British Teddy-boys, with shoes the size of Volkswagens and a heavily built-up hairstyle razored square across the neck. The American tennis manager Jack Kramer also played an important part in shaping our appearance, even though his palpable influence was confined to the apex of the head. His flat-top haircut was faithfully reflected by what occurred on top of our own craniums, where each hair rose vertically to the level of a single, imaginary horizontal plane and then stopped dead. Even Halyard, normally conservative in his attire, turned up one day with the top of his head looking as if it had been put through a band saw. Griffiths set up a barber shop in the prefects' room and gave us his skilled attention, checking the results with a tee-square. Well greased with Brylcreem, the side panels of our haircuts were left to grow long and be swept back with an octagonal, many-spiked plastic rake which looked like the inside of an Iron Maiden for butterflies. At the back, above the straight-as-a-die bottom line, a muted duck's arse effect occured, further echoing the just-vanished bodgie ideal and directly presaging the incoming cultural onslaught of *77 Sunset Strip*, among the first programmes to be shown on Australian television.

Continuing to read downwards, we come to the drape-shape jacket. The emphasis was on heavily padded shoulders and a waistless taper towards a hem line on the lower thighs. Cut to my personal specifications, the drape of my own jacket was so tastefully judged that you had to look for several seconds before noticing how a supernumerary set of shoulders, sloping at a steeper angle, started where the real ones ended. Shirt and ties were something assertive from a shop near Museum station called Scottish Tailoring, the pink, cerise or Mitchell Blue shirt flecked with white and the multi-banded iridescent slub tie cut square at the bottom like a decapitated coral snake. Scottish Tailoring also supplied the peg-top bottle green slacks with the fourteen-inch cuffs and the personalized fobs. Socks were usually chosen in some contrasting colour to the shirt. I favoured mauve socks myself, since they interposed an arresting bravura passage between the bottle green cuffs and the quilt-top ox-blood shoes with the half-inch-thick crepe soles. Moving, the shoes made a noise like cow pats at the moment of impact. Stationary, they allowed their occupant to lean over at any angle. You will understand that I am describing a representative outfit for day wear. In the evening I dressed up.

Somewhere else, in the parallel universe inhabited by the Australian equivalent of the middle class, boys of my age must have been learning to feel at ease with their advantages. Doubtless I would have found theirs a world of stultifying conventionality, had I known it. But I never knew it. The essence of a class system is not that the privileged are conscious of their privileges, but that the deprived are conscious of their deprivation. Deprived I never felt. I had neither the insight nor the power of observation to realise that there might be another breed who recognised each other simply by the untroubled, unquestioning way they shared good manners, well-cut clothes and shoes that never wore out. I didn't feel disadvantaged. I just felt lost. Conforming desperately with my nonconformist outward show, inwardly I could find nobody to identify with – certainly not Marlon Brando in *The Wild One* or James Dean in *Rebel Without a Cause*. The inarticulacy of those two heroes would have been a blessed retreat. Instead I was the captive of my fluent tongue. The effort of being continuously diverting left me limp. I never doubted that those were the only terms on which I would ever be accepted.

Close friends would probably have been there had I really wanted them. But that would have taken time from the daily task of playing to the gallery. To that, the only alternative I could ever countenance was solitude. Very occasionally I went out with Gary on the pillion of the BSA 500, but by now the refurbished one-lunger was disturbingly fast. Even in top gear the separate ignition strokes were still audible, but the vacuum behind me swelled my shirt out like a spinnaker, the airstream was hard on the eyes and when we heeled over in the corners I thought the speeding asphalt was coming up to hit me in the ear. Eventually he sold the 500 and bought a BSA 350 OHV which he started to adapt for racing. No matter what he did with it it would never be as quick as the AJS 7Rs that dominated its class, but it was still a demanding machine with expensive tastes. There was no longer much room in his life for me.

My mother and I still went to every change of programme at both Ramsgate and Rockdale Odeons so we were seeing at least four movies a week. She sat there dutifully through the war films, even though she despised most of them. She got really angry at John Wayne in *The Sands of Iwo Jima*. Musicals she couldn't take, but she still sat there, generously keeping me company while I envied Gene Kelly and doted on Cyd Charisse. She even sat still for Betty Hutton, though she would rather have had her teeth drilled. In fact the only film she ever walked out of was *Hot Blood*, an epic of gypsy life in which Cornel Wilde and Jane Russell stared significantly at each other through the flickering light of the campfire, very occasionally raising their arms above their heads as if to check up on the current state of their own armpits, although it turned out that they were only getting ready to dance. My mother and I quarrelled frequently but we reached a comforting unanimity on such matters as what constituted a lousy picture. She could be very funny about poor Mario Lanza. She took her revenge over antipathetic film stars by getting their names wrong. Muttering imprecations at Dolores Day and Susan Hollywood, she was good company as we walked home through the night along Rocky Point Road. For years the mere mention of Lizabeth Scott, renamed Elspeth Scott, was enough to send us both into hysterics. I wish our closeness could have been at least partly due to a conscious effort from me. On the contrary, it was only our apartness that was fuelled by my will. She knew that I was doing badly in my last years at high school. I knew she was right, but didn't want to admit that I had made a mistake. When we clashed, the talk and the tears went on for hours, leaving both of us exhausted.

So at most it was a family of two, except for Christmas, when we always went to visit Aunt Dot in Jannali. Aunt Dot laid on a Christmas tree and an enormous Christmas dinner, eaten as usual at noon on Christmas day. The fatted calf scarcely ranked among the *hors d'œuvres*. Everything was still as scalding hot as the day Grandpa spat the zac. The same trifles, plum puddings and lemon meringue pies. Decorated with cotton-wool snow, brittle globular doodads and strings of tinsel, the tree shed dry green needles and presents for myself. Another highlight of the trip was a visit around the corner to some distant relatives called the Sturrocks. The size of troglodytes and older than the hills, they crouched in the stygian depths of their weatherboard house and croaked greetings. All their lives they had gone on putting on clothes without ever taking them off. I believe they were spontaneously combustible, like those people in Dickens. The whole of Christmas was a solemn ritual but my mother and my aunt needed to be close even when they got on badly. Their brothers had never been much use to them, so they supported and comforted each other as their losses mounted. I would have been proud of both of them if I had had any sense. Lacking that, I withdrew into myself and counted the hours until I could be alone again.

At school and church I got by as an entertainer, but it was a solitary's way of being gregarious. I was never really at ease in company. Nowadays I am at last blessed with friends so close that I don't even feel the need to try, but at the time I am talking about such friendships belonged to other people. I observed them enviously from a distance. It was only in my own company that I could switch off the act. Until the Glaciarium closed down I used to go skating alone there twice a week all through the winter, on Wednesday afternoon after school and for two sessions on Saturday. I bought a second-hand pair of Puckmaster ice-hockey skates. They were a typically bad buy, although not as bad as the football boots that were three sizes too big and finished my Boys' Brigade soccer career before it began, since I had to run some distance before the boots started to move. The hockey skates were merely clapped out in the heels and soles, so that that the screws pulled out and the blades parted company from the boots at critical moments. But on the days when my skates stayed together I was perfectly content, circulating endlessly while ogling that prettiest of all sights, the line formed by the behind and upper thigh of a girl skater. I never went to classes and could perform no tricks more complicated than a 'three', but I had a flash turn of speed. During the fast skating periods I could run quickly enough in the turns to lay my inside hand on the ice – the surest way of pleasing the crowd, especially if another skater removed your fingers. As usual, I was trying hard to look good, but there were also moments of genuine, monastic solitude. Talking contentedly to myself I would circle with the crowd, zigzagging to hold my speed down and tucking one hand inside my windbreaker, like Napoleon. Perhaps Napoleon found out that he had chicken pox the same way I did. It was a hot day outside, the ice was covered with an inch of slush, there were thousands of people jamming the rink, the loudspeakers were playing 'Don't Let the Stars Get In Your Eyes', and I discovered I had a little bubble on my stomach. Two little bubbles. Scores of little bubbles. I left immediately, guilty with the realization that I had infected the whole Glaciarium. It closed soon after, probably as a direct result. Since there was no other ice rink nearer than San Francisco, I hung up my skates.

But there was also my bicycle. Simultaneously with my first long trousers had arrived a scarlet 28-inch frame Speedwell to replace the old brown 26-inch frame rattletrap on which I used to tilt quixotically with the privet hedges. The frame of the new bike was not fully tapered but with my eyes half closed I could almost call it a racing bike, especially after I had it equipped with white-wall tyres and three-speed Sturmey-Archer hub gears. At the beginning the saddle was flush with the cross bar. By the time of my final year in school the saddle was extended to its full height. I had given the bike's appointments a lot of thought. The gear-change trigger was placed next to one of the brake levers at the end of the ram's horn handlebars, so that changing down was like firing a gun, while all I had to do to change up was flex my knuckle. Impressively clad in striped T-shirt, sandshoes and khaki shorts with rolled-up legs, I rode many miles every weekend. I could be at Mascot aerodrome in a few minutes, at the George's River bridge in half an hour. Sometimes I rode all the way to the National Park, just so that I could coast down Artillery Hill. Boys got killed trying that: it was a long, long hill. The idea was to go down without ever touching the brakes and at the end to go streaking across the dam without any change in the stoic expression. No expression could have been more stoic than mine. The speed of the airstream was enough to distort my features until they looked like what happened to the rocket crew in *Destination Moon*, but underneath I was still heroically stoic. It was an important test, which I passed, although typically I was unable to do so without posing.

So I got used to travelling alone. It was hard on my mother, who earlier on had always been good at setting up interesting trips. She would sort out the details of trains, buses and boats, so that without effort I would find myself beside her watching the aborigines diving for coins at La Perouse, or howling along through the latticed girders of the Hawkesbury River bridge in the Newcastle Flyer. On the boat to Bundeena she got seats for us in the prow so that I could lean daringly over and watch the porpoises as they appeared, disappeared and reappeared in our bow wave, sinking to spin around each other and rising in quick succession to blow a squirt of aerated water that sprinkled your delighted face like angel spit. Now *there* was a gang worth joining. My mother told me that there was nothing in the sea, not even sharks, that could hurt them, and that there was nothing they wanted to hurt. Those were the days when she could still tell me things. The breeze caught her hair and pulled it back. She looked like Garbo in *Anna Christie*. When the water grew shallow enough for the sand to be clearly visible the porpoises peeled away and left us together.

But now I knew it all and couldn't bear to be told, not even by myself. I shouted down my own conscience when it tried to inform me that I was well on the way to securing a Leaving Certificate which would scarcely rank as a dishonourable discharge. Even English had gone completely sour on me. I had my name down to take the English Honours paper. Big joke. I was fully qualified to answer anything that might be asked about Erle Stanley Gardner or Leslie Charteris, but beyond that I was perfectly clueless. None of the dozen books a week I had been taking out of the local Public Library had anything to do with literature. Nor was the teacher assigned to the Honours class likely to spot the discrepancy between my knowledge and the tests about to be made of it. He was, in the first place, a librarian. He was, in the second place, geriatric. He might have been Mary Luke's older brother. Where Mary started every lesson with instructions on how to make a Bunsen burner, Dewey – short for Dewey Decimal System – always began by showing you how to open a new book from the centre so that reading it would not distort the spine. The book's spine, not yours. He was probably sound on that one subject but on anything else he was a dead loss. While he burbled aimlessly for his allotted hour, I spent the time memorizing all the parts of the Moto Guzzi V-8 racing motorcycle engine. But I was already well aware that not even so prodigious a feat of memory would do me any good. It was the older boys, the ones who could do the maths, who would go on to design and construct the beautiful machines. While I read about cars, they were already buying them, taking them apart, putting them back together and driving them around. On the other hand, I was no longer any good at English either.

I entered the examination hall with the same feelings the RAAF pilots must have had when they flew Brewster Buffaloes into action against the Japanese – underpowered, outgunned, fearful and ashamed. I left the examination hall fondly recalling how well I had felt going in. The mathematics papers I had expected to find incomprehensible, but it was unmanning to find the English Honours paper equally opaque. It was full of questions about people I had never heard of. Shakespeare's name I recognized almost instantly, but who was George Eliot? What had he written? I could do none of it. Simpler than going home would have been to catch a tram to the Gap and jump off. I spent weeks reassuring my mother that everything would be all right, while simultaneously indicating that if everything turned out not to be all right it would be no true measure of my real ability or future prospects. But when the results appeared in the *Herald* the bluff was over. I got an A and five Bs. The A was in English: it meant that I had failed my Honours paper outright but had been above average in the ordinary paper. Since the average mark for the ordinary English paper had been set to coincide with the linguistic attainments of Ginger Meggs this did not count for much. The five Bs meant that I had wasted my time for a lustrum each in five different mathematical subjects – a total of twenty-five man years straight down the drain. About all that I had managed to achieve was matriculation. It sounded like micturition and meant even less. Practically anybody could matriculate. But you needed several more As than I had achieved if you were to get a Commonwealth Scholarship, and without one of those there was not much hope of acquiring a university education. I was a total failure.

There was no longer any hope of dissuading my mother from the conviction that she had been right all along. Even in the dust and flame of the débâcle, it was obvious that English had been my best subject, or at any rate my least worst. In the mathematical subjects which had been supposed to further my engineering career I had scored almost nothing. I fought back with all the petulant fervour of one who knows that he is in the wrong. In my heart I had long known that the other boys would be the engineers. But where did that leave me? What was the thing I was supposed to do, now that it was proved I could do nothing else?

At this point, like the Fairy Godmother, the Repatriation Commission stepped in. The Australian government never got around to doing very much for war widows, but in a weak moment it had developed a soft spot for war orphans, who could claim a free university education as long as they matriculated. Far from having to meet Commonwealth Scholarship standards, they needed only to obtain the number and quality of passes that might be appropriate for an apprentice bottle-washer. By this absorbent criterion, I was in. All I had to do was apply. Even then I almost managed to persuade myself that I wanted to go to the University of Technology. If I had prevailed in this wish my mother would undoubtedly have ended it all under the wheels of a trolley bus. Luckily the Repat wasn't having any. Sydney University it had to be. They advised an Arts course. Since I thought this meant drawing, at which I had always been rather good, I signed on the dotted line.

In retrospect it seems incredible even to me that I had come so far and remained so ignorant. It was not just that I was nowhere compared with an English sixth-former or an American prep school graduate. I was nowhere compared even with my fellow Hurstville alumni who had gone to Sydney High. When I met Elstub on the train he was reading *The Age of Anxiety* and I was reading *Diving to Adventure*. Knowing nothing, I scarcely suspected what I was missing. Barely realizing what a university was, I looked forward to it as something vague on an indeterminate horizon. The immediate task was to survive as an office boy in the L. J. Hooker organization, my first proper job. In my senior high-school years I had tried several different jobs during the school holidays. The most disastrous was as a shop assistant in Coles, where I rapidly discovered that I was incapable of dealing with impatient customers without becoming flustered. Merely to discover that the anodised aluminium tray I was supposed to wrap was wider than the wrapping paper was enough to set me darting about distractedly in search of wider paper or a narrower anodised aluminium tray. In just such a frenzy I ran into a display stand on which were carefully arranged hundreds of cut-glass bowls, dishes and plates. The stuff proved to be amazingly durable, which raised questions about the composition of the glass. Instead of shattering, it bounced. But it bounced everywhere, and before the last piece had stopped rolling I was on my way home. I had a similar job in Herb Horsfield's Hobby House, but rather than sell wind-up toys to wind-up customers I retreated into the toilet and read *The Caine Mutiny*. When Herb finally realized that he was making no sales at all when I was in charge he reluctantly opened discussions about terms of separation. He quite liked me, which was foolish of him in the circumstances.

L. J. Hooker's was a bigger thing all round. By this time my mother was in despair of my ever accomplishing anything. She had no idea what a university Arts course might be but she had every reason to suppose that I would make a hash of it. L. J. Hooker's, on the other hand, was the fastest growing real-estate firm in Australia. If I applied myself I might work my way up. If only to blunt the edge of the disappointment in her eyes, I resolved to knuckle down.

In the three months before university started, I would prove myself as an office boy to myself, my mother and the world.

The main office of L. J. Hooker's was situated in Martin Place, just near the Cenotaph. I got off the train at Wynyard every morning, walked to the building, descended to the basement, hung up my coat, picked up my scissors and applied myself to the thrilling task of cutting out all the L. J. Hooker classified ads in that day's *Herald*. It took most of the morning. The rest of the day I pasted them into a big book. At set intervals I also delivered mail all around the building, thereby giving myself the opportunity to die of love for the boss's secretary, a tall, ravishingly voluptuous girl called Miss Wiper. Every day, delivering the mail to her, I would greet her with a suave one-liner gleaming from the polish of twenty-four hours' sleepless rehearsal. 'Hi, patootie,' I would pipe casually, 'how goes it?' Her answering smile invariably floored me completely. I would enter her office looking as relaxed as Ronald Colman – if you can imagine Ronald Colman wearing quilted shoes the size of small cars – and leave it crawling and sobbing. It seemed to me at such moments that my love was being answered. Actually, I now realize, something more interesting was happening. A kind woman was enjoying, mischievously but without malice, the spectacle of awkward young manhood searching for a voice and manner. Where is she now? What lucky man did she marry?

But love for Miss Wiper is an insufficient explanation for how thoroughly I became alienated from the task. If I had been blessed with a gift for self-knowledge, I would have clearly recognized myself to be unemployable. As it was, this and many other attempts had to run their disastrous course before I at last learned that I am good for what I am good for and for nothing else. It was only by an accident of timing that I was able to resign from Hooker's before I got the boot. Every Friday after work I had to take the mail – which was all contained in a special large envelope – across Martin Place to the GPO and drop it in the slot. Then I had to take another large envelope full of copy for the weekend's classified advertising around the corner to the *Herald* building and leave it at the desk. On the Friday before the week I was due to leave, I paid both these calls, hopped on the train at Wynyard, and was off to Kogarah for the usual weekend of quarrels, movies and long, lonely bike rides. Since we had no telephone, I did not have to answer for my latest achievement until Monday morning, when I got to the office and found a note on my desk from Miss Wiper asking if I could come up and see her as soon as it might be convenient.

Pausing only to comb my hair for half an hour, I translated myself to her office, the first lines of an off-hand speech already vibrant on my lips. She forestalled me with the information that it was L.J.H. – meaning Mr Hooker himself – who was requesting my presence. I had barely time to die the first nine hundred of a thousand deaths before I was in the great man's office and face to face with him across a desk which I at first thought was tapered at the sides, until I realized it was so big that my stunned vision was being struck by the perspective. There was nothing on top of the desk except L.J.H.'s folded hands and two empty envelopes. 'The famous Mr James, isn't it?' enquired L.J.H. This was the time to tell him that I was not the famous Mr James at all, but was in fact Group Captain the Baron Waldemar Incognito of the Moldavian Secret Service on a sensitive diplomatic mission which, alas, demanded that I should leave immediately by the nearest window. Unfortunately the words would not come, partly because my tongue had spot-welded itself to the roof of my mouth. 'Luckily the GPO and the *Herald* both got on to us while there was still time,' L.J.H. reassured me. 'A pity, in one way. You realize our weekend classified advertising involves several hundred thousand pounds' worth of business. It would have been the biggest mistake any office boy had ever made anywhere in the world. You would have been in Ripley.' By Ripley L.J.H. meant a newspaper feature called *Believe It or Not*, in which the readers were asked to marvel at such phenoma as a man who had cut down a gum tree with his teeth, or an office boy who had put half a million pounds' worth of classified advertisements through the wrong hole.

L.J.H. stood up. He looked very large. He also, I was pathetically relieved to note, looked very kind. He had his hand stuck out. At first I thought he was inviting me to read his palm, but then I realized he was saying goodbye. 'Something tells me that we'll be hearing more from you one day. Perhaps in some other line of work. You're going to the university, I believe.' It was a statement, not a question, but it gave me a chance to say something. 'Nyengh.' L.J.H. generously chose to ignore this further evidence that he was dealing with a

Venusian, just as he had chosen to ignore the distilled water dripping from my hand. 'It's a good life. You'll find yourself there.' I was on my way out, going backwards. The oak door was shut. I was alone with Miss Wiper. Silently she offered me a Mintie.

13. LET US REJOICE, THEREFORE

Freshers and freshettes arrived at the university a week before full term in order to be inducted into the academic life by means of lectures, displays, film shows and theatrical events. The period was known as Orientation Week, a title which confused me, since I failed to see why the Far East should be involved. The university motto was *Sidere mens eadem mutato*, which loosely translated means 'Sydney University is really Oxford or Cambridge laterally displaced approximately 12,000 miles.' In fact the differences were enormous. For one thing, there were few colleges: the overwhelming majority of students arrived in the morning and left in the evening. In the Arts course you could read several subjects, rather like the American system. The way to pass exams was to reproduce the lectures. Personal supervision – the heart of the Oxbridge system – scarcely existed. There was a Union for debates and a certain amount of strained singing in which *Gaudeamus igitur* featured prominently, but on the whole the emphasis was on pushing forward to get one's degree. With careers as lawyers or upper-echelon school-teachers in mind, the Arts students were even more dedicated to exam passing than anyone else. There was a day shift and a night shift, both toiling away nervelessly towards their nine passes. It took some of them the maximum allowable nine years, but they all got there. Nobody who wanted to pass ever failed, not even the beautiful, elegantly groomed, ineffably dumb girls from Frensham who had been sent along to acquire some elementary culture before resuming their inexorable progress towards marriage with a grazier. Any real originality of mind or behaviour was confined to the astrophysics department or the medical school, which both ranked high in world standing. The huge Arts faculty placed as little emphasis on the human imagination as was consistent with the study of its products.

Even for Australia, the late 1950s were an unusually apolitical, conformist period. Nevertheless a certain amount of eccentricity took place. There were about two dozen illuminati who dominated the student newspaper *honi soit*, edited and contributed to the magazines *Hermes* and *Arna*, and produced, directed and acted in plays put on by SUDS (the Dramatic Society) and Players (the other dramatic society). Making a career out of failing first year Arts on an annual basis, this coherent little group were hard to miss during Orientation Week, since they were continually trotting up and down Science Road in order to take turns manning the publicity booths relating to their various activities. The booth for *honi soit* was called the Flying Saucer. A circular plywood creation with a pointed roof, it was only about six feet in diameter but at the moment of my arrival it was crammed with these exotic creatures, the like of which I had never seen. Nor, I think, had they seen anything quite like me. I had turned up in my school blazer, but in order to indicate that I was a man of parts I had pinned my Presbyterian Fellowship badge to the lapel, alongside the Boys' Brigade badge in my buttonhole. A brown briefcase contained sandwiches. My haircut looked like an aircraft carrier for flies.

But at worst they were seeing an extreme example of a known type, the clueless fresher. I, on the other hand, was seeing something I could not even compare with other examples of itself. I hadn't known that people were allowed to look like this. The women had long, stringy black hair, heavy eye make-up, and smoked cigarettes no hands. The men smoked their cigarettes in long holders. They affected flannel shirts, corduroy trousers, and the kind of long-nosed desert boots which I was subsequently informed were called brothel creepers. During this first encounter I could see nothing of these people below waist level, since only their upper works showed above the counter of the Flying Saucer. But their tightly packed heads, arms and torsos were sufficiently extraterrestrial to leave me numb with awe. 'My God,' cried the shortest of the men, 'it's a Christian! Come and work for *honi soit*. We need a broad spectrum of opinion. You could offset the influence of Wanda here. She's a witch.'

The girl referred to as Wanda coughed her assent, projecting a small puff of ash. 'My name is Spencer,' said the same short man again. He had jug ears, horn-rimmed glasses and a crew cut. 'Sign here and report for duty at the office tomorrow morning. It's around that corner. A sort of hut arrangement in Early Permanent Temporary. Here is a sample copy of the paper. Those badges are distorting the shape of what would be a perfectly good jacket, if it were a different colour and cut.'

Threading my way in a daze through the other booths, a good quarter of which were magically staffed by the same raggle-taggle team I had just met in the Flying Saucer, I entered the Union building, mechanically bought a tie dotted with the University crest, and sat down in the reading room to look at my sample copy of *honi soit*. Half of it seemed to be written by Spencer. There was a short story by him of which I could make little and some poems of which I could make even less. One of the poems was about Rimbaud's cigar. Who was Rimbaud? Yet in another way I saw the point instantly. The vividness of the language was extraordinary. Even when crammed into meticulously symmetrical verse forms every sentence sounded like speech. I can't say that my future course was set there and then, but neither can I say that it wasn't. I was so excited that my badges rattled. There were sparks coming off my lapel.

Later that day I attended the Sex Lecture and laughed knowingly along with all the other nervous virgins. I joined both Film Group and the Film Society, though I had no idea how they differed. I joined almost everything. I wondered where I could buy a pair of brothel creepers. Every time it all became too much I retreated to my bolt-hole in the Union reading room and looked at *honi soit* again. The cartoons were amazingly good. They were signed 'Huggins'. Everybody who counted seemed to have only one name. Every other leather chair in the reading room was similarly occupied by a freshman looking, I was relieved to note, not much more at ease than myself. Indeed few could smoke as confidently as I, although everyone was trying. It was like a bush fire in there.

I headed for home bamboozled with smoke, and strange, unfocused dreams. At tea I blew smoke into my mother's face and explained that at university one was expected to join in a wide range of extracurricular activities in order to broaden one's outlook. I sketched reassuring verbal pictures of how I would explore caves with the Speleological Society and jump with the Parachute Club. My mother doubtless had the look of someone whose troubles are only just beginning, but my mouth was too far open for my eyes to notice anything.

Next day I turned up at the *honi soit* office bright and early, several times tripping adroitly on the short flight of steps. I was

wearing my new brothel creepers, bought on the way up the hill from
Central Station. My old ox-blood quilt-tops were in my briefcase. I
had chosen a pair of brothel creepers with very long toes. They must
have looked, to the independent observer, rather like the footwear of
a peculiarly unsubtle clown. Certainly it was hard to climb stairs in
them without turning sideways, so my arrival in the office proper
was somewhat crab-like. The Flying Saucer crew were all in there,
plus a few more I was seeing for the first time. Wanda was still
smoking no hands. Spencer was sitting at a typewriter. A tall man
looking like an illustration of a kindly young history master in an
English public school was standing beside him.

'Good morning,' said Spencer without ceasing to type. 'This is
Keith Cameron.' The tall man said, 'How do you do. Sandwich?' 'You
aren't expected to take one,' said Spencer. 'Cameron is merely being
polite. Wanda you already know. The man in the suit is John Bottomley.' Bottomley was conservatively tailored for the year 1908. He
wore spats. 'The man in the other suit is Jim Howie.' Howie was
dressed and groomed for the grouse moors. 'Wanda will show you
how to edit copy. Meanwhile Cameron and I will get on with this
diverting lampoon for the next issue. On behalf of us all Howie and
Bottomley are hatching a plot to unseat the editor, who is an idiot.
For a blessing he is not present. A no-confidence motion concerning
the editorship will be put at a special meeting in the Wallace Theatre
this afternoon at three o'clock. Here is Maurice Grogan.'

Grogan swung into the office by one hand, which was reverse-
gripped around the upper door frame. He wore nothing on his
superbly muscular body except a Speedo the size of a G-string, a pair
of the kind of sandals known as Hong Kong thongs, and a beard. He
jumped up on a desk and crouched, gibbering and snickering.
Nobody seemed to notice. I sedulously copied everybody else's indifference while Wanda showed me how to sub-edit the readers' letters.
To do this she had to use her hands – my first evidence that they
were not paralysed. When she pointed things out she did not always
point to the right place because her eyes were screwed up. Ash fell
from her cigarette, which she allowed to grow remarkably short
during the course of her lesson. I was afraid her face would catch
fire. Meanwhile the conspirators conspired and the creators created,
both colloquies being punctuated by low growls and high-pitched
squeals from Grogan. As they worked, Cameron and Spencer kept

up an exchange of allusive wit that I found at once daunting and exhilarating. Spencer called something Firbankian. Who, what or where was Firbankian? I was lost, yet not in the usual way of feeling that I ought to be somewhere else. Somehow I knew that I was in exactly the right spot.

'Shall we lunch at Manning or the Forest Lodge?' asked Spencer. 'Let's remember,' said Cameron, 'the importance of remaining sober.' 'Not as important as having a drink,' said Bottomley. 'And besides, we'll never get the fool out anyway. A gesture is the most we can hope to achieve.' With me attached, the whole caravan moved across Parramatta Road, up a flight of steps, and along the street to a pub called the Forest Lodge, which during opening hours was the daytime headquarters of the artistic set. We all trooped through the back gate while Grogan swarmed over the wall. Again nobody took any notice. I was later to learn that Grogan was Spencer's steady date. Spencer was bisexual but least unhappy with Grogan. The same applied to Grogan vis-à-vis Spencer. For a long time I was incapable of grasping any of these facts, being under the impression that homosexuality was some kind of rare disease. I am glad to say that incomprehension gave way to tolerance without any intervening period of bigotry. But enlightenment lay far in the future, and for the time being I was as innocent as Queen Victoria when young.

As in all Australian pubs at the time, the beer came in two kinds, New and Old. New was made yesterday and Old was made the day before. I asked for a schooner of New, manfully not betraying the fact that it was the second drink of my life. It differed from the first drink in that I was able to sip it without gagging. It still tasted like camel's pee. I closed my eyes so that nobody would notice they were crossed. But my ears were functioning perfectly. They had never had so much to listen to. The brain between them could process only the odd scrap of the information that was streaming in through the aural receptors. I had never heard such conversation. What kind of car, I wondered, was a Ford Madox Ford? What sort of conflict was an Evelyn War? At the mention of *Decline and Fall*, I advanced the name of Gibbon. Cameron gently explained that the book in question was written by the aforesaid War, spelt Waugh. Had I not read anything by him? Who was my idea of a good modern novelist? I said Nicholas Monsarrat. There were snorts all round at this. All present snorted audibly. Wanda snorted visibly. Spencer cast his eyes to the sky. But

Cameron saved my face by insisting that there were good reasons for admiring Monsarrat, especially in his less famous works such as *HMS Marlborough Will Enter Harbour*. I would find, however, Cameron assured me, that Waugh's early novels were unbeatable for comic invention. 'How can you talk about Waugh when I'm reading Firbank?' Spencer asked a cloud. 'Here's Huggins.'

Through the gate walked the most artistic-looking young man I had ever seen in my two days' experience of artistic young men. He was all pale suede and corduroy. The ends of a loosely knit scarf dangled almost to the ground. He had a folio under his arm. Surrounding a face so handsome it was like a cartoon, his hair was blond and abundant. He was smoking a cigarette about two feet long. Within seconds he was seated, sipping at a beer glass held in one hand while he sketched with the other. He did a group sketch of everybody present. I was staggered – by the speed of his hand, by the quality of what it produced, and by the fact that I was included in the result, which I was allowed to keep. That night I pasted it on to my wall at home, airily explaining to my mother that it was the work of my friend Huggins, whom I knew quite well, since he was a close acquaintance of mine, and had in fact sat beside me during the vitally important meeting in which the editor of *honi soit* had retained his position only by a hair's breadth. Actually, I now realize, any condemnation emanating from my new acquaintances had the effect of vociferous advocacy, just as anything they favoured was automatically doomed. Spencer's speech had clinched the issue. He mentioned Cocteau, Kleist and Lord Alfred Douglas. The chairman imposed a gag and put the motion to a vote. It was lost by 560 votes to eight. I was one of the eight.

From that day my university career proceeded on two separate paths, one of them curricular and the other not. In my new desert boots, but still retaining my Fellowship badge, I attended lectures in my four first-year subjects, English I, Modern History I, Psychology I and Anthropology I. One among hundreds, I sat taking elaborate notes. I see no reason to mock myself in retrospect for so slavishly writing everything down: nearly all of it was news to me, and some of it was to prove permanently useful. The lectures on phonetics, for example, were a painless way for a writer to pick up essential knowledge about what sounds really rhyme even when they look as if they don't, and what sounds really don't rhyme even when they look as if they do. Twenty years later I am still drawing on that knowledge every day. Nor was I in any position to scorn elementary lectures on the time-shift in *A Passage to India*, since I was not yet fully divested of the impression that E. M. Forster's principal creation had been Horatio Hornblower. As for *A Portrait of the Artist as a Young Man*, I certainly needed help there, having been only dimly aware that Ireland was a Catholic country.

Modern History helped to make me less clueless on such points. The English component of the History course was occupied mainly with Tudor constitutional documents. To the suitably unprepared student it could not have been duller. But the European side of things introduced me to the Anabaptists, the Medici, the Habsburgs and a charming group of bankers called the Fuggers. Even here, though, I had trouble establishing a perspective. What had been so wonderful about the Renaissance? Why had Burckhardt bothered even to the extent of being wrong about it? But my pen raced on, unhampered by the mind's doubts. I didn't even know enough to know that what I now knew meant nothing without the knowledge that was meant to go around it.

Anthropology lectures were full of references to Evans-Pritchard, Radcliffe-Brown and Margaret Mead. The set books had titles like *Growing Up in New Guinea*, *Structure and Function in Primitive Pago-Pago* and *Having It Off in Hawaii*. Every time evolution got a mention, the girls in the audience who belonged to Sancta Sophia college would put a conscience-saving mark at the top of the page and discreetly cross themselves. Since they ran to angora twin-sets, this last move would involve a gentle but tangible-looking self-inflicted pressure on their cosily enclosed bosoms, which in several cases were of notable size and shape. Watching one especially pretty Catholic girl called Noeleen Syms thus delicately caressing her own breasts, I sucked so thoughtfully on my biro that I was favoured with a sudden, solid mouthful of black ink. For the next week I had lips like a silent movie star and teeth like the Mikado.

Psychology was taught by a faculty composed exclusively of mechanists, behaviourists and logical positivists. They would have made Pavlov sound like a mystic had he been foolish enough to show up. He must have heard about how boring they were, since he never appeared, but it was not for want of having his name invoked. The whole faculty salivated *en masse* at the mere mention of him. As so often happens, dogmatic contempt for the very idea of the human soul was accompanied by limitless belief in the quantifiability of human personality. On the one hand we were informed that there was no ghost in the machine. On the other we were taught how to administer tests which would measure whether children were well adjusted. But quite a lot of solid information was embedded in the pulp. Since there was nothing I did not write down and memorize, the real information was still there years later, when all the theoretical blubber surrounding it had rotted away. A synapse, after all, remains a synapse, even after some clod has tried to convince you that Michelangelo's talent can be explained in terms of the number and intensity of electrical impulses travelling across it. Or do I mean a ganglion?

Thus I applied myself. At that time a genuinely important man, Professor John Anderson, was head of the Philosophy Faculty and still delivering his famous lectures on logic to first-year classes, but typically I had failed to set my name down for the only subject that might have stimulated a mental component more intricate than mere memory. As it was, I did not sustain the full impact of Anderson's realism until some years later. For the time being it was taxing enough to absorb elementary information about palatal fricatives, gametes, Dyak kinship patterns and the theological significance of Zwingli. Walled in behind a stack of books with titles like *We of the Wee-Wee* and *Dropping Your Lunch in the Desert*, I sat at the back of the Wallace theatre with a fairly steady set of companions. Most of them had already graduated out of school blazers into sports coats, but it was plain that in their case raffishness would go no further. Less square than the out-and-out exam passers, they were still not bohemians. They were ex-GPS and lived in fashionable harbour-side suburbs like Bellevue Hill and Rose Bay. Without exception they were on their way to becoming lawyers. For them, Arts was a couple of easy years before the real work started. Some of them drove MG TCs. Their real life happened away from the university, but they talked about it while they were there. Admiring their relaxation, I was glad to be in with them and vaguely hoped that some of their ease would rub off on me.

On the way to lectures, during lectures and after lectures they all watched girls, awarding points for prettiness of face, size of chest, etc. Twenty years later they are probably still talking the same way and doing the same things. They were lucky enough to get set in their ways early. I warmed to them because they knew exactly what they were and liked being it. Their self-assurance, I need hardly add, was no virtue in itself, and to admire it was an admission of inadequacy on my part. Doubtless I would have warmed to the *Waffen-SS* for the same reason. Luckily the group in question happened to be harmless. Gilbert Bolt was the ringleader, mainly through being even less energetic than the rest of them. Leading from behind was a technique I had not previously encountered. Somehow, without lifting a finger, he made ordinary things amusing. He looked half asleep most of the time. Raising an eyebrow about a millimetre was his way of advising me to calm down.

Perhaps the Bellevue Hill mob were my anchor to windward, because simultaneously I was becoming more and more involved with the aesthetes. Except for the Film Society, I soon came to have no other extracurricular activity. Nor did I last long as an active member of the Film Society. Their screenings took place at lunchtime in the Union Hall, a highly atmospheric neo-Gothic nightmare of a place which was unforgivably pulled down a few years later. Everybody was there. Members of the Film Society sat in the minstrel gallery while the common herd sat in the hall proper. Before the house lights dimmed an old 78 of Bunk Johnson and George Lewis performing 'When the Saints Go Marching In' was played over the public address system. I was proud to be among those in the gallery but it was fated that I should join the majority below. There were two full-sized 35mm projectors. We manned them with a crew of two, stripped to the waist because of the heat. I found it hard to keep the carbon arc burning at the right intensity. When the picture got dark, I overdid it with the readjustment, so that the picture got too bright. I never noticed a stoppage until the film melted. On the screen, Alan Ladd and Virginia Mayo would turn to stone and be suddenly overwhelmed by bubbling gravy. A junior member was supposed never to be left alone in the box but in practice the senior crew member was often outside in the gallery palpating his girlfriend.

If I had had help, the fourth reel of *Simba* would probably never have got away from me. The take-up reel fell off its spindle, leaving me a clear choice of shutting down the projector or else letting the film pile up on the floor. I chose the second course, unaware of just how much volume a reel of film occupies when unwound. When it was time for the next reel change, my senior colleague, whose name was Pratt and who was sitting outside in the gallery, retrieved his hand from his girlfriend's blouse and opened the door to the box. He was expecting to see me and the projectors. Instead he was confronted with a pulsing, writhing wall of celluloid. I was somewhere inside it. It was at least half his fault. But screening *Tales of Ugetsu* with its reels in the wrong order was entirely my responsibility, since I was in charge of film preparation that day. I suppose I marked the reels wrongly. Hardly anybody noticed the difference, but I realized that it was time to dismiss myself from the Film Society and join its public.

Anyway, I had started to begrudge any of my spare time that was not spent with the bohemians. The Union Revue would have been enough on its own to win my allegiance to their cause. By some act of folly Spencer and Cameron had been placed in charge of the revue for that year. They called it *Flying Saucers*. Between them they wrote all the scripts. They also appeared in most of the songs and sketches. The decor, by Huggins, was brilliant when you could see it. Spencer, however, had designed the lighting. Little would have been visible even if those Film Society members who were operating the dimmers had contrived to stay sober. There was great emphasis on dry ice, so that slow billows of mist crept from the stage into the auditorium, which gradually came to resemble a polar landscape in which people had been embedded up to the neck. Ultra-violet light made the actors' teeth glow green through the white fog. Instrumental music came from an electronic synthesizer played by Pratt. Vocal music was by Palestrina. There were at least two sketches about Virginia Woolf. A third sketch might have been about her, but was more probably about Gertrude Stein. Grogan played Alice B. Toklas, or it could have been Vita Sackville-West. Wanda was either in the cast or kept crossing the stage for some other reason. Bottomley and Howie, sharing the one pair of large trousers, purported to be a mutation. They mouthed abstract dialogue, partly as a forecast of how language might deteriorate in the aftermath of an atomic war, partly in defer-ence to the fact that nobody had got around to actually writing the sketch. A tall, beautiful girl called Penelope White came on wearing a gown composed of shaving mirrors. She announced, in a voice like a chainsaw hitting granite, that her song had not been written yet, but that Spencer had asked her to recite a poem. She recited it.

I subsequently learned that it was by John Crowe Ransom. During her recitative, Spencer stood on one leg in the background, softly tapping a gong.

Interval was longer than the first half, which in turn was longer than the second half, although it was hard to tell when that was over. The audience, except for myself and my companion, had left long before. My companion was a girl from Kogarah Presbyterian Church Fellowship called Robin Warne. Afterwards I took her home to Carlton, telling her, during the long train trip, that Spencer and Cameron believed in pitching their work at a level which would force the audience either to confess itself inadequate or else translate its prejudices into violence. I quoted Spencer to the effect that an audience should be challenged, not coddled. When Robin announced that she hadn't understood or enjoyed a single moment of the evening from start to finish, I countered with Spencer's favourite word: 'Precisely.'

She burst out laughing when I tried to kiss her and didn't speak to me the following Sunday, but I didn't notice. I was too busy planning that year's Kogarah Fellowship revue, which I called *Unidentified Flying Objects*. As producer and director I appointed myself sole script writer and cast myself in every sketch. Lacking adequate supplies of dry ice, I set fire to some rags in a plastic bucket. Graham Truscott, decorated with a joke moustache of his own devising, was in charge of sound, which consisted of a jewel from my recently begun modern jazz collection – an EP record featuring Maynard Ferguson and Clark Terry engaged in a long attempt to damage each other's hearing. I had tested this particular disc a few hundred times on my mother and could vouch for its challenging effect. As the trumpeters interminably wailed and shrieked, I improvised monologues in which such names as Ford Madox Ford and Ronald Firbank figured prominently. The audience stormed the exits.

That same week, the Fellowship newspaper, of which I was editor and leading contributor, was largely devoted to a long article extolling the virtues of atheism. I had cribbed this almost word for word from the preface to *Androcles and the Lion*, one of the set books for English I. Shaw had enchanted me with his rationalist blarney. It was fitting that my shallow faith should have been uprooted by a toy shovel. The Reverend C. Cummings Campbell asked me along for afternoon tea at the Manse. Still coughing from his evening at the one and only performance of *Unidentified Flying Objects* (handicapped by a pair of lungs which had been poisoned at Ypres, he had been among the last to fight his way out of the hall) he nevertheless managed to contain his anger. Instead of booting me immediately into the street, he began by gently suggesting that I might care to off-load some of my more onerous responsibilities, such as the editorship of the Fellowship newspaper, until I had worked out of my system what was plainly 'the influence of that man Anderson'. As usual I was careful to resign a split second before being fired. I told him that I did indeed need time to think, and that perhaps it would be better if for the nonce I were to absent myself altogether. He heaved what would have been a sigh of relief if it had not turned into a coughing fit. My last vision of all things Presbyterian was of the piece of sponge cake – it had pink icing – which I had parked uneaten on the edge of my saucer.

Showing my usual capacity to walk away without a qualm, I left it all behind upon the instant: the bugles and the drums, the vaulting horse and the oak pews, Christine Ballantine's eyes like a pleading fawn and Mrs Pike's voice like a strangled fowl. I had no doubts that I was through with it all for ever. My cocksureness must have been terrible to behold. Night after night I reduced my mother to tears with my intellectual arrogance. Copied sedulously from Spencer, but potentiated by an insensitivity that was all my own, my forensic style was as intransigent as Vyshinsky's. Ferociously I attacked my mother's lingering, atavistic determination to go on believing in something. If she didn't believe in anything specific, I insisted, why couldn't she just believe in nothing? Triumphantly I refuted her arguments, never recognizing that they were true feelings and amounted to a deep intuition of the world, which in the long run we must see to be purposeful if we are to live in it at all.

I suppose that first year at university was just about the most ridiculous phase of my life. It was love again, of course, but this time I was in love with all of them. I copied Spencer's walk, talk and gestures. I copied the way he wrote. I copied the way Keith Cameron read: Spencer, lost in the toils of a fully bisexual love life and a chronic deficiency of funds, hardly ever read anything except science fiction. I soon realized that his *pronunciamentos* on literature in general were based on the most evanescent acquaintance with its individual products. But Cameron, who already had a BA degree and was qualifying to begin an MA, had an impressive private library of modern literature. I devoured it author by author. Spencer had told me *Four Quartets* was the greatest thing written in recent times. I practically memorized it, but was bewildered to find that Spencer had switched his allegiance to Edith Sitwell. Cameron was less capricious. His level head was the necessary corrective to Spencer's influence. Huggins I admired for grace, ease, creative fertility, and plethora of beautiful girlfriends. He was always promising to let me have one of them when he had finished with her, but somehow it never came about. This was lucky in a way, because I would scarcely have known how to behave. I had a girlfriend of my own, an Arts I student called Sally Vaughan: sweet, pretty, decent and intelligent. There was a lot of heavy petting going on but she was a Catholic, I was an idiot, and there was nowhere to take her anyway. She lived with her parents in Mosman, across the harbour. I still went home every night, although later and later as the year wore on, especially after I had discovered in myself a liking for the effects produced by several schooners of New consumed one after the other.

In the Forest Lodge I drank with the Bellevue Hill mob and the aesthetes. With Spencer, Huggins, Grogan and Wanda (Cameron was a teetotaller) I visited my first King's Cross cafés and became acquainted with wine. There was more of the same stuff at Lorenzini's, a wine bar where the university writers made contact with the intelligentsia of the town. Lex Banning, the spastic poet, was often to be found there. But the place where all the half-worlds met was the Royal George Hotel, down in Pyrmont. The Royal George was the headquarters of the Downtown Push, usually known as just the Push. The Push was composed of several different elements. The most prominent component was, or were, the Libertarians – a university free thought society consisting mainly of people who, like the aesthetes, failed Arts I on a career basis, but in this case as a form of political protest against the state. Endorsing Pareto's analysis of sexual guilt as a repressive social mechanism, the Libertarians freely helped themselves to each other's girlfriends. They had their own folk singer, Johnny Pitts, a hairy dwarf who every few minutes would flail his guitar, launch into a few bars of some barely comprehensible protest song about working conditions on an American railroad, and fall sideways.

The next most prominent component was the aesthetes themselves, minus Keith Cameron but plus some specimens who were no
longer to be seen around university, their nine years having finally run
out. Without exception they were on the verge of writing, painting or
composing something so marvellous that they did not want to run
the risk of injuring it by rational analysis. As well as the Libertarians
and the aesthetes there were small-time gamblers, traditional jazz
fans and the homosexual radio repair men who had science fiction
as a religion. A pick-up jazz band played loudly in the bar. The back
room had tables and chairs. If you stuck your head through the door
of the back room you came face to face with the Push. The noise,
the smoke and the heterogeneity of physiognomy were too much to
take in. It looked like a cartoon on which Hogarth, Daumier and
George Grosz had all worked together simultaneously, fighting for
supremacy.

Nothing feels more like home than the place where the homeless
gather. I was enchanted. Here was a paradise beyond the dreams of
my mother or the Kogarah Presbyterian Church Fellowship. Here was
Bohemia. I had friends here. Everyone in the Push borrowed money
from everybody else. Happily I joined the circuit, forming a bad
habit I was not to conquer for many years. Even in the rare evenings
when Spencer or Huggins did not turn up, there was always Bottomley to talk to and borrow from, since this was the place where
he made contact with his fellow gamblers. One of them was six feet six
inches high and nicknamed Emu. Apart from his being permanently a
thousand pounds in debt and in fear of his life, there was nothing
remarkable about Emu except his mistress, but she was very remarkable indeed.

Her name was Lilith Talbot. About thirty years old, she was
classically beautiful, with a discreetly ogival figure and a river of
auburn hair. She was softly spoken and always elegantly dressed –
two qualities which by themselves would have been enough to make
her unique in those surroundings. What she saw in Emu was one
of the great mysteries. Some said, crudely, that it was a matter of
physiology: others, that it was an attraction between opposites. I
adored her, first of all from afar, then from progressively closer to.
She was openly delighted with my naive worship of all these people
whose every secret she had known for years. She was probably also,
I now realize, secretly delighted with my absurdly affected mimicry

of Spencer. She accused me of being in love with him. I hotly denied
the charge, even though it was partly true, and counter-attacked,
greatly daring, by telling her that I was in love with her, which was
wholly true. I tried to content myself with the prospect of a Platonic
relationship. Not only was she entirely loyal to Emu, but Emu had
friends who were almost as frightening as his enemies. The world
of crime started just where the Push finished, and often the edges
overlapped.

By this time my first poems were coming out in *honi soit*. They
were, of course, the most abject pastiche, but my first appearance in
print led me to an excess of posturing beside which Nerval walking
his lobster would have been as inconspicuous as the Invisible Man.
A symphony in corduroy velvet, smoking cigarettes the length of a
blow-gun, I casually sprinted into Manning House, spread out a dozen
copies of the paper, and read myself with ill-concealed approval. Even
the patience of the Bellevue Hill mob was strained. They voted that
I should no longer be heard on the subject of literature. Since the
aesthetes grew equally tired of hearing their own opinions coming
back at them, I was left with only Sally to berate during the day,
and Lilith to harangue in the evening. They were bemused and
long-suffering respectively. Heinrich Mann, writing about Nietzsche,
remarks at one point that self-confidence often precedes achievement
and is generally strained so long as it is untried. No self-confidence
could have been more strained than mine. Underneath it, needless
to say, lay gurgling indecision. The contradictions were piling up to
such an altitude that it was getting hard to see over the top of them.
On the one hand I was a petty bourgeois student, on the other a
libertarian bohemian. Sobbing into my beer in the Royal George,
I predicted doom for myself in the forthcoming examinations. By
day I nursed my hangover and meticulously took notes, wondering
what the Push was up to. What was I missing out on?

When the exam results came out, I was deeply shocked to find
that I had passed in both Anthropology and History, was listed in
Order of Merit for English – i.e., midway between a pass and a credit
– and had secured an outright credit in Psychology. Obviously the
examiners had been moved to find their own lectures being returned
to them in condensed form. Apart from Huggins, a star student in
Architecture, none of the aesthetes had ever done as well in a lustrum
as I had done in a year. I was neck and neck with the boys from

Bellevue Hill. This made me feel guilty and alarmed. Which was I, a conformist or a nonconformist? I could feel my own personality coming apart like the original continental plates. Getting drunk was no solution, even though my mother was charmingly willing to accept the consequent behaviour as evidence of fatigue brought on by too much study. As I collapsed in the porch at midnight, having fallen over every garbage bin on the way down the street, I would explain to her that the Habsburgs had been too much for me. In a dressing gown with the hall light behind her, she looked down at her son, doubtless wondering what he was turning into. I was wondering the same thing.

Could there be such a thing as a virgin sophisticate? Had there ever been a man of the world who came home every night to his mother? Fate resolved this latter anomaly with brutal speed. My number came up and I found myself conscripted for National Service.

14. BASIC TRAINING

National Service was designed to turn boys into men and make the Yellow Peril think twice about moving south. It was universally known as Nasho – a typically Australian diminutive. Once you were in it, four years went by before you were out of it: there was a three-week camp every year, plus numerous parades. But the most brutal fact about Nasho was the initial seventy-seven day period of basic training, most of which took place at Ingleburn. Each new intake of gormless youth was delivered into the hands of regular army instructors who knew everything about licking unpromising material into shape. When we stepped off the bus at Ingleburn, they were already screaming at us. Screaming sergeants and corporals appeared suddenly out of huts. I stood clutching my Globite suitcase and wondered what had gone wrong with my life. While I goggled at a screaming sergeant, I was abruptly blown sideways by a bellow originating from somewhere behind my right ear. Recovering, I turned to face Ronnie the One.

His real name was Warrant Officer First Class Ronald McDonald, but he was known throughout the army as Ronnie the One. Responsible for battalion discipline, he had powers of life and death over all non-commissioned personnel and could even bring charges against officers up to the rank of Captain. His appearance was almost inconceivably unpleasant. A pig born looking like him would have demanded plastic surgery. His brass gleamed like gold and his leather like mahogany, but the effect was undone by his khaki drills, which despite being ironed glass smooth were perpetually soaked with sweat. Ronnie the One dripped sweat even on a cold day. It was not just because he was fat, although he had a behind like an old sofa. It was because he was always screaming so hard. At that moment he was screaming directly at me. 'GEDYAHAHCARD!' Later on a translator told me that this meant 'Get your hair cut' and could generally be taken as a friendly greeting, especially if you could still see his eyes. When Ronnie was really annoyed his face swelled up and turned purple like the rear end of an amorous baboon.

For the next eleven weeks I was running flat out, but no matter how fast my feet moved, my mind was moving even faster. It was instantly plain to me that only cunning could ensure survival. Among the university students in our intake, Wokka Clark was undoubt-edly the golden boy. Already amateur middleweight champion of NSW, he was gorgeous to behold. But he couldn't take the bullshit. What happened to him was like a chapter out of *From Here to Eternity*. They applauded him in the boxing ring at night and screamed at him all day. That summer the noon temperature was a hundred plus. Ronnie the One would take Wokka out on the parade ground and drill him till he dropped. The reason Wokka dropped before Ronnie did was simple. All Ronnie had on his head was a cap. Wokka had on a steel helmet. The pack on his back was full of bricks. After a few weeks of that, plus guard duty every night that he wasn't boxing, even Wokka was obeying orders.

You couldn't fight them. Even the conscientious objectors ended up looking after the regimental mascot – a bulldog called Onslow who looked like Ronnie's handsome younger brother. It was like one of Kenny Mears's games of marbles: nobody was allowed not to play. I could appreciate the psychology of it. The first task when training new recruits is to disabuse them of the notion that life is fair. Otherwise they will stand rooted to the spot when they first come up against people who are trying to kill them. But my abstract understanding of what was going on impinged only obliquely on the concrete problem of getting through the day without landing myself in the kind of trouble that would make the next day even more impossibly difficult than it was going to be anyway.

Something about my general appearance annoyed Ronnie. There were a thousand trainees in the intake but I was among the select handful of those whose aspect he couldn't abide. I could be standing in a mess queue, Ronnie would be a dot in the distance, and suddenly his voice would arrive like incoming artillery. 'GEDDABIGGAHAD!' He meant that I should get a bigger hat. He didn't like the way it sat on top of my head. Perhaps he just didn't like my head, and wanted the whole thing covered up. The drill that I had learned in Boys' Brigade saved my life. When it came to square-bashing, it turned out that the years I had spent interpreting Captain Andrews's commands had given me a useful insight into what Ronnie was likely to mean by his shouts and screams. When Ronnie yelled 'ABARD HARGH!' I knew almost straight away that it must mean 'about turn'. Thus I was able to turn decisively with the many, instead of dithering with the few.

On the parade ground Peebles drew most of the lightning. So unco-ordinated that he was to all intents and purposes a spastic, Peebles should not have been passed medically fit. But since he had been, the Army was stuck with him. After a month of training, when Ronnie shouted 'ABARD HARGH!' 999 soldiers would smartly present their backs and Peebles would be writhing on the ground, strangled by the sling of his rifle. For Peebles the day of reckoning came when he obeyed an order to fix bayonets. This was one of Ronnie's most frightening orders. It had the verb at the end, as in German or Latin. In English the order would have sounded something like: 'Bayonets . . . fix! Bellowed by Ronnie, it came out as: 'BAHAYONED . . . *FEE!*' The last word was delivered as a high-pitched, almost supersonic, scream. It was succeeded on this occasion by another scream, since Peeble's bayonet, instead of appearing at the end of his rifle, was to be seen protruding from the back of the soldier standing in front of him. After that, they used to mark Peebles present at company parade every morning but lose him behind a tree on the way to battalion parade, where he was marked absent.

My kit, not my drill, was what got me into trouble. For once in my life I had to make my own bed every morning, without fail, and lay out for inspection my neatly polished and folded belongings. Since the penalty for not doing this properly was to have the whole lot thrown on the floor and be obliged to start again, I gradually got better at it, but I never became brilliant. National Servicemen had to wax and polish their webbing instead of just powdering it with blanco. It was a long process which bored me, and the same fingers which had been so tacky at woodwork were still likely to gum up the job. The problem became acute when it was my platoon's turn to mount guard. Throughout the entire twenty-four hours it was on duty, the guard was inspected, supervised, harassed and haunted by Ronnie the One. The initial inspection of kit, dress and rifle lasted a full hour. Ronnie snorted at my brass, retched at my webbing, and turned puce when he looked down the barrel of my rifle.

'THASSNODDAGHARDRIVAL!' he yelled. He meant that it was not a guard rifle. 'ISSFULLAPADAYDAHS!' He meant that it was full of potatoes. I looked down the barrel. I had spent half a day pulling it through until it glowed like El Dorado's gullet. Now I saw that a single speck of grit had crept into it.

In the guard-house we had to scrub the floors and tables, white-wash the walls and polish the undersides of the drawing pins on the notice board. When we went out on picket we could not afford to relax for a moment, since Ronnie could be somewhere in the vicinity preparing to do his famous Banzai charge. At two o'clock in the morning I was guarding the transport park. It was raining. Sitting down in the sentry box, I had the brim of my hat unbuttoned and was hanging from the collar of my groundsheet, praying for death. I had my rifle inside my groundsheet with me, so that I could fold my hands on its muzzle, lean my chin on the cushion formed by my hands under the cape, and gently nod off while still looking reason-ably alert. I had calculated that Ronnie would not come out in the rain. This proved to be a bad guess. I thought the sentry box had been struck by lightning, but it was merely Ronnie's face going off like a purple grenade about a foot in front of mine. I came to attention as if electrocuted and tried to shoulder arms. Since the rifle was still inside my groundsheet, merely to attempt this manoeuvre was bound to yield Peebles-like results. Ronnie informed me, in a tirade which sounded and felt like an atomic attack, that he had never seen anything like it in his life.

The inevitable consequence was extra kitchen duty. I can safely say that I did more of this than anybody else in the battalion. While everybody else was out in the donga learning to disguise themselves as ant-hills and sneak up on the enemy, I was in the kitchen heading a crack team of cleaners composed of no-hopers like Peebles. The kitchen was as big as an aircraft hangar. All the utensils were on an enormous scale. The smallest dixies would be four feet long, two feet across and three feet deep. Lined with congealed custard and rhubarb, they took half an hour each to clean. The biggest dixie was the size of a Bessemer converter and mounted on gimbals. I was lowered into it on a rope. When I hit the bottom it rang like a temple gong. After the kitchen sergeant was satisfied that the dixie was shining like silver he pulled a crank and I was tipped out, smothered in mashed potato.

It must have been while I was inside the dixie that I missed out on the chance to volunteer for Infantry. That was how I found myself in the Assault Pioneers – the one specialist course that nobody sane wanted to be on, since it involved land mines, booby traps and detonators. In the long run the lethality of the subject proved to be a boon. National Service was winding to an end by that stage – ours was to be the last intake – and the government didn't want any mother's sons getting killed at the eleventh hour. So instead of burying mines for us to dig up, they buried rocks. While our backs were turned, they would bury a hundred rocks in a careful pattern. We would move through the area, probing the earth with our bayonets, and dig up two hundred. It wasn't as glamorous as being in, say, the mortar platoon, but I came to appreciate the lack of excitement, especially after we were all marched out to the range and given a demonstration of what the mortar specialists had learned.

The mortars in question were the full three inches across the barrel – not the two-inch pipes that had little more than nuisance value, but really effective weapons which could throw a bomb over a mountain and kill everything within a wide radius at the point of impact. A thousand of us, including the colonel and all his officers, sat around the rim of a natural amphitheatre while the mortar teams fired their weapons. All looked downwards at the mortars with fascination, except for Ronnie the One, who was down with the mortars looking upwards, tirelessly searching for anyone with too small a hat. Team after team loaded and fired. The bomb was dropped into the mortar and immediately departed towards the stratosphere, where it could be heard – and even, momentarily, seen – before it dived towards its target, which was a large cross on a nearby hill. You saw the blast, then you heard the sound. It was a bit like watching Ronnie having a heart attack on the horizon.

Every team did its job perfectly until the last. The last team was Wokka Clark and Peebles. They had to do *something* with Peebles. If they had put him in the Pioneers he probably would have bitten the detonator instead of the fuse. It went without saying that he could not be allowed to drive a truck or fire a Vickers machine gun, especially after the way he had distinguished himself on the day everyone in the battalion had had to throw a grenade. (One at a time we entered the throwing pit. The sergeant handed you a grenade, from which you removed the pin. You then threw the grenade. When he handed Peebles a grenade, Peebles removed the pin and handed the grenade back to him.) The safest thing to do with Peebles was team him up with Wokka, who was so strong that he could throw the base plate of a three-inch mortar twenty yards. All Peebles had to do was wait until Wokka had done the calibrations and then drop in the bomb. He must have done it successfully scores of times in practice. He did it quite smoothly this time too, except that the bomb went in upside down.

If you were to rig a vacuum cleaner to blow instead of suck and then point it at a pile of dust, you would get some idea of what those thousand supposedly disciplined men did a split second after they noticed the bomb going into the mortar with its fins sticking up instead of down. They just melted away. Some tried to dig themselves into the earth. Some started climbing trees. But most of us ran. I was running flat out when an officer went past me at head height, flapping his arms like a swan. Ronnie stopped the panic by shouting 'HARD!', meaning 'halt'. The noise could have been the bomb going off, but since it was unaccompanied by shrapnel it seemed safe to pay attention. Everyone turned and looked down. Ronnie picked up the whole mortar, base plate included, shook out the bomb and handed it to Peebles. Silence. Wokka still had his hands over his eyes. Peebles dropped the bomb in the right way up. The mortar coughed. There was a crackle in the sky and a blast on the hill. Then we all marched thoughtfully back to camp.

By now I had made a career out of being a private. Having made the mistake of supplying all the right answers in the intelligence test (since it was exactly the same test that I had been studying in Psychology I, this was no great feat) I was at first put under some pressure to become an officer, or failing that an NCO. But it soon became clear to all concerned that I was a born private. I had revived my joker persona as a means of ingratiating myself with my fellow conscripts. I had no wish to lose their approval by being raised above them. Nor was I morally equipped to accept responsibility for others. But I did manage to get better at being the lowest form of life in the army. I was a digger. I learned the tricks of looking neat without expending too much energy. And although it would have been heresy to say so, I actually enjoyed weapons training. I had the eyes to be good at firing the .303 rifle, but not the hands. Yet I relished being instructed on it. And the Bren was such a perfect machine that there was avid competition to specialise. I never got to the stage of wanting to sleep with one, but must admit that there were times when, as I eyed the Bren's sleek lines, I discovered in myself a strong urge to fiddle with its gas escape regulator.

The weapons sergeants were all regular soldiers with combat experience, usually in Korea. There was virtue, it seemed to me, in listening when they talked. They were wise in their craft. Every few intakes one of them got shot by a National Serviceman. None of them wanted to be the one. After surviving a long encounter with half a million glory-hungry Chinese it makes no sense to be finished off by some adolescent pointing his rifle at you and saying, 'Sergeant, it's stuck.' They were particularly careful when it came to instructing us on the Owen machine carbine. This was the same gun I had once carted around Jannali. The Owen cocked itself if you dropped it and shot you when you picked it up. It disgorged fat, 9 mm slugs at a very high rate of fire and the barrel clawed up to the right during the burst. If due precautions were not taken, the man on the left of the line would mow down everyone else, including the instructor. The sergeants were very cautious about whom they put on the left, and always stood well to the left themselves. Some of them stood so far to the left they were out of sight. Without exception they refused to let Peebles fire the thing at all. They parked him behind his usual tree on the way to the range and faked his score.

I also enjoyed drill. Einstein once said that any man who liked marching had been given his brain for nothing: just the spinal column would have done. But I wasn't Einstein. Since most of one's time in the army is wasted anyway, I preferred to waste it by moving about in a precise manner. It was better than blueing my pay-packet at a pontoon game in the lavatories. As fit as I would ever be in my life, I could fling a Lee Enfield .303 rifle around like a baton. When I was ordered to volunteer as Right Front Marker for the exhibition drill squad, I sensibly said yes. Saying no would have immediately entailed being lowered into the big dixie, so it was scarcely a courageous decision.

The drill squad was one of the star items on the big day. Visiting brass and proud parents lined the parade ground. Dressed in white singlets, khaki drill trousers, gaiters and boots, ninety-nine strapping examples of bronzed young Australian manhood all took their time from me. We looked like an erotic dream by Leni Riefenstahl. Ronnie gave the orders in his usual mixture of Urdu and epilepsy, but by now I could read his mind. Miraculously dry-handed in the heat, I put the .303 through its paces. It was all a matter of not worrying. Just let the body remember. It wasn't until the routine was over and we were marching off to a storm of applause that the thought occurred to me: they had done it. They had got what they wanted out of me. But on the other hand I had got what I wanted out of them. I had acquired my first real measure of self-sufficiency, which is something other, and quieter, than mere self-assertion, and probably the opposite of being self-absorbed.

That night the whole drill squad was given leave. Blazing with brass and polished green webbing, I got off the train in Sydney after sunset and headed straight for the Royal George, marching an inch above the pavement in my mirror-finish boots. There was a roar of scorn as I entered the back room. Cries of 'Fascist!' rose from all sides. But for once I was sure of myself. Nobody looking as unappealing as the Libertarians was in a position to sneer at the starched perfection of my KDs. Johnny Pitts flailed his guitar, launched into a few bars of some barely comprehensible protest song about American militarism, and fell sideways. Grogan, saluting wildly, jumped up and down on a table. Once again he was clad in nothing but G-string Speedo and thongs. Spencer was pretending to be dazzled by my beauty. Everyone was in character. It all passed me by, because I had noticed that Emu was not present. Lilith Talbot was unaccompanied.

I suppose it was just my lucky night. Emu, it transpired, was somewhere in the Blue Mountains, hiding from some people who had threatened to dip him by the heels in Hen and Chicken Bay, a part of the harbour much favoured by grey nurse sharks. From the goodness of her simple heart, Lilith told me straight away that it would be a pity if we did not take advantage of this opportunity to complete my basic training. But it could happen only once, and there must never be a word to anyone, or my death would follow shortly upon hers. Did I understand that? Transfixed by the shape of her mouth, I nodded dumbly. We walked out of the room together – a sound tactic, since it looked too intimate to be anything but innocent. And if I couldn't believe my luck, all those other helplessly doting males would be doing their best not to believe my luck either.

On the ferry to Kirribilli we sat on a bench in the prow. It was a warm night in late summer. The breeze would have ruffled Lilith's hair if her hair had been less heavy. A junk-yard of light, Luna Park spilled ladders of pastel across the water, the Big Dipper roaring like a wounded dragon. Under the deck of the Harbour Bridge, the ultra-violet beacon that guides the big ships through the dark sent out its cobwebs of lapis lazuli above our heads. I made Lilith look up at it. She let me kiss her. I didn't know it was allowed. I kept expecting a squad of MPs to appear and place me under arrest.

But there was just us. Walking up the hill was like being shown into Olympus by a resident. Everything she had on must have weighed about two ounces all told. A pale-blue cotton dress and a pair of gracile high-heeled white sandals were all that I could see. I didn't know what to do with my hands, but somehow everything was all right. It went on being all right when we got to her place. Really the house belonged to Emu. It was his one tangible asset. Lilith had a room in it of her own, although even here there were signs of Emu's pre-eminence. A crate of empty beer bottles against the wall could belong only to him. The same applied to the 16 lb shot on top of the cupboard. In a previous incarnation Emu had been GPS shot putt champion.

Lilith opened the curtains towards where the sun would be when it came up. It seemed that nothing but darkness was there now. But when she turned out the light, there was still enough illumination to reach her. She took her dress off over her head and stood there while my eyes began the long task of getting used to seeing what before they had only imagined. For Lilith, her own beauty was a sufficient reason to exist. I would like to be able to say that we celebrated her loveliness together. In fact I hardly knew what I was doing. She was more tolerant than I was capable of realizing. I had no idea of delay, and would not have been able to do much about it even if I had. It was all too exciting. What an older and wiser man would have made last for hours was all over in seconds. I gave a spasmodic lurch and kicked the cupboard. The shot rolled off the top of it and fell into the crate of beer bottles. I was too pleased with myself to care. Lilith Talbot is among my fondest memories. And you can stop thinking that she's a figment of my imagination. Of course she is.

15. VERY WELL: ALONE

The last week of basic training was spent on bivouac at Singleton. The whole battalion camped out in the donga. Our company was instructed to storm and fortify the top of a mountain. My Pioneer platoon was ordered to dig a command post out of the virgin rock. Since there was no dynamite, we had to do it with picks and shovels. After six days the command post was three inches deep. If the battalion had been commanded by leprechauns it would have been an ideal headquarters. I didn't care. I could still taste Lilith. Periodically there was a tremendous hullabaloo as a pair of RAAF Sabre jets went past below us. They were pretending to strafe the infantry who were fitfully shooting blanks at each other down in the valley.

Around the campfire at night I was the expert on sex. I was still a long way away from learning that the main difference between an adult and an adolescent is the ability to keep secrets. I betrayed Lilith dreadfully, even to the extent of telling them her real name. But everybody else was too drunk to notice. The mortar platoon kept us in fresh meat. Accidentally on purpose they blew a cow to smithereens. One moment it was grazing contentedly and the next it was spread all over the landscape. Every platoon got a smithereen each. We roasted it over the fire and washed it down with wine bought in bulk from a vineyard in the next valley. The wine was so raw that it left your tongue looking like a crocodile-skin handbag.

A fat soldier called Malouf had stolen my position as chief joker. He sang a hundred choruses of 'Old King Cole' and fainted into the fire. But in my new role of sex expert I had enough confidence to serve out my time. It was steep up that mountain. We slept under ground sheets rigged as pup tents. It was advisable to pitch your tent in close contact with the trunk of a stout tree, otherwise you could end up as part of an avalanche. With my feet sticking out of one end of the tent and my head out of the other I looked straight up at the stars. There were stars between the stars. The mountain air was unmixed, as in Dante's Paradise: you could see to the edge of the universe. The Southern Cross was so brilliant that it dripped. You could have picked it out of the sky and hung it around a young nun's neck. I had never felt more alive. From miles away below came the occasional snapping of dry sticks and what sounded like the muffled howl of a wombat being raped. It was Ronnie, Banzai-charging the sentries.

Buoyant with well-being, I returned to civilian life. Between the top of Margaret Street and our front gate my mother came to meet me. I knew that look, so my mental defence mechanisms were already going into action when she told me that Gary Meldrum had been killed the day before, racing his motorbike at Mount Druitt. I learned the details later on. He had been leading a pack of AJS 7Rs when his telescopic front fork collapsed on a bend. The bike went up in the air with its throttle stuck open and when it came back down again he was lying underneath it. The chain cut his throat and he died instantly.

I walked my mother inside and made her a cup of tea. I didn't feel anything at all except a sense that I was falling upwards from the past. It was all going away from me. I could feel a vacuum plucking at the back of my shirt. After the funeral service at Kogarah Presbyterian Church I cried noisily in the street but it was the kind of reflex that would have pleased the Sydney University Psychology Department, since it was unconnected with anything going on in my head. I began to suspect that I might have nothing in there except scar tissue, or else a couple of loose wires that should have been touching each other but weren't.

Being a mother's boy is a condition that can be fully cured only by saying goodbye to mother. Nevertheless I did not entirely revert. I was soon having my bed made for me again, but I managed to keep something of my new-found independence. Justifying callousness as necessary for survival, I did pretty much what I pleased. The rest of my university course was a steadily accelerating story of possibilities explored and studies neglected. Lilith and I were just friends again, alas. On the other hand she had spoiled me for little girls who, in the charming jargon of that time, did not come across. So I left Sally Vaughan in tears, went in search of something less complicated, and had my wishes granted often enough to ensure that the moment of real involvement in somebody else's life went on being put off into the indeterminate future, whose outline looked as hazy as ever. All that I could be sure of was that some form of writing would play a part in it.

I went on to become literary editor of *honi soit*, with a page of my own to look after every week. Almost invariably I filled it with my own productions. Some of them were so pretentious that even today I can't recall their tone without emitting an involuntary yell of anguish. But a certain fluency accrued from the sheer exercise, and inevitably a certain notoriety accrued along with it. There was a shimmering before my eyes. Narcissus was beginning the long process of getting his reflection in focus.

The need to be approved of aided my progress, if progress it was. I never stopped admiring the talent of Spencer and Keith Cameron, but gradually at first, and then quicker all the time, my own activities took a different course. The desire to amuse overcame the desire to shock. By my second year I was already writing a good proportion of the Revue, and by my third year I was writing almost half of it. Against my will but according to my instincts, I recognized that when I mimicked Spencer's mannerisms I made no connection with the audience, and that when what I wrote was my own idea, the audience laughed. I tried to hold them in contempt for that, but could not quite succeed. So I tried to hold myself in contempt instead, but could not quite succeed at that either. It was already occurring to me that in these matters practice might be wiser than theory.

If only everything had been clearer. If I had read Sartre at that stage I might have learned that the obligation to create one's life from day to day was an inescapable responsibility. Luckily I read Camus instead. Here was my first mature literary enthusiasm: instead of merely having my prejudices confirmed, I was disabused of them. Camus offered consolation by telling you that yours was not the only personality which felt as if it was lying around in pieces – every life felt like that from the inside. More importantly, he offered a moral vision that went beyond the self. 'Tyrants conduct monologues above a million solitudes.' I looked at a sentence like that until my eyes grew tired. It wasn't poetry. So why was it so poetic? How did he do it? And where could I buy a coat like his? I tilted my head to the same angle, practised lighting a Disque Bleu so that the flame atmospherically lit the lower half of my face, and planned to die in a car crash.

The immature enthusiasms continued along with the mature ones. I went crazy for Ezra Pound. I unhesitatingly incorporated the manic self-confidence of his critical manner into my own prose. Since my ignorance far outstripped even his, I was lucky not to fall further under his spell. Once again instinct was wiser than thought. Even when I was drunk with awe at the sheer incomprehensibility of the *Cantos*, I was simultaneously delighting in the clear, strong, sane talent of MacNeice. When I came to read Yeats I soon saw what real grandeur was, and realized that Pound's grandiloquence was not it.

The Great Gatsby helped teach me what a real prose style was like. I read it over and over. Even at that early stage I could see that if it came to a choice between Hemingway and Fitzgerald, I would take Fitzgerald – not just because his cadences were more seductive, but because he was less sentimental. I never let it come to the choice, preferring to admire them both. I went mad on the Americans generally. e. e. cummings made me drunk. Mencken's sceptical high spirits seemed to me the very tones of ebullient sanity. It went without saying that there was no question of being interested in Australian culture as such. Nobody, as far as I knew, had given it a thought in the last twenty years.

Having finished reading Keith Cameron's library, I started reading the university library, which was named after someone called Fisher. In those days Fisher Library was housed in a building which looked like the little brother of Milan Cathedral and formed part of the Quad. But even when I was wearing a groove up and down the library stairs I was always careful not to read anything on the course. If the syllabus said Beaumont and Fletcher, I read Mencken and Nathan. If it said Webster and Ford, I read Auden and Isherwood. Life would have been so much simpler had I done what I was asked that today I never stop wondering why I didn't. Two or three of the English lecturers were of world class. I assiduously contrived never to learn anything about Old English. I faked my way through that part of the course by memorizing the cribs. It was only my ability to conjure a fluent essay out of thin air that got me admitted to the third year of the honours school. That, and the incidental benefit of reading Shakespeare morning, noon and night. There, for once, I got the horse before the cart.

Psychology I gave up at the end of the second year, just before it gave up me. When it came to statistical analysis, I was helpless. A deep spiritual aversion to the whole subject might also have had something to do with it. Not even Freud appealed. I could see the poetic fecundity of his imagination, but as an actor in a real-life Oedipus play I felt free to question his teleological sophistry. Undoubtedly, my father having mysteriously been killed, I had inherited exclusive rights to my mother's favours. But to suggest that either of the two survivors had in any way desired such an outcome was patently ludicrous. I got through the psychology examinations on a 'post' – i.e., a *viva voce* after having written a borderline paper. I would not have been granted even the 'post' if it had not been for my clinical case study. During the course of the year we had to assemble an elaborate case study of some real person. My clinical study was little Toni Turrell, sexy Shirley's sister. Five minutes into the Wechsler-Bellevue intelligence test I realized that little Toni was a hopeless moron who would yield up the same personality profile as a block of wood. So I excused her from any further tests and cooked up the whole thing. It was, if I may say so, a brilliantly convincing job. 'Toni: A Case Study' was my first attempt at a full-length fictional work. (This book is the second.)

Anthropology also moved to a natural demise at the end of the second year. It was only a two-year subject anyway. Having absorbed the contents of *Frigging Around in Fiji* and regurgitated them at the appropriate moment, I was rewarded with the minimum pass. Education I, which I sat in my second year, I failed outright. I can see now that this result was an instinctively correct estimate of the subject's importance, but at the time it fitted in with a familiar pattern. Since my mind, or at any rate my heart, was already on some other path, I was not as worried as I might have been about the growing evidence that my attention was wandering from my work. But for my mother the whole meandering dereliction was all too disturbingly recognizable, especially now that I was more often arriving home early the next morning instead of late that night, and then late the next night instead of in the early morning.

Between second and third years I tried to recoup my position in the parental eye by getting a job in the long vacation. I was accepted as a trainee bus conductor. The buses were green Leyland diesels operating out of Tempe depot. The easy routes went overland to places like Bexley and Drummoyne. The difficult routes went through the city. I found the job fiercely demanding even on a short route with a total of about two dozen passengers. I pulled the wrong tickets, forgot the change, and wrote up my log at the end of each trip in a way that drew hollow laughter from the inspectors. The inspectors were called Kellies, after Ned Kelly, and were likely to swoop at any time. A conductor with twenty years' service could be dismissed if a Kelly caught him accepting money without pulling a ticket. If a hurrying passenger pressed the fare into your hand as he leapt out of the back door, it was wise to tear a ticket and throw it out after him. There might be a plainclothes Kelly following in an unmarked car.

Days of fatigue and panic taught me all over again that I am very bad at what I am not good at. We worked a split shift with four hours off in the middle of the day. Effectively this meant that we were on the job twelve hours a day, since there was nothing else to do with the four hours off except hang around the depot. I got so tired I used to sleep the whole four hours on a bench in the billiard room. Once I conked out with a lighted Rothmans in my hand. I dreamed of a bushfire burning down Jannali school with Miss Turnbull still inside it. I woke to face a cloud of smoke. The whole front of my shirt had burned away. The billiard room was full of conductors and drivers who had been placing bets on when I would wake up. The white nylon singlet I had been wearing under the shirt was scorched the colour of strong tea.

I lasted about three weeks all told, which meant that I hardly got past probation. The routes through town were more than the mind could stand even in the off-peak hours. In peak hours the scene was Dantesque. All the buses from our depot and every other depot would be crawling nose to tail through town while the entire working population of Sydney fought to get aboard. It was hot that summer: 100° Fahrenheit every day. Inside the bus it was 30° hotter still. Hammering up Pitt Street in the solid traffic at about ten miles an hour, the bus was like the Black Hole of Calcutta on wheels. It was so jammed inside that my feet weren't touching the floor. I couldn't blink the sweat out of my eyes. There was no hope of collecting any fares. At each stop it was all I could do to reach the bell-push that signalled the driver to close the automatic doors and get going. I had no way of telling whether anybody had managed to get off or on.

My one object was to get that bus up Pitt Street. Passengers fainted and just hung there – there was nowhere for them to fall. The air tasted as if it had just been squirted out of the safety valve of a pressure cooker full of cabbage.

In those circumstances I was scarcely to blame. I didn't even know where we were, but I guessed we were at the stop just before Market Street. I pressed the bell, the doors puffed closed, and the bus surged forward. There were shouts and yells from down the back, but I thought they were the angry cries of passengers who had not got on. Too slowly I realized that they were emanating from within the bus. The back set of automatic doors had closed around an old lady's neck as she was getting on. Her head, wearing a black veiled hat decorated with wax fruit, was inside the bus. The rest of her, carrying a shopping bag with each hand, was outside. I knew none of this at the time. When I at last cottoned on to the fact that something untoward was happening and signalled the driver to stop, he crashed to a halt and opened the automatic doors, whereupon the woman dropped to the road. She was very nice about it. Perhaps the experience had temporarily dislocated her mind. Anyway, she apologized to me for causing so much trouble. Unfortunately the car just behind turned out to be full of Kellies. Since it would have made headlines if a university student had been thrown off the buses for half-guillotining a woman of advanced years, I was given the opportunity to leave quietly. Once again this failed to coincide with my own plans only in the sense that I had already resigned. In fact I had made my decision at about the same time as the old lady hit the ground.

16. FIDGETY FEET

Nor, in my last year, did I prove to be any better as a student than I had been as a bus conductor. I no longer saw fit to attend any lectures at all. But my extracurricular activities flourished, following the principle that I could be infinitely energetic in those areas where it didn't matter. The Revue that year had my name in the programme thirty-two times. As well as writing most of the sketches, I was assistant producer to a man called Waldo Laidlaw, an advertising executive who was prominent in fringe theatre. Spencer and Keith Cameron despised Waldo's stylishness but I couldn't help being fascinated. He ranked as the local Diaghilev. Under his aegis, the Revue's costumes and décor took on an unmistakably self-confident look – a fact which could be easily detected by the naked eye, since Waldo was in favour of turning the lights right up. Most of the numbers I wrote were so embarrassing that I can't recall them even when I try, but others had the sort of half-success with the audience that fans the desire to go further.

By now I was writing a good half of *honi soit* every week. The letters column was full of protests about things I had written. The letters of protest were nearly all written by me. A certain kind of cheap fame accumulated, in which I pretended not to wallow. More significantly, the *Sydney Morning Herald* asked me to review books. The editor was Angus Maude, who at the time was serving out the bleak years after Suez, before returning to Britain and resuming his climb to influence. I owe Angus Maude a great deal. The bread of exile must have been bitter enough without having my cocksure ignorance to cope with on top of it. The first reviews I wrote for him were too pig-headed to be publishable. His simplest course would have been to forget the whole idea. But by a series of gentle hints he induced me to write within the scope of what I knew, so that I could turn out a piece which, while it did not fail to be dull, was at least seldom outright foolish.

Tom Fitzgerald, editor of a new literary-cum-political weekly called the *Nation*, was the next to pick me up. He had already hired Huggins. Fitzgerald treated me with great patience. A man of real learning, he also had the gusto to value keenness even when it was uninformed. In Vadim's, the King's Cross coffee bar where he held court, I would join the table late at night and pipe fatuous comments from my position below the salt. The other, more venerable literary men present stared deep into their glasses of Coonawarra claret or hurriedly reminisced, but Tom went on being tolerant even after the catastrophic week when I succeeded in reviewing the same book both for his magazine and the *Herald*. The Gaggia espresso machine hissed and gurgled. The six-foot blonde waitress swayed and swooped. Huggins blew in with a sheaf of new drawings. This was the life. The Royal George started seeming less attractive, especially when you considered that Emu was likely to be sitting in it. He had a new way of staring at me that made me feel cold and sticky, like a very old ice-cube.

Getting my name in the papers helped ease the transition from the last year of University to the first year of real life. My honours degree in English was scarcely of the highest grade, but there was no need to tell my mother that the result was really less impressive than it looked, and besides, in the same week that the results came out the *Herald* offered me a job. I was only to be assistant to the editor of the magazine page of the Saturday edition, but it felt unsettlingly like success. As if to redeem myself for betraying their uncompromising standards, I spent many evenings that summer with Spencer and Grogan, bucketing across the Harbour Bridge in Grogan's wreck of a Chevrolet to crash parties on the North Shore. Unfortunately I found it less easy than they did to hate what was to be found there. The young men of the North Shore might exceed even the Bellevue Hill mob in their partiality for cravats and suede shoes, but some of the girls were uncomfortably appealing. I resented their gentle manners but not from superiority. What unsettled me about the people of the North Shore was the way they all knew each other. I was, am, and will continue to be until the grave, incurably envious of all families.

But I was flattered to find that my name was already known.

While Grogan was being thrown out and Spencer was being aloof in a canvas chair beside the swimming pool, I would be queueing at the wine cask or holding forth near the barbecue. It seemed to me that the girls hung on my words. It seemed that they were positively leaning sideways to drink them in. Then the lawn would swing up and hit me. After just such an exploit a girl called Françoise drove me back to town. She was a diplomat's daughter. Infuriatingly she could read Latin, French and German, looked marvellously pretty, and would not let me sleep with her. She offered something called Friendship instead, which I grudgingly accepted. After vomiting into the glove compartment of her Renault Dauphine, I felt I owed her the time of day.

My year at the *Herald* can be briefly recounted. The editor of the Saturday magazine page was a veteran journalist called Leicester Cotton. He was a sweet man whose days of adventure were long behind. We shared a partitioned-off cubicle just big enough to hold two desks. While he got on with choosing the serials and book excerpts which would fill the main part of the page, it was my task to rewrite those unsolicited contributions which might just make a piece. All I had to do was change everything in them and they would be fine. Apart from the invaluable parsing lessons at school, these months doing rewrites were probably the best practical training I ever received. Characteristically I failed to realize it at first. But gradually the sheer weight of negative evidence began to convince me that writing is essentially a matter of saying things in the right order. It certainly has little to do with the creative urge *per se*. Invariably the most prolific contributors were the ones who could not write a sentence without saying the opposite of what they meant. One man, resident in Woy Woy, sent us a new novel every month. Each novel took the form of twenty thick exercise books held together in a bundle. Each exercise book was full to the brim with neat handwriting. The man must have written more compulsively than Enid Blyton, who at least stopped for the occasional meal. Unlike Enid Blyton, however, he could not write even a single phrase that made any sense at all.

But the contributors most to be dreaded were the ones who came to call. Down-at-heel, over-the-hill journalists would waste hours of Leicester's time discussing their plans to interview Ava Gardner. Any of them would have stood a better chance with Mary Queen of Scots.

Even the most sprightly of them was too far gone to mind spoiling the effect of his wheeler-dealer dialogue by producing in mid-spiel a defeated sandwich from the pocket of his grimy tan gaberdine overcoat. One character used to drop in personally in order to press for the return of articles which he had never sent. Another was in charge of a pile of old newspapers so heavy that he had to drag it. He was like a dung beetle out of Karel Capek. Our office was a transit camp for dingbats. Every form of madness used to come through that door. It was my first, cruel exposure to the awkward fact that the arts attract the insane. They arrived in relays from daylight to dusk. For all the contact they had with reality, they might as well have been wearing flippers, rotating bow ties, and sombreros with model trains running around the brim.

No wonder Leicester was relieved when his old journalist friend Herb Grady dropped in. Herb Grady bored me stiff with his endless talk of old times but at least he looked normal. He used to come in every morning about an hour before lunch, which he took in the Botanical Gardens. He was retired by then, so I assumed that the small leather case he always carried contained sandwiches and a Thermos of tea. I could imagine the tea growing cold even with its silver shell as Herb reminisced interminably on. Leicester didn't seem to mind, however. Then one day, as Herb was getting up to leave, the hasp on the leather case snapped open and the sole contents fell clattering to the floor. It was a single ice-skate.

Probably because I found the work easy to cope with, I felt as if I were marking time. Like most people who feel that, I hung around my old haunts. That year I directed the Union Revue. Despite my tenaciously lingering pretensions, those items emanating from my pen attained a hitherto unheard-of perspicuity. I also discovered within myself a knack of delegating authority – which essentially means recognizing your own limitations and deputing others to do well what you yourself would only muck up. The show was called *A Rat up a Pump*. It came in on budget and showed a profit. The audience, if it did not go home happy, at least stayed to the end. At the back of the hall I preened unobtrusively, praying that one of the actors would get sick so that I could go on instead. The one who did was the cast midget. Since all the sketches he was in depended for their point on his diminutive stature (he was about 18 inches high in his elevator shoes) trying to get his laughs was something of a challenge.

It was the only challenge of that year. Even Françoise finally yielded, although wisely she never ceased to be suspicious. I rather liked the idea of being thought of as a shit – a common conceit among those who don't realize just how shitty they really are. In retrospect I wonder that she put up with me for a single day. The boredom must have been tremendous, since on top of all my other affectations I was going through an acute Salinger phase, starting off as Holden Caulfield and ending up as Seymour Glass. She managed not to burst out laughing when I casually declared my intention of learning Sanskrit. She no doubt guessed that some other influence would drive that remote possibility even further into the distance, although it could have given her no pleasure to discover that my next persona, when it arrived, had been borrowed from Albert Finney in *Saturday Night and Sunday Morning*. Lurching from the cinema with my hands crammed into my pockets to guard them from the Northern cold, I waited for my breath to form a cloud before my face. Since it was ninety in the shade, this was not on the cards, but the Flash of Lightning was a long time hanging up his cape.

Things were getting a bit too easy. On the other hand, there was growing evidence that they were also getting a bit meaningless. There was nothing I knew worth knowing. Françoise was a model of tact, but occasionally she would unintentionally reveal that she had actually read, in the original language, some of the authors upon whose lack of talent I pronounced so glibly. Unable to fool her, I could not hope to go on fooling myself. Slowly it began occurring to me that the ability to get things done was a combination of two elements, the desire to do them and the capacity to take pains. The mind had to be both open and single. I had always shared the general opinion that Dave Dalziel, one of my student contemporaries, was faintly ludicrous, since he was so fanatical about films that he kept notebooks in which every film he saw was graded according to twenty different criteria. Then he suddenly started making a film using all his friends as actors. It took a year to complete. I had turned down his invitation to write the script. Someone else did it instead. When I saw the film I was envious. It was no more awful than my own work. More importantly, it was *there*. Abruptly I realized that Dave Dalziel was there too. What he had done once he would do again. It also occurred to me that those who had laughed at him loudest were the least likely ever to do anything themselves. Not that Dave kept his public short of reasons to shake their heads over him. One weekend about a dozen car-loads full of aesthetes and theatricals drove south to hold a bush picnic near Thirroul. I was braced in the back of Grogan's Chevrolet along with Bottomley and Wanda. Spencer was in the front seat, navigating. Navigation consisted of tailing the car in front – never easy with Grogan driving, since he was unable to go slower than flat out. Despite looking as of it had been gutted by a hollow charge, the Chevrolet could do a true eighty. Dave's Jaguar Mk IV went past us as if we were standing still. Dave was standing back to front on the driving seat with his head, shoulders and torso all protruding through the sunshine roof. He was waving a bottle of wine at us. That night around the campfire I learned that his long-legged girlfriend had had one foot on the accelerator, one hand on the wheel, and the other hand inside Dave's trousers. Something else he told me that night was that he believed his future lay in England. He seemed to know exactly where he was going. Thoughtfully I helped to put the fire out by hurling on it and crawled into a sleeping bag with Wanda. Kissing her was like cleaning an ash-tray with your tongue.

Huggins came back from a trip to Europe. In London he had actually met T. S. Eliot. Within a month he was on his way to New York, riding in one of the Boeing 707 jet airliners which had by now succeeded the old Stratocruisers, Super Constellations and Douglas DC-7s in the eternal task of shaking our house to its foundations. In Huggins I could clearly see the reality of talent, as opposed to the rhetoric of pretension. What he said he would do, he would do. What he did was in demand. He was on his way.

Something told me it was time to move. I still don't know what it was. Is it restlessness that tells us we are not at rest? Such questions invite tautologies for answers. Actually we all got the same idea at once. It was just that I was among the first of that particular generation to make the break. Suddenly everyone was heading towards England. We were like those pelagic birds whose migratory itinerary is pricked out in their minds as an overlay on the celestial map, so that when you release them inside a planetarium they fly in the wrong direction, but still according to their stars. I drew my severance pay from the Herald and bought a £97 one-way passage on a ship leaving at the very end of the year. As I should have expected, my mother, when I gaily informed her of my plans, reacted as Dido might have done if Aeneas had sent a barber-shop quartet to tell her that he had decided to leave Carthage. She was simultaneously distraught and insulted. But my callousness won out. Plainly I would get my way even in this. How could I be sure of that, unless I had been spoilt? So it was all her fault, really.

In that summer of 1961 I was seldom home to be made impatient by what I considered her unreasoning grief. During the week I slept on sundry floors, infested the coffee bars, and swam with Françoise at Brontë and Bondi. At the weekends I went North with the Bellevue Hill mob to Frank Clune's old house at Avalon. Gilbert Bolt's cousin used the place as a weekender. Consisting mainly of verandas, it could sleep half a dozen people comfortably and a dozen uncomfortably. We swam all day at Palm Beach, got drunk at night, and were woken in the morning by the whip birds and the kookaburras. The girls wore sandals, white shorts, T-shirts and a dab of zinc cream on their noses. Walking back from the shops with meat for the barbecue, they were apparitions in the heat haze, dreams within a dream. I never drew a sober breath. The mosquitoes who found a way inside my net at night got too drunk to find their way out again. On Christmas Eve I woke at ten in the morning with a shattering hangover to find that my bare feet, which had been tilted skyward over the rail of the veranda, were burned shocking pink on the soles.

The last days ticked away. I packed in an hour, carefully ignoring all advice about warm clothes. The ship sailed on New Year's Eve of 1961. She was called the *Bretagne* – an ex-French 29,000-ton liner now flying Greek colours. The point of departure was the new international terminal at Circular Quay. After nightfall the farewell party swarmed all over the deck. All around the quay echoed the confused noises of music, laughter, sobbing and regurgitation. The water around the ship was lit up so brightly it was as if there were lights below the surface. It was a cloudy pastel green, like colloidal jade. The deck was jammed. Hundreds of people were leaving and thousands had come to see them off. Johnny Pitts should have been going. His intention had been to go to Cuba and 'fight for anarchy'. Unfortunately in the place where his passport application required him to state his profession he had put 'Anarchist'. So he was not allowed to leave.

But the whole Push had turned up anyway. If the Push didn't crash it, it wasn't a party. They brought the Royal George jazz band with them. All the Bellevue Hill mob were there. One of the two rugby players sharing my cabin was of their number. Some of the Bellevue Hill mob were there to say goodbye to me as well. Spencer and Keith Cameron, Wanda and Bottomley turned up specifically to wish me luck. My mother was there. Françoise was there too, not saying very much. Probably she was still pondering my valedictory oration of the day before. On Bondi beach, with her neat body sheltering me from the sandy prickle of the Southerly Buster, I had intrepidly told her that I would be gone five years, and advised her to forget me. I suppose I expected to be admired for this heroic stance. As with all instinctive role-players, my first expectation was that other people would recognize the scene and play their part accordingly. Nor, to be fair to myself, could I see why anybody should miss me. Excessive conceit and deficient self-esteem are often aspects of each other.

The last crane-loads of shish kebab and moussaka came swinging aboard. The party was reaching its frenzied height. The jazz band shouted 'Black Bottom Stomp'. I stood crammed into a bunch with my mother, Françoise, the ever-polite Keith Cameron and half a dozen other well-wishers. Every other passenger was surrounded by a similar tight circle. Suddenly a narrow path of silence opened towards us through the crowd. She always had that effect. It was Lilith. She might have said 'Armand Duval, where are my *marrons glacés*?' but all she said was 'Hello'. After suavely introducing Françoise to her as my mother and my mother as Françoise I steered her to the rail.

'Won't Emu miss you?' I croaked offhandedly.

'He knows all about you,' she said, looking down into the bright water. 'Don't worry. I told him that if he killed you I'd never speak to him again.'

'Why did you let me?'

'I just liked your slouch hat. What do you call that thing in it again?'

'A bash.'

'Anyway, by the time you get back, I'll be old.'

'Don't be silly,' I said, believing her. She turned around and looked up at the deck of the Harbour Bridge. I followed her gaze. She was looking at the blue cobweb. Then we did one of those quick, awkward kisses where each of you gets a nose in the eye.

Then she was gone, the crowd making a path for her as it always did. A siren went. They piped all visitors ashore. Drunks fell off the gangplanks. Could my loved ones tell from my eyes how much less I felt than they did? Catching my streamer as she stood with thousands of others at the rail of the dock, my mother was as brave as if she had never done this before. Which ship was it that she was seeing? Was it her husband or her son who stood at the other end of the swooping ribbon that grew straight, then taut, then snapped?

The lake of white light between the ship and the wharf grew wider. Behind the crowd on the roof of the dock I could just see Grogan jumping up and down. He appeared to have no clothes on at all. As the year turned, the tugs swung the ship's prow down harbour. From the stern I watched the lake of light divide into two pools, one of them going with me and the other staying. Passing between the Heads was like being born again.

17. THAT HE SHOULD LEAVE HIS HOUSE

The voyage was too tedious to be described in detail. Apart from the one occasion that I stepped over the border into Queensland, it was the first time I had ever been outside the confines of NSW But the sense of adventure was nullified by the living conditions on the ship. Even a luxury liner is really just a bad play surrounded by water. It is a means of inducing hatred for your fellow men by trapping you in a confined space with too few of them to provide variety and too many to allow solitude. The *Bretagne* was all that and less. Every acceptable girl on the ship was being laid by a crew member before the ship was out of the Heads. This was a replacement crew who had all been flown out from the Persian Gulf. The previous crew had walked off the ship at Melbourne after one of the officers had shot an albatross.

With my two footballing companions I inhabited a phone-booth-sized cabinette on Deck Z, many feet below the water line. One wall was curved. It was part of the propeller shaft housing. If one of us wanted to get dressed the other two had to go back to bed. After we cleared the Barrier Reef we ran into a gale and spent a day heeled over at about twenty degrees from the vertical. One of the footballers chucked into the washbasin. The contents of his stomach, which had included two helpings of rhubarb crumble and custard, congealed in the basin. When the ship righted itself the surface of the solidified chunder remained at an angle, not to be removed until we docked in Singapore.

In Singapore we went by trishaw to Raffles, where I grandly ordered a round of lager for the three of us. The bill came to £47 – nearly all the money I had. What little cash was left over I spent on a taxi to Changi. The gaol was full of Chinese pirates. They were guarded by Gurkhas. The Gurkha warrant officer showed me around. In this place the Japanese commandant had deliberately withheld supplies of rice polishings while the POWs wasted away from vitamin deficiency. In this place my father had weighed as much as I had when I was ten years old. I tried to imagine him having the dead flesh cleaned out of his ulcers with a heated tea-spoon. I could not. It was all gone. He was gone. In Changi I realized that I would never find my father as he had been. It was no use looking. One day, in my imagination, he would return of his own accord.

On the way out of Singapore harbour the captain misunderstood the pilot. The ship went the wrong side of a buoy, hit a sand bar and turned towards the wharves. The anchors were dropped and the brakes were applied to the chains, but the ship's momentum was not easily checked. The links of the chains glowed cherry red. When they were hosed down the water was instantly transformed into geysers of steam. On the dock the stevedores in black shorts and flat conical hats looked up to see a 29,000-ton liner coming straight at them. They headed for the tall bamboo. The ship stopped just in time. A diver went down to check the damage. He surfaced to announce that one of the propeller shafts had a kink in it. Guess which one.

At reduced speed the ship limped across the Indian ocean. The Greek entertainments officer entertained us by organizing Greek dancing displays, in which the prettier girl passengers showed us the skills they had learned from the crew during the day. The skills they had learned from the crew during the night we were left to imagine. Greek dancing consists of a man holding up a handkerchief, striking a masculine attitude, and performing some extremely boring steps until a girl grabs hold of the other end of the handkerchief and performs some steps even more boring than his. Then a lot of other girls hold hands with each other and perform some steps which make everything you have previously seen look comparatively exciting. I would much rather have done lifeboat drill, but all the lifeboats had long ago been painted into position so that not even dynamite could possibly have released them. This was an additional factor to be considered when you tried to imagine – or rather tried not to imagine – the number of sharks who were following in our wake, passionate for leftover baklava.

For some reason the swimming pool, just when we needed it, was emptied, never to be filled again with anything except beer cans thrown into it by the circles of formation drinkers who sat cross-legged on the deck chanting 'Who took the cookie from the cookie jar?' Then the ship stopped altogether. The temperature was roughly that of the surface of the sun, which didn't look very far away. Praying for release at the ship's rail, I watched a turtle go past on its way to the Red Sea. That was where we were supposed to be going, but we weren't. That night, as every other night, the film was *The Naked Jungle*, in which Charlton Heston and Eleanor Parker battle the killer ants of South America. The next day there was Greek dancing. The day after that, the ship moved.

Aden was a revelation. Until then my belief in God's indifference had been theoretical. In the Crater of Aden there were things on show that might have made Christ throw in the towel. Certainly there were wounds he would not have kissed. Beggars whose faces had been licked off by camels proffered children whose bones had been deliberately broken at birth. Catatonic with culture shock, the passengers of the good ship *Bretagne* bought transistor radios and binoculars. With the radios they could drown out the hum of flies and with the binoculars they could look somewhere else.

The Suez canal still featured some wrecks from 1956. Lacking the cash to join an expedition to Cairo, I stayed on the ship as it crawled through to Port Said. Nasser's MiGs went by, up above the heat. I was down inside it. Port Said was like Coles or Woolworths, without the variety. Three products were on sale, all of them cranked out by a factory on the edge of town. They sold fake leather whips, fake leather wallets, and fake leather television pouffes. The fake leather was made of compressed paper. The passengers of the *Bretagne* emptied the shops, which filled up again just behind them. Nasser's police were omnipresent, making sure nobody got hurt. Nobody was going to interfere with you as you purchased the wherewithal for whipping yourself and counting your money while watching television. You were safer than in St Mary's Cathedral. The only danger was of being driven mad by Nasser's charismatic gaze. His portrait was everywhere.

We missed out on Tangiers because of the pressing urgency to keep a date with the dry dock in Southampton. But we did have half a day in Athens. On the Acropolis I watched one of my compatriots carve his name into the Parthenon and heard another ask where the camels were. The girl passengers raced into town to buy hats with pom-poms and handkerchiefs for Greek dancing. But I felt no less ignorant than my compatriots. The stone drapery on the caryatids seemed to give off its own illumination, as if the bright sun penetrated the surface before being reflected. It infuriated me that I couldn't read the inscriptions. Their clear, clean look only increased my suspicion that the real secrets of the tragedies and the Platonic dialogues, which I had thought I knew something about, lay in the sound of the language, and that until I could read that I would know nothing. I was right about that, but confirmation lay far in the future. Now there was nothing to do except return to Piraeus and commit myself into the hands of the sons of Pericles for the last leg of the voyage. I don't suppose the lump of rock outside the harbour would have looked any more significant if I had known that its name was Salamis.

The *Bretagne* wasn't much of a ship. On her next voyage back to Australia she hit the bottom of the harbour again, this time in Piraeus. She caught fire and burned out. There was nothing left but the hulk, which had to be blown up. But her job was done. She had got me to England. In the Bay of Biscay on our last afternoon at sea she ran before the gale, clumsily hurdling the enormous swell. By midnight she was in the Channel. Undetected from the bridge, I crouched out on deck in the prow, waiting to see the lights of Southampton. They materialized about an hour before dawn. They were just coloured lights and it was very cold. I had never been so cold. White stuff was falling out of the sky. At first I thought it was manna. The ship ground to a halt and waited for morning. It shook gently to the vibration of the girl passengers saying farewell to the crew. I went back down to Deck Z, lay on my bunk, and wondered what would happen next.

What happened next is another story. This story I had better break off while I still have your patience, if I do. The longer I have stayed in England, the more numerous and powerful my memories of Sydney have grown. There is nothing like staying away for bringing it with you. I have done my best to tell the truth about what it was like, yet I am well aware that in the matter of my own feelings I have not come near meeting my aim. My ideal of autobiography has been set by Alfieri, whose description of a duel he once fought in Hyde Park is mainly concerned with how he ran backwards to safety. Perhaps because I am not even yet sufficiently at peace with myself, I have not been able to meet those standards of honesty. Nothing I have said is factual except the bits that sound like fiction.

By the time this book is published I will be forty years old. When

I left Sydney I boasted that I would be gone for five years. I was to be gone three times that and more. During that time most of those who came away have gone back. Before Gough Whitlam came to power, having to return felt like defeat. Afterwards it felt like the natural thing to do. Suddenly Australia began offering its artists all the recognition they had previously been denied. It took a kind of perversity to refuse the lure. Perhaps I did the wrong thing. Eventually fear plays a part: when you are too long gone, to return even for a month feels like time-travel. So you try to forget. But the memories keep on coming. I have tried to keep them under control. I hope I have not overdone it, and killed the flavour. Because Sydney is so real in my recollection that I can taste it.

It tastes like happiness. I have never ceased to feel orphaned, but nor have I ever felt less than lucky – a lucky member of a lucky generation. In this century of all centuries we have been allowed to grow up and grow old in peace. There is a Buster Keaton film in which he is standing around innocently when the façade of a house falls on him. An open window in the façade passes over his body, so that he is left untouched.

I can see the Fun Doctor juggling for us at Kogarah Infants' School. One of the balls hits the floor with a thud. Then what looks like the same ball lands on his head. I can hear the squeak that the mica window panels of the Kosi stove made when I scorched them with the red-hot poker. When Jeanette Elphick came back on a visit from Hollywood they drove her around town in a blue Customline with her new name painted in huge yellow letters along the side: VICTORIA SHAW. On Empire Night when we threw pieces of fibro into the bonfire they cracked like rifle shots. Every evening for weeks before Empire Night I used to lay my fireworks out on the lounge-room carpet, which became impregnated with the smell of gunpowder. Peter Moulton kept his fireworks in a Weetabix carton. On the night, a spark from the fire drifted into the carton and the whole lot went up. A rocket chased Gail Thorpe, who was only just back from therapy. She must have thought it was all part of the treatment.

At the Legacy Party in Clifton Gardens I got a No. 4 Meccano set. On hot nights before the nor'easter came you changed into your cossie and ran under the sprinkler. At Sans Souci baths I dive-bombed a jelly blubber for a dare. If you rubbed sand into the sting it hurt less. Bindies in the front lawn made you limp to the steps of the porch and bend over to pick them out. Sandfly bites needed Calomine lotion that dried to a milky crust. From Rose Bay at night you could hear the lions making love in Taronga Park. If the shark bell rang and you missed the wave, you were left out there alone beyond the third line of breakers. Every shadow had teeth. Treading water in frantic silence, you felt afraid enough to run Christ-like for the shore.

At the Harvest Festivals in church the area behind the pulpit was piled high with tins of IXL fruit for the old age pensioners. We had collected the tinned fruit from door to door. Most of it came from old age pensioners. Some of them must have got their own stuff back. Others were less lucky. Hunting for cicadas in the peppercorns and the willows, you were always in search of the legendary Black Prince, but invariably he turned out to be a Redeye. The ordinary cicada was called a Pisser because he squirted mud at you. The most beautiful cicada was the Yellow Monday. He was as yellow as a canary and transparent as crystal. When he lifted his wings in the sunlight the membranes were like the deltas of little rivers. The sun shone straight through him. It shone straight through all of us.

It shone straight through everything, and I suppose it still does. As I begin this last paragraph, outside my window a misty afternoon drizzle gently but inexorably soaks the City of London. Down there in the street forlorn umbrellas commiserate with each other. In Sydney Harbour, twelve thousands miles away and ten hours from now, the yachts will be racing on the crushed diamond water under a sky the texture of powdered sapphires. It would be churlish not to concede that the same abundance of natural blessings which gave us the energy to leave has every right to call us back. All in, the whippy's taken. Pulsing like a beacon through the days and nights, the birth-place of the fortunate sends out its invisible waves of recollection. It always has and it always will, until even the last of us come home.

FALLING TOWARDS ENGLAND

To

Chester and John Cummings

I had already noticed with various people that the affectation of praiseworthy sentiments is not the only way of covering up reprehensible ones, but that a more up-to-date method is to put these latter on exhibition, so that one has the air of at least being forthright.

Proust, *Le Temps retrouvé*

All censure of a man's self is oblique praise. It is in order to show how much he can spare.

Johnson

Preface

This is the second volume of my unreliable memoirs. For a palpable fantasy, the first volume was well enough received. It purported to be the true story of how the author grew from infancy through adolescence to early manhood, this sequence of amazing biological developments largely taking place in Kogarah, a suburb of Sydney, NSW, Australia. And indeed it *was* a true story, in the sense that I wasn't brought up in a Tibetan monastery or a castle on the Danube. The central character was something like my real self. If the characters around him were composites, they were obviously so, and with some justification. The friend who helps you dig tunnels in your back yard is rarely the same friend who ruins your summer by flying a model aeroplane into your mother's prize trifle, but a book with everybody in it would last as long as life, and never live at all.

As for the adults, they were shadows, but that was true to how children see, and my mother, in particular, was too much of an influence on my life for me to appreciate at that age – or at any subsequent age, for that matter. Her quiet but strenuous objections to *Unreliable Memoirs* arose from my depiction, not of her, but of myself. Apparently I was not the near-delinquent portrayed, but a little angel: to suggest otherwise reflected badly on her. The insult was not meant. Perhaps I should have pointed out more often that without her guidance and example I might have gone straight from short pants to Long Bay Gaol, which in those days was still in use and heavily populated by larcenous young men who had chosen their parents less wisely.

Unlike my mother and my father, who were robbed by history of a rounding to their youth, I had come peacefully to my middle years and wanted to celebrate my good luck, or at any rate atone for it, by evoking a childhood blessed enough to be typical. But the typical, for even the most high-minded male child, does not exclude the revolting. I tried to leave some of that in. One might argue that I should have made a more thorough job of it. A Scots lady ninety-three years old sent me a charming letter saying that when young in Ayrshire she had done all the things I did. The book must have been read aloud to her, by someone who knew which pages to pass over in silence.

To tell my story in the belief that I was remarkable would have been sufficiently conceited. To tell it in the hope of being universal was possibly even more conceited, not to say pretentious. He who abandons his claim to be unique is even less bearable when he claims to be representative. But at least he has *tried* to climb down. There is a story by Schnitzler, called 'History of a Genius', about a butterfly so impressed by how far it has come in one day that it resolves to dictate its autobiography. Yet Schnitzler, so greatly generous about human beings, sells the butterfly short. The butterfly's only mistake is to imagine itself unusual. The story of its day would be well worth having, and all the more so if it realized that millions of its fellows shared the same career. Usual does not mean ordinary. A butterfly's compound eyes, which can see in the infra-red, are no less extra-ordinary because every other butterfly has them. The same applies to human memory. When I hold my hands as if in prayer and roll a pencil between them, I can smell the plasticine snakes I made in Class 1B at Kogarah Infants' School. There is nothing ordinary about that.

Far from being all done in a day, my own story is of a late developer: one who, deficient in natural wisdom, has had to learn everything by trial and error. In this book my errors continue, but in a different context. In Sydney I had come of age but still had a lot to learn. In Europe I forgot what little I knew. London in the sixties, it was generally believed, had sprung to life. Lost somewhere in the hubbub, I either marked time or went backwards. Readers who grew up faster, wherever they did so, might still recognize in these pages something of what they went through in order to become what they now are. Those whose personalities were handed to them in one piece might shake their heads. There are such people, and often they are among the saints, but they are denied the salutary privilege of remembering what they once were, before they knew better. It is possible that they are also denied knowledge of where the human comedy begins, in the individual soul. But I wouldn't want to be caught suggesting that the past dissolves in mirth. Things happen that can't be laughed off. Our hero is a bit older in this book, and the same ways are not necessarily so winning.

Not that I have registered here the full squalor of my past derelictions, some of which I can't begin to recall without an involuntary yell to quash the memory. But to confess would be an indulgence, and there are bigger sinners growing old in Paraguay. Young Australian men living in London drank a great deal but broke nothing except the hearts of young Australian women. Feminism as a mass movement was imminent but had not yet arrived; women were still exploitable; and men duly exploited them. For the sons of the Anzacs this wasn't a very noble chapter, and the girls who suffered, should they read this book twenty years later, might justly complain that I have glossed it over. For them to know that the crassness of their young men was waiting for them at home was bad enough, without encountering more of the same when they arrived abroad. Some of them might find their faintest outlines here, sharing a false name, catching someone else's bus to work in Lambeth or Fulham. No disrespect is intended: quite the opposite. The full complexity of the human personality is something I no longer presume to sum up, or even to suggest.

I can't remember having been *consciously* insensitive. I can hardly remember being consciously anything, except cold. It was all a bit like being on the moon: you moved forward because you were falling forward. The clear path is revealed later, looking back. Which doesn't mean that one disclaims responsibility for one's actions. We are what we have done; and besides, we can't deny it without giving up our pride. 'For my part, since I have always admitted that I was the chief cause of all the misfortunes which have befallen me,' wrote Casanova in his old age, 'I have rejoiced in my ability to be my own pupil, and in my duty to love my teacher.' Did knowing himself to be vain make him less vain? Leaving the metaphysics to others, he died writing his life story – which, considering the other things he might have died doing, was not the least dignified way he could have gone. What a swathe he would have cut through Kogarah! A thought to keep the reader's expectations in proportion as I begin this account of my impact on England, drawn there by gravity like a snowflake to the ground.

C.J.
London, 1985

1. SOFT LANDING

When we got off the ship in Southampton in that allegedly mild January of 1962 I had nothing to declare at customs except goose-pimples under my white nylon drip-dry shirt. This was not because I had been prudent in my spending but because I had spent the last of my money in Singapore, plus twenty pounds I had borrowed from one of my cabin mates – and which I still owe him, come to think of it. The money had gone on a new suit which I didn't actually have with me in my luggage. The tailors in Singapore's Change Alley had taken my measurements and promised to send the finished suit after me to London. This had seemed like a sensible arrangement, so I had handed over the cash, thereby depriving myself of any leeway for a spending spree later on in Aden. I thus missed out on the chance, seized by most of the other Australians of my own age on the ship, to be guided by the expertise of Arab salesmen in the purchase of German tape recorders and Japanese cameras at a fraction of the price – something like five-fourths – prevailing in their countries of origin.

In the crater of Aden, while my compatriots knowingly examined the Arabic guarantee forms for machines whose batteries were mysteriously unavailable, I hovered in the heat-hazed background, sullenly attempting not to catch the remaining eye of a beggar whose face had otherwise been entirely chewed off by a camel. It had been very hot in Aden. In England it was very cold: colder than I had ever known. The customs men did a great deal of heavy-handed chaffing about how you cobbers couldn't really call this a winter, ho ho, and what we would look like if there really was a winter, har har, and so on. Their accents were far funnier than their sense of humour. They all seemed to have stepped out of the feature list of an Ealing comedy for the specific purpose of unpacking our luggage and charging us extra for everything in it. My own luggage consisted mainly of one very large suitcase made of mock leather – i.e., real cardboard. This compendium was forced into rotundity by a valuable collection of tennis shorts, running shorts, Hawaiian shirts, T-shirts, Hong Kong thong rubber sandals, short socks, sandshoes and other apparel equally appropriate for an English winter. The customs officer sifted through the heap twice, the second time looking at me instead of at it, as if my face would betray the secret of the illicit fortunes to be made by smuggling unsuitable clothing across half the world.

As the people all around me were presented with huge bills, I gave silent thanks for being in possession of nothing assessable for duty. The ship's fool – a pimply, bespectacled British emigrant called Tanner who was now emigrating back the other way – was near tears. In Aden and Port Said he had bought, among other things, two tape recorders, a Japanese camera called something like a Naka-mac with a silver box full of lenses, a portable television set slightly larger than an ordinary domestic model but otherwise no different except that it had a handle, a stuffable leather television pouffe for watching it from, a hi-fi outfit with separate components, and a pair of binoculars so powerful that it frightened you to look through them, especially if you saw Tanner. Most of this gear he had about his person, although some of it was packed in large cardboard boxes, because all this was happening in the days before miniaturization, when an amplifier still had valves. The customs officer calculated the duty owing and confronted him with the total, at which he sat down on his boxed telescope and briefly wept. It was more money than he had in the world, so he just signed away the whole mountain of gear and walked on through a long door in the far side of the shed.

A few minutes afterwards I walked through the same door and emerged in England, where it was gently snowing onto a bus full of Australians. There was a small cloud in front of my face which I quickly deduced to be my breath. The bus was provided by the Overseas Visitors' Club, known for short as the OVC. The journey by ship, the bus ride to London and a week of bed and breakfast in Earls Court were all part of the deal, which a few years later would have been called a Package, but at that time was still known as a Scheme. The general thrust of the Scheme was to absorb some of the culture shock, thus rendering it merely benumbing instead of fatal. As the bus, which strangely insisted on calling itself a coach, headed north – or west or east or wherever it was going, except, presumably, south – I looked out into the English landscape and felt glad that I had not been obliged to find my way through it unassisted.

The cars seemed very small, with no overhang at either end. A green bus had 'Green Line' written on it and could therefore safely be assumed to be a Green Line bus, or coach. The shops at the side of the road looked as if they were finely detailed painted accessories for an unusually elaborate Hornby Dublo model railway table-top layout. Above all, as well as around all and beyond all, was the snow, almost exactly resembling the snow that fell in English films on top of people like Alastair Sim and Margaret Rutherford. What I was seeing was a familiar landscape made strange by being actual instead of transmitted through cultural intermediaries. It was a deeply unsettling sensation, which everybody else in the coach must have shared, because for the first time in twelve thousand miles there was a prolonged silence. Then one of the wits explained that the whole roadside façade would fold down after we had roared by, to reveal factories manufacturing rust-prone chromium trim for the Standard Vanguard. There was some nervous laughter and the odd confident assurance that we were already in the outskirts of London. Since the outskirts of London were well known to embrace pretty well everywhere in the south of England up to the outskirts of Birmingham, this seemed a safe bet.

A few ploughed fields presented themselves so that the girls, still pining for members of the ship's crew, might heave a chorus of long sighs at the bunny rabbits zipping across the pinwhale corduroy snow. After that it was one continuous built-up area turning to streetlight in the gathering darkness of what my watch told me was only mid-afternoon. Enveloped in many layers of clothing, people thronging the footpaths seemed to be black, brown or, if white and male, to have longer hair than the females. High to the left of an arching flyover shone the word WIMPEY, a giant, lost, abstract adjective carved from radioactive ruby.

There was no way of telling, when we arrived, that the place we were getting off at was called Earls Court, In those days it was still nicknamed Kangaroo Valley but there were no obvious signs of Australia except the foyer of the OVC, crowded with young men whose jug ears stuck out unmistakably from their short haircuts on either side of a freckled area of skin which could be distinguished as a face, rather than a neck, only by the presence of a nose and a mouth. Here I was relieved to find out that I had been assigned to the same dormitory room as my cabin mates, at a hostel around the corner. So really we were still on board ship, the journey from the OVC foyer around the corner to the hostel being the equivalent of a brisk turn around the deck, while carrying a large suitcase.

The snow was falling thickly enough to replenish a half-inch layer on the footpath, so that my black Julius Marlowe shoes could sink in slightly and, I was interested to notice, be fairly rapidly made wet. It hadn't occurred to me that snow would have this effect. I had always assumed snow to be some form of solid. In the hostel I counted up my financial resources. They came to just a bit more than ten pounds in English money. Ten pounds bought quite a lot at that time, when eight pounds a week was a labourer's living wage and you could get a bar of chocolate for threepence, a chunky hexagonal coin which I at first took to be some form of washer and then spent a lot of time standing on its edge on the bedside table while figuring out what to do next. Improvising brilliantly, I took some of the small amount of money over and above the ten pounds and invested in an aerogramme, which I converted into a begging letter and addressed to my mother, back there in Sydney with no telephone. Her resources being far from limitless, I did my best not to make the letter too heartrending, but after it was finished, folded and sealed I had to leave it on the radiator for the tears to dry out, after which it was wrinkled and dimpled like an azure poppadum.

Dinner in the hostel made me miss the ship-board menu, which until then I would have sworn nothing ever could. What on earth did a spotted dick look like before the custard drowned it? A glass mug of brown water was provided which we were assured was beer. I sipped fitfully at mine while everybody else watched. When I showed no signs of dengue fever or botulism, they tried theirs. Having rolled inaccurately into my bunk, I discovered, like my two cabin mates, that I couldn't sleep for the silence of the engines.

Next day there was still a tendency to cling together. I was in a three-man expedition that set out to find Piccadilly Circus by following a map of the Underground railway system, starting at Earls Court station. To reach the station we had to travel some way on the surface, keeping a wary eye out for hostile natives. It was a relief to find that in daylight at any rate a sizeable part of the local population was Australian. At that time the Earls Court Australians had not yet taken to carrying twelve-packs of Foster's lager, and the broad-brimmed Akubra hat with corks dangling from the brim was never to be more than a myth, but there was no mistaking those open, freckled, eyeless faces, especially when they were sticking out of the top of navy-blue English duffle-coats religiously acquired as a major concession towards blending into the scenery. My own duffle-coat was bright yellow in colour and would not have helped me blend into anything except a sand dune, but luckily it was hanging in my cupboard back in Kogarah, Sydney. Or unluckily, if you considered how cold I felt in my light-green sports coat with the blue fleck. Or would have felt, if I had been less excited. But we were going down in a lift through a hole in the ground to another hole in the ground which would take us under London to Piccadilly Circus. Piccadilly! I even knew what it meant. It was a tailor's term, something to do with sleeves. No doubt the tailors had started a circus when times got tough.

Knowingness evaporated when the tube train pulled into the station. The train was so small that for a moment I thought it was a toy – another component of the Hornby Dublo table-top layout, except this time under the table. You almost had to bend your head getting into it. The electric trains in Sydney were sensibly provided with four feet of spare headroom in case any visiting American basketballer wanted to hitch a ride without taking off his stilts. He might have stood out because of his colour, but at least he wouldn't be bent over double. In this train he would be bent over double, but at least he wouldn't stand out because of his colour. Half the people in the crowded carriage seemed to be black or dark brown. They were dressed just the same as the white people and often conspicuously better. I had entered my first multiracial society, all for the price of a tube ticket. If I had come from an apartheid country, I would have had a kit of reflexes that I could have set about modifying. But coming from a monotone dominion whose Aborigines were still thought of, at that time, as something between a sideshow and an embarrassment, I had nothing to go on except a blank feeling which I hoped was receptivity. A sperm whale feeding on a field of squid – not giant squid, just those little squidlets that form its basic diet – cruises along with its mouth open, taking everything in. That was me, open-mouthed to new experience. The sperm whale looks the same when drowning, of course: going down and down with its gob wide open and the pressure building up and up. By Knightsbridge we were making nervous jokes about a journey to the centre of the earth. The escalators leading to the surface at Piccadilly were like sets from *Things to Come*. Then we popped out of the ground and stood rooted to the mushy pavement by the Sheer Englishness of it all. 'Coca-Cola' said a wall of neon, glowing as if day were night – a fair assessment of the overcast morning.

But Eros was sufficiently evocative all by himself and we set off for Buckingham Palace with high hearts, going by way of Nelson's Column and the Admiralty Arch. The Mall showed pink through the churned slush, St James's Park was a spun-sugar cake-scape with clockwork ducks, and a flag on the Palace indicated that She was at home. The Guard obligingly began to change itself just as we arrived, the Coldstreams handing over to the Grenadiers. Tourism was still under control at that time so it was possible to catch the odd glimpse of the participating soldiers, instead of, as now, seeing nothing except the rear view of Norwegians carrying full camping apparatus and holding up cameras to fire blind over the hulking backpacks of other Norwegians standing in front of them. Needless to say we did not regard ourselves as tourists. Whatever our convictions, we were children of the Commonwealth, not to say the Empire. One of us rather embarrassingly stood to attention. It was not myself, since I was a radical socialist at the time, but I understood. It was something emotional that went back to Chad Valley tin toys, Brock fireworks and the every-second-Christmas box of W. Britains lead soldiers. I remembered my set of Household Cavalry with the right arms that swivelled and the swords held upright, except for the troop leader whose sabre stuck out in line with his extended arm while his horse pranced. When his arm worked loose and fell off I wodged it back on with a gasket of cigarette paper. I can remember remembering this while the band played 'British Grenadiers', and can remember how wet my eyes were, mainly from the cold that was creeping upward from my feet. At first they had been numb. Now they felt like something Scott of the Antarctic might have made a worried note about in his diary if I had been a member of his expedition. As the officers on parade screamed at each other nose to nose from under their forward-tilting bearskins, it began occurring to me that the climate was going to be a problem.

Or part of a larger problem, that of money. There was more

sightseeing in the next few days, with the National Gallery putting everything else in perspective. Indeed it put its own contents into perspective, since here again, even more strikingly, there was a discrepancy between the actual and what had been made familiar in reproduction. The Rokeby Venus, for example, was supposed to be the size of half a page in a quarto art book, not as big as the serving window of Harry's Café de Wheels at Woolloomooloo. She looked a bit murky at that stage – they cleaned her a few years later, and perhaps overdid it – but her subtly dimpled bottom, poised at the height of the viewer's eyes, made you wonder about Velázquez's professional detachment. Though most of the rooms in the gallery were still a mystery to me, I was confident enough, or ignorant enough, to decide that Art with a capital 'A' was going to be a source of sensual gratification on all levels. At the Tate Gallery I was relieved to find that the Paul Klee pictures were roughly the same size as in the books. But just to reach the galleries by tube was costing money, and meanwhile time was running out.

There was a grand total of eight pounds left and it didn't help when I lost the lot, along with my prize yellow pig-skin wallet, at Waldo Laidlaw's wedding party. Arriving out of the sky in his usual grand style – absolutely nobody else you knew could afford to fly – Waldo instantly married one of the girls from my ship. Apparently it had all been arranged back in Australia. The party was in the as-yet-unfurnished shell of a ground-floor flat in that part of Camden Town where you could overlook Regent's Park if you could find your way on to the roof. In Waldo's words, overlooking it was easy, because you couldn't see it. All the Australian advertising types were there, the women unattainably well-groomed and the men sporting Chelsea boots, an elastic-sided form of footwear I had not previously encountered. I was the only one dressed for the Australian summer, with three T-shirts and a pair of running shorts on under my Hawaiian shirt and poplin trousers. Feeling the heat of the crowded room, I took off my jacket, left it in the bedroom on the bed with the overcoats, and prepared to dance.

A hit record called 'Let's Twist Again' was playing over and over. Several people among the sophisticated throng had already reached exhibition standard in dancing the Twist. I think I could have matched them through sheer inspiration, but my shoes were in bad shape and tended to stick where they were, cruelly restricting my rate and radius of swivel. In the kitchen there were big tins of brown water you could open with your thumb. I treated the stuff with the contempt it deserved, pronouncing its alcoholic content to be minimal. Pronouncing its algolic contender be mineral. Pronouncing my own name with difficulty. After kneeling in the toilet for some time with my head resting in the bowl I felt fighting fit again and all set to lie down. It was then that I found my wallet missing and did my best to spoil Waldo's celebration by telling him that one of his guests must have lifted it from my jacket. It was courteous of him to arrange a lift home for me instead of throwing me in the canal. When I sobered up a couple of days later it became evident that the wallet must have first of all dropped through the large hole which had developed in the bottom of my jacket's inner pocket and then fallen through the detached lining into the street before I even got to the party. It was still a good jacket otherwise though, with leather buttons like scout woggles.

So the week at the OVC hostel was all used up. One of my cabin mates, the one who had stood to attention in front of Buckingham Palace, moved out to fulfil his ambition of becoming a British officer who would protrude from the top of a rapidly moving armoured car while wearing a beret. At Sydney University he had been an actor but it was now clear that this training had always had no other purpose except to further the attainment of his real aim in life. Though his hyphenated surname would probably have got him the job anyway, it couldn't have hurt his chances that he wore clothes like Dennis Price and talked like Terry Thomas. I had little patience with his hunger for military tradition but hated to see him go. My other cabin mate was in London to study music. Having made his arrangements, he now moved off and started doing so. Talking grandly of my intention to take a small flat in Knightsbridge, I managed to get some loose change off him before he left, but not enough, and since he was the very man I had touched in order to finance the Singapore suit I could scarcely dun him for a more substantial contribution. A postal order from home would be another week arriving. The snow in Hyde Park was not deep enough for me to build an igloo and my suitcase, although absurdly large when carried, was too cramped to live in. So I lugged it around another corner and occupied the living-room floor of two girls from Sydney's North Shore who had known me at university. After a year in London they were still in Earls Court. I was in no position to mock their lack of enterprise. They were well brought up, well spoken, well equipped and well organized – too well organized to put up with a permanent hobo camp on their parlour carpet. Curmudgeonly, this reluctance, because each evening after helping to drink their wine I generously offered to sleep with either or both. But they shared their meals with me, stuffed my shoes with paper before drying them in the stove, advised me on the purchase of a blue duffle-coat, and helped me look for somewhere to live.

Gently they discouraged my notions of seeking a maisonette in Bayswater or a mews house in Belgravia. There was a bed and breakfast boarding house in Swiss Cottage that wanted only three pounds ten shillings a week. When my postal order came, the girls very kindly drove me there. It was a long way from Kangaroo Valley and when their Volkswagen Beetle splurged away along the overlapping lines of grey slush I stood in the snow beside my mock-leather suitcase and felt that I was ashore at last. My boats were burning and I was too far inland to see the flames. I resolved to grow a beard.

2. BEYOND THE VALLEY OF THE KANGAROOS

My new home was nondescript, in the strict sense of there being nothing to describe. Wallpaper, carpets and furniture had all been chosen so as to defeat memory. About twenty people were in residence. Most of them were failed South African and Rhodesian farmers with an accent so harsh it made mine sound like Sir John Gielgud's. You met them not only at breakfast but in the evening as well, all sitting together watching *Tonight* on television and shouting at the black man who sang the topical calypso. We were downstairs together because there was nothing we were allowed to do upstairs in our rooms alone. The list of rules forbade cooking in one's room, taking already cooked food to one's room, or taking food that did not need cooking to one's room. No visitors were allowed in one's room at any time for any reason: if one died, one's body would be allowed to decompose. Breathing was allowed as long as it made no noise. The same applied to sleep. Anyone who snored would wake up in the street. The proprietor had not made the mistake of retaining the original thick internal walls. They had been replaced by twice as many very thin ones, through which he and his lipless wife could accurately hear, and, some lodgers whisperingly warned me, see.

The danger of noisy sleep, however, was largely obviated by the difficulty of sleeping at all. One blanket too few had been carefully provided, and the central heating, although it visibly existed, was cold to the touch and had to be topped up by a two-bar radiator which failed to glow the first time I switched it on. When I nervously complained about this it was pointed out to me that the radiator was on a meter. Having never seen a meter before, I had thought that the grey machine squatting heavily in the corner was part of the house's electrical system. In a way it was, but making it function was up to me. I put in a shilling and the radiator came on. Gratefully I took off my top layer of T-shirts and running shorts, preparing for bed. The radiator went off. When I put in a florin the radiator glowed and fizzed for a bit longer but what the meter really liked was an enormous half-crown piece, a beautiful coin whose aesthetic appeal was enhanced by its then considerable purchasing power. I hated to see it go, and felt even worse, an hour or so later, when the meter, by instructing the radiator to dim out, signalled that it would like another coin the same size. The whole idea of paying to keep warm would have struck me as ludicrous if I could have stopped shivering. My teeth chattering like castanets, I doubled the thin pillow over my head to muffle the noise, so that it must have seemed, to my landlady poised outside in the corridor, as if I had ceased rehearsing for the title role in *Carmen* and started pain-training a rattlesnake.

My plan had been to take a low-paying menial job during the day and compose poetic masterpieces at night. After due reflection I decided that it would be preferable, at least initially, to take a high-paying job in journalism and sacrifice a small proportion of the masterpieces to expediency. From the editor of the *Sydney Morning Herald*, Angus Maude, I had a letter of introduction to one of the *Herald*'s previous editors, John Douglas Pringle, like Maude an Englishman but unlike him now back in London and editing the *Observer*, a newspaper whose every issue I had devoured in Australia six weeks late, and which I was now able, with admiration increased still further by understanding, to read on the day of publication. I had vowed never to use this letter of introduction, which Maude had pressed on me against my declarations of artistic purity. Crammed randomly among the socks in my giant suitcase, it had become rumpled, but a glass ashtray heated at the radiator soon ironed it relatively smooth. Cleaning up the scorched ashtray with my toothbrush took somewhat longer. Armed with the letter and with a tartan tie thoughtfully added to the Hawaiian shirt, I went to see Pringle at the *Observer*'s building in Blackfriars. Eyeing my incipient beard with what I took to be grudging appreciation of its bohemian *élan*, he asked me what languages I could read and I said English. He asked me what I wanted to do and I said write features. As I ashed my duty-free Rothmans filter on to his carpet, he pointed out that he already had a building full of young feature writers who could read at least one foreign language, wrote perfectly acceptable English and had the additional

virtue of knowing quite a lot about Britain, since they had been
brought up in that country, i.e. this country. My ejection from his
office followed so shortly upon my entrance into it that the two
events were effectively continuous. What made it more galling was
that I could see his point. There wasn't really very much I could
contribute to British journalism. On the other hand there probably
wasn't very much it could contribute to my artistic development, so
perhaps this was less a set-back than a reprieve.

Back at what I had by now learned to call my digs, the problem
of laundry loomed large. Open at the foot of my bed, the giant
suitcase had nothing left in it that had not already been classified at
least twice as too dirty to be worn, and some of my socks were
twitching where they lay. So I bundled the whole heap into one of
the landlady's threadbare pillowcases and crunched off along a pavement of newly refrozen slush to the nearest launderette, otherwise
known as the coin-wash, or – inaccurately but more evocatively –
the bag-wash. (Strictly speaking it was only a bag-wash if you left
somebody else holding the bag, and if you stayed to tend the machine
yourself it was a coin-wash, but as usually happens, the fine semantic
point gave way before the attractions of sonority.) The launderette
had two rows of seats down the middle, back to back, so that everyone
could watch his or her machine. The place was jammed and I had
to wait for both a machine and a seat. During the waiting time I
read the instructions. Large coins would be required for the machine
and smaller ones to obtain a cup of soap. When my turn finally came
I loaded the machine with a convincing nonchalance, poured in a
cup of soap and sat down between two South Africans who were
smiling to themselves. I could tell they were South Africans because
(a) when they talked across me it was like being beaten up, and (b)
two people from any other nation would have arranged to sit beside
each other if they wanted to conduct a conversation. After ten minutes
of going *gwersh gwersh* my machine proffered an explanation of why
my companions had been smiling, snorting and clubbing each other
with verbal truncheons of crushed Dutch. The window in the front
of the machine having whited out completely, the flap in the top
popped open and a gusher of suds began gouting out, enveloping
the machine and advancing inexorably across the floor. It was an
albino volcano. The South Africans were beside themselves and I was
between them. They even laughed with that accent. Finally the woman

in charge of the establishment came wading through the foam and added the antidote, some form of contra-detergent which killed the suds off inside the machine. I was handed a squeegee with which to contain the gleaming cloud around it.

After the second rinse, my clothes were ready to be slopped into a plastic basket and transferred to a centrifuge which would rid them of excess water. I was interested to note, during the transfer, that my shirts had taken on some of the colour of my socks. The South Africans had noticed this too and were reaching across my temporarily empty seat to hit each other with rolled-up copies of the *News of the World*, having apparently given up hope of reducing each other to unconsciousness by voice alone. The rattle of the centrifuge drowned out their merry cries. Next came the tumble drier, which required a large coin for half an hour's tumble. It had a bigger window than the washing machine and gave you a better show, but at the end of it most of my clothes still felt wet, so I put in another coin and set them tumbling again. Resolving to bring a book next time – Prescott's *The Conquest of Mexico* in three volumes would be about the right length – I occupied myself with observing how the yellow tint of the window was making my whites look tea-coloured instead of the pale bluish-grey they had been when I put them in. When the drier at last finished its second stint I opened the window and found that all my drip-dry shirts had indeed gone slightly saffron in colour – clearly as a preliminary to catching fire, because they were so hot I could hardly touch them. There was a riot of harshly accented laughter in the background.

When I got the shirts back to what I hated to call home, they proved to be not just aureate in hue, but brittle in texture. I put one of them on and a cuff broke off. The nylon polymer had been transformed into some friable variety of perspex. Another worrying aspect was the pillowcase, which I should have washed along with its contents. I would have to sleep holding my nose. But at least my personal linen was now fragrant enough to allow me a night out with the Australians at a party in Melbury Road, on the Holland Park side of Kensington High Street. This was perilously close to Earls Court, which I had vowed never to enter again, but as an evening's distraction it beat watching television with the Voortrekkers. The previous evening there had been a play about a black African freedom fighter earning the respect of the security police by his bravery. Whenever the weary policemen stopped hitting him there were shouts of protest from my fellow lodgers. The uproar reached a climax when the black was allowed to make his dying speech without being assaulted. 'Thet's what's *rewning* Efrica,' said a voice from a winged chintz chair, 'litting a keffir talk to them like thet.' Another chintz chair agreed. 'Thet's right,' it said. 'They mist not be allowed to answer *beck.*'

Far from sure why I had come to England at all, I was nevertheless certain that it hadn't been in order to hang out with my compatriots, but unaccountably I now craved their well-modulated tones. With a gallon tin of brown water under each arm I climbed the stairs to the top-floor flat of a house in Melbury Road which had held a large Australian expatriate contingent since the time of the Pre-Raphaelites, one of whom had rented the studio in the back yard. There were fifty duffle-coats draped over the banisters and about a hundred people frantically twisting inside the flat itself, data which suggested that each couple had arrived sharing the one coat. The girl to whom I had sworn eternal fealty was half the world away and I was feeling friendless, but this new style of dancing, in which the partners did not actually touch each other, was a heaven-sent opportunity to move in on other men's women. I had been practising the Twist in my room and because of the necessity to remain undetected by the landlady's sonar I had developed a finely calculated frictionless style, in which my feet trembled noiselessly on the spot while the rest of my body alternated between drying its back with an imaginary towel and pointing out the approach of hostile aircraft. All this was done in a closed-eyed trance, but I can't believe that I looked any more ridiculous than the rest of the men and certainly I inflicted far fewer injuries through inadvertent karate blows with the flying feet, although my rapidly and randomly extended pointing fingers were admittedly apt to make contact with somebody else's eyeball. A polite squeal resulting from just such an infringement brought me face to face with one of my erstwhile girlfriends, who had already been in London for a year, working as an editorial assistant for a publisher. Unfortunately she had embraced Catholicism in the interim, which turned out to mean that I was not allowed to embrace her. It was quite an accommodating broom cupboard that I backed her into – much larger than the sort of thing we had been used to in Sydney – but she warded off my beer-breath, bristle-chin importunities with a regretful knee and insisted on going home with the English publishing type who had brought her, some woofling galah with a Morgan.

Next evening I took her to see *Hiroshima mon amour* and we became the only couple in history ever to see that film and not get into bed together afterwards. We sat on it instead. Her bed-sitting room in Chalk Farm was cosy enough if you didn't mind the cruci-fixes. 'You saw nothing in Hiroshima.' You can say that again. She looked prettier than ever in all that wool. Even her tights were made of wool. It became clear that they would stay in place. But she was generous with something more substantial – practical assistance. Rupert, the goof in the Morgan, was looking for a freelance copy-editor. With my *Sydney Morning Herald* training I could do it on my head. Helping myself to more of her wine, I explained my firm intention not to compromise. But the duty-free cigarettes were running low and at this rate even my bed and breakfast would soon be too expensive. A temporary sell-out might be advisable. Having finished off her reserve bottle of banana-skin Beaujolais, I took the typescript she had given me and set off on foot through the cold, foggy night towards Swiss Cottage. Navigating by a sure Australian instinct for the lie of the land, I saw quite a lot of Maida Vale, and got home in good time to be locked out.

The typescript was for a children's book about dinosaurs. 'As massive as a modern home and weighing many tons, Man would have been dwarfed by these massive creatures . . .' I spent the next two days sorting out tenses, expunging solecisms and re-allocating misplaced clauses to the stump from which they had been torn loose by the sort of non-writing writer for whom grammar is not even a mystery, merely an irrelevance. Short of rewriting the thing entirely, I couldn't have done the job better, so it was with confidence that I posted the doctored script, together with a covering letter stating that a mere thirty pounds a week would be about the right rate, in view of the fact that I would be working only casually, in between my own literary projects.

Hampstead Heath was a slush curry of dead leaves but lent itself readily to the creative meanderings of young writers with high expectations and cold hands stuffed into duffle-coat pockets. In the next few days I joined this ambling band, ploughing a lonely furrow to criss-cross with theirs. On a park bench padded with newspapers I sat shivering while a new kind of poem formed in my notebook. It was a poem I could understand. Until then, most of my poems had been devotedly incomprehensible. Now they were becoming comprehensible, a transformation that would have allowed me to detect their sentimentality if they had not been so true to my feelings, which were sentimental. But I was warmer than I would have been in my room, and when inspiration failed I could always make the short pilgrimage to Keats's house. It looked compact and elegant among the leafless trees – compact and elegant like him. He wrote the 'Ode to a Nightingale' there, but although I was mad about his odes at that time, the ode I was maddest about was the one on Melancholy. *Sudden from heaven like a weeping cloud.* I thought of that line when I was walking down Frognal and the rain caught me with nowhere to hide. So I got back home soaked, just in time for the evening post, which informed me that I hadn't got the editorial job. Apparently what I had written in my covering note – that the thing needed rewriting entirely – was what I should have done. So once again I had been saved from selling out. Drying myself in front of the radiator while the meter ate half-crowns like Smarties, I tried to feel relieved, but it was getting less easy all the time.

3. SOUL FOR SALE

Never, I had vowed, would I sell my soul to an advertising agency. Not even if I was starving. Not even if I had no ceiling over my head. Yet starvation was only one step down from the breakfast I was getting every morning, and the ceiling over my head had South Africans on the other side using it as a floor. Waldo invited me to a party he was throwing for all his flash new friends in English advertising. I went along in order to be disgusted by their materialist values. There were plenty of materialist values on display, starting with the traffic jam of early production model E-type Jaguars parked out in the street. The men were reasonably easy to sneer at, with their elastic-sided, chisel-toed Chelsea boots and girlish length of hair. As usually happens in such circumstances, the real challenge was presented by the women. One of them was called Brenda and she was so glossily pretty that it was hatred at first sight. Unfortunately she was clever and funny too, so it was not easy to remain hostile. She was married to some pipe-sucking Nigel who tried to interest me in how David Ogilvy had once told him that if you fouled the air in somebody's bathroom, all you had to do was strike a match and the atmosphere would instantly return to its pristine sweetness, even if the bathroom were as big as an aircraft hangar. I can remember this with such clarity only because I was in the process of falling in love with his wife at the time. But she was married, and would have been even more frightening if single. It was clear just from what she had on her that it took a lot of money to run such a woman. The time had come for a modification of values. Faust was ready to negotiate. Casting Waldo as Mephistopheles, I drew him aside and asked him how to set about becoming a copy-writer. Since he had had to endure my callow jibes against his profession many times in the past, it was big of him to answer this question with useful information instead of the horse laugh. Apparently there was a vacancy coming up at Simpson, Sampson, Ranulph and Rolfe. He would get me through the door and from then on it would be up to me.

Reassured, I danced a few times with Brenda and tried not to be disappointed when she had to leave early with a gouged eye. She and Nigel climbed into a ludicrously small new car calling itself a Mini. With my bump for technology I could tell straight away that such a glorified toy would never catch on, but still I couldn't imagine anything more desirable than being in a very small car with a girl like Brenda. All it would take would be a few scintillating jingles, and vroom-vroom. 'You'll *piss* it in,' said Waldo. 'Just remember to cover your mouth when you belch and don't stub your fags out on the Axminster.'

Waldo was as good as his word and I had barely a day to prepare my spontaneous utterances before reporting to St James's Square and being ushered into the suave presence of SSRR's senior partner and creative chief, the legendary P. H. S. 'Plum' Rolfe. He had Hush Puppies on his feet and a tweed tie around his neck, but the tie was loose and his feet were on his desk, so it was possible to relax – something I would not otherwise have found easy to do, because I was a bit worried about my wardrobe. The suit from Singapore had still not arrived and by now I had begun to wonder if the green sports coat and the wrecked shoes were quite the thing, especially as my scorched drip-dry shirts tended to shatter no matter how carefully I buttoned them up, making my facade look like a vandalized housing development unless I not only arranged the tartan tie to cover the damage but contrived to keep it that way while lounging casually in a chair. But Rolfe seemed to like my poems. While he was opening my old Sydney University magazines to the places marked, I tried a few rehearsed spontaneous utterances and he liked them too. It was ever more encouraging when he turned out to like the unrehearsed ones still better. He told me to send him a five-thousand-word essay on why I wanted to be an advertising man and then come back again in a fortnight.

Having written the essay that same evening, I went next morning to the Mayfair branch of the Bank of NSW and raised a £50 overdraft on the strength of being a hot job prospect for a top agency. Since I had no account at the bank and was clearly opening one only in order to see the assistant manager and touch him for a loan, it will be appreciated that my powers of persuasion were benefiting from a surge of confidence. No doubt the beard helped. Looking less like an oversight by now and more like an act of defiance, it must have presented an overwhelming challenge to the assistant manager's bourgeois inhibitions. I should have asked him for a hundred.

A small part of the ensuing desert of vast eternity I was able to spend marching from Aldermaston with Waldo's advertising contingent. Actually we didn't march from Aldermaston. Like 90 per cent of the marchers we marched from just outside London, but it was called marching from Aldermaston and felt wonderful. That was the whole point, I need hardly say: feeling wonderful. The whole thing was essentially a religious festival. It wasn't politics, it was performance. I was aware of this even at the time, since my radical socialism, which in my own eyes made me an implacable outsider like Bakunin, necessarily included a deep hostility to the Soviet Union, which I already knew, long before Solzhenitsyn's revelations, to have been a murder factory on a scale barely hinted at by Khrushchev's speech to the 20th Party Congress in 1956. No amount of stupidity on America's part could allay the uncomfortable feeling that unilateral nuclear disarmament had no more in common with multilateral nuclear disarmament than insanity had in common with sanity. But solidarity between opposites being possible for as long as it remains ineffective, the party got bigger and louder while you watched. I danced along with the Ban-the-Bombers because they were the nicest people. I even sang with them, which was the ultimate tribute to their sweetness, because those songs were terrible. 'Ban the Bomb, it's now or never Ban the Bomb, for ev-er more!' Actually I just moved my lips. Like a Shadow Cabinet Minister pretending to sing 'The Red Flag' at a Labour Party Conference, I was too bashful to pronounce the words. But I was there, acting out a fantasy because it was more fun than what I knew to be truth. Brenda was there too, of course, and the chance to stride along beside her would have taken me on a pilgrimage to Lhasa if necessary. It turned out she had all the same doubts as I had but was there because of Nigel, who was there because everybody else was. If the sixties ever had a real beginning, an emblematic event that set the tone for an epoch, that was it – thousands upon thousands of nice people all behaving as if the irritable shrugging off of awkward facts was a kind of dance. Indeed just such a dance soon came in on the heels of the Twist, and was called the Shake.

Flushed with virtue, I turned up in St James's Square on the appointed day with my shirt cuffs protruding just the correct inch from the sleeves of my green jacket, an adjustment made easier by the fact that they had parted company from the actual shirt. The Singapore suit, had it arrived in time, would undoubtedly have been an advantage, but once again Mr Rolfe looked reassuringly bohemian, smoking with no hands while he leafed through my essay. He had never read a more convincing case, he said, for how primal creativity could be combined with a job in advertising. He had no doubt that I could write Australia's answer to *Paradise Lost* in the evenings while concurrently promoting cornflakes all day. What he and Messrs Simpson, Sampson and Ranulph were after, however, was someone who wanted to do nothing else except promote the cornflakes. They wanted someone for whom the poetry was not separate from the cornflakes, but actually *in* the cornflakes and *of* the cornflakes. Like Frosties, I suggested: the sugar wasn't separate from the cornflakes, it was in them and of them. Rolfe said I had hit it exactly, but didn't give me any extra points for the insight. 'Face it,' he said, smiling without dropping the cigarette, 'you aren't modest enough to be corruptible. Getting rich isn't what you're really after. You'd always be writing something for yourself on our time.' He had the great gift of making you feel that you had been turned down because you were too good, so I didn't start feeling miserable until I was outside in the square, where I had a hallucination, startling in its clarity, of Brenda retreating into the distance while waving to me from the passenger seat of a speeding Maserati. The pavements, though cold to my perforated shoes, were dry for once, so I walked all the way home to Swiss Cottage, feeling more ill, broke and woebegone all the time. The Singapore suit was waiting for me when I got there. It had been forwarded from the OVC and was wrapped in thick brown paper through which several peep-holes had been torn, presumably by customs officers. The conviction nagged me that if I had been wearing it I would have got the job. At least it would ensure that I got the next job.

Unwrapped, the Singapore suit was impressive for its weight of cloth. When I put it on and stood in front of the sliver of glass which the landlady evidently supposed to constitute a full-length mirror,

I looked the image of bespoke respectability. You had to hand it to those oriental tailors. They might be flatterers – 'What muscular forearms,' they had whispered as they plied the tape measure, 'what powerful thighs' – but they knew how to cut cloth. Then I lifted my arms to adjust the mirror, and discovered that I couldn't see. The shoulders of the jacket had immediately risen to engulf my head. When I put my arms back down, vision returned. Perhaps I had just moved too suddenly. Tentatively I lifted my right arm. The right shoulder of the jacket went up past my ear. Ditto for the left side. Even more slowly I lifted both arms. Blackout. There was no spare cloth in the armpits: the gussets, or whatever they were called, were missing. Presumably it was the Singapore style of suit, designed for a subtle oriental people not much given to gesture. Anyway, if I kept my hands by my sides it looked quite good.

4. INTO THE HINTERLAND

There was enough left of my overdraft to finance a change of residence. My Swiss Cottage landlady, clearly not charmed by the misshapen ashtray or whatever had happened to her pillowcase, had raised the rent, perhaps also because the end of winter was in the air, with a congruent diminution of revenue from the electricity meter. It was time to rent my first bed-sitting room. In those days a bed-sit all to yourself could be had for three pounds a week, a significant amount less than I was paying at Swiss Cottage. As I compose this sentence, it costs about thirty pounds a week in London to share a two-room flat with three other people and each of them wants to interview you personally before okaying you for the short list, after which the final selection is by written examination. Even allowing for the way money has declined from twenty times its current value in as many years, lonely life was more possible then. Nowadays the young and broke are lucky to sleep on the pavements, while the unlucky ones get chatted up in a pub by a kind-looking chap, taken home to his place, strangled, cut up into small pieces and flushed down a drain. Comparatively little of that was going on in my time. John Christie had merely killed the sort of older people that nobody would miss. The sort of younger people that nobody would miss were not yet on the scene.

Pretty well the worst that could happen to you was to answer the wrong advertisement, which I duly did, ending up in a first-floor horror of a room at the high end of Tufnell Park Road. The other side of the Heath was not necessarily the other side of the world. Kentish Town was only just up the hill and already showing signs of gentrification. But gentrification hadn't touched my room. Putrefaction, yes. Trying to guess what colour the wallpaper had been before the attack by the brown virus from beyond the planets, I vowed that my stay in the Tufnell Park area would be a short one. Somehow, if necessary by a temporary submission to capitalist values, my fortunes would be transformed, after which it would be a small flat in Knightsbridge with easy access to Harrods food hall.

Or perhaps a large flat in Chelsea. At about this time I presumed on my slight acquaintance with Joyce Grenfell to get myself invited around to Elm Park Gardens for a much needed proper lunch, involving such luxuries, long missing from my diet, as beans, lettuce and other foodstuffs coloured green. It was our second meeting. I had first met her when I was a member of the Sydney University Journalists' Club and she had come to Australia on a theatrical tour. We had sent her a luncheon invitation which she threw us into a panic by accepting. Since then I had written her a barrage of tiresomely clever letters which she had been kind enough to answer – probably, I am now able to see, as a means of doing penance, because her nature was so saintly that she looked on duty as a blessing. Semibearded and weirdly clad, I sat there in the otherwise immaculate kitchen of her flat, explaining revolutionary socialism while consuming her food. She asked me if there was anything I needed. What I needed was an independent income in five figures, but to my credit – there was so little to my credit that I feel justified in the boast – I didn't put the bite on her. Instead I informed her that everything was going according to plan. I had shaken myself free of materialist values and the results were already showing in my poetry. Some recent examples of this I read to her unasked. She countered by trying out one of her new sketches on me. It was the one about the old lady who posts the dead rabbit through the car window. I laughed helplessly, but while walking home suffered from bitter afterthoughts. Her work was so obviously the finished product, whereas everything of my own, though it struck me as masterly in the hour of its composition, seemed fragmentary only a few days later. The contrast was made doubly galling by my secret agreement with Ken Tynan's published opinion that the Grenfell school of revue was irredeemably genteel and therefore belonged in the dustbin of history, along with the plays of Terence Rattigan and of almost everybody else except Brecht. You could tell that she was a historical back-number by the way she lived, with all those carpets and cushions and a portrait of her mother by Sargent up on the Regency-striped wall. There was even a woman to wait on table. Comfort and good manners stood revealed as an expression of privilege, and the fact that the privilege had all been worked for just went to show.

None of that back in Tufnell Park, at the cutting edge of the bohemian experience. Though spring was on its way, there were still enough cold nights left to demonstrate what was involved in the change from electricity to gas. Over the basin – an early Sung dynasty ceramic artefact which had been pieced back together by a blind archaeologist – there was an early-model Ascot gas water-heater with several levers which had to be swivelled in the right order when the thing was ignited. If the correct procedure was observed, the machine merely exploded. But if you got it wrong you could be in serious trouble. Even the radiator, or fire, ran on gas. It consisted of a single lattice-work pipe-clay heating element standing vertically in the cusp of a metal reflector, which would have thrown the heat forward had it still been shiny, but which was now, and obviously had been for a long time, black enough to absorb any bold calorie that might threaten to escape from the barely pink glow of the clapped-out element operating at full throttle. For cooking, there was not only the mandatory free-standing gas ring but a proper stove, this latter item having been billed as a luxury extra which could well have warranted the bed-sit being advertised as a flat with kitchenette.

The first hour of the first night revealed that all the bedclothes provided were insufficient to keep my feet warm. Lying there fully dressed with the blankets bound tightly around my feet and knotted, I reluctantly calculated that the gas fire would have to be left running as well. With my feet still bound I hopped over to the gas meter, inserted half a crown, lit the fire, hopped back to bed and lay down. After twenty minutes the element had done little more than assume the colour of a raspberry ice lolly, so I hopped over to the stove, lit that too, left the door open so that the heat would pervade the room, hopped back to bed again, and was just manoeuvring myself into the horizontal position when the fire and the stove both gave a mutter, sputter and guttural pop. It was a total flame-out. The Swiss Cottage electricity meter had been merely a gourmet. The Tufnell Park gas meter was a gourmand. It was Moloch. Obviously it melted the cash payments down for their constituent bullion and gave no more gas than was in the coins themselves.

Winter was almost over but abject poverty was clearly only just beginning. My book-buying habits were no help. From Australia I had brought only one book with me: *Studies in Empirical Philosophy* by John Anderson. The scrupulous realism of Anderson had been either a direct influence on, or a cause of reaction in, almost every Sydney University student of recent years except me. Typically I had failed to avail myself of his instruction while he was still giving it out free every day in the form of lectures. But on board ship, with the man himself safely dead, buried and falling ever further behind, I had submitted myself at last to his magnetic force. Though I was to be a long time making myself proof against the urge to escape from reality into righteous anger, and am perhaps not entirely immune from its blandishments yet, the example of Anderson's critical scepticism struck deep. 'It will be a sign of renewed progress, then,' wrote Anderson in his devastating critique of Marxism's philosophical pretensions, 'when we see revolutionists divesting themselves of the idealistic elements in their philosophy and embracing a consistent realism. Meanwhile, it is the philosopher's business to be realistic, to attack idealism wherever he finds it, to consider constantly what is the case.' Anderson's was the voice of reason. But the voice of poetry had not lost its power to intoxicate, especially as embodied in the works of Shakespeare, whom I now rediscovered with a fervour explicable only in terms of my new geographical proximity to his old stamping grounds. True, Tufnell Park had not been the location of any of his several theatres. Indeed if you were to construct a map showing all those purlieus of London even tenuously relevant to Shakespeare's life, there would be a large blank area of which Tufnell Park would be the centre. Not even in the rarely performed *Henry III Part 4* does anyone say 'Brave friends await full-armed at Tufnell Park.' Nevertheless I heard the whispered echo of his light tread everywhere, and when, in a Charing Cross Road second-hand bookshop, I found a set of the four-volume Nonesuch Shakespeare in the small format, the consideration that it cost exactly as much money as I had in the world was outweighed by the sensuous allure of the gold-stamped buckram half-bindings, marbled boards and opaque paper. Although it rated nowhere as a scholarly text, the set when stood upright on my rickety linoleum-topped bedside table helped to make my cell look intentional in its austerity, as if it belonged to St Jerome rather than Caryl Chessman. The effect was further enhanced by the purchase of Louis MacNeice's personal copy of *Practical Criticism*, by I. A. Richards, which I found spine-upright on a trestle table outside the bay window of a small bookshop in Bloomsbury. On the end-paper was the price in pencil, half a crown, and MacNeice's signature in faded ink. Perhaps the bookshop owner could not read. I bought the book for its resonance as an association copy and added it to my table-top library.

Even when bought as bargains, this library's constituent volumes were costing me money I didn't have. To compound the felony, the very books which were eventually to teach me a measure of humility had at first the effect of encouraging me in the opposite, so that I pursued the life of the mind as if the world owed me a living. If the mind develops at all in such circumstances, it is likely to do so leaving certain gaps, one of which will be the failure to realize that to borrow money without the intention of paying it back is a form of theft. I, on the other hand, believed that property was theft – a more glamorous idea altogether, and one which encouraged the notion that if you could induce an acquaintance to give you some of his property in the form of money you were practically a policeman. Luckily I was circumscribed in my begging from friends, first of all by a shortage of friends and then by their own shortage of cash. Sources of small-scale loans with which to pay back large-scale loans were drying up. But I was determined to live the artistic life, and there were quite a few extremely artistic activities which could be pursued at no expense, if you were prepared to walk there instead of ride. Every time the National Gallery held the British people to ransom by announcing that a Leonardo cartoon would go to America unless they stumped up, I would walk to the gallery, study the great drawing on display, and generously insert into the collection box some small-denomination aluminium coin from Singapore or Port Said. If the Whitechapel Gallery held a Barbara Hepworth retrospective I would trek down the Holloway Road to the East End and spend hours caressing her brass volumes and bronze volutes with a famished eye. The famished stomach I placated with fish and chips bought from a glorified roadside whelk-stall just near the gallery. The stall featured a lot of other weird stuff along with the whelks, including what looked like cross-sectional research samples of a prehistoric worm colony trapped in a glaciated bog. These, I was told, were jellied eels. While I was being told this, a small bow-legged man in a flat cap came shambling up, purchased some of the jellied eels, and began, with quivering, palsied hands, to cram them into his asymmetrical maw. He assured me, between noisy mouthfuls, that a life-long diet of jellied eels had made him what he was.

Kenwood House was another free treat, not just for the pictures but for the Adam interiors. I began to have an eye for the clean sweep and jocund formality of the plaster ceiling in a grand English house, perhaps impelled by the contrast it presented to my ceiling in Tufnell Park, which looked as if a loosely stretched and seriously crumpled old tarpaulin had been stuccoed with night-soil. Whether Kenwood House had an eye for me was another question. Certainly my appearance would have startled the original owner if he had still been around to greet his guests. Winter by now was transforming itself into spring by way of a transitional period consisting mainly of mud. The air, if not exactly balmy, was too warm for a duffle-coat, so I was wearing my new combat jacket, bought from one of the many army-surplus stores along Holloway Road which were still occupied with distributing the excess production stimulated by the Korean war. This combat jacket was not the American quilted kind which actually kept you warm. It was more the British kind whose chief function was to get dirty. But clad in it I could imagine myself looking interesting and dangerous; not a man to be messed with. Anyone taking due note of my now more-than-half-formed beard might have decided that I was a man who could be depended upon to mess with himself, but to distract the world's attention from my head there was what was going on around my feet. These were enveloped in a pair of shoes given to me by Joyce Grenfell. She said that they had been given to her husband but that they had not fitted. She was a woman who never lied in her life. In this one case there might have been an element of diplomatic inexactitude. I suspect that they had fitted, but that he had rejected them for another reason. With thick uppers and an invulnerable three-ply sole, they were well made – far and away the highest quality footwear that I would enjoy for many years to come – but they were tanned a colour so reddish it was almost strawberry. It was another episode in my long history of unsuitable shoes, a story which is not yet closed and would need a book of its own. Let's just say that even now, when I have learned to dress as plainly as possible, I still get so impatient with the whole time-consuming business of covering up exposed skin that I will buy the first thing that catches my eye, and that when it comes to shoes the first thing that catches your eye is the last thing you should ever put on your feet. It is almost better to be an impulse shirt-buyer than an impulse shoe-buyer. I have worn shirts that made people think I was a retired Mafia hit-man or a Yugoslavian sports convenor from Split, but I have worn shoes that made people think I was insane.

Anyway, when I turned up for my next attempt to land a job, that was how I looked – like Judas Iscariot deserting across the 38th Parallel in shoes stolen from a clown. A wine merchant called T. H. Lawrence (I remember it wasn't D. E. Lawrence but was something equally unlikely, so it must have been T. H. Lawrence) placed a classified advertisement for a young man to learn the wine trade. Required qualifications would be a degree in the humanities, physical strength, and an interest in fine wines. The first qualification I certainly had. The second I still had in part, despite the effects of eating fat-fried food every night in a dark room. The third was more of a problem. At the time I left Australia it was already on the verge of becoming one of the great wine countries of the world, but I won't pretend that I was in any way *au courant* with the incipient viticultural break-through. My idea of a fine wine was one that merely stained your teeth without stripping off the enamel. In Britain I had discovered Woodpecker cider and resorted to wine only when it was on offer free at Melbury Road parties, where it usually issued from a large green bottle marked with the name of the Hungarian composer Janos Riesling. Nevertheless I had picked up a certain amount of technical chat and reckoned I could get away with a short interview if I kept it laconic. Since the address was that of a country pub in Kent, I eschewed the Singapore suit. Also the red shoes were the only ones I currently possessed. To wear them in combination with the Singapore suit would be to set up a contrast in colour which even I could see was a blow to the optic nerve. If I kept my arms to my sides, the dark cloth of the Singapore suit lulled the viewer's eyes as they travelled down my person, which only made the dissonance more stunning when it was revealed that I was standing in two bidets full of strawberry soda. The combat jacket made for a more meant-looking ensemble, in my opinion. This opinion could have been mistaken but I doubt that it would have made any difference if I had arrived suitably attired for an investiture. When I finally fetched up at T. H. Lawrence's rustic hostelry after long, lost detours up and down winding hedge-lined single carriageways, the proprietor came to the door, took one look at me and quite obviously loathed what he saw happening on the lower part of my face.

'Oh dear,' he snapped. 'Beard.' Generously I stood nonplussed, instead of retaliating, which I could have done by pointing out how hard his blue blazer and handlebar moustache were trying to make me think of the Battle of Britain, an effect undone by his extreme brevity of stature. He might very well have flown against the Germans, but only on the back of a pigeon. I either managed to bite all this back or else never thought of it, probably the latter. Scott Fitzgerald's Nick Carraway says at some point that any demonstration of complete self-confidence draws a stunned tribute from him. Even today, when some oaf who has confused rudeness with blunt speech tells me exactly what he thinks, I tend to stand there wondering what I have done to deserve it, instead of telling him exactly what I think right back. In those days I was even more easily wrong-footed, not having begun to realize that the boor has a built-in advantage which can be countered on the spot only at the cost of becoming a boor oneself. I used to worry about having no quick answer, and was thus bereft of self-esteem as well as of speech. So when T. H. Lawrence asked me what I thought of the recent French and German vintages I was not best placed to give a convincing summary. My mumbled generalizations got me as far as the bar, but there he poured a glass of yellowish white wine and asked me to taste it.

'This is a 1960 Trockenbocken hock from Schlockenglocken,' he rapped, or words to that effect. 'Selling it through my club for a quid a bottle. What do you think?' I sniffed it, said it had a nice nose, sipped it, said it had a nice bottom, and sank the rest of it in one. 'You know bugger-all about wines,' announced T. H. Lawrence matter-offactly, in the clipped tones of a veteran Spitfire pilot telling the duty officer that the new boy on the squadron had made an unauthorized solo pass over Rhine-Hopstein airfield at nought feet, copped a packet of light flak, and flown straight into a petrol tanker. 'Wasted your time coming down here. Wasted mine too. Cut my hedges for lunch and we'll call it square.'

Starting either side of the pub's gravelled forecourt, hedgerow stretched in each direction along the roadside for as far as the eye could see. With the clippers provided, I went at it and in less than an hour had trimmed a surprising amount of hedge – something like one and a half square yards. T. H. Lawrence the wee Wing

Commander didn't help by periodically emerging from his ops room to laugh good-naturedly at my efforts and confess his wonder that an Ossie (*sic*) should be so inept at the kind of activity which must be fairly standard in the Backout or Backthere or whatever it was called, har har. Like many Englishmen of his class and IQ, the Sanforized Squadron Leader was either incapable of pronouncing the word Aussie correctly – i.e., with a 'z' sound instead of an 's' – or else did not want to, for fear of spoiling the priceless joke whose other elements included the Outback, kangaroos, and the hilarious fantasy of people walking around upside-down. 'I expect you Ossies see plenty of kangaroos in the Backout when you're walking along upside-down' was a standard line, invariably preluded, postluded and punctuated by self-applauding shouts of laughter from a large mouth held six inches from my face. T. H. Lawrence's version of the same theme differed only in that his mouth was held six inches from my chest. Stripped to the waist and seething with misdirected fury, I clipped like a maniac and got the whole hedge trimmed in time for a late lunch.

My lunch was served on a trestle table in the open air. A piece of stiff white cheese smeared with yellow pickle had been clamped in a vise of partly refreshened bread. There was also half a pint of brown water. These victuals were brought to me with a practised display of weary magnanimity by the abbreviated Air Commodore himself. I had been hungry and thirsty until I saw these things. But the sun was almost warm and there was the additional pleasure of watching the farmers arrive for their midday break. It was a highly traditional sight. You got the sense that it had been going on for a millennium. From Lagondas, Graber-bodied Alvis Grey Ladies and V-8 Aston Martins they emerged barking in tweeds. 'Nigola!' they yelled. 'Over heah, Nigola! I say Nigola! Over *heah*!' Yet their wives and mistresses made me want to keep my eyes open, even if my fingers were in my ears. Merely quacking while their menfolk bayed like hounds, they looked all the more desirable for their daunting self-assurance. In London I had seen nothing like them. Perhaps it was the district. More probably it was spring. Sitting out there with those wonderful, hand-woven, gentleman's-relish women under the same sun, I was made invisible by my appearance, like a satyr in an old engraving who blends with a gnarled-tree-trunk and its attendant shrubbery. Thus I could catch the perfume of their corduroy and cashmere as they yelped to each other about banging along to Harvey Nichols for a spree. Lust and envy made their usual explosive mixture in my soul. If one of those long-striding creatures had smiled at me I would have thrown back my head and given the warrior-call of the bull ape. But nobody infringed my frustrated privacy except the miniature Marshal of Air Vice, Group Captain T. H. 'Taffy' Lawrence, Distinguished Self-Service Restaurant and Bar.

'Finished? Good. There's a path around the back. Show you.' I thought he was showing me a quick way to the railway station, but it turned out that he was showing me the back boundary of his property, another hedge almost as long as the one in front. I could have done a bunk the minute he left me alone. Defiant, defeated anger required that I stay and make a job of it. By the time I had finished, the afternoon was almost spent, but the countryside was still a pretty sight as I walked back along the winding single-lane road to the station, occasionally leaning back sourly into the hedge while fast cars full of contented, well-dressed, well-fed people treated the road as if they owned it. Which, of course, they did.

5. CRACKING THE SECRET CODE

Just when you think things are as bad as they can get, suddenly they get worse. Not that there was a shortage of jobs. Though the reader of today might find it difficult to believe, in 1960s London there was casual white-collar work to burn. I, however, seemed incapable of getting in amongst it. By now I had my name down with the Professional and Executive register and it was amazing how many interviews they sent me off to that I mucked up by talking too much, talking too little or talking just the right amount but to the wrong person. I merely throw in this observation for the benefit of any younger reader, or for that matter any older reader, who has never got a job after an interview. Neither have I. An interview is where you sell yourself, and some of us are just bad salesmen, with no gift for correctly assessing the demand before we start matching it with a supply. If a clerk's job was on offer, I came on strong, filling the air with abstruse literary references, when the only references the interviewer wanted were from some previous employer saying that I had performed clerical duties to his satisfaction and not stolen the clock. If the vacancy was for an editorial assistant, on the other hand, I underplayed it, saying little and looking tough, like a one-time boundary rider who, despite the circumstances of cultivated leisure implied by his now possessing a suit made in Singapore, could still mend a fence or trap a frilled lizard. It was a disaster either way, but the second method at least had the virtue of rendering the interviewer visible at all times. Employing the first method, I had always to hold the cuffs of the Singapore suit's sleeves in a surreptitiously clenched fist while making an expansive, genius-betokening gesture, otherwise the man I was talking to would disappear as if by magic. Not long afterwards I would disappear myself, but there was nothing magic about that.

Back on the street, spring was well established and the girls of

London were prettier than they had ever been or would ever be again. They were saying goodbye to the old austerity without having quite yet said the full, mad hello to sixties fashions at their most demented. Skirts were on their way up the thigh but had not yet reached the waist. Hair was back-combed but had not yet attained the shape and consistency of a lacquered crash-helmet. Stiletto heels were long and sharp but not yet like needles, so that if a girl trod on your foot you were able to hop about in pain instead of being pinned screaming to the dance-floor. There was a new exuberance abroad, atomized libido was misty in the air, and I was out of it. No money, no prospects. Just debts, purple gums and a pair of shoes that lit up in the dark like dachshunds with scarlet fever.

But there were too many casual jobs on offer for me to go on missing out, even with my talent for being the man off the spot. Just when the only funds remaining were half a dozen Woodpecker cider bottles worth threepence each for the returned deposit, a classified advertisement led me to a London University annexe in Bloomsbury where questionnaires were being coded. A dozen casual coders were required, degree essential and qualifications in psychology desirable. Having majored in psychology at Sydney University, I was taken on as the dozenth coder. Fifteen minutes later and I would have dipped out. This I could be sure of, because, fourteen minutes after I signed on, a candidate turned up who looked as mathematically gifted as Max Planck, an impression not dissipated by the slide-rule sticking out of his pocket. It was a nice change to stand there and see him turned away, instead of being turned away myself. The man in charge, a handsome young tweed-jacketed Rhodesian called Robin Jackson if it wasn't Jack Robinson, showed signs of regretting how things had transpired, but quixotically decided to stick by the arrangement already made. Banzai. I was in, at the lavish emolument, for the six weeks the job would last, of ten pounds a week before stoppages. What stoppages were I had no idea, and for the moment was too busy to ask.

The completed questionnaires contained the answers of thousands of people to hundreds of questions. These questions ranged from concrete enquiries about age and gender to a whole last page of abstract stuff about attitudes and values, whether liberal or otherwise. As I now remember it, which is vaguely, a statistically random sample of students was being assessed for demography, motivation, goals, height above sea level, etc. No doubt I was pretty hazy about it all even at the time. The typical respondent started off by saying he was a nineteen-year-old male and ended up rating the possibility of God's existence on a scale from one to five. In other words it was a snare for Snarks, a sieve to measure water, a machine to count sand. But to convert the written answers into a given range of symbols was a mechanical matter for anyone who had ever spent a couple of years fooling around with Personality Profiles, Thematic Apperception Tests and that old standby of university psychology departments world wide, the Minnesota Multiphasic.

We all sat around a large, polished mahogany table with Robin handing out new sheaves of uncoded questionnaires and stacking the ones we had finished into a heap. After the first hour I was on automatic pilot and using up some of the spare energy by inspecting my fellow workers as they toiled. Half of them, I was pleased to note, were females. One of these, sitting at the end of the table to my left, was a very elegant young Indian woman in a gold-trimmed sari the colour of bleached pomegranate. Her name, too sonorous to be forgotten however long I live, was Saraj. Perhaps my heart would have gone out to her if Millicent had not been sitting directly opposite me. But Millicent would probably have had the same effect if she had been sitting upstairs. She radiated so much sensuality that I could still see her after I had closed my eyes.

This is neither the time nor the place to give my conclusions about the physics and metaphysics of sexual attraction. For one thing, it would take a separate volume. For another, I doubt if anything I had to say would be of sufficient originality to warrant the effort, not to mention the trouble. Most inhibiting of all, I seriously wonder if I have yet reached any conclusions, or ever will before I die. When I do die, and come to that check-point inside the gates of Hell where the horrible Minos circles himself with his tail as an indication of the infernal level to which the new entrant is assigned, it will be no secret between me and him that during my time on Earth I suffered from – or enjoyed, if that is the preferred formula – inordinate susceptibility to female beauty. It will be the second thing that he asks me about. His first question will not demand an answer. 'Hello there, cobber! Must be a relief to be walking the right way up with no kangaroos around out there in the back! Brought your tube of Foster's? Har har.' But the next question will be harder to dodge.

I suppose it was a case of arrested development. From childhood onwards I had seen beauty in women as a revelation of universal truth, and now, in what should have been adulthood, I still did, which meant that adulthood felt like childhood, with childish behaviour as an inevitable consequence. There is a lot to be said for idealizing those we adore, but not if it means neglecting to listen to what they have to say. A good-looking woman, as well as being the incarnation of a Platonic concept, is quite often a human being as well. One of the cockney photographers who were at that time just beginning their rise to fame recently told me that his success with some of the world's most gorgeous women was almost entirely due to patting them on the bottom – or, as he put it, patinum honour bum. Having looked like goddesses all their lives, they had never met a man who patted them on the bottom, although they had met hundreds of men who wrote poems in their honour. Sitting at home beside my suitcase in Tufnell Park I wrote many a poem about Millicent. I never made the mistake of showing them to her, but all day at work I did my best to impress, and my worshipping eyes must have had the unswerving fervour of Hitler's. My consolation, when I got things in perspective a bit later – about fifteen years later – was that she would probably not have been interested even if I had looked and sounded less like an aspiring disciple of Christ who had been rejected on grounds of mental instability. She had, after all, recently married a young doctor who called for her at work one day seemingly specifically to convince me of his close physical resemblance to Alain Delon. Perhaps it *was* Alain Delon, whose career was at that time only just starting to boom. Perhaps the reason I thought that he merely looked like Alain Delon was the tears in my eyes. Not that Millicent required anything beyond herself as a stimulus to induce weeping. Merely to glance at her was to feel the tear ducts fill and spill like cisterns after spring rain.

Her eyes would have been too big if they had not been pale blue. The planes of her face were too classically defined for lips so romantically lush, but the clarity of her cheeks showed that there was more life in her than could possibly remain calm – the blood flooded under them like a peach ripening before your eyes. Her straight dark hair was so strong that wisps of it would fight loose from the ribbon tying it back, so that occasionally, without looking up, she would have to lift one long-fingered hand to clear her vision. This movement would bring certain sections of her upper figure into play. There were several opportunities a day to see the whole of her statuesque form in motion. I preferred to avoid these by either closing my eyes or else averting them, lest I emit, as I did on that first afternoon, an involuntary groan of such intensity that Saraj offered me a Beechams Powder. Millicent had the kind of hips known as child-bearing by those people who try vainly to remind us that all these splendours are laid on exclusively for the purpose of reproducing the human race. But it was Millicent's breasts which struck me at the time as constituting unarguable proof that the Man Upstairs was trying to find out how much he could get away with without causing a mass rebellion. Indeed at one point during a mix-up at the coat-rack in the corridor, Millicent's breasts struck me physically. It felt like being run through twice with an angel's tongue. But to arrange another such accident would have caused comment, and anyway idealism shies from reality, even when, especially when, the reality matches the dream. All day and every day I confined myself to dreaming. When Millicent's hand was raised to restore a stray strand of hair, there was a slight shift of the breast on that side. It was enough to make me cram the corner of a questionnaire into my mouth and bite it to stop squealing.

Occasionally, about once every thirty-four minutes on average, Millicent would get tired of coding, put down her pencil, lift both her clenched fists high behind her head, and yawn. As an alternative to swallowing a questionnaire whole I coded furiously, branding female orphans who lived with foster parents in Wandsworth and studied bookkeeping at the polytechnic as male upper-middle-class Oxbridge history graduates with an interest in blood sports. There is also a possibility that I was trying to impress her with my coding. I was probably trying to make her think: 'My God, can that boy *code.*' In other words, I was acting like a virgin. Hating myself for it too, because I wasn't one, was I? But I was starting to forget what not being one was like, and was not yet experienced enough to know that for any man short of senility or satyriasis, virginity is a recurring condition, and not the worst from which he can suffer, although only self-possession can make it graceful.

Since I had self-obsession instead, I was not best equipped to maintain my equilibrium. Writing badly by night and coding badly by day, I was getting less enjoyment than I should have done out of my first long taste of being alone and paying my own way, or some of it. But not even the most determined cultivation of chaos can prevent the occasional outbreak of order. Having been advised by Robin that the Courtauld Gallery was just around the corner, I began spending some of my lunchtime there. The Italian primitives would probably not have said much to me even if they had been first rate: my appreciation of painting was fated to work backwards from a starting point in recent times, so as yet I found the Renaissance, when I visited the National Gallery, an elaborate preparation for Rembrandt, whose main achievement in turn was to have done all that could be done with darkness, so that one day the Impressionists would show the same exhaustive virtuosity with light. But the Courtauld's Impressionists and Post-Impressionists *were* first rate. The great names were represented by only a few paintings each, yet these were capital works without exception. For the first time I got beyond admiring the individual painter and became immersed in the individual painting. There was a comfortable leather bench on which I sat and stared at Manet's *Girl at the Bar of the Folies-Bergère* for half an hour on end, not always in the hope that Millicent would walk in and catch me there looking intense. After the first few weeks the accumulated evidence that she was never going to visit the Courtauld Gallery had become overwhelming.

As with many scatter-brained women her handbag was a bin, out of which she would produce, when the teabreak conversation flagged, one of those cube-shaped paperback novels by which American authors in elevator shoes take revenge on their country for its having rendered them illiterate. In Millicent's case it was always the same novel, called something like *The Insatiables*. She would take squares of fudge out of the bin and melt them in her lovely mouth while it formed silent words as she slowly read. She is probably still reading that book and I would be surprised if the fudge hadn't taken its toll, although not disappointed. Usually we do not want people to flourish after they have proved that they can live without us, but Millicent was a special case. And to think I never got near her – except when, instead of the fudge, she produced from her bin one of the ten cigarettes to which she rationed herself each day. I would always lean across the table and light it for her. The table was eight feet wide, but before the filter tip of each lucky Dunhill had settled into position between those sumptuous lips I would have lit a match and be sliding

across that polished mahogany like a speed skater falling headlong
and face downward on the fleeing ice.

My own cigarette ration was more like twenty during working
hours, with twenty more each evening. By the time I eventually quit,
about twelve years ago, I was smoking eighty cigarettes a day. People
who scoff at this figure have never noticed how quickly a true addict
smokes a cigarette, so that the burning tip, instead of being a shallow
glowing cone, is like a red hot wire. Also you get to the point of
having two cigarettes going at the same time, until you reach the
terminal stage when you have three of them in your mouth at once,
recoiling in sequence like guns in a turret. I finally quit when I found
myself at two o'clock one morning assaulting a cigarette machine
which had taken my last four coins and given nothing in exchange.
The machine will probably never forget my deadly flurry of right
uppercuts and left jabs, but that's another story. Even when confining
myself to a comparatively moderate forty a day, however, I must have
been a spectacle, with butts piling up around me and my beard
turning yellow around the mouth. On my right hand, only the little
finger was the colour of skin. The thumb and three remaining fingers
were a startling mixture of orange-peel and gold leaf. It didn't take
a genius to figure out that the nicotine must have been turning me
the same colour inside as outside. All it took was someone capable
of mature reflection.

More important in the short term, which for a long time remained
the only term I could think in, was that the cigarettes ate up a large
proportion of the money I had left over after paying the rent and
buying the ingredients for my evening meal of bacon and sausages
cooked in the fat of a similar meal cooked the evening before. The
last duty-free Rothmans was far behind on the horizon, like a ship
disappearing towards a more affluent world. For a while I still smoked
the same brand, but with tax added to the price they would have
been far too expensive even if my first pay packet had not revealed
the full meaning of the word 'stoppage'. It meant heart-stoppage.
Some form of emergency tax had been imposed until such time as I
qualified for a rebate. Presumably one qualified for a rebate by being
able, for several weeks consecutively, to read the amount which had
been withheld without succumbing to cardiac infarction. This was
all a bit much, especially coming on top of the weekly National
Insurance slug. I had thought that National Insurance was meant to

insure me, but judging from the size of the compulsory contributions the idea was to insure the nation. So I switched to Players No. 6. A lot shorter than Rothmans, they were the tiny kind of cigarette that children smoked at matinees. In recompense my daily consumption shot up to sixty, with consumption sounding like the operative word. If coughing was a sign of literary ability, I would soon be up there, or down there, with Keats and Kafka.

Summer arrived, the job ran out, and the team dispersed, some of them to take an early holiday before starting serious work. Millicent walked out of my life, swaying gently at the hips: a new recruit for the growing army of the untouched, another chapter in the history of what never happened. I took the loss stoically, screaming only when alone. One of those naturally grave young men to whose air of tranquillity I aspired in vain, Robin had impressed me with the seriousness of his enforced exile, something with which voluntary exile has little in common. I was merely on a long holiday. He was banished. But all the more devotedly he studied to be a lecturer in English literature, showing remarkable tolerance for my views on the subject, which he was well aware owed their fluency to a culpable superficiality in the actual business of reading the books. It is never heartwarming, when you are three-quarters of the way through *The Wings of the Dove*, to be told by someone who has read only three pages of it that it is not worth reading. Robin not only mastered his justifiable impatience, he actually helped me line up another casual job, just around the corner in Gordon Square – something about counting up all the foreign students in Britain. But the job didn't start for another two weeks, during which I would be once again flat broke.

Telling people I was on a fortnight's holiday and would soon be drawing pay again, I raised almost enough scratch to smoke and drink continuously, provided I got plenty of sleep during the day. Much of this sleep I got in the parks. I slept in Hyde Park near the Serpentine, St James's Park near the pond, Green Park, Regent's Park and Holland Park. Daringly ranging further afield, I slept for several hours in the grass at Richmond while deer cropped up to a few feet all around me, so that I woke up looking like a chrysoprase cameo. Most adventurously of all, I slept in the meadow at the Mill in Cambridge.

One of my old Sydney fellow students and drinking mates had

already been up at Trinity Hall for a year, reading the second part of the Modern Languages tripos as an affiliated student. During his last summer in Sydney we had been on stage together in the Union Revue, I playing Abdullah Tracy, the Arabian millionaire detective, and he making a show-stopping appearance as the rhythm and blues belly-dancer, Fatima Domino. After the show we would join the Downtown Push at whatever party they had crashed and get drunk enough together to forget the waves of indifference which had emanated from the audience. The last time I had seen him, on the drunken night before he sailed for England, he had been wearing full Push battle order, right down to the suede desert boots worn shiny on the toes. Our faces six inches apart, we had shouted farewell on the understanding that the Poms would never suck him in. Now, in Cambridge, he was suddenly in a three-piece suit and sounded like the Queen broadcasting to the Commonwealth. His new accent cut me off at the knees.

Even with his old accent I would not have found it easy to understand what he was talking about, Apparently there were sound academic reasons why he was still up, when everybody else had gone down. Otherwise he would already have gone down and not come up again until Michaelmas, or Candlemas or possibly Quatermass. But being obliged to stay up was nothing like as bad as being sent down. There was a big difference between being sent down and going down. That was one of the first things one learned when one came up. When I heard him use the word 'one' I began to suspect that he had been drugged, tied to a chair and brainwashed. But after a few pints of brown water in the Eagle, plus a few more in the Little Rose – Pepys's pub, he explained with enthusiasm and difficulty – it was more like old times. He hired a canoe at the Mill and we paddled to Granchester, where a lot of young people were sitting around. These, it was explained to me, were not up. A succession of pints at Granchester was cut short by afternoon closing time, whereupon we paddled back to the Mill. Up at Granchester the church clock had stood at ten to three but down at the Mill it was ten to five. Up, down, up, down. The itinerary was out of Rupert Brooke, the echolalia out of *Four Quartets*, the situation out of hand. On the meadows there were some girls sitting down who were also not up. For a while we lay down and then later on we got up. It was in this condition that I fell into Corpus Christi and looked up at where Christopher

Marlowe, no mean piss-artist himself, had had his rooms. I was led into Trinity Great Court as Byron had once led his bear. In the main court of King's I was held steady until the Chapel stopped moving. The sun was gone out of the sky but the twilight was like day, so that the dark, honey-soaked biscuit of the stone – long overdue for the thorough cleaning it has since received – looked like an edible cut-out against the brushed azure. A trembling cut-out. Up, down, up, down. A small old man who looked like E. M. Forster shuffled by. It was E. M. Forster.

That evening we ate in an almost empty hall, called Hall. But the Hall of Trinity Hall was not the same as the Hall of Trinity. Trinity Hall was not a Hall at all. Trinity Hall was a college. This was merely its Hall. It was Trinity Hall's Hall, that's all. I was wearing a borrowed gown which kept tripping me up while I was sitting down. I had to keep getting up to fix it, whereupon I would fall down. Brown water was served by a man in a white jacket who helped me when the potato salad got into the sleeve of my gown. Up at the high table, called High Table, there were men looking down on us. These men, I was told, were Don's. Don's what? It was agreed that I was too tired to contemplate going up to London until next morning, so I slept that night in my friend's rooms. We went up a set of stairs, called a Stair, and fell down in a set of rooms, called a Set. My companion slept in or near his bed but I was not envious. I was perfectly comfortable with my left arm hooked over the towel rail and my head in the washbasin, although every half hour or so there was a terrible noise, like a man singing the first few bars of 'Celeste Aida' into a bucket.

6. STATISTICAL CATASTROPHE

Having seen an old friend fall so conspicuously on his feet should have tipped me off that I was falling on my head. Incredibly this was a fact that I had still not faced. It was finally brought home to me by an episode which strikes me even now as so shameful that I have to struggle, as I begin to tell it, against the urge to hide behind chalk-white make-up and a putty nose. But whereas it is simply good manners to make a story about one's ordinary human failings as entertaining as possible, one's extraordinary human failings require less self-indulgent treatment. What I did next couldn't be glossed over with ten coats of hand-rubbed Duco. I took a job on, mucked it up, panicked and ran. That's the long and the short of it. There was a girl involved, but that makes it worse, because she in no way approved of my behaving badly, and the only reason she couldn't help me behave better was that I didn't listen. Remorse, remorse. But let's not jump the gun.

Once again the job was in Bloomsbury, just around the corner from Woburn Walk, in one of whose bow-windowed little houses W. B. Yeats had once written poetry, and in another of whose bow-windowed little houses Ezra Pound had once played the bassoon. Whether the second activity helped or hindered the first has always remained an open question, but to the inward ear of my imagination this was a mighty conjunction of creativity, as if Goethe and Beethoven, instead of slipping through each other's grasp, had settled down in the same street to write *Faust* as an opera. I couldn't walk past those bow windows without shivering, and indeed still can't. Twenty years ago the shiver was at least partly caused by apprehension. The job had something wrong with it. It was too easy.

My employer was some official outfit called the Association for Commonwealth Institutes, if it wasn't the Institute for Commonwealth Associations. Its headquarters were in the usual Georgian terrace house. From the architectural viewpoint, Bloomsbury had been raped twice, once each by the Luftwaffe and London University. The attack by the university had been the more merciless, but there were still a lot of Georgian terraces left. Few of them, however, were quite so elegant as the one housing the Institute for Associations. With the credit obtainable from friends on the basis of my prospective first week's wages minus stoppages but plus rebate, I bought a pair of black chisel-toed Chelsea boots to go with the Singapore suit. Entering the building, I felt that I needed only a bowler hat and a tightly rolled umbrella to make me look the complete establishment figure. If I had had the hat, hanging it on the hat-rack in the hall without being rendered temporarily headless by my suit would have entailed a pretty energetic combined jump up and lunge sideways, yet the idea was sound. Even the beard, after suitable attention from a pair of nail scissors, looked like something that might have been approved of by the navy, instead of fired at on sight.

Once having entered the building, I bent to my task. This I did literally, because the task was spread out on one of those familiar large mahogany tables, except that this time I was on my own. The task was a large chart in which I was to enter, against the names of all the institutions of higher learning in Britain, the number and provenance of all the Commonwealth students attending them. At the end of the scheduled two months, the task would be completed by my tallying the total number of entries, thus to give a set of figures which could be read out by the responsible minister in answer to a parliamentary question already tabled. A cinch. Nothing to it. All it needed was a level head.

For years after the disaster I tried to convince myself that a level head was something I possessed naturally and that I lost it only because of Pandora. In cold retrospect it becomes apparent that a man with the Medusa touch will wreak havoc whether he has help or not, but at the time of the explosion, and for as long as the debris was falling, I couldn't help believing that the whole débâcle had at least something to do with Pandora's legs. Pandora's legs had the rest of Pandora on top of them, which didn't make things any easier. The man in charge, a nice old thing in a three-piece suit with a watch-chain, had explained the chart, shown me how to analyse the data sheets, made a few sympathetic remarks about how my new shoes must have been hurting, and left me alone. It was all plain sailing

for about an hour, and then Pandora opened the door to ask me if
there was anything I wanted. Instantly I wanted Pandora. Her severe
expression only added to her appeal. Those career-girl glasses were
something cruel: when she looked at you it was like having your
photograph taken by the police. Their frames were so big that she
was getting both your profiles to go with the full face. But her
mouth was all the more intriguing for being set in a firm line. From
there on down she was Jaeger twinset, pearls and plaid skirt with a
safety pin, but it was all put on over a figure twanging with whip-
lash energy. Millicent's sensuality, the memory of which now began
a rapid retreat into the past, had been languid, passive, receptive.
Pandora's was the other thing entirely: avid sinuosity on a hair-trigger.
And whereas Millicent's legs had been merely poetic, Pandora's were
rhapsodic. They came tapering down out of the hem of that glorified
Black Watch kilt like a pair of angels nose-diving with their wings
folded, did a few fancy reverse curves of small radius so as to recreate
the concept of the human ankle in terms of heavenly celebration,
and then swooped at an only slightly less vertiginous angle into a
pair of black lacquer stiletto-heeled court shoes with little bows near
the toes. Stiletto shoes had come on even further in the previous few
months, to the point where prospective airline passengers were asked
not to wear them. Airliners kept crashing in the Andes and when the
search party finally managed to cut its way through the jungle it
would find the usual fuselage full of skeletons, except that at least
one of the skeletons would be wearing stiletto shoes which had to be
extracted from the metal skin of the pressure cabin with a pair of
pliers. Pandora's heels were like that. Looking at her for the first time
with roughly the emotions of the Flying Dutchman meeting her
namesake, I suddenly and strangely remembered a more than usually
weird case study in Havelock Ellis about a man who got his rocks
off by lying down and having women stand on his vital areas without
removing their buttoned boots. If Pandora were to co-operate in
such a venture, there could be no doubt that the experience would
prove terminal, but what a way to go. Pinned like a butterfly. This
ambiguously disturbing prospect was made even more unsettling by
her air of severity. Though she didn't look as if she would be much
interested in your pleasure, an interest in your pain was clearly not
to be ruled out.

I was maligning her, of course: it was just the glasses. Having foisted one of my fantasies on Millicent, I had immediately set about foisting a different fantasy on Pandora. But there could be no doubt that the detachment of her manner was more effective than a provocation. To indicate that there was nothing I wanted, I raised both hands as if to fend off help, while saying: 'No worries.' What I said came out muffled, but her reply was witheringly clear. 'Is there something wrong with your clothes? What happened to your head just then? You looked like Charles I.' I told her the story of the Singapore suit, a would-be self-deprecating routine which by then, after so much practice, was in a high state of polish. Any normally equipped English-speaking female could be depended upon to laugh aloud at least twice during this comic *tour de force*, but Pandora didn't crack a smile. This was particularly galling in view of the fact that her line about Charles I had been pretty good. Not perhaps a miracle of invention, yet tellingly delivered from the dead pan. Pans didn't come deader than Pandora's pan. I was gibbering. What could I do to break the pack ice on that minatory face?

The answer was nothing, but I didn't find that out before trying everything. There was a Howard Hawks season at the National Film Theatre. I took her to see *His Girl Friday*, one of the funniest films ever made. She sat there like a world champion poker player. Her studied indifference might have had something to do with the way I rolled in the aisle. (Anyone who rolls from side to side in the aisle might be doing so naturally, but to roll up and down the aisle is an affectation.) If that was so, however, why did she agree to go out with me again? And she always said yes to going out, just as she always said no to any form of physical contact. When I asked her if it was the beard she said it wasn't. Then what was it? One night we went to the Royal Court to hear Lotte Lenya sing Brecht and Weill. Lenya's voice was in rags from laryngitis and the tube trains arriving and departing under the theatre sounded like a fault in the earth's crust, but the acrid lilt of 'Surabaya Johnny' proclaimed the inexorability of desire. Pandora invited me back to her flat for coffee. I told myself to stay calm and it would all drop into my lap. It did, too: a steaming hot mug of Nescafé. Nothing else. Perhaps it was a tactical error to give her my standard lecture on the evils of capitalism. I gave her the short version – less than three-quarters of an hour – but before it was half over she was saying 'Really?' in the middle of each sentence as well as at the end. When I tried to kiss her on the way out I rammed her spectacle frames. It was like being thrown against a windscreen.

History was leaving me behind. John Glenn went into orbit but I stayed earthbound. Britten wrote his *War Requiem*. Basil Spence built Coventry Cathedral, which briefly held the title of Most Hideous Building in Britain before the new London Hilton pipped it for top spot. The Mariner unmanned space mission left for Venus. The Moulton small-wheeled bicycle appeared on the streets of London, giving the miniskirts of its female riders a further boost towards the belt. When a girl's tights came towards you on a Moulton, they were making scissor movements at eye level, especially if you were on your knees sobbing with lust. The air was pulsating with libido, but somehow Pandora hadn't heard the news. I knocked myself out trying to impress her. There is no point trying to impress women – if they are listening to you at all, then they are already as impressed as they are ever going to get – but this fact takes some of us a long time to learn and even then it is easily forgotten in the stress of frustration. Pandora wasn't impressed with what I knew. An Oxbridge education had equipped her to say 'Really?' on those occasions when she was told something she didn't know already. When Pandora said 'Really?' it was like being flicked in the face with a wet, sandy towel. Equally clearly she was not impressed with my looks, clothes or earning potential. No doubt it was out of fairness that she always paid her share, yet her manner implied that she was subsidising a gypsy. So there was nothing left to impress her with except a revolutionary new method of calculating the number of foreign students.

Why this did not impress her mystified me at the time. My formula was a breakthrough in sociologico-statistical methodology comparable to those diagrams by Pareto showing causes and effects all linked up with arrows. With four different coloured pencils I approximated the increment against the asymptotic co-ordinate. The chart looked like Stravinsky's holograph manuscript of *Le Sucre du printemps* overlaid by a computer print-out of the Walt Disney Organisation's payroll. My employer, Mr Niceold Thing – soon, if all went well, to be Sir Niceold Thing – dropped in to see how my work was going and pronounced himself dazzled. 'But doesn't this slow everything down terribly?' he asked. 'Only,' I explained patiently, 'in the initial stages. It takes a few weeks to do the transpositions, but then all you have to do is read off everything in the right-hand column and you get the whole answer in a few minutes.'

He wasn't as convinced as I was, but he needed to be only half as convinced as I was to be convinced enough. Instead of ordering me to forget the new method and just get ahead with the old one, he retreated looking trustful but worried – never a good sign in a commander. He probably blames himself for what happened and I must say that there are moments when I agree with him. They are weak moments. Pandora, after all, told me outright that I was breaking a butterfly on a wheel, or words to that effect. 'Making a meal of it, aren't you?' Without lifting my head I converted the five Sierra Leone students at the Bradfield Polytechnic into a green Greek gamma with a pink circle around it. 'Just put down the tea, smart arse,' I retorted. It was part of my new plan to relax her with obscene banter. It wasn't working any better than the old plan, but it wasn't working any worse either, which made it a potential step forward.

'Would you like a cake?' she asked with what sounded like less than total indifference to my destiny.

'Sticky cake or crumbly cake?' I riposted, edging the pink circle with yellow.

'No, not cake. *Cake.* Cake-Akela. Thought you might be hot.'

I looked up to see that she had brought two bottles of the familiar American beverage in its sensually draped and fluted bottle. This was tantamount to a love-tryst. I followed it up immediately and once more crunched the bridge of my nose into her spectacle frames. If she had not been turning away as I lunged forward with my eyes closed, the hinge where the ear-piece joined the main frame would not have cracked open and spilled the tiny brass pivot. A long way above me as I crawled around looking for it, she kept saying 'Really' without the question mark, which made it sound even worse.

Getting her back to the mood of relative abandon in which she had voluntarily brought me a fizzy drink took weeks. My first English summer was now at its blazing height. For an hour on end the sun would shine. In the parks at lunchtime the English males would bare their potato-white bodies to what they had heard described as ultra-violet rays. Pandora appeared in a new range of dresses which apparently she usually wore only when in Cannes or Nice with Daddy. When we walked in Lincoln's Inn Fields the allegedly pitiless sunlight did nothing to unfreeze her cryogenic face, but at least it silhouetted her legs through the thin gingham so that I could see the shapely shadows heading upwards. When I tore off my shirt, the remnants of my Australian tan made a remarkable impression on her. No impression. None. In desperation I switched back to the indoor approach and took her to see the Lycergus Cup in the British Museum, hoping that the sunlight slanting through its delicate green and pink calyx would touch some deep, repressed, Dionysian impulse in her Apollonian soul. It didn't.

Not making it with Pandora, I was fatally distracted from the more portentous truth that I was not making it with my job either. By the time the awful facts sank in, it was too late. There was no hope of assembling my multicoloured symbol-scramble into an intelligible order: not in the time available, and probably not within the foreseeable duration of the known universe. Neither was there time to go back and start again with the ordinary method. Somebody normal might just have managed it, but my morale had collapsed. With the parliamentary question only ten days away, I turned up at work, looked obliquely at the chart, sat down and wrote poems. Every time my employer stuck his head through the door, I brusquely assured him that any moment now, with a stroke of a pencil, the scheme would yield its results. Pandora no longer made her daily appearance. Putting my hand on her bottom in the British Museum had been a terminal mistake. She was looking at the Elgin Marbles and for a blessed second I thought that I was feeling them: cool, firm, curved even in their planes. Then her favourite word, only this time with an exclamation mark, echoed through the museum like a polite gun-shot, or a door that had never really been open clicking finally shut.

There was only one honourable course: to go to the boss and make a clean breast of my failure. So I took the dishonourable course. On the third last day before the deadline I did not go to Bloomsbury. I went to Birmingham instead. On the credit side of the ledger – the sole positive entry – may be put the fact that I didn't do a midnight flit from my digs. Fronting up to the landlady fair and square, I paid her a month's notice and no arguments. A committed sherry-drinker who was invariably blotto by eleven in the morning, she failed to recognize me, which made it easier. Toting the cardboard suitcase, wearing the Singapore suit, sweating into the Chelsea boots which already had holes in them, I headed for Euston and the train that would take me north to sanctuary. The ticket cost me the last cash I had, but I was cleaned out in the metaphorical sense only. My soul was heavy with the fluid of a molten spine. After such knowledge, what forgiveness?

7. THE BIRMINGHAM DECISION

Head of the Department of Psychiatric Medicine at the University of Birmingham, Professor William Trethowan had a wife, two teenage daughters, a son in short pants and an unexpected bearded visitor holding a cardboard suitcase. 'What's wrong?' was the first thing he asked. I shrugged. 'What happened to your head just then?' was the second thing he asked, but in a detached manner, not pressing for an answer. He had an apparent lack of concern which people in trouble who found concern inhibiting would seek out, so I was far from being the first unannounced runaway to darken his door. At Sydney University, where I had first met him, his house had been a hostel-cum-clinic for highly strung would-be poets. An eminent English doctor of medicine who talked like George Sanders, played jazz trumpet, was generally interested in the arts and had a wife both keen and competent to produce the first Beckett and Pinter plays Sydney had yet seen – it was a challenging proposition for Australian students who were accustomed to a solid show of philistinism even from the Arts faculty. My neurotic but divinely gifted friend Spencer had arrived for dinner at the Trethowans one April night and not left until August.

I can give Professor Trethowan his real name and occupation because there was nothing professional about our relationship even at this, the lowest moment of my life, when I must have so closely resembled one of the case studies that could never be discussed outside his office. When I asked for refuge and time to think, he gave me both freely, plus unlimited access to his precious collection of old Vocalion 78 rpm records featuring Benny Carter. If I had asked to have my confession heard he would no doubt have granted that wish also, but whether from a Protestant upbringing or an innate suspicion of my own theatricality I have never been able to believe in that particular method of purging a sin. In my experience the sin is still there afterwards. Whenever the late and unlamented Albert Speer said 'I should have known', I always recognized my weaker self staging a carefully underplayed tantrum in which maudlin exhibitionism palmed itself off as atonement. Of *course* he should have known. That was his crime: deciding not to. Yet although I could honestly plead innocent to any charges of mass murder, the relative puniness of my transgression did not alter its absolute reprehensibility. For a while I contemplated emigrating back to Australia. At that time an Australian visiting Britain had all the advantages of British citizenship, including the opportunity to emigrate home again at a cost of only ten pounds sterling. Many of my compatriots who ran out of funds and hope used this escape route. Even as I thought of it, a change in the law closed the loophole for good, as if to ensure that I should not outwit my destiny. So there was nothing left except suicide.

As the last of summer strove tenaciously to keep the potted plants alive in the pedestrian areas of Birmingham's new Bull Ring shopping complex, I would trail my way from one zebra crossing to the next, tour the art gallery, gaze at the Pre-Raphaelites (not as many as in Manchester, but more than enough) and consider the various possible means of my forthcoming voluntary exit. There is something about the Pre-Raphaelites which makes me contemplate self-inflicted death even when my conscience is clear – something to do with the way they managed to predict every shade of lipstick on a modern cosmetics counter. But this time I was definitely, or at any rate pretty seriously, planning to rid the world of my presence. Adopting a mysterious smile which enjoined complicity, I presented my four-volume Nonesuch Shakespeare to the younger daughter and my cherished association copy of *Practical Criticism* to the elder. I was saying goodbye to the treasures I had laid up on earth. Now nothing remained except the final act. When I sat down to write the letter which would explain this decisive step to my mother, however, I had a lot of trouble with the opening paragraph. It wasn't easy to hit the right tone.

There was another difficulty. Either I loved life, or I couldn't take my misery seriously enough. Perhaps there was, and is, a connection. To be incorrigibly ebullient might entail a congenital inability to assess the shambles around us in its correct importance. Since on this occasion the shambles had been wholly caused by me, I could hardly escape being at least shaken. It never came to choosing between

the sleeping pills and the slashed wrists, but there was food for deep
and severely troubled thought. My first thought, now that I had
resolved not to end it all, was of how to get my books back, but on
second thoughts I decided to regard their loss as a down payment
on the appropriate propitiatory offering to the gods. This matter
decided, it began occurring to me that my grand schemes for working
by day and writing by night all had a fundamental flaw – my lack of
qualifications for working by day. Unless the task was of the simplest
and most undemanding, my mind wandered. Even at that stage, after
so many years of evidence, I had not yet realized that there could be
no task simple and undemanding enough, but at least I now resolved
not to take on anything which could not be successfully tackled by a
ten-year-old child. I had overestimated the age bracket, but the idea
was right.

Another right idea was to negotiate my way back to some sort of
institute of higher learning. For the lost soul, the university is the
modern monastery. On top of that, it had started to dawn on me
that my years as a student at Sydney University had been fruitful in
everything except actual study. I needed time to read seriously, and
working all day was no more favourable to heavy reading than it was
to writing. Also I hadn't been able to get out of my mind a story my
Cambridge friend had told me about the poet Gray. It was to do with
his epoch-making switch from one Cambridge college to another. At
Peterhouse they had made an apple-pie bed for him once too often,
so he had crossed the road to Pembroke. That journey of about
twenty yards was, apart from one brief visit to a country churchyard,
the biggest thing that ever happened to him. I needed to be somewhere where a twenty-yard walk was an adventure and you could
spend your life polishing a single elegy. Dreaming of Cambridge
should normally have been an activity on a par with my previous
plans to take a flat in Belgravia. But strangely enough I had a possible
way in, or up. My capacity for wasting time at Sydney University had
attracted the amused attention of the Reader in English, George
Russell. Humanely learned in Old English, Middle English and the
European Middle Ages generally, he had a lot of information to
impart; all of which I managed to ignore. I still recollect with shame
how, in a seminar, he opened Ernst Robert Curtius's *European Literature and the Latin Middle Ages*, raised his hands above it as if he were
breaking communion bread, and called it a great book. The shame

springs from the fact that twenty years were to go by before I bothered to find out that he was right. But he must have thought I had promise. Every week Françoise and I were invited to his house and there I was gently but firmly introduced to classical music. In return for being allowed to assail George and his wife Isabel with my Thelonious Monk LPs, I was obliged to at least consider the more accessible quartets of Vivaldi. Always I got dead drunk on George's well-chosen wines. My comportment must have been less brutish than I remember, because he told me – or rather told Françoise, so that she could tell me when I sobered up – to get in touch with him if the day ever came when I wanted to settle down and read seriously, an activity for which he thought I had a considerable, if entirely unexplored, talent. At Pembroke College, Cambridge, they might possibly take me, he ventured, on his recommendation. His own career at the college had been so distinguished, he neglected to add, that even if I turned out to be an utter goof they would still be in profit.

At the time, and for a long time afterwards, I thought nothing of this offer, believing that the cloisters were no framework for a serious artist. But in Birmingham, living on charity, with autumn crowding glumly in and nothing in view except further proof of unfitness for everyday life, the serious artist was ready to think again. So I composed a densely packed airletter to George Russell begging him to get me in out of the cold. It was a carefully phrased effort, a concentrated masterpiece of the epistolary art, and I sincerely trust that he never kept it. He must have acted on it immediately, because within two weeks Pembroke wrote to offer me a place. They had been just as unquestioningly welcoming to Gray, of course, but with better reason, because although he probably cut no great figure as he came sulking across the road with an armful of his bedding, he at least had a few elegies under his belt.

Thus was I offered on a plate what many native-born Britons have to strive for and often in vain – a fact of which not one of them has ever sought to remind me. God knows what George Russell said. He must have told them I had discovered the lost books of Tacitus, squared the circle and was on the verge of developing a unified field theory. But my assumption that to be given a place would ensure an automatic grant proved incorrect. The responsible authorities wrote to say that I could indeed receive a grant, although only after being

resident in London for three years. This meant at least two more
years of proving myself unemployable. There was nothing for it except
to go back south and begin my sentence. Professor Trethowan and
his wife, gracious as always, refrained from cheering aloud when I
announced my departure. They merely looked very, very happy, as if
a weight had been subtracted from their shoulders and added to their
refrigerator, which I had been helping their children empty for too
long. If it occurred to me that I had been a shameless free-loader, I
merely added the realization to my burden of guilt, as you might toss
an apple-core into a skip full of rubbish. 'When you finally get to
Cambridge,' said my host in farewell, 'head straight for the Footlights.
It's your sort of thing, believe me.' I don't think, at this distance, that
he meant my future was on the stage. I think he meant that it wasn't
in the cloisters; but I prefer to regard this remark as one more
instance of his acute psychological insight. The Viennese essayist
Friedrich Torberg once poured out his troubles to Alfred Adler, who
told him that with so much going wrong he had a right to feel
lousy. Torberg immediately felt marginally, but crucially, better. Bill
Trethowan had the same knack. He knew I had a bad conscience and
he didn't pretend that it could easily be made good. The gnawing
conscience, the agenbite of inwit, helps us know ourselves. Showing
an unprecedented measure of dignity, I refrained from putting the
agenbite on him for my bus fare. Instead I took his daughters aside
and fixed a price for the books I had already given them. Kisses all
round and I was gone, hoping I looked like a devil-may-care vaga-
bond. If only we could really tell what impression we make. Probably
there would be no living.

The bus from Birmingham's Digbeth deposited me in Hammersmith's Talgarth. Digbeth, Talgarth: it sounded like one of those
Anglo-Saxon chronicles which mercifully exist only in fragments. I
was a stranger in a strange land, a wanderer reduced to his essentials,
with only a suitcase for shelter and the light of my red shoes to steer
by. Yet fortune, ever ready to rub in the message that what she holds
back from the deserving might be given to the undeserving if she is
in the mood, chose this moment to smile. There was a party on at
Melbury Road. In quick succession I was offered a place to sleep and
a job which might have been tailor-made.

My benefactors were dancing together. One of them was Babs, an
Australian girl actually living in the top flat of Melbury Road at the

time, and the other was one of her several English admirers, a dandruffy man in a crumpled three-piece suit who had trouble getting people to remember that he was called Trevor. His main problem was that nobody understood what he did. Computers were his field and he talked a lot about how they were going to revolutionize the world, to the point that ordinary people would have a computer in the house, and so on. All this would have sounded like nonsense even if he and Babs had not been dancing the Shake while he was saying it. But he had a room for rent in his flat, available as of now. When I asked him where the flat was, it was as if I already knew the answer, and was only seeking confirmation. 'Tufnell Park,' he said. 'Up and coming area.' Babs, who was now twisting while Trevor was shaking, was even harder to hear because she was going up and down instead of just vibrating, but I gathered that a job in one of the Lambeth public libraries would be open from the next Monday and with her recommendation I would be a dead certainty. She had worked there herself the previous year and the librarian would do anything she told him to. Trevor, to whom the same clearly applied, nodded vigorously, but that could have been the music. 'All you have to do is put books on shelves,' shouted Babs. 'For you, it's tailor-made.' My recent experience of tailors might have warned me, but there was too much noise and too much beer. There was a plastic barrel of it in the kitchen with a little spigot that you could lie under.

Trevor had one of the new Minis. With my suitcase across the back seat and my soused body hanging in the front passenger's seat belt like the corpse of an executed revolutionary, I went back to Tufnell Park. Nor was it even a different part of Tufnell Park. Trevor's flat was just around the corner from where I had been before. I felt like a rat going back to Tobruk, to a place I returned to only in order to be bombed out of. Page 45 of the *London A-Z* had become my map of the world. But my allotted room couldn't have been cosier. Beside the bed there was space for the suitcase if it stood upright. There was also space for me if I stood upright, as long as I stood upright on the bed. Time for that tomorrow. The problem now was to lie down without getting hurt. I started by kneeling and then did the difficult next bit by twisting myself sideways so that my mouth hit the pillow at an angle which allowed breathing. You can tell when it works because you wake up again next morning.

On the weekend before my new job started I paid two important calls. The first of them was to say goodbye to Pandora, who told me that she was under the impression I had said goodbye already. It transpired that she and Niceold, to save the minister from parliamentary embarrassment, had worked together for two days and a sleepless night in order to accomplish what I had failed to do in two months. When I laughed nervously at this information she used her favourite word with no emphasis at all, like a death knell tolled by a cracked bell underwater. I backed out on all fours with a last, long, longing, hopeless look at her intractable ankles. The second call was on Joyce Grenfell and wasn't much more successful. My account of recent events drew the bare minimum of appreciative laughter. Never one to preach, she none the less made it known that in her view those who regarded themselves as gifted had fewer, not more, excuses for behaving badly. Characteristically she had seen through at a glance to the centre of my self-indulgence. Satan's opening remarks are almost always about how talented we are. As I left her, I was already chewing over the implications. They were too many to swallow that day or, as I can now see, that year or that decade, and perhaps the lesson has not fully sunk in even yet.

There were several Lambeth libraries, of which the one with the putative sure-fire job for me was in Brixton. A bus from Holloway Road went straight there, taking only nine years for the journey. By the time I got there I would have needed another shave, so the beard was a plus. Clad in the Singapore suit, I evidently impressed the librarian, whom I will call Mr Volumes because at this distance I can't remember anything about him except the way he spoke. He spoke very loudly. Even for a road-worker wielding an unjacketed pneumatic drill he would have spoken loudly, but in a librarian his voice was truly startling. In all other respects he was a shambling buffer but then this stentorian voice came out. 'YOUNG BARBARA SAID YOU WERE JUST THE MAN. WAS SHE RIGHT? EH? EH? WHAT?' I did a lot of nodding, got the job, was shown out of the office into the reading room, and stepped on the delicately tapering right hand of Lilith Talbot, who was kneeling down to shelve some books with a lithe grace never employed on shelving books up to that time.

In Sydney, Lilith, the glamour girl of the Downtown Push, had memorably divested me of my virginity, something which had been of no use to anyone. As the personal property of the notorious gambler Emu Coogan she had not been able to go on with our affair – or that was what she had said, perhaps letting me down lightly. But now, in despair at Emu's continued indebtedness to the standover men (apparently he had spent a night chained upside-down to one of the Mosman wharf pilings, listening to the rising tide) she had run away to England. Her intention was to recuperate from years of stress. Instantly I saw my own role in her recuperation.

She didn't see it the same way, so I had to reconcile myself to our renewed friendship remaining chaste for the immediate future. Meanwhile I did everything I could to ensure that my presence bulked large in her life. During the morning shelving session we would shelve as a team. 'CANOODLING AGAIN, YOU TWO?' Mr Volumes insinuated gleefully, whereat the sleeping tramps at the reading table would come up out of their chairs mumbling automatic apologies. This was embarrassing but it helped get the idea into Lilith's head. Also I took her out a lot, principally to the National Film Theatre. She sat through a whole Vincente Minnelli season, each film prefaced by a long free lecture from me, delivered on the bus. Walking back across Waterloo Bridge in the first fogs of winter, I would deliver a further monologue concerning the finer points of what we had just seen. She seemed appropriately grateful for all this instruction, which she was getting for almost nothing. Out of my weekly wage, after stoppages, I paid for all my own cigarettes and cider, on top of most of my rent. All Lilith had to do was buy the NFT tickets and provide the occasional small loan when we dined out together.

Dining out meant shepherd's pie and bitter at the Anchor, Bankside. The Anchor was a little sooty brick Georgian pub on the Embankment. You could sit on the wall outside and look across the river to St Paul's. The tiny house from which Christopher Wren had once done the same thing was a few yards along on the left, on the same site as a previous house where Catherine of Aragon had spent the night on her way upriver to marry Henry VIII. Lilith and I sat there in our duffle-coats looking out over the Whistlerian nocturne, with no sound in the cold air except the muffled drunks in the pub, the dimpled gurgle of the tide turning, the chugalug of the barges, and the slurred drone of my voice telling her about the genius of Arthur Freed and the exact difference between Fred Astaire and Gene Kelly. Framed in the hood of her duffle-coat, her angelic face looked as if it were receiving a revelation. It always did, of course.

Long practice at listening to the gratuitous political lectures of the Downtown Push had taught her to yawn with her mouth closed, with no tell-tale flaring of her poetically sculpted nostrils.

My campaign to get Lilith back into bed would have run into trouble even had she been compliant, because there was nowhere to go. Her bed-sit in Maida Vale was on the fourth floor of a red-brick terrace house inhabited on the first three floors exclusively by landladies. It must have been some sort of landladies' training college: they were all in there, learning how to pick up the sound of illicitly creaking bedsprings and stockinged male feet on the stairs. They had echo-sounders and infra-red detectors. The layout *chez* Trevor was theoretically permissive but in practice hopeless. Trevor's large room contained Trevor's electronic gear, Trevor's weirdo junior-scientist friends, and Trevor. He slept there on a convertible divan: one of those things that doesn't look much like a sofa, but after you fiddle with it for a while it doesn't look much like a bed. To uproot Lilith from polite drinks in the living-room and lead her off into my adjacent roomette could be for one purpose only, especially when you considered that unless we climbed straight away into my bed we would have to squat on it like Indians. After a gallon or so of Woodpecker the obviousness of such a move might be lost on me, but Lilith was not only sober, she was, like all genuinely sexy women, decorous. Anyway, even this slim possibility disappeared when Trevor evicted me. Accurately pronouncing me a defaulter on my payments, he rented the room to a girl folk singer. I could kip on the floor of his living room until I had found somewhere else. He was very nice about it, but also very firm. I think he had hopes of getting somewhere with the folk singer, who sang the standard Weavers repertoire with a Roedean accent. Her name was Ninette and that was the name of her LP: *My Name is Ninette*. She made semi-regular appearances on the Bernard Braden show on the BBC and was thus well enough off to afford a new inner-spring mattress to go on top of the one provided by Trevor for what had previously been my bed. The mattress came wrapped in a sixteen-ply paper bag. Autumn had by now become winter in all but name, Trevor's fan-heater did more for his bed than for my area of the floor, and the insulating properties of the paper bag were obvious. So I moved into it.

8. THE MAN IN THE BROWN PAPER BAG

In Trevor's living room, my suitcase against the wall served as a headboard. Folded clothes made a pillow. Beyond, into the centre of the room, stretched the brown paper bag, forming my bed. Wriggling into it took some time, but once inserted I could settle down in comparative warmth for a long night of turning from one side to the other. It was the hardness of the floor which compelled frequent movement. A lot of this I could do in my sleep, because my body, albeit much abused, was still young and supple, and I have always had Napoleon's gift of falling asleep at will, although unfortunately it has not always been accompanied by his gift of waking up again. The problem resided not in how the hardness of the floor affected my sleep, but in how the noise the paper bag made affected Trevor.

As he lay there in the darkness on his enviably luxurious convertible divan, it was as if, somewhere nearby, a giant packet of crisps was being eaten by one of those cinema patrons who think that they are being unobtrusive if they take only a few crisps at a time and chew them very slowly. When Trevor could bear no more he would switch on his modernistic tubular bedside light, wake me up and tell me to be quiet. Invariably I would discover, upon waking, that my bladder, which was already showing signs of being weakened by the steady inundation of cider, demanded emptying. So I had to get out of the paper bag, go away, pee, come back and get back in, thus creating a double uproar. When Trevor switched his light off again I would lie there trying not to move. Only a dead man or a yoga adept can keep that up for more than twenty minutes. Judging that Trevor was asleep again, I would essay a surreptitious turn to one side, making no more noise than a shy prospective bride unwrapping a lace-trimmed silk nightgown from its tissues. This movement completed, for a long time I would lie there, inhaling and exhaling as shallowly as possible and waiting until the sound of Trevor's steady breathing deepened into the second level of sleep. Only then would I make the necessary full turn on to the other side. A man tearing up a thin telephone directory while wading through dead leaves would have been hard put to be so silent. But if, after these manoeuvres, I dropped off to sleep, it was inevitable that an involuntary shift of weight would sooner or later produce the full effect of a large, empty cardboard box being attacked by a flock of woodpeckers. I can be sure of this because sometimes the noise woke me as well.

Even after the student-codifying catastrophe and the subsequent agonizing reappraisal, my powers of self-deception were still in healthy shape, but it was not easy to convince myself that mere lack of sleep lowered my performance at the library. I preferred to think that it was the frustration caused by not sleeping with Lilith. Having convinced myself of this, I did my best to make her see reason. In no sense of the phrase was she having any. Probably she had already guessed that I was an irredeemable incompetent. Certainly Mr Volumes had rumbled me early on. The evidence was hard to miss. I always arrived late. Oliver Goldsmith, accused of the same thing, pointed out that he always left early. Lacking his self-confidence, I merely looked sheepish. 'YOU MUST KEEP TIME, YOU KNOW,' Mr Volumes told me and the rest of the borough. Lilith had been transferred to another branch so there was nothing exciting to look at except the tramps who came in to get out of the cold. They would sit at the big leather-topped table pretending to read *Country Life* but it was obvious that the blood-bag eyes couldn't focus on anything except a bottle of methylated spirits or a tin of boot polish. You could make bets with yourself about which disease they would succumb to first, cirrhosis or gangrene. Once a month they were rounded up and hospitalized so that their socks could be removed surgically. Skin ingrained with dirt has the anomalous effect, in the right light, of looking expensively tanned, as if by the Riviera sun: an observation which, once I had made it, depressed me deeply. But the real killer was boredom. Stamping the cards of borrowers, I ran out of answers for the little old ladies who wanted to know if they had already read the book they were thinking about taking out. The smart ones used a perzonalised coding system. One of them would put a small inked cross on page 81 of every book before bringing it back, so that later on in the library she could turn to that page and, if she saw her mark, be reminded not to take the book out again. Another would draw a circle in red pencil around the last word on page 64. There were hundreds of them at it all the time. If you picked up a book by Dorothy L. Sayers or Margery Allingham and flicked through it, you would see a kaleidoscope of dots, crosses, blobs, circles, swastikas, etc. It was interesting but not interesting enough. When I met Lilith in the evening, I complained about having trouble concentrating. She advanced the theory that for someone whose destiny was to read and write books there could be no profit in being obliged all day to do nothing except pick them up and put them down. I took some comfort from this advice, although the historic evidence should have suggested that it was fallacious. Jorge Luis Borges and Archibald MacLeish had each pursued a successful literary career while working as a librarian. Philip Larkin was currently doing the same, although I didn't know that. Admittedly Proust had been a disaster as a librarian but that was mainly because, instead of turning up late, he never turned up at all. When Mr Volumes began hinting, in his subtle way, that I might think of pursuing a similar course, I did my long perfected number of resigning one step ahead of the boot.

Jobless in winter in a paper bag. My discomfiture had a Miltonic ring to it. But now that I was merely working through a sentence towards the day of release, defeat was easier to shrug off, or even to cherish as a token of my rebellious nature. There is also the possibility that I was clinically certifiable at the time. Sex starvation was in its downhill phase and something had gone seriously wrong with my teeth. The half-dozen of them that I had already lost didn't hurt, but those remaining in my head rarely did less than give a sharp twinge when I sucked anything – air, for example. Under Lilith's influence I was now attempting to vary my egg, bacon and sausage diet with the occasional helping of steamed greens, but the treatment was a holding operation at best. The connection between the teeth and the brain is intimate and potentially devastating: that much I knew. But you wouldn't catch me going to a dentist. I was too smart for that.

Breathing carefully through the nose – never an easy trick for a chronic sinus sufferer – I auditioned for a new job at a light-metal-work factory off the Holloway Road. The supervisor wore a grey lab coat, had a short back and sides haircut polished with a buffing wheel, and favoured blunt speech. 'I'll speak bluntly,' he rapped. 'Don't like your general appearance. Don't like the beard. Don't like the fingernails. Should have worn a suit, not that jacket. Shouldn't wear a jacket like that unless you're in the army. If you have to wear a jacket like that, should wear it tomorrow, not to your interview. Interview, you should be standing up straight, not slouching like that. Shouldn't be smoking. I'm not smoking. Why are you? Hope we won't be seeing those shoes again . . .' The roar, clank, thump and *chong chong* of the stamping machines out on the factory floor drowned some of this out but not enough. I listened stunned, which was obviously the desired reaction, because I was taken on, as a general workman, at nine pounds a week before stoppages. Young British-born readers with qualifications but no job will doubtless wince to read of an immigrant with a job but no qualifications. All I can say is that things were different then. The economy was already collapsing but everybody thought the noise was bustle.

With proof of my employed status I found new digs around the corner from Trevor's, in Tufnell Park Road proper. Since it was by now clear that Tufnell Park was my Berlin and my Paris, it was only fitting that I should become resident in its Kurfürstendamm or Champs-Elysées. From the awe-inspiring single-storey edifice of Tufnell Park tube station, Tufnell Park Road swept down majestically for half a mile until it met Holloway Road in a *carrefour* blazing with the glamorous white light of the launderette. At No. 114 I was exactly halfway down the road, and thus equidistant from the only two points of interest. My room was in the basement, with a window opening not so much on the back garden as under it, so that I looked out into a cross section of the earth. But the rent was a more than reasonable thirty shillings a week. In fact it was a snip. Mrs Bennett had not kept up with the times. She was eighty plus and walked with a stoop, which meant, since she was not very tall in the first place, that I often didn't see her before falling over her.

Not seeing her was made easier by the darkness. Her connections with the outside world had been broken on the day when her fiancé sailed away to the Middle East on the same ship as Rupert Brooke. Out there he had suffered the same fate, but without writing any poems. Understandably the modern world had ceased to interest her from that moment, and she had declined to keep up with its inventions, including any lightbulb more powerful than forty watts. The chintz furniture was well dusted but so faded that it was virtually monochrome. No doubt it was all still a riot of colour to her eyes.

In the corridors and on the staircase it would have been easier to find one's way by the weak light of the frosted bulbs if only the wallpaper had been a brighter colour. But it was all brown: brown on brown with dark brown wooden trimmings. Sometimes through the layers of varnish you could see the ghost of a William Morris print, like jungle under a flooded river full of mud. Once, while she was waiting, it must have been a bright little house he would have been glad to come home to. Then she went on waiting without an object and it all turned dark. I could sympathize, but things got very tricky on the stairs, which I had to spend a certain amount of time groping up and down because the toilet was on the floor above. If you ran into her in the dark, no matter how slowly you were going, it usually meant a tumble. For her a fall would probably have entailed multiple fractures, but she was so low down that she acted as a fulcrum. It was always the rest of us – everyone in the house at some time or other – who took the dive. This wasn't so bad if you were going upstairs at the time, but if you were heading in the opposite direction it could involve a sudden plunge into the brown void, with a good chance of cracking your head against a skirting board the colour and consistency of petrified gravy.

With its narrow bed, single-bar radiator and burnt-umber decor, my little room was an unlikely setting for happiness, yet Lilith took one look at me in my new context and immediately granted the favours so long withheld. Perhaps she had been touched by the spirit of Christmas. The snow began early that year and a good deal of it had already occupied the top half of the vista through my window, above the half filled with dark earth. She had come a long way by bus to cook me my weekly lifesaving meal of liver and greens. I was knackered from a hard day in the factory. Also, chary of the effect that the cold air had on my bared teeth, I wasn't doing much talking. This was probably the key factor. Eloquence might get you started with a woman but it is often taciturnity which seals the bargain. Shakespeare has a line about it – somewhere in *Henry V*, I think. Those who can rhyme their way into a lady's favour do always reason themselves out again. Not being able to say anything, I couldn't say the wrong thing, which left Lilith, undistracted by importunities, free to decide that in such a depth of winter there was no further point in leaving her beautiful body lonely. There is also a slim chance that I was an irresistible object of pathos, but experience suggests that even the warmest and most generous woman can be moved to tears of compassion without feeling impelled to take off her clothes.

The only real explanation, however, is that I got lucky, not only then but for the rest of my life. Right through that epic of a winter she came to me several times a week. The first love affair I had had which lasted long enough for me to get used to it, it did wonders for my confidence. It probably did wonders for my arrogance, too: her queenly bearing could not, as I recall, prevent my taking her for granted unless she issued the occasional verbal reproof. Innate tolerance – plus, no doubt, vivid memories of Emu Coogan's impecuniosity – made her slow to remonstrate, so I got away with what seemed a lot even at the time, and strikes me in retrospect as something close to white slavery. When I packed her off home on the last bus it was only common sense to give her the poems I was sending out, each batch of them accompanied by a folded self-addressed envelope and placed inside another envelope addressed to an editor. To expect her not only to post the letters but to buy the stamps for each envelope was possibly a bit much. She did it without complaining. Hearing no protest, I took everything and gave nothing.

Some stupidities only time can cure. What could be gained by experience I gained then; or the essentials of it anyway, and the deep self-doubt that inhibits and cripples was obviated at an early stage. Which is not to say that I was permanently immunized against all anxiety. In future liaisons, that particularly humiliating version of impotence known as first night failure was always to be a hazard. But when it struck, it did so in perspective, as an embarrassment rather than an affliction. All it means, if you wilt that way with a lady, is that you haven't yet really met her. You're not trying to make love to a woman, you're trying not to miss an opportunity. I have heard men say that such a thing has never happened to them. The claim, I think, speaks as much against their imaginations as for their virility, but no doubt they are telling the truth. The truth might even redound to their credit: never to be unmanned could be a sign of manhood. Those of us who can't plausibly make the same boast have at least some comfort. We find out the hard way, if that's the appropriate phrase, whether the lady has a forgiving soul. Since no other kind of woman is worth getting mixed up with, the man who crumples at the first sign of impatience should be glad to consider himself forewarned, if not forearmed.

In this case the question became academic after the first evening, and for a long winter that should have been a disaster I put on satisfaction like a weightlifter putting on muscle. Without Lilith I might have been not just unhappy, but dead. The winter deepened into the worst since 1947, then the worst since the year after the Great Fire, then the worst since the last Ice Age. The cleared snow formed long ridges at the sides of the roads. These ice ridges turned dark with dirt: burial mounds for long ships, they were pitted like breeze blocks. With thousands of tons of water lying around in frozen form, the anomalous consequence was a water shortage. So many pipes burst that the system just packed up. You had to draw your household water from a stand-pipe in the street. The residents of 114 Tufnell Park Road took turns to do this on behalf of Mrs Bennett, whose only recorded journey outside the front gate was instantly defeated by the frozen snow-ridge at the road's edge. It was taller than she was. After gazing for a while into that threatening escarpment of refrigerated lucent suet, she turned back bewildered.

Bewildered and coughing. Many old people died younger than they should have, that winter. If they were poor they died of hypothermia. If they were well enough off to keep their radiators going full-time, it was the acid fogs that got them. The fogs, the last great fogs that London was ever to see, were Dickensian epics through which I groped home from work each evening, lucky to be young and mobile. The bus that brought Lilith to me would arrive an hour late, its headlights diffused by the fog into opalescent radiance. Mrs Bennett was always glad to see Lilith and usually arranged to be on the stairs so that we could both fall over her. But soon her cough confined her to her room. For a while I was mildly afraid that she had withdrawn because of the shock induced by my poems, which she had asked to see – or had at any rate agreed to be shown – yet had obviously found to be not quite the sort of thing she had grown used to at the time when dear Rupert was into cleanness leaping. Eventually her cough became audible even through the ceiling and thus disabused me of my typically solipsistic notion. You had to be above a certain age to cough like that but anyone who qualified could be sure that there would be nothing temporary about the affliction. Once it started there was only one way of stopping it. Each droplet of fog had a molecule of sulphuric acid attached. The fog looked romantic if your beautiful girlfriend had stepped off a bus and was materializing out of it towards you with the dark outline of her duffle-coat taking shape against the nacreous cloud. To the old people it was breath-taking in a different way. Mrs Bennett was only one of the many who tried to hide from it in the bedroom. But the mist with the sharp taste got in through the old warped door jambs and the place where the window sash would no longer sit square.

Even had she been in sight she would probably still have been out of mind. Her star lodger was too busy being the horny-handed proletarian and tireless young lover. Actually the demands of the first component of this dual role often threatened to inhibit my achievements in the second. After a night spent shivering – if Lilith had been there, my room seemed colder than ever after she was gone – I arrived already tired at the machine shop, where the warm air that would otherwise have been welcome was offset by the continual uproar. The machines were devoted to taking $6' \times 4'$ sheets of metal and punching or drilling various patterns of holes in them. Punches went CHUNK CHUNK and drills went YERK YERK. An acre of machines doing both these things produced a clamour which one's ringing ears might have analysed as CHUNK YERK CHUNK YERK if one's body had not been vibrating. Physically walking on air from the interminably reiterated percussion, I heard the sound as CHU-CHU-CHUNK (CHERK YUNK!) YER-YER-YERK (UNK UNK!) ERK ERK, or sounds to that effect. The machine operators, who had been doing the same sort of work since the Second World War or even earlier, watched the flow of cutting oil and the glittering spillage of metal waste with understandable indifference. Once upon a time the perforated plates had been going into Lancaster bombers and there was point to the work. A team from *Picture Post* had come to take photographs of them cheerfully doing their bit. Now the perforated plates were going into the backs of slot machines that sold Kit-Kats and packets of Smiths Crisps. Alienation, as defined by the young Marx but better described by the older William Morris, was a palpable presence. Where Marx and Morris had both been wrong, however, was in the assumption that men alienated from their labour must necessarily be denatured. The machine-operators all drove second-hand but immaculately kept Rovers or Riley Pathfinders and had enough spare cigarettes to 'lend' me about a packet a day between them. I was the alienated one and opium was my religion.

My job was to help a man called Fred load as-yet-unperforated metal plates of specified gauge on to a trolley, wheel them to the machines, unload them in sequence, load the finished plates and wheel them back to the racks in which they were stored vertically until shipment. At the beginning and end of this chain of events there was a mildly thrilling moment when Fred picked up and put down the heavier plates by means of a Ferris hoist which ran on a rail in the roof. It was controlled electrically from a hand-set. Fred pressed the buttons on the hand-set and I steadied the plates so that they didn't swing around and swipe anybody. You couldn't call Fred's job skilled labour, so as his assistant I scarcely rated as a dogsbody. This situation was made no easier by Fred's personality. A dedicated racist, he lurked outside the machine-shop door at lunchtime so that he could shout 'ANY COCONUTS?' to the West Indian girls in transit between the steam laundry and the greasy spoon. Even worse, from my angle, he liked to shout racist jokes to me while we were working. He had a theory that all Australians were descended from Aborigines, and that any Australian immigrant into Britain was therefore part of the universal black conspiracy to deprive the British working class of employment. Compounded by the Wagnerian banging and jangling, his sentiments had the same effect on me as the iron band tightening around Cavaradossi's head. Fred's first word was always 'EAR!', by which he meant 'Here!' He kept yelling that until I paid attention. 'EAR! (CHU-CHU-CHUNK) THIS JEW (CHERK YUNK!) ANNA NIG-NOG (YUNK CHERK!) SO EASE ALL BLACK FROM A BOO POLISH (YER-YER-YERK) . . .' Fred didn't put me off the cockney accent, which had already influenced my own, no doubt with ludicrous results. But he would have gone a fair way towards putting me off the proletariat, if I had really believed that it existed. In fact my belief in such things was only theoretical, and even the theory was a fag-end. It had always been transparently obvious to me that there could be no such thing as the masses. There were only people. Even Fred was unique. That was the awful thing about him.

Thus the little factory chuntered on, with Fred and me pushing and pulling our trolley endlessly around its inner perimeter. Meanwhile the rest of the country was gradually coming to a standstill. For some reason which nobody has ever been able to figure out, the British consider themselves to be living in a tropical climate into which any intrusion of snow, no matter how brief, is always regarded as Freak Weather Conditions. The railways, for example, are invariably brought to a halt by any snowfall heavy enough to make the rails show white instead of silver. The drivers in their Hawaiian shirts and dark glasses climb down from their cabins and quit. The trains are not allowed to move again until the commuters have had a day's rest and the tabloid newspapers – even more cretinous than the Australian equivalents – have had a chance to run headlines about the Freak Weather Conditions. (BRR! SAYS BR: IT'S SNOW-GO!) It will be understood, then, that in the winter under discussion the trains vanished for weeks on end. So did most of the livestock. The sheep were so far down that the army was using echo-sounders to find them. Then somebody had to look for the army. It would have been a good story if it had ended at the proper time. But it all went on and on. History, however, has to be truly disastrous before it impinges on your personal odyssey. For me, with my new assurance, the snow was just a backdrop. Secure within, I was looking outwards for the first time.

The owner of the business arrived in a Bentley to tour the shop floor, his blazered school-age son in attendance. They paraded like royalty, with their hands behind their backs. Only the blunt-spoken supervisor got his hand shaken. It was because his hand was clean. In Australia the air would have been thick with first names. I really was in another country, an observer as flabbergasted by exotic ritual as those first Portuguese in China whose astonished narrative stands out even in Hakluyt's vast codex of the strange. Fascinated, I neglected to steady a batch of steel plates which Fred had just picked up with the hoist. The swinging load knocked him backwards off his feet and on to the trolley, where he lay pondering the implications while the plates shook themselves out of the grip of the hoist, crashed to the concrete on their edges a few inches from his head, and, considerately tilting away from him – instead of, as they might equally well have done, towards – accumulated thunderously on the floor like playing cards in Valhalla. At this point, but for an entirely unconnected reason, the supervisor cut the power in the machines. The owner wished to address his work force. The clangour stopped with a reverse shock, an inburst of sound, a downroar. Fred, never quick at adjusting to circumstances, was still yelling. '. . . UCKING NIG-NOG GIT, YOU'RE AFTER MY JOB!' The owner and his son left hurriedly, even as the blunt-spoken supervisor headed towards me, his eyes narrowed with purpose.

9. *SOLVITUR ACRIS JAMES*

Out in the countryside, the corpses of sheep and the hulks of abandoned trains emerged from the melting snow. Spring came to Tufnell Park. It was too late for Mrs Bennett, whose cough had already stopped by itself. Not going to her funeral was a sin of omission easily committed – all I had to do was not ask the precise time it would take place. Also I was busy looking for work. But my conscience was uneasy at the time, and although it never became exactly inflamed on the subject I can still say that my dereliction lived with me as a matter for regret. Perhaps I had been put off death at an early age. Certainly I had a revolutionary socialist's contempt for ceremony, which I construed as empty posturing, and never more so than when the chief participant was, as in this case, dormant. Nowadays I set much less store by my independence of mind, and indeed doubt whether it really exists. Yeats's question about custom and ceremony has at last sunk home. In those days I was either a different man or – something even harder to understand and absolve – a glib version of the same one. The old lady had not only been kind and gracious, she had taken positive delight in the idea that the feckless young writer under her roof had been so thoroughly compromising such a well brought-up girl. One of those rare people who, having missed out on a blessing, are glad instead of bitter to see it conferred on others, Mrs Bennett in death deserved something better from me than the cold shoulder. But she was dealing with someone impatient of mere formalities.

So was Lilith, who wanted to be married. If she had wanted to marry me I would probably have panicked, because a sound instinct told me that I was far from ready. But she wanted to marry Emu, which gave me an opportunity to be peeved. She made the announcement after we had seen *Les Enfants du paradis*. 'If all the people who live together were in love,' said Baptiste, 'the Earth would shine like the Sun.' Lilith had been my Garance. 'When I want to say yes, I can't say no.' How lucky I had been to meet my woman of the world and find it all so easy. Lilith, no less lovely than Arletty, sat beside me, looking as happy in the reflected light as a woman could who had just paid two bus fares, bought two cinema tickets, and was about to pay for two bus fares more. All the way home on the slow bus past the now shrinking roadside ranges of dribbling black mousse I explained the significance of what we had just seen, how it was all an idyll. In my little room she took me to her with special tenderness, which should have told me that this had been an idyll too, and must now end. Typically, though, I had to be told what I might have guessed.

Hypocritical jealousy is more enjoyable than the genuine article but I still managed to work myself up into a state. Lilith, however, remained calm. Her mind was already on its way home, and soon her body followed it. The time had come for her to be married, so she went where it would happen. It was as if her mission in my life had been completed. She had got me through the winter without my succumbing to vitamin deficiency: my gums were purple only when I smiled, and I couldn't do much of that even in spring, lest the air get at my teeth. She had also got me through that dangerous second stage of virginity, the stage in which we are only technically no longer chaste, and callow anxiety is compounded by a little learning. I still had a lot more to find out about women, but I was on the right track. It was only much later that I could be sure of this, however, because there is a wrong track which runs beside the right track for a long way.

Released from stability, which youth finds hard to bear even when beneficial, I was suddenly mobile, like the unfrozen landscape. The whole country woke up to an ecstasy of self-consciousness. There were political scandals, quasi-satirical television programmes, hit singles to make the dead dance, and the rise of the miniskirt to ever less prudent lengths of shortness. Cabinet Ministers were disgraced for love, thugs robbed a mail train and were hailed as heroes, unmasked traitors were admired for their complex personalities, the harlot's cry from mews to mews had the exultant confidence of Callas singing 'Casta diva', and the Beatles mouthed and mimed to fame in screaming theatres whose seats had to be heat-dried afterwards because they were soaked with the love-juices of pubescent girls.

Urgent messages of change came from everywhere, the most insistent of all from my teeth. With my bad conscience blacked out by stabbing pains from molars and incisors, I went on National Assistance to tide me over. When the assessor came to look at me in my room I sat opposite him in the brown darkness with my mouth closed, making signs of need with eloquent hands. Touched, or afraid of infection, he signed the papers and skedaddled.

At a Melbury Road party I met an Australian dentist who impressed me by being able to tell I had toothache by the way I was dancing. He was dancing himself at the time, opposite a wonderfully proportioned girl from Curl Curl. She had a freckled face and a jersey miniskirt whipping softly around her hand-span waist to the sensual pulse of John Lennon's rhythm guitar. She was a red rag to a bull. 'Flash me the fangs for a sec,' said the dentist, matching her step for step as she trod successively on imaginary cigarette butts. 'Shit a brick, you'd better get down to see me pronto.' Next morning – still drunk from the night before or I never would have made it – I arrived at his surgery in Shoreditch to be greeted by the girl from Curl Curl, who turned out to be not only the receptionist but the nurse. She performed this double function in a white uniform of mini length, with white patterned tights below. Her employer, whose name was Barry, conformed in every respect to the paradigm Australian dentist I had been warned against, down to and including the 3.8 Jaguar parked outside. For the English chattering classes, stories about Australians had begun to serve as a mild form of licensed anti-Semitism, a function they retain. One of the stories then current was about the typical Australian dentist who spent a year in London pulling every tooth in sight, thereby defrauding the National Health and making possible the purchase of a 3.8 Jaguar, in which he and his beautiful nurse then decamped to the south of France and retired. Barry had the car and the beautiful nurse but in other ways he didn't fit the stereotype at all. For one thing, he showed no urge to extract any teeth that were not already an obvious lost cause. Instead he fought to save them, despite my generous offer to surrender them without a struggle. 'Nar,' said Barry, 'you don't want to lose that eye tooth. I'll just kill the nerve and go down the hole into the root. Give her a good cleaning out. Nothing a cavity likes more than a good probe, right, Noelene?' If you wonder how I can recall the way Barry talked, it's because trauma etches the memory. Freud's theory of repression is doubtless right – how could we tell if it was wrong? – but in my case it ceases to apply when the subject turns to teeth. Back almost to the beginning of my life, I can remember everything that happened at the dentist's. Mostly what happened was my imagination running out of control, but that made the experience no less frightening. While writing the first volume of this work I was not yet ready to face the full degrading facts of my dental history. I think that by now I can handle it, but if you get the impression in the next few paragraphs that their author is looking into the pit of his own nature, you will probably be right.

It started in Kogarah when I was about seven years old. That dentist, whose own teeth weren't much of an advertisement, should never have told me that the extraction of my abscessed molar wouldn't hurt. It did, distinctly. I felt betrayed, and received no comfort from the dentist, who had received a squirt of pus in the eye. Outrage at his perfidy motivated me to a brilliant career of truancy which ensured that I did not visit any dentist again until all my remaining first teeth were extracted in one go, under gas. When I woke up I was given limitless lemonade and ice cream as a reward for bravery. In fact my bravery, after a week's delaying tactics including a furniture-fracturing tantrum, had consisted of agreeing to accompany my mother to the surgery on a bus instead of in the police car which she had indicated would otherwise have to be called in. But the Shelley's lemonade was balm to the plundered gums and the Street's ice cream was a portent of all the sweet things I would now be able to eat when my mother wasn't watching. The Jaffas, Fantails, and Minties which had extracted so many of my first teeth with such precision now riddled my second teeth with cavities. Since I would rather have suffered toothache than go for a check-up, the sweet things got an uninterrupted opportunity to make a cave-system out of the choppers of whose straightness my mother was so proud. She couldn't understand how it was happening. (She probably couldn't understand how so much small change dematerialized from her purse, either.) When a tooth was giving me hell I would try to plug it temporarily by taking a good deep bite into a chocolate bar. Finally there was too much pain to live with and I was introduced, after only token escape attempts, into the surgery of a special dentist for young people, Mr Jolly. He had his chair rigged up as a cowboy saddle with stirrups and you were encouraged to wear toy guns. These latter were supplied by the receptionist if you didn't own any.

With a Ned Kelly cap-pistol holstered low on each hip I felt a bit self-conscious sitting there, not just because I was sixteen years old but because of a dim awareness that my mouth might present an offensive sight to a man whose whole ambience was so radiantly clean. Upon looking into my open maw Mr Jolly reacted only by catching his breath and turning pale. In the first session that was all he did – look around, poke about a bit, and get his nurse to mark up the cavities on a mouth-map – but after it was over I rewarded myself, at the nearest newsagent's, with a Hoadley's Violet Crumble Bar. At the next session a week later he did a bit of drilling, but not much. Such was his method: to proceed slowly and build confidence. He was also very generous with the local anaesthetic. This accorded well with one half of my ambivalent feelings about the hypodermic syringe: on the one hand I demanded to be as desensitized as possible, on the other I hated needles. He overcame my negative tropism by giving a small preliminary injection to dull the impact of the second, larger one. Further injections followed if there was any suspicion of a reawakening tingle from my fat lip. The cumulative effect rendered me numb to the waist. He could have sawn my head off and I wouldn't have felt a thing.

Since my accursed imagination was still alive, and even more terrified of the drill now that I had only its sound from which to deduce what it was doing, he could never step on the accelerator. Any time the noise of the rotating bit rose above a low buzz, I would be arching up out of the chair like a strychnine victim while making, from the back of my throat, the strangled gargles of a turkey choking. These noises had a galvanizing effect in the reception area outside, where the waiting children and their anxious mothers erroneously inferred that the current patient had got the drill tangled in his vocal cords.

At that rate there was no hope of filling even one cavity per session. On average it took four trips to plug each hole, with the gap stopped by a temporary filling until the big day came when the cavity could receive its permanent filling of amalgam. Before the amalgam went in, the cavity had first to be lined. The lining included some alcohol-based component which, if it fell on your tongue, burned like Mexican food, but with the mouth jacked open there was nothing to be done except hope the inserted rubber pipe would suck it away along with the spit. Then the amalgam was smeared in, a few flakes at a time, on metal spatulas, like paint from the palette of a slap-happy but somnambulistic Post-Impressionist gradually going mad with the *impasto*. At the subsequent session the hardened filling was polished and the next cavity made its first, tentative encounter with the shy tip of the lethargically turning drill. Since I had something like thirty-four cavities to fill – I can remember for certain that there were more holes than I had teeth – it will be appreciated that the course of treatment stretched over what is called, in Australia, a considerable period of time. Finally all my teeth had been shot full of lead. I had a mouth like two sets of knuckle-dusters. The *pièce de résistance* was fashioned from a nobler metal. It was a heart-shaped gold filling in one of my front teeth. Mr Jolly worked on that one like Benvenuto Cellini on the statue of Perseus. By the time it was in position I had finished high school and was ready to begin university. Mr Jolly told me that of all my unsatisfactory aspects as a patient, the most depressing was the way he couldn't start work on my mouth each week without first cleaning out the debris of chocolate, toffee, liquorice and mashed peanuts from around the very fillings he had spent a good part of his career painstakingly inserting. I got the impression that he wouldn't have minded seeing me take a bit of the pain myself, yet he never succumbed to the temptation. He must have been a saint.

Barry wasn't that but perhaps his straightforwardness was a virtue. Where Mr Jolly would do everything to put fear at rest, Barry would tell you the worst and challenge you to run. 'This next bit's going to hurt like buggery.' He was right every time. Within minutes of each session starting I was making inner vows not to come back next week, but he had a way around that. 'I'm going to leave that molar wide open so the muck inside can dry out, but if you don't come back soon the bludger'll go septic and you'll die in agony.' He did about a year's work in three weeks. Most of my back teeth were beyond hope but the front ones looked like the full allocation unless I laughed, which I didn't feel like doing for some time. The last and hardest job was to clean up my gums. After every few scrapes I flew around the surgery like an open-mouth balloon. The girl from Curl Curl pinned me with a body-slam and the job was done.

'You'd feel a lot less scared,' said Barry, saying goodbye for ever, 'if you understood your real problem.' Wet-eyed with relief, gratitude and remembered pain, I asked him what that was. 'You're a coward.'

10. FAIRY MILD GREEN LIQUID GODMOTHER

While having my mouth fixed I had changed residence. Farewell to Tufnell Park. Even through the dull ache in my mouth I could taste the thrill of a new era. Youth was at the helm. London had begun to swing. Films were being made in which it was assumed, almost always erroneously, that the story would be more interesting if the people concerned were to run instead of walk. Nothing could be more up to date than to be a young man with a beard and strange shoes, carrying a suitcase, free-wheeling, on the move. I moved all the way up the road and around the corner, into a loft made available by a nice young married lady who charged a reasonable rent. My pyramid-shaped hutch, which could be entered only via a ladder starting in a top-floor room full of her children, was half the size of the room I had left behind and had even fewer built-in facilities, but by moving two blocks I had entered Kentish Town, so for all practical purposes I was in Hampstead. As part of the same upwardly mobile thrust, I had landed another white-collar job, and this time I wasn't coding reports or filling up charts. I was coding reports *and* filling up charts.

Market Assessment Enterprises had third-floor offices just off High Holborn on the Gamages side of Grays Inn Road. Gamages is gone now and I suppose Market Assessment Enterprises, or MAE, has long been wound up, because it was a happy-go-lucky outfit that was far too much fun to work for. Except for the recently ex-Oxbridge Jeremys and Nigels who owned the company, the work force consisted exclusively of young fringe-dwellers who worked for no other reason than to finance their intense night life. There were some outstandingly pretty girls, fashionably dressed in high white plastic boots yet always cadging each other's cigarettes. There were young men in sharply cut suits with flared trousers – the first hint of the Carnaby Street look – but they couldn't afford to eat lunch.

The low-paying jobs were in the office, coding the reports. The even-lower-paying jobs were out in the street, where you stood with your report sheet and asked randomly selected people from the passing crowd whether they preferred the cap of the plastic bottle of green liquid detergent fully detachable from the plastic bottle or else attached to the plastic bottle by means of a short plastic attachment. In reality the selection of respondents wasn't random at all, because the only people who would consent to answer such questions were mental defectives or people with such inadequate personalities that any form of conversation came as a blessing. For the first day I tried to be honest but it was hopeless. The only man who gave a coherent set of answers to all twenty-five questions turned out to come from Sweden. Rather than discard the one answer-sheet that made sense, I wrote down that he came from Swindon. It then occurred to me, as it had independently occurred to all my colleagues, that if you could make up the man's address you could also make up the man's answers and even the man himself. The whole thing could be done in the pub.

Employing the same skills which had scored me a perfect mark for my Clinical Case Study in the Sydney University Psychology exams, I produced, at the end of my first week, a set of reports which ensured my promotion to the office staff proper. This meant that I could sit in the office and take the fantasy a step further by coding the incoming reports so that they would be ready for transfer to punched cards. Everyone sat at small desks, as if at school, but talked at the top of his or her voice, as if the school were in the grip of some permanent rag day. The light of spring poured through the windows and illuminated Moira, the girl in the next desk to my right. Moira's physical presence disturbed me in a way that I knew I remembered, but couldn't remember exactly how. Then I suddenly realized that she reminded me of Sonia Humphries, the girl who had sat beside me in the double front-row desk of Class 1B at Kogarah Infants' School in 1946. The resemblance was furthered by Moira's notable deficiency of height. Measured vertically, she lacked inches. Measured around the chest, however, she did not. Moira was the first girl I ever found both attractive and out of proportion. Up to then I had always been drawn towards a classical balance of forces, but

Moira made her combination of diminutiveness and excess seem like a romantic challenge. Besides, she was keen – always a potent influence on judgment. Halfway between a garden gnome and one of those country and western singers off whose straining denim shirt-fronts the rhinestones jump like popcorn, she thought I was wonderful and I found it hard not to agree.

Down in the pub – where she regularly paid for her round of drinks after helping me pay for mine – she would sit on the edge of her seat with the toes of her sling-backed shoes just reaching the floor and tell me horror stories about her lover, a company director called Eric. Eric's company, it transpired, dealt principally in goods which had fallen off the back of a van. One of the tell-tale signs of the now efflorescent sixties was how the much-touted outbreak of classlessness was matched by an obsession with status, so that any fly-by-night operator would call himself a company director merely on the strength of having had his mohair suits made to measure. Apparently Eric had rescued Moira from her old job as a knife-thrower's assistant in Brighton, but she soon found Eric's idea of looking after her almost as bad as watching the knife-thrower take a stiff drink to steady his hands between the matinee and the main performance. So Moira had run out on Eric and was now covertly occupying an under-eaves bed-sit in Lamb's Conduit Street. While she was telling me this, the evening sunlight flooding through the clear upper panes of the pub windows lit up her beehive of red hair, her freckled face and her chaste white blouse, which didn't seem to drape vertically anywhere except at the back. Just as it was occurring to me that Lamb's Conduit Street wasn't very far away, Moira insisted that I accompany her there immediately. I complied, doing my best to stroll in a casual manner while she trotted beside me. It further occurred to me that all this was too simple. I was right about that, but first there was a short interlude while I enjoyed the uncomplicated delight of a perfectly straight-forward woman. In her little room, decorated only by a chianti-flask lampstand and a suitcase rather like mine, Moira asked for nothing except to give love while having money borrowed from her. She was infinitely exploitable. It should have dawned on me sooner that my predecessors in her favours would be unlikely to let such a bonanza go by default.

What I couldn't hope to guess in advance, however, was the extent and fervour of Moira's gratitude. The mere fact that I did not beat her up was enough to establish me in her mind as a gift from heaven. With desperate urgency she granted me her body as a reward. Amazed to discover that there was someone in whose universe I rated as a kind man, I did my best, through evening after evening, to keep up with her frantic insatiability. My landlady grew ever more waspish as I telephoned once again to say I would be home very late. Sometimes I arrived home so weary, and so fuddled from the cider with which Moira had kept me primed, that I had trouble climbing the ladder from the children's room up to the loft, and would sit there among the teddy bears until I got my breath back or dawn broke, whichever was the sooner.

The only, but real, trouble with Moira was that there was nothing else she wanted to do. I took her to the NFT to see Chris Marker's *Letter from Siberia*, a documentary film whose exuberantly serious tone of voice still influences everything I do twenty years later. At the time I was knocked sideways. The details of the majestic final sequence are fresh in my mind today. 'There isn't any God, or curses,' said the narrator as the rocket took off, 'only forces – to be overcome.' I didn't agree even then, but I sat transfixed by the rhythm of that voice – the strong view lightly stated. It wasn't words plus pictures. It was words times pictures. At some length I told Moira just how badly the world needed to forget John Grierson and his whole boring tradition. Moira, however, just wanted to get me alone so that she could go on being grateful in the only way she knew. Hazlitt was only half right when he warned his fellow writers that they will dream in vain of the analphabetic woman who will love them for themselves. There is such a woman. What he should have said is that if we find her she will bore us. Moira would have been the ideal concubine if an ideal concubine had been all I wanted. To find out that I wanted something more, or at any rate something else, was disturbing. A fantasy had been made actual and had scared me in the process.

Things got scarier still when I tried taking a night off. The next day at the office Moira was red-eyed from lack of sleep. Just while I was pondering how to disentangle myself from her pneumatic embrace without destroying her newly established faith in mankind, my problem was solved for me. A man walked into the office, stood over her desk, and nodded towards the door. He didn't look quite violent enough to be Company Director Eric but he didn't look like Canon Collins either. She left with him without saying a word.

I went after them down the stairs and she must have heard me, because on the last landing before the street I found her facing me. I accused her, with more relief than rancour, of having carried a torch for Eric all along. She told me that the man wasn't Eric. It was the knife-thrower. She was married to him. Then she gave me an uncharacteristically reticent kiss, clattered down the remaining stairs and went out of my life.

I got fired the same day, after a statistical fault in a report about a red plastic tomato-shaped tomato sauce container led to an investigation. The people out in the street had faked their questionnaires as usual, but at least they had built in a few believable discrepancies. For three long and light-headed weeks I had coded the questionnaires while blacking out from the previous night's encounter with Moira. Husbanding my vestigial energies, I had neglected to put in the inconsistencies required by verisimilitude. The result was too perfect, too simple to be believed: rather like Moira herself.

11. THE WARPING OF THE NINTH

Failure felt like liberty, so heady was the air. Not only had I to change jobs, I had to change residence as well. Moira had been and gone like Julie Christie in *Sparrows Can't Knack* or *The Loneliness of the Long-Distance Liar*. Another one just like her would be along soon if you waited, and twice as soon if you moved on. All the new films were the same one with a different title: middle-aged entrepreneurs with second houses in up-and-coming Marbella were making money by convincing the young that money didn't matter and the moonlight flit equalled romance.

My landlady, who had probably wanted nothing from me except a sounding board for her justified complaints about her pig of a husband, had not got even that. Instead of bidding me good riddance she put me in the way of a new job and a roof to go with it. An old Oxford chum of hers was starting up, from an address in Chelsea, a prestige publishing house cum second-hand book service. In the first-floor library of his double-knock-through Georgian house I sat to be interviewed, my arms in the sleeves of the Singapore suit held carefully to my sides. He did all the talking. Visions of the future were conjured up: we would be a combination of Bertram Rota and the Officina Bodoni. He would be the management and I would be the staff. Within a short time I would be a company director. Salary would be a matter of agreement from time to time, but I could take it for granted that I would not want for money, make sense? Each of his successive verbal flights was tagged with the rhetorical question 'make sense?', short for 'Does that make sense?' And at that moment it did make sense, although I should have been more worried about the white foam at the corners of his mouth. A no-longer-young semi-titled Englishman is not necessarily suspect just because his complexion is as purple as beetroot and his eyes pop, but if he spits foam without noticing then it is a safe bet that there are other things he isn't noticing either.

His name was Maurice Dillwick. The name Dillwick was famous, not because of him but because of his father, one of those hereditary peers who defy probability not only by donating their services gratis to the public weal but by being rather good at it. The old man had organized shadow factories during the war, organized their demobilization afterwards, helped nationalize the coal industry, helped rationalize the steel industry, and acted as the kind of benevolent Lord Chamberlain whose civilized tolerance served to perpetuate an inherently stifling institution and thus enfeeble the English theatre for longer than necessary. His was a greatly successful life in all respects but one: his son, though clever, was not quite clever enough to distinguish a passion from a fad or a vocation from a phase. While his father lived, Maurice was kept on short commons, rarely being given more than a few hundred thousand pounds at a time with which to pursue his career as a racing driver, a film director, an explorer or a spy. When the old man hit the soup one day in the House of Lords dining room, Maurice inherited so much money that not even he was able to lose it all at once, so each new enthusiasm could be pursued until he got tired of it. At the time of my recruitment he had already been a publisher for a year.

Not a lot of publishing had been accomplished in that time. That was where I would come in: with my fresh approach, uncluttered by stiffly traditional practices, I would give the project a no-nonsense internal structure. In being stimulated to these fantasies about my prowess, Maurice was perhaps aided by two extraneous factors. One was that George Russell had responded to yet another request for a reference, sending, by return air-letter, an encomium which would have sat extravagantly on the shoulders of Pico della Mirandola. (That I ever wasted my professor's time by such demands is of enduring shame to me, and that I should have drained his energies in connection with this particular mare's nest is something I will have to answer for at the last trumpet.) The other document in my favour was a letter from *Encounter*, signed by Stephen Spender himself, accepting my suite of five poems about porpoises. Maurice was almost as impressed by this as I was. He immediately had me cast as the Christopher Brennan of my generation. (From his days as proprietor and editor of *Negozio nero*, an international arts magazine which had cast its net even wider than *Botteghe oscure* but with less accuracy, Maurice had retained an acquaintance with the principal names in the not very long honour roll of Australian literary history.) As a man of letters I would give the new firm – called provisionally Editions Dillwick – not just an internal structure but an antipodean boldness. He appointed me a company director forthwith.

Promoted from staff to management within a week, I still had no cash in hand but was compensated by being given a back room of the house in which to set up my suitcase. My room, like every other room except the second-floor suite in which Maurice slept and dressed, was piled waist-high with stacked books, the stock of a second-hand book dealer whom Maurice had saved from going bust. The second-hand book dealer was an ageing but still sexually active old poet called Willis Cruft who had once, in Alexandria during the war, written apocalyptic verses which Tambimuttu had found bad enough to publish in *Poetry London*. Nowadays Cruft did not ask for much in life except enough cash to drink wine, run a string of Chinese girlfriends and attend the occasional Sibelius concert at the Festival Hall. Maurice having bought his stock from him for an indeterminate sum, Cruft was obliged to wait around in the hope of extracting some petty cash from time to time. Meanwhile, as a company director of Editions Dillwick, he was included in our three-way talks on how the books piled on the floor might be dispatched to the waiting world. His certain knowledge that there could be nothing immediate about this process was tempered by the necessity of not dampening Maurice's enthusiasm. Realism and feigned optimism thus fought an eternal war in his features, which were already deeply cragged by decades of too much wine, too little success and whatever had gone on in Alexandria.

We three directors of Editions Dillwick sat down around a tea-chest full of the standard edition of Bernard Shaw (the red binding, lacking three volumes) to plan the company's future. Maurice called this convocation the Think Tank. Two hours went by while Maurice discarded all our suggestions for the design of the firm's letterhead. More unsettling was that he discarded his own suggestions with equal vehemence. It quickly became apparent that Maurice could not hear an idea without becoming enthusiastic about it, and that he could not become enthusiastic about it without turning against it. What was not yet apparent was that he was like this in large matters as well as in small. But when the builders arrived it all started to become clear, to others if not to me.

Maurice had contracted a building firm called Piranesi Brothers to refurbish the house throughout while the books were still in it. In Maurice, the newly emergent Habitat design ethos had found its ideal lay exponent. He wanted all the old wallpapers out, all the wood stripped and stained, and every plaster surface painted white. The inevitable result was spots of paint-stripper, varnish and white emulsion all over the green New York edition of Henry James (spines of some volumes cracked). Maurice accused the Piranesi Brothers of plotting to work slowly and ruin his stock. The Piranesi Brothers would retire to the first-floor bathroom, barricade themselves in and privately agree that Mr Dillwick was a nutter. Little did they know that Maurice was taping everything they said and compiling a dossier for the future court case. When they drove off in their Dormobile to another job, Maurice would trail them in his green Jensen to find out where they went, then conceal himself and take photographs of them as they hatched plots to spatter Pamastic all over our priceless second editions (endpapers slightly foxed) of the *Complete Poems* of Alice Meynell. It was about this time, acting from an instinct far quicker than lagging thought, that I wrote off to the LCC telling them they would be wise to come through with my Cambridge grant straight away, because I had no other plans and might well become a burden on the social services.

According to Maurice, the Piranesi Brothers were conspiring to cheat him. According to common sense, they were merely, like all small building firms, running several contracts at once in order to turn an honest profit. But common sense had no chance against Maurice's superior intellect. The dossier grew ever fatter. It bulged with photographs, legal documents and transcriptions of taped telephone calls. Finally even Maurice must have begun to notice that he was overwrought, because he gave himself a holiday. 'I'm *bored* with these builders,' he averred, foam much in evidence. 'I have to get away and think about the overall *shape* of the company. I've been pushing myself too *hard* on a day-to-day basis, make sense?' It didn't, because he hadn't, but if that was the way he felt, who was I to argue? Having bought a new Jensen just like the old one except for a sparkling set of Borrani wire wheels, he disappeared towards the south of France, leaving me in charge.

In charge, that is, of a house full of loose books and frustrated builders. Willis Cruft sensibly declined to consider any advice I might have about how the situation could be retrieved. Correctly diagnosing Editions Dillwick to be an irredeemable folly, he gave himself to Sibelius and the relay of Chinese girls still flying in from Hong Kong. I should have listened to him when he said that things would only get worse on Maurice's return. I preferred, not very passionately, to believe that they would get better. Meanwhile I was in the position of Grand Admiral Dönitz in the few days between Hitler's suicide and the surrender of Germany – I was exercising supreme power over a shambles. To my credit I did not keep up the telephone surveillance on the Piranesi Brothers. My dereliction was in clear breach of Maurice's departing orders, but I would have felt contemptible doing it and anyway I couldn't work the Grundig. To my shame, on the other hand, I went on spending my expense money – there had still been no vulgar talk of salary – instead of handing Maurice my resignation. Handing him my resignation while I was in Chelsea and he in Antibes would not have been easy, but to stay on was taking candy from a baby.

My typical day was spent making tea for the decorators and standing close behind them so I could catch a dollop of varnish before it fell on the cover of *The Apes of God* (reprint, two signatures out of order, otherwise fair) and halved its already negligible value. In the evenings I wooed an Australian girl called Robin who had a marvellous clear skin and was teetering on the verge of deciding not to be a strict Catholic. To encourage her in that direction I took her to see every Buñuel movie in town. When *Los Olvidados* was on at the Chelsea Arts cinema I took her there two nights running but still couldn't slide my hand between her breasts without getting my wrist tangled in the chain of her crucifix. My large talk about being a director and chief executive of Editions Dillwick didn't work the trick either. The letter from the LCC which I had hoped would excuse me two years of waiting for Cambridge only excused me one year. My determination was plain, they said, but it would have to wait until the October after next to attain its object. This was a disappointment. Another letter capped disappointment with disaster: Stephen Spender wrote to say that the number of poems accepted for *Encounter* was now so great that he could see no prospect of printing mine in the foreseeable future. He could, however, arrange to have them published immediately in another magazine, whose name, if I remember correctly, was *Periphery*, or perhaps *Margin*. I wrote back to say that I preferred the original arrangement, which I regarded as a promise, and that the unforeseeable future would do me fine. Perhaps my language was too forceful, because I received no reply. The word 'galah' is an acceptable term of mild remonstrance among Australians. The English, not knowing what a galah is, tend to take offence.

Downcast, I forgot to be the anti-Catholic polemicist and company director. My real self, such as it was, showed through. Robin must have decided either that she liked it or that she might like it after a few things had been done to it, because she hung her scalloped-edged white slip over the back of a chair and took me to bed. Or rather, I took her to bed, the bed being mine: there were books stacked all around it and I spent a lot of time reassembling the collected works of Hugh Walpole after Robin fell over them on her way back from the bathroom in the dark. She looked marvellous dressed in a towel and a crucifix. It made me feel like the hero in one of those *Nouvelle vague* films that were coming out just about then. I lay back like Jean-Paul Pierre or Pierre-Jean Paul or whatever the twerp's name was, the sheet tucked around my waist and a cigarette dangling dangerously from my lower lip.

Very dangerously, as it turned out. The damage to the sheet was extensive and I could easily have burned Robin to death. There was worse. Availing myself of Maurice's stereo, I had been listening half a dozen times a day to his two-disc set of Beethoven's Ninth conducted by Toscanini. The adagio, in particular, sent me into a trance. What delicacy, and yet what drive! How little rubato and yet how supple! It was in just such a mesmerized condition that I left the two records on top of the switched-on amplifier while I took Robin to the pub, there to help her overcome her inhibitions about drinking by showing her what an entertaining fellow I became when inebriated. Having helped me home, Robin was the first to notice that the Toscanini records had acquired crinkled edges. As well as making me feel iller – iller, that is, than how ill I felt from the whiff of molten vinyl, as well as how ill I was already feeling anyway – their patent unplayability made me feel inadequate. Doubtless Maurice had too many toys: but I was in a position of trust, 'Position of truss,' I explained tearfully to Robin. Late that night, without her knowledge, I zigzagged down the corridor through the cairns of books and transferred the warped discs from the top of a stack of albums to the bottom, partly from the slim conviction that the weight would flatten them out, mainly in the pious hope that Maurice would never twig. After all, he had so much stuff.

Robin understood when I told her that I had to go to Italy. Françoise, the girl I had left behind in Australia, was now studying in Florence and could no doubt arrange accommodation while I spent a week recuperating from vinyl poisoning. I could tell that Robin understood because she didn't physically oppose my going, and in those days I construed absence of explicit opposition as a whole-hearted endorsement. I was careful to borrow some spending money as additional evidence of her goodwill. The petty cash left behind by Maurice would cover the plane ticket, and I planned to hitch-hike after I got to Milan. But there would be cigarettes to buy. Robin was the first to appreciate that a New Wave hero must have his cigarettes, which in Italy, I had heard, were hard to obtain. In my jeans, T-shirt, combat jacket, beard and dangling cigarette I reckoned I looked the sort of tough customer the Italians would take seriously. To complete the ensemble I had a bang-up-to-date pair of new shoes. Black winklepickers so long in the toe that the distance from the front of my foot to the front of the shoe was greater than to the heel, they looked dazzling down there. Even while staring straight ahead I could see the toes of my shoes in my peripheral vision. Equipped to kick the brains out of a fly, I had to walk with my feet slightly sideways, like a ballet dancer. Somehow I reached Gatwick, boarded a Dan-Air DC7-C charter flight, and headed for that far-off country the British call Europe.

12. FIORENZA, FIORENZA

Everything went fine until Milan, because the pilot was making all the hard decisions. After that I was on my own. Immediately people started behaving very strangely. I had already attracted a few sideways glances from some of the Italians on the plane, but here in the actual Italy the Italians stared openly. They formed groups so as to co-ordinate their unblinking scrutiny. At first I thought it was the shoes, but the immigration official couldn't see them from inside his glass booth, and he stared too. Did I bear a startling resemblance to the lost king Vittorio Emmanuele IV? Not too fanciful a notion, because it rapidly became apparent that the focus of interest was the beard. I had the only beard in Italy. (No kidding: the first modern native Italian beards were grown after the Florence floods, still some time in the future.) As I herringboned along in my winklepickers with my beard collecting dust, I must have struck the locals as a failed cross-country skier making fun of Garibaldi.

Another drawback was that nobody spoke English. As I was later to learn, you need only ten words of their language and the Italians will gladly help you with the rest, but at that stage I had only three words and a punctuation mark: 'Autostrada del Sole?' I was looking for the Highway of the Sun. When I said this phrase with an interrogative inflection while doing my gestural imitation of a six-lane highway, people crossed themselves. Some of them crossed the street. But a few brave souls pointed the way, so that after about two hours of doing my frog-man walk through the killing midday heat I had reached the highway at a spot where it looked like I might get a lift, if one of the hurtling cars would only stop. After another two hours one did. It had an English driver: a Unilever accountant who said he could take me as far as Piacenza. While I drank two bottles of orangeade out of a six-pack and the entire contents of a flask of mineral water, he explained that it wasn't just the beard which kept me rooted to the hard shoulder, it was also that hitch-hiking was forbidden. Dimly I remembered Françoise having told me that in her last letter. Receiving advice, ignoring it, and then later finding out the hard way how good it was, has been the story of my life. One of these days the Good Samaritan might fail to materialize, or might not have any orangeade with him when he does.

Just outside the Piacenza exit my saviour set me off at a point where I might conceivably pick up another lift south, but he warned me not to bank on it. After an hour and a half of watching Fiats, Lancias and Alfas go by both ways like an exchange of bullets, I got the point and started walking towards town. It was a long way and I was grateful when a three-ton truck heading in that direction slowed down and stopped just ahead. The old hooked thumb had worked at last. When the driver leaned out, he doubled my relief by speaking English.

'You want a lift?'

'Yes, actually.'

'Yes, actually. You from England?'

'Australia.'

'Australia. I hear your accent now. I was in Australia, at the Snowy River Project. I do not like Australians. Here in Italy we do not like the beard. I drive into town, get some of my friends, we come back and fix you good.'

On the other side of the roadside ditch there were cabbages growing among which I hid, but after about another hour it started looking probable that he would not come back, so I began walking again, this time without the extended thumb. The land smelled like piss but that could have been the way I felt. Having to turn my feet sideways even to limp successfully, I had a terrific pain in the ankle, so by the time I got to Piacenza railway station I had barely enough strength left to get my wallet out. Spending all my remaining money on a ticket to Florence was rendered needlessly complicated by the fact that none of the ticket-sellers had ever heard of the place. At last their supervisor showed up and set them straight by informing them that the city they had always referred to as 'Firenze' was in reality called Florence. It took a long time to sort out and I missed a train while it was happening, but the next train had a name – *accelerato* – that sounded fast enough to make up the difference.

It transpired that *accelerato* was the Italian word for 'stopping at

every station and going very slowly in between so as not to overshoot'.
I arrived at Florence long after dark and reached Françoise's *pensione*
near the Medici Palace long after that, having frequently lost my way
through being obliged to turn around and disperse the crowd following my beard. The landlady took one look at me and immediately
appointed herself Françoise's guardian. I was allowed into Françoise's
cool, terracotta-tile-floored room long enough to wash the dust from
my face, but the landlady stood in the doorway with her powerful
arms folded and large chin raised high, thereby abetting an already
remarkable physical resemblance to Mussolini. I ended up sleeping
on the floor of a partitioned-off section of a decrepit palace down
behind the Piazza della Signoria. The owner of the flat, a spotty but
sweet girl called Barbara, was an old school friend of Françoise's
from Australia. I don't owe Barbara any money – Françoise paid the
rent – but I owe her a lot for her time and concern, and it worries
me now that I didn't realize that then. When I met her again in
London the following year, I was short with her, instead of taking
the trouble to hark fondly back as she expected. Eventually too many
such incidents rankled enough to make me change my ways – to the
extent, anyway, of never taking any favours that I would not have
time to be grateful for. It sounds like a cold man's rule and I'm afraid
it is, but I was even worse before I thought of it.

My ill-judged arrival had put Françoise in a false position. Nowadays you have to go pretty far south in Italy before you encounter
the widespread belief that any foreign girl is a whore unless her father
and two brothers drive her around in an armoured car. In those days
the whole of Italy was like that. Françoise, clearly a well brought-up
girl, had been highly thought of in the *pensione* and therefore subject
only to the usual relentless innuendo from the male guests, actual
attempts at molestation and rape being confined to the street, down
which, since she did not look notably foreign, she walked at the same
hazard as any other presentable woman – i.e., young male pests,
known locally as *pappagalli*, followed her in cat-calling groups, while
older male pests appeared suddenly out of doorways or lunged from
cars in order to run a lightly touching hand over her bottom and
whisper obscenities in her ear. Though all this was standard stuff to
which she was well accustomed, I would shout with anger when I
saw it happen. I should have been angry with myself, because it was
my advent which had ensured that the *pensione* was no longer her

refuge. Françoise was now known to keep open company with a young man not her husband. Moreover, he had a beard, unacceptable shoes and shouted a great deal. The landlady, by dint of a long speech delivered in front of the assembled guests during which she profiled in true *il Duce* style with her chin as high as her forehead while they burst into spontaneous applause, made it clear to Françoise that I was to be met outside if at all.

To shave off the beard would have reduced the city-wide brouhaha to more manageable proportions, but my dander was up. We radical socialists could always be relied upon to take a stand when there was no hope of budging the status quo and every chance of embarrassing our friends. Françoise would have been well justified in washing her hands of me but she was a born educator. Angry, unbalanced and flailing as I was, I still found the great city opening up before me. She knew just where to take me. In the Uffizi I was stood in front of the Giotto madonna, the Portinari altarpiece by van der Goes, the Leonardo Annunciation and the two wide-screen Botticellis. In the Bargello I met Michelangelo's Brutus face to face. (He was on the first floor in those days: they put him downstairs after the flood.) To the Accademia for Michelangelo's slaves and to the Medici chapel for his times of day. Across the river to the Brancacci chapel, where I pretended to see, and perhaps already saw, the difference when Masaccio took over the job of painting the walls. It was Orientation Week all over again: the edited highlights, at which I still might have gagged unless wisely led. But Françoise was a real teacher and for once I was a serious student. It was a serious city. The surf of forgotten faces in the Gozzoli and Ghirlandaio frescoes I might conceivably have laughed off. Michelangelo's *terribilità*, when it transfixed me through the stone eyes of Brutus, shook the soul. It was so like being looked at by Françoise's landlady.

My self-esteem took a battering. Part of being overwhelmed by a big new subject is the shame of realizing that you knew nothing about it before. Helping me to feel worse were the twin facts that I ended up alone on Barbara's floor every night, and that whenever Françoise took me to meet her friends it rapidly turned out that everybody wanted to speak Italian except me. Or, rather, including me, except that I didn't know how. Up until that time I had been pleased, not to say proud, to remain monolingual. Now came the climb-down. I can even remember the moment. It was at an early-

evening drinks party on a grassy little hill behind a big house on the
other side of the Arno. The men had their sleeves rolled up in the heat
and the women were bare-shouldered in cool silk dresses and high-
heeled sandals. Françoise and her friend Gabriella were arguing with
Franco, an economics lecturer at Florence University and notable
contributor to the kind of film magazine, just then becoming prominent, edited by Bellocchio's cousin or Bertolucci's brother. Franco
had reacted against Wölflinn's line on the *cinquecento* to the extent
of proclaiming Andrea del Sarto no good at all, whereas the women
thought that the cartoons in the Chiostro della Scala were rather
marvellous. I had my own, perhaps half-baked, opinions on this
matter, but by the time I had persuaded Françoise to translate them,
the conversation had moved on to the merits of Fellini, with specific
reference to *Otto e mezzo*. Franco thought the film a fraud. Gabriella
disagreed. Françoise strongly disagreed, as well she might, because
we had seen the film together the previous evening, she for the
second time and I for the third, although it had been my first time
without the aid of subtitles. I disagreed so strongly that I took
Françoise aside, not really hurting her arm that much, and urgently
briefed her on my position. When we turned back to the conversation,
Franco and Gabriella were yelling at each other simultaneously, but
I forced Françoise to interrupt them and advance my argument. They
greeted it with raised eyebrows and embarrassed shiftings from foot
to foot. It was because of the irrelevance of Fellini's transcendental
imagination to the question of who might succeed Palmiro Togliatti
as leader of the Communist Party.

Experiencing inarticulacy for the first time since the cradle, I was
so frustrated that I dug the toes of my winklepickers into the hill and
stood there bouncing with unexploded energy, like a woodchopper on
his plank waiting for a signal that never came. That same night,
Françoise sat down beside me with a volume of Dante and construed
a few lines of the *Inferno* to begin showing me how the language
worked. *Per me si va tra la perduta gente.* Through me you go among
the lost people. A line that crushed the heart, but in the middle of
it you could say *tra la.* It was music.

Thus it was, when I reached Milan on the return journey and
was unable to pay the airport tax because of having bought too many
cigarettes at the railway station, that I was able, out of my ten-word
vocabulary, to come up with the one word required: *Disastro!* I said

it repeatedly with much wringing of hands, until an Indian passenger booked on my flight gave me 1,000 lire and waved aside all talk of repayment. I have liked Indians ever since. The alternative would have been to cast myself on the mercy of the Italian airport police, who all looked as if they were closely related to a certain truck driver in Piacenza.

Back in London, my problems had not gone away. Indeed while I had been away they had joined forces. Robin was cheesed off with me for some reason; Willis Cruft was accusing me of having cut him off from the petty cash; the builders had not only given up but taken to using the back garden as a storehouse for spare equipment; and Maurice's mother was on the premises to inform me that I must leave for Glyndebourne immediately. Rapidly adapting Maurice's dinner jacket to my differently arranged proportions, the grey-haired but energetic Lady Dillwick had her mouth full of pins half the time, but she spent the other half telling me that since Maurice had arranged to take a party to see *Capriccio* and then decided that he would rather go off to the Côte d'Azur instead, it was up to his substitute to fill in. Lady Dillwick's decisiveness was aided by her technique of not letting anyone else finish a sentence. This habit was later to be made familiar by Britain's first woman Prime Minister, but at the time it was a new one on me. As I stood there in my underpants while Lady Dillwick took up her son's satin-piped black trousers by about six inches, I did my best to disqualify myself for the task. 'I'm not even sure where Gly . . .' 'Maurice ought to realize that I've better things to do with my *time* than get him out of these messes.' 'How will I know wh—'

'Those pointed shoes won't be suitable at all.'

Maurice's patent leather pumps were three sizes too big for me so Lady Dillwick padded them with Kleenex. Trepidatiously setting off, I reached the taxi before the heels of the shoes left the house. Lady Dillwick waved me away with an air of 'There, that's *that* taken care of.' I had begun to get an inkling of why Maurice was the way he was. At Victoria I met my companions for the venture. They were a bald, decrepit avant-garde publisher, his beautiful but plastered interior-decorator wife, and his large, ageing, Central American senior editor, a woman who eked out an Elizabeth Bergner voice by wearing wooden jewellery and an ankle-length fur coat – rarely a wise idea in summer, even if the summer is English. On top of daring to import such marginal American writers as Alexander Lobrau (*The Beatified Deserters*) and Brad Krocus (*Absorbent Gauze Swabs* and *Violators Turned Away*), the publisher was currently notorious for staging the first of those Happenings by which London was now establishing its pioneering position of being only just behind New York. I had read about how he had invited fashionable society to a dark room off Shaftesbury Avenue full of actors pretending to be tramps and drunks, through which noisomely struggling mass the perfumed invitees had to find their way while the air filled with finely sprayed water and taped traffic noise. The assembled notables all agreed that this experience was somehow radically and liberatingly different from everyday life in the street outside. Unfortunately the publisher, who like so many promoters of the youth craze was in a state of advanced middle age compounded by bibulous excess, had got the idea that in an ideal world all the Happenings would join together with no intervening periods of the quotidian. He now had the brainwave, for example, of getting down to Glyndebourne without any of us purchasing a train ticket. If you did, you were a spoilsport. I'm sorry to say that I was craven enough to go along with this, instead of doing what I should have done, namely spoiling the sport. When we got off the train it turned out that we had to cheat on the bus too, with each of us pretending that someone else was paying. I was still blushing with shame and fear halfway through the first act of the opera. Then I started paying attention to one of the most hypnotic sounds I had heard in my life. It was the sound of the Central American senior editor, massive in the seat beside me, telling her string of wooden beads like a rosary.

During the picnic dinner at the interval my companions all had the chance to have a good laugh about how the emergency stitching in my trousers had started to come adrift. I did my best to divert their attention by explaining that this whole den of privilege and ridiculously attenuated pastiche would be enough reason in itself to start a socialist revolution forthwith. My fervour masked awkwardness. What with the difficulty I was experiencing in keeping my shoes on and my trousers from unfurling like the inadequately reefed sails of a pirate ship with a drunken crew, I had begun to feel a bit self-conscious. But most of the other men present were reassuringly scruffy. Here was my first lesson on the resolutely maintained untidiness and ill-health of the English upper orders. In baggy evening dress and old before their time, they displayed gapped and tangled teeth in loosely open mouths. Gently shedding dandruff, they lurched across the lawn. When they stood at the bar they looked like Lee Trevino putting. Here also would have been my first lesson in opera, but I found the piece too tenuous to grasp except for the Countess's long soliloquy, during which even the senior editor was charmed into interrupting her death-rattle. Doubtless the way Elisabeth Söderström looked was a help to me in focusing on how she sounded, but I would probably have been captured even had she been less graceful. For a few minutes I got a glimpse into an unsuspected realm of lyrical subtlety. Then the brusque rattling of the wooden beads began again.

Back to Victoria we scaled, one of my trouser legs now forming a black concertina above its canoe-like shoe. That was the night I should have packed it in: random pin money and inappropriate pay-offs did not add up to a salary, and keeping paint-spots off stacked books was the work of a scarecrow. Instead I stuck around. Robin, whose frown of welcome had soon melted into resignation, was there most evenings to cook a meal and help me move the heavier items of builders' equipment. It was a place to live; it was the sort of sinecure, I told myself, that artists had always taken with a clear conscience; and it was certain that Maurice, when he got back, would be better or at least no worse. So I let another three weeks of lightly disguised idleness go by. Luckily for appearances, if not for my conscience, I was actually hard at work transferring an unsaleable almost complete edition of John Galsworthy out of the way of the plasterers when Maurice's Jensen announced its arrival outside by ramming the builders' skip with its left headlight. Tanned the colour of butterscotch and still wearing his Côte d'Azur walking-out dress of rope-soled canvas shoes, lightweight seersucker slacks and a pale-blue T-shirt with a little white anchor, Maurice came bounding up the steps to announce that the positioning of the skip was evidence incontrovertibly establishing the conspiracy between the Piranesi Brothers and the team of Russian spies which MI5 had asked him to keep tabs on in Cannes.

Apparently that was why he had been gone so long. From his unobtrusive vantage point at a table beside the swimming pool in front of the Majestic, he had been surreptitiously photographing the Russian film delegates as they took their constitutional along the

Croisette each morning, make sense? Then it had emerged, in response to discreet enquiries, that a beautiful woman called Valentina Pirenucci was booked into the same hotel as the Russians. As Maurice excitedly began telling me about the love affair that he had almost had with her – he was being set up, he could see that now – he pushed a cigarette through the screen of foam joining his lips and lit it more than halfway down, almost at the filter. He looked accusingly at the flaming ruins of the cigarette. Then he looked accusingly at me. He wanted to know what I had accomplished. Apart from getting to Glyndebourne and back alive while dressed as Groucho Marx, I had accomplished nothing, so there was not a lot I could say. He looked at me as if I was part of the conspiracy. He was right. I was. Anyone who did any kind of business at all with Maurice was only helping him further into confusion. The decent thing to do was to get out straight away, and I had not done it. Now, too late, I tried to make up for my opportunism. But I had still not finished packing my bag that night when I heard, drifting along the corridor from Maurice's locked bedroom, the sound, horribly distorted, of the adagio of Beethoven's Ninth Symphony, conducted by Toscanini. Maurice had discovered the final piece of evidence. It all made sense.

13. LIKE A BURNISHED THRONE

Charlie came to my rescue, unfortunately. In that great age of the company director, Charlie was the company director epitomized. He had a one-man import-export business. He could get things for you. If you had things you didn't want, he could take them away. Around the Chelsea pubs he was a conspicuous figure, not just because of a major squint but because of his promiscuous taste in fast foreign cars. Peter Sellers had a new car every week but Charlie had a new one every day. On Monday it was a Maserati with a body by Touring of Milan and on Tuesday it was a Mercedes-Benz 300SL with gull-wing doors. None of the cars really worked, but he didn't own them long enough for them to stop working entirely. They stopped working entirely for the people he sold them to. While he was driving them, they went, just. 'Hop in,' Charlie would say from an out-of-date yet eternally beautiful Zagato-bodied 2 + 2 Ferrari. After you had hopped in, you would wonder why the car was going so slowly. You couldn't wonder it aloud because of the noise kicked up by the chain-driven overhead camshafts. At the next pub, Charlie would explain convincingly how everything would be all right tomorrow, once the drip-feed venturi to the rocker-boxes had been greased. 'Fancy another jar? Your round.'

Charlie said I could live on one of his boats: the one moored at Twickenham. The rent sounded stiff but he reassured me by saying that the boat was an ocean-going job. 'None of your put-put boats what fart about on a river.' As we headed west in an off-white Lancia Aprilia drop-head with my suitcase in the back, I had visions of a modest but comfortable state-room on the sort of yacht that would not be ashamed of itself if anchored in the lee of Niarchos or Onassis. And indeed *The Relief of Mafeking* was the biggest thing in the basin, but only because it was a coal barge. An ocean-goer in the sense that it had long ago made regular trips to and from Newcastle by sea rather than canal, my new home was so broad in the beam that it was practically circular. Charlie soon had me convinced that this was an advantage. 'Your so-called sleek lines can't give you this, mate,' he said with an expansive gesture in the living space between decks. 'What you've got here is width.' As we stood there with our heads bowed, I had to agree that there was width. What there wasn't was height, but I failed to remark this, being too excited by the prospect of the well-joined planks below and above. I hardly needed Charlie to tell me that there was no workmanship like that nowadays. He showed me how the Calor gas cooking ring worked, warned me that the toilet might be a bit tricky, and left me to unpack. Standing on deck to wave goodbye, I felt like Horatio Hornblower on the bridge of his first command. Lesser boats crowded the basin, in which the tide was so low that some of the water was hard to distinguish from mud. Presumably the smell would be less piercing when the water rose, and meanwhile the Lancia was a reassuring sight as it roared away, stopping only once while Charlie lifted the bonnet to tinker with the engine.

Flushing the toilet was no problem as long as the tide remained out. All you had to do was kick the foot-crank twenty or thirty times until with a loud *kerchunga* the bowl emptied into the bilges. When the tide came in, however, I was saddened to discover that the same process emptied the bilges into the bowl. By that time it was late at night and it had started to rain. The drumming of the rain on the deck was at first a comfort. But after a not very long time there was the less snug sound of the rain that was coming through the deck and dropping on my floor. It happened only where the fine workmanship of the planks was no longer reinforced by caulking. One such place was in the exact centre of the cabin, so that the puddle formed at the apex of the curved floor and distributed itself very evenly in all directions. A carefully positioned bucket could only delay this process, and anyway I didn't have one. So I went on deck in the driving rain, got down on my knees and found the hole. An old piece of canvas stretched across would soon fix that. There were no old pieces of canvas. I laid out one of my tea-coloured nylon drip-dry shirts and weighed it down around the edges with some bits of wood whose nautical name echoed vaguely in the memory. Belittling pins? Bollocks? The whole operation took no more than twenty minutes, so I didn't really get that much wetter than I would have if

I had stood in the centre of my cabin all night directly under the leak.

Next morning another drawback revealed itself. My new home was a long way from the centre of London. Unless Charlie turned up on some errand or other I would have to go in by train or Green Line bus. For a few days I waited for Charlie but it was becoming imperative to find a job, so finally I spent a whole morning getting to town and putting my name down to be considered by London Transport for a job on the tube. They were looking for guards, not drivers. This suited me. I couldn't drive a car but thought that I could probably guard a train, and perhaps work on the odd poem between stations. I could see myself being cheery, useful, a good man in a crisis. Trollope had designed the pillarbox. Keats, Chekhov and Schnitzler had all been doctors. T. S. Eliot had worked in a bank and Wallace Stevens for an insurance company. I would be a tube guard. Obviously I would be overqualified but I was willing to forget about that in return for a steady income and travel privileges – these latter being particularly welcome to someone living a long way away by water on a ship that could not sail. The next day, in the Singapore suit and the winklepickers, the beard trimmed with nail scissors, I sat down, with almost a hundred other candidates, for the intelligence test. Judiciously I soft-pedalled the brainy stuff, neglecting to mention my degree and doing my best to keep Schopenhauer's name out of it. I must have done all right because after half an hour's wait I was sent into another room for the psychological test. This time there were only about fifty candidates. The examiner sat at a desk. You were signalled forward to occupy the seat opposite him when the previous occupant had been dismissed, after a greater or shorter time. Obviously the long interviews were the more successful ones. Some of the interviews were as short as five minutes. Mine was the only one that lasted a minute and a half. I can remember the questions now. 'Why did you leave your last job?' 'Why did you leave the job before that?' 'And the one before that?' I can't recall my answers, except that they were short at first and grew progressively shorter. His closing statement, I thought, revealed a lack of sensitivity which helped to explain why, as a psychologist, he had risen no higher than the underground railway. 'You have failed the psychological test and we are unable to offer you a position.'

Failing to get down that hole was my low point. Or so I thought, assuming that the task was easy. Actually such jobs – being a postman is another one I still covet – demand exactly the sort of elementary yet responsible alertness that the congenital dreamer is least qualified to give. There is a consoling passage in *Dichtung und Wahrheit* about our capabilities being forecast by our dreams, although it might just mean that Goethe would have made a lousy tube guard. But I was still far short of a full self-appraisal. I was also short of cash. Robin, who worked in a Baker Street bookshop, trekked out to Twickenham often enough to keep me from dying of malnutrition, but the fares and the food used up a disheartening proportion – disheartening even for me, let alone for her – of whatever was left over from keeping herself alive. Where was Charlie?

He arrived one morning at the wheel of a Lagonda, handed me a parallel text of *Les Fleurs du mal*, and told me to bring my tooth-brush because we were going to Paris. If I helped him load some furniture into his van in London and unload it in the Flea Market in Paris, there would be something in it for me and I would see the City of Light. The noise of the Lagonda drowned the actual mention of how much the something was. Lagondas were not supposed to be noisy. This one had gearbox trouble. But the van, to which we transferred at Charlie's lock-up garage in Fulham, worked well enough. It was a little blue Bedford tailgate number whose rear tray we carefully filled with solid English furniture – old rosewood military chests and stuff like that. When we reached Dover, I was impressed but not surprised to hear Charlie tell the British customs men that the gear, all French originally, had belonged to his French-born great-aunt, long resident in England, who had recently died tragically of cancer, of the rectum in point of fact, so that the residue of her worldly goods was now returning to her bereaved half-sister in Auteuil. While this was being said I sat there reading Baudelaire as instructed, no doubt to give the impression of being part of the household. At Calais, Charlie told the French customs men that the stuff was all English, of negligible value as you could tell from the chipped inlays, and that it was on its way to furnish the flat of the eccentric new Paris bureau chief of the *Financial Times*. Behold his artistically gifted son, soon to be studying French literature at the Sorbonne. Charlie got most of this across with gestures but there was quite a bit of French mixed in. I was so dumbfounded that I must have looked artistically gifted, because the *douaniers* waved us through. Since the furniture plainly *was* English, and therefore not part of *le patrimoine*, perhaps they didn't care whether Charlie was profiteering or not. Anyhow, we were soon bowling happily down the *route nationale*, with the poplars strobing away on each side.

Under a bright sun we made good time but it was a bit bumpy. Some of the lashings in the back came unstuck so I was standing up there to keep a chest of drawers and a cupboard from knocking into each other when Charlie tooted the horn and I looked ahead and saw Paris. The city lay low among the hills like a dry lake of violet talcum with a little pistachio model of the Eiffel Tower sticking up. It was the Eiffel Tower. Delirium at first glance.

At the Flea Market our consignment of furniture sold out straight away. Charlie handed me my commission: a wad of jokey paper napkins with coloured pictures of people like Richelieu and Mazarin. The wise move would have been to hand the money straight back to him and thus clear up what I would soon owe for rent, but instead I toured the open-air bookstalls along the banks of the Seine, bending over the green-painted bins like a starving parrot over a box of seeds. Books in French scarcely counted as a wise purchase, since I couldn't read more than the odd word of them, but I was working on the assumption that one day I would be able to. Charlie had friends in Paris with whom we had dinner. I didn't enjoy it much because they spoke little English and looked as if they had been left out of a crime movie starring Jean Gabin because they were too sinister. This especially applied to the women. Charlie's *mauvais garçon* squint fitted right in. The rest of him fitted in too: he spoke the international language of where to get things. I couldn't keep up. But the wine I handled quite well, needing, when I bunked down on somebody's floor, scarcely any help to undress. A less clouded happiness came next morning, when I sat outside a café at the crossroads of the Boulevard Saint-Michel and the Boulevard Saint-Germain, drank cognac and watched the girls on their way to work. I had never seen so much prettiness all in the one place. Charlie explained how they did it, with their small wages all going on clothes and nowhere to live except a cold-water broom cupboard. 'Your actual Frog bird,' he announced, 'has got eyes of her own.' Though my own eyes were as yet untrained, I could see straight away that the silk-and-cotton-clad shop assistant clicking along on her way to the Galeries Lafayette was an entirely different proposition from her London counterpart, teetering towards C & A in a black-lacquered hair helmet, cadaverous white face-mask, laddered tights and a skirt no bigger than her belt. It was the difference between *chic* and shock. Calling myself studious, I ogled unashamed, until Charlie said it was time to go.

Zonked by the cognac I slept all the way to London. At Fulham, Charlie climbed into the Lagonda and went somewhere else, so with his strong hints about the desirability of a prompt rent settlement still echoing in my ears I got back to the barge by Green Line bus in time to discover how the deck looked after the tide had gone far enough out to prove the theory – common among the basin's regular inhabitants, I now learned – that *The Relief of Mafeking* had been incorrectly moored. The tide was back in again but a lot of the caulking on deck had gone missing from between the planks. I found some of it in my cabin. My bed, which had been a mattress with a blanket on it, was now a mattress with a blanket and bits of tar on it. Luckily they were too old to be still sticky.

Paying a return visit as arranged, Françoise arrived at Gatwick and with her usual cool head found her way, against all the odds, to my floating palace. I would have met her at the airport, but for some reason Robin wouldn't lend me the money. The tide was out and the yacht basin wasn't looking its best. There was something particularly depressing about how the brown milk bottles sticking up out of the mud were full of water. Standing at the foot of the gangway, Françoise looked out of place in her blue silk blouse, pale-grey straight skirt and hand-made high-heeled suede sandals. She had always had the gift of bringing order and elegance to her surroundings. This new challenge, her expression suggested, might be beyond her. Showing her down to my quarters, I made a nervous joke about Pandora and the Flying Dutchman, before remembering that Pandora was the wrong name to mention. So I switched the frame of reference to Cleopatra's barge.

It didn't rain, so at least we didn't get wet. But without rain there was no relief from the heat. The tide came in and did something to tame the smell, but it did nothing for the toilet, which turned out to be the final insult. In a few days Françoise did a lot to make the place habitable and my intake of foodstuffs less toxic. I was eating salads and there was a pillowcase on the pillow. But a toilet that worked in reverse was too much. Until it should be time for her charter flight back to Italy, she went to stay with the girls in Melbury Road.

Gallantly I carried her suitcase. There was a party going on when we arrived. Robin was there, looking a bit distant for some reason. Françoise didn't look very tolerant either so I danced with a tall girl called Joanne who had recently got off the boat. I told her that I had recently got off a boat too. Just when I had got her laughing at the story about the blow-back toilet her boyfriend moved in on her, so I found myself talking to an old acquaintance from Sydney called Nick Thesinger. At Sydney University Nick had been the star actor of his final year just as I was starting off as a freshman. He had left for England with the high hopes of his friends filling his sails, although he himself had always been realistic enough to guess that London needed Australian actors the way Newcastle upon Tyne needed coal from Newcastle, NSW. So it had proved, and within a year he had been forced into supply teaching, to eke out what he called 'a small competence' of money from home. But school teaching had soon become more than just a living. 'At Stratford, I'd be lucky to carry a spear a year,' he explained. 'At the dear old school I'm simply *forced* to play Macbeth, Hotspur and Richard III every morning, with Hamlet for lunch and Lear in the afternoon. One's thespian urges aren't just satisfied, darling. The relevant glands are *squeezed dry*.' His teacher's salary plus the small competence enabled him to keep a set of rooms just off Baker Street. He had a spare bedroom, into which I was invited to move as soon as was practicable. As to rent, the sum mentioned was more than I had, yet so would have been any other sum no matter how small, because next morning everything I had left went on getting back to the barge and leaving a token pay-off for Charlie. You couldn't really have called it a midnight flit. For one thing, it was daylight. For another, the rent I owed him was more than offset, in my opinion, by the psychic and perhaps physical damage inflicted by the leaking ceiling and the retrodynamic dunny. I drew up a sort of account sheet explaining all this, weighed it down with a few coins, packed my bag and headed down the gangplank towards the Green Line bus stop, watched by a large woman with piled-up ginger hair who was sunbathing in bursting bra and colossal pink satin bloomers on the deck of a small launch which at first appeared to be listing under her weight, but which on closer examin- ation proved to be stuck in the mud with one side propped up by the rust-eaten remains of a wrought-iron bedstead. The nautical phase of my life was over.

The musical phase now began. Like Françoise a born teacher, Nick was one of those opera fanatics with the gift of putting you on rather than off. In Australia I had discovered jazz because nobody at Sydney University could very well escape it. Classical music had come to me later and piecemeal. On swimming parties to Avalon with the Bellevue Hill mob at weekends, I had acquired their taste for such stirring stuff as Haydn's trumpet concerto and Beethoven's Seventh. In London I had become intimate with Beethoven's Ninth in the manner already related. More happily, Joyce Grenfell had taken me to the Festival Hall to see the Borodin Quartet play Beethoven's late quartets and Klemperer conduct Bach's Brandenburg concertos. I say 'see' rather than 'hear' because I couldn't take my eyes off the Borodin cellist's tapping foot or Klemperer's right index finger, especially the latter. As the old master sat there in his wheelchair, it was the only part of him that could still move.

But these were scattered experiences and no trained voice had been involved save Söderström's in *Capriccio*, heard intermittently through the machine-gun beads of my companion at Glyndebourne. Nick gave me an immersion course, starting with two scenes in *Der Rosenkavalier*: the Presentation of the Silver Rose and the last act trio. From the first day of this exposure, the bathroom rang to my imitation of Sena Jurinac, Elisabeth Schwarzkopf and Teresa Stich Randall. Lacking the vocal equipment to impersonate any of these women singly, I compromised by providing a vigorous pastiche of all three singing together. Pleased instead of panic-stricken at what he had wrought, Nick moved on to Verdi. From an old set of *Trovatore* the gold-rush chest-voice of Zinka Milanov reached to thrill me. Wagner was introduced through Lotte Lehmann and Lauritz Melchior singing the love duet from *Tristan*. Next came Wotan's farewell and the magic fire music from *Die Walküre*, conducted by Knappertsbusch, whose always-advancing quietness I was taught to value above the vertical clamour of Solti's complete *Ring*, released on Decca that very year. My prejudice against Solti – justified, I still believe, in the case of Wagner – was to remain fervent for years afterwards, until the lyrical flow of his *Eugene Onegin* made me think again. But prejudices were part of the enthusiasm, just as jealousy is part of passion. I went opera mad, and all because of Nick. He knew where to drop the needle – an especially important qualification in the matter of Wagner, with whom it is an invariable rule that the most immediately accessible bits are never at the edge of the disc.

Then there was Mozart. 'Lisa della Casa,' Nick would say, lying back in a winged chintz-covered chair with his eyes closed and his fingertips together, 'is a bear of very little brain, but you have to remember that *so was Wolfgang's wife.*' And at that moment, on the highlights record drawn from the wonderful old Erich Kleiber set of *Le nozze di Figaro*, the lady in question would sing the first notes of '*Dove sono*' for the tenth time on the trot. I wallowed like a hippo. It was a mud-bath in concentrated beauty. One doesn't love literature, said Flaubert. Though he said so because he was re-inventing it and the labour hurt, he would have been right anyway. Music we can love.

But the gramophone was merely an adjunct. The main means of instruction was the opera house itself. We were in the amphitheatre or the gods at Covent Garden almost every night. The nights we weren't, we were at Sadler's Wells, getting into training with the English version for something that would show up in the real language at the Garden later on. Nick was in no doubt about the Englishing of a foreign opera: it was strictly a leg-up for getting to grips with the original, in which the language was not just inseparable from the melody but formed its living spine. During the intervals of *Falstaff* we would adjourn to the bar so that Nick could discuss with his friends how Tito Gobbi or Geraint Evans was handling the big challenge. Nick's friends called each other 'love' a lot but they were all omniscient, so I assumed that they had good reasons for booing Galina Vishnevskaya at several points during *Aida*. Later on, however, I started to wonder whether it hadn't been because she was showing too much leg.

Because Nick's friends were queer without exception. Or, rather, with one exception: me. Whether through innocence or an opportunistic disinclination to complicate such a rich source of free enlightenment, I failed for a long time to rumble Nick's true sexual allegiance. The young sailors who arrived at midnight and disappeared into his bedroom would reappear at breakfast. Perhaps he was picking up extra money teaching a workers' extension course. Noises of wrestling came through the wall at night. Perhaps he was practising judo. At long last I realized why Nick wore such a forced smile when Robin came to call. Indeed it was Robin who told me. She also told me how unfair I was being. It wasn't just because I had nothing with which to pay the rent that I was getting away with paying no rent. Nor did all those tickets for Covent Garden grow on trees. Even when you sat so high in the gods that the stage looked like a postage stamp crawling with ants, it still cost a lot of money to be present on the night Birgit Nilsson kept drilling Brünnhilde's climactic notes right through the middle while Valhalla, which was supposed to fall, got caught in the scrim up which the Rhine, in the form of projected green light, was supposed to rise. She sang like a train coming while the set malfunctioned all around her. It was heroic art and it all had to be paid for. Nick was allowing himself to be taken advantage of, but I was still taking advantage. Once again it was time to move on.

Yet I was moving on with two acquisitions that would serve me well. One was an awakened love for the exultant human voice. The other was a reinforced tolerance for homosexuality. Previously I had never been against it, but had shared the usual delusion that it must be some sort of disease. After living with Nick and receiving the benefit of his knowledgeable, critical, yet wholeheartedly dedicated love of music, I came to believe that it was a necessary and valuable part of life. Two of my great heroes, Proust and Diaghilev, would have convinced me eventually. Proust's article about Flaubert, or that marvellous essay by Diaghilev in which he takes Benois to task for the deficiency of his historical view, would have been enough to persuade me that there is a quality of intellect, a generous precision of humane judgment, which, so far from being damaged by inverted sexual proclivities, is probably enhanced by them. But the job had already been done by a not always happy, always smiling school teacher who so munificently showed me where to find, at the start of the second side of the Beecham set of *La Bohème*, the duet in which Victoria de los Angeles and Jussi Björling celebrate the beatific prospect of going to bed together. I still find it difficult to believe that Nick and his sailors felt the same way, but to believe otherwise would be an impertinence. Some people are different from the rest of us, and so are the rest of us.

14. BACK TO SQUARE ONE

Homosexuality was not Dave Dalziel's problem. Many people called him mad, but nobody ever called him queer. You would have been able to tell he had arrived in England just by how the girls at Melbury Road went starry-eyed. They stopped giving each other haircuts copied from Mary Quant advertisements and started making group appointments at the hairdresser. Dalziel, for as long as I cared to remember, had drawn women like mosquitoes to a sleeping man. It wasn't because he was good-looking, although he was. It wasn't because he cleaned his nails and dressed in spruce clothes, although he did. It was because he was obsessed. Dave Dalziel was movie mad. He was determined to be a film director, although there had been no Australian film director since Charles Chauvel, mainly because there was no Australian film industry. Very well, an Australian film industry would have to be created.

Meanwhile Dalziel was in Europe to learn more about the craft of his art. He had a short-subject script to shoot and a rich friend, Reg Booth, who would finance the project at the price of being allowed to star. Actually Reg was rich only in comparison to the rest of us, so the money had to be deployed with great care. Dalziel worked all day on preparing this movie. In what spare time he had he saw other movies. He breathed, ate and slept movies. As a consequence, women went silly about him. It was because he had no time to be silly about them. The rest of us chased women and looked foolish doing it. He let them chase him and looked fine. I would have hated him for it if he had been less good company, but if you allowed for his occasional patch of near insanity he was too funny to pass up. Like all truly entertaining talkers he rarely told jokes. He just had a way of putting things. There was a big party on the top floor at Melbury Road to mark the official end of summer. Dalziel suddenly materialized and addressed me as if we had parted only the day before.

'I hear you've been living with a horse's hoof,' he drawled. It emerged that he and Reg had just taken a flat in Warwick Road, on the other side of Kensington High Street, and were looking for a third man to share the rent. 'Here's your chance to play Harry Lime. Also we need someone to keep the landlady quiet, who is a MONSTER. How would you like to slip her the pork sword?'

He always talked like that. The metaphors were so mind-boggling that you found yourself doing what he wanted. A dominant personality doesn't have to believe in its own will. All it needs is the inability to recognize the existence of anybody else's. My suitcase and several string-handled paper shopping bags full of books were downstairs in the hall. Dave, Reg and Robin helped me carry them to Warwick Road, although Robin, to my annoyance, clearly would have been glad to carry the whole lot just to be near Dave. Reg won't mind my saying this, because many times in the following year we bent elbows at the pub for the specific purpose of discussing Dalziel's demoralizingly unfair share of charm, which we were agreed gave rise to, or was possibly even caused by, grave simplicities in the brain. Reg also won't mind my saying that his script was no world-shaker. Even as I moved into the Warwick Road flat, principal photography was about to begin. From the way Mrs McHale, the middle-aged and bitterly irascible landlady, stood permanently by the staircase with her arms folded, you could tell that a top-floor flat with three heterosexual young Australian men in it was already well beyond the limits of what she would ordinarily be prepared to put up with. If her lips had been any more pursed they would have fallen off. You could also tell, from the way she tapped her prominently veined and sinewed foot, that she thought the young men had too many visitors even in normal circumstances – especially female visitors, whose presence necessitated her taking up an invigilating position on the landing outside our flat so that she could make frequent unannounced entrances through the door compulsorily left open. In the week before the camera turned on page one of the script there were a lot more visitors of both sexes. Mrs McHale's foot became a blur. Young actresses auditioning as extras arrived in mini-skirts which Mrs McHale clearly regarded, not without reason, as tantamount to nudity. Men with silver boxes full of hired equipment and tea-chests full of scavenged props endangered the threadbare carpets and crappy wallpaper which Mrs McHale cherished as if the Victoria and Albert Museum could be restrained from appropriating them to its collection only by armed force. We called her Hearty McHale, in the way that a wrathful deity is given nicknames to make it less awful. What she was calling us was beyond guessing, but at the annual World Landladies' Rally in the Munich beer hall she would no doubt have plenty to say when her turn came at the banked microphones. 'They get like that,' said Dave wisely, 'when they don't get enough of the veal dagger.'

Applying listlessly for jobs during that period, I had plenty of spare time to help with the movie, and for acting as substitute focus-puller while playing a small part I got ten pounds for each week of the fortnight it took to shoot. The film, written by Reg with additional dialogue by Dave, was a mystery about an unnamed man, played by Reg, who works as a hit-man for the Organisation and then finds out that the Organisation is trying to eliminate him, etc. Called *The Man from the Organisation*, it would have been the least mysterious mystery in the world if not for my focus-pulling, which gave some of the shots – the really vital ones, too expensive to be done again – an extra quality of ambiguity. Yet my acting was precise, even pedantic. In the key scene where I impersonated a passer-by in the street who turns to look at the seriously wounded hero, I walked the prescribed eighteen paces, paused for the three seconds required, and turned looking puzzled, exactly as instructed. Next day's rushes showed how exact I had been. You could see me silently counting to eighteen, moving my lips as I counted to three, and then looking as if I had been asked to expound Heisenberg's uncertainty principle. 'You'll have to do it again tomorrow unless we can get George C. Scott,' said Dave, making a note. 'Asking you to play someone you're not is like asking King Kong to play the Moonlight Sonata.' He was right. In later years my acting has improved, if only in the sense that I have got better at being myself.

During that hectic fortnight I learned a little about filming and a lot about Dalziel. I could see now that he wasn't always mad. Sometimes he was just concentrating. When he ignored what you were talking about and started a new conversation in the middle of your sentence, it was because he hadn't heard you. He attacked one crisis after another without any sign of artistic temperament. In sharp distinction to the rest of us, he didn't behave like an artist at all. He behaved like a truck-driver who has to get a load of perishable goods to a certain destination by a certain time. His creative resources were considerable, but invisible because fully committed. There was nothing left over with which to pose. Perhaps the logistic demands of his medium had matured him early. In my own medium, which makes few practical demands beyond the securing of an adequate supply of stationery, coming down to earth takes longer. But here again, and as usual, it was probably a matter of personality. Dave was simply the way he was. Once his single-mindedness had looked like dementia. Now it looked like obduracy. It didn't take a prophet to realize that one day it would look like talent.

Photography completed, *The Man from the Organisation* moved into what Dave called its post-production phase. In other words work stopped completely while they figured out how to pay for the editing. Reg was no longer rich and had to get a job as a driver with a luxury hire-car firm. This came in handy for allaying the spleen of Hearty McHale, because when Reg temporarily parked a Daimler or a Bentley in front of the house she got the idea that at least one of us was in funds. Reg spoiled it all one evening by forgetting to take off his cap. Dave, with characteristic practicality, had already arranged a short-term job in a Hammersmith builder's yard called Cornwall's Erections. He had underestimated, however, the physical labour involved. At sunset he would come reeling home too tired to wash off the grime. Usually there was some adoring woman who had been hanging around with no other aim in life beyond swabbing the caked dirt off his shoulders and bowed neck. When there wasn't, Reg and I took over. Even with these emollient side-benefits the job was clearly another case of Dalziel's extraordinary dedication to the task in hand. It made me feel queasy about borrowing money from him. Most of what I had earned from filming was already owed, which induced an anxiety that made me smoke more. Nor could it be denied that Warwick Road was situated less in Kensington than in Earls Court. I was back to where I had started, except lower down. Winter was almost upon us and I felt like the pariah of the pack. Even Robin, most generous of attendant angels, was looking at me with a curled lip.

Luck landed me my best job yet. A long, insane letter I had written to Penguin Books suggesting that they publish my collected

trasty, making the women's faces look like Kabuki masks, while the photographers looked like East End criminals. There were pictures of East End criminals looking like company directors. In the text there was invariably a lot of talk about the disappearance of class divisions, the adduced evidence being that a pacey young designer from Tower Hamlets had married a duke's daughter. There would be a picture of the duke's daughter wearing the young designer's designs. Located without any connecting tissue inside the perimeter of the bleached-out facial area, her enormous black-rimmed eyes and grainy grey mushroom mouth looked surprised at her own daring: three blots on white cardboard. The vacant were being given *carte blanche* to adore themselves. Once the enviable had looked human but hard to get at. Now they looked inhuman and further off than ever.

For those of us with our noses pressed to the glass, the reality of the swinging new era was a dance party to which you brought your own bottle. But as the news about the allegedly effervescent London reached Australia, ship-loads of would-be revellers and social revolutionaries came sailing towards the putative action. Inevitably they all ended up at the bottle party. People I had left Australia to get away from started turning up in bunches – intellectuals who had read three books; writers who had read no books at all and would never write one either; pub singers who would forget the words of their sea-shanties unless you were unlucky. They filed on to the buses at Southampton and debouched into Earls Court by the well-drilled platoon.

Less organized on principle but no more reticent, those members of the Downtown Push who were still young enough to travel arrived in dribs and drabs. The woodwork was the whole world thick but out of it they came crawling, still full of theories about the repressive mechanisms of a society which allowed them to indulge their every whim. Grecian Ern Papadakis arrived, his famous book on Trotsky as yet unpublished, mainly because it remained unwritten. Not far behind him came Ross Peters the Prestige Pie-eater, an expert on Reich's orgone theories who had once received a letter from Reich himself. These men were legends and had the women to prove it: lank-haired, taciturn creatures with approximately depilated bare legs, their shoulders hunched from constant listening.

One night at Melbury Road, half cut and wholly content in the midst of the writhing throng, I had just finished shaking to a Beatles track when I was horrified to hear the actual living squeal of Johnny Pitts, the Push folksinger who had for ten years unsuccessfully attempted to emigrate from Australia so as to go to South America and – I quote the wording of his passport application – fight for anarchy. At last they had made the mistake of letting him out, and now he was here. As usual he thrashed his guitar, whined a few bars about bad working conditions in some American correctional facility, and fell sideways. Somebody put the Beatles back on and the crowded room danced again, but it had been a bad moment. Sitting exhausted in a corner with a woman kneeling at each arm and another soothing his forehead from behind, Dalziel suddenly looked haunted. The past was catching up.

But you could always outrun it. One place we ran to was the Iron Bridge Tavern, deep in the East End. Queenie Watts and a friend of hers called Shirley sang jazz there every Saturday. We used to go down there in Dingo Kinsella's apology for a car. Dingo was a spidery journalist serving a one-year stretch in the London bureau of one of the Sydney newspapers. This meant that he was being paid an Australian salary, which in turn meant that he was, by our standards, wealthy. If he had drunk less seriously he would have been driving a Facel Vega at the very least. As things were, he locomoted in what must have been the last roadworthy example of the old upright Ford Popular. A car that had never been popular with anybody I knew of, it held all of us in acute discomfort. Dingo drove the way he drank, as if he wanted to die. But since the Popular's top speed wasn't much higher than that of a walking man, we were all agreed that it was worth the risk. Every Saturday, Dingo would give three toots on the horn and we would all pile out of the house to go looking for the car in the next street. Hearty McHale refused to let him park the machine even momentarily in front of her salubrious establishment, lest property values should be lowered still further.

On the way down the long East India Dock Road to the pub the car would weave from side to side in a sine curve of about ten feet amplitude and a hundred feet pitch. At the Iron Bridge we would listen to the happily shouting trad band until time was called and we were thrown out. On the road home the car ran straight and level, because when Dingo got blotto beyond a certain point he seized up solid. Turning corners remained a problem, which we could sometimes solve by getting him to close his eyes and talking him through it. In a faster car this would have been fatal. To us it was just part of what Bruce Jennings might have called a Rewarding Experience for the Young People.

15. THE GREEN GLADIOLUS

Dressed as a deliberate caricature of an English gentleman from the late gasolier period, Bruce Jennings had been in London longer than anyone and was both appalled and delighted that the rest of Australia now seemed bent on joining him. He was appalled because, without being in any way servile, he had submitted himself to Europe and was by now ten years deep into a love affair that the new arrivals looked determined to consummate in five minutes. He was delighted because they provided him with raw material. I suppose Reg and myself were included in his field of observation. But Jennings' interest in Dave was more than just clinical. He recognized a fellow talent. His memories of home sharpened by exile, Jennings was the first Australian writer-performer to exploit the Australian idiom for its full poetic value. He had a fine ear and the learning to back it up. Dave, though an avid general reader, had only the ear. But Jennings valued Dave's ability to fish a phrase up out of childhood and throw it flapping on the table. 'Fair suck of the pineapple,' Dave would say in protest when I tried to hit him for a quid at Wally's, and Jennings' eyes would go shiny. He'd forgotten that one.

Wally's was the greasy spoon in a lane behind Warwick Road. It served plates of fat. You could have sausages in your fat or fried eggs in your fat. You could have the sausages and the fried eggs together, but it meant you got more fat. We ate at Wally's most evenings because the price of cooking at home was a stream of protest notes from Hearty McHale about noise, smells, smoke, fire and the lettuce leaf so vandalously trodden into the hallway carpet. Wally's was a strange place to find the fastidious Jennings – who was known to take luncheon at Rules in the company of his admirer, John Betjeman – but he dropped in a couple of times during the period when he and Dave were discussing the possibility of a movie. I secretly laughed this possibility to scorn, not yet having realized that the ability to plan in the long term, while retaining the capacity to tell a long-term plan from a wild dream, is crucial to success in any of the collaborative arts. I thought they were both a bit nuts.

Jennings left you in no doubt of his brilliance, though in some fear that his monologues might never end. A career drinker, he would stand balefully in the middle of a party, the only man present in a Turnbull & Asser shirt, antique Chavet tie, pin-stripe double-breasted Savile Row suit, Lobb shoes, black fedora and a monocle. 'Des is the name,' he would loudly confide to an invisible interlocutor, 'Des Esseintes.' And indeed he was the hero of *A Rebours* to the life, a Count Robert de Montesquiou *de nos jours*, creating himself as a work of art. He didn't have the living tortoise inset with turquoises but no doubt it was on order. Meanwhile he had everything else, and I was wide-eyed even as he stood there swaying. When he fell to the floor he would usually take a couple of people with him. Laid to rest on a sofa, he would sleep until the party thinned out. Then, with just the right-sized audience, he would start a closed-eyed, resonant muttering which might consist of nothing but brand-names and radio jingles from the far Australian past. 'Rosella Tomato Sauce . . . Twice As Nice If Kept On Ice . . . Sydney Flour is our flour, we use it every day . . . I like Aeroplane Jelly, Aeroplane Jelly for me . . . You'll sleep tight 'cause you'll sleep right, on a Lotusland inner-spring mattress . . .'

Years later I was to realize that this was the most original side of his mind talking. He was rediscovering and reordering an Australian language which had never had any pretensions beyond the useful and had thus retained an inviolable purity. It was the language written on bottles of cough medicine and packets of junket powder: a vocabulary without any value beyond common currency, and therefore undiluted by aesthetic pretension. With a sure instinct reinforced by his dandy-ish collector's erudition, he had realized that not all the ephemeral was evanescent – that there was such a thing as a poetry of trivia, uniquely evocative for a country whose art was hag-ridden by a self-conscious striving towards autonomous respectability. Jennings was already well embarked on a salvage expedition to raise a nation's entire cultural subconscious. The obtuse among his country's intellectuals – a high proportion – thought he was lowering the tone, and belittled him accordingly. He armoured himself by polishing his façade still more brightly. Delacroix, said the doomed Jean Prévost in his wonderful book about Baudelaire, was a dandy not because he wanted to impose his superiority but because he wanted to defend it. Similarly Jennings retreated ever further into his own effulgence, taunting his detractors with the dazzling pages of an open book – the lexicon of their lost youth.

At the time, however, I couldn't get interested in any of that, since it concerned Australia, and Jennings' Australia, through being so vivid, only lit up what I was still trying to leave. It was Jennings' Europe that attracted me. Jennings could tell you what Satie had said about Ravel. I knew what Hemingway had said about Gertrude Stein, but Jennings knew what Gertrude Stein had said about Picabia, because he owned the letters. He also owned a Picabia. For Jennings, the side-trails of the old international avant-garde were a stamping ground. I thought then, and still think now, that it is more important to be familiar with the major artistic works than knowingly conversant with the minor artists, but Jennings wasn't as easy to fault there as one might have thought. Just because he knew a lot about Honegger didn't mean that he was an ignoramus about Haydn. Jennings was formidable. I didn't envy him his talent, being conceited enough to believe that I had some of my own. I did envy him his well-stocked mind. Actually I should have envied him his talent too: stocking your mind isn't the same as stacking crates in a warehouse. It's a gift.

So is being a landlady. Either you run the show, or the show runs you. Hearty McHale was determined to be mistress in her own house. It followed ineluctably that we were on borrowed time. We were careful to have no parties. We rarely cooked anything more complicated than half a pound of frankfurts. But we were an epicentre of unpredictability. Hearty McHale's mental equilibrium depended on a silent house full of closed doors, with nothing moving except rent. The only acceptable noise in her establishment was the restrained clamour made by money as it transferred itself from the tenant's wallet into the owner's bank account. From there, according to rumour, the loot went to Spain and was sunk into a block of flats affording a view of the sea to any British mountain-climbing holiday-maker equipped with powerful binoculars.

Such was the system which our mere presence disturbed. If we had been trainee Trappists we might have lasted longer. As things were, the crisis came closer every day. In the evenings I would stagger upstairs with heaps of Penguin books for my growing library. When one of these heaps collapsed in my arms, an extruded copy of *The Psychopathology of Everyday Life* inflicted minor but detectable damage on the hallway rubber plant. Hearty McHale reacted as if I had thrown a phosphorous grenade. She had already warned me that the beams under my area of the floor were not designed to hold up the British Museum reading room. Books, however, were a negligible irritant compared with women. Reg had a very quiet Australian girlfriend whom he planned to, and subsequently did, marry. Mostly he visited her instead of she him, but she turned up in Warwick Road on two occasions and for Hearty McHale two meant two hundred. Robin came to me at least once a week because it was not practicable for me to take to her the clothes that needed ironing, darning, mending, replacing, etc. Unless these missions of mercy could be accurately timed by the synchronization of watches and the use of semaphore from the top window, they necessarily entailed the ringing of the downstairs front doorbell, which Hearty McHale interpreted as the prelude to nuclear attack.

But it was Dave's female admirers who tipped the already precarious balance. When he loved them and left them, some of them failed to get the point, and came looking for him. Reg and I spent a lot of time sitting in the kitchen with a lissome yet decidedly hysterical actress called Bambi who was reluctant to believe that Dave had had to depart suddenly for Easter Island. Leaving one cigarette still smouldering in the ashtray on the kitchen table, she would light several others while compulsively searching the flat. Reg would trail her, catching the ash in his cupped hands before it hit Hearty McHale's moth-eaten though purportedly invaluable carpet. Dave was curled up in the loft above the bathroom. He was so tired after a day's work at Cornwall's Erections that he didn't care where he slept, so it was all right for him. But it was tough on us, and finally we rebelled. Perhaps we were offended by what he could afford to turn down. An evening came when we declined to stall Bambi and she caught him still in the bath. It was the luxury bubblebath we gave him each Friday. Friday was payday and we would count his money as he lay in deep foam after another dedicated week of selfless toil. Taking the sponge from me and the loofah from Reg, Bambi arrogated to herself the task of cleansing and anointing the exhausted hero. Reg and I retreated to the kitchen for half a bottle each of

Woodpecker cider, a few hands of gin rummy and some ill-disguised fits of jealousy. When Hearty McHale burst in, her pulsatingly veined feet were about six inches off the linoleum, thus indicating the speed she had attained going up the final flight of stairs. She evinced the special fury reserved for when it was Dave who was receiving the female visitor. Brushing our feeble reassurances aside, she headed for the bathroom, with Reg and me close behind her and making as much noise as possible so that Dave might take warning. The bathroom door was locked from inside but Hearty McHale had a ring of duplicate keys, like a warder. She threw open the door. Bambi was nowhere to be seen. Dave sat there in deep white suds looking suitably shocked. Some of the items in his pile of discarded clothes were suspiciously diaphanous at a second glance but otherwise there was no sign of anything untoward. Had he lowered her out of the window on a rope of knotted towels?

The long, interrogative silence was broken by the splutter of Bambi surfacing. Mesmerized by her cap, epaulettes and half-cup brassière of glistening foam, I had a pang of envy that I can still feel as I write this. Reg positioned himself to catch Hearty McHale's falling body but she was made of sterner stuff than that. The network of veins stood out in relief from the tops of her feet like the roots of gum-trees on the bank of a dry creek, but if standing on your dignity is what really matters, you can even have apoplexy in the upright position. Skinflint means what it says.

16. AUTUMN OF THE EXPATRIATES

So we got notice one day and a new home the next. It was the house in Melbury Road, whose palatial ground-floor flat had suddenly become vacant after the landlady's husband died of old age. The landlady, who had run an all-female orchestra during an earlier incarnation, instantly moved into the basement, where she kept open sherry for any of the orchestra's alumnae still capable of dropping by. Her name was Geraldine and she was, for a landlady, unusually accommodating, probably because of her close spiritual connection with 'hot' music, a renowned sweetener of the soul. An already heavily peopled house was thus made free to rival the demographic density of Shanghai. There were three floors of Australian girls above us, Geraldine and her heavily lisping visiting female ex-clarinettists below us, and Dibbs Buckley living in the backyard studio with his gorgeous wife Delish – a name whose accent fell on the second syllable because it was short for delicious.

The back-yard studio had been added when the house was owned by one of the Pre-Raphaelites – either Holman Burne-Jones or Edward Everett Hunt, I can never remember which, having conceived, as you might have gathered, a hatred for the Brotherhood and all their works which has endured to this day. But the Pre-Raphs knew how to look after themselves. The studio was a split-level pavilion befitting Buckley's status as incomparably the most successful young Australian expatriate. Sidney Nolan had taken decades to break through but Dibbs, while the dust from the rubble was still rising, made his entrance through the same hole with a Qantas bag over his shoulder. The Marlborough Gallery was selling his pictures as fast as he could paint them, which was very fast indeed, because he worked in sequences. Golden-haired, rugby-nosed and as restless as a surfer on a wet day, he chose a theme, painted every possible variation on it, and then sold his sketchbooks and preliminary drawings along

with the pictures. Before sending the drawings off for sale he would
deck them out with quotations from his current reading. Privately I
thought this practice a slightly premature assumption of immortality
but publicly I smoked his expensive cigars and drank his even more
expensive imported Australian beer, while doting, like every other
red-blooded male of Dibbs's acquaintance, on the seraphically lovely
Delish – an admiration which in my case she didn't pretend to
reciprocate. Mortification was eased by the fact that she plainly didn't
care much for any of us. Unusually for a woman, she didn't favour
even Dave with a soft eye. She would smile at him occasionally, but
it was only a refrigerator door opening.

Delish was a van Eyck angel in jeans and T-shirt, but she had a
hard business brain and could spot anyone who would waste her
husband's time a mile off. Dibbs's propensity to sit around drinking
and yarning with his less luminous fellow countrymen she regarded
as a tolerable, or at any rate inevitable, subsidiary urge, but she had
a clock running somewhere in the background and always made sure
he was dead on time for dinner with Sir Kenneth Clark. At the end
of the day's work, if the late autumn weather was fine, we would
gather around the great oak in front of the studio to drink away our
respective memories of Penguin Books, luxury cars that broke down
on the M1, the rigours of Cornwall's Erections and an enormously
demanding sequence of paintings about Christine Keeler and Mandy
Rice-Davies. The arguments were more heated than illuminating.
Dibbs would hail the greatness of Matisse, I would explain that
Matisse was essentially derivative, Dibbs would correctly insist that the
circa 1906 Matisses in Leningrad were of an unparalleled grandeur,
and I would pour scorn all the more eloquently for not having been
to Leningrad and knowing nothing about the subject. Meanwhile
Dave had the blacked-out look he got when he was mentally working
on a screenplay and Reg wondered openly how these egomaniacs
could breathe the same air. It was a pleasant pastime, which for the
rest of us went on after Delish had appeared, whispered in Dibbs's
ear, and taken him inside. But when, half an hour later, the two of
them would emerge transformed – Dibbs in a dinner jacket with his
aureate locks carefully tousled, Delish in silver sandals and some
dream of a plum-juice silk sheath held up by nothing but her perfect
breasts – the pastime was shattered by reality. They were off to the
opera and we weren't. The dregs in the tins of beer tasted like aloes.

But the air of prosperity emanating from the back-yard studio was contagious. Before winter had taken its grip, Dalziel had signed off from Cornwall's Erections and signed on as a supply teacher. Reg handed in his chauffeur's cap and took the same route to respectability. Though they never knew what school they would be teaching at tomorrow there was usually work, and, more important, always a decent pay-packet. Australian supply teachers were in good repute, especially if they taught English, because among the natives the ability to spell and parse their own language was already becoming scarce. Each morning the three of us left for work looking the height of bourgeois conformity. My beard was still in place but the effect was tempered by Reg's spare tweed jacket, which he eventually let me have at a low price after I had burned a hole in the sleeve. At the end of the day we would converge again out of the cold, exhaling puffs of steam but with enough spare energy to get on with real life. I worked at my poems, Reg chipped away at the opening sentence of a novel which might well be finished by now, and Dave, with Dingo's willing co-operation, transported the increasingly less rough assembly of *The Man from the Organisation* from one borrowed editing room to another. Dinner was meat – not hunks of meat, as in Australia, but pathetic scraps of meat, as in Britain – which the girls upstairs transformed into edible dishes by heating it in secret ways and adding bits of stuff to it. There was a lot of wine. The evening usually grew into a party. Life had acquired a certain rhythm.

Spencer disrupted it. When left behind in Australia, he had been bisexual, broke, and an expert at wasting his outstanding verbal gift. Now, suddenly, he was married to an heiress, had arrived in London by aircraft, possessed money to burn, and was set on making the West End the jumping-off point for an assault on world theatre. He wanted me to collaborate with him on the writing of a revue. Once written, the show would be financed by his wife's father, whose name in Australia was synonymous with a brand of fly-paper which hung in every home. For almost fifty years (Pam, Spencer's wife, was a child of the tycoon's third, or it could have been fourth, marriage) money had been accumulating in the family vault with the tempo and volume of flies hitting sticky paper across Australia's three million square miles of hot rock. Now the cash would be put to creative use. Spencer explained all this to me while he manoeuvred a second-hand but sumptuous Armstrong-Siddeley Sapphire towards the terrace house he and Pam had taken in Hampstead. A whole floor of the house had been fitted out as a study. High-quality cigarettes and alcohol, purchased on Spencer's Harrods account, stood within reach of a casual hand. The typewriter was the size of a grand piano. Here we settled down one Saturday and discussed what we were going to write. We were still discussing it on Sunday. Pam did the cooking, which consisted principally of examining the tin of jellied pheasant until she found the instructions for getting it open. Spencer and I did the talking. Nobody did any actual writing but it was early days and careful planning was held to be a virtue. The show, provisionally called *The Charge of the Light Fandango*, would galvanize the comic theatre out of the complacency into which it had been plunged by the inexplicable success of *Beyond the Fringe*. Spencer and I found it hard to agree about most things but on that point we concurred: the audience must not be truckled to. The current fad for undergraduate irreverence, we knew, merely flattered their philistine self-satisfaction. We would provide something less palatable.

But success lay in the future – rather further in the future than either of us could possibly imagine. Meanwhile here was a quasi-creative way of justifying a succession of drunken winter weekends. One could get smashed and call it a theatrical experiment. Theatre, always absurdly overvalued in London, was at that time spoken of with religious awe. Some of the older actors deserved the worship they attracted. I saw Gielgud in *The Cherry Orchard* and thought him as good as the play. Somehow I got to Chichester and saw Olivier's Othello. When he ripped the crucifix from his neck and flung it aside, you knew that it had flown straight down the gangway to his dressing room and hung itself on a hook: the physical energy was volcanic but precise, like his articulation of the words, which his super-spade accent coated with bitter chocolate but did not blur. *Put out delight and den put out delight.* Exactly what he did put out, the sexy devil.

Alas, it was already the twilight of the great actors. The producer was the new king. This was all right if the gimmick fitted: Peter Hall's *Troilus and Cressida*, previously known as Shakespeare's *Troilus and Cressida*, lost nothing by being put on in a sand-tray and Dorothy Tutin looked good barefooted, kicking granular silicon all over the Americans in the front stalls. For Peter Brook's all-leather *King Lear*, however, Paul Scofield had been encouraged to adopt a gravel voice.

From the circle of the Aldwych I couldn't hear what he was talking about. He looked like Tugboat Annie on a wet night and sounded like a cement mixer. Even worse, the director had run the first three acts together without an interval. There was no way of knowing this fact in advance unless you had bought a programme and I had bought a couple of extra pints of bitter instead. In the exact centre of a very long row of people, by the end of the first act I was ready for a pee. By the end of the second act I was ready for emergency surgery. When the third act followed without a break I knew that something would have to be done, possibly *in situ*. I held out as long as I could and then started crawling across people's knees. On stage, Gloucester was having his eyes put out. In the circle, there was a man struggling desperately sideways towards the exit through an entanglement of legs, like one of those American footballers in training who have to run very fast with knees high through piles of tyres.

I made it to safety approximately in time, but as I stood there – or, rather, reeled and swayed there like a man watering his lawn with a hose which had been unexpectedly connected to a powerful artesian well – it began to strike me that the capacity of my bladder was perhaps incompatible with the quantities of liquid I was attempting to put into it. Over the next decade I attempted to solve this problem by forcing even more liquid in, on the assumption that this would enlarge the receptacle. Common sense, which might have suggested that this was the wrong approach, was vitiated by the method itself. When I finally embraced abstinence it was because of the simple urge to work a longer day. Thus, without joining Alcoholics Anonymous, I was at last able to leave Piss-Artists Notorious. But that's a much later story. At the time we are talking about, I was a man out of control, sobbing with relief in a urinal while the lights were going out on the Third Servant as he fetched flax and whites of eggs for Gloucester's bleeding face.

The return to my seat in the audience was effected by the same route employed on leaving it. At least nobody mistook my perform- ance for part of the production. But following hard upon producer's theatre came the theatre of group improvisation, one of whose hall- marks was that the actors were practically never on the actual stage, but were continually roaming up and down the gangways looking for trouble. New York's Living Theater had come to town and its

collectively inspired cast spent the whole time in the audience provoking hostile bourgeois response and thus unveiling the insidious
nature of US imperialism, although there was rarely any mention of
the especially insidious aspect of US imperialism represented by the
Living Theater. London's typical literary couple – he a novelist, she
a cookery correspondent or vice versa – would sit dutifully attentive
in their aisle seats while a naked six-foot white actor with a beard,
or a naked six-foot black actor without a beard but with an earring,
thrust his bottom in their faces as a challenge to their honky values.
Afterwards they would invite him home to insult them further,
consume all the liquor in their stripped-pine drinks cabinet and
violate their teenage daughter.

Dibbs and Delish Buckley varied from this practice only by
inviting the whole cast. Our nostrils invaded by an unfamiliar sweet
odour, Dave, Reg and I went out into the yard one chill night and
found it inhabited by murmuring people in fancy dress, passing,
after one dainty puff each, an oddly defeated-looking roll-your-own
cigarette around in a circle. Having included herself for some reason
in this silent pow-wow, Delish looked especially exotic, like a Dior
mannequin in a hobo camp. Unasked yet vociferously confident, I
joined the circle, making sure, when the butt got to me, that I dealt
with it properly. I sucked it to a stub in two jumbo drags. 'Who is
this asshole?' whispered a huge black man standing by the oak tree.
I knew he was black because I couldn't see him against the dark
trunk and I knew he was huge because the voice came from high up.
Delish gave me one of those downward waves of the hand with
which she customarily apologized for the provincial behaviour of her
husband's hangers-on. She had beautiful hands, incidentally: deeply
tanned but glowing with that edible, enviable golden health which
Modigliani gave his odalisques while he was dying. Cruel one, I
pursue thee over the rolling billows. Horace said that. Someone must
have put him through it.

17. THE DEEP TAN FADES

The foundations of Delish Buckley's profound tan had been laid in Australia. That much went without saying. She and I had both been exposed to the same intensity and duration of ultra-violet. Even though she had done most of elegantly splayed spine-bashing on the high-toned beaches north of Newport, whereas I had been mainly confined to the humbler inlets stretching south from Bondi to Cronulla, it had been the same free sunlight for both of us. But Delish's tan was now being topped up by regular visits to the Bahamas, St Tropez and – the Buckleys practically discovered the place – Bali. Her tan was intact. Mine was a memory. In Australia, even during winter, one had always had, when one examined oneself before the mirror, a tide-mark around one's waist and upper thighs. When naked, even at one's most wan, one had always looked, at the very least, as if one were wearing a nifty little pair of white panties. But after the second year in London the hallowed demarcation line paled away, never properly to return. Stripped to the waist on a summer's day in Holland Park, the most you could acquire was a mild pink blush. Jamaicans in Fair Isle beanies laughed as they danced past your outstretched form. At night the pink rash itched like an authentic burn but declined to alter the skin's pigmentation. The melanin remained unmoved. You woke in the morning looking more than ever like a peeled raw potato about a week old, with a certain subtle tinge of azure to its chill whiteness. For the girls, the disaster could be staved off with a sun-lamp or, failing that, a timely application of Tan-Fastic. For the men, most of whom could barely afford to keep an ordinary electric bulb burning, there was nothing to do except become resigned. Turning pale was part of one's commitment to the great adventure.

As so often happens in matters of morale, to give up the symbol led to a wholesale erosion of the reality it stood for. When the

Chindits in Burma lost hope, they gave up shaving, and when they gave up shaving they would die of a cut finger. When we lost our tan, the emblem of our bronzed Aussie robustness, we tended to yield along the whole front of general fitness and healthy diet. Dalziel was an exception: he had never smoked and always drank less than other people so that he could give them orders in a credible voice. The rest of us smoked as much as our credit would stand. My borrowing requirement for cigarettes always ran at an unreal proportion of salary. Each time I shifted to smaller cigarettes, I upped the frequency with which I demolished them. By now I had left Players No. 6, the kiddies' cigarette, far behind, and was smoking some brand that looked as if it should have been dangling from the lower lip of a hamster. But I sucked them in like short lengths of spaghetti.

The steady kippering of my insides had so far led to only intermittent convulsions – the average coughing fit was easily quelled by squeezing my head between my knees – but my wind already showed signs of impairment. If I ran a hundred yards for a stationary bus I couldn't get up the stairs after I had caught it. Like most people who smoked umpteen cigarettes a day, I tasted only the first one. The succeeding umpteen minus one were a compulsive ritual which had no greater savour than the fumes of burning money. To have experienced the full thrill, one would have had to have been one's own girlfriend, for whom mouth-to-mouth contact clearly had the same effect as sucking the exhaust pipe of a diesel truck. Smoking so many more cigarettes than you felt like smoking was supposed to indicate an addiction to nicotine, but I suspect that in my case it was merely gluttony. Call it an addictive personality if you like, but since the age of nought I had never been able to get enough of anything. First it was milk and then it was marshmallows.

Just after the war my mother was invited to an RSL social evening in Kogarah. Whereas any man who had served in any capacity could be a full member of the Returned Servicemen's League, she, a war widow whose husband had died on active service, had to wait to be invited into the RSL hall as a guest. Such was the position of women in Australia at that time. One of the most prominent dignitaries of the local RSL lived in our street. He had spent the war as a quartermaster at Singleton, with special responsibility for latrine-boring equipment. My mother's inclination was to wish a plague on the whole business, but she wanted to give me a night out, and the social evening had a special supper for children. A highlight of the supper was marshmallows. Several of the children ate half a dozen of these each and felt sick. I swallowed two dozen and felt fine, except when my breathing stopped. Picked up from where I was writhing on the floor, I was held aloft by giant hands and slapped vigorously on the back. Nothing happened for some time, and then a pink-and-white mass of congealed marshmallows the size and splendour of a shampoo-soaked satin cushion from Zsa-Zsa Gabor's boudoir hit the floor with a sticky plop.

This pattern was to recur. I had better be silent about the ticklish matter of a certain famous pie, except to say that if that brand of meat pie had not been meant to be eaten in excess, its pastry would not have been so enticingly soggy, and that if the pie had not been meant to be regurgitated, the cubes of meat gleaming through its sludge of gravy would not have been so purple. But the RSL marshmallows and the meat pies happened in Australia, as an occasional alternative to good home cooking, and where the effects of *gourmandise* could be offset by exercise. In London there was no home cooking worthy of the name. When you were in funds you ate out. But only the people whose faces appeared in such publications as *Town* and *Queen* could afford to eat in restaurants serving food which would leave them looking and feeling better instead of worse. 'A way of life based on the glossy magazine,' Harold Macmillan had said in a bid to touch the common pulse, and his very words told you how remote the idea was from everyday experience.

When we felt rich, we ate in the local Angus Steak House, where a bland but plump piece of animal was accompanied by reasonably crisp chips and a half tomato cut with a toothed circumference, like a rubicund cog-wheel. When we felt less rich, we might eat at a certain British chain of hamburger restaurants devoted to serving nothing else. In recent years, perhaps encouraged by competition from McDonald's, the British hamburger has become a credit to the nation. At the time of which I speak, it looked like a scorched beercoaster or a tenderized disc brake. Flanked by chips which, if picked up individually on a fork, either shattered or else drooped until their ends touched, the British hamburger lay there sweltering under its limp grey duvet of over-fried onions. When you cut it up, put the pieces in your mouth and swallowed them, the British hamburger shaped itself to the bottom of your stomach like ballast, while inter-acting with your gastric juices to form an incipient belch of enormous potential, an airship which had been inflated in a garage. This belch, when silently released, would cause people standing twenty yards away to start examining the soles of their shoes. The vocalized version sounded like a bag of tools thrown into a bog.

The British hamburger thus symbolized, with savage neatness, the country's failure to provide its ordinary people with food which did anything more for them than sustain life. In Italy, for the same price as a typical British hamburger meal including sweet, a builder's labourer could eat like a king – rather better in fact, because pasta dishes gain from being kept simple. Françoise, short of lire herself, and with her slim resources cut in half by my presence, always took me where the poor ate well. In Britain this opportunity was not on the cards. It was said that a poor man could eat well in Britain if he ate a British Railways breakfast three times a day, but British Railways was already in the process of putting its breakfast beyond the reach of the average wage-earner – a process which was to culminate, after the name-change to British Rail, in a successful effort to put the same breakfast beyond the reach of the Duke of Westminster. A more practical alternative to the British hamburger – more practical than climbing on a train just to eat – was the workers' café, or kayf. Alas, not every district had one of these. At their best, the kayfs had a certain style. Men with flat caps, donkey jackets and chipped finger-nails could fill up on beef and two veg plus spotted dick with custard. At their worst, the kayfs sliced the beef with the same sectioning equipment used to prepare laboratory specimens for mounting on a microscope slide. Even worse than the worst, there was Wally's, still bubbling away like a tub of hot fat in the lane behind Warwick Road, only a few hundred yards away from Melbury Road across Kensington High Street. All too often we would end up at Wally's because we were collectively too broke for any other solution except one: the last, the zero option, which was to eat at home.

This wasn't so bad when the girls on one of the floors above us did the cooking, but they weren't always available. Most evenings we would send an ambassador upstairs to explore the possibility of having our food cooked for us. Usually the girls would invite us all up and help transform our scrawny chops or dreadful packets of sausages and streaky bacon into something edible. But increasingly often they were lost in the throes of preparing a beef Stroganoff or a casserole, the centrepiece of some candle-lit dinner party for English suitors in charcoal pin-stripe suits. It got to the point where the girls would be wearing full-length gowns and jewellery. The Ruperts and Christophers would arrive in cabs full of roses. The stench of flowers on the stairs drove us back defeated into our all-male domain, where there was nothing to do except fend for ourselves, with predictable results. Supermarket food bred a supermarket mentality. I myself could account for a pound of pork sausages at a sitting. I don't know exactly what was in the sausages, but I did know that a block of ice cream made by the same firm didn't taste significantly different.

Though Dalziel made sure he got to a health-food restaurant once a month, the rest of us ate junk because it was easy and I ate more junk than anybody because to keep on eating was easier than stopping. For brief spells the supervisory care of an accompanying woman led to a saner diet, but the only reason this happened was because letting her look after the food was easier than looking after it myself. It was the line of least resistance, and usually it led downwards. I had not yet begun to put on weight, but the possibility was there, like the side of a hill getting ready to slip. There was a falling feeling, especially in the scalp. My comb had hair in it. When the others told me I had a bald patch I told them it was an enlarged crown, but with a shaving mirror held at an angle over my head like a halo I looked into the bathroom mirror and saw a would-be tonsure about the size of a florin. American graduates in hair technology called this the 'O' effect. The 'O' effect at the back of my head was being approached by an 'M' effect at the front, where my temples, when I pulled the hair back from them with the edge of my hand, were retreating as I watched. Add this combination to my wrecked mouth, my all-over pallor and an escalating inability to make any sudden move without coughing for ten minutes, and you had a lot to worry about. And when you had a lot to worry about, the thing to do was to have a lot to drink.

Everybody I knew drank all the time, so I wasn't unusual in that. But I was unusual, I now see, in so easily getting drunk. I couldn't see it then because I was always either drunk or recovering. What I had was a ridiculously light head. I had no more business drinking alcohol than someone allergic to cheese has eating pizza. Unfortunately I liked the feeling of getting tight. When we all went down to the pub in the evenings, I discovered with intense pleasure that the revoltingly cheery horse-brass décor was already out of focus after the second pint of brown water. After the third pint I could barely articulate, and like most people in that condition I found articulation a matter of urgency. Trying to say something of extreme importance, I dimly registered that my tongue was moving slowly. So I started to say the same thing again, as if repetition would get the message across. At closing time it was a hundred-yard walk home for everybody else and about half a mile for me. Every few seconds I would spot the rest of the blokes and try to join them, but couldn't find them again until I had bounced off a brick wall or a parked car. The hangover next morning would be an epic. Overnight dehydration shrivelled my eyes to raisins. Every morning my tongue was like a small sand dune abraded by a hot wind.

Nowadays, more than ten years after swearing off the demon rum, I can take half an inch of wine with a meal without seizing the bottle from the waiter and tilting it to my pursed lips. Strictly speaking, therefore, I was never an alcoholic. I didn't need to be. Just as most people who take cocaine are not drug addicts, but behave so badly that they might as well be, so did I manifest every characteristic of the true booze artist. Except one: my leg wasn't hollow. Or to put it another way: my head wasn't hard enough to let my leg fill up. I got paralytic too quickly to do myself any major damage. The authentic toper bombs his brain cells with a bottle of Scotch a day and you never notice until they take him away for a liver transplant. Me you noticed in the first few minutes. All the more unlikely, then, that the delicately poised Leslie should even contemplate an emotional alliance.

Yet it happened, although so briefly that I doubted its occurrence immediately afterwards. Probably I doubted its occurrence even during, and thus hastened its end. Though she was undemonstrative to the point of shyness, it was all too obvious that she was letting me into her life as a distraction from heartbreak. A long love affair with a married man was either reaching the usual conclusion or had entered one of the usual off-again hiatuses preceding the usual conclusion. The older and more experienced man having lost his charm, the way was open for the younger and less experienced man to pose his more easily thwarted threat. The door to her affections opened so suddenly that I can forgive myself for falling through it, but not for flailing straight across the room and toppling out of the window. Leslie would have had a civilizing effect on me, given time. We made our first private-life contact not at Harmondsworth or in the Kombibus but at the London Library in St James's Square. I was there doing research into authors' photographs. Each week I gave myself a whole day at the London Library to dig up previously unused, easily distinguishable pictures of, say, Maxwell Anderson, Sherwood Anderson and Robert E. Sherwood. This took about twenty minutes. The rest of the day I would read. I read many volumes of the proceedings of the Nuremberg Tribunal, thereby saddening myself deeply but gaining a valuable inoculation of disillusionment – the precondition for a realistic happiness. Just on cue to help me test this theory out, Leslie showed up in one of the metal-floored book-stacks so that I could clank casually around the corner of a wall of shelves and meet her face to face. She was collecting references for one of the Peregrines she was editing. Peregrines were seriously highbrow Penguins and Leslie was a seriously highbrow person. Being that, being a woman and being in publishing, she was also seriously underpaid, but her little basement flat in Pimlico was a delight. Well used to not noticing my surroundings, I noticed these. Like everything about her the interior decoration was lightly done but not too dimity. There were postcard pictures of Colette and Simone de Beauvoir, of Alma Mahler-Werfel and Lou Andreas-Salomé. Not even names to me at that time, they crowded Leslie's mantelpiece with what she presumably took to be friendly faces. Virginia Woolf was up there on the wall, like a sad horse sticking its head in through a window. Sipping tea, I made myself at home. Helping myself to her vodka, I made myself too at home, but that didn't matter at first. The bull had arrived in the china shop but the proprietress welcomed the diversion.

A lot went on in two weeks. With Robin either out of town or safely ironing a large pile of shirts, I took Leslie to see the newly reconstituted complete print of *La Règle du jeu* at the Academy. She knew much more about Renoir than I did but imparted the knowledge more mercifully than I would have done had the positions been reversed. She had read modern languages at Somerville and had a wall full of Pléiade and Insel Verlag thin-paper editions to prove it. I scanned their immaculate spines with the mixture of desire and fury with which I still look at closed books even today. Eight years had gone by since she had come down from Oxford but she still went there every second weekend. The name Geoffrey was mentioned. I imagined some weedy countertenor in a long black academic gown. Casting myself as the iconoclast – it didn't take much effort – I trampled on her tentatively expressed nostalgia for the cloisters, the libraries and the crocus-bordered lawns. In view of the fact that I was heading for just such a haven myself, this was the yelping of a dog in the manger, but it jolted her from her melancholy. During tea at the Tate one Saturday afternoon I gave her my complete diagnosis of Britain's post-imperial ills. In the setting of Rex Whistler's light-fantastic murals, my oration must have sounded wonderfully incongruous. Certainly it got her attention. Resting her chin on those porcelain wrists she stared at me absorbed, as if Lenin had mounted a soapbox in Kew Gardens.

Since I was too young for her in every way, the law of diminishing returns would have set in eventually, but for the nonce she was not bored. Horrified, but not bored. What put her off, then? Perhaps it was a combination of things, tolerable as separate symptoms yet adding up to a syndrome that no woman of refinement could long countenance. My nicotine-gilded right hand might have been a draw-card on its own: the man with the golden arm. Smoke must have given my lank hair and beard a cosy smell, like the snug of an old pub. My British hamburger breath spoke challengingly of the modern Britain. Hush Puppies having attained a ubiquity which made me less defiant about associating them with the repressive footwear of the sahibs, I had bought a pair, saving money by choosing a brand called something else. Judging by how, after the first hour of having had them on, the sweat of my feet reacted with their unbreathing uppers, my new shoes should have been called Mush Puppies. After a week they were Slush Puppies. Yet Leslie was able to laugh about them as I left them outside in the area under the wrought-iron staircase.

What she couldn't laugh at, however, was the way I started turning up half-cut as soon as I thought she was in the bag, and then getting fully cut while I was with her. She might have pointed out, correctly, that it was an insult. Instead she just drifted out of reach. Before I could wake up to what was going missing, our friendship was back to where it began. I supposed then, and still prefer to suppose now, that I wanted it that way, and so hurried the business to its conclusion.

There is, of course, always the possibility, however vanishingly small, that she simply didn't like me, but that sort of thing happens only to other men, doesn't it? No, she was too serious, too intense, too honest, too much. After my first evening with her I was already writing poems about saying goodbye for ever. It was a bit of a blow to find out that she felt roughly the same way, yet hurt pride was lost in the relief. Writers much more exalted than I am have the same weakness. Think twice before you get mixed up with a writer, and ten times before you marry one. Writers want things to be over, so that they can write the elegy. Gray toured that churchyard on the run.

18. PRELUDE TO THE AFTERMATH

You could tell how winter became spring by the way the pile of manuscript paper representing *The Charge of the Light Fandango* doubled in size, from two pages to four pages. There had never been four pages to match them. Spencer and I had once written obscurely but here was the evidence that we had grown out of all that. Now we wrote impenetrably. We were producing the first truly post-Cubist material in the history of comedy. Any idea that made us laugh we would hone and refine until it didn't. Then we would try it on Pam to make sure that it met our standards. If she looked sufficiently bewildered, it was in. If she laughed, we took it back for a rewrite.

Despite the unnerving proximity of the lost Leslie, I was also feeling pretty cocky at work. Sir Allen Lane had given over the day-to-day management of Penguin to a whizz-kid called Tony Godwin. Actually Godwin was already in his forties but it was a symptom of Britain's post-war condition that anyone given power before his hair turned white was called a whizz-kid. Godwin's hair was worn long and thick to frame his Caribbean suntan, with a candy-stripped high-collared shirt, kipper tie and waist-hugging charcoal mohair suit all conspiring to connect the heavy head with the lightweight shoes. A star player in a gentlemen's game, Godwin was clearly very bright. His neglect of the back catalogue was to have deleterious effects in the long term, but there were enough attendant lords who could have looked after that aspect if they had seen its urgency. In the search for new titles, however, he was truly adventurous. He brought in a young editor called Tony Richardson – no relation to the film director – who took the unprecedented step of commissioning a book about the Beatles. I liked Richardson's company. More surprisingly, since he was so fastidiously quiet, he liked mine, and over coffee in the canteen would take time to explain his concern with trivia. Instead of dismissing popularity as a sure sign of the meretricious, he wanted to find out what lay behind it. Laden with first-class academic honours, he was properly suspicious of mere trendiness – the word was new then – but equally averse to the ivory tower, which he thought was a dead weight. The energy of the ignorant fascinated him. He was a deep young man but it turned out, alas, that a lot of his reticence was economy of effort. He was ill, and soon died. Hardly having known him, I missed him, and some people who knew him better never quite got over the loss.

So the two big ideas I had discussed with Richardson I took to Godwin himself. Penguin had published the occasional science fiction novel in the worthy British tradition but there were vast American sources which remained untapped. There was a boom on the way and Penguin could get in first. The same applied to books about the movies – not boring studies by Paul Rotha about Film or Cinema, but books about the movies. I wrote Godwin a long memo on the subject. To his credit he took me out to lunch on the strength of it. I must have put my case badly. Proving to him that I was a fanatic in both fields was probably a mistake. Dismissing his driver and taking the wheel of the big Jaguar himself, he drove us to a secluded pub. Seizing my opportunity before he got the car into third gear, I spoke continuously, but instead of raving about twenty different science-fiction writers with names like Cordwainer Simak and swooning over twenty different film directors with names like Ray Siodmak, I should have been judiciously enthusiastic about a maximum two of each. 'We might do a bit more science fiction,' Godwin said, in a tone of voice that told me my cause was lost, 'but I don't need a buff who knows all about the neglected minor novels of Kohl and Pornbluth. I need an editor who can see a big project all the way through without wasting my time and the company's money.' Dandyish himself, he perhaps took my beard as a sign of unsoundness. He would have been right, of course. 'Pohl and Kornbluth,' I said feebly, knowing that he had slipped up on purpose as a contribution towards letting me down lightly. Still, the pub lunch had made a change from the canteen. In the canteen I would have had a tray full of ordinary food and some excellent views of Leslie. In the pub I got a piece of stale French loaf with a dead shallot laid out on it, a dollop of shepherd's pie like a rhino's diarrhoea, and a good solid dose of rejection. By and large it is our failures that civilize us, but one doesn't want to take that principle too far.

Up until that point I had taken a relaxed attitude to my job, but from then on I became positively somnolent. With the arrival of spring it became easier to get a good day's sleep just by resting my head on the desk. Come autumn I would be back in those groves of academe outside of which, it was becoming increasingly clear, I was unqualified to function. Meanwhile there was one last summer of hard labour to be lived through. The *vie bohème* at Melbury Road reached its peak, and, as usually occurs when happiness is perceived as such, began instantly to melt away. On weekends we drank at Henekey's in the Portobello Road. Ella Fitzgerald sang at the Hammersmith Odeon. Callas and Gobbi were in *Tosca* at Covent Garden. Not even Nick Thesinger could get in but we all saw the show on television, which was black and white in those days but made Callas look all the more dramatic. The girls on the top floor had a television set that gave you quite a good picture if you hit it with your clenched fist at the right angle. I spent hours in front of it and would have been hard put to disagree with anyone who accused me of wasting my time. Only a decade later did it turn out that I had been engaged in formative studies.

As a luxury we would dine out at Jimmy's in Soho. Jimmy's was a basement restaurant in Frith Street. Bianchi's, the restaurant favoured by successful people in journalism and television – not yet collectively known as the media – was further along the street and two floors up. It was said that those two floors were the longest climb in London. It cost more than ten times as much to eat at Bianchi's as at Jimmy's and I liked things well enough below ground. The place had started life as an air-raid shelter but had gone down since. Yet the low price of the lamb chops was not reflected in their taste, which was made only more piquant by the number and size of the caterpillars in the salad. On Sunday afternoons, with attendant women reading heavy newspapers on the sidelines, we played soccer with a tennis ball in Holland Park, adding our profane cries to the clattering of the peacocks who otherwise carried the full burden of disrupting the open-air concerts.

Reg went missing from the team when he got a message from Sydney saying that an ex-girlfriend had died after an illegal operation. Though it was nothing to do with him, he blamed himself for having been away, a reaction which suggested – correctly, as things turned out – that he would be going home for good. In those last pre-Pill days, the possibility of a back-street abortion was the unstated but inescapable sub-text of the revels, whether you were a shy tyro in Sydney or an experienced roué in London. One of the girls upstairs at Melbury Road was caught out during my last few weeks in residence. Her English company director suitor was long gone. I got the job of taking her to the appointment, waiting for her in the dark parlour which served as a reception area, and taking her home when the deed was done. Her sense of loss afterwards would have been food for the moralist. Yet what struck me, and strikes me still, was her fear beforehand. I wish I could have said better things. Thank God for changed times. The contraceptives weren't hard to live with if a lady didn't mind playing hostess to a small floppy frisbee full of hair-gel and a gentleman didn't mind dressing part of his anatomy as a bleached frogman. But a misfortune could bring misery. The way out of the misery could bring tragedy. Women took that way out because the alternatives were impossible. Today people need to be reminded that the choice is not between legal abortion and the supposedly edifying effects of bringing up an unwanted child. The choice is between legal abortion and illegal abortion. To know something of what an illegal abortion was like, you didn't need to have seen a girl's corpse after an unsuccessful operation. All you needed to have seen was a girl's face on the way to a successful one. They never put the appointment in their diaries. They always wrote the address on a piece of paper, so that they could throw it away afterwards.

Society was to blame. Actually, on this point, it was, but I held it to blame on most other points as well. My radicalism, now further fuelled by semi-regular reading of the *New Left Review*, found expression at the London School of Economics, where I turned up unasked to the weekly student debates and joined in from the floor. The standard of articulacy was not high. Neither was my standard of logic, but that deficiency made me more prolix instead of less. Harry Pollitt's son Brian, an ex-President of the Cambridge Union, was the star guest one night. He had inherited his father's politics but a privileged education had obviously softened them. When my turn came to speak I pointed out, truly if not wisely, that egalitarianism would remain a dream as long as places like Cambridge existed. Pollitt agreed that Cambridge should be levelled forthwith but put in a plea for the retention of King's College Chapel. He had his

tongue in his cheek and knew it. I had my head up my arse and
didn't, but to some of the less perspicacious students present I must
have sounded like the more committed revolutionary. After the
debate, two of them approached me and told me proudly that while
earning extra money on the building site of a new housing development they had been deliberately fiddling with the wiring so as to
hasten the downfall of capitalism. With sudden visions of some old
lady switching on the immersion heater and blasting herself to
kingdom come, I instructed these teenage saboteurs to get down
there next morning and put things right pronto. Shivering in the
summer midnight as I waited for a bus back to Kensington High
Street, I resolved to abandon the revolution then and there. This
might sound like easy come, easy go. But I doubt if I was ever the
sort of harebrained dabbler with ideas who turns up in Dostoevsky
and Conrad. My convictions were strong enough. Yet my instincts
were even stronger, and they were all against any notion that ends
can justify means. I had what it took to be feckless, but *realpolitik*
was beyond me. So it needed only a little event to overcome a big
idea. Many reluctant liberals would have similar tales to tell about
their retreat from radical certainty. There is no mystery involved. The
solidarity of the Left is a mirage. The common ground between
revolutionaries and parliamentarians is made of air. Its transparency
can be rendered apparent by a very small fact. You can be in a
demonstration, someone near you will bend to pick up a stone, and
you will realize that you are in the wrong place. Being obliged to
remember from that day forward that your fine ideas weighed less
than a pebble will never be comforting, but always salutary.

Not having yet informed Penguin that I would soon be doing a
bunk, I shamelessly took my annual holiday as a reward for all my
hard work. Françoise was waiting on Florence railway station and
her joy at seeing my beard again can be imagined. This time there
was no question of compromising her reputation at the *pensione*.
Instead we took a room at Lastra a Signa, a suburb on the edge of
town, where I compromised her reputation with the entire district.
The room was an ex-bathroom which had been converted by adding
extra tiles to the ceiling. The landlady made it clear that only the
recent double hernia sustained by her hod-carrying husband had led
her to even consider offering this wonderful abode to an unmarried
couple. Unlike her husband, however, she had the forbearance not

to join the crowd of menacingly staring locals who followed us in the street. Usually he was in the forefront, no doubt to make up with persecuting zeal for the compromise which had been forced on his wife by his economic weakness. For a man with a serious physical disability he certainly knew how to spit. It was like that terrible scene in *L'Avventura* when Monica Vitti gets followed around by a town's whole population of deprived males. Françoise's good looks, however, though sufficiently startling, were not quite enough to explain the element of potential homicide informing that massed masculine gaze. It was my beard that had tipped them over the edge. They probably didn't like my shoes, either – a new ox-blood pair with gold buckles at the sides. The shoes had cost not much more than five pounds, so I don't suppose the buckles were real gold. But they weren't superfluous. They were holding down the straps. It was the straps that were superfluous.

Incipient hatred of all Italian males was staved off by deeper acquaintance with Leopardi and Enrico. Leopardi had been dead for some time but his poetry, painfully construed by me with Françoise's patient assistance, was a revelation. Enrico's paintings perhaps lacked the same hard-won authority but he was alive. He was the lover of Françoise's friend Faith, a fine-boned English modern languages graduate who had come to Florence in search of Petrarch and stayed on to live with Enrico. They had a farmhouse on a winding road out past Fiesole in the northern hills. Enrico helped buy the food for Faith to cook. He also helped cook it. He had a *boules* court set up in the back yard, near the chicken coop. His Italian was fast and funny yet so clear that I could feel my grasp of the language improving as I listened. He spent a lot of time on helping me to speak it – far more time than any truly committed artist would have had to spare. The truth was that his temporary job as an art teacher was becoming a full-time job and that both he and Faith had fallen victim to happiness. Instead of achieving their ambitions, they had improved their lives. It was all such a waste, I would tell them as I drank their wine. Françoise agreed with this analysis, or anyway didn't disagree.

Back in England, I found Dalziel on the point of leaving for Africa. A job as head of the Nigerian Government Film Unit had come up and he had decided that a couple of years spent making a documentary every two weeks about politicians giving speeches would still be better experience than living on hope in London. The rough cut of *The Man from the Organisation* got him the job. The Nigerians thought it was a true story but liked the close-ups. I hated to see him go, but in only a few days I would be gone myself. Dibbs had already left for New York, where his sequence of paintings featuring Delish on a massage table had created a sensation. The masseur was variously Freud, Einstein, Kafka and Elvis Presley, with appended texts from each. Dave shared my scepticism but characteristically cut through to the heart of the matter. 'If he spent less time writing down quotable quotes he could learn to draw,' said the new head of the Nigerian Government Film Unit while packing his canvas hold-all. 'But he's got the colour. Especially that sky blue. It looks just like home.' Warning me not to get lost in the books, Dalziel moved out. His parting words were typically lyrical. 'Don't put a dent in the beef bayonet.' Until three replacements moved in I had the flat to myself. At Penguin I had given my notice, which was eagerly accepted. Leslie seemed to mind least of all. They would have been even keener to see my back if they had known how close I had come to supplying Bertram D. Wolfe's photograph for the cover of a book by Bernard Wolfe. At least I hadn't sent them Virginia Woolf. But only a frantic sprint down the corridor and a degrading last-minute tussle with the art-editor had averted the same sort of catastrophe which I had been hired to prevent in the first place.

Down at the Iron Bridge I told Dingo all about it as part of a campaign to amuse him on his last night. Unaccountably he had decided that the place to be an Australian journalist was Australia, so he was not attempting to renew his appointment. He told me all this through the din caused by an ancient male singer who upgraded his performance of 'Mule Train' by hitting himself on the head with a tin tray. Not notably more smashed than usual, Dingo sold me the Ford Popular for a shilling. A non-driver, I didn't want it for transport. I wanted it for a monument. By dead of night, Dingo steered it to the designated spot, and there we left it to rust – in front of Hearty McHale's. The first phase of my career in London was thus summed up as having had nuisance value and nothing more. I went home to an empty flat.

My suitcase looked eager to be away. Stained white with dried rain, even my shoes were itching to be gone. By now they were Gush Puppies, but they would take me to safety. On the flag-stones of ancient courtyards they would find a sure footing.

MAY WEEK WAS IN JUNE

I realise very well that the reader has no great need to know all this; but I need to tell him.

Rousseau, *Les Confessions*

I wear a suit of armour made of nothing but my mistakes.

Pierre Reverdy, quoted by Ernst Jünger
in *Das zweite Pariser Tagebuch*, 21 February 1943

I've never made any secret of the fact that I'm basically on my way to Australia.

Support Your Local Sheriff

Preface

Somebody once said that a trilogy ought ideally to consist of two volumes. Unfortunately he never said anything else, so his name is forgotten. When I set out to write *Falling Towards England*, the second volume of my unreliable memoirs, I honestly meant it to be the end of the enterprise. Gradually it became clear, however, that my entry into the University of Cambridge marked the beginning of a further episode, whose events, while less than awe-inspiring on the scale of cosmology, would suffer distortion if compressed into a few chapters. I could have made more room at the back of the book by cutting the front, but it was already cut. The nuances, after all, were everything. It would not have been enough to say that I was a failure in London. One had to convey the way failure felt: how the clothes slept in to keep one warm looked wrong next day, how a letter of rejection could be distinguished from a letter of acceptance before it was opened, how one drank to quell one's nagging conscience about having borrowed the money with which to drink. In the next generation, young people needed a heroin habit to live like that. I managed it through sheer talent. Cambridge was my way out, if not up.

Once again, though, the raw story would not have been enough. God, said Mies van der Rohe, is in the details. In Cambridge, I began to find my way, but simply to say so would have been to muff the point, because I found my way by getting more lost than ever. It was just that this time, by a bigger than usual dose of my usual extraordinary luck, I was given the chance to become confused in a fruitful, or potentially fruitful, manner. In London, entirely through my own bad management, I had been hunted from pillar to post. In Cambridge I could develop my propensities, such as they were, to the fullest extent possible, and all at once. The result was chaos. Fortunately there is a natural law, whose mathematical basis I don't pretend to understand, which says that chaos isn't always just random. It can have patterns in it. The story in this volume – while being, as before, no more faithful to the facts than the ego finds convenient – is as true as I can make it to the pattern which emerged when my half-formed personality was put back into the scrambler. I won't dignify the process with the name of self-discovery. The self scarcely altered. It might even have become more conscious of itself than ever. But the panic was over. I was still broke, but I had landed in the lap of the only kind of luxury I have ever cared about – a wealth of opportunity. Where once every move had been forced, now there was nothing but choice. For too long the Flash of Lightning had not been free to deploy his cape or put on the mask with the stretched elastic knotted at the back to keep it fitting tightly under the strain of his amazing acceleration. Now once again he was off and running in six different directions.

Cambridge was my personal playground. It would be useless to pretend otherwise. I would be surprised if nostalgia for those easy years did not drip from the following pages like sweat. The place hasn't changed much since. The old Footlights clubroom, together with the whole rat-infested district of which it was the hub, was bulldozed to make room for the Lion Yard development, enraging some but probably saving the city from another outbreak of bubonic plague. The buses have changed colour, there has been a massacre of elms, the old Eagle is ominously surrounded by scaffolding, the Pakistani restaurant on the ground floor of the Friar's House has become a souvenir shop, and fancy goods are now sold in the back room of the Whim where I once sat by the hour writing in my journal. As always, committees of dons do more than the worst developers to inflict horrible buildings on their beautiful city. Yet Cambridge – like Florence, the other main location of this epic – stays what it was. My life didn't. In Cambridge, in the sixties, my course was altered and fixed, for good or ill. For this reason, though I still spend a good deal of time there, the place is always in the past to me, as epoch-making as my first pair of long pants, and almost as glamorous. The spires, the lawns, the spring alliance of jonquils and daffodils: I hardened my heart against these things, and they all went to my head. Byron kept a low profile in Cambridge, confining himself to booze, broads and leading a live bear around on a string. I was less inclined to hide my light under a bushel. The days of our youth are the days of our glory. He said it, and I believed it.

C.J.
London, 1990

1. GENTLEMEN, SPORT YOUR OAKS!

Arriving in Cambridge on my first day as an undergraduate, I could see nothing except a cold white October mist. At the age of twenty-four I was a complete failure, with nothing to show for my life except a few poems nobody wanted to publish in book form. Three years of hand-to-mouth existence in London had led me nowhere but here. For all I knew, Cambridge was receiving me with open arms. They could have had flags out. There could have been a band playing. It was impossible to tell. The white opacity came all the way to my eyeballs. Outside the railway station I stood holding my cardboard suitcase. I couldn't see the station and I could barely see the suitcase. Having been in Cambridge only once before, for a short drunken visit that started well but ended in a haze not unlike, in its texture, the one through which I now groped, I had only the dimmest memories to go on of how to get to town.

Luckily I remembered, when I reached the war memorial, that the statue on top of it was pointing roughly in the right direction. I had to climb the memorial to find out what the direction was. After that I was on the right track to the city centre, where there was enough light to distinguish people from letter boxes. The letter boxes, in my perhaps embittered view, had warmer personalities than the people, but the people, although not notably less taciturn, at least knew how to give directions if they felt like it. I asked a nice little old lady the way to Pembroke, which was to be my college if I ever found it. At first she snarled at me, perhaps because I had located her partly by touch. It took only about a quarter of an hour to calm her fears, however, after which she pointed the way down Pembroke Street and told me to turn left at Trumpington Street. I turned left too early – probably into Tennis Court Road – and ended up at the Fitzwilliam Museum, which I mistook for Pembroke until put right by the man at the desk inside. Before I could get myself and my suitcase back out through the revolving doors he managed to regale me with his entire repertoire of jokes about kangaroos, koalas, dunnies, and walking upside down in the outback, ha ha. As an Australian expatriate I had grown used to the fabled English sense of humour but preferred to steer clear of it when possible, for fear of laughing too hard.

On the far side of the street I found, by stepping into it, a gutter the size of a small canal. This I slowly followed to the left, occasionally crossing the footpath to check the texture of the buildings with my carefully extended right hand. The ashlared front wall of a college crustily identified itself to my fingertips. When stone became wood, I guessed it must be the front gate of Pembroke and turned towards an egg-yolk halo which materialized in the form of the Porter's Lodge. The porter, called Keeps if not Waits, knew an Aussie (which he mispronounced Ossie) when he heard one and was fully informed about kangaroos, koalas and the necessity of walking around upside down when down under, ha ha. Having exhausted the subject and me along with it, he directed me to my set of rooms, D6 in the old court, known as Old Court, above the dining hall, known as Hall. Having asked for 'the smallest possible set of rooms consonant with my playing the clarinet', I found that I had been given an oak-panelled suite which would have been large enough to accommodate Benny Goodman, and his big band along with him. It scarcely needs saying that I couldn't play the clarinet at all, but on the day I made the written application I must have been toying with the idea of taking up that instrument. As I stood beside my suitcase in the middle of the sitting room, a handsome young man in a silk brocade dressing gown appeared suddenly beside me with a silence made possible by monogrammed leather slippers. 'Abramovitz,' he said, holding out a pampered hand. I knew that this wasn't my name so I guessed that it must be his. 'I live across the corridor. *Love* that beard. Don't worry, I'm not bent or anything. Just philanthropic. Let me show you the form.'

At least five years younger than I, Abramovitz carried on as if he were fifty years older. He was reading law and naturally assumed that the only reason I was reading English for a second undergraduate degree was in order to give myself time for plenty of extracurricular activities. He advised me to step around to the Societies Fair in the Corn Exchange before I decided finally on trying out for the

Footlights. He himself believed the Union to be the only thing that counted if one had one's eye on high government office. I asked him if he was going to be Prime Minister. 'No, Disraeli was the last of our boys they'll ever let in there. Chancellor of the Exchequer: that's the spot.' He explained to me what to do about laundry, of which, as usual, I had more needing to be done than done. He also showed me how to sport my oak. A heavy rolling outer door, the oak was meant to signal that the occupant was at home to nobody, although it was left unclear whether this applied to Abramovitz.

His advice turned out to be good, however. The Societies Fair was indeed a cornucopia of activities, like Orientation Week at Sydney University but on the scale of the Earls Court motor show. Here was my chance to get interested in heraldry, beagling and riding to hounds. Each activity had a booth attended by undergraduates in the appropriate costume. The dramatic societies stood out through having a more abundant, although scarcely lavish, presence of under-graduettes. Careful not to squander my whole grant at once, I did not actually join these dramatic societies there and then, but spent a lot of time standing around being told why I should. Some of the girls from the ADC I thought especially persuasive. But the dramatic society whose booth most impressed me was the Footlights. It con-sisted of one bare trestle table. Behind it sat a solitary, fine-drawn, bored-looking individual in a tan cashmere jacket. 'How do I join?' I asked. 'You don't,' he said through a barely controlled yawn. 'You audition.' Informing me that his name was Idle, he handed me a roneoed set of instructions saying where, when and how. The auditions were some time off and the chances of selection seemed very slim.

My theatrical urges were further stimulated by the purchase of a gown. Throwing my bearded chin upright and drawing the gown's black drapes around my shoulders, I looked like a Wittelsbach crown prince going mildly ga-ga or a close friend of Count Dracula in search of a meal. When I appeared that evening in Hall there was a hush on the benches and some of the freshmen seemed to feel vulnerable in the area of the neck. Actually I would have done better to dine off them than off the food. This latter proved useful only as a discussion point. The entrée wasn't tender enough to be a paving stone and the gravy couldn't have been primordial soup because morphogenesis was already taking place. 'How *about* this shit?' said a rotund American whose name turned out to be Delmer Dynamo. 'You can bet they're eating something else up *there*.' He angled his pear-shaped head towards High Table, where, surveyed by a plaster bust of William Pitt the Younger, the dons were Dining in Fellowship. They weren't exactly joined together with cobwebs but you couldn't have called them vibrant. It wasn't their age, so much as their well-being, that impressed. Even at a distance you could tell that the dark wine was helping the venison go down to their profound satisfaction. I wondered which of them was the Senior Tutor of Supervisors, whom I was due to meet next day. Or was he called the Senior Supervisor of Tutors?

When I turned up next day to meet him, all the other freshmen in the college turned up too. The Senior Tutor, whose full title turned out to be the Senior Tutor of Junior Supervisors, was obviously shy, but equally obviously he had overcome this disability by a meticulous attention to social punctilio. He made small talk and expected every-body else to do the same. Five minutes after shaking hands with him I found myself left alone with an Iranian biochemist whose name sounded like a fly trapped against a window. This sudden conjunction was blessed with our mentor's assurance that we would have a lot in common. What we had in common was a small glass of sherry and a large measure of awkwardness. I cursed the Tutor for this instead of doing the sensible thing and asking a few questions about biochem-istry, a field in which my interlocutor was later to become eminent. If I had asked a few questions about the Senior Tutor I would have found out that he was the world's leading authority on Propertius. Surrounded by distinction, both actual and potential, I was exclusively occupied with not dribbling sherry into my beard. With that, and with the inexplicable presence of Abramovitz. 'What are *you* doing here?' I asked when I had manoeuvred my way to his side through the crowd: 'I thought this was for freshmen.' 'But I *am* a freshman,' said Abramovitz happily. 'I came up the day before you did.' It struck me on the spot that if the English had spent their lives preparing to fit into one of these places, then the only smart thing to do was not to bother about fitting in at all, and I can honestly say that from that moment on I never wasted any time trying. I wasted time doing other things, but not doing that.

Drinks next day with the Master once again featured the full cast, and once again the tipple was warm sherry. The Master was a retired pure mathematician who had no pretensions towards social ease. Wearing a full-length gown, he stood glumly in the centre of the room while we milled around him in our short gowns. Throwing a glass of sherry down my throat and plucking another from a passing silver platter, I assessed him as a nonentity and was duly rewarded for my acumen by finding out, twenty years later, that he had been on the committee which approved the funds for the first Manchester computer just after the Second World War. Being in possession of that information at the time might have induced enough awe to offset the aggrieved loneliness with which I drank. Apart from the biochemist with the buzzer for a name and the omnipresent Abramovitz, the only face I found familiar was that of Delmer Dynamo. His pear-shaped head, I could now see, was situated on top of a pear-shaped body, which his black gown caused to resemble a piece of fruit going to a funeral. 'How about *this* for a wing-ding?' he shouted conspiratorially. 'You can blow it out your ass. Have you met the Dean yet?' I replied that I was due to meet the Dean the next day. 'You're gonna dig it,' averred Delmer. 'Mind you, he hasn't got this bozo's carefree verve.'

Delmer was only almost right. The Dean, whose name was the Reverend Meredith Dewey, was indeed a picture of inactivity as he sat back in a winged leather armchair and expended just enough energy to keep his pipe alight. But unlike the Master he had overt characteristics. For one thing, his room was full of rocks. The Dean was an amateur geologist who picked up souvenir rocks every time he travelled abroad in order to attend some less-than-crucial ecumenical drone-in. Indeed there were irreverent suggestions that he would accept the occasional invitation – like the one from the Pan-African Convocation of Pastoral Curators in Accra – just so that, between papers and seminars, he could go forth unto the hills and root around for chunks of granite. Doubtless these imputations arose from envy, but only a historian of mining engineering would have been envious: the Dean's rooms were on the first floor and for many years had been arousing concern among the female staff in the linen room below. As they toiled over the ironing of our sheets and pillowcases, they had to live with the mental picture of the creaking ceiling finally bursting open and the Dean's massive collection descending on them like the temple of the Philistines after Samson gave it the push. When you sat facing the Dean you were surrounded by about thirty million years of the Earth's petrified history. While he dutifully enquired after your spiritual welfare you could fill the time by wondering how he got the stuff through customs. There was no problem about how he carried it. Though of only medium height, he had shoulders like Charles Atlas and could obviously lug a tote-bag full of pitchblende for miles. But when those decolonized *douaniers* opened up his luggage and found it crammed with unrefined ore, why didn't they suspect him of stealing their uranium?

The sleepy holiness of his appearance was the only explanation. I told him about my atheism and socialism. His eyelids grew as heavy as sandstone, a large piece of which was poised on a sideboard for purposes of comparison. 'Convinced about that beard, are you?' he enquired tentatively, then lapsed into silence while I explained about radical socialism. I interpreted his apparent torpor as a sherry-fuelled sloth. It was only later on, when I found out how sharp he was, that I realized he was politely but immovably bored rigid at meeting his ten thousandth young saviour of the world. With his direct line to an earlier and better qualified envoy sent on the same task, the Dean was in the position of a senior manager who is required, for form's sake, to go on interviewing candidates after the job has been filled. He released supplicatory puffs of smoke heavenward, tapped his fingertips together, and snuck lazy, longing sideways looks at an inviting lump of lignite.

Overseeing my studies in English was Dr Stewart Frears. Professor Frears, as he later became, was, although the senior English don in the college, only a lecturer at that stage, but he was already an authority on the Metaphysical poets, to which his learned and common-sensical approach had already been more than enough to attract regular vilification from Dr Leavis. In life as in death – between which two states he was currently hovering – Leavis was the most contentious name in Cambridge. Like an old volcano that goes dead in its central crater but unpredictably blows hot holes through its own sides and obliterates villages which thought themselves safe, Leavis was dormant yet still bubbling. Frears caught more than his fair share of the lava and perhaps this accounted at least partly for a pronounced nervous tic. He would periodically click his teeth and twitch his head sideways almost to one shoulder, like a violinist trying to smash his instrument no hands. He won't mind my recalling this trivial affliction because later on it disappeared. (All the many recipients of routine libels from Leavis got a bit flak-happy in one way or another but in almost every case the trouble cleared up after the old warrior passed on to that great Organic Community, which, despite his vehement assurances that it once existed on Earth, has its foundations only in the cloudy soil of the Empyrean.) While it was still happening, however, Dr Frears's flicking tic inevitably attracted some of the attention I was supposed to be directing towards the post-Elizabethans. Actually, to do myself the discredit I had coming, I was having a hard time getting interested again in the Metaphysicals. I had passed through my first Donne period in Sydney and was not to go crazy about him again for another decade or so. In short, I had done Donne. Currently, I was much more under the sway of the Cavaliers, the Romantics and any other historical group except the one I was supposed to be studying. Reading off the course was my temperamental habit. Nowadays I devour whole literatures in sequential order, making notes and writing essays all the way. It's because I don't have to. When I did have to, I couldn't do it.

So it wasn't just my supervisor's neck-snapping twitch that put me off George Herbert. But even had I been as respectful of Herbert as I am now – anyone who tells you that Herbert is negligible beside Donne doesn't understand Donne either – I would have had trouble articulating a clear analysis of *The Temple* if my interlocutor were continually threatening to catch a fly between his cheek and shoulder. I got increasingly nervous about turning up for my weekly supervision. As usual, I lied my way out of trouble, inventing various ailments. Shoving a piece of cotton wool behind my lower lip and pretending to have an abscess was perhaps the silliest trick. Even my better wheezes were schoolboy stuff and the man in charge wasn't fooled. He could have had me rusticated. It sounded like being castrated with a rusty knife and it hurt even worse, because it meant being thrown back into the harsh world where you had to earn a living. Instead, very generously, he passed me further down the line, to those junior dons who were still, as he put it, 'in the first fury of their supervisions'. It sounded too much like work but at least I was still along for the ride.

And the ride meant Footlights. The club held two smoking concerts (called smokers) each term. The first smoker of the first term was the chief audition smoker for new members. The club room was above MacFisheries fish shop in Falcon Yard, off Petty Cury. Required dress was a dinner jacket, which for purposes of the audition I hired. There was no point in buying one outright at that stage, because if I had not got in, there would have been no occasion for wearing it until I graduated. I played Noël Coward in an old Noël-Gertie routine written long ago in Sydney by my three-piece thoroughly Anglicized Australian friend, who had first invited me to Cambridge two years before and was now on the point of graduating. He was a member of Footlights but for some reason had never used the sketch himself. Perhaps he never found a suitable co-star. I was luckier. Though I made Noël Coward sound like Chips Rafferty, I was spurred on by a Gertrude who, although an Australian like me, could act well enough to be believable as anything. Her name was Romaine Rand.

Slightly older than I and already equipped with a degree from Melbourne, Romaine had descended on Sydney University while I was still a second year student. Tall, striking and already famous for her brilliantly foul tongue, she had pursued graduate studies, libertarian polemics, and, for a brief period, me. At the risk of sounding even more conceited than usual, it is important that I record this fact, for a reason which will shortly emerge. At the time I was having published, in the literary pages of the Sydney University student newspaper *honi soit*, a lot of articles, poems and short stories conveying omniscience, poise and worldly wisdom. Publication was not difficult to arrange, because I edited those pages. Correctly intuiting at a glance that I was grass-green in all matters and emerald-green in the matter of sex, Romaine, at her table in the Royal George Hotel, took bets with the Downtown Push that she could seduce me within twenty-four hours. Next day the news reached me before she did. When she appeared, striding like a Homeric goddess, at the door of the cafeteria in Manning House, I cravenly escaped through the side entrance and hid behind the large adjacent gum tree. The rumour that I hid *up* the tree was false but slow to die.

The following year I was a senior and had developed some real confidence, or at any rate had become convinced by my own swagger. This time it was I who pursued Romaine. When the old Union Hall of beloved memory was pulled down and replaced by a new theatre of unparalleled hideousness, I found Romaine sitting behind me at a matinee performance of one of the inaugural plays: some frail, panting comedy by Anouilh which was now receiving the *coup de grâce* from a hunting pack of Australian accents. I held hands with her in the dark: quite a trick when the woman is sitting in the row behind you. It was easy, I told myself, to detect the shy vulnerability which lay beneath this woman's strident show of independence. Consolingly I stroked her palm with my fingertips. They were a bit sweaty, but she didn't object. Later on I walked her home along Parramatta Road. I did my most accomplished heart-winning athletic feat: the one where I grabbed a lamp-post with both hands and stood straight out sideways into the passing traffic. She looked impressed. Running with sweat from these exertions, at her flat I invited myself to take a shower, and did not lose the opportunity to show off the muscular development of my torso, which in those days was arranged with most of the wide bits at the top. Again she looked impressed. Guess what? I didn't get her into bed.

The reason I am telling you all this is that Romaine herself blew the whole story long ago. After she became, deservedly, world famous, she seized the first chance to get back to Australia and tell the most chaotic journalist in the country – whose prose, when he had worked as my assistant on *honi soit*, I had always felt honour-bound to rewrite – the full story of my crummy seduction technique. She evoked my lamp-post lateral extensions and shower-booth biceps-flexing in such hilarious detail that not even the journalist's slovenly verbosity could dull the comic effect. As a champion of truth, a leading light in the struggle against male chauvinism and sexist hypocrisy, Romaine had a right to say all this. I was more appalled by what she didn't say. *She didn't say that she had chased me up that tree.* All right, behind that tree. She didn't say anything about betting the Downtown Push that she could deflower me in twenty-four hours from a standing start. Nothing. Not a word.

But all this was before and later. For the moment, I was standing back to back with Romaine on the tiny Footlights stage, she with her notable bust strapped down under an old A-line satin frock suitably modified – Romaine was always a dab hand at the household tasks against which she later rebelled on behalf of womankind – and I resplendent in watered-down hair and made-up velvet bow tie holding together the collar of one of my old off-white drip-dries. The rented DJ with its stove-pipe pants descended into a brand new pair of black bootees with zips up the inner ankle. Romaine had a cigarette holder the length of a billiard cue and I held my cigarette from underneath, like a Russian spy. With our nostrils given an extra arch of fastidiousness by the smell of halibut rising through the floorboards from the marble display tables of MacFisheries below, we mouthed brittle dialogue. I was awful, she was great, so we both got in. Romaine thus became one of the very first female members of the Footlights, because that was the smoker at which Eric Idle – the slim, dapper and unnervingly deep young President – finally managed to realize his long-laid plan of extending the franchise to the other half of the human race. Up until then, women could appear in Footlights revues only as guests, and most of the dons who congregated around the club's small but thriving bar made it piercingly clear that they had preferred the era of good, straight-forward transvestism, with properly shaved legs and no nonsense about it. Keeping her gratitude well under control, Romaine eyed some of the assembled senior members with manifest disdain. 'This place is jumping with freckle-punchers,' she told me confidentially, so that only about thirty of them choked on their drinks. 'You can have it on your own.'

So we immediately split up again. Companionship between Romaine and myself had never been easy, because each of us suspected the other of the desire to conduct a perpetual monologue and neither was inclined to act as the feed-man, or feed-person. In my view she argued exclusively from the emotions and in her view I must have epitomized the kind of arrogant male who would hold such an assumption. Apart from and below all that, however, was a deeper reason: in those days ambitious young Australians left their country in order to discover themselves as individuals. Clinging together when abroad was the last thing they wanted to do. The idea that the Australians in England roll logs for each other has always been exactly wrong. Most of them wouldn't roll a twig. I could barely name two of them who would roll me into an open grave.

Romaine took one look at the English Tripos requirements, declared them infantile, and by force of argument got herself registered as a PhD student. The University Library, in keeping with the vaguely pre-Columbian threat of its appearance, swallowed her up like a tomb. Perhaps it had absorbed all the other women in Cambridge too. There seemed to be very few of them, and fewer still who were available. From the two women's colleges, Newnham and Girton, only a handful of girls took enough time off from their studies to appear in the vicinity of the dramatic societies. These brave rebels would attend Footlights smokers but otherwise they were to be observed only near Sidgwick Avenue on their way to and from lectures. On ordinary nights in the club there was scarcely a woman to be seen, except the occasional up-and-coming, or more likely down-and-going, actress from a touring company who would take a late-night snort after the evening performance in the Arts Theatre. The relative absence of a civilizing female influence made it all the easier to get disgustingly drunk. One was allowed to run up a bar bill. Mine became a bar booklet. The door of the Footlights closed at night long after the front door of my college, so after navigating my way from Petty Cury to the street behind Pembroke I had to climb over the back wall. Climbing in (called Climbing In) was an experience that varied from college to college. Though frowned on, it was an accepted practice. Undergraduates couldn't walk through town after dark without their gowns or else the Beadles would challenge them and, if necessary, give chase. The Beadles wore bowler hats and most of them had RAF moustaches. Wind resistance, however, did nothing to slow them down. But once you had reached the walls of your college there were no patrols to stop you climbing in. The occasional drunken undergraduate who impaled himself on a railing spike received no punishment beyond the scar. When King's had a physically handicapped undergraduate it installed a small handrail on one of the walls near the river so that he could climb in without drowning. It was all very English: a rule made to be broken, as long as you didn't kick up a fuss. Within the first two weeks I became adept at scaling the back wall whatever my state of inebriation, crossing the roof of the bike shed and dropping to the ground beside a huge cylindrical metal skip in which rubbish was placed for incineration. In the third week, however, I was so drunk one night that I dropped in the wrong spot, with a noise like a huge gong being softly struck. I woke up inside the skip several hours later, a bleak dawn sky overhead.

2. THE DEAR OLD COLLEGE

College life had its attractions. Had I been a few years younger, I might have fallen for them headlong. For undergraduates coming up from public schools, the colleges were no doubt too familiar in their accoutrements to be especially impressive. By public schools, of course, I mean private schools. A boy from Eton might have found even King's or Trinity the same old thing on an only slightly larger scale: the same turrets, crenellations, lodges, fenestrations, cloisters, clerestories, porticos and porters. Those freshmen who came from State schools, however, now met with a concentration of custom and ceremony which had the wherewithal to overwhelm them. It didn't have to hurry. It had all the time in the world. Since I was still a radical socialist, I had no trouble analysing how the system worked. The idea was to tame the intelligent upstart by getting him addicted to privilege. The beautiful architecture had a political function. In Paris, Haussmann's great boulevards were only incidentally grandiloquent: their real purpose was to provide the widest field of fire for the artillery and the quickest access for the cavalry to anywhere the workers might stage a rebellion. In Cambridge, the lovely façades, the sweeping lawns, the intricate crannies opening on distant vistas, were meant not just to lull but to disarm: nobody who had once lived in these emollient surroundings would ever again feel sufficiently alienated from society to be anything more troublesome than a reformist. Gradualism was implicit in every carefully repainted coat of arms and battered refectory table. To remain a revolutionary in such a context you would have had to have treason in the blood, like Kim Philby. Such, at any rate, was the theory, or what I took the theory to be. My college, as I tried my best not to call it, was hardly prodigal with the creature comforts but it knew how to make life convenient. To get my laundry done, all I had to do was put it in a box and leave the box at the head of the staircase. In the course of time, a box of fresh laundry would magically appear in the same place. There are men in British public life to whom this has gone on happening into old age. They are under the impression that their laundry is taken care of by a force of nature. Such coveted hidey-holes for gentlefolk as the Albany in Piccadilly aren't selling the luxury of the Savoy: they are selling the invisible services of the dear old college. The oak-panelled walls are there to remind the inhabitants of school and university. The laundry box is there to reassure them that there is still a linen room somewhere which they will die without ever having to visit.

All this I could anatomize with the piercing insight of Marx and Engels. But I put my laundry into the box just the same. It was too handy to pass up. Similarly the bedder was an institution which could not be defended but was impossible to forego. The bedder was a woman who made your bed. Many of us were ashamed that a woman who might otherwise have been employed doing useful work for society, not to mention fulfilling herself spiritually, was earning a pittance by squaring up our crapulous sheets and blankets. Not many of us ever met her, however. I met mine just once, and just long enough to learn that she valued the work without necessarily valuing me, whose standards of hygiene she found questionable. 'I have to speak frankly, Mr James,' she quacked unprompted. 'Frankly, the best thing to be said for you is that Mr Abramovitz is even worse, frankly.' Her name was Mrs Blades and she looked tough enough to need no defending. So I decided to put off the moment of going to the barricades on her behalf. Very soon I left my bed unmade without giving it a thought, and came back in the afternoon to find it made without giving that a thought either. After all, the same thing had happened at home for the first eighteen years of my life.

Similarly, my initial impressions of the food served in Hall were soon modified. At first I had thought the food was terrible and that I would never be able to eat it. After a few weeks I had come round to the opinion that the food was terrible but that I could eat it. Here again, the arrangements were just too convenient to pass up. Breakfast was there for the taking. I rarely took it. Usually I got up just in time for lunch. It didn't taste of anything, but that could have been the fault of my mouth, fur-lined after a heavy evening. For dinner, you had your choice of first or second sitting, as on board ship. The advantage of the first sitting was that the High Table was empty. At the second sitting, if you looked up from your plate of burnt offerings and denatured vegetable matter, you were faced with the spectacle of the dons Dining in Fellowship off a haunch of venison while they circulated the claret with the speed of happy children playing pass-the-parcel. On the other hand the second sitting enabled you to linger over an extra half pint of acceptable bitter before gravitating to the graduates' parlour for a noggin of port or three. Either way, I could get from my rooms to dinner simply by dragging on a gown and falling downstairs. Falling off a log would have been harder, and I wouldn't have got fed.

This cosy, effortless taking-on of sustenance had an irresistible appeal, especially considering that I was under no compulsion to fraternize with my fellow undergraduates beyond rubbing gowned elbows with them at the long low table. I entered the Junior Common Room only, if ever, to read the newspapers. My in-college hangout was the graduates' parlour, where one could sign for one's drinks and comport oneself almost as a don. Another Australian affiliate, Brian C. Adams, overdid this to the point of not even hanging up his gown. He stood around pontifically in full drag, his accent, during the course of one term, losing all trace of antipodean colouring, and acquiring, during the course of a second term, an affinity with that of Princess Margaret. '*Eigh-ow*,' he would neigh, '*rarely?*' He meant 'Oh really?' but the expression emerged like a chicken which had been strangled in a letter box and then pushed out through the slit. Not that Adams was stupid. He was merely quicker than most to go native. He was arrogant, but at least he was honest. Reading English like me, he was after first class honours, and said so. His unprompted disquisitions on critical theory made me wonder if I would be able to get a third even if I worked. He had already read everything, and was now reading it again. He talked learnedly about the Spirit of the College, I suppose with some justification, because he never left its front gate except to attend lectures in Sidgwick Avenue, visit the University Library, or sit at the feet of F. R. Leavis in Downing. In Pembroke, the Gray Society was a literary organization which met monthly to hear a paper. Brian C. Adams became secretary of the Gray Society before I had even heard that it existed. In Australia, while still an undergraduate, he had published a slim but substantial critical work, *Johnson's Boswell: the Man-made Self*. Two copies of this booklet promptly appeared in Pembroke College Library, with the signature of Brian C. Adams on the donor's bookplate. Brian C. Adams was a College Man.

If, however, you had gagged him, stripped the gown off him, and viewed him from a suitable distance, Brian C. Adams might just conceivably have been mistaken for an ordinary human being. The true embodiment of the College Spirit was Delmer Dynamo. Though his satirical verbal assaults on the college food and facilities never ceased, it was clear that Delmer had found his promised land. His tailoring becoming more gentlemanly by the week, he would manoeuvre his low-slung posterior into position against the open fire of the graduates' parlour, part the rear wings of his Savile Row tweed jacket, and toast himself like a marshmallow while lovingly discussing the Dean's proclivities, real and imagined. 'The question isn't how he gets his rocks *in*,' Delmer would announce loudly. 'The question is how he gets his rocks *off*.' Delmer called the graduates' parlour the grad pad, a designation which eventually all its habitués, even the English, took up. There could be no doubt that the grad pad's cosiest amenity was Delmer himself. He was in there like the furniture. Similarly he was as prominent in Hall as Spenser's portrait or Pitt's bust. Every graduate was invited once a year to dine at High Table. Delmer wangled it three times in his first term. Dining on offal down in the pit, we would look up at him while he sat there being waited on. He would be attacking the venison while the stringy beef was attacking us. At assimilating himself to the English establishment, Delmer Dynamo left Disraeli looking like Guy Fawkes. It was because he was so interested. He knew all the college gossip. Few dons could resist the way he talked about their colleagues. The college was a microcosm which he took at its own estimation, as a macrocosm. Not even the Dean could do without Delmer, who had mugged up the whole history of Pembroke's most precious architectural possession, the Wren chapel. 'Sometimes I can't believe that boy's Jewish,' the Dean was heard to say. 'He really does know an *awful* lot about stained glass.' The Dean would invite Delmer to sherry and show him geological treasures kept in thin glass-topped drawers in locked cabinets: slivers of silver, chips of chalcedony, amulets of anthracite, lollipops of lapis lazuli. Delmer feigned interest far into the night, plugging his yawns with a fat Havana cigar. The Dean liked Delmer's cigars, of which Delmer's father, once a term, sent him a dove-tailed box the size of a small suitcase.

The Master and his wife asked Delmer to dinner in the Lodge, where Delmer, maddened by the Madeira, announced his intention of willing his personal library to the college. He was lucky that the Master laughed the offer off. Delmer's book-buying already represented a large, if indiscriminate, investment. In receipt of all the rare book catalogues, he chose from them almost at random, and within a seemingly unlimited budget. If he purchased a set of, say, Maria Edgeworth better than the one he already had, he gave the old one to the college library, where the bookplate marked 'From the collection of Delmer Dynamo' was soon familiar. Delmer's declared aim was to rival the learning, taste and munificence of the legendary Aubrey Attwater, who, at the turn of the century, had been the college humanist *par excellence*, a byword for fine wine, fine bindings and fine manners. Delmer founded the Aubrey Attwater society, electing himself both president and secretary. When it turned out that he was also the entire membership, he prorogued the next meeting *sine die*, but without giving up on his ambition to emulate Attwater's luxurious indolence. For Delmer, college was more than a context. It was a niche, a cradle. It was an egg cup.

I saw the point but wanted something else. Perhaps my brain just wasn't subtle enough for me to sit around until all hours amidst the softly lit oak panelling while discussing why Selwyn was an obscure college, Sidney Sussex was more obscure, and Fitzwilliam was even more obscure than either. In my view, the differences between colleges were impossible to detect. I had, and still have today, enough trouble telling the difference between Cambridge and Oxford, too many of whose products flatter themselves that they have been stamped by the one with some indelible hallmark which informs the discerning that they did not go to the other. No doubt Pembroke had enjoyed more than its fair share of poetic talent – as well as the aforesaid Spenser and Gray, Christopher Smart and Ted Hughes had both been there – but the fund of creativity wouldn't be added to by feeling smug about it while warming one's behind at the fireplace of the grad pad. Without feeling disloyal to my college, I felt under no compulsion to make it my sole stamping ground. A wider stage beckoned: fairly begged, in fact, to be occupied.

Like Oxford, Cambridge was, as it still is, an aggregate of colleges. The university as a whole existed only in two ways: one, as a means to examine the undergraduates, and two, as a display case for their extracurricular activities. Into these latter I purposefully entered. Actually, I did not have much of a plan, but since I was four or five years older than most of my fellow undergraduates – a big gap at that age – I was, although unusually immature, a bit less unsure of myself than they were, and in my principal activity, writing, I had the immense advantage of having been at it a while longer. Cambridge was full of aspiring writers. To publish their works, there was a whole range of periodicals: the weekly newspaper *Varsity* and the irregularly appearing but dauntingly historic *Granta* were only the two most prominent. There were poetry magazines with names like *Pawn*, *Solstice*, *Inverse*, and – a token of seriousness, this – *Poetry Magazine*. There was a stapled, cyclostyled weekly called *Broadsheet* which reviewed everything: the penniless prototype of the listings magazines which ten years later were to strike it rich. The *Cambridge Review*, for which William Empson had once written and in whose letter columns the Leavisites would still occasionally immolate a colleague, was put out by graduates, but otherwise the whole immense publishing effort was produced by a few young men, and fewer young women, all *in statu pupillari*. They were in constant search of publishable material. They were about to meet the right man. They had the demand and I had the supply. In prose even more than in verse, I was still trying to bring my style under control, but in comparison to all the other hungry young geniuses I had the odd scrap of solid information to offer along with the strained metaphors and the overloaded syntax. When I reviewed a film, for example, I could quite often refer to other films by the same director. All those tickets to the National Film Theatre, paid for by my dear lost love Lilith Talbot, were now to have their effect. The great age of the undergraduate film buff had not yet arrived. Nowadays every university in the country boasts a dozen young aspiring film critics who know everything about their subject, even if, because they have seen so many films so fast, they know nothing about anything else. In my day, such a range of reference was less common. I was a harbinger. For *Varsity*, reviewing *Muriel*, I launched into a survey of Resnais's entire *oeuvre*, including the rarely seen *Nuit et Brouillard*. For *Broadsheet*, reviewing *Cuba Si!*, I questioned whether Chris Marker in a state of certainty could ever be as interesting as he was in *Letter from Siberia*, when he was in a state of doubt. Other undergraduate would-be cultural journalists might have been cleverer than I was – as I was later to discover, several of them were – but they hadn't been alive long enough to have that kind of scope. Beyond that, I had the virtue of my chief drawback. My childish imagination was still vivid with the gaudy bric-a-brac which had helped to form it. I wrote about Tarzan and Jane as if they were still real to me. They were, so I sounded convinced, and to sound convinced is the first and longest step towards sounding convincing. My prose pieces gave the effect, strained for though it might be, of a sort of panoptic pop. For the undergraduate editors, always too short of publishable contributions, I was a gift horse who ran off at the mouth.

Soon I was appearing in every publication. The poetry magazines I supplied from the dog-eared back catalogue of finished masterpieces that lined my cardboard suitcase. Here again, there were other undergraduate aspirants more talented. But they were in the first phase of their development and I was in the second of mine. I had got to the point where I would keep working on a poem until it sounded, to my ears at least, like a finished product, not just a promise. It hardly needs saying that my judgment was often faulty: no amount of finishing touches will compensate for a bad design. Much of what I then published seemed to me so immature in retrospect – and retrospect began only a few years later – that at one recent stage I seriously planned to buy up all surviving copies of the relevant magazines and burn them. But at the time it must have seemed, and not just to me, that my work had an authority lacking in the average undergraduate's contribution. It would have been surprising if this had not been so. The poets and editors – all the editors were poets and most of the poets were editors – were admirably poised in their reserved demeanour but they were terribly young. They wore tweeds and corduroys. One of them smoked a pipe and ate seed cake with his sweet tea. Another hid his acne with his hand. The occasional poet-editor was a classless *arriviste*, called something like Steve Bumption, who wore a white leather jacket and talked about Graphics, but at that point trendiness had barely impinged. 'Graphics,' he would say, 'is where it's *all happening*.' But he was saying it into a void. It was all happening in Carnaby Street, not in Cambridge. Mostly the young people who ran the university literary scene looked and sounded as if they belonged in a wartime BBC radio studio along with C. Day Lewis and Louis MacNeice. They crouched beside the gas fire in their rooms pasting up the layout of the next issue on the threadbare carpet while they drank Nescafé from chipped mugs. Doubtless they had ambitions of their own but this failed to occur to me when I burst in and brow-beat them into running a two-page layout of what I cheerfully assured them was my best stuff. Since I never took 'no' for an answer, their only way to reject my work was to accept it and then try to forget it. I wouldn't let them forget it. Even in that first year, about two-thirds of everything I submitted got published, which, since I submitted a lot, was a lot. My self-assurance must have been a bit tough on the nerves of some of the young poets who had been around for two years already and might have hoped to shine unrivalled during their third year. None of them sought to make me aware of this, or even, in my hearing at any rate, objected to a colonial taking over. There might, of course, have been the odd snide comment I missed. There probably wasn't much I didn't miss, come to think of it. I had never been much of a one for the hidden message. Nor did it occur to me that a lack of editorial resistance might not necessarily be a good thing. What I really needed was discouragement.

Fate decreed that in the theatrical field, if in no other, I would soon get what was coming to me. At the second Footlights smoker in the first term I was on stage in half a dozen different sketches. The Footlights club room, while it had a curtained stage, had no deep wings or any other means of concealment while you waited your turn to go on. Under the windows on the Falcon Yard side of the clubroom there was a wooden bench where you had to wait. It was *de rigueur* to look up at the stage and pretend to enjoy the act preceding yours. As I write, I can feel the curve of that wooden bench under my buttocks: it grew so familiar. Like the oiled stench coming up through the floor from MacFisheries below, and the thump of the dancing feet coming down from the Yacht Club through the ceiling above, the pinch of the bench evoked a cocktail of fear and triumph. You couldn't have the triumph without feeling the fear first. Thus the basic structure of any theatrical experience was laid out cold. Without having in any way begun to refine my sketches – it still hadn't crossed my mind that they would have to be constructed at least as carefully as poems – I went out to the little stage often enough to make an impact. Also I had an angle. My stuff was literary. With the aid of an unsuspecting Canadian who played Alice B. Toklas, I performed a sketch I had written about Gertrude Stein. Nobody really understood it – I'm sure of that because I didn't either – but at least the number had a tone of its own. At that time, the Footlights was going through one of its recurring periods of looking for a new style. A few years before, *Cambridge Circus*, essentially a Footlights May Week revue with a bigger budget, had conquered London and eventually the world. The Footlights, which had recovered from the success of supplying half the cast of *Beyond the Fringe*, was once again plunged into the necessity of not repeating itself. In London, the satire boom was already commercialized to the point where joining it would have looked slavish. The challenge, as always, was to find your own voice, and the problem, as always, was to find out where that had been mislaid. The club was full of precociously accomplished young performers but as yet they had little to say. I had a lot to say, even if I was not accomplished. This put me in the dangerous position of playing uncle: my worst role. Like most people who organize their lives badly, I just love giving advice.

The Footlights committee were advised by their new recruit to climb on a train and go up to London to see the opening night of *The Charge of the Light Fandango*. The revue I had written with my erstwhile Svengali and long-term collaborator Spencer had found a backer: Spencer's father-in-law. My share of the writing had largely been completed before I came up to Cambridge. Employing the odd weekend *exeat*, I had attended a few rehearsals and helped Spencer to rewrite those of our songs and sketches which threatened to be insufficiently obscure. The cast were all Australian expatriates with high hopes. Some of them had been abroad long enough to be wondering if the big break would ever come. Spencer himself had high hopes, strangely enough. His dedication to obliquity was unimpaired but somehow he expected that his efforts to alienate the audience would meet with rapturous applause. Less forgivably, I expected the same result. I not only should have known better, I *did* know better: but I had been caught up. Any theatrical event has a momentum of its own: any theatrical event except *The Charge of the Light Fandango*. The Lyric Theatre, Hammersmith, had been hired at colossal expense. The Footlights committee were sitting with me in a box. To say that the disaster unfolded would be to exaggerate its pace. The disaster developed at the speed of stale cheese growing blue hair. It was all low points, but perhaps the lowest was a song about a jewel robbery which Spencer and I, greatly pleased with our own ingenuity, had written to the tune of Ravel's *Bolero*. Six of the cast were meant to sing it while tip-toeing in intricate patterns around the stage. If they had merely forgotten the words it would have been a mercy. Pummelled by the waves of indifference from the auditorium, however, they remembered the words, but in the wrong order. Since the choreography was cued by the lyrics, the actors were soon out of sequence. Eventually two of them were out of sight, having taken craven advantage of their proximity to the wings. It was hard to blame them. The song was a *tour de force* and nothing else.

The whole show was like that. It was all technique. Even at that time I half-realized it: a pretty drastic self-appraisal after more than a year's work. The Lord Chamberlain, who at that time still exercised his baleful influence on the British theatre, had insisted that my best sketch be left out. It was an all-purpose Queen's speech, in which the sovereign assured some foreign country that her best wishes, warm blankets or aircraft carriers were on their way towards it. The idea was that she could cross out what did not apply. When the Lord Chamberlain crossed out the whole thing, I tried to convince myself that censorship had wrecked our chances. The dutiful chuckles of the Footlights committee should have told me the truth. They stayed to the end, in sharp contrast to the majority of the audience, which drained away steadily throughout the first half, leaving the second half to be watched only by friends and relatives. The party afterwards was a wake in all respects except the failure of Spencer's father-in-law to realize that he was the corpse. Either he enjoyed losing money or else he was simply relieved about not having been on stage. It would have been disloyal to renounce my expatriate colleagues, who had all tried hard. Also I honestly felt (self-deception always feels particularly honest) that we had done something new and challenging. Privately, however, far back, in a dark part of my mind which admitted light but was slow to reflect it, I was getting ready to begin again. In Sydney, though I had found Spencer's influence overwhelming, I had always harboured secret desires to establish a contact with the audience. In Cambridge, the undergraduate thespians, however green, shared the same impulse. The polite young men I was with wanted to be entertainers and so did I. On the train back up to Cambridge we talked about something else. They were so kind and tactful that they frightened me. Where had they got it, this sensitivity to the pain of others? School must have been Hell, like the trenches in the First World War, which could have been the subject of the reviews that *The Charge of the Light Fandango* got next day. I read them in the Junior Common Room and resisted the temptation to rip them out of the newspapers so that nobody else would see them. This forbearance might have been, had it been conscious, a correct guess about the tactical advisability of not reacting to criticism. In reality, however, I was so drained of energy that the effort of tearing a sheet of newspaper would have left me breathless.

Luckily a chance to work off my embarrassment offered itself straight away. Footlights was not the only institution to stage smokers. Some of the colleges had an annual smoker of their own. These college smokers were staffed almost exclusively by Footlights members who were not necessarily members of the college concerned. In other words, the Footlights were pulling a fast one. The relevant university bye-law, fiercely enforced by the proctors, allowed the Footlights only two smokers per term plus the annual May Week revue. In order to work up the best material from the twice-a-term Footlights smokers into a form which might possibly make it into the May Week revue, the Footlights infiltrated the college smokers. Any Footlights member who wasn't enrolled at the college concerned was invited in as a guest. A sufficiently fanatical Footlights performer could thus tread the boards in the club room, in his own college and as a guest in every other college, so that he was in a constant rhythm of rehearsing and performing for as long as the academic year lasted. In a college smoker, especially, he would get plenty of practice at playing to a wider audience, because a college smoker could be attended by anybody from that college or any other college, since the tickets were on the open market.

Of all the college smokers, the most reliably successful was the Pembroke smoker. When Peter Cook had been up, agents from London would attend the Pembroke smoker and try to purchase the material. On one occasion Cook sold the whole show to the West End. The effect of his professionalism, though not necessarily of his originality, had lingered on. It was a hard act to follow, and when the Footlights committee suggested that I might like to direct the next Pembroke smoker I was not hasty in saying yes. Without question I was the natural choice. The only other Footlights member from my college was some kind of scientist who had been elected to the club by accident after giving what the audience had taken to be a brilliant impersonation of a man who had forgotten a terrible script. When the fact finally percolated that the script had really been terrible and that he had, indeed, forgotten it, he settled down for three years of enjoying the bar facilities and left the field clear for me. But although I had no doubts about the desirability of going back to basics and learning to please an audience, I had several doubts about whether this was the right time to do it. First of all, there was the question of my studies, which so far were non-existent. Also my confidence was not at its highest. The quality of the silence with which the audience had greeted *The Charge of the Light Fandango* was still ringing in my ears like a blow to the side of the head with the flat of the hand. I could still hear every cough, every wild, bitter laugh of disbelief, every bang of the safety exit double-doors as the steel bar across them was hit loudly by the uncaring fist of another customer baling out like a test pilot from a prototype spinning to its doom. Finally, the doors had been held open by the usherettes. They had nodded knowingly. I didn't want to see that knowing nod again.

I was talked out of my gloom and into the job. Actually, the show couldn't lose. Eric Idle was in it and he knew all the ropes. Above all, he knew that what really mattered was the wine. Into Pembroke's old library, called Old Library, were carried many boxes of a cheap but acceptably smooth Beaujolais from Peter Dominic, who also supplied the glasses. Many of these were broken on the first night by the Hearties. The show ran for four nights and everybody came. The Hearties were merely the noisiest element. Large, boat-rowing types with low foreheads, thick necks and annoyingly pretty female companions imported from London, they laughed at everything, including the love songs. Everyone else enjoyed the show too, although most of them would have been hard put to give a clear account of it afterwards. All the men were in black tie and all the women in evening gowns. Some of the male dons would have liked to have been in evening gowns also, but they confined themselves to lipstick and rouge. The stage, constructed from beer crates for the occasion, was only about six feet square and stood uncurtained in one corner of the room, so that you could make an entrance through the door leading to the book-stack. The rest of the room was packed with small low tables tightly surrounded by increasingly happy people. The oxygen was quickly used up. So was the wine, except that our waiters kept replacing it. The heat was terrific. Breathing neat nitrogen, with only an unlimited supply of plonk to stave off dehydration, the entire audience was already drunk before the lights went down on the first act. Even the dons were shouting. But the level of physical behaviour remained decorous if you didn't count the periodic attempts by the Hearties to smash their table by dancing on it.

The show, I am bound to say, merited an enthusiastic response. A cast of all the best Footlights guest artists did their stuff, topped off by Romaine Rand's fabled striptease nun routine, making its first appearance since the Sydney University revue several years before. For its reincarnation in the Pembroke smoker, she had hand-sewn a whole new Carmelite nun's habit. She wore a particularly daring bikini underneath. Luckily, the Dean didn't see the show until the last night, when he bit through the stem of his pipe. Though Romaine pulled the walls in, really there was nothing in the show which did not go down a storm, mainly because the audience was clinically intoxicated, but partly because, in my role as producer, I had arranged the running order with some care, making sure that the up-beat songs came at the end of the half and stuff like that. I even got away with my own monologue. A whimsical little number about two railway locomotives in love, it went on for so long that the Hearties, from a sitting start, managed to reduce their table to matchwood before I was half-way through. But the show had built up too much impetus to be easily stopped. Since the whole of the university's theatrical establishment turned up over the course of the four nights, this small success could be counted as my first tangible impact on the broader Cambridge scene. For anyone with the right set of personal inadequacies, an applauding audience is a wine far more heady than anything that you can buy in a bottle. I was especially pleased to see the women putting their hands together admiringly. The wine having flowed freely for the cast as well as the audience, it was with a fond eye made foolish that I peeped low around the corner of the book-stack door while some other act was on stage and checked out those pretty faces looking up, lit as if they were spectators at a ballet by Degas. I felt love. I felt grief. I felt sick. Where had they been?

Wherever they had been, they were gone again when the fifth day dawned and there was no more Pembroke smoker to draw them out of their hiding-places. A life without women made it hard to be temperate. Theoretically, I was undeviatingly loyal to my near-fiancée,

Françoise. Having left Australia the year after I did, she was now studying in Florence. Italy was a long way away. My close Catholic acquaintance, Robin, was still in London, but even London needed an *exeat* and Robin was going through one of her recurring phases of being reconciled with the Church. Questions of fidelity aside, to know a girl in Cambridge would have been the answer, but where were they? The few that I clapped eyes on seemed capable of transferring themselves from the Sidgwick Avenue site to the safety of their Newnham sitting rooms within a matter of seconds, or else cycling back up Castle Hill to Girton as if competing successfully in the Tour de France. Perhaps I should have paid more attention to my personal appearance. Many a young man has worn himself to a frazzle practising verbal approaches when what he should have done was wash his hair. But even supposing I had squeaked with cleanliness, who would have seen the shine? Sitting through lectures at Sidgwick Avenue was too high a price to pay, and if the undergraduettes weren't working there, they were working in the University Library, the faculty libraries or their rooms. Study was all they ever did. Abramovitz had the answer but it took his kind of unembarrassable self-confidence. He toured the schools in Station Road where the foreign girls came to learn English, picked himself a strapping German with paradigmatically chiselled Aryan features, brought her back to his rooms and gave her English lessons. The fee was not in cash but in kind. Through Abramovitz's frequently sported oak, the squeals of his guest penetrated with ease. What was he doing to her in there? When I met him in the gyp room while brewing tea he would explain, trembling with repletion, that he was doing his bit for historic justice. 'I've *enslaved* her, dear boy. It's the guilt. She's putty in my hands.' I think he taunted her during the throes of need. Anyway, there was a big scandal when his ancient bedder – the same Mrs Blades who was my bedder too – tottered into his bedroom one morning and found half a dozen loosely knotted, awesomely heavy condoms festooned all over the decor. The one draped over the lampshade had started to fry. Presumably Mrs Blades had seen one or two of those things before, back around the time of the Battle of Jutland, because when she eyeballed six of them at once the shock of recognition drove her backwards all the way down the stairs and across the court into the Dean's office, where she had hysterics among the haematite. Convulsions amid the chrysoprase. She passed out into the porphyry. The Dean proclaimed the matter out of his spiritual jurisdiction and got in touch with the Chief Rabbi, who happened to be Abramovitz's uncle. Abramovitz should have had another year of living in college but he was told that next year he would have to take digs in town. He was lucky not to get sent down. He had luck running out of his ears so maybe the reprieve was just normal. Abramovitz was among the blessed. Some of the English he taught Helga apparently got her into a lot of trouble back in Stuttgart. 'Wasn't it remarkable,' he asked me years later, 'how *much* she looked like Heydrich?'

3. SLEEPING TIGER

Preparing for Part Two of the English Tripos was supposed to take me two academic years, and the first was already gone in a drunken haze. As usual, I had done quite a lot of reading. Again as usual, little of it was on the course. I had started teaching myself French by construing Proust a sentence at a time – the complete job was to take only slightly less than fifteen years – but to satisfy the examination requirements I would have done better to teach myself a bit more English from the English Moralists, some of whom I could not recognize even by name, let alone by their opinions. The unspoken policy in Cambridge was to give affiliated students like myself a long rein in their first year, although a certain proportion – mainly Americans, strangely enough – persisted in regarding the long rein as enough rope, and hanging themselves with it. Suicide from loneliness was unnervingly common. One of the many hazardous prospects of a bedder's job was to enter a young gentleman's oak-panelled sitting room in the morning and find him suspended from the central light-fitting. This possibility was rendered less likely in my case by the news that I too, like Abramovitz, might have to spend the following academic year lodged in the town, where oak panelling was less lavishly supplied. I was also officially advised that during the long vacation it might be profitable to attain at least nodding acquaintance with the curriculum, and thus stave off the already likely possibility that I would receive a degree classified so low it would be tantamount to a certificate of mental disability. But all these admonitions were easy to take lightly now that it was May Week in Cambridge.

May Week, one need hardly point out, took place in June. Only if it had been called April Week would it have taken place in May. Your first academic year in Cambridge is so arranged that you must learn to appreciate your surroundings in winter, when the trees are waterlogged traceries and the buildings are doomy silhouettes between sky and fen. Captain Cousteau diving without lights saw more colour under a continental shelf than you will see in Cambridge between November and March. Also he kept relatively dry. So you either hang yourself from despair inside one of the venerable edifices or else learn to love them for their shape alone. The perfect little lidless cube of Clare College unpacks its form most reluctantly, but eventually most completely, when the grass of its courtyard is covered with a tablecloth of snow. In Garret Hostel Lane, the dark chimneys of Trinity's south wing are already cut out clearly against the sodden clouds. The trick is to see the brilliance of the set design before the spotlights are switched on. After that, not even the blind could miss it. When spring pumps the water out of the panorama, the lawns of King's light up and throw their radiance into walls that suddenly look as edible as wafers. The blue sundials in the courts of Caius reveal what they have been mimicking: a clear sky. The Wren library in Trinity fills up with sunlight underneath, a baroque hovercraft on fire. The backs of the colleges are like Dresden reborn in a garden, like an Ideal Chateau Exhibition on a toytown Loire. The whole undergraduate population takes to the punts. Released from their examinations, the girls whose very existence you had begun to doubt reveal their delicious corporeality in thin cotton frocks vaporized by sunlight. Horrible young men in blazers and straw boaters momentarily attain the fluent beauty of a river party by Renoir, before their neighing voices – 'I say Simon! Simon! Don't let those oiks nab that punt!' – shatter the illusion. The illusion forms again. Everyone is outdoors. Everyone except those concerned with the Footlights May Week Revue. They are inside the Arts Theatre, facing the horrendous prospect of not being loved.

That first year I calamitously failed the audition to join the cast, but got the job of assistant stage manager. Being a bit older than anyone else involved, I was in a potentially humiliating position, but felt, with the flop of *The Charge of the Light Fandango* still reverberating in my dreams, that a stretch of being humble couldn't hurt. It could be argued that Cambridge was already eroding my spirit of protest. A more likely explanation, however, was that I had temporarily suspended my self-assertiveness in order to submit myself to a new discipline. I was falling back in order to jump better. The French, I had just learned from Proust, had a phrase for it: *reculer pour mieux sauter*. I couldn't pronounce it very well, but it sounded like the right idea.

As a Footlights May Week revue assistant stage manager, I was diligence personified. The previous year's revue had apparently been only one step up from a fiasco. It had tried to ape its successful predecessor *Cambridge Circus* without the wherewithal in either personnel or material. This year's had improved the position to the point of being merely something of a dud. Romaine had been coaxed out of the library to join Eric Idle at the head of an accomplished cast, but good material was at a premium, and most numbers were little better than workmanlike. But being little better than that, they were never worse than that either. The music, in particular, seemed astonishingly inventive and accomplished to anyone who, like myself, had spent several years arduously fitting lyrics on to ready-made melodies because he didn't know anyone who could write new ones. In the Footlights there were young men who could read and write music. In the depths of my conceit I didn't really believe that any of these youngsters could write words better than I could, but when it came to putting black dots between staves – or between keys or whatever it was that they did – there was no question that they had me whipped. Nearly everybody could sing. Even those who could only speak could speak in tongues. They could do accents, for example, which I couldn't, and indeed still can't. So there was an air of professionalism about the whole business, to which I contributed with some ruthlessly efficient assistant stage management. When the show was touring the provincial towns, the set had to be secured to the stage with sixty-four separate screws. I had them all colour-coded. With one of those pump-action screw drivers I could do the whole job in the dark. When Idle sprinted on stage as the Olympic torch-bearer, his flaming torch had been primed by me with exactly the right amount of inflammable fluid. When Idle came sprinting off again, barely had the lights snapped out before I had propelled Romaine, dressed as a Russian peasant woman and sitting in an old armchair on top of a wheeled platform, smoothly into position for her appearance as Tolstoy's widow. The whole lexicon of backstage terminology – tabs, flats, spots, dimmers – was easy on my lips. On the entire tour I made no mistakes at all. It turned out that I was saving them all up for the opening night in London.

Perhaps the venue spooked me. Once again, by the cruellest

coincidence, it was the Lyric, Hammersmith. The memory still haunted me of how the audience, during the early stages of *The Charge of the Light Fandango*, had fought among themselves at the crowded exits. That night at the wake, I had poured Spencer's bereaved father-in-law a full glass of whisky because he had been still too stunned to say 'when'. This night I must have been reliving that night, because when the time came to prime Idle's Olympic torch with inflammable fluid I overdid it by a pint. As he ran on, his torch was already sending flames almost to the proscenium arch, and before he was half-way through his monologue there were fireballs falling all around him. Trouper that he was, he kept going to the end, but the audience found it harder to laugh as it became more likely that his incipient demise would entail theirs. Shortly before the end of the number the torch, as if disappointed at having failed to burn down the theatre, sputtered out, just in time to ruin Idle's punch-line, which depended on its still being alight. When he came running off into the wings he cursed me with admirable restraint, but by now I was rattled, and I pushed Romaine's trolley into the blackout with too much force, so that it rolled several feet past the marked position. When the fixed spotlight which should have illuminated her was switched on, it illuminated a circular area of empty stage instead. She delivered the first part of her monologue in total darkness, during which time, it transpired, she had got out of her chair and begun the job of pushing the trolley back towards the right position. When the lighting operator at last figured out what had gone wrong, he killed the fixed light and picked her up with a follow-spot, thereby revealing her toiling away like Mother Courage at the exact moment when she was describing what it was like to be paralysed on her death bed. The audience was either sophisticated enough to be wondering politely how Brecht had got into the act, or else had correctly judged that something was amiss.

The show would probably have been no great smash hit anyway, but I had helped scotch what chance it had. The notices were death threats. David Frost, acting as a guest critic in *Punch*, was generously kind, but a turkey, once cremated, declines to be a phoenix. Though the revue ran for the scheduled two weeks, it was full only from Thursday to Saturday, with hellish matinées during which the cast ran some of the sketches backwards to see whether the old age pensioners would notice. I got some valuable training in how to keep slogging away at a show after it had been pronounced dead. Also, I was getting paid: the first real money I had ever made in show business. Though the stipend wasn't very large, it was larger than the one I earned next. When the show folded, there was still a lot of the Long Vacation stretching ahead, and before I could get to Italy I would need to earn the fare. One of the regular staff at the Lyric told me that the circus at Olympia had an opening for a roustabout. I applied for the job and got it before I found out that the opening was at the back of a tiger.

My job was to clean out the tiger's cage. In later years, when telling this story, I didn't always remember to mention that the tiger was removed from the cage before I got in there with my bucket and short shovel. Actually there wouldn't have been much danger if the tiger had stayed put. He had probably thrown the occasional scare into Clive of India, but to Clive James he posed no threat. So old that only his stripes were holding him together, he had teeth that couldn't dent the tennis ball with which he had been provided. Already safer than if he had been stuffed, he was rendered definitively innocuous by drugs. Some form of tranquillizer was fed to him in his morning hunk of raw meat, zonking him to the point where he couldn't suck his tennis ball without dribbling. The trainer plus three assistants removed the savage beast from its cage by rolling two long poles under the dozing corpse and lifting it out like a litter full of rag and bone. Then in I would go, a man in control of his fear, showing the ice-cool nerve of those who work close to the big cats. In I would go and scoop up those sadly depleted droppings. The poor shagged-out old moggie could scarcely shit a pretzel. The stuff was a sort of dark green, if you're wondering. Or perhaps, in that mysterious part of the brain which Baudelaire conquered like a new country, one of my memories has taken colour from another.

*

Flashback

When I was about twelve years old in Sydney I was allowed for the first time to attend the Royal Easter Show on my own, carrying two whole pounds with which to buy sample bags. I bought the Minties sample bag so that I could assemble the Minties cardboard gun, which was meant to fire cardboard discs but could fire lead slugs if you doubled the rubber band. Having assembled the gun, I ate all the Minties. I bought the Jaffas sample bag and ate all the Jaffas. So my stomach already had a lot to deal with before I bought not just one Giant Licorice sample bag, but two. My plan was to take one of the Giant Licorice sample bags home to my friend, Graham Gilbert, who was bedridden with German measles. Before I had finished eating the contents of my own Giant Licorice sample bag, this plan was already starting to fade, and during the long wait for the Doll's Point bus that was to take me home I ate the contents of the second bag as well. There was an incredible amount of licorice in a Giant Licorice sample bag, and all of it was black. There were logs of black licorice, straps of black licorice, coils of black licorice, cables of black licorice. By the time the bus came I had eaten everything and could make my way only with caution up the stairs to the top deck. Just past Brighton-le-Sands the road along the beach met President Avenue. From the junction it was an easy walk to Kogarah, so that was where I usually got off. It was where I got off this time, too, but not as usual. I pressed the upstairs bell to halt the bus at the next stop, but I couldn't move without feeling strange. The conductor appeared on the downstairs rear platform and looked up the staircase to see who had pressed the bell in an irresponsible manner, a misdemeanour to which a statutory penalty was attached. As I swayed at the top of the stairs I could see him in the stair-well mirror, so he must have seen what I did next. I vomited. I did the big spit. In the resulting avalanche, large fragments of Minties and Jaffas appeared merely as reinforcement, like gravel in liquid concrete. The basic thrust of the whole thing, the burden as it were, was an unspeakable tide of half-digested licorice. Yet what struck me with most force, even as the first wave of the descending onslaught struck the conductor, was how strange it was that what had gone in black had come out green. It was a dark green, admittedly: a green deeper than bottle green, thicker than heavy jade. But still it was green. From where I crouched heaving at the head of the stairs, it all went bouncing down like a baroque cascade of duckweed nougat. When, void and light-headed, I started walking home, the bus was still there: all the passengers had been ordered off because the conductor had refused to continue.

*

But that was to digress. I like to think that in adulthood I have acquired a certain polish, and that if I were now offered two sample bags full of Giant Licorice I would have the will-power to turn one of them down. There is no use pretending, however, that my sensibilities were either refined or usefully mortified by squeegeeing the effluent of a senile feline whose only contribution to the big cat act was a slow hop on to a stool and another slow hop down again, the two manoeuvres being separated by a growl in response to a crack of the trainer's whip. The growl sounded like a long yawn from the audience, a comparison which could readily be verified. It wasn't much of a circus, yet I rarely failed to watch the performance. The show didn't run to a trapeze act but there was a good-looking and sumptuously shapely girl in a silver-spangled scarlet leotard who climbed up a rope into the roof, hung on by her teeth to a short silver bar, and then spun rapidly round. It's an old act – Degas and Lautrec both did a picture of it – but it never fails if the girl has the right equipment, and Pearl had. She was billed as Pearl the Girl in a Whirl and in addition to her athletic attainments she demonstrated an excellent understanding of my poems for someone whose usual reading matter was the novels of Barbara Cartland. Pearl was all strength. When she flashed her teeth you tended to cross your legs involuntarily. But underneath the finely tuned muscles there was something tender. Unfortunately the ringmaster thought so too. Pearl was his mistress. When the circus broke up they left for Benidorm together. I left for Florence, this time able to pay for my own ticket, with only a small subsidy from Robin so that I could buy two cartons of duty-free Rothmans filters – which in Italy were as good as gold, because the Nazionale cigarettes produced by the state tobacco monopoly tasted like burning polystyrene.

Another wise precaution was to remove my beard. This transformed my reception in Florence almost as much as it transformed my face, which emerged pale, small and pointed at the bottom, like a talking turnip. Some of the things it said were in the local language, which with Françoise's encouragement I had mastered to the point of being able to speak platitudinously on the subject currently under discussion, instead of the subject that had been changed five minutes before. In those last few beautiful summers before the floods, the young university people of Florence had an open-air party every evening as the sun went down behind the cypresses lining the informal garden of some villa on the other side of the Arno, usually on the slope leading up between the Gardens of Boboli and the Piazzale Michelangelo. Sunset left the horizon rimmed with a light like crème de menthe. Young men wore cravats, allegedly of English origin, thus adding extra casualness to their tan lightweight suits, the jackets of which were hooked on one shoulder in the warm air. Young women wore silk and sandals. To indicate nonconformity they smoked like old trains. Feminism had not yet arrived but the girls were already feeling, if not their power, certainly the need for it. They could all talk a streak. One of them, called Adriana, was so witty she literally took away your breath: you were scared to respire in case you missed a wisecrack. Incorrectly judging her eyes to be too small, she drew circles of mascara around them, which made her look like a pangolin. At dinner in Gabriella's apartment across from the façade of the Pitti Palace, Adriana would palpitate on the spot with the fecund splendour of her own verbal invention, her cigarette waving around her head like a magic wand, ashing gaily into the ice-cream pudding. 'The sweet is my ashtray,' she would cry in her own language: 'it sounds like my autobiography.' Gabriella ate the affected area, as a gesture of apology for her money and titles. Larger gestures would be demanded later, but this was before the young Italian intellectuals had taken their rebellion much beyond a daring thesis reinterpreting Gramsci, or an interest in the poetry of Pier Paolo Pasolini. When crocked on Chianti they sang the old songs of the partisans. With the hangover came the eternal question of who would be appointed whose research assistant when and where. '*Bella ciao*,' they sang rebelliously, '*bella ciao bella ciao bella ciao ciao ciao*.' But the system was hard to buck. If music could have changed the antiquated Italian university system it would have had to be the kind of music that changed Jericho. Even Gabriella must have been concerned about how and where she would fit in. If she was worried, though, it was hard to tell. In addition to the apartment opposite the Pitti Palace, Gabriella owned a villa in the country. She was an aristocrat. Her hospitality was extended not only to her friends, but to the friends of her friends, such as myself. She had nobility. There is nobility in every class but if an aristocrat has it she finds it easier to exercise it. My beliefs, at the time, being dead set against privilege in all its forms, I found it disturbing to like her style. Though not beautiful, she had the grace that brought beauty towards her.

Everyone was at his best near Gabriella. Françoise's fine intelligence burst into flower, and Adriana became a semantic fountain. Keeping, or trying to keep, up with what Adriana said was the best possible training, a linguistic advanced motorist's course. A supplement to the course was La Lucciola Estiva, the Summer Firefly, an open air cinema in the dry pebbled bed of the Arno which showed the comedies of Ugo Tognazzi and Nino Manfredi on a continuous basis. L'Immorale, a comedy directed by Pietro Germi and starring Tognazzi, was the first Italian film whose dialogue I was able to follow. Tognazzi played a soft-hearted amoroso who kept two wives and a mistress ecstatically happy by lying to all of them while he ran from one to the other on a split-second timetable. He never missed a trick. Remembering every birthday and anniversary, he always bought the correct flowers, turned up on time for the intimate little dinner by candlelight, knocked himself out being wonderful with the children. Finally, in a post office, while mailing three separate sets of letters and postcards, he expired quietly from a heart attack. The audience laughed helplessly at his demise, so perfectly was the film paced. I saw it three times and enrolled it among the all-time film masterpieces. Perhaps it wasn't, but the thrill was authentic: the state of grace when we break through into understanding a new language is, after all, only the recurrence, this time fully conscious, of the long euphoria in which we first attained comprehension of the tongue to which we were born. For those of us who work with words, a periodic return to that initial urgency is essential. Don't listen to the pedant who says that because you have not mastered the whole speech of another language there is no point learning to read it. Smatterings are well worth having. They help strip the world bare again of its cloaking vocabulary. Dante's few lines about how paper burns took me back to the first principles of evocation in a way all of Shakespeare's plays could not, because with Shakespeare I had forgotten that the word and the thing are different things. Florence was my unofficial university. In my few weeks there I read more than in the whole of the previous year. My whitewashed room in the Antica Cervia, an obscure locanda behind the Palazzo Vecchio, was like a warehouse of sand-coloured BUR paperbacks. Two streets further down towards Piazza Santa Croce was the Trattoria Anita, a cheap restaurant favoured by whores, pimps and cigarette-smugglers. There I read and ate, spattering the pages of Cesare Pavese with spots of meat sauce. In the Biblioteca Nazionale I was part of the furniture, taking short lunches so that I could wolf down Sapegno's history of pre-Renaissance literature, the notebooks of Leopardi and the major works of Benedetto Croce. Very little of this would come in handy when I sat the Italian paper in Part Two of the Cambridge English Tripos, but my guardian angel was still working overtime to protect me from utilitarian values. His representative on Earth was Françoise, who seemed duty-bound to push the right books in front of me so that I could devour them. What satisfaction she got out of my single-mindedness I didn't bother to ask. The question never occurred to me, any more than it occurred to me to wonder why she didn't choose between her several other suitors, all of them serious and one with a very large Mercedes. Perhaps that was my secret. Having left ordinary self-absorption behind, I was a self trying to absorb all creation, and must have been as hard to ignore as a vacuum cleaner.

Michaelmas term was already a week old when I caught a crowded train north to Milan. Reading Eugenio Montale's first book of essays, I scarcely noticed that I spent the whole journey on my feet. The plane was delayed by a day. The airline paid for a night in a cheap hotel but such necessary extras as cigarettes ate up my remaining cash and when asked for the airport tax I was once again embarrassingly not able to produce it. The last time that had happened to me, a nice man from Calcutta had taken pity and offered assistance, no strings attached. This time there was no Indian Samaritan on hand to overhear my entreaties and fork out the money. All the Indians were back in India. The airport tax official, noting the book I was carrying, must have independently decided that a foreigner's incipient love of the world's most lovely language should be encouraged by subsidy. Dumb luck. Don't think it doesn't bother me now, how my falling bread always landed with the buttered side up. It even bothered me then. But there was a mass of compensatory trouble waiting for me in the chill air of the fens. In my Junior Common Room pigeon-hole was a series of progressively more curt notes from the Dean requiring my presence at once. Either he was digging a mine-shaft down into the linen room and needed help, or I was in deep shit.

4. UNQUIET FLOW THE DONS

I nearly got thrown out. Squatting gnome-like in his rocky grotto, the Dean examined the bowl of his pipe as if he had not yet given up hope of discovering small but valuable mineral deposits within its charred circumference. Mature students of a certain theatrical *réclame*, he informed me, could get away with a lot, but to come up late for term, without a previous written application, was to invite rustication at the very least. Also it was just plain bad manners. To one *in statu pupillari* such as myself, he explained, the college was *in loco parentis*. Gazing at the Dean as he sat framed among feldspar, I found it hard not to reflect that he was about as loco as any parent could well get, but this unworthy thought was chased away by my uncomfortable realization that he had a point. Offering my apology on the spot, I pleaded, with some truth, that the educational stimulus of Tuscany had distracted me from my normal loyalties. The Dean accepted these protestations with a Christian heart, though it was clear that Italy for him meant either the presence of the Scarlet Woman or an absence of suitable rocks. Perhaps the customs officers had once opened his bags in the Brenner Pass and found them full of Carrara marble. This year, he told me, I would not be offered a set in college. He understood that there was a room going at the Eagle, in the centre of town. The Eagle being a pub, it scarcely counted as approved lodgings, but it would do until I found something better. He made it sound as if I had better find something better pretty quickly, or else die of privation. He did not, on the other hand, offer the alternative of staying on in college until something classier than a room at the Eagle should become available. 'Trot along,' he insisted, 'and rent it straight away.' My packed suitcase, he added, was in the care of the housekeeper. Naturally I could eat in Hall as usual, but perhaps it would be an advantage both to myself and the college if I no longer had to scale the walls after dark. There was such a thing as dignity, and too many nights spent in the incinerator skip could entail its loss. 'One can only advise,' he puffed.

He left me to find out for myself that the incinerator skip knocked spots off the Eagle as a place of abode. The Eagle was the most romantic pub in Cambridge, if not the whole of England. During the war, bomber crews from all over East Anglia had come to the Eagle to spend, in hilarious conviviality, what was statistically likely to be one of their last evenings alive. Riding on each other's shoulders, into the deep-red linoleum ceiling of the saloon they burned the numbers and nicknames of their squadrons with naked candle flames: a portent, doubly hideous for its innocence, of their own fate, and a grim token of the fiery nemesis they were bringing every night to the cities of Germany. To this day I can't enter that room without hearing their laughter, which becomes steadily more unmanning as I grow older. All my sons. Twenty years ago I was not all that much older than they had been when they were snuffed out. It was a hall of fame, a temple of the sacred flame, a trophy room for heroes. Unfortunately my room was somewhere above it, and not quite so grand. The door to my room opened off the first-floor gallery which ran around the courtyard where the coaches had once stopped. When I opened the door and stepped into the darkened room, I fell across the bed and smacked my forehead smartly on the opposite wall. Luckily the wall, under many geological layers of plaster and paint, was sufficiently resilient to absorb most of the impact. It was also quite moist. When I found the light switch, a twenty-watt bulb dispelled just enough of the gloom to reveal that the moisture was not my blood. It was rising damp. It was also descending damp, with a good deal of transverse damp mixed in. The smell of mould was tropical. The temperature of the air, on the other hand, was arctic. There was a two-bar electric fire, one of whose bars worked reasonably well for half its length. I had lived like this in London. I had no wish, and no capacity, to live like this again. Squeezing my cardboard suitcase into the space not occupied by the bed, I lay down in the half-light and tried to decide whether I was near tears or had simply begun, like my new surroundings, to deliquesce. There was a pillowcase on the pillow but there was something on the pillowcase. It was wet dust.

I had not really been punished. Nobody ever was. The ancient universities looked after their own. When a currently famous poet lived on my stair at Pembroke, he not only invited women friends to stay the night and the next night as well, he advertised the fact by encouraging them to dry their stockings out of his window, which overlooked the old court, called Old Court. After about a year of indecision, the Senior Tutor for Junior Supervisors finally grasped the nettle. He knocked timidly on the poet's seemingly permanently sported oak. Nothing happened. The Tutor went away. The next day he went back and knocked again. Still nothing. The day after that, he knocked again. At last the oak rumbled open to reveal the poet, stark naked with his arms thrown apart, shouting 'Crucify me!' Within seconds the Senior Tutor was having tea with the Dean. Together they decided that nothing had occurred, even though blasphemy, as the celebrated case of Mark Boxer had recently demonstrated, was the only reason why anyone ever *was* sent down. The Tutor went on to become the Master, the poet went on to become Poet Laureate – I name no names – and the Dean went on. Continuity was the keynote. Any amount of eccentricity was tolerable as long as not publicized. If my friend Boxer, rather than publishing a mildly secular poem in *Granta*, had practised voodoo in his rooms, he would have gone on to get his Gentleman's Third, instead of being carried symbolically out of Cambridge in an open coffin. But merely to state his case is to show the truth. To be thrown out was to be kept in. Oxbridge had you even when it let you go. Oxford threw Shelley out but kept his name. You can get sprung only on probation. It drives some alumni bananas, so that they write whole cycles of plays and novels about how they don't really care about not having become dons. One of the several candidates for the dubious title of Cleverest Man in England always tells his interviewers that the one real failure of his life was his not being elected a Fellow of All Souls. Can you imagine, say, Leonardo da Vinci, who had a reasonable claim to the title of Cleverest Man in Italy, confessing his disappointment at being refused membership of any institution at all, no matter how exalted? Though I had reason to be grateful to Cambridge, I was already thanking God that it hadn't caught me young, before the world had given me some measure by which to get its insidious cosiness into proportion. As things stood, I had the memory of how Masaccio's frescoes looked on the wall of the Church of the Carmine in Florence to remind me of what intellectual distinction was really like. The dons could impress me with what they knew, but it took more than their port and walnuts to impress me with what they were.

And some of them were as crazy as loons. To give a star student free board and lodging for life might well protect his future productivity from quotidian distraction but it is rarely good for the personality and can lead to behaviour patterns indistinguishable from those that get people in other walks of life locked up. Either Trinity or Trinity Hall, I forget which, elected a History Fellow in the 1930s who seemed set fair to be the next Edward Gibbon. From that day forward he never did anything except walk the streets with a bundle of old newspapers under his arm. If they had always been the same newspapers he might have retained some historical interest. You could have stopped him and found out what the *Daily Express* had said about Ribbentrop. But he changed the newspapers at random, just as he never took the same route twice on his endless walks to nowhere.

A don didn't need to be carrying a bundle of newspapers in order to manifest an unhinged walk. It was a Fellow's privilege, when crossing a courtyard, to walk diagonally across the grass instead of, like everyone else, keeping to the flagstones around the edge. Dons whose behaviour was near normal in all other respects would exercise this grass-treading privilege even when it would have been more convenient to everybody, including themselves, if they had not. In summer they would amble across the grass and then wonder loudly why they had been followed by a large party of tourists from Osaka. The answer was obvious: the tourists from Osaka had not been able to judge from the Fellow's gowned appearance that he was any more uniquely privileged than a bad imitation of Batman. But the Fellow's training had equipped him to deal only with the abstruse. Though he could deliver a learned paper about Ulrich von Wilamowitz-Moellendorff's refutation of A. B. Drachmann's theories about *Antigone*, or preferably compose a scathing review of somebody else's learned paper on that subject, he couldn't deal with the proposition that the really smart way to preserve the grass would be to deny access not just to most people, but to everybody. One don, in a college I had better not name, walked diagonally across the grass even in winter. This would have made sense if he had worn wellingtons. He invariably wore the patent leather dancing pumps which had been bequeathed to him by Ivor Novello. The snow could be three feet deep and you would see his tracks going through it like the wake of a caribou. The short cut would have made some sense if he had been saving mileage at the beginning of a route march to Land's End. He was only going as far as the Porter's Lodge to see if there was any news of the Jamaican steel band he invited over every year to play calypsos to him in his rooms. Blessed with a large inheritance, he had a healthy bank balance which the gift of a suite of rooms, all found, did nothing to diminish, but his emotional propensities were more questionable, although rumour had it that not all the members of the steel band were asked to remove their clothes, only some. The rest just took off their overcoats and galoshes.

In Cambridge there was a good deal of High Table homosexuality, some of it still struggling in the closet but a lot of it out in the open and dancing around on tiptoe. Recently the full story has been told of how the homosexual mathematician, Alan Turing, most gifted of all the many Queens of King's, saved Britain's life in World War II. With a then unusual combination of mathematical and engineering genius – two departments which the English educational system had always worked hard to keep separate – Turing devised the mechanism by which radio signals encoded through the German Enigma machine could be read in time to produce the stream of useful, often vital, secret intelligence known as Ultra. It was the society outside Cambridge which hounded Turing to an early grave. Cambridge itself, even if it did not precisely cherish him, at least offered him its tolerance and protection. Even more than Keynes's or Wittgenstein's, Turing's case, it seems to me, is decisive. Though it could be said that Cambridge was equally tolerant and protective of a whole succession of Foreign Office and MI5 prodigies who subsequently turned out to have been drawing an extra salary from the Soviet Union, nothing can alter the fact that Hitler, who threatened the whole of civilization, owed his defeat in a large part to a high-voiced but not very predatory invert who threatened nobody, and that the dons of King's, who knew all about Turing's proclivities, did nothing to sabotage this desirable outcome. Where victimless crimes are concerned, tolerance is an absolute good. Cambridge will probably never get round to formally approving homosexuality, but the type of homosexual involved perhaps prefers a blind eye to public acknowledgment, and meanwhile a tacit understanding seems to provide liberty enough. In my time as an undergraduate, however, I sometimes had to concentrate very hard on how horrible most of the boat-rowing heterosexuals were if I was to offset my distaste for some of the more epicene dons, of which Footlights had a full quota among its senior membership. Dating from the long era when every May Week revue had been a big-budget exercise in make-up and drag, they would turn up at term-time smokers and form a swooping group at the back of the room, muttering archly at the pretty pass to which things had come. One of them was among the nicest men I had ever met, but I didn't go for his pals. They obviously thought I was too butch to be plausible, and I was constantly afraid of being knocked flat by their flailing wrists. I bottled it up, though. Human nature is various, and I have never been pleased enough about my own nature to be fully contemptuous about anybody else's, provided he isn't homicidal. These weren't that: they were just a bit high-pitched. The kind of undergraduates who swarmed around them certainly weren't being misled, unless sugar misleads ants.

In order to be weird, however, a don didn't have to carry bundles of old newspapers, cross snow-filled courtyards diagonally with only his head showing, or make up his eyelids with the very lightest touch of blue shadow. Some of them could maintain an unbroken recti-tude of deportment while still going comprehensively haywire, especially if they were involved in the humanities. Cambridge science having done such earth-shattering things, it was sometimes suggested that non-scientists were suffering from an inferiority complex. If so they kept it well hidden. A more likely explanation concerns the relative difficulty of keeping work separate from life. A physicist can't live his physics. A humanist can live his humanism and after too much Madeira might find it impossible not to. One of the young Cambridge philosophy dons specialized in aesthetics and made sure you knew it. He dressed the part, wearing a black leather jacket, tight trousers and high boots. He had not, at that stage, produced any of the substantial writings in which he has since expounded his view-point, but such was the level of personal invective he maintained in conversation that you always knew where he stood. He stood on his opponent's throat. He was a Leavisite, junior model. He had taken his master's principles of literary criticism and applied them to the other arts as well. Thus it came to light that in each field of artistic endeavour there were only three or four master practitioners, all the others being enemies of civilization. In music the three or four were reduced to one: Wagner. I once heard this terrifying young man say that one of the many great things about Wagner was that when you realized his true greatness it obviated the necessity of listening to pipsqueaks like Puccini. I searched his face for a sign of humour but could see nothing except certainty. It was Leavis that had made him certain. On the rare occasions when the black-leather Wagnerian could be tempted into print, it was usually an encomium in the *Cambridge Review* for some collection of addle-pated late essays by Leavis, or else it was a passionate attack on a book, any book, by someone who, at some point in the past, no matter how distant, had disagreed with Leavis or merely failed to endorse his every opinion. Even Wagner came second to Leavis.

Leavis himself, though nearing the end of his career, was, as I have mentioned, still active around Cambridge and more irascible than ever, particularly against his disciples. To do him credit, he could never be depended upon to go on lapping up the hosannahs of his sycophants indefinitely. At some unpredictable moment he would turn on his arselickers and deliver a series of stunning kicks to their pursed lips. Later on, almost with his dying breath, he publicly repudiated the Wagnerian for having 'misrepresented my views'. Far from having misrepresented Leavis's views, the Wagnerian had endorsed them even at their most fatuous. When Leavis wrote his last-gasp, break-through essay in which Tolstoy was discovered to be a great novelist, the Wagnerian, either having forgotten about the existence of Matthew Arnold or else never having heard of him, announced that nobody had dared to proclaim Tolstoy's eminence so courageously before. With his tongue thus applied to the heel of his master's boot, the acolyte was ill-prepared to receive its toe in his teeth. The Wagnerian never fully recovered. He took to wearing a Harris tweed jacket and ordinary shoes, and not long ago, at a dinner party in a private home, I caught him red-handed listening to other people instead of just laying down the law as of old.

Really he shouldn't have taken it so hard. Leavis's views were almost impossible not to misrepresent, because they were designed so that only he could hold them. This was partly true even in the early, fruitful part of his career, and became completely true later on, when dogma took over from doctrine. Those who opposed him he merely insulted, but to support him invited vilification, and anyone who arrived at one of his conclusions before he did suffered treatment that differed from character assassination only in being prolonged like torture. When he gave his famous Dickens lectures the hall was jammed. I was there along with the worshippers, the admirers and the merely gullible. Brian C. Adams was sitting in the front row, with two fountain pens ready in case one of them ran out. He was doing his best to appear critically detached but there was no mistaking his look of exaltation when Leavis came trotting briskly in. Leavis was Seriousness personified. He even had a serious way of being bald. Though I had, and for some years to come retained, respect for the intensity of his commitment, I suppose I was the only person present who actively disapproved of him. There were plenty who detested him, but they had stayed at home. I wanted to see at least the vestiges of the mental force he must once have had in order to cause those decades of fuss and bother. I hadn't tried to enrol in his seminars because I had passed the age of being caught up in his rhetoric. This will sound like light-mindedness to all those Cambridge graduates – many of them now prominently placed in the theatre, radio, television and journalism as well as the academic world – who think that Leavis made them serious about literature. But literature would have made them serious about literature. They met him at an impressionable age, and they have matured since only to the extent that his influence has been ameliorated by the thing he preached of but saw with such distorting strictness – life. It depends not just on who your mentor is, but on when you meet him, and I no longer needed Leavis to tell me that Shakespeare was a greater poeter than Shelley. If Leavis had had something to say about the kind of poet Shelley would have been had he lived to middle age, I might have listened. But the good Doctor dealt in absolutes. Nevertheless I was prepared, as that bald-eagle head bent over its pile of notes and cleared the gaunt throat in its open collar, to admit that he had something, if he had.

What he had, alas, was a long series of attacks on all those critics who had made the unpardonable mistake of calling Dickens a genius before he did. Humphry House came in for an avalanche of abuse, clearly because Humphry House had given half his life to Dickens while Leavis had still been proclaiming that only *Hard Times* merited serious attention. The names Graham Hough and John Holloway also kept cropping up, although their connection with Dickens was not clear. 'We know what to think of Dr Hough,' sneered Leavis, as though no further explanation were necessary. 'We know what to expect from Dr Holloway.' Perhaps Hough and Holloway had not only been prematurely pro-Dickens, they had also been anti-Leavis, or, even worse, pro-Leavis without permission. Then a strange thing began to happen. The names Hough and Holloway went on cropping up, but they cropped up mixed up. 'This is the kind of misrepresentation, I need hardly point out, which we have learned to associate with the name of Dr Houghoway.' Not long afterwards there was a reference to Professor Hollohough. Some of Dr Leavis's pages seemed to be in the wrong order. He shuffled them, apparently at random, and read on. This should have been a touching, if not exactly comic, grace-note to the performance, but the outpouring of venom forbade sympathy. As the hour neared its end, there was a peroration against Edmund Wilson, who had pioneered the movement which, long before Leavis got around to joining it, had brought the critical appraisal of Dickens into line with public appreciation. 'We doubt Edmund Wilson's qualifications to discuss Dickens,' said Leavis, and although I am quoting from memory the memory is so indecently vivid I would swear by its accuracy. 'We doubt Edmund Wilson's qualifications,' he wound up triumphantly, 'to discuss *any* literature.' Beside me, an Indian girl student in a sari noted it down: 'doubt E. Wilson quals. discuss *any* lit.' In a blessed life, that moment was as close as I have so far come to witnessing clerical treason in its pure form, dogma distilled into a pathogen. One day I might write a book about how I think cultural memory is transmitted, and perhaps I had better put off discussing this sad business until then, but for now I should say, in order to stave off charges of frivolity, that I thought any amount of frivolity preferable to the Leavisite parade of seriousness. Better Lord David Cecil at his most fruitily fluting than Leavis's Vyshinskyite tirade, his inquisitorial denunciations. The hall was full of students who would have profited immensely from reading Edmund Wilson's literary criticism, which was, and is, full of discovery and judgment. Wilson's appreciation of Dickens was just what they should have been encouraged to read. Instead they had been given an excuse to do something for which students need no encouragement: not to read.

Not much of a reader on the course myself, I was in no fit state to climb on a high horse. Helping me to contain my rage was the suspicion that this event was more parody than reality. The Leavisite brand of *odium theologicum* had all the characteristics of totalitarian argument, right down to the special hatred reserved for heretics. But the patterns of thought which had filled the concentration camps of Europe proper had arrived in England in the mercifully diluted form of university politics. The ruckus surrounding Leavis, though too nasty to be a farce, was not toxic enough to be a tragedy. You could always have gone somewhere else. Leavis himself could have gone somewhere else, but fought to stay on in Cambridge. It couldn't be said while he was alive, and is still considered bad taste when said now, but the reason he was shut out of university preferment had little to do with his supposedly challenging originality. It was personal. People will submit to having their opinions contradicted, but not to having their characters attacked at the same time. They can't watch their fronts *and* their backs. They would rather shut the door. So Leavis, as he put it, became part of the real Cambridge: the Cambridge in spite of Cambridge. He was part of the landscape. You became accustomed to seeing him walk briskly along Trinity Street, gown blown out horizontal in his slipstream. He looked as if walking briskly had been something he had practised in a wind tunnel. Not long before he died I was in Deighton Bell's second-hand bookshop looking over the rain-ruined books of the literary booze-artist John Davenport, who must have left the library doors open on the stormy night of his suicide. Suddenly Leavis's wife, Queenie, appeared at my shoulder. 'Nasty piece of work, Davenport,' she muttered, having no reason to know me from Adam. 'While he was up here he was the leader of a *particularly odious set.*' Seeing me buy Davenport's cracked and stained Pléiade edition of Rimbaud, she nodded approval. Almost any teacher, no matter how intransigent his or her views, can be moved to tears by the sight of a student voluntarily purchasing a book, but the light in Queenie's eye was one of reminiscence. 'With Frank it was Laforgue. He nearly broke us, buying up those Frenchmen. On to it quite independently of Eliot. In France you couldn't get him past a bookshop. We were there a lot when we were young.' She sniffed for a while at a row of damaged books which Davenport had failed to return to the London Library. Then she left. In later years I have remembered that chance encounter as part evidence that in matters of the spirit the truly dangerous poisons are refined from flowers. In her husband's youth she must have found him as easy to love as in his last days I found him easy to loathe. I tried not to hate him, though. Of all the moral lessons he had to teach, the one that stuck was the one he taught inadvertently. In his later books he libelled his literary opponents so scandalously that when he tried to condemn Stalin he had no harsh words left over. If he had been asked to give his opinion of Hitler and Himmler, he would not have been able to summon up any terms of disapprobation that he had not already lavished on Houghaway and Hollohough. He had given up his sense of reality, and all in pursuit of the very study which, he went on insisting, was the only thing that could give you a sense of reality. He was a self-saboteur.

5. YANKS ON THE CAM

You can make a good case for even the weirdest don if he stimulates the young to anything, if only anger. At my age I didn't need the goad. Though I was still too idle a student to put much time into the business of seeking out a sound teacher and listening to what he had to say, at least I recognized such a one when I heard him. Theodore Redpath, for example, was an old man by then and his lectures on tragedy didn't sparkle. You had to strain to listen. But when he talked about Sophocles he was responding to the Greek text. His little book on Tolstoy took in all the Russian scholarship. He was unspectacular, but I had come just far enough to know that he was worth listening to, and precisely because he had no big ideas. He talked nothing except sense. Younger undergraduates couldn't be blamed for wanting stronger stuff. In Pembroke, the star students in English were nearly all Americans. Some of them went to hear George Steiner, recently installed at Churchill College, talk eloquently about how the crisis of Western civilization had reached a point where it would be better if everybody stopped talking. Others went to hear Leavis talk about how the crisis of western civilization had been made worse by Steiner. Some of them went to hear both, took verbatim notes from each, intercalated the results and served up the synthesis in their weekly essays. Sharing practical criticism seminars or group supervisions with the Americans, I would marvel at the seriousness with which they took it all. But there would be ample time for them to become less gullible later, and for the time being their all-fired keenness was probably more fruitful, and certainly more attractive, than my indolence. They had a hard enough time fathoming the English, so my own transitional persona must have seemed as out of focus as a chameleon crossing a kilt.

They, to me, looked perfect. Whether Ivy League WASPS, New York Jews or third generation Polacks and Bohunks with names full of 'c's and 'z's, they were fully in character and inexhaustibly supplied with authentic all-American dialogue. They were all very bright, of course, which helped. Fulbright scholars and Phi Beta Kappa almost to a man, they were reading the second part of the English Tripos, like me. Unlike me they had degrees which had been won by hard work against deadly competition at Yale, Princeton, Harvard, Columbia and Amherst. Of the Ivy League types, the outstanding example was Stradlington Westwood Blantyre III, called Strad for short, like an expensive violin. And indeed he was a finely tuned instrument, though built like an upper East Side brownstone. Six feet four in his triple-welted brogues, he had grown a moustache out of shyness and looked apologetic that it had hidden no more than his upper lip. The expression 'modest to a fault' had been invented for him. President of Triangle when at Princeton, he had a fine line of songs and monologues, but could be forced on to the Footlights stage only at gunpoint. The only male graduate who could cycle past Newnham and make its inhabitants appear at the windows spontaneously – the rest of us could not have obtained the same results had we thrown tear gas – he never noticed the sensation he caused. Every day he was invited to tea at Girton, more than once by the dons themselves. He was actually *invited* to that heavily defended castle full of unattainable females. The rest of us would have been picked up by the searchlights and fixed machine guns before we had even cut our way through the barbed wire and reached the moat full of alligators. But what did he do when he got there? He discussed Thackeray. As the inmates passed him cucumber sandwiches with trembling hands, he quietly made clear that there was a fiancée waiting for him at home. Pending his graduation and marriage – the two events were apparently scheduled to take place simultaneously – energies left over from study were expended on rowing. He rowed for the college and would probably have done the same for the university if he had not been so intelligent. In the grad pad after Hall, when the affiliated students would stand around drinking port or coffee in a vain attempt to quell memories of what they had eaten for dinner, I would accuse Strad of wanting to do all the right things. 'No,' he said, after thinking it over, 'I just want to do things right.'

He thought himself conventional but made an art of the conventions. I admired his good manners and perhaps he relished my lack of them. At any rate he took me some way into his secret life. One afternoon, in his rooms, he poured me another inch of Bourbon and put an LP on his record-player. 'It is important to be *cool*,' he said, with characteristic terseness. 'These three women are called the Supremes. Notice how *cool* they are.' While the sublime riffs and harmonies of 'You Can't Hurry Love' came lilting into my life for the first time, Strad was rolling a peculiar-looking cigarette. 'Now let's hear that again while we take a drag on this object, which we call a *joint*.' I would like to say that the experience was transformative, but like most first-time pot-smokers I missed the point through not taking a sufficient quota of air. The Supremes were enough to get me high all by themselves, however. Strad was like that: he played it dead square, but there was always another side to him. His façade had facets.

Of Delmer Dynamo I have already given a preliminary description, but he, too, was many-sided, if someone so bulb-shaped could be that. In his second year he had put out shoots and tendrils. He had not relinquished his sardonic commentary on the college and its facilities. (Famously he had said 'blow it out your ass' within earshot of the Dean, but had got away with it because the Dean, misled by the American pronunciation of the word, had thought that Delmer was making some arcane reference to a biblical animal.) Delmer had, however, embraced English cultural values with the determination of a Greek ship-owner angling for election to White's. He was a college man yet more than a college man. He was practically a college building. His large supply of money from home was poured into first editions of George Eliot and the novels of Dickens in the original monthly parts. In his rooms there was a matched pair of Purdey shot-guns, one of which had not been fired, and the other of which, by Delmer's own account, had been aimed at a partridge and accounted for a beater. There was fly-fishing equipment. Where once there had been a rack of Savile Row suits and tweed hacking jackets, there were now two racks, while on the appropriate pegs and shelves, specially installed, there were Burberry overcoats with detachable linings, oiled Barbours, opera capes, deerstalker hats and green wellingtons.

Late night discussions in front of Delmer's fireplace were fortified with a hamper from Fortnum and Mason's. Most impressive of all, kept in a small car park off Trumpington Street, was Delmer's car. It was a Bentley with a very rare H. J. Mulliner double-shell body

of aluminium. A measure of Delmer's Englishness was that he did
not call aluminium 'aloominum'. Delmer's newly anglicized diction,
seemingly acquired from manuscripts which P. G. Wodehouse had
rejected as too characteristic, shed any last overtones of self-mockery
where his car was concerned. 'Care for a spin, old bean?'

Strad, who adored Delmer, warned me to play along. 'He's serious.
Don't call him on it or he'll crash the goddam thing.' The big
drawback was that Delmer couldn't drive. He had an international
licence but he must have bought it off a crooked cop in Atlantic City.
In the car park, Strad and I had to wait a long time while Delmer
tried to turn the key. Not in the ignition: in the door. When we got
into the car there was another long wait while he got it to start. 'Tally
ho!' he cried, when the flooded carburettor at last coughed life into
the engine. 'Wizard prang! Now let's toodle off into the landscape.'
Then he couldn't get out of the car park. With too much pride to
let anyone else try instead, he crabbed toward the exit, backed up,
twisted the wheel, lurched forward again, but couldn't line the front
wheels up with the way out. Part of the trouble was the driving
position. With his feet on the pedals he had to tilt his head back in
order to see over the walnut dashboard. Eventually it was time for
Strad to go rowing, so he got out. That left me. After a while I got
out too and tried to guide Delmer between the posts. It didn't work.
Though the engine of the Bentley wasn't very loud even when revved
in desperation, there was a terrific silence after Delmer switched it
off. He climbed out, shut the door, and looked for a long time at his
most expensive acquisition. His hands were in his pockets. I got the
impression that if they hadn't been he would have punched a dent
in the front door. The lustrous toes of his ox-blood shoes, which had
been handmade in St James's, were twitching. But the revenge he
took on his recalcitrant purchase was not physical. Recrimination
had gone beyond that. With his hands still in his pockets he threw
back his head and cried out to Heaven. 'BLOW IT OUT YOUR ASS!'

Strad and Delmer both slaved over their books like gladiators in
training, but always with a sense of their limitations. Strad would
one day go to work in the family publishing firm, Delmer in the
faculty of English at Columbia. They would serve literature, not
create it. JFK, their best hope and only President, was dead; the
Vietnam war, though still rated officially only as a police action,
already beckoned with an evil welcome for contemporaries who had

been less lucky; they were troubled for their country and grateful for small mercies. But Bob Marenko was Captain America. An Amherst Phi Bete who as a high school tight end had already been scouted by every team in the newly formed National Football League, he had turned his massive shoulders on sport in order to put his head down and charge at literature, fourth down and goal to go. In his rooms he had two copies of Yeats's collected poems, one to be kept sacred and the other to be marked up. In the marked copy every line was underlined and annotated in the margin. 'Elision of "the" and "indifferent" conveys casualness of swan after consummation, while abruptness of terminal word "drop" mimics action. Develop.' Unsurprisingly for one so young and keen, Marenko's own poems aped those of his idol, yet you couldn't fail to be impressed by the sheer number of them. He never sent them out for publication in the university newspapers and magazines. Instead he passed them around the college, listening attentively to criticism before going back to his rooms and writing far into the night. It was clear that if he did not become a great poet he would become a great critic. The latest books and articles by Harold Bloom, Northrop Frye, Yvor Winters and Stephen Marcus were all collected and cross-referenced by Marenko as if they were jazz records. He felt the same way about jazz records, but they had to be modern. Thelonious Monk was about as far back as Marenko's tastes went, and he really started to feel comfortable only with John Coltrane, whose interminable solos could be listened to and argued about until dawn broke. Marenko wanted to discuss things. Above all, he wanted to discuss Vietnam. He was serious about it: much more serious than the anti-war agitation which was by now building up throughout the Western lands. If Marenko thought it was a just war, he would put his head down and run at the Viet Cong. If he thought it was unjust, he would put his head down and run at his own government. Hence the necessity to talk things over. The debates lasted half the night every night, except when there was live jazz to be heard. Every Wednesday night there was a guest soloist at the Red Lion in Lion Yard, usually a good, solid British sax player such as Ronnie Ross, Art Themen, Don Rendell or Kathy Stobart. Colin Edwards, a townsman, was the resident drummer, and Mike Payne, a retired Vampire pilot, played the bass. For a few shillings it was a feast of danceable mainstream music. On top of that, once in a great while an American legend came to town. Duke Ellington

came to Great St Mary's and gave his Sacred Music concert, which
proved to be a bit too sacred for my taste, while Marenko merely
found it antediluvian. I tried to explain that Ellington's great period
had been in the early 1940s, when every three-minute recording was
like a miniature symphony. Marenko's eyes were suffused with pity.
But when Thelonious Monk played at the Union, even Marenko got
excited. We went with Delmer. Monk-mad myself, I did my best to
understand as the mighty man – backed by a susurrating post-bop
rhythm section in which the drummer seemed to hit nothing except
the cymbals and the bass player did everything he could to avoid the
beat – punched clusters of notes apparently at random and climaxed
a half-hour rendition of 'Monk's Dream' by jabbing all his fingers
into the lid of the key-board. 'Jesus H. Christ on a crutch,' said
Delmer at interval, 'this guy is stoned.' Marenko tried to set Delmer
straight. 'I can relate to how you might feel that, Delmer,' said the
star student compassionately, 'but the aleatory component was always
implicit in Monk's music. He's merely taking that element to its
logical conclusion.'

'Blow it out your ass,' Delmer replied. '*I'm* going *home*.' Marenko
and I stayed for the second half, during which Monk twice missed
the piano altogether. But over cocoa late that night Marenko was
persuasive about our having witnessed an important step in modern
music. Marenko's passionate erudition was hard to resist. He knew
so much, and cared so much more. Long before dawn, he had me
convinced that every move of Monk's hands had been a miracle of
controlled self-expression. Late next morning we were waiting outside
the Blue Boar Hotel in Trinity Street to pay homage when Monk
checked out. When he appeared, he wasn't precisely being carried by
the drummer and the bass player, merely supported by them, but his
feet were only vaguely in contact with the ground and his eyes looked
like blood capsules. 'Where we *at*, man?' I heard him enquire softly.
'Still in England,' muttered the bass player. 'Stay cool till we're in the
car.' Monk's toes were touching the pavement but they were dragging
behind his heels. His puce eyeballs rolled upwards to look at the
narrow brim of his black felt hat while his lips, between his tooth-
brush moustache and his vestigial goatee, imitated a little doughnut.
'Where we *at*?' he moaned.

Marenko took this setback philosophically, the way he took everything. Dutifully he would enlarge his world view to fit the world. In

college I spent more time with the Americans than with the British because the Americans were more interested in everything, including Britain. They certainly made better Europeans. They worked hard at their languages and got across to the continent in every vacation. They looked on self-improvement as a sacerdotal obligation. Democratic without being philistine, studious without feeling superior, the Americans were my solace inside the college. Outside the college, I necessarily spent much of my time with the natives. By that stage, I was publishing poems and articles in every issue of *Varsity*, *Granta* and the *Cambridge Review*, with the overspill going into the aforesaid gaggle of evanescent literary magazines unread by anybody except the committed *literati*. These latter life-forms were now becoming easier for me to classify into their various weights and types. There were flashbacks called Algernon who dressed and sounded as if they were auditioning for a tea party thrown by Harold Acton or Maurice Bowra. There were ultra-grey ex-grammar school types who wrote something called Concrete Poetry and were called Ken. Both groups, had I but known it, were on their way up in the world. The Algernons were all from minor public schools. In the new mood of classlessness they could plausibly carry on as if they came from major ones. (As the cachet enjoyed by the editorial staff of *Private Eye* had already demonstrated, the principal effect of the sixties social revolution was to make young men who had been to Shrewsbury feel less miserable about not having been to Eton.) The Kens were amassing points for their future careers: a BBC general traineeship would fall most easily to the *curriculum vitae* which showed evidence of artistic endeavour, if not actual achievement. Over the secret desires and lurking ambitions of both Algernon and Ken I rode rough-shod. Algernon wrote crepuscular sonnets and Ken assembled, probably with tweezers, microscopic unpunctuated stanzas from which the ghosts of ideas gestured feebly, like lice in raindrops. There was a lot of white space left over, which I filled. My verse was still a long way from the clarity which I was eventually to realize should be my aim – I would rather my work were thought prosaic than poetic, and there are some who would say that I have been granted my wish – but compared with the eye-dropper out-squeezings of my undergraduate rivals it was a torrent of candour. Also, after a year's practice, I had become almost impossible to turn down. Having grown another beard even more farouche than its predecessor, when I fronted up

at an undergraduate editor's door I must have looked less like an
aspiring contributor than someone who had been hired to collect a
debt. I was only about five years older than the average final-year
literatus but in your twenties a lustrum is like a canyon. Most of
these young scribblers, I guessed, would one day give up, whereas I
had already diagnosed myself, correctly, as having the disease in its
chronic form. I was a lifer. Being that, perhaps I should have sent
my work out to the professional magazines, but if these amateurs
resented my crabbing their act they didn't show it. Not that I would
have noticed if they had, because I spent as little time socializing
with them as possible. If, to them, I was just too insensitive, to me
they were just too callow. Except for the Algernons, who were living
in Echo Park, all that concerned them was Experimental Writing,
and I had come far enough to know that there is no such thing as
experimental writing. There is only writing. The arts do not advance
through technique, they accumulate through quality. One evening I
went to a literary tea in Newnham. The editor of a magazine called
something like *Samphire* had invited me as guest of honour. If the
editor had been male, I need hardly state, I would have found
the invitation much easier to refuse. All the Cambridge poets were
there, the Algernons in their velvet jackets and the Kens in their
anoraks. During the muffled course of a desultory conversation in
which tea-cake crumbs were carefully retained in the cupped hand,
Anselm Hollo was proposed as a touchstone contemporary poet. My
contention that they would all be better off learning MacNeice's
Autumn Journal by heart was greeted with tolerant smiles by the
Kens. The Algernons were more ready to entertain the notion but
they were outnumbered. The balance was shifting. Revolution was in
the air. An aerosol can of crazy foam was passed around. We were
supposed to close our eyes and shape the foam between our hands
while improvising on the theme of primal creation. One of the Kens
squirted the crazy foam into his long hair. I left, not because I didn't
like them but because what they had on their hands, under the crazy
foam, was time, and time was what I was already running out of.

At such moments I wondered whether I had any legitimate business being in a university, which is, after all, a place where young
people discover themselves. Those who have already done so should
clear out. These misgivings were reinforced by what went on in
the Union debating chamber. Abramovitz was elected Secretary of the

Union in the first term of his second year: the fastest climb to power on record. I attended his inaugural debate with some vague intention of speaking from the floor. I was ready to lie down on it and go to sleep before the paper speeches were half over. Though Abramovitz himself conducted the proceedings suavely enough, the frolicsome puns and points of order from the resident wits would have tried the patience of a saint. A moustached madman called Peregrine Sourbutts-Protheroe kept jumping to his feet and proposing that the motion be put, or that the point of order be promulgated, or whatever. Since the motion was some balls-aching foolery along the lines of 'That this House would rather rock than roll', I was all in favour of its being got out of the way as soon as possible, but apparently Sourbutts-Protheroe was out of order. He certainly looked it. Instead of the black tie favoured by the committee he wore full white-tie evening dress, except that he also wore plimsolls. Abramovitz informed me that Sourbutts-Protheroe was tolerated for the amusement he provided. The humourless, keen to be thought otherwise, love to laugh but need to be told when, so they are always glad if a clown dresses the part. With my eyes closed I listened in despair as the evening wore on. It was just possible that something serious could be said in such a context of bad jokes and braying laughter. But something funny never could. I vowed never to speak in a university union debate. In later years I was to rescind that vow several times each in Cambridge and Oxford, but always with subsequent regret for a largely wasted evening. If only they would cut the malarkey and get on with the oratory. Nothing speeds up your heart like speaking on your feet.

There was plenty of opportunity for that in the Footlights, where I continued to meet young British people who were to influence my life deeply. Some of them have become well-known since. I will try not to single them out merely on that basis. Stylistic gymnastics ensue when one tries to drop a name softly, while simultaneously indicating that one was present at the birth of, and perhaps even helped breathe life into, the future star. ('The name Marlon Brando didn't mean much then, but when he watched you act you knew that someone very special was analysing your every move, your every vocal inflection,' etc.) Besides, some of those who impressed me most have never become stars, but have lived normal lives instead: a destiny to be preferred, in my opinion, unless the strength of inner compulsion leaves no choice.

Eric Idle had gone down to begin a professional career as a performer on stage and screen. Since the road to Monty Python was longer and harder than most of the journalists who write about the subject are capable of taking in, he won't thank me for saying that he had future stardom written all over him. He was a consummate performer. He was, however, still somewhat short of material at that time, having not yet found his true comic vision, which was within him, but needed a context to bring it out. His successor as President of Footlights was Andy Mayer, whose originality was already fully established, and probably had been when he was still in the cradle. Mayer must have lacked the neurotic requirement for the limelight, because nowadays he is happy to work behind the camera. At the time his precocity floored me. He went on stage with his own stuff, and it was unique. So was his style of delivering it. A smallish young man with a huge Beatles-style helmet of dead straight dark hair whose fringe was cut square across the eyes so that he had to tilt his head back to look at the audience, he had a weird sort of negative timing which made pauses go on longer than they should, except when, as he often did, he got a big laugh, which he would try to talk straight through, as if he couldn't hear it. Staccato and legato at the same time, his monologues were short and apparently incoherent collages of verbal fragments. A routine in which he pretended to be an American evangelist had me simultaneously roaring with laughter and breathless with admiration, wondering how he packed so much in. 'Jesus Christ! Remember the name. Said. (Long pause) Or is *said* to have said. (Longer pause) God! (Inconceivably long pause) I put it to you that he *noo*! *I* dunno. (Looks at watch, nods into wings.) So! (Extends forefinger, finds it fascinating, becomes transfixed, shakes head.) Write away! Write away *right* away to the following *ad*dress . . .' There were only about a hundred words in the piece but it took him five minutes to get through it, so panic-stricken was the audience. They would hold on to each other and howl.

Pronounced by so young a man, these comic ramblings, when I stopped laughing to reflect, stung like a reproach. My own monologues were still running at about ten minutes minimum and Mayer was taking half the time to say twice as much, with four times the effect. When it was announced that President Johnson's daughter,

Lucy Baines Johnson, was engaged to be married, I presaged the nuptials with a monologue which was my first really big hit in the Footlights. But the emphasis was on 'big'. Cast in the form of a running commentary, as if the wedding ceremony were a football match, the piece went on and on like a novel by Thomas Wolfe before Maxwell Perkins had persuaded him to cut it down to merely mammoth proportions. The foreign policy of the United States was starting to worry me almost as much as it was starting to worry my American friends. I had a lot to say on the subject. Partly because my American friends were present in the audience, my 'Lucy Gets Married' monologue went down a storm in the Falcon Yard club-room, but it was a long storm, with several lulls included. Chastened by Andy Mayer's gift for brevity, I trimmed my masterpiece by several minutes before going public with it in the Pembroke smoker. At the cost of sacrificing some of the more obviously political content, the laugh lines were brought closer together. What I was then engaged in, I realized much later, was the first stage in a laborious process of learning to remove the connecting tissue so that the argument could be unified by tone rather than logic. In the long run this painfully acquired discipline would enable me to write a thousand-word article which sounded as if I was just saying it (detractors who called my television column in the *Observer* a cabaret turn were exactly right) but at the time it was painful to go on and die, and even when I had a hit, like 'Lucy Gets Married', the hit could be alarmingly hit and miss. A laugh that I got on Thursday night wouldn't be there on Friday night. What had I done wrong? I had produced the show successfully enough – the wine had once again done its work on the audience – but I was less adept at producing myself. This was to remain a pattern. When it came to criticizing and arranging the work of others, the shaping spirit operated in good order. When it came to my own work, the enthusiasm of invention made me deaf to my own better judgment. Always I had to go into hiding and lick my wounds before I found the wherewithal to improve. When I did improve, it was often in the wrong direction, towards a more polished performance, when what I needed to do was to perform less: the deader my pan, the better my words worked. An anti-talent, I needed a non-style.

Romaine Rand: now *there* was a performer. After her striptease nun routine the previous year, I was well aware that her absence from the Pembroke smoker would not be tolerated. The Hearties would dismantle the place if she did not show up. By now I was in digs on the Newnham side of the river, having got out of my room in the Eagle only just in time to avoid being consumed by the killer mould. My new room was rented from a nice young couple of graduate scientists who needed the money. Apart from my habit of smoking in bed while drunk, from their viewpoint I must have been the ideal tenant, because I was busy in Footlights almost all the time. They seldom saw me, and my memory of them is hazy. I changed my sheets about once a term, but never slept in them long enough on any given night to turn them any very deep shade of grey. A pot of jam that I left with its lid off for two or three months was mysteriously removed. Apart from that there was no interference with my freedom. Rather better organized as usual, Romaine lived in a Newnham hostel not far away. Her sitting room had a diamond-leaded casement, through which, from outside the building, I debonairly inserted my upper body before launching on an eloquent appeal for her participation in the Pembroke smoker. Walled in by stacks of books about Elizabethan rhetoric, she tried to stave me off by pleading pressure of work. I had the answer to that. Since, as I have related, she had managed to persuade the university authorities that she should be allowed to forget the Tripos and register for a PhD, it was *my* year for sitting examinations, not hers. Then she tried to stall me by saying that she didn't have a number ready. I countered by telling her that it would be enough for her just to show up and go on. It didn't matter what she did, but if she wasn't there then I was a gone goose. This appeal to her compassion was unavailing, because although Romaine's emotions were powerful, they came and went, and this was a Tuesday, whereas her day for compassion was Wednesday. Tuesday was her day for patriotism. When I pointed out that if the Pembroke smoker flopped it would be bad news for Australia, she began to melt, and when I wound up by suggesting, in broad terms, that no essay in the art of cabaret and intimate revue could be fully alive without the galvanizing influence of her genius for improvisation, it became clear that I had finally touched her heart. Her day for self-obsession was every day. Since the same went for me, it had taken time for me to switch the centre of attention from me to her, but having once got around to it I could congratulate myself on my cunning. 'Don't get your hopes up,' she said dismissively, already engrossed again in the exquisite scholastic filigree of *Love's Labour's Lost*. 'I'm fucked if I'll work my tits off for a pack of dick-heads who row boats.' She promised, however, to put in an appearance of some kind. Romaine had her drawbacks but her word was her bond. She had said she would be there, so I was saved. It was with an inexpressible sense of relief, then, that I backed down the gardener's ladder up which I had climbed to her window. Although elated, I was careful not to hurry. Her sitting room was only on the second floor, but the gravel driveway looked as hard as a proctor's heart.

Though Romaine did indeed turn up on the first night of the Pembroke smoker, she terrified me by announcing that she intended to do nothing except sing 'Land of Hope and Glory'. She had brought the sheet music for this, so that our piano player could accompany her. She was also carrying a dark blue straw hat with a stuffed bird on it. She put in a request to go on last, so that she would have time to practise her piece out in the corridor. My own view was that it was her look-out. The standard of numbers was quite high that year. We had a jazz quartet powered by the compulsive mainstream drumming of Colin Edwards, who was moonlighting from his regular gig at the Red Lion. Under the low ceiling of the Old Library, with the audience far gone into the rapture of the deep, that band sounded like a destroyer passing close overhead. All the Footlights who had aspirations towards being included in the May Week revue were parading their audition pieces in highly polished form. I'm bound to say that I held my own with them. In my capacity as producer, I chose to place my 'Lucy Gets Married' monologue as the second last number. By that time the Hearties at the back of the packed room were sitting on each other's shoulders and swinging playfully at each other with empty wine bottles. Down at the front, flanked by two Girton girls in taffeta, the ruffles on the expensive dress shirt of Delmer Dynamo were hanging limply wet, like cabbage bleached by steam. The audience were all so tight that Sir Alec Douglas-Home could have read out the university bye-laws and gone over like Max Miller. At the end of my monologue, I was swept off the stage by a tidal wave of applause. As Romaine went past me in the dark, I tacitly challenged her to top that. For a long while nothing much happened. I peeked around the door. The preliminary cheering had died down to a provisional rhubarb. Some of the Hearties were laughing at

Romaine's hat, but all the rest of the audience were refilling one another's wine glasses while she handed her sheet music to the piano player, gave him whispered instructions, stood back, folded her hands, cleared her throat, and nodded for him to begin the accompaniment.

The result was chaos. She sang 'Land of Hope and Glory' with her lips out of synchronization with the words. When she sang the word 'hope', her mouth was pronouncing the word 'land', and so on. The effect was uncannily funny, as if the world had come loose from its pivot. I saw the normally staid Strad Blantyre pass out from laughter. He was out of his chair and on the floor as if the room was being sprayed with bullets. People were holding on to one another and crying. Delmer Dynamo was removing his clothes by tearing at them, like a sea-lion strangling in its own skin. When Romaine finished the song they made her sing it again. This time she added illustrative gestures, but they were out of synchronization too. She marched on the spot when she should have looked maternal, smiled winsomely when she should have looked martial, laughed when she should have wept. The audience rocked back and forth as if lashed by the gale of their own laughter. When I led the rest of the cast on for the closing number it was like setting up a Punch and Judy show after the battle of El Alamein. I did my best to look proprietorial, as if the whole idea had been mine. This strategy must have worked at least partly, because from that day forward I was able to run up debts on my college bills, and an *exeat* was always easy to obtain. When I said I had important business in London, I was believed. I had become a tolerated eccentric. This had been, was, and probably still is, one of the undeclared side-benefits of the Cambridge system. Within broad limits you can make as big a fool of yourself as you like, and still be put up with. In that respect, on the day when the ancient universities become efficient they will cease to be productive. Misfits and failures should have room to flourish. The proposition is made no less valid by the haste with which the misfits and failures spring forward to agree with it.

6. MEET KEITH VISCONTI

My important business in London consisted largely of misbehaviour. Charter flights had made Italy cheaper to get to but no nearer. Meanwhile my old life in London could be reached for the price of a student rail fare. Some of my cronies, including the incipient film director, Dave Dalziel, had gone home or gone away, but others had stayed on to enjoy what had become self-consciously an Era. Among these latter was my erstwhile girlfriend, Robin, whom I had helped to become a lapsed Catholic. Since then her personality had flowered, to the extent that the nuns who had brought her up would have sent her to Hell on the strength of her clothes alone. Also she danced well, in a sort of silent frenzy. She was one of those people whose whole bodies have a feeling for popular music, and that was the time when popular music had a feeling for bodies. If you believed the glossy magazines, Swinging London was a place where you could run along the King's Road and meet Julie Christie running the other way. People you knew, or anyway people known by people you knew, were working as extras in Antonioni's *Blow-Up*, and sending out reports of how David Hemmings was being pressed flat between ravenous women. The barriers were down, the hunt was up, the game was afoot. Actually it wasn't quite like that. The youth scene consisted, as it always had, of awkward parties with alcohol still the strongest stimulant, apart from desire. This last, however, was rampant, and was flogged on to a new fervour by the music. The music really *was* good. Every new Beatles LP moved things on to a new plane of rhythmic sensuality, as if we were all ascending from floor to floor in a transparent building that swayed more as you climbed higher. Though Robin had good cause to distrust me, in these circumstances she lacked the fanaticism which would have been necessary to fight me off. Her tiny flatlet in Pimlico had a yard consisting of precisely four paving stones. The yard, hilariously called an area, was hemmed in by a wall taller than a man. At three o'clock in the morning I would be up and over that wall like a commando and sobbing at her closed door. What could she do but let me in? Other young women were harder to persuade but the occasional one succumbed, probably because it was too dark to know quite what was going on. In the aftermath I was not always a gentleman. Even more shamefully, I thought I had an innate right to thoughtless behaviour. The *Zeitgeist* had given my Bacchic urge a blanket endorsement. The quantum leap in the efficiency and convenience of contraceptive methods amounted to a mandate. Rubber, however elastic, had been to some extent a restraint. Now the wraps were off. If you looked closely enough at the Pill, it glowed with a green light.

On the loose in London, I could fancy myself as a rake. Fancying myself was easier in those days than it became later. Quite a lot of my hair was still on top of my head. My chest, though it showed signs of slipping, had not yet begun to accelerate. As a line-shooter I was indefatigable. I could fall in love in ten minutes and tell her about it for ten hours. I wrote poems on the spot and read them out unasked. Most of what I said, I believed. When I told some pretty dancer that she was a revelation, it was true. True at the time. I had commitments elsewhere but elsewhere was somewhere else. My trick, or condition, of being able to compartmentalize my life allows me to be active in several fields at once. This was already coming in handy as far as writing went: I could write during the day, go on stage at night, and each activity would benefit from the other. But from the moral viewpoint there was another sense in which I needed to be watched. It took me a long time to learn to watch myself, possibly because I didn't much like what I saw when I did.

The return of Dave Dalziel helped to restore my capacity for dedication. Without him, London might merely have been where I went to do a cheap imitation of Christopher Marlowe in his cups. Dalziel had come back out of Africa, and he demanded allegiance. Being a model of seriousness, he got it. He was a man dedicated to his art. That his own art lay mostly in the future merely testified to its purity. In Nigeria, he had put in a punishing year and a half as head of the government film unit. Apart from a couple of local assistants, whom he had to train, he was the whole staff. One of the loveliest of the Australian expatriate girls, a brunette of Irish extraction unbelievably called Cathleen O'Houlihan, had flown out to marry him. Knowing his record, and stung by jealousy, I doubted if the alliance would last, yet I couldn't deny the magnificence of the gesture. It was a leap in the dark. Nigeria was already in a recognizable preparatory stage of the civil war which was later to make the name Biafra notorious. At that time, nobody outside Africa could tell an Ibo from a Hausa. According to Dalziel's letters, however, the lay-out was terrifyingly simple. The Ibos were smart and everybody else hated them for it, so sooner or later there would be a massacre. Meanwhile the Nigerian politicians wanted nothing from the government film unit except to be filmed individually in close-up at all times, even at night. 'You can't turn an empty camera on them, either,' wrote Dalziel. 'They show up at the lab and demand to see the negative. These guys are *very easy to see* in the negative.'

As conscientious as ever, Dalziel had got on with the charade while sedulously maintaining his lines of communication to London, in the hope of snaring a job that would get him out of Lagos before people started cutting one another up. Utterly without side, he had a great gift for true friendship with the black Africans and didn't want to be there when the inevitable happened. It was already happening when he and the now pregnant Cathleen landed in London. They took a small house in Brixton, where their parlour soon became a gathering point for refugees from Nigeria. You could meet people who had run government departments who would now count themselves lucky if they were allowed to clean trains. I met a tubby, middle-aged, smiling woman there whose whole family had been massacred before her eyes. She was smiling to hold her face together. Cathleen organized the tea and cakes. I listened to the baby in her stomach. It sounded keen to join the party. I had known Cathleen when she had first arrived in Sydney like an inspiration out of an emerald background, an Iseult Gonne transported in space and time. Now she was a wife and soon to be a mother. Dalziel had a new air of – what was it? – sanity. Something was going on that I felt left out of.

Dalziel still had plenty of the old insanity left, however. In Nigeria, on the few days of the month when he was not required to film politicians as they queued up to appear one at a time in front of the camera, he had managed to shoot the footage for a twenty-minute short subject about the only traffic jam in the history of Lagos. It wasn't the most thrilling topic in the world, but the film was put

together with such craftsmanship that Dalziel was easily short-listed
for the newly created job of running the British Film Institute's
Production Board. The successful applicant would be given the task
of providing spiritual guidance and practical assistance for aspiring
young film-makers. At the interview, Sir Michael Balcon correctly
judged Dalziel to be the authentic article, and he was hired. Not even
Balcon, a great man with the generosity to relish talent in others,
realized just how authentic his new protégé would prove to be. Dalziel
was so selfless in his efforts to aid young hopefuls that a mere salary
seemed small reward: he should have been canonized. Certainly he
had a saint's patience. Some of the aspiring young film-makers were
patently crazy. In a few fateful cases Dalziel found this fact difficult
to detect. Thousands of applications had poured in from people who
wanted to make a film. Many of them loftily left blank the space in
the application form reserved for an outline of the film they wanted
to make. It transpired that they didn't want to be pinned down by
the restrictions of the system. Dalziel was sceptical enough to realize
that they wanted the status of film-makers without having to go
through the taxing business of actually achieving anything. But if an
applicant seemed to have an idea that was even halfway decent,
Dalziel would put it up to the board, get a budget, and supply the
incipient Fellini with everything he needed, which usually included
talent. Like many people with abundant creative energy, Dalziel found
it hard to imagine what it was like to be without it. If a young would-
be film director stood there without saying anything, Dalziel thought
that it was because the hot new prospect was so bursting with ideas
as to be inarticulate. If a young would-be film director not only stood
there without saying anything but smelled as if he hadn't taken a
bath in a long time, Dalziel thought that it was because the hot new
prospect was so bursting with ideas he was not only inarticulate,
he was beyond being concerned with the petty details of personal
hygiene.

I have gone only half way towards describing Dalziel's principal and most troublesome protégé, Keith Visconti. Though Keith's
anabasis from the status of comprehensive school expellee to potential
cinéaste should not be derided even in retrospect, there were several
reasons to think that on top of being illiterate and odoriferous he
was also clinically insane, with overtones of petty larceny. He had,
however, an inborn knack for thinking in sequences. He understood

the essential grammar of eyelines and reverse angles without needing to have it set out for him in diagram form. Of no fixed abode, he seemed to live out of the gabardine overcoat which he wore at all times. It shone in a way that any piece of cloth does when it is dirty enough. Clutched tightly against the coat, because too big to fit into either of its bulging pockets, was a ten-minute show reel, made on short ends, which featured a friend of his, dressed unconvincingly as a waiter, serving another friend of his, dressed even more unconvincingly as a businessman, with a cup of coffee. Despite the implausibility of casting, sets and costumes, the action all happened in the right order. This was enough to convince Dalziel that Keith Visconti was a genius, an impression that Keith said nothing to contradict. Keith never said anything. He just stood there in his grotty overcoat, silent and immobile. Dalziel was thus able to read into his new pupil all his own qualities of inventiveness, lucidity and scruple.

The film Keith wanted to make was about a businessman and his wife, or perhaps mistress – the relationship was not specified – sitting in a restaurant and being served coffee. The woman is mysteriously drawn to the waiter, who has perhaps played a role in her earlier life, or perhaps might play a role in her later life, or perhaps both, if not neither. Leaving questions of motivation aside, Keith's screenplay was a small miracle of carefully calculated specificity. Every close-up was thoroughly notated as to expression, the line of the eyes, the intensity of the light. The fact that the whole thing was written out, with very few of the words correctly spelled, in pencilled block capitals on scraps of paper from varying sources, some of the pages being stuck together with gravy stains, did nothing to dissuade Dalziel from the view that here was a talent from Heaven, a technically endowed avatar on the scale of Pushkin, Mozart, Schubert or Seurat. Lacking Dalziel's purity of soul, I was more easily able to spot that Keith was a potential head-case. Actually I was wrong, too. There was nothing potential about Keith's mania. During his first visit to Dalziel's house, he had helped himself to half the contents of the refrigerator. Cathleen had smiled on this bohemian trait but had been startled to notice, after he left, that several of her brassières were missing. She uttered a clear warning. Dalziel was too caught up to heed it and I was too craven. I was on the set as an unpaid grip when filming began on *Expresso Drongo*. This was Dalziel's working title for the project and showed that he had not lost his sense of humour. But there were some signs that he might have lost his judgment. Keith did at least twenty takes on every shot. Something always dissatisfied him. In the hired studio, it would be the angle of a light. In an exterior shot, it would be the intensity of the sun. He would squint at it as if it were the wrong size. He would complain that his leading actress had moved when she clearly hadn't, because she never did unless told to. All of this would have mattered less if Keith had not arrived late each morning for work. His excuse was lack of funds. Since the film's tight budget ruled out subsidized meals, Keith borrowed from Dalziel against the eventual profits. Taking this handout as his right, Keith complained that there was nothing left over to pay the cost of public transport, so he had to walk, which in turn was very hard on his shoes. His shoes certainly bore out this contention. Once they had been a rather good pair of brogues, but at that time they had probably belonged to someone else. Now they had cracks, thus exposing Keith's socks to the air, with penetrating results. He had feet like dead dogs. The film was four days behind schedule after three day's shooting, a ratio which it was to maintain and eventually exceed. Dalziel was slow to admit the possibility that it was in Keith's interests to spin things out. *Expresso Drongo* was Penelope's tapestry. To put it more plainly, it was Keith's meal ticket. Even after Dalziel caught on, he allowed this state of affairs to continue, hoping that he would be able to work his influence. That, as he saw it, was his job. A less generous man would have hit the silk sooner.

Keith's leading lady was called Nelia. Close interrogation had revealed that Keith's knowledge of the cinema was virtually zero, but apparently he had once seen a French film and been impressed that one of the actresses had been billed under her first name only. Nelia was Keith's discovery. Dalziel objected that the name would only serve to confuse the enormous public which the completed film would undoubtedly attract. Keith dug in his worn-down heels. As out of anything else, there was no talking Keith out of casting Nelia in the twin roles of wife and/or mistress. One of these personages – the one who waited outside the restaurant before coming in, as opposed to the one who waited inside the restaurant and did nothing at all – she played in a blonde wig, which cost a large proportion of the film's budget. The film lacking a wardrobe mistress, Nelia took the wig home with her every night and brushed it herself, presumably for hours, because it shone with a rare lustre. When quizzed closely by Dalziel, Keith avowed, in a few words widely spaced and reluctantly enunciated, that his relationship with Nelia was purely professional. It was hard to see how things could have been otherwise. Keith was so dirty that he had small plants growing on him. Any kind of physical contact with him was clearly out of the question. And Nelia was a zombie. You could simply park her in a chair, go away, come back hours later and she would still be sitting there. She was quite pretty but in a way so lacking in animation that even I had trouble idealizing her.

Characteristically I managed it. To those of us who are artists at daydreaming, resistance from the medium is an invitation to invention. Nelia had neat features, a sweet figure, and an uncanny gift of stillness. To my mind it was more than enough. Soon she was my Anna Karina, my Jeanne Moreau, my Monica Vitti. I had ample scope to nourish these fantasies. Each day on the set I tried to make myself indispensable by shifting silver boxes about and helping to place the lights, but when Keith got started on his usual twenty takes there was plenty of time to become acquainted with Nelia if she wasn't in the shot, or even if she was. I could get nothing out of her except a hint that she liked tennis players. 'Tony,' she would murmur, looking at the sports page of some subhuman newspaper it took her all day to read. 'John.' Convincing myself that she had mystery, I perched near her as often as possible, rather hoping that I would be asked to massage her neck, which must have ached from the combined effort of sitting and reading. I thought I was getting somewhere when she asked me to scratch her back: not the whole of her back, just a particular spot in the middle, about three inches below the shoulder blades. I did that several times a day for about a week. Finally I dared to be romantic. 'Is that *the* spot?' I murmured. 'The special place?' In a hitherto unheard-of burst of vivacity she turned her face towards me, instead of just speaking straight ahead as usual. 'No, it's them bras Keith give me,' she said. 'They fit funny.' Years later I learned that she was a notorious tennis groupie who was as much a part of Wimbledon as the strawberries and cream, or the rain. Exhausted players who had fought their way through to the last sixteen would find her waiting for them in their hotel rooms. She would be wearing nothing but a blonde wig. They called her New Balls Nellie.

Not everyone who wants to make a film is crazy, but almost everyone who is crazy wants to make a film. It is just one of the things that crazy people want to do, like starting a law suit or sending long, unsolicited letters to people in the public eye. A letter from a nutter has a recognizable format and orthography, as if all letter-writing nutters have to go through some kind of Top Gun nutter-letter-writing academy. Usually – I think I've said this before, so maybe I'm going nuts too – the letter is written in green ink and its many pages are tied together with a bootlace in the top left-hand corner. Even if typed, however, the letter will continue after the signature in a PS which will run around the edge of the filled page in a dense spiral until the whole of the margin is packed tight. This will occur no matter how many leaves the letter consists of – rarely fewer than twelve – and even if the verso of each leaf is left blank. Usually it isn't. Every space is filled up. Though the combination of energy and futility can be depressing to contemplate, at least the nutter letter can be written on a low budget. The nutter movie costs thousands of pounds at the very least, and if the nutter hasn't got the money himself then he will have to get it from someone else. As the officer designated to provide tyro film makers with operating capital, Dalziel was in the position of a man giving away free meat in Moscow. He was on his guard, but he was handicapped by his correct perception that the partition between talent and obsession is often thin.

The ambiguous case of Keith Visconti would have sapped Dalziel's confidence if it had not been for the continuous, reassuring presence of our old friend and compatriot Alain le Sands. Born Alan Syms in Brighton le Sands, only a mile away from my own home suburb of Kogarah, this conspicuous figure in the history of modern Australian cinema had gone to school and grown up without either my or Dalziel's ever having met him. At the University of Sydney I still didn't meet him, but Dalziel acquired him like a shadow. As I related in the first volume of these memoirs, Dalziel knew the names of the director, cameraman and editor of all the films he had ever seen. Alan Syms knew all those things too. Dalziel made the initial, fateful mistake of assuming that there must be some kind of affinity between himself and this intense young man who followed him everywhere. It turned out that Alan Syms also knew the names of the assistant director, the make-up artist and the second unit focus-puller. By the time it emerged that Alan Syms not only possessed this information, but was incapable of restraining himself from conveying it unasked, it was too late. That light of excitement in Alan Syms's eyes was the effulgent stare of the true film buff. The eyes were large, with contracted black pupils blazing in the dead centre of the very white whites. They never blinked. His mouth was similarly always wide open. It was equipped with large square teeth, like freshly cut tombstones. Alan Syms talked in a high, piercing shriek. Everything he said was otiose information about movies. He carried a card index.

Alan Syms was one of the main reasons Dalziel left Australia. When Alan Syms showed up in London, changed his name to Alain le Sands and started passing himself off as the leading light of the Australian New Wave, he was one of the main reasons why Dalziel left for Nigeria. At FBI guest lectures given by distinguished visiting American film directors such as John Frankenheimer or Delmer Daves, Alain le Sands would turn up and dominate question time. In a voice like a descending German dive bomber, he asked Frankenheimer for details about his assistant editor on *Seven Days in May*. When Frankenheimer visibly failed to recall exactly who his assistant editor had been, Alain le Sands provided the man's name, address and marital history. It was at this point, I am certain, that Dalziel began to find Lagos attractive. While Dalziel was away, Alain le Sands perfected his act by equipping himself with a screenplay for a short subject. By the time Dalziel got back, Alain le Sands had his film half-made. His own funds – which, judging from his varied supply of leather jackets, must have been not inconsiderable – were all used up. His few friends had been fleeced. He needed completion money. He made Dalziel's life a misery, demanding that the incomplete film be seen and assessed. He would telephone Dalziel in Brixton at three o'clock in the morning, waking up a whole houseful of Nigerian refugees. Finally, for a quiet life, Dalziel agreed to see the incomplete film at a small screening room in Soho. I happened to be in town and was present for the event. Dalziel had stipulated that Alain le Sands himself not be in attendance, so there were no witnesses except Dalziel, myself, and the projectionist, who was the first one to say 'Shit'. The film was entitled *He Alone*. It was subtitled '*un film de Alain le Sands*'. Dalziel was to relate this fact so often afterwards that Alan Parker picked the joke up and made it famous, but I was there at the birth and it was no joke. *He Alone* starred Alain le Sands himself, in a role closely modelled on that played by Charles Aznavour in *Tirez sur le pianiste*. Dalziel, who had wanted to *tirez sur* Alain le Sands for many years, groaned deeply in the dark. Yet Alain le Sands was no slavish plagiarist of Truffaut. Plot, characters and entire scenes had been faithfully copied, but he had an incompetence that was all his own. The deliberate jump-cuts of the *nouvelle vague* were translated by Alain le Sands into simple errors. Playing a young hero of threatening charisma, Alain le Sands would leap instantaneously from one side of the room to the other, his cigarette growing longer on the way. His sleeves would unroll and roll up again from shot to shot. As he advanced threateningly down a hotel corridor, he appeared to be walking between a set of railway lines. They were the dolly tracks of the camera. The cameraman must have been blind not to see them and adjust the framing accordingly. Perhaps he was too busy compensating for an evidently advanced case of Parkinson's disease. The camera shook as if mounted on a billycart. Unfortunately this imposed awkwardness of filmic style gave the central character none of the vulnerability of its model. Alain le Sands was playing the Aznavour character as if he were Robert Mitchum. He was being hunted, but he was not afraid. The point was thus neatly removed, leaving a vacuum. Close-ups were held for a long time. He smiled in every one of them, looking like two cement footpaths which had been freshly laid side by side. Dalziel watched in fascinated horror, audibly calculating the thousands of pounds the thing must have cost. Though it lasted only about fifteen minutes you could practically smell the burning money. Dalziel vowed that whoever else's cash was thrown on fire, it wouldn't belong to the BFI Production Board.

When Dalziel and I emerged shaking into the cold light of Soho, Alain le Sands was waiting for us on the pavement. 'What did you think of it?' he screamed. 'Hopeless,' said Dalziel. 'What are your criticisms?' shrieked Alain le Sands. 'There aren't any,' Dalziel replied wearily. 'It's just hopeless. Nothing works. It's a waste of time. A turkey. Forget it.' Alain le Sands made a strange move sideways. 'Yes, but how about some *constructive* criticisms?' The word 'constructive' was still echoing off the Georgian facades when we noticed the camera crew across the street. Alain le Sands had captured the whole scene. Luckily he could not afford to wear a radio microphone. We couldn't see a sound man. But unless his cameraman was even more incompetent than usual, he had got the picture. Dalziel commendably did not throw his coat over his head as we got into his car. It was a Jaguar 2.4 that was rather like his clothes: bought second-hand off a barrow but it looked terrific. It wouldn't start. The screaming face of Alain le Sands filled my window until the engine fired. 'God knows what he'll do with the footage,' said Dalziel as we pulled away. 'Keith's going to be a relief after that.' We spent the afternoon and early evening watching Keith Visconti shoot the big scene where the woman seated at the café table reveals that she takes sugar as well as milk. Six hours and a carton of sugar cubes dissolved like memories.

My key role in London's upsurgent film *milieu* made me even more determined, when back in Cambridge, to see every movie that came to town. I could not physically watch more movies than I had been watching already, but my newly acquired identity of quasi-film-maker gave new legitimacy to my pretty well constant attendance at the Cambridge cinemas, of which there were at that time half a dozen, most of them showing double bills. Across the river and up the hill, the Rex cinema showed – back to back and without let-up except for a few Pearl & Dean commercials – old and at the time almost entirely forgotten Hollywood programmers and films noirs with titles like *Dateline Homicide* and *Make My Tombstone Thick*. If you counted in the Arts cinema and the film societies, which together took care of the recherché present and historic past, Cambridge offered a chance to see just about every film ever made. I saw them all. In the late mornings I would write and deliver poems. From early afternoon on I was rarely out of a cinema except when I was in Footlights, and most of my time there was spent watching television. Armed with my practical knowledge I analysed every cut and change of angle, communicating my conclusions gratuitously to those sitting near by, even if they were strangers. I was forever drawing the attention of innocent civilians to what I took to be fine points of technique. Most of the time, I have since realized, I was simply wrong. Competent technique is what mediocrity has in common with genius, so there is small point in getting enthusiastic about it. Unless he is an outright hack, a journeyman will be just as careful as Fellini to make his shots match – often more careful. Buñuel, the most inventive of all film directors, resolutely declined to interest himself in any matter he thought merely aesthetic. But a little knowledge, though not always injurious to a practitioner, is invariably fatal to a critic. In recent years I have worked on documentary films at every stage of production and post-production. For any television documentary with my name in the title I have spent at least as much time in the cutting room as on the actual shoot, and often twice as much. I have turned a sentence around to fit pictures and I have asked for a shot to be run backwards to fit words. That kind of finicky labour is an experience for which there is no substitute. Youth, energy and appreciative passion, no matter how blessed they are with insight, aren't enough. There is no comparison between what I know now and what I used to know. Nowadays, after seeing a film or television programme, I wouldn't dream of praising its director until I had seen what he had done with other writers, and especially with other producers. I have seen a producer direct the whole movie. I have seen a cameraman save a director's career. But in my early innocence I fell for the *cinéaste* line full length. A fan of *Al Capone* and *Invitation to a Gunfighter*, I would point out that the director of both these masterpieces, Richard Wilson, had been the assistant editor on *Citizen Kane*, and that this fact should not be ignored when trying to account for their peculiar excellence. Though this wasn't a bad point, I was only a step away from sounding like Alain le Sands. Raise my voice three octaves, build up my teeth with white plaster, and I could have been him.

7. THE OSTRICH ALTERNATIVE

Obsessions are what we have *instead* of normality. They aren't a version of it, they are a surrogate. My obsession with the moving image was what I was having instead of working on the set books. Out of the three terms of my second and last year as an undergraduate, one and a half had gone by before I could bring myself even to sit down and assess the magnitude of what I had not yet done in the way of preparing to satisfy the examiners. When I finally faced the issue, I quickly realized that I would have a better chance of satisfying them if I offered them my body. To present them with the contents of my mind would be an insult. My first move was to write one of my classic letters to my mother telling her that I was studying hard and not to worry about a thing. More than usually specious, this work of fiction helped get me in the mood for works of fiction composed by other people, such as Dickens and Thackeray. But merely not feeling negative wasn't the same as feeling positive. Enthusiasm was lacking. Why did it have to be Dickens *and* Thackeray? And why were Dickens's novels so very long, not just in thickness but from page to page? He piled it on as if I had all the time in the world to take it off. Jane Austen had had a far better idea of how much time a busy poet and performer had to spare. There was also the advantage that in previous incarnations, while being an aesthete at the University of Sydney or a down-and-out post-Beatnik bohemian in Earls Court and Tufnell Park, I had actually read some of her books. Acquiring a working knowledge of her *oeuvre* was thus on the cards. I resolved to concentrate on Jane Austen and thereby reap the benefits of the informed insight that cuts deep, the sharp focus. Whether a sharp focus on Jane Austen would come in handy when discussing the novels of, say, Dostoevsky, was a point that remained moot. A moot point I could always deal with by crossing the river, climbing the hill and hiding from the reality of afternoon in the sweet, artificial night of the Rex.

Most of the films I saw there were like me: rootless, unsung, wandering the universe like a spaceship with a dead crew. When *The Manchurian Candidate* was withdrawn from the screen after the assassination of President Kennedy, it showed up nowhere in the world except at the Rex, where I saw it at least ten times. I could, and at the drop of a hat would, analyse its camerawork exhaustively, but in a more reliable part of my addled brain I must have realized that it was the words which really counted. I learned George Axelrod's perfectly turned screenplay line by line. At that time and for years to come, the muttered question 'Why does your head always look as if it's coming to a point?' was a secret password among those who shared the Manchurian connection. I, however, was the only person I ever met who could correctly recite the key line in *Breakfast at Tiffany's*: 'I've never had champagne before breakfast before. With breakfast, often. But never before before.' The line was Axelrod's, not Capote's. I also knew that the best line in *The Big Sleep* – 'She tried to sit in my lap while I was standing up' – was not Raymond Chandler's. Years before it was rediscovered as a cult classic, the all-time off-beat Hollywood sleeper *The Night of the Hunter* would also show up only at the Rex. The print was full of splices yet the photography retained its lustre and, more importantly, the narrative still flowed. Bowled over by Charles Laughton's talent as a director, I still had enough sense to realize that James Agee's screenplay was the vital contribution.

The second time I saw *The Night of the Hunter* at the Rex – once again I was in flight from Dickens – I was one of only three people in the audience. The others were two of the most beautiful people I had ever seen in my life. Both of them were Indians, and before I introduced myself I had mentally transferred to them the title of a piece by Duke Ellington: the Beautiful Indians. The beautiful girl was called Karula Shankar and the young man, if possible even more beautiful, was called Buddy Rajgupta. They looked like a tourist advertisement for Nirvana. It turned out, however, that they were students like me. In some respects they were even my kind of student. They, too, were in flight from the size of Dickens's novels. In other ways they were not students like me at all. Apart from their physical allure, they seemed materially comfortable to a degree unparalleled among the undergraduate population. This I deduced before we had even reached what Karula called Buddy's pad, whither I had been invited back for coffee. Buddy's casual Western clothes he might have worn at a Hyannis Port lawn party and Karula's sari was so subtle in its colours that you had to check your eyes for teardrops. Surely it was a film of water which was supplying the prismatic interplay as she rustled silkily along? No, it wasn't. In the middle of her superb forehead a tiny upright ellipse of scarlet spoke of the mysterious East. Her voice, however, spoke of Sarah Lawrence or Vassar, with the occasional word strongly emphasized, as if she had suddenly moved closer. 'You don't play *bridge*, by any chance?' Already lost, but not so far gone as to have forgotten that a competence at bridge might be hard to fake, I said I didn't. 'Man, have you ever met the *wrong* people. *We* play it *all* the time. We'll have to *teach* him, won't we?' Buddy said nothing for a long while as we walked. I could tell he was thinking. Finally he said: 'Yeah. OK.'

Buddy's pad was behind a heavy door in a neo-Georgian brick facade somewhere near Newnham. I can remember a gravel drive and an overhanging elm which must be gone by now, because the Dutch elm beetle went through Cambridge like silent wildfire later on and missed hardly a single candidate for extermination. I imagine the spacious layout of Buddy's pad has gone too. There can't have been many subsequent undergraduates who would have been able to keep up that level of classy carelessness. By student standards the place was enormous, colossal, outlandish: it was Grand Central Station, the Grand Salon of the Louvre, the Great Hall of the People in Peking. Actually I suppose the main room was only about thirty feet by twenty, but even among all the divans and cushions there definitely would have been room to swing the tiger whose skin was on the floor. The general arrangements were for a Rajah who had been brought up in the Ritz, which was apparently pretty well what had happened. Family photographs indicated that Buddy's fore-bears had driven at Le Mans, flown in the King's Cup, hunted from howdahs, played host to the Mountbattens. Pretending not to be impressed by all this was made easier by the books, which were loosely shelved by the thousand, and all interesting. Such American avant-garde publishing houses as New Directions and Evergreen were fully represented. These imprints I at least recognized. Others were new to me. Proud of my one-volume collected Nathaniel West, I was rather put out to see his separate novels all lined up in the original American editions, their paper wrappers intact. Undergraduates like to believe that they read adventurously but few of them do. Mostly they follow two curriculae: the official one, and the unofficial one which prescribes books supposed, by general consent among their generation, to be of epoch-making interest. Buddy was a genuine extracurricular reader. He had his own taste and followed it where it led. Nor was he one of those paid-up exquisites who read minor writers because the major ones are insufficiently obscure. He was in search of originality in all its forms. The quest was made only the more impressive by his off-hand manner. Nowadays he would be called laid-back. At that time the word for him was cool. Even in conversation, he never ran to catch the bus. 'Have you read Agee's film criticism?' he asked. 'Yes,' I lied. Buddy crossed slowly to his shelves, took down the relevant book, leafed through it, found some paragraph that he had been looking for, silently read it, closed the book and handed it to me. 'You should,' he said.

And I did. That year I read almost everything on Buddy's shelves. Constant attendance at the cinema never cut into my reading: only into my official reading. Unofficially I would rather read than sleep. The Cambridge second-hand bookshops always beckoned. By the second week in any term I was usually too broke to buy anything. The University Library, needless to say, was out of the question: it was full of students who were actually studying, a sight which would throw me into a panic. So every few days I took an armful of books back to Buddy's pad, there to exchange them for more. Occasionally I was a fourth in bridge games but I never learned: the Beautiful Indians were too good at it to remember what it was like not to be able to play, so they couldn't teach me. Several times I was paired off with an Italian graduate economist called Mario who could memorize the whole pack at a glance no matter how it was shuffled. I came to dread the moment, usually no more than halfway through a hand, when Mario, Buddy or Karula said something like 'That's it, then,' and they all laid out their cards, having foretold how the hand – or round or rubber or whatever it was called – must play itself out. I had no sense for cards and got no better. Even today, playing gin rummy with my small daughter, I am notoriously easy meat, and have been since she was seven years old. If I make a fool of myself at gin, it can be imagined what a figure I cut at bridge. I just couldn't do it.

Reading I knew how to do: except, of course, when it was prescribed. Buddy was the same way. As far as I remember he never sat for the examinations, and might well already have been sent down without his noticing. Already, on that first afternoon, I envied him his insouciance, although I was too obtuse to realize as yet that it was only part of an aristocratic principle whose other main component was a deep sense of social obligation. Downing the proffered martinis as if they were water, I conveyed to Buddy and Karula my radical convictions, explaining to them the economic problems facing their country and how easily these could be solved. 'Man, that's *crap*,' Karula murmured from her sleepily curled position in a heap of paisley cushions, as if Liberty's had been bombed and geraniums were growing among the ruins. Buddy, smoking a black Russian cigarette so delicately that it seemed never to grow shorter, either listened to my monologue or thought of something else. Perhaps he was thinking of his country, in which, he slyly neglected to tell me, his father was a liberal publisher who had many times laid his life on the line for democracy and would expect his children to do the same. It was a typical Cambridge undergraduate evening: ignorance spoke out confidently while experience waited for it to catch up. Night fell and deepened. Karula rose from her cushions and made for the kitchen. She constructed large, American-style hamburgers. Eating a hamburger without putting down my martini glass made it difficult to talk, but I coped.

It never occurred to me that I should at least have offered to leave the Beautiful Indians together. Anyway, towards midnight I was given the job of escorting Karula home. She lived right in the centre of town, in a suite of rooms in a gingerbread house in a little lane, no wider than a thin man, leading off Market Square. It took a long time to get there because I found her a bit of a handful to escort. In fact I found her at all only with difficulty. The martinis must have had something in them. Alcohol, perhaps. Probably it was the way they made them in India. I tripped over gutters, detoured into bushes, fell down holes in the road. I peed behind a parked Mini and missed it. Karula, perfectly sober, was in hysterics. When we finally got to her place it turned out that she had forgotten her front door key. Luckily her room was on the ground floor. We jemmied her window without much trouble – Karula's peals of oddly accented laughter covered the noise of splitting timber – and I boosted her though. There was so much sari that I didn't really touch her. It was like pushing an unfolded parachute into a dumb waiter. But I felt her. The sweet heat of life. She was lovely and she wasn't mine. I wanted all the lovely women to be mine. If not all, then a few. If that was too much, then just one. Here, now. This instant. I sat down and had a little cry. 'Shit, man,' came that bewitching voice from inside the window, 'go *home*.' But where was home? Far, far away. Using the cool wall as a guide, I edged toward the street light at the end of the alley. So cold in England, even when it was warm.

8. WELL INTERRUPTED, PEMBROKE

Let me not convey an impression of time completely wasted. If I had been enrolled to read a science subject and had dodged work in such a fashion, I would have been cheating. But in retrospect it seems possible that I only *felt* fraudulent. Eschewing the set books with unequalled diligence, I read everything else. From the conversations that lasted until dawn, I remembered what I heard in the rare intervals when I wasn't talking. The awkward truth, when it comes to the humanities, is that knowledge, taste and judgment get into us by uncharted routes. Late one night in Footlights, alone with the sputtering black and white TV set, I saw and heard Jacqueline du Pré playing the Elgar cello concerto. I saw her before I heard her, and went mad for her smile as I never did for Elgar, but another barrier between me and classical music softly crumbled. Until then I had been convinced, wrongly, that the main stream of great music was in the symphonies and the operas. After that, I started looking for it in the right place, in the concertos and the chamber music. It was her passion that did it. We live more by example than we think. Strong evidence for this view was provided by the disconcerting fact that I was a bit of a role model myself. Undergraduates who were shy about their intellectual or artistic ambitions looked up to me because I was blatant about mine. They believed that I knew a thing or two and I'm bound to say that I agreed with them. When the JCR of my college was invited to send a three-man team to compete in the television programme *University Challenge*, that I should be included seemed natural not just to me but to everyone. The rank of captain being offered, I made no demur. My second-in-command was an American called Chuck Beaurepaire, who was a walking, shouting encyclopaedia. Delmer Dynamo and the other Americans avoided him because of his knack for making his interlocutor redundant. He talked all the time and nothing he said was refutable, because all of it was facts. A formidable practitioner along those lines myself, I had been known to go toe-to-toe with him for a full half-hour before pausing to draw breath, whereupon he swept inexorably into the gap. Beaurepaire talked the way Alexander gave battle. He went straight at you. 'Watch out for Chuck,' whispered Delmer loudly one night in Hall. 'He's got another hole to eat with. The mouth *never* gets tired.' Beaurepaire was sitting only about three places away and should have heard, but he was talking. 'Johnson has the legislative record. Viewpoint of social benefits, Great Society biggest thing since New Deal. Just has a dumb name. Should've called it something else. Fair shake. Free lunch. Whatever. Know what Johnson said about J. Edgar Hoover? You don't? Tell you. Listen, this is great. They asked him why he didn't fire Hoover, right? Johnson said he'd rather have Hoover inside the tent pissing out than outside pissing in. My father was *there* when he said that. Johnson was on the Hill when Jack Kennedy . . .' Beaurepaire delivered all this in a sustained bellow that made all around him look into their stew as if a tunnel might open through it and lead them to salvation. But from the viewpoint of Pembroke's team for *University Challenge*, to have Beaurepaire on tap was like being offered the assistance of Otto Skorzeny to pull a bank-raid. The third member of our team was a nice young man whose name I have forgotten. He had been chosen because he knew something about science. Beaurepaire knew all about that too, so the young man never needed to open his mouth, and, being shy, didn't try. Let us call him Christopher, because if his name wasn't that then it was Nicholas. His family had a nice house outside Manchester, where we all stayed the night before we recorded the show next day. In those days, Granada Television ruled the ionosphere with *Coronation Street* and an unrivalled array of classic small formats like *University Challenge*, *All Our Yesterdays*, *What the Papers Say* and *Cinema*, which was to be the first programme I ever regularly presented when, some years later, I tentatively essayed what has turned out to be my principal means of earning a living. At that time, however, I had been on television precisely once. It had happened in Sydney.. Television itself had been new to Australia. I was one of a team of Sydney University students ranged against a team of journalists in a game of bluff. We had scored precisely no points. I forget the rules, but I never got over sitting there for half an hour without saying a word. This time, I resolved, would be different. In one of

Christopher's guest rooms, I lay awake looking at the hammered beams and white plaster of the low ceiling. Outside in the grounds, the moon shone on the lake. I didn't want Christopher's inheritance. I didn't even want, or not very much, Christopher's mother, which was quite mature of me, because she was exactly the stamp of unassuming but self-assured gentlewoman most calculated to arouse greed and resentment. Her husband, I had guessed, must have been that object covered with coats and hats that we passed in the hall. Anyway, he hadn't joined us for dinner, which, excusing herself, she did not change for, merely adding tiny pearl earrings to her ensemble of cable-stitch roll-neck sweater, corduroy trousers and penny loafers. Quality unencumbered by finery, her *soignée* allure was the unfussiest possible interplay of form and content. Serene. What a word. There was nothing ruffled about her image until it reached my eyes. 'You *will* look after Christopher tomorrow, won't you?' I nodded conspiratorially while Beaurepaire told her about the Tennessee Valley Authority.

Next day we were up against an all-girl team from St Hilda's, Oxford. I'm sorry to say that we creamed them. Christopher just sat there and I almost did the same. Beaurepaire was magnificent. Bamber Gascoigne, moderating the programme, could barely begin a question before Beaurepaire answered it. 'It was unhistorical of Keats . . .' Gascoigne began. 'Balboa!' shouted Beaurepaire over the zap of his buzzer. He had instantaneously figured out, not only that the question must concern Keats's mistake in putting Cortez on a peak in Darien, but that the question would be about whom he should have put there instead. Bitterly reflecting that 'Silent, upon a peak in Darien' neatly summarized the condition and location to which everyone who knew Beaurepaire would like to see him translated, I was nevertheless pleased that we were cleaning up, and the last bonus question was a personal triumph for myself. The right answer depended on knowing that Leonardo's 'Last Supper' had been painted on a wet wall. Having seen it helped. A man of the world, I struggled not to look too pleased as we swept to victory. The camera probably saw the struggle. Personality is the thing it catches. Everything else it lets go.

You have to realize that in those days the whole country watched every episode of *University Challenge*. They watched it in working men's clubs. The Queen Mother watched it, knuckles white, running to the telephone to place bets. At the time of writing, television in Britain is still, by the skin of its teeth, a communal event – the best reason for being involved in it – but twenty years ago there was no question about it. If you were on television in prime time, the whole population of the country was looking through the same small window right into your face. That night we, the winning team from Pembroke, were given dinner by Bamber and the programme's producer at the Midland Hotel. The losing team was nowhere to be seen. The producer's beautiful researcher had a nice, fresh, land-girl sort of smile which bore up pluckily under a verbal onslaught from Beaurepaire that left Bamber looking thoughtful, as if wondering whether it was all worth it. Somehow I knew that he really thought it was, even if it cost him this, a bad evening out with the cocky youngsters. It wasn't just the money. It was the thing itself. The millions watching. The show. I vowed to myself that they would never get me. Never, never would I succumb to the lure of television. Its mereness I found offensive. Television didn't transform you. You just sat there. Look at Bamber Gascoigne, just sitting there while two pretty girls from the next table leaned over his shoulder – leaned *on* his shoulder – to get his autograph. *Four* pretty girls. It was a moment of truth. Even Beaurepaire stopped talking. Silent, upon a peak in Manchester.

The following week we came back for the next round, against another Oxford college, Balliol. Once again we stayed at Christopher's house the night before the big day. Christopher's father was still nowhere in the picture. Christopher's mother either changed for dinner or else had been wearing that black jersey silk bias-cut scooped-neck top all day, along with the straight plum velvet skirt and the ankle-strap sandals. While Beaurepaire blew a gale I drowned in her eyes. I resolved that when we returned victorious the next evening, I would dare. I had been reading a biography of H. G. Wells which said that when a guest at a country house party he already had a map of the sleeping arrangements in his pocket before he got off the train, with the distances all worked out so that he could get the mother and the daughter before dawn: a brace with one barrel. Along the corridor at dead of night, knock softly on her door, and begin with a discussion of her son's personality problems, currently being exacerbated by unshielded exposure to the overweening self-confidence of Beaurepaire. As she leaned elegantly sideways in the tempest emanating from the latter's tireless lungs, I essayed a small sympathetic smile and was rewarded with a soft lowering of eyelashes like two black moths making a deck landing on stretched silk. I went into battle against Balliol as if her handkerchief was tucked into my tunic, or was fluttering, as it were, from the point of my couched lance.

Boy, did we lose. And it was all my fault. The Balliol blokes knew more than the St Hilda's women and were a lot quicker at hitting the buzzer. Their captain was practically a psychic. He guessed the question before Bamber's mouth was fully open and his reflex speed on the buzzer was like one of those small Australian boys who can bring down a dragonfly by spitting at it. But Beaurepaire was magnificent. He kept us in there, matching the Balliol top gun volley for volley as the afternoon blazed to a climax. The two teams were dead even when it came to the last question, which was about music. I heard two bars and knew it was Verdi. I heard four bars and knew it was *Otello*. I hit the button while the Balliol captain's overdeveloped thumb was still in the air. Beaurepaire hit the button too but the answer was already out of my mouth. '*Otello!*' I shouted. 'It's *Don Carlo!*' shouted Beaurepaire, louder. Louder but too late. Bamber wrapped it up. 'It was *Don Carlo*, as Chuck Beaurepaire said. Clive James should have waited. Congratulations, though, Pembroke, on being such close losers . . .' I think I bore up reasonably well. I was told subsequently – I am still told today by anyone I meet over the age of forty – that the tears which I thought were jetting from my eyes merely made them shine, and that if it had not been for my mouth, which went all square like a baby ready to howl, nobody would have known that my world had collapsed.

As we discovered the previous week, losers, no matter how close, did not get invited to the Midland Hotel. All the way back to Christopher's house I explained that the bit of *Don Carlo* they had played was almost identical to the bit in *Otello* just before the whole cast sings at once. Beaurepaire was sulking. Keats would have mistaken him for stout Cortez. Christopher's mother opened the door to us. She looked wonderful. So did her husband. It transpired during supper that he had just got back from Canberra, where he went regularly in order to talk about investments in minerals. 'You're making a mistake, I think,' he told me, 'in selling us the stuff outright. It would be wiser to impose conditions so that nobody could buy anything without processing it out there. That way you'd get a bigger industrial base. At the moment you're just giving it away. The Japanese can't believe their luck.' This was an opportunity for Beaurepaire. His mouth was off and running. I looked at Christopher's mother. I looked at those lashes. They were spread wide while the eyes they protected looked adoringly at her husband. He certainly was quite impressive, if you don't mind them modest as well as handsome, intelligent and rich. 'It must be a bore for you,' I managed to choke out, 'changing planes in Sydney. Must be a hell of a long flight.' He nodded. 'It would be if we didn't have our own. Gives me a chance to keep my hours up.' It turned out that he had flown Meteors in Malaya. I felt terrible. It should have been *Otello*. That bit just before he kills himself, where the strings well up and weep, would have been just right.

9. WANTING AND FOUND TESTED

Sexual starvation was the undergraduate's prescribed fate. I considered myself hard done by, having to share it. After all, I was a man of experience: perhaps not precisely a boulevardier, but withal no sprig. I had experimented, and intended to experiment further. In my opinion I was still at a formative stage. I did not yet consider myself responsible enough to settle down. How could I be, when I was scarcely responsible enough to settle a bill? Without wishing to emulate Prince Aly Khan or Porfirio Rubirosa, I yet believed that there was a certain amount of adventuring which a man should regard as his duty; that I had at least made a start; and that if allowed a fair chance I might well make my mark. Consider the evidence. There was my chequered past. There was my long-term liaison in Italy. There was, to make me feel interestingly treacherous, my intermittent imbroglio with Robin in London. But in Cambridge there was, resoundingly, nothing. At the time the number of male undergraduates known to be cohabiting with females could be counted, with difficulty, on the fingers of one hand – with difficulty because the hand would be trembling with envy. A detached observer might have felt that I was already getting my share. As far as I am able to assess the truth by looking back, however, my sense of deprivation was genuine, even though it arose from a compulsively, and possibly psychopathically, inadequate capacity to realize that out of sight should not mean out of mind. People loyal to me I was loyal to only when I was with them. This went double for women. I have learned better since, but very slowly, and the fact that I had to learn it, instead of having the instinct conferred on me by nature, has been a grief to me, although never so much as it has been a grief to others, who always had to grieve first before I noticed that grief might be appropriate.

There was also the consideration that I was very energetic, a condition which time has since gone a long way towards curing completely. Whatever my psychological compulsion towards putting it aimlessly about, sheer physical randiness was a powerful potentiating agent. If the result was priapism, Cambridge might have been specifically designed to put a stop to it. Men of that age, in that epoch, wanted their women attractive or not at all. There being, in the first place, few women *in statu pupillari*, the number of them who might arouse desire by their appearance was few indeed, and these received a volume and concentration of male attention which in some cases ruined them for life. The actresses were the worst. After a season with the ADC and a single appearance with the Marlowe, girls who started off with the self-effacing temperament of voluntary aid workers ended up carrying on like Catherine the Great. Being cast in a play was the merest interlude between bouts of theatrical behaviour extending deep into everyday life. They made entrances. They stormed out. They had the vapours. They did all these things going in and out of the University Library. There were exceptions, but the one I had to go and fall for wasn't among them.

From the wooded slopes of Highgate by way of Golders Green and Tel Aviv, Consuela Schleppkis, though rather younger than I, was at the triumphant end of a university career during which she had taken the starring role, and most of the notices, in every major ADC and college production. A prima donna on stage, she was even more so off it, and after the drama critic of the *Cambridge Evening News* named her as Actress of the Year she went over the top like a regiment. Previously, though she had been unable to cycle up Castle Hill towards Girton without making innocent passers-by suspect that she might be Lady Macbeth, she had been subject to brief bouts of normal behaviour. Now she would take notes in a Sidgwick Avenue lecture theatre with such an air of commitment that the lecturer would break off to ask her if anything was wrong. Actually commitment was what she needed and later on she duly got it, but in the meantime her histrionic intensity was no excuse for my stupidity, whose only mitigating factor was her personal appearance. Consuela would have been a personable girl in any circumstances. In the Cambridge context she was like Marilyn Monroe in Korea. She was slim and dark rather than plump and blonde, but the effect was roughly the same. Blessed with a clear-skinned oval face dreamed by Modigliani in his last fever, she moved well when she was not self-conscious. She rarely wasn't, but moved well enough even so. As the spring of my second year approached, Consuela was rehearsing an open air production of *As You Like It* in the gardens of Clare. Leaning on a hedge, her forehead in her hands, concentrating on her lines, she was so graceful that she made you – or me, at any rate – forget that no one can really lean on a hedge without falling through it. I besieged her with poems. Some of them still seem to me to be pretty good even today. Others were trash. She took them all as her due. They were burning in the fire when she finally invited me to an early tea at her digs near Fenner's. The weather was already warm, but she said we would need a fire if we were going to take our clothes off. Already unnerved by the knowledge that she had asked everyone in Cambridge theatrical society whether it would be wise to sleep with me, I was reduced by the inspiring spectacle of her silky body to incurable impotence. Unaware then, and for some time to come, that what a gentleman should do in such circumstances is to forget himself and think of a few things the lady might like – which is, come to think of it, pretty well what a gentleman should do in any circumstances – I tried everything except ringing up the Fire Brigade. An immediate, frank confession of inadequacy might have enlisted her sympathy to the extent of getting her to drop the play-acting, which would have been a help.

Finally I tried to bluff it out, if that's the appropriate expression. At first Consuela lay back with a show of drowsy, patient sensuality, as if Madame Récamier were receiving Châteaubriand in her boudoir and his dotage. This was not a bad number but unfortunately she must have read somewhere about the possibility of a smouldering simper. She unleashed several of these in succession, decorating them with a flare of the nostrils which would have made the Dalai Lama's robe strobe, but which reminded me of a wild horse I had seen in Taronga Park zoo when very young – when I was very young, that is, the horse being obviously mature, not to say virile. I think it was one of those zebras that have no stripes, but do have a very long and large penis, which, when ready for use, extends so far from the lower abdomen that it will hit the ground unless its owner is standing over a hole. This recollection made me feel even more inadequate than I was feeling already. Desperately I tried to think of stimulating things. Again, here is a technique to which, reputedly, men in that situation often have recourse, but which has little to recommend it. If one is already in the presence of an actual incitement to desire, trying to think of an alternative incitement to desire can only emphasize the discrepancy between one's psychological quandary and the fierce simplicity of one's real-life position. To the part of the mind that watches the mind at work, the disjointure reveals itself as fundamentally absurd. Nothing is sillier to one's superego than to observe one's ego grinding away at the sweaty task of trying to flog one's recalcitrant id into action. I was already far gone in the interior turmoil of this metaphysical confrontation when Consuela put the lid on it by shifting to a new role. She became solicitous, as if I had some rare disease. I got the impression that I had only days to live. Her large and lovely eyes were full of horror and wonder at how God's behest had worked itself out by striking me down, thus depriving her of a great earthly love, but perhaps – who knew? – compensating her with a lasting memory of spiritual grace. If she had left the room, put on a nurse's uniform and reappeared at the foot of the bed holding a hurricane lamp, she could not have done a better impersonation of Jennifer Jones. By now I was ready for the hospital anyway, and would have been glad if she could have left it at that. Unfortunately she saw a further possibility in the scene: a direction in which she might, in actor's parlance, *stretch* herself, since it had long ago become clear that there was no chance of stretching me. She became scornful, as if Lupe Velez, on her famous first tempestuous visit to Errol Flynn, had thrown herself naked on the floor only to find her passion rewarded with a lecture on stamp-collecting. Tossing her head, Consuela made a sudden exit to the bathroom. A bathroom was already a very impressive accoutrement for an undergraduate to have, but the spectacle of Consuela exiting into it was awe-inspiring. She then made an entrance out of it, apparently without having done very much in there except pause for breath and learn her lines. 'It doesn't matter,' she snapped, tossing her head again and gazing fixedly out of the window. 'Let's just say it doesn't *matter.*' What had she seen out of the window? Lohengrin arriving on a swan? It scarcely seemed possible, since the curtains were still drawn. But a certain amount of light was coming through them. Consuela liked looking at light. She liked standing in it. She looked very beautiful there: long-haired, small-bottomed, heroic in her tragedy. My clothes were all over the room. Getting into various bits of them, I couldn't help noticing that I was always looking at her back. 'Look,' she said at last. 'It just doesn't bloody *matter*, OK?'

There was still quite a lot of the afternoon left. Too miserable even to go to the movies, I spent it at the Whim, the Trinity Street coffee bar in whose back room the aesthetes gathered. Except for the Footlights, who were only there in the afternoon when the clubroom closed, everybody in the university's artistic world would use the Whim all day as a headquarters, clearing house, comfort station, watering hole and gossip exchange. The Whim worked on the French café system: you could sit for a long time over a single cup of coffee as long as you didn't mind paying too much for it in the first place. I enjoyed writing there because there was a good chance of being interrupted. This time I worked steadily on a poem – it was one of those threnodies which claim that to say goodbye is inevitable because the ecstasy is too intense to last – without encouraging anyone to join me in conversation. Indeed, I made a point of not lifting my head. A couple of hours went by like that. The place was jammed with its late afternoon regulars when Consuela made an entrance. In full drag as a tempestuous gypsy princess, she was pretty enough to stop a speeding train. A whole room full of aesthetes ceased talking about themselves and looked at her. Meanwhile she was looking at me. She shook her head. She threw it slowly back, raised her clenched fists to her forehead, and rocked as if her body was in the throes of rejecting a brain implant. Then she lowered her arms, looked at me again, shook her head slowly, and made an exit. Everyone looked at me. If she had left it at that, they all might have at least remained in doubt, but over the next few days she told everyone the details individually.

In retrospect I must concede that I was in no position to fault her on that point, because until much later in my life I was terribly indiscreet. Telling myself that to spill beans was a necessary component of a wonderful, warm, openly Antipodean personality, I exchanged gossip with the best of them, which necessarily meant that I also exchanged it with the worst of them. If people asked me intimate questions I would tell them the answers. I told people all about myself. Less forgivably, I told people all about other people too. I can't even say that the concept of privacy eventually crept up on me. It was forced on me, by other people's pain – or, to be less complacent and more accurate, by my pain at earning other people's justified disapproval. In this regard I have become a different person: infinitely more guarded, unforthcoming to the point of paranoia. To embarrass someone by revealing his secret to someone who might damage him with it seems to me, in my later incarnation, a crime worse than breaking wind at an investiture. Having learned something of what malice can do, and of how candour plays into its hands, I am now a clam. In those days I simply blabbed. But I still thought that Consuela was impermissibly revelatory about our unproductive tryst. She did everything but hire a sky-writer. Everyone in town knew. The women who sold cream cakes in Fitzbillie's knew all about it. More than twenty years later I was still meeting perfect strangers who sympathized with me over my fiasco with Consuela Schleppkis. Let me take this opportunity to set the record straight. The truth is that my failed affair with Consuela rankled for a while, but nowadays, far from being still sensitive on the subject, I try to show that I enjoy a good joke against myself, before I go quietly away somewhere to be sick.

There was ample excuse for being unmanned. The Tripos examinations were imminent, and I was scarcely prepared to answer the essay paper, let alone the specialized papers on Swift, on tragedy and on God knew what else. On Jane Austen I had done just enough background reading to convince myself that I knew less about the foreground than I had thought. The mandatory foreign language paper was at least possible now that I had learned some Italian, which enabled me to avoid the French option. Emboldened by having started to get somewhere with Italian, I made renewed efforts to teach myself French, but I was at an early stage, possibly having overtaxed myself by choosing A la recherche du temps perdu as a primary reader. After six months I was about halfway through Du côté de chez Swann and still looking up every second word in an old Larousse. If I had known then that I would turn bald before I got through the whole thing I would probably have given up. A lack of sense of proportion is one of the big advantages of being young: when we grow out of it, we leave possibilities behind along with the absurdity. Proust remains my idol of idols to this day – and I could not, or at any rate would not, have written that last sentence without his influence. His willingness to generalize about life enthralled me even when I myself knew little about life worth knowing. His specific, concrete observations I admired but thought I understood how he did them. It was the *aperçus*, the aphoristic insights driving deeper than observation, which continually surprised me. His every sententious formulation I underlined in ballpoint, until the tattered, coffee-stained *Livre de poche* was fat with dog-ears and looked blue when it fell open. It was one of the books I carried everywhere in those spring days when I was theoretically gripped by examination fever. Examination lassitude would have been a more accurate expression. It was as though I had been bitten by a tsetse fly. As time grew shorter, I moved slower. Having kept well away from the Footlights May Week revue – I had neither auditioned for it nor volunteered any ancillary services beyond handing over a few scripts – theoretically I was unencumbered with extracurricular commitments. Thus free to plan my time constructively, I did little except make plans. I constructed elaborate flow charts of what I needed to do, when what I really needed to do was do something. Quietly getting crocked in his college room, my supervisor, nicknamed the Baby Don because his name was Ron Maybey, greeted me with only partly feigned admiration on the one occasion I could bring myself to turn up. 'Remarkable track record,' he said. 'Far as I can tell, you haven't actually *completed* a weekly essay in two years. Fancy a sherry?' It was gallows humour. I should have been in a blue funk.

But the sun was out, the girls were out with it, the punts were on the river and I was lying casually on its far bank, opposite the back lawn of King's, on the edge of the meadow. The pampered cows and expense-account sheep of King's were behind me, grazing plumply among the buttercups. Before me was the prettiest stretch of waterway in the world, bounded on the far side by the austerely satisfying facade of Gibbs's Fellows Building, with whose central arch I would always position myself in line so that I could see through it to the dry fountain in the middle of the front lawn. Wearing nothing but a pair of shorts, I could lie there working on my flow charts. When I broke into a sweat from all that effort I could roll into the river and swim lazily about, just quickly enough to dodge the punts. Of the young men who propelled the punts – of their honking voices, their self-satisfied features and their clothes purchased for a touring production of *Charley's Aunt* – I felt no more tolerant than I had the previous year, but all anger subsided at the sight of their precious cargo. Elegant fingertips of first and second year undergraduettes would trail past at eye level as I lay limp, submerged to the nostrils.

The third year undergraduettes, needless to say, were all in their rooms studying for the examinations which, it periodically occurred to me, I would, at this rate, plough like a plane crashing. So I hauled myself out of the water, temporarily put aside the latest master plan for concentrated study, and tried to sketch out a few thoughts relating to the set books.

One of the special papers was on Swift, and there I thought I had the glimmering of an idea. Swift's prose appealed to me so strongly that my enthusiasm had survived a crushingly boring lecture from the current American academic expert on the subject. On a brief visit paid for by some memorial lecture fund, this worthy had packed one of the Sidgwick Avenue lecture theatres with an audience of dons, graduate students and final year undergraduates all eager to hear him on the subject of Swift's sense of humour. By the time the visitor – I recall him as being the Hale Professor of Raillery at Yale, but I must have got that wrong – had finished isolating, exemplifying and analysing what he took to be Swift's techniques of comic invention, anyone present with even a vestige of a sense of humour was, or should have been, praying for death. The professor was a bore on a Guggenheim, a long-range drone, an international ballistic fossil. I spent the whole hour drawing little pictures of hanged men. I was kept from falling unconscious, however, by constantly renewed surprise at the gales of laughter which greeted the professor's every creaking sally. When he quoted something by Swift that he said was meant to be funny, they laughed. Sometimes it *was* funny, although not after he got through reading it out, because he always added a bit of explanatory acting – including, especially, a shrewd, quizzical twinkle which he evidently assumed to be the facial expression Swift might have adopted when regaling fellow members of the Scriblerus Club with a passage of improvised invective. When the professor said something on his own account that was clearly meant to be funny also – you could tell it was a joke because he did everything except lay his index finger alongside his nose – they laughed even louder. It occurred to me that an academic audience – not necessarily individually, but in the aggregate – is like the audience for serious music when faced with the challenge of reacting to *A Musical Joke*. They kill themselves laughing because the only other possible response would be to ask for their money back. They roll in the aisles because they lack the nerve to take to their heels. This was a very depressing conclusion to reach and for a while I blamed Swift himself. Swift himself would have been quick to blame mankind. His misogyny I found off-putting until I read the journals to Stella and Vanessa. The professor was convinced that there could not have been anything between Swift and the girls except a rich exchange of good jokes. This was enough to persuade me that the truth might be different, and I soon turned up enough textual evidence to be certain that the sly old boy had been screwing both of them. Apparently there was still much learned discussion about whether Swift's use of the phrase 'a cup of coffee' was, or was not, a veiled reference to sexual inter-course. Whole academic careers were devoted to this supposed conundrum. To me it looked like the most easily penetrated code since Pig Latin. 'Can't get over that last cup of coffee we had on the floor,' Swift would write, or words to that effect. 'Get ready for three cups of coffee in a row tomorrow night.' Vanessa and Stella were equally scrutable in their replies. 'Must have at least six cups of coffee with you as soon as possible. Love and kisses.' To my mind, the Hale Professor of Raillery at Yale and all his academic kind were wilfully missing the obvious.

It could be said that my mind was not in a very objective state, but whatever the accuracy of its judgments, affection for Swift was fully restored, and I actually got around to reading extensively not just in his major works but in the poems, pamphlets and correspon-dence. I even read some of the relevant scholarship and criticism. This was the first time in my life that I had ever studied an author against his background at the time I was supposed to, and I was disturbed to find that although I achieved growing intimacy with the author I couldn't make any sense at all of the background. Of the many experts on Swift beside the Hale Professor of Raillery – who had long ago departed by Pan Am Boeing 707 to spread his message of cheery bathos to a helpless world – the big cheese was Professor Irvin Ehrenpreis, whose lumbering two-volume work on Swift was mindbending in the completeness of its scholarship. Professor Ehrenpreis knew about every philosophical concept and rhetorical convention current in that part of the eighteenth century. He knew about animism, dualism, Deism, dynamism, Platonism, pleonasm, Whiggery and buggery. Though Professor Ehrenpreis didn't write badly, it was evident to me, in my cocksureness, that he had soaked his brain in the period to the point of its falling apart like dead meat left too long in tap water. According to Ehrenpreis, Book IV of *Gulliver's Travels*, the book about the Houyhnhnms, reflected Swift's attitude to the current Platonic, or was it neo-Platonic, concepts of man, God, society and whatever. According to me, Gulliver felt about the Houyhnhnms the way Swift felt about Sir William Temple and all the other English aristocrats whose high civilization he admired but on whom it shamed him to dance attendance. The Yahoos were Swift's people, the Irish. He couldn't live with them, but he found little solace, and much more humiliation, in his position of court wit to the English gentry. I had it all worked out. I even drew a little chart.

Actually, after all these years, I still have an inkling that I might have been on the right track. Certainly the scholars and critics were on the wrong track when they suggested that Swift's great writings had been dictated by some sort of synthesis of current thought. That works of art can be inspired only by individual passion is something I am even more sure of now than I was then. Gulliver's love for the Houyhnhnms is made painful to him by their contempt for the Yahoos. His divided feelings are real feelings – Swift's feelings. If I had the time, the qualifications and the academic ambitions I think I could defend that case now. On the eve of the Tripos examinations I was sure I could. I was a man with an idea, and I was angry. Burning in my brain was the memory of the range of gesture and facial expression employed by the Hale Professor of Raillery when he was being amusing about Swift's imitating a horse's whinny and transcribing the sound as the word Houyhnhnm. No doubt that was how it happened, but I knew in my blood and bones that Swift had dedicated his adult life to never being in the same coffee house with a man like the Hale Professor. I was Swift's champion. In my examination paper his great, tormented spirit would rage, laugh, despair and exult.

Unfortunately it happened exactly like that. Casting my eye down the front page of the examination paper, I noted the request to interpret Book IV of *Gulliver's Travels*. Instantly my pen was flying. In a fine frenzy, pausing only to call for another quire of writing paper, I spent the whole three hours answering that one question. We had, however, been instructed to answer four questions. I had left the examination schools, and was standing outside in a pool of summer light trapped by blonde stone buildings, before I quite realized that I had condemned myself to scoring a maximum of twenty-five per cent on that paper even if, which was unlikely, they liked what I said. Instead of cramming for the next day's paper, I spent half the night composing a letter to the examiners begging them to believe that I had failed to read the instructions. The idea that the ability to read instructions was one of the things we were being examined on didn't occur to me at the time.

Ballsing up the Swift paper set the tone for my whole effort in the examinations. The novel paper went only just better. With some ingenuity I answered the questions on the Russian novel by making references to nobody except Jane Austen, but there is a limit to how much you can say about D. H. Lawrence when you have read only *Pride and Prejudice*. As for the English moralists, I was still ignorant as to who they might be, let alone about what they had said. Today it surprises me when I recall how incapable I was of getting interested in anything that smacked of distilled wisdom. If it wasn't Proust, I didn't want to hear it. I valued spontaneity above all else, as if concentration could not be spontaneous too. On my shelves now, collections of aphorisms sit like containers of radioactive material. Just to mention the French, there are Montaigne, Pascal, La Rochefoucauld, Vauvenargues, La Bruyère. Of the Germans and Austrians, there are Goethe, Lichtenberg, Schnitzler, Kraus, Altenberg, Polgar. The pregnant sentence affects me like a lovely woman in the same condition. When Sainte-Beuve said that Montaigne sounded like one long epigram, it was high praise. Thomas Mann's great son Golo is my favourite modern historian because he sounds so like Tacitus, packing a loosely troubled world into a tense neatness. Envious in my youth of what seemed easy, in later years I find nothing more thrilling than the formulation so loaded with meaning that it burns the mind. Only last year, catching Raymond Aron's enthusiasm for Montesquieu, I devoured the *Lois* as if it were *The Lady in the Lake*. My memory is not especially good and as a linguist I am doomed to remain a mere dabbler, but by now I am so drenched in that type of writing that I can quote it off the cuff more easily than I can spit. If only I had had such a facility to draw upon when I sat those examinations! My ignorance of the British moralists might not have been so glaring if I could have imported a few names from the continent. Hobbes, Hume, Locke: how to sum them up, when they had needed such large volumes to sum themselves? I sucked my pen. On the other side of the room, Consuela Schleppkis wrote like a woman possessed. She called for more paper as if she wanted to start her own magazine. I doodled. The clock ticked like a bomb.

On the Italian paper, on the other hand, I lavished a fatal fluency. If Montesquieu had been in my mind to aid me, I might have said something sensible about Machiavelli. I could read *The Prince* in the original, but I had nothing original to say about it, because I had found Garrett Mattingly's theory – that the book was a satirical parody – too attractive not to adopt. An acquaintance with the other masterpiece, *The Discourses on Livy*, would have told me that Machiavelli, far from doing a roguish cabaret number, was founding a tradition of political realism for the modern age. Only in my prose translation of Dante did I really know what I was doing. Françoise had taken me line by line through every dramatic passage in *The Divine Comedy*, so when one of those passages came up it was a cinch. To that extent my satisfaction with the paper was justified, but I should have realized that I would be lucky to get half marks for the whole thing. Allowing myself a measure of elation, however, was the only alternative to despair. I pretended, in the Whim and on the river bank, that I had everything under control. On the day before the last paper, the essay, I lounged at apparent ease under a cloudless sky whose chalky light blue matched the sundials of Caius. The cows and sheep masticated bucolically behind me. King's College chapel waited for its choir, which duly crossed the stone bridge to my right, the top hats of the smallest boys barely clearing the parapet as they all marched *en croc* for a date with Bach. Was Cambridge getting to me? I had a strange feeling of not wanting to leave – doubly strange because I had approached the examination like someone setting out to be expelled. The prospects of being asked to stay on to do research were dim. I rolled impressively into the water, sank like a hippo under a passing punt full of girls, and damned near killed myself ramming my head against a bicycle stuck in the muddy bottom. It must have been one of the pedals that gashed my scalp. There wasn't much pain but there was quite a lot of blood. It was cowardly not to get it stitched.

Marenko, who knew about first aid, stuck a field dressing on my wound, so it was with my head in a sling that I faced the essay paper next day. I should not have been so surprised to find that I could do it. Who couldn't? The choice of set topics was so wide that even an examinee who had been compelled to silence by all the other papers would have been able to find something to say this time. The only way of stuffing it up completely would have been to get in a dither about which topic to choose. Luckily one of my pet subjects was right there on the paper. I had read Hannah Arendt's book *Eichmann in Jerusalem* when it had been serialized in the *New Yorker*; I had followed both sides of the subsequent controversy; and I had reached my own conclusions on the validity of the catchphrase 'the banality of evil'. One of the set topics was exactly that: *The banality of evil*. My pen fizzed for the full three hours. The invigilators brought me some more paper like coal-heavers feeding a ship's furnace. My pen overheated. On the only occasion when I paused to look around, Brian C. Adams was staring at me as if I was his nemesis. My own fond opinion of what I had written was that I could have published it as a piece in a weekly. More importantly, I got the thing finished before the bell rang. Unfortunately this fact only served to remind me that on scarcely any of the other papers had I actually managed to answer the prescribed number of questions within the allotted time. Elation induced depression. If only I had been prepared for the whole examination, instead of for just one paper! Outright failure had probably been warded off, but a low 2:2 was the most I could expect and a third was on the cards. As I left the hall, my gown felt like a shroud. Suddenly I didn't want to give all this up.

All this included May Week in its full splendour. Examinations out of the way, the lawn parties flowered. The June sun shone on them as if intent to prove that once in a way it could co-operate. As a minor luminary in the areas of theatre, literature and related arts, I had a fair sheaf of invitation cards – their timings mutually arranged by the hosts so as not to clash – but anyone with half a brain could figure out where the next party was and just walk in uninvited. The basic layout was the trestle table set up on a college lawn. In the men's colleges, mostly the table was bedecked with nothing more grand than a bowl of fruit punch, the bowl borrowed from the college kitchen and the punch concocted according to loudly touted formulae promising instant oblivion to all who drank. Though for some imbibers this proved to be the case, if you kept your head you could move from one party to another and never reach the point at any of them when the ladle scraped the bottom of the bowl and came up with nothing in it except apple skins and orange pips.

If the girls were throwing the party, there was often something to eat and usually something better than punch to drink. I went to a white wine effort in Newnham which not even the presence of Consuela could ruin. She had such a triumph in *As You Like It* that she even forgot to cut me. I watched the production in Clare Gardens and had to admit that as well as looking maddeningly pretty she was actually pretty good. As a rule undergraduates don't act as well as actors and she was no exception: but quite often they speak better, through being less inclined to make the lines their own instead of the author's. Shakespeare, especially, rewards good speakers who are indifferent actors, whereas bravura actors who speak badly can only do him an injury. Consuela spoke surprisingly well for someone so histrionic. She took a long time to come on. There was an ornamental pool in the middle of the Clare Gardens acting area. Consuela held her head so proudly high that I thought she might walk into the water, but the lines fell like pearls.

> *Ros:* But why did he swear he would come this morning, and comes not?

I could feel the eyes of a hundred of her friends on the back of my neck. No doubt I was being self-conscious. Why not? Everybody else was. It was the right place and the right time. Around the pool, among the flower beds and between the hedges, the young, would-be, not-for-long actors deployed their hired costumes as they had been taught by some preposterously solemn young director who wanted to be Peter Hall or Trevor Nunn. In their element, the theatrical dons at the back of the natural auditorium threw decrepit fond looks at Orlando. They thought him charming. In that weather I thought them charming. They had their place in this enchanted forest. Absurdly I was sorry that I must soon lose mine.

Buddy threw a party in his back garden. Among the guests were what he described as one or two people from London. The champagne was endless. Under its influence I was able to predict that the young man with the huge mouth would never make it as a popular singer. Susannah York was there. She was so beautiful that I burst into tears. Luckily I was lying down by then, so nobody noticed. Karula dipped a napkin in the iced water of a champagne bucket and spread it over my face. I could see the sun through it. That should have been the most lavish May Week party. It was topped for opulence by Delmer Dynamo, who took over the whole back lawn of Pembroke and slew the fatted calf. Befitting his position as President and sole member of the Aubrey Attwater Society, Delmer had outfitted himself for the occasion in cream ducks, cricket boots, candy-striped blazer, straw boater and a monocle. The ensemble would have been suitable for receiving the Prince of Wales on board the deck of a steam yacht, somewhere around the turn of the century. Delmer could keep his monocle in place only by tilting his head so far back that he was shouting upwards, as if at a passing Zeppelin. Marenko, Strad and some other Americans wore rented white tuxedos with carnation boutonnières. As a barbershop quartet they stood in the rock garden and sang 'The Whiffenpoof Song'. The Master and all the college dons were there. The Dean, somehow managing to keep his champagne glass empty without removing the pipe from his mouth, gazed upon Delmer with transparent fondness. Obviously the college would be sad to see him go. Equally obviously the college did not feel quite the same in my case. Finding myself trapped with the Dean, I was further unsettled to detect in his eyes a look which suggested that he considered himself trapped with me. He sought refuge in the past. 'Brilliant boy, Oppenheimer. Jew, of course, but a real gentleman. Rutherford didn't want to let him into the Cavendish, you know. Said he was too weak on the experimental side. But Thomson believed in him. Young Oppenheimer was really, *really* interested in my minerals. You should have heard him talk about birefringence. Brilliant, brilliant boy. You don't get many like that now. There's Dynamo, of course, but on the whole they're a poor lot now.' The Dean was making it plain that my very existence was an insult to his dream. His whole speech, the longest I had ever heard him give, was an exhalation: one long sigh.

I sighed myself when Delmer shyly confessed that his college had offered him an extra year just so that he could read in preparation for his graduate course at Columbia. 'Hot shit, man,' he crowed. 'They coughed up.' His monocle gleamed in the sunlight. He had done quite a lot of work and deserved his good fortune. I would have found it easier to be warm with fellow-feeling if it were not for the chill wind which I could feel blowing even in the fragrant, stationary air. Where else in the world would I ever fit in except here, where I had never felt the least urge to fit in? And truly I had no social ambitions in Cambridge beyond the tattered pink velvet jacket of the Footlights presidency. The Footlights committee had decided that if I could stay on for a year the jacket was mine for the asking, but the only way for me to remain a member of the university would be to enrol as a PhD student. For that I didn't have the finance, and without at least a 2:1 result in the Tripos I wouldn't be accepted for registration even if I had the money. So it was all over. In the grad pad, Brian C. Adams commiserated with me. 'You hit the books at least a year too late,' he said sympathetically. 'Still, all that Footlights nonsense should come in handy if you apply for the BBC. Let me buy you another glass of sherry. The Amontillado's really rather surprisingly fine.' Brian C. Adams was taking it for granted that he would get a first. So was everyone else taking it for granted that Brian C. Adams would get a first. There was a rumour that the College was considering taking him straight into Fellowship, so that he could sit up there eating venison where he belonged. Belonging must be a good feeling. Usually it was a feeling I got in or near Footlights, but the May Week revue, when I went to see it on the first night, only made me feel left out. Romaine was in it. She did the 'Land of Hope and Glory' routine with predictable results. There were people rolling about in the aisles like eels. Andy Mayer did his holy roller commercial. 'Write away *right* away . . .' I tried to be elated when my own material went well. It didn't always and it mocked my physical absence even when it did. As far as I was concerned – which on this evidence wasn't far – Footlights was unfinished business. In the Whim I sat anonymously, writing the kind of valedictory ode which treats personal disappointment as if it were the heat death of the universe.

Packed and all set to go, I turned up at Senate House to read the examination results with an air of fatalism which would have done credit to Sydney Carton, the only Dickens character I had managed to mention in the novel paper. (I had read the Classics Illustrated comic of *A Tale of Two Cities* when still a pupil of Kogarah Infants' School.) When I saw that I had got a 2:1 I thought it was a misprint. When Brian C. Adams saw that *he* had got a 2:1 he thought the same. Eventually his fellow members of the Gray Society calmed him down by pointing out the truth: that he was simply too good for the Tripos and should have been doing a PhD all along, like Romaine Rand. For the first few days after he came out of shock, however, nothing except Nembutal would keep Brian C. Adams from throwing himself from his casement window into the courtyard. Exactly balancing his despair was my euphoria. I couldn't see how I had done it, until Ron Maybey the Baby Don, breaking all the rules, told me. 'Never *seen* such a spread of marks,' he said, with evident disapproval. '*Very* good score on the essay paper. Nothing at *all* on the Swift paper. Should be impossible. Ought to get something for writing your name. Think that worked for you in the end. They decided that you'd gone mad that day. No excuse at all for the novel paper. One of the examiners wanted to have you sent down for it. You be staying on?' He was the only don, whether infant or adult, who had ever been sincerely interested in what I was writing, so I told him that I hoped to snare a research grant and be President of the Footlights simultaneously. 'Don't see why not,' he said. 'But I shouldn't actually *tell* them that when you apply. Stress the academic side. Sherry?'

Suddenly it was all at least possible. I applied for a research grant on the basis of a burning desire to evaluate Shelley's reading of the major Italian poets. The university wouldn't actually decide whether or not it was going to finance this scheme until September. Meanwhile I told the retiring Footlights committee, who were about to leave on tour with the revue, that my research grant was in the bag. They handed over the pink jacket, which I stored with the rest of my stuff in the Pembroke linen room. My conscience was reasonably clear, as far as I could tell without actually examining it. If I didn't get the grant, I could always give the jacket back. In the interim it seemed appropriate to go where Shelley had gone, at least up to the point where he drowned himself. Françoise was in Florence. To get there would be expensive. Luckily Robin was still in London. After hitting her for a small loan, I booked myself on the student charter flight which I have already described in my book *Flying Visits*. The reader will permit me the indulgence of making cross-references to my own work when I confess that the journey was never one I have been keen to repeat even in written form. I was exaggerating only when I said the plane swerved to avoid the Matterhorn. It didn't swerve except when it was taking off. Most of the students really *were* seventy-year-old Calabrian peasant women wearing black clothes and carrying string bags full of onions, and I really *did* have a nun sitting beside me who clutched my sweating palm as we came crabbing in to land. It was the way cheap flying was in those days. Today, the nightmare is in the crowded airport. When you get airborne you're relatively OK. Then, the flight was in the lap of the gods. One of David Hockney's early paintings had such a strong appeal for me that I kept a reproduction of it pinned to my wall wherever I moved. I liked its bright colours and cunningly innocent outlines, but most of all I liked its title: 'The Flight into Italy'. Knowing that there was a chance I might have something to come back to made the letting-go all the sweeter, of course. If you can manage it, safe danger is always the best kind.

10. ATTACK OF THE KILLER BEE

Once again, Florence was my principal destination, but this time I had to go to Venice first, a detour I begrudged. Françoise was there on a fortnight's study leave, to read manuscripts in the Marciana Library in the Piazza San Marco. Proust said that after he got to Venice his dreams acquired an address. For me the impact was, as you might imagine, nothing like so subtle. Never fond of the *Vedutisti* painters – Guardi, I thought, used too much lipstick and Canaletto was patently unreal – I was expecting a picture postcard. I knew all the jokes about Venice, of which the best was Robert Benchley's telegram home: STREETS FULL OF WATER PLEASE ADVISE. The exquisite, I had persuaded myself, held no appeal. Give me the chiselled jaw and marble biceps of Florence every time. Thus prepared to be indifferent, I was in an ideal condition to be floored. Before the *vaporetto* was halfway down the Grand Canal I was already concussed. Heat focused by a nacreous sky like the lining of a silver tureen dissolved the surface of the water into a storm of sparks, which were projected as wobbling bracelets of pure light on the otherwise maculate façades of crumbling plaster and rotting marble. The whole place was being eaten alive by liquid luminosity. It was a vision of eternity as soluble as a rusk, God's love made manifest as a wafer in the world's wet mouth. Françoise had rented a little room just behind the Piazza San Marco. I set up house on her floor. While she read in the library I made a library desk for myself on a café table at the city end of the Rialto, just to the left of where the steps of the approach to the bridge formed a natural rostrum from which the characters of *The Merchant of Venice* might step down into the main acting area. The tourist season being at its height, most of the people who came stepping down were Americans. 'Isn't it *weird*?' a woman in a baseball cap asked another woman in a baseball cap. 'When they say *Accademia* I can understand *them* but when I say ACADEMY *they* can't understand *me* at all.' The baseball caps were appropriate because both women were the shape of a baseball. Nothing could break the spell. There I sat reading, periodically lifting my head to confirm all over again that Canaletto had been so literal he might as well have used a Hasselblad. Trying out for the Regatta, the *Bucintoro* swept by with whomping oars, a ceremonial dream boat dripping gold. Every gondolier sang like Gigli. From Françoise I borrowed a volume of Leopardi's *Zibaldone*, the elaborate notebooks in which the great, crippled poet kept track of his vast learning. Religiously looking up every unknown word in a dictionary, I eventually broke through the almost tangible barrier that separates being only just able to read from being able to read with reasonable ease. I started to keep a notebook myself. Dignified with the name of Journal, it would run to a dozen volumes in the next nine years. 'Volumes' is a grand word for tatty exercise books. They must be somewhere amongst my junk. One day I must look into them and see what I thought important. Puerilities, I imagine. But the *soi-disant* journal doubled as a commonplace book, and to that extent it was useful. The habit of copying out was a good one to acquire. Though the main idea was to build up fluency in reading a foreign language, the beneficial side-effect was to fix a lot of good stuff in my head, if only at the level of the half-forgotten. The waiters soon learned to approach me only when I signalled. For a while I thought they were smiling tolerantly because as sons of the Most Serene City they were pleased to see a visitor inspired by intellectual effort. Later I learned that they were being even more tolerant than that. Like all the personnel of the service industries in Venice, they lived in the industrial satellite towns, commuted to work, and would have preferred to bring me a fresh glass of iced coffee every thirty seconds. They needed the tips.

When Françoise got out of the library we would have lunch in a cheap restaurant called the Trattoria al Vagon. You could get there by walking from either St Mark's or the Rialto. The path was a maze in either case, crossing little bridges from island to island, and never turning a perfectly square corner within the island itself. We always had to allow half an hour for getting lost. Years later I tried to find the al Vagon and couldn't. Perhaps it was never there. It was so good and cheap that it might have been a dream. The pasta was always *al dente*, an expression which could be pressed into service as the name of a ferocious gangster. Lui Medesimo ('he himself') was Al Dente's conceited sidekick. Françoise generously laughed at these heavy jokes while I drank her share of the claret to top up mine. Even for her, who preferred to stay sober, there was always the sense that we were living out a carnival scene by Longhi – another painter whom I had previously despised, and of whom I was now starting to see the point.

Yet again, though, it was the Renaissance that carried the heavy charge. Hungry as always for the main event, I was disinclined to be sidetracked by the quirky, the decorative or the merely pretty. Two minutes' walk from the al Vagon, Verrocchio's equestrian statue of Bartolomeo Colleoni rode sternly through the Piazza San Giovanni e Paolo. There were pigeons on his helmet and a barge full of empty coke bottles in the canal at his feet, but his *grandezza* was only increased. To every Australian schoolboy of my generation, Bartolomeo Colleoni was the Italian cruiser sunk by HMAS *Sydney*. The *Sydney*'s bows were subsequently built into the stone harbour wall near Kirribilli pier under the north end of the Harbour Bridge. But in Venice I could see the real Bartolomeo, the *condottiere* four centuries into his immortal ride, his image more immediate than the man himself, or any man alive, even me. The contained energy of that bronze horseman kept me occupied for what seemed like hours. Probably it was less than that, but certainly I stared longer than Byron did, who in one of his plays – either *Marino Faliero* or *The Two Foscari*, I forget which – let slip the opinion that the grim rider was made of marble. It is very doubtful if Byron ever went out of doors in Venice. Recovering in his room between visits from insatiable noblewomen, he would totter asymmetrically to the window, check that the Grand Canal was still there, and turn back wearily to the rumpled couch. Poor bastard.

Françoise believed in her mission to civilize me. When the white heat of the early afternoon sky had eased to a tolerable azure, we would tour the outlying churches by *vaporetto*, on the hunt for Bellini. Most of his capital works were in the Accademia or else in churches close to the centre, but there were others further out, and anyway even his minor canvases were major. Until then, I had been under the impression that all Bellini had ever painted was Madonnas in blue anoraks nursing babies the size of high school children in front of a green shantung antimacassar, with distant landscape an optional extra. Now I saw the range of his humanity, his old men and infantile angels all shaped from pure colour, the painterly monumentality organically complete. In my journal I solemnly noted every painting, enrolling Bellini on my growing list of indispensable seminal figures. His namesake the composer was already on the list. So was Liszt. The honour roll was meant to be growing shorter, but no matter how ruthlessly I pared it down, there was always another genius around the corner demanding to be let in. My appreciation of Tintoretto was not much enhanced by being in his home city, which because of its wet walls has never been kind to the fresco, tempting the business-minded painter towards too-big canvases it took a football team of assistants to help him fill. Most of Tintoretto's best paintings were done on a smaller scale and eventually exported: I had already learned to admire him elsewhere. Titian's last manner, however, was well represented in the Venetian churches. 'Like Shakespeare's sonnets and Beethoven's late quartets,' I remember telling my journal, 'Titian's valedictory paintings have a divine carelessness.' Veronese, I decided, was in Paris and London: to all intents and purposes he had left town. Lacking the means to get out into the surrounding Veneto, we saw little of Tiepolo. I decided to like him anyway: Giambattista, that is, not Giandomenico. I was very strict in my judgments. Françoise, who had heard my unshakeable convictions revised before, patiently upheld the reasonable viewpoint – a propensity which, modest to a fault, she considered her limitation. She also, I need hardly add, paid for the museum tickets, the *vaporetto* rides, most of the meals, and the bus trip to Padua.

Padua was dominated by Donatello's equestrian statue of Gattamelata, a work which I instantly declared inferior to Verrocchio's Bartolomeo Colleoni. This judgment I have since found no good cause to revise, although nowadays I would be less likely to share it with a trattoria full of German tourists. Giotto I had, until then, respected only because Dante thought well of him. Though the big Madonna in the Uffizi was obviously the start of something, I had been able to get interested in the trecento only as a prelude to the quattrocento, which, in its turn – I was suffering from a developmental view of the arts – was clearly only the muted overture to the cinquecento. Françoise had argued wearily against this dogma until it became plain to her that mere reason was powerless. Only evidence would convince me. This was the evidence. In the Arena chapel I stood stunned as the drama unfolded all around me. Drama was exactly what it was, of course: what Giotto had rediscovered, after its thousand years without a voice, was the intensity between human beings. Oscar Wilde had once stood in the same chapel. He, too, had been impressed. You could tell how overwhelmed he was. He was the only English-speaking person to have visited the chapel in the last two hundred years who had not signed his name on the wall. All around the circumference of the chapel, the frescoes were thoroughly mutilated up to the height of an upstretched hand. These graffiti depressed me much more than the missing Mantegnas. Falling out of an erratically flown B-25, practically the only bomb to have hit the historic centre of Padua had gone straight through the roof of the Ovetari Chapel and atomized Mantegna's biggest-ever fresco cycle. But that was just a misfortune of war, a bad spin of the wheel. Vandalism was an endemic human failing. Italy had too many paintings to look after and too little public money with which to hire people to look after them. I didn't mind so much when pictures got stolen: usually they were ransomed back the following week, with tax advantages to both sides. When paintings got razored I became agitated. The German and Dutch galleries had installed alarm systems whereby no masterpiece could be approached without the offender being instantly gagged, bound and arrested. In the Italian galleries even the guides regularly fingered the paint surface. You would see some idiot bodging his finger into a Botticelli. A reformed vandal with a bad conscience, I began to get very touchy about seeing paintings touched, or even breathed on.

Arriving in Florence just in time for the kind of weather that encouraged the inhabitants to leave, we took a room at the Antica Cervia. The Santa Croce *quartiere* behind the Palazzo Vecchio was the old stamping ground of the *popolo minuto*, in the sense that this was where the little people had been stamped into the ground by a commune which, however egalitarian, had never quite succeeded in distributing its power down as far as the penniless. Still radical enough at that stage to be rather thrilled by my discovery of Gramsci's prison letters, I fancied myself as fitting right in when we dined at the Trattoria Anita with the prostitutes and pimps. In Italy it was a point of style to be a bit red. *Sinistra* was such a thrilling way of saying left wing. *Lotta continua!* The struggle continues! Though theoretically clean shaven at the time, I grew a two-day stubble and tried to look dangerous as I leaned forward over the *spaghetti al sugo*, my intense eye-contact with Françoise perhaps having been unduly

influenced by the steely look Giotto had given St Francis. I made it
clear to her that the clientele of the trattoria were essentially *my*
people: vagabonds, snappers-up of unconsidered trifles, the wretched
of the earth. In point of fact most of them scarcely even rated as
petty crooks. The boys with the gold chains around their necks who
scratched their crotches all the time thought they had done a hard
day's work when they succeeded in selling each other a carton of two
hundred contraband Marlboros. Otherwise they spent a good deal
of time wistfully annoying foreign girls in the hope of forming a
profitable liaison, but their hearts and minds weren't in it. The true
pappagalli would put energy and invention into being pests. This
bunch preferred not to work up a sweat. On principle, in the first
few days, they eyed Françoise suggestively, challenging her to restrain
what they obviously hoped might be an irresistible impulse to cast
reason and her clothes aside. After having absorbed the accumulated
evidence that she was unlikely to jump into their laps, they relaxed
again into their customary torpor. The energy of those brave young
men was all for show and their women didn't even bother to show
it. To classify them as hookers paid them a compliment. It was a
courtesy title. They were too lazy to lean against a wall successfully.
Most of the time, when they weren't eating, they sat in the back of
a bar complaining in concert about the ladders in their fishnet
stockings. A potential customer needed radar to find them.

The only real proletarians present were Anita and her family, who
worked their guts out from daylight to midnight, on a profit margin
so slim that if a tomato went rotten it was a disaster. Anita could
think of nothing more exciting in life than the possibility – a very
slim one, given the inefficiency of Italy's educational system – that
her clever young daughter might go to university and learn to speak
well like Françoise. The daughter, universally called *La Tempesta*, was
almost old enough to wait on table. Neither Anita nor her equally
hardworking husband wanted the apple of their eye to spend her
whole life doing what they had done and their two sons were already
doing. These were the kind of proletarians whose only dream was
to become part of the bourgeoisie. Gramsci started sounding less
convincing. I was still reading him, but not in the restaurant.

Now that I no longer had to, I read all day. Françoise was studying
manuscripts in the Laurenziana, in a magnificent reading room at
the head of a staircase by Michelangelo. Scorning the gloom of the

libraries, I made my base at a bar in the Piazza della Signoria, just in front of a house designed by Raphael. Alas, he had designed it without an awning. As the daily heat increased from merely intense to overwhelming, I changed base to a better-shaded bar near the Badia, whose graceful tower was my personal landmark. The heat was still too much so I transferred to the Biblioteca Nazionale, having decided that the gloom of libraries might be all right after all. In fact there was plenty of light inside, along with the tolerably cool air. With the Arno only fifty feet away, I could sit at a desk for hours on end, reading my way through the collected works of Benedetto Croce, who wrote so much that he made Ruskin look as parsimonious as E. M. Forster. This autobiography is not meant to be a precise intellectual history, which I doubt if anyone can write about himself without fudging the facts. Ideas, even if they come from books, are modified by experience in ways too indirect to be assessed at the time or recalled accurately afterwards. I can state confidently, however, that those weeks in the library in Florence were crucial to my mental development, to the extent that such a thing has ever taken place at all. Croce, in particular, played a vital role in making me feel better about being mentally *un*developed. Formally laid out in his capital theoretical volumes on aesthetics and poetry, and richly applied in countless ancillary volumes of criticism and cultural history, his central concept of the naive artistic impulse had a strong appeal, perhaps because I was, as I still am, unusually naive myself. For Croce, the individual creative talent was irreducible. A peasant who could crack a good joke might have it, whereas an educated man who gave his life to poetry might not. The high arts and the low arts were united to the extent that they were inspired. Within the unity conferred by inspiration, all categories were illusory. This was good news for a reader whose devotion to the high arts was continually being sabotaged by the attraction of the low ones. But Croce offered no easy consolation. His position was not an indulgence. It was the outcome of a lifelong, untiringly rigorous process of examining his own omnivorous enthusiasm with a cool detachment. The vehicle of his thought was the proof of his grandeur: his prose, so transparent as to be beyond style, flowed like a river without ever being carried away by itself – or so it seemed. His effect on me, as I progressed from reading with a dictionary to context-reading to reading with ease, was like learning to swim. As I read his pages by the hundred and then the thousand, I tried to remind myself that any great stylist sounds like an oracle until a big enough historic fact contradicts him. After all, I had been equally impressed by George Bernard Shaw until I realized just how wrong he had been about Hitler and Stalin. But Croce's anti-totalitarian credentials were impeccable. Also he was writing in a foreign language. Undoubtedly there was a self-congratulatory element in my thrilled response. Part of the thrill lay in being able to read at all. Careful not to make Leopardi's mistake – he read so much that when he tried to straighten up one day he found he couldn't – I would get up from the desk once an hour, go outside, sit on the river wall and look downstream towards the Ponte Vecchio. Drained by the heat trapped in its etched upper valley, the river was little more than a collection of shallow pools. In the late afternoon sun they lit up white. Fishermen standing in them were silhouettes expounding theorems by Pythagoras. It occurred to me, not as forcefully as it might have, that Florence was my real university, from which Cambridge was the vacation. I was out of phase with my own life. Never would I be able to relax, except when effort was called for, whereupon I would go to sleep. Did this mean that on the day I died I would wake up? *Speriamo.* Here's hoping.

Françoise was there to temper my fanaticism. In theory, a born teacher likes nothing better than a keen student, but there are limits. When we toured the country villas of the Medici, a bronze nymph or satyr disporting on the edge of a fountain would inspire me to give a lecture on the virtues of Giambologna until I found out that it was by Pierino da Vinci. Unabashed, I would give another lecture on Pierino's limitations. Françoise was a very good photographer. That year she posed me against all the fountains of the city and environs, securing a set of pictures remarkable for their composition and for the fact that my mouth was closed. My spoken Italian was not yet good enough for me to join in easily when she was with her friends, so she had to suffer the full spate of my eloquence in English when we were alone. We weren't alone all that often. Her student contemporaries were as gregarious and welcoming as ever, with an extra sense of group identity engendered by the worsening conditions in the universities. Everyone you knew was a red that year. Even Gabriella went to the Communist Party open air festival in the gardens at the Cascine. The dazzling Adriana had changed her thesis topic from Cesare Pavese to Rosa Luxemburg. Older and wiser heads

– they had begun to call themselves that more stridently, now that the young were calling them reactionaries – insisted that the growing hubbub was just another case of *fantapolitica*: fantasy politics. To a certain extent that was true, but underneath the posturing there were real grievances. The universities were corrupt. Most of the faculty were behaving like absentee landlords. Even the best students could see no career prospects. *La Sinistra* had become a vocation in itself. It had its own language, its own literature, its own cinema. At its best, the Italian left-wing cinema was capable of an analytical *tour de force* like *The Battle of Algiers*, which I saw three times in a row, resolved to emulate its hard-bitten detachment. But Gillo Pontecorvo was a sophisticate who could read history as a tragedy. The young revolutionaries could read it only as a comic book. Most of them believed that the United States had caused the Second World War. All of them believed that the United States had sabotaged the Italian popular revolution after the war was over. The alleged prosperity of modern Italy was a sham. The elected government was Fascism in thin disguise. It was all the fault of the Americans. The question was simple. Why was the government powerless? The answer was simpler. Because capitalism was powerful. Students gathered around the café tables to examine the implications of this obvious fact. Young men dressed in the Italian bourgeois version of the English aristocratic manner discussed how the wealth of their fathers might be redistributed. Taking drinks in the gardens of her villa under an evening sky strangely rimmed with green radiance behind a picket fence of silhouetted cypresses, Gabriella and her coruscating friends were a cut above all this but they had the same frustrations and the same passions. Adriana being politically passionate was a sight to behold. She was an aria without an orchestra. *Ma donnEEna, figOOrati!* she would wail, the ash from her cigarette powdering the evening air. Watching, I moved my lips silently to match hers, the rhythm of her lilting voice. How could it be translated? But little *lady*. Figure it *out*. The second, stressed syllable of *figurati* was hooted, as in the word 'hoot'. What mad music! I called for madder music, and for stronger wine. Both were immediately forthcoming, especially the wine. Thoroughly committed by now to the study of my second language, I was already realizing the benefit I would reap even if I got nowhere: my first language would stand revealed for what it was, a mechanism so complex that it lived. The revelation was intoxicating. I had to sit down suddenly, right there on the parched grass. The Italians, products of a culture in which drunkenness was almost unknown, politely pretended that they thought I might be ill.

During a brief pause in the political discussion we would all go to the movies at the Summer Firefly. A short walk along the dry bed of the Arno near the city end of the Bridge to the Graces, the Summer Firefly charged you almost nothing to get in but broke even by screening old movies at very low standards of projection. At ten o'clock on an August night the heat was killing, but it beat being inside. Indeed the Summer Firefly beat anything. It was the best cinema I was ever in. At first glance an al fresco flea-pit, in its capacity to generate a careless rapture it exceeded even the Rockdale Odeon, the Hampstead Everyman, or that little place in the Rue St Severin where they used to screen old Humphrey Bogart movies in *version originale*, back to back, for ever. One of my all-time favourite Westerns, *3.10 to Yuma*, was the Summer Firefly's staple item. Under the title *Quel treno per Yuma* it cropped up every second week, running about fifteen minutes less than its proper length because the print was full of splices. Glenn Ford and Felicia Farr would suddenly switch positions on screen like electrons changing levels. The fact that I already knew all the dialogue by heart in English, however, made the story easier to follow in Italian. We all sat there happily shouting advice to Van Heflin while the other stars, the astronomical ones, sharpened overhead in the deepening purple. At the climactic point where Glenn Ford leans out of the hotel window so that Richard Jaeckel can see him and ride off to tell the rest of the gang, the image on the screen, which had already been flickering weirdly, settled down to show the bottom half of one frame and the top half of another. Glenn Ford's chin and collar were on top of his hat. Electing myself spokesman, I went back to advise the projectionist, who was facing away from the screen while entertaining three friends. They all had glasses of wine in their hands and seemed quite happy to be told that a disaster was taking place. '*Disastro nella proiezione!*' I assured them. '*Glenn Ford si è convertito in una pittura cubista!*' Grammatically questionable, but it worked the trick.

The Summer Firefly's seats were rusty metal folding contraptions that could easily capsize in the gravel if you laughed too hard. The walls of the roofless auditorium were composed of plaited brushwood, intermittently penetrated by children, whose faces appeared like cherubic visitations, abruptly withdrawn when swept by the beam of the usherette's weak torch. Half drunk but fully happy, in the Summer Firefly I hung suspended within reach of the perfect life. It was an illusion, of course: it always is. It can only happen when you have no responsibilities, which is itself an illusion.

On the coast at Viareggio and Forte dei Marmi we swam until August became a slightly more bearable September. Considering the waves to be beneath the contempt of an Australian surfing hero, I sat on the unsatisfactory sand reading the poetry of Eugenio Montale. It was a good location in which to become acquainted with *Ossi di Seppia* – cuttlefish bones. Montale's poetry was difficult for the right reasons. It was reticent, unrhetorical, compressed, permanent. Memorising it line by line, I was put in my place by the increasing weight of what I had absorbed. '*To vanish,*' I mistranslated, '*Is thus the adventure of the adventures.*' During this same educational interlude a Sarah Lawrence graduate student called Lisa joined us, as if to remind our bold young radicals of just how powerful a force American cultural imperialism actually was. She looked like Angie Dickinson, spoke Italian almost as well as Françoise, and was writing a thesis on Castiglione. She drove an Alfa Romeo Giulietta Spider hired with the first example any of us had ever seen of an American Express card. When she appeared on the beach in a black bikini, the boys put off the revolution until the next day. Watching Lisa and Françoise standing waist deep in the flat Tyrrhenian was one of my lasting visions of that impeccable summer. Everything went right. Even the life-transforming message was carried in on cue. Back in Florence at the Antica Cervia, there was a knock on the open door. The proprietress stood there in the compact heat of the gloomy corridor. She was illuminated like a figure of destiny by one of those twelve-watt bulbs of which every Italian landlady has an endless supply, so as to be able to replace them when they burn out once every hundred years. She held a letter forwarded by my college. It informed me that I had been registered for a PhD and that a study grant would consequently be forthcoming.

This news, it was agreed, was too good to deal with on my own. The first instalment of the grant was too far off to borrow on the strength of it. I was hugely in debt to Françoise, whose own finances would have been strained enough without me. Dalziel had offered me three weeks' work on *Expresso Drongo*, which he assured me was making good progress. I would have to go back to London. The Italians would not let me go without a party. More precisely, it would be a dinner: a kind of Last Supper. My perpetual beatific smile must have convinced them all that I was touched by grace. The dinner would be at a special restaurant serving nothing but game. The game was one of the secondary results of the Italian hunting season, whose principal product, as usual, had been an impressive pile of wounded hunters and extinct passers-by. When the bell rang to start the Italian hunting season, devotees of *la caccia* drove at full speed into the woods and shot everything that moved. Since the animals were sensibly lying low, most of the victims were people. Advancing at random through the woods, the hunters – whose minds, like their expensive guns, were on a hair trigger – fired when they thought they saw something. Often they had seen each other. They also killed civilians in nearby villages. The occasional wild animal got hit, but only by a fluke. One man blasted a rabbit that was already hanging from another man's belt. So much frantic vehicular traffic on the woodland roads, however, ensured that a considerable amount of wildlife was run over. The leading all-game restaurant in Florence, I was assured, would be plentifully supplied with pheasants, wild geese, stags, bucks, oryx, ibex and its *pièce de résistance*, wild boar. I was promised the most tearful send-off since Dante went into exile.

With Françoise safely dispatched to the library, I spent my last afternoon in Florence luxuriating in sorrow on a stone bench just in front of Santa Maria Novella. I had been inside to commune with one of my heroes, Paolo Uccello, whose frescoes in the Green Cloister had recently been uncovered after about a decade *in restauro*. For once in my life, I told myself, I could take credit for experiencing an emotion appropriate to the circumstances. I knew that I would come back to the city, but that I would never be so happy here again as I had been in this short time. Open in my lap was the *Inferno*, at the great passage where Farinata talks about his banishment. His dignity, I persuaded myself, was mine. I felt that I, too, was a knight in a suit of armour.

Would that it had been true, because at that moment a bee stung me. The bee must have been lurking between my bare forearm – the sleeves of my shirt were rolled up – and my waist. When I shifted my arm slightly, the bee was trapped, and reacted the way bees do. I felt as if a length of stiff copper wire had been shoved into my arm and momentarily fed with the total electric power of an underground railway system. The stab of pain was so disproportionate that I didn't complain until it was over, so instead of emitting an abstract scream I cried 'Jesus Christ!' at a volume that stopped the traffic. It turned out that almost nobody in the square was Italian. A whole busload of English Carmelite nuns stared at me as if I were a blasphemer. They had a point. It was a long way to come to hear the Lord's name taken in vain at ear-splitting volume on the front steps of His own house. A representative of the British Council crossed the square to wonder if I might consider moderating my tone. Only the Americans noticed nothing untoward. They probably thought my outcry had been part of some religious ceremony. The pain was already gone, leaving nothing more than an American man in a baseball cap saying to another man in a baseball cap: 'You mean we gotta spend another three hours in *this* place?' I forgave them, having surmised – correctly, as it turned out – that America was merely first in achieving a level of average income so high that even the mentally underprivileged were able to travel, and that shortly all the other industrialized countries would start exporting idiots too. My senses had never been so sharp. I was clairvoyant. When I met Françoise for drinks at the café near the Badia, I was giggling. When we all arrived at the game restaurant I was already hilarious. The whole bunch was there. The joint was jammed but we had a long table to ourselves. Wild boar with wheel-marks across their backs were hanging from the rafters. I thought it was too funny for words. For the first hour I was the life and soul of the party, in my opinion. My conjectures as to which bits of the wild boar were concealed by the thick gravy were widely received as brilliantly original after Françoise had translated them. Then I got sick. Bee venom and wild boar had done something to each other that a gallon of chianti couldn't fix. In the toilet I was sad to discover that there was no throne I could kneel beside so as to be sick into it. Instead, there were those glorified holes in the ground. Those porcelain efforts that look like plaster casts of the footprints of square elephants. Flush with the ground and they flush all over your feet. Very, very hard to be sick into accurately. Very HAH! That wasn't so bad. Not accurate, though. Not ACK! ACK! I was there a long time. Beppe and Sergio, two of my closest friends in my whole life, arrived to find out how I was. I was OK, but where were the others? They were all my closest friends. Get them all in here. Bring the girls in too. Just a second. YAARGH!

The two guys held me while I tried to regurgitate the wild boar, from which not all the hair, it now became apparent, had been removed. If this kept up, I was going to be sick. The third time that I was helped back to the table, there were suggestions that I should be taken to hospital, but I refused to go unless it was guaranteed that there would be a toilet there. I had seen Italian ambulance crews in action. Manned by volunteers in white Franciscan cowls, the ambulance would scream to a halt at the scene of an accident and immediately the situation would be transformed. Victims lying there with broken backs would be thrown into the ambulance. People bleeding to death from wounds that needed only a tourniquet would be given artificial respiration instead. The volunteers were businessmen with a commendable urge to perform some community service, but they would have done better to sweep leaves. Without the protection of anonymity, they would have stood a good chance of being indicted for murder, if ever the eight differently uniformed Italian police forces could have got out of each other's road long enough to prevent the next crime instead of just arriving abruptly on powerful motorcycles to be photographed beside the results of the last one. No, I didn't want any of that. Just leave me sitting here like a grinning corpse and I'll be fine. Talk among yourselves while I look as if I'm getting ready to vomit a live pig into your lap.

Having thoroughly spoiled my own party, I succumbed to a case of raving, perambulating semi-malaria from which I did not emerge until late next night, when the bus from Luton airport arrived at Victoria. Only then, when all the other passengers were waking up, did I at last fall into a fitful sleep.

11. FULL VELVET JACKET

It should have been an heroic return. After a mentally improving sojourn beyond the Alps, I was coming back to Cambridge in triumph, at the university's invitation and expense. The reality was less exalted. With my trusty cardboard suitcase full of dirty washing I scaled the outer wall of Robin's ground-floor flatlet in Pimlico. It was after midnight. Safely hidden in the tiny area, I tapped at her door-length window very quietly, so as not to wake the neighbours. I tapped for an hour without waking her either. Finally the window swung open and I was greeted by the glistening point of a carving knife. It was Robin's flatmate, an English drama student called Alison. Though her terror was not feigned, it was, I thought, excessive. Robin, I was informed, was staying the night at her boyfriend's place in Notting Hill. What boyfriend? Peeved, I set up camp on the floor of the kitchenette. There was plenty of room if I kept my legs folded. When that became impossible, I opened the cupboard under the sink and put my feet in there. Not kicking over the cans of Ajax was harder when I slept. I had to stay awake and concentrate. For three weeks it wouldn't be so bad.

Turning up for work on the set of Keith Visconti's film, I found that there had indeed been developments. Dave Dalziel assured me that the key scene where the girl must decide whether or not she wants milk in her coffee was now in the can. Unfortunately the young actor playing the waiter had temporarily ceased to be available. A childhood friend of Keith's, he was being questioned by the police in relation to an incident at New Cross in which the contents of a van full of the new Japanese portable TV sets had gone missing. He was being questioned, that is, during the previous several months of filming. Now that he had finished being questioned, he had vanished. Apparently some of his friends were looking for him. Not childhood friends like Keith. Other friends. Nelia knew all about it, but she wasn't saying much – not, I think, out of secrecy, but because she couldn't raise the energy. She had started reading a magazine and the effort was wearing her down. It was called *Woman's Realm*. She could just about get an issue finished before the next one came out. Besides, Keith was making her work all the time.

With Dalziel's constant advice, Keith had been using Nelia to get all the close-up reaction shots he could while the search went on for either the original waiter or someone who looked like him. By now it had become apparent that the waiter's scenes would have to be shot again with a different actor. Keith had offered to produce another of his lifelong friends but Dalziel had vetoed this. A proper actor had been hired: one of the Australian expatriates who had been left swallowing engine oil in the burning water after *The Charge of the Light Fandango* had pointed its propellers at the sky and gone roaring down to the bottom. Keith objected that the actor did not look English. Dalziel overruled him. 'I don't think this guy looks especially Australian, do you?' Dalziel asked me this in tones that compelled agreement. The actor, on top of the body of the Man from Snowy River, had the face of Lew Hoad, but I concurred in the judgment that his national origin was impossible to guess. The actor was unimpressed by what I had done for him. All he could remember was *The Charge of the Light Fandango*. Understandably there was a certain *froideur* when he found that my daily presence was part of this deal too. So I did my best to stay out of the way. After doing my bit to shift lights and carry silver boxes I would go outside and sit waiting at the kayf across the road. The studio was in a back street behind Olympia, so it was not a very salubrious kayf. I was writing poems about Florence. They were full of Medici pomp and Machiavellian circumstance, of tasselled banners and blazing trumpets, the sweet waistlines of Paolo Uccello handmaidens and the crackling flames of Savonarola's pyre. All this I wrote about while sitting under a chalked menu announcing that spam fritters with two veg could be followed by spotted dick with custard. Outside the dirty window, rain that for some reason would only make it dirtier fell thinly but persistently, like a small annoyance. The yawning discrepancy between the place I was writing about and the place I was writing about it in, however, seemed to help. I told myself that it was always best to be physically elsewhere from one's spiritual concern: thus recollection was left free to focus. How, for example, would I have come to value the stylish, precisely calibrated density of a tiny Italian *espresso basso* if it were not for the contrast provided by this giant mug of English tea? Tea leaves floated limply on its vast surface. Under the surface there were more tea leaves. A mug of tea of that size and consistency took a minimum of ten minutes to drink, even when cold. If I sipped carefully, opening my pursed lips to the width of a vein, I swallowed only about half a pound of tea leaves, leaving a mulch three inches deep in the bottom of the mug. Yes, this was the real England that Richard Hoggart had talked about in *The Uses of Literacy*. When Raymond Williams complained in *Culture and Society* of the healthy working class traditions that were being lost, this was what he meant.

Dalziel didn't really have enough for me to do during the week. On the weekends it was a different story. His sister was in town. Beryl Dalziel was a sculptress. Like her brother's, her career lay in the future. Unlike him, she did not travel well. Dave Dalziel was famously capable of getting organized. He had a filing system for his correspondence. Some of the clothes he bought off market stalls would have looked incongruous on any man less personable, and the Jaguar he had so proudly bought for a song showed increasing signs of having been overhauled at some stage of its career by someone who might have been a childhood friend of Keith Visconti, but on the whole Dave Dalziel was a scrupulous realist. He did not cause trouble to others. He could get himself from country to country with all his belongings, get the telephone connected, hire a plumber. Beryl Dalziel could do none of these things. She needed help.

Above all, she needed help moving. During the three weeks I was involved with her peregrinations, she changed flats four times, twice on the one weekend. These moves would have been complicated enough if her innumerable suitcases and steamer trunks had been full of air. She claimed to have put her sample sculptures in storage on arrival, but I was convinced they were in her luggage. They were the heaviest bags I have ever carried. In fact there was no question of carrying most of them, even with Dalziel on one end and me on the other. They had to be dragged. Moving her out of the upstairs flat in Maida Vale which we had moved her into on the previous weekend, Dalziel and I began by taking each end of one of the smaller suitcases. I remembered that a week before I had thought it contained nothing except machine tools. This time it must have been packed with uranium. Luckily it was I who was holding the bottom end, or it might have been Dalziel who bore the brunt, with incalculable consequences for the future of the Australian film industry. The thing accelerated down the thinly carpeted stairs. Ignoring Dalziel's exhortations to stop it with my body, I stepped smartly aside while the case boomed past and slammed into the window seat on the landing, staving in its plywood-panelled front. We rearranged the cushions so that the damage hardly showed. The next case we took a step at a time, positioning it vertically and edging it out until it dropped on to the next step down with a thump that shook the house. The landlady was out. Landladies were always out when Beryl took off. She timed it that way. How she managed it when there weren't at least two grown men around was another question, or yet another question. It was already another question how the cases we were taking down had grown even heavier since we took them up. It took an hour and a half to move all twelve cases. We saved the biggest of Beryl's bulk carriers until last. A metal steamer trunk bound about with clasps and hasps, it looked as if it was waiting for a cargo ship. On each side, B. DALZIEL was painted in yellow letters two feet high. I remembered this object vividly from former journeys, but there had been a change. Previously merely backbreaking, it was now immovable. Dalziel and I both got behind it and shoved with all our strength. The trunk reacted like the Albert Memorial. We tried again, this time applying the pressure more gradually, on the theory that a steady build-up would break the air seal holding the bottom of the trunk to the threadbare carpet. We had our eyes closed with the strain, so it wasn't until we had given up that we noticed Beryl had lain down on the bed with her thumb in her mouth.

From long experience, Dalziel recognized this behaviour as a sign of guilt. He demanded that the trunk be unpacked and the contents manhandled separately. His sister sulked. The clock ticked. Not for the first time, I wondered how different my personality – and therefore, presumably, my life – might have been had I grown up with siblings to contend with. Dalziel still had flashes of the old insanity but essentially he was a reasonable man. His sister was essentially unreasonable. Was he like that because of her? Was she like that because of him? It was getting dark. At last she gave in. She unlocked the trunk. It was full of house bricks. 'For my kiln,' she explained. 'Want to do porcelain.' All the other bags proved to have their share of bricks too. Eventually we got everything into the hired Dormobile and set off for Beryl's next address. On the way, at Dalziel's insistence, the bricks were dumped into a builder's skip.

After three weekends of intense body building, my cardboard suitcase was like a feather draped over my crooked index finger when I turned up in Cambridge to claim my inheritance. The place was infested with a new intake of undergraduates, all self-consciously parading in their new gowns, which, had they but known it, were due to be replaced in short order by old gowns whose more experienced owners had seen an opportunity to update their kit. Cambridge was a bit like being in the army: you had to know the lurks. By now I was a lurk man, like Sergeant Bilko. This was nothing to be proud of, so I tried not to be proud of it. As a graduate student I was less of an anomaly than I had been as an undergraduate, but I was still a pretty weatherbeaten customer to have hanging around an institution dedicated to forming the characters of young people and furnishing their minds with knowledge. All I can say now is how I felt at the time; that somehow the fact that I was a few years older than my fellow clerks was cancelled out by my feeling a few years younger than they would have felt had they been a few years older. One day I would catch up with myself and then everything would come out even. Meanwhile, I had been granted the immense privilege of being allowed to live in unapproved lodgings. To put it another way, the college didn't want me making life miserable for any of its registered landladies. With the first instalment of my study grant safely in the bank, I paid back the college what I owed in loans. This left nothing like enough to pay back Footlights what I owed in bar bills, but since I was now President of the Footlights I calculated that I could sway the committee to excuse me my debts until such time as I could pay them back with inflated currency. Retrieving the pink jacket and the rest of my junk from the Pembroke linen room, I staggered along King's Parade, turned right into Benet Street, and moved into the Friar's House, just across from the Eagle.

The Friar's House looked like the best address in Cambridge. It was a half-timbered edifice which had no doubt been built by the eponymous friars. You could tell it went back a long way by all the angles it leaned at. My room was on the first floor. I hadn't been in it thirty seconds before I found out why the rent was so cheap. In those days the ground floor of the Friar's House was occupied by the most popular Pakistani restaurant in Cambridge. I like the smell of curry – rather better than I like the taste of it, in fact – but the fabric of the Friar's House, being so old, was porous. Without going downstairs, I could recite the menu. Another shock was the hitherto unannounced presence of Romaine Rand, who had already taken another room on the same floor as mine. Indeed it was the room *next* to mine. It was the big front room facing on to the street. In something less than a week, Romaine, who in another time and place might have run the sort of salon that Goethe and the boys would have swarmed around like blowflies, had already transformed her room into a dream from the Arabian nights. Drawing on her incongruous but irrepressible skills as a housewife, she had tatted lengths of batik, draped bolts of brocade, swathed silk, swagged satin, ruched, ruffed, hemmed and hawed. There were oriental carpets and occidental screens, ornamental plants and incidental music. The effect was stunning. Aristotle Onassis had married Jackie Kennedy in vain hopes of getting his yacht to look like that. Romaine, however, once she had got her life of luxury up and running, did not luxuriate. She had a typewriter the size of a printing press. Instantly she was at it, ten hours a day. Through the lath-and-plaster wall I could hear her attacking the typewriter as if she had a contract, with penalty clauses, for testing it to destruction. As well as finalizing her thesis, apparently, she was working on a book. She definitely would not be available for Footlights, so I could forget it. 'Only a few of them are funny,' she announced, 'and *none* of them can fuck.' I slunk back to my bare room. There was, or were, the flat metal frame of a single bed, a stained mattress, the curried floorboards, a bulb without a shade, and my suitcase. I resolved that I, too, would transmogrify my environment. Picking out a section of the wall where a shelf might go, I tapped it with a testing forefinger. About a square foot of plaster fell off and brained a cockroach.

Making large plans to decorate my eyrie on a scale that would put Romaine to shame, I set off next morning for the Do It Yourself Hire and Supply shop in Hills Road. Somehow I never found it. At the cinema, the DIY Hire and Supply advertisement had always been the one I had most trouble identifying with. It featured an old man with a Ringo Starr haircut who smiled at you while boring holes with a Black and Decker drill. I was well aware of what would happen if I tried to smile at anybody while boring holes. Searching with decreasing urgency for the DIY centre, I happened on a second-hand bookshop and went in there instead. It wasn't a very good second-hand bookshop – mostly its stock consisted of the sort of unsellable item which people nowadays palm off on Oxfam in order to feel charitable – but I had already cleaned all the other second-hand bookshops out. It was a mystery how I managed, on less than no income, to go on building an impressive personal library. From my habit of writing the date when I purchased a book under my name on the front flyleaf, I can now tell that I bought several volumes of Rilke's letters at about that time. Since I would have been able to read no German more difficult than the extracts from *Till Eulenspiegel's Merry Pranks* which had been included in my elementary German textbook at Sydney Technical High School, I must have bought those volumes in the expectation that I would learn the language later on. By that criterion, no purchase was beyond my reach. I brought my trophies home to the Friar's House and lined them up along the edge of the floor where the bookcase would go once I had bored the holes in the lengths of wood that I would be buying in the near future. Until then, late at night when I came home from the Footlights, I lay reading under the dozen blankets I had obtained on a loan from the ladies in the Pembroke linen room. A cold autumn would have made sleep difficult even if there had been a functioning power point for the electric fire I had bought before finding out why it was so cheap. Making sleep impossible, however, was the noise of Romaine's typewriter. Through the trembling partition dividing our two rooms came the frenzied uproar of a belt-fed Mauser MG42, firing long bursts from a concrete pillbox.

She was getting somewhere and I wasn't. Footlights was only one of the distractions that kept me from attending to my principal business, which was meant to be Shelley and his readings of the Italian poets. The luckless man chosen to supervise my PhD thesis was Professor Graham Hough, of whose distinction I was uneasily aware. I went to see him in Darwin. From the time it took me to get there, he might as well have been in Darwin, Australia. Actually Darwin College was only just across the Cam. A hundred yards along Trumpington Street towards Pembroke, turn right down Silver Street, cross the bridge, and I should have been there in five minutes. It took ten times that because I was thinking. When I got to the bridge I looked downriver and thought for a long while. The wooden lattice of Queen's Bridge spanned the river like a quietly exultant reproach.

According to an (inaccurate) legend, Isaac Newton had designed it, the cocky prick. He hadn't only known what he was doing, he had been mad keen that everybody else should be appropriately cowed, the asshole. During the long vacation I should have got enough of a grip on my subject to make it sound worthwhile for my supervisor to find out about it himself so that he would be able to check up on me as the work advanced. Unfortunately, what seemed a good idea had remained merely a good idea. I had a few citations to suggest that the influence of Dante and Petrarch had been not just thematic, as Shelley himself proudly admitted, but technical, at the level of imagery and rhythmic strategy. Hough wanted to know how this last item differed from the metrical patterns which it was already known that Shelley had taken over wholesale from his Italian models. Sure I was right, but being short of information – always a dangerous state for anyone who is trying to sell someone else on an idea – I struggled to adduce chapter and verse. Hough was patient. As a prisoner of the Japanese in Malaya, he had been through more trying times than this. Younger students than myself might be torn between the brimstone of Leavis and the fireworks of Steiner, but Hough's realistic solidity was what I valued most in a teacher of English. As much for the theoretical dabbling it eschewed as for the pure reason it espoused, I thoroughly approved of his little book *Essay on Criticism*. A poet himself, he wrote the civilized verse of a man who had been far enough into the pit to admire the scenery on the way back out. I didn't want to muck him around. With sherry-fuelled eloquence I conjured visions of the deep studies I would pursue. If not convinced, he was at least lulled. I got the impression that he might be on the verge of nodding off. It was my suggestion, not his, that I should come back when I had something on paper. Instantly he was on his feet with his hand out. I went to shake it, but it was going past me to the door handle.

On the way back to college to pick up my mail, I took the long way around past the pond and over the meadow. At the Mill I stood communicating with the ducks. The river was already closed down for the winter. Raindrops prickled on the dark water just above where it filled with cold light as it curved out to leap through the sluice. It was the kind of thing Leonardo da Vinci liked to draw. Leonardo hadn't been here, of course, but nearly everybody else had. Not only Rupert Brooke had been down at the Mill, Rutherford had sat here on the wall and watched the atoms pursue their unbroken curve. John Maynard Keynes had looked into that clear declension and seen the economic consequences of the Versailles Treaty. Wittgenstein had seen the silence of what cannot be expressed, Alan Turing the soul of a machine. Apparently there was now some crippled young man at King's who was working on a unified field theory that would explain absolutely everything. Surrounded by these exemplars of mental effort, I couldn't even be sure that I would do the work I had cut out for myself. Worse, I was sure I wouldn't. Somehow I would be drawn aside, into something else. All the ducks knew enough to stay well upstream of where the surface of the water moved faster and lost its comforting darkness. I couldn't stay out of the light. If I had been a duck I would have been down the sluice. I wouldn't even make it as a web-footed waterfowl. Those ducks got on my nerves so much that I wrote a poem belittling their pretensions.

My duck poem took two days of undeflected concentration. If something was irrelevant, I could do it. While I was supposed to be studying the poems of Shelley, I was writing mine. By this time *Granta* was practically my private newsletter. I still contributed, with grand condescension, to *Varsity*, but I was growing sick of its inability to set up my carefully finished copy without including all the same misprints which disfigured the news stories sent in dramatically from the telephone booth around the corner by would-be Fleet Street pie-eating hacks who were all cheap excitement and no sentence structure. The snapping point came when I reviewed Joseph Losey's desperately unfunny comic film *Modesty Blaise*. I compared the undraped Monica Vitti to the Rokeby Venus. It came out as the Rokesby Venue. I might have stood for this if anybody concerned had been ashamed, but student journalists don't learn to take pains until they have to, and perhaps that's the way things should be. It's hard enough crawling out of your shell, without being driven back in by sneers and quibbles. Uncomfortably aware that I had been hanging around too long, I left the junior reporters to get on with it and switched my feature-writing efforts to *Granta* on the semi-fulltime basis necessitated by my having accepted a post as its new arts editor. Taking on this task was sheer folly but I was sick of being at the mercy of undergraduate newspaper editors. Those who edited the magazines had a greater sense of responsibility than the *Varsity* tribe. They also had a bad habit of leaving the printer to get on with it while they toasted muffins in each other's rooms, but at least, as one of them, I would be able to accept my own stuff without demur and make sure that it got laid out with appropriate prominence: nothing too strident, mind, just plenty of white space to set off the body copy, the occasional full-page photograph to remind the readers of who they were dealing with, and a caption prominent enough to make sure that they didn't get my photograph mixed up with anybody else's. Like all previous and subsequent literary editors of *Granta*, I began with confident hopes of securing contributions from world-famous literary figures. If my letters were answered at all, it was in the negative. Jean-Paul Sartre said '*Non*.' The fact that he had said the same to the Nobel Prize committee was small comfort. Dalziel gave me a good piece on the films of John Ford. It needed a lot of subbing, because he had written it in spare time he didn't have, now that the BFI Production Board was pressing him hard to finish *Expresso Drongo* even if Keith Visconti had to be fired.

The one advantage of being Granta's literary editor turned out to be intangible when it really mattered. At the invitation of the Italian department, the great poet Eugenio Montale came to town and sat in the Senior Common Room of Magdalene to be interviewed by the head of the department, Professor Limentani. The room was jammed with members and students of the Italian department plus a couple of hundred others who had all forced their way in to pay homage. Starved of oxygen, Montale sat there under his distinguished cap of silver hair being asked several questions by Professor Limentani. The Prof spoke in a voice that might have just been audible to anyone with an ear-trumpet who had been sitting in his lap. Tired after a long journey, Montale must have thought that to whisper at great length to a huge room full of strangers was an English national custom, like riding to hounds. He whispered too. About two hundred and fifty people all dying of nitrogen narcosis were in there for an hour struggling silently for position so that they could watch two Italian men of advanced years moving their lips. Not for the first time, the extent to which an academic organization could bungle a big event made me wonder if undergraduates got sufficient credit for the extracurricular things they accomplished. I wrote an article about the occasion for *Granta*, subbed it myself, laid it out and left it for the editor to see through the press. When the issue came out, my article was there pretty much as I had written it, except that almost every detail was in the wrong place. All the paragraphs were out of order, so that Montale – now known as Montela, although sometimes as Mantabe – left Cambridge in the middle of the article before arriving at the end. My critical remarks concerning his famous poem about the lemon trees were attached to a quotation from his equally famous poem about the sunflower. My name was the only item which appeared correctly, thereby ensuring that the blame for the mess would be entirely mine.

At about this time, Florence was hit by a flood that killed a lot of people, played havoc with the artistic patrimony, and transformed the city's way of life. I felt guilty about not being there to help, but not as guilty as I felt about setting out to spread enlightenment and ending up adding to the confusion. There wasn't much I could do about bringing people with lungs full of mud back to life. I felt ashamed of my powerlessness, but the shame was abstract. To have my name on a page of nonsense felt as shameful as having run someone over. Françoise was in Oxford, to start a Bachelor of Philosophy course. After having taken her doctorate with the maximum possible marks – a feat unheard-of for a foreigner, and rare even for a native – she had providentially left Florence before the catastrophe. I was relieved that she was safe. But that, as Gatsby says of Daisy's love for Tom, was only personal. Those columns of pied type were hard to get over. I sent a copy of the magazine to Françoise at Somerville and by return of post she was kind enough to commiserate, although her suggestion that nobody would notice the difference did not have the soothing effect that she intended. No doubt things would have gone better if I had been at the press. I couldn't be everywhere. Certainly I couldn't be at my desk. Shelley would have to wait for a bit.

As usual the thing that demanded most of my attention was Footlights, only now more than ever. In my capacity as President I was in constant attendance. There were more committee meetings than usual because I was intent on delegating every task of day-to-day administration. To delegate successfully, I had to call a meeting, so that everybody could be told what to do. The secretary looked after the finances, the cabaret director looked after the cabaret bookings, the Falconer looked after the clubroom. This left me free to sit in the bar until late at night looking after general policy. My first big policy decision had to do with Prince Charles, who had arrived at

Trinity with the whole of Fleet Street just behind him in a succession of hired coaches. It was evident that Footlights concerts and revues, unless an embargo was imposed on his name, would consist of nothing but sketches about Prince Charles. The press was already a gruesome warning of what to expect. Traditionally nuts on the subject of the heir to the throne, they had now gone berserk. Student journalists who had dreamed of joining the World of Paul Slickey were now given good reason to think again. Their heroes, in the flesh, turned out to possess not even the inverted glamour of sleazy corruption. Nothing more complicated was going on than the usual behaviour of a pack of sharks in a feeding frenzy. Determined not to be a prisoner of his fate, their quarry took part in a smoking concert in Trinity. Fleet Street, for which any Cambridge theatrical event is always a Footlights revue – usually misspelled 'review' – ran headlines about his appearance with Footlights. (FOOTLIGHTS CHARLES – PICTURES). Sensibly he didn't come near Footlights. The roof would have fallen in. Thus he solved half the problem himself. The other half was for us to solve. Informing the committee that they would have to agree in advance to pass the motion *nem. con.* – otherwise the mere fact of there having been a discussion would have become a story too – unilaterally I imposed the embargo. This was the right thing to do, but while doing it I felt the sinister thrill of unchallenged power. Luckily I managed to remind myself in time that as President of Footlights I was not the Shah of Persia, just *primus inter pares*. At very most, as the Dean of Pembroke might have put it, I was *in loco parentis* to those *in statu pupillari*.

Helping to remind me on this point were the club smoking concerts. There was a new bunch of multi-talented performers coming up who had me beaten to the wide, especially when it came to music. Reading for the Classics Tripos at St John's, Pete Atkin was a shy young man with rimless glasses who had an unfair amount of natural authority on stage, as if being in the limelight saved him from self-consciousness. He wrote shapely melodies which, while being completely original, partook of every musical tradition from Buddy Holly back to Palestrina. Footlights had always had a strong musical element. There was always someone who knew all about jazz and someone else who knew all about pop. John Cameron could score for a big band *before* he got to Cambridge, so it was no surprise that he led one after he left. Daryl Runswick was a music scholar in

Corpus Christi who could put away the bow and pluck his bass like Ray Brown: later on he was to accompany Frank Sinatra at the Festival Hall. Robin Nelson could write a parody of a Bach cantata that sounded like a Bach cantata. But Atkin knew everything. He was particularly erudite on the subject of Tin Pan Alley. He knew Rodgers and Hart note for note and word for word. The same Mercer and Arlen songs that were my touchstones he could play and sing straight through from memory. Though he wrote excellent lyrics for his own tunes, I was ruthless in planting the notion that he might perhaps consider setting one or two of my own efforts. Cuckoos laying eggs give more subtle hints than I did. Believing then, as I still believe, that a song lyric should be at least as disciplined as a published poem, I produced, in that first flush of collaboration, intricately symmetrical stanza forms which Atkin could inject with music only at the cost of making it evident that he had been required to use a syringe. It was easier to loosen up the syntax when we worked the other way around, with me concocting a lyric to fit a tune he had already written. After a while we met somewhere in the middle, roughing out both melody and story at a preliminary session around the piano. The piano was on the Footlights stage. Late nights in the Footlights grew later. If Atkin had known that we would write hundreds of songs over the next eight years, he might have struck for regular hours. I had a way of catching people up in my enthusiasms. But I don't think he would protest, looking back, that I turned him aside from his studies. Talent will out. It has a mind of its own.

Some people have so many talents that their idea of being normal is to have only one. Russell Davies was also from St John's. He had already taken a double first in the Modern Language Tripos without realizing that he had sat the examinations. He thought they were application forms. It didn't occur to him to ask what he was applying for. When people asked him to do things, he said yes. He could do everything except say no. The only reason he was so late getting to Footlights was that he had been asked to play by every jazz band in the area. He played a different instrument in each band. He could play the tuba, the trombone, the trumpet, the saxophone and the piano. When he got to us, it turned out that he could write, draw, sing, dance and act, all better than anyone else. He hadn't quite realized that he could do these things. There hadn't been time.

With Atkin and Davies both around, things were already looking promising for the next May Week revue, of which I intended to be the producer. I had already ruled myself out as a performer. In this company I would be outclassed. As the year developed, St John's proved to be a bottomless cornucopia of gifted new recruits. Atkin and Davies had a friend unromantically named Barry Brown, who wrote and performed surreal monologues. Together they all put on the St John's Smoker. There was an interloper from Emmanuel called Jonathan James-Moore who looked and sounded like a retired colonel invented by Saki. They all seemed to have the kind of stage presence that many professional actors spend a lifetime acquiring, but today they would be unanimous in admitting that they paled into the decor when the spotlight came up on Julie Covington. The decor was in the St John's bike shed, annual home of the St John's Smoker. Atkin and Brown had discovered Covington at Homerton Teacher's College. Spotlit against inaccurately draped black curtains in the smoky, crowded depths of the bike shed, her prettiness was sufficient on its own to induce a reverent hush. The reverent hush deepened to religious awe when she began to sing. Student singers who could hold a note were rare. Student singers who could hold an audience were radium. Talent-shopping from the back of the mesmerized crowd, I foresaw a whole new era of student revue opening up, in which the lyrical element, formerly an occasional by-product of make-up and drag, would be fundamental.

Inspired to a minimum of half a dozen new song lyrics per week, laboriously I commuted to Oxford by train so that I might read them aloud to Françoise. Her room in the Somerville graduate house had the rare luxury of central heating, but I made a practice of reciting all my new lyrics on arrival, before removing my duffel coat. Unaccompanied by music, they were perhaps harder to appreciate than I surmised. The Oxford and Cambridge Ski Club had booked a hotel in Zürs am Alberg for an off-season week in early December. Françoise was going and she suggested that if I wanted to write and recite lyrics without being interrupted by a long train trip via Bletchley, I should come to Austria. Picturing what the officers of the Oxford and Cambridge Ski Club would undoubtedly look like – RAF moustaches and white roll-necked pullovers with Olympic rings on them

– I scornfully declined. What would a radical socialist be doing mixed up in an upper-crust activity like skiing? On my return to Cambridge, Marenko told me that he was going to Zürs. Blantyre was going too. Even Delmer Dynamo was going. I told them I couldn't ski. 'Blow it out your ass,' said Delmer. '*Anyone* can ski. You just point the things down the *hill*, for Christ's sake.'

12. HELL BELOW ZERO

Somehow the Oxford and Cambridge Ski Club got to Austria by train. The club had no officers – it was just a letterhead – so the mass movement was more of an instinctive migration than an organized journey. The Americans caught the train at the last minute. They had planned to go in Delmer's car. It turned out that nobody knew how to fill it with petrol. The filler cap had a combination lock which Delmer had not had occasion to open before because he had never driven the car far enough to run out of fuel. Also there was nowhere to put Marenko's skis. Delmer feared that a roofrack would damage his precious hand-rubbed paintwork. Apparently he had expected Marenko's skis to be much shorter. This was a reasonable assumption. Marenko's skis were made of metal and went on for ever, like two lengths of railway line.

Unseasonably, the snow at Zürs was fresh and deep all the way down into the valley. After hiring boots and skis I headed for the baby slope. I was alone. Françoise had been skiing every year in Australia since the first rope-tow had been put in at Thredbo when she was a child. Instantly she was off and gone. Strad ski'd like a gentleman. He went with her. Delmer spent the whole of the first day buying all his gear instead of hiring it, which promised great things. When he finally emerged from the most expensive ski-shop in Zürs, he was carrying a lot of big boxes and already wearing a sensational pair of boots. In those last days of lace-up boots, experts might wear clip-ons, but scarcely anybody had clip-ons made of plastic. Delmer's were not only brilliant red plastic with silver clips, they had knurled screws, screwed knurls, grommets, gauges and three-way adjustable furbelows. 'Get *these*,' crowed Delmer. 'Tomorrow I'll be out of *sight*.'

But by then I had seen Marenko. As I lay there sobbing where I had fallen off the T-bar at the top of the baby slope, I had seen him high above me on one of the lower, slower stretches of a black piste. Unmistakable in his dark glasses and the black one-piece overall of an SS tank commander, he came bouncing down through a mogul field in a dead straight line, slamming from hump to hump, both his poles held by their middles in one hand while he adjusted his collar with the other. What was worse, he saw me. After disappearing behind a clump of trees like a gannet into the sea, he suddenly reappeared on the last, allegedly elementary stretch of red piste on the other side of the T-bar. At first he was going at a scarcely believable velocity, but what was really unbelievable was how smoothly he translated all that impetus into stasis. Changing direction at the last possible second so that he curved up the hill and around the top of the wheel at the head of the T-bar, he just leaned over and stopped, his poles still in one hand. 'This goddam ski-pass keeps flapping loose,' he said. 'Nearly strangled myself up there on the Death's Head. How *you* doin'?'

Though it hurt me to say so, I had to tell him that I wasn't doing very well. For some reason he didn't seem to realize this. He told me to take a run down the slope while he watched. Take a *run*. I took a crawl. Snow-ploughing rigidly with my nose between my knees, I headed downwards at one mile per hour, coming to a halt altogether if someone else had fallen in front of me. Marenko ski'd backwards beside me. 'Don't try to stop the skis,' he said. 'You're choking them. Let them run.' Momentarily I let them run and headed for the village. Between the baby slope and the village was a road. On a collision course from the right came a skidding bus with chains on its wheels and a driver whose arm was across his eyes. Luckily there was a barrier of snow-caked slush at the high edge of the road. While I lay in it face down, sobbing in a muffled manner, Marenko told me I was wasting my time on the baby slope. 'You're a natural,' he announced. 'Tomorrow we'll get you up there on the Death's Head.'

The next day dawned clear and bright, unfortunately. I had been hoping for a blizzard. Everybody was going up to the Death's Head except Delmer. At breakfast he had announced his intention of starting slowly. 'Gotta break in the new boots, men.' And indeed the new boots looked as if they needed breaking in, almost as much as his ensemble needed toning down. A blue and crimson effort with a colour-coordinated beanie, it aroused expectations of speed which Jean-Claude Killy might have found it difficult to fulfil. No stretch pants had ever been so stretched. On the back of the quilted jacket appeared the words DOWNHILL ACTION HI-FI CHALLENGE. On the breast pocket the words RACING TEAM CLUB encircled the face of a snarling tiger. If Delmer had been the right shape for all this it would have helped, but there would still have been a problem. The famous new boots supported him so well that he couldn't bend down far enough to get his skis on. Strad had to help him into them. Delmer looked impatient. Once the skis were on and the bindings were closed, he fell over. All this happened in front of the hotel. 'Blow it out your ass!' shouted Delmer. Some passing Austrian ski-masters, whose walking boots looked as if they had put their legs down the throats of live wolves, looked curious. 'Was hat er gesagt?' 'Weiss nicht.' We helped Delmer out of his skis and he waved us away, promising to join us later, after the micro-wedge plinth mounting on his boots had been recalibrated to match the barometric pressure.

The idea that Delmer had been wise to cop out early grew on me as we rose in the cable car towards the peak of the mountain known as the Death's Head. My imagination was working overtime as usual. The cable car stopped well short of the peak. The tree line was still in clear view below and the slope looked quite gentle compared to the north face of the Eiger. I hoped it was from the cold that Françoise was trembling. She had advised me to go to ski class but I had shouted her down, keen as usual to take no advice, however sensible, until bitter experience had rendered it imperative. 'This is more like it,' said Marenko. This is more like what? I subvocalized. My lips were too cold to move. I just breathed very quietly through my nose and tried to look at only the first few yards of the slope. The angle it was at looked ridiculous enough by itself, without considering the cliff it turned into a bit later on. The only stroke of luck was that even the vertical bits were covered with fresh snow. 'You can't hurt yourself,' said Marenko. 'If you fall over you'll stop eventually.' But I was already gone, sliding on my face, held back by nothing except the minimal resistance of the snow through whose surface my nose was trowelling a thin furrow. 'Stop!' shouted Marenko as he sliced past at full speed beside me. The clear contradiction between what he was saying now and what he had said just before had obviously not had time to strike him. 'Get your skis below you and you'll stop!' My skis were above me and I wasn't stopping. Marenko cut in underneath me and brought us both to a halt with me crumpled upside down against his ankles. 'That's a good start,' he said, fishing with one of his poles for my left ski, which had come off. 'Shows you're not afraid of the slope.' Françoise and Strad appeared beside us, looking worried. 'You two go on,' said Marenko. 'I'll give him a few pointers.' They wanted to stay but I insisted. I didn't want anyone else to be there while I was being given the pointers.

Each hour that ensued seemed like a bad day. I cried all the time. The tears never fell. They just tinkled in my eyes like Christmas decorations hanging in a window. Before I knew how to traverse across packed snow, Marenko was making me traverse across deep powder. I crashed into snow drifts with both my skis off. The automatic ski brake had not yet been invented. The skis were attached by thongs to your boots, except when the thongs came undone. Mine always did. The bindings, when Marenko rescued the skis from further down the same drift, or from the top of the next drift down, were caked with snow, which at that altitude turned to ice faster than a gloved fingertip could scrape it out. The bindings weren't today's forgiving, apparently simple affairs that you can just step into after a token gesture of knocking the snow off the bottom of your boots with the tip of a stick. They were spring and cable bindings which would not close unless all the snow had been brushed out of them and any hint of ice on the bottom of your boots had been scrupulously removed. Wallowing in a drift, I found these requirements impossible to fulfil. Marenko patiently waited, doubtless thinking about Yeats, while I waded out of the drift towards a firm footing. 'Good training,' he said. 'Just like my first year at Aspen.' He couldn't seem to grasp that the reason I was just lying there was that I couldn't move. 'Don't worry if you feel tired,' he said, blowing on his dark glasses. 'It's just fatigue.'

Though we were on a red piste, which was theoretically much easier than a black piste, there were narrow stretches that I wouldn't have contemplated trying to snow-plough down even in a snow-plough. I took my skis off and walked. On the wider stretches, however, Marenko insisted that I try to do parallel turns. The main difficulty, I found, was to go slowly enough in the first instance so that the turn could be initiated under some sort of control. I was already falling before I turned, so all that the turn did was to alter the direction of the fall. The instruction to lean out into the valley I found impossible to obey, because I had already fallen towards the mountain. The skis having become crossed while my body continued to move, *then* I leaned out into the valley, but by that time I was fully airborne. It was a parallel turn only in the sense that my flailing form was parallel to the snow. On the beaten piste the resulting impact was audible and painful. It was much nicer falling into the drifts. I began to look around hopefully for the next drift. Eventually fatigue reached the point where Marenko began to notice. The piste was about to narrow into a mogul-ridden swoop to the right, with its right edge curving up into the mountain and its high left lip masking a sudden drop to the foot of a clump of pine trees. You could tell how steep the drop was by the fact that only the top halves of the trees were visible. I looked at all this but it must have been clear that I wasn't taking it in. We sat down for a while and Marenko gave me a piece of chocolate. 'You're going great,' he said. 'Only another hour and you'll be down.' At this point Françoise and Strad appeared. They were on their third or fourth run down the mountain. 'He's going great,' said Marenko. All I had to do was sit there until they got bored and went away. Instead I somehow got the idea that it was now or never. In such cases the rule should always be: never. When in doubt, don't. Françoise and Strad fishtailed neatly down the chute and waited at the bottom, looking up. Marenko *schussed* in a sweet straight line, his arms held out to the sides like a falling crucifix as he bounced from hump to hump of the frightening moguls. He spun on his skis about two-thirds of the way down so that he was going backwards, drifted to a stop beside the others, and waved a pole to indicate that I should follow.

I should have taken my skis off and walked, but I was too tired. And they had made it look so easy. I started to traverse across towards the outer edge of the piste. After an inspired snow-plough turn I was traversing the other way. But the second turn, which took me some way up the high wall to the right, was of such large radius that it didn't slow me down at all, so when I headed back to the left I was going at full clip. 'Too fast!' shouted Marenko. 'I *know*!' was my agonized reply. Heading up and out over the high left edge of the piste, I tried to stop myself by sitting back. Thus lightened, the skis moved even faster, so I was actually lying down in mid-air as I sailed out into space. 'Death,' I thought. 'This is it. Here it is.' Pine tree branches snapped off in quick succession. They sounded like a pom-

pom firing. Their thickness, as it happened, might have been precisely calculated to break my fall instead of my back. My skis came off in the tree, so when I bombed into a drift I was not only moving just slowly enough to survive the impact, I was spared the usual humiliating search for lost equipment. By the time the others materialized below me, having beaten a path through the trees, I had reassembled my stuff and was able to make a brave show of having meant the whole thing. Marenko, in his way, helped. 'You've done the hard part now,' he said. 'Nice work.'

Marenko's teaching methods were, of course, the worst possible for a beginner. Having ski'd most of his life, he had no idea of what it was like not to be able to, and thought that you were incapable from mere recalcitrance, which could be overcome by exhortation. Natural athletes are rarely the best teachers. The person who can teach you something is the one who remembers how he learned it. There was another inhibiting factor. Skiing is a technical sport which has little to do with strength. At that stage I was still quite strong and all too ready to try turning the skis by brute force. It can work only on gently sloping, packed snow. For the last part of the run, some of that was available, and even after my day of torment I was foolish enough to believe that I was getting somewhere. The other three took it slowly so that I could keep up. I fancied that I looked part of the group as we came sweeping down past the baby slope. I rather hoped that Delmer would be there to marvel, but at first there was no sign of him. Then Strad spotted Delmer's beanie. It was sticking up out of the snowdrift at the bottom of the slope. The weatherbeaten, superannuated ski-masters who tended the baby slope were gathered round the beanie. One of them was poking the snow with a long thin stick. Muffled sounds could be heard from under the snow. I recognized Delmer's catchphrase, modulated into fluffy softness as if shouted through a pillow. '*Was hat er gesagt?*' one of the ski-masters asked us. '*Macht nichts,*' said Strad. '*Er sagt nur dass er OK ist.*' I was amazed. I never knew Strad spoke German.

Strad didn't like to show off. He was reluctant to reveal that he was capable of anything until circumstances forced him into it. My own character being incurably different, I envied him his ability to keep his light under a bushel. For me, being able to do something meant that I had to prove it, and being unable to do something was a taunt from Fate. Being unable to ski would have been more bearable in, say, Barbados. In a ski resort it was intolerable. I resolved to dare all. Next day Delmer appeared in full ski kit but without his boots. He had bought himself a pair of yak's hair *après-ski* bootees, and with these crossed in front of him he settled down in a deck chair to cut the pages of his New York edition of Henry James, which had just arrived in a crate. Until the technology had been sorted out, he announced, we would never catch him putting on skis again. His place in the ski class – he had booked himself in for a week of advanced lessons – he kindly gave to me. The ski-masters advised me to swap it for elementary lessons. It was a blow to the ego to be skiing with the children but when they did it better than I the message sank in. Drawing on my usual reserves of fanaticism, I set to work on mastering the stem turn. I mastered it so well that in later years, when the stem turn went out of fashion, it took me an age to unmaster it, and even today, in moments of stress, I find the back ends of my skis drifting apart by that tell-tale inch which brands my generation of skiers more surely than the waffle pattern left by thermal underwear around the thickening waistline. At the end of the week I could get down the red piste on the Death's Head without taking my skis off. It wasn't much of an achievement – there was a six-year-old girl in a crash helmet who would go past me three times while I was coming down once – but it made me absurdly content. What I liked best about skiing was how it made loneliness legitimate. Raised in the hot sun, my idea of romance was to feel cold. North was a thrilling word to me. Balzac said that a novel should send the reader into another country. My dreams were like that. They still are.

On the snow I didn't know what I was doing. As compensation, there was a concert at the end of the week. From the hundreds of student skiers, those who thought they could do a turn came shyly forward. There was the amateur magician with the duff patter and the American girl with the guitar who could sing all the songs Joan Baez sang except that they sounded different and she couldn't remember any of them all the way through. 'Oh Gard, I'm sorry. No, wait . . . No. It's gone.' In this context I was able to shine. I hit them with my 'Lucy Gets Married' number and followed it up with my new one about the lost H-bomb. The Americans, in particular, were delirious. By then the concern with the Vietnam imbroglio had built up to the point where even the Ivy League Americans – and these were certainly those – had doubts about their country's role as a world policeman. As an Australian at a British university telling American citizens how they ought to behave, I was in an anomalous position if I stopped to think about it. It was a less anomalous position than being upside down in a snowdrift, so I didn't stop to think about it. I just rode towards the laughter like a heat-seeking missile. This was the first time I had played to an audience outside Cambridge. I might have been encouraged by the results if I had envisaged a career as a performer. At that time I thought of my own appearances on stage as nothing more theatrical than a form of writing with a light shining on it, like a goose-neck lamp on a desk. It was just a form of expression. I wasn't even sure what form it was. It wasn't acting. I didn't even memorize the stuff. I just read it out. Timing was for real performers: it usually struck me as artificial even when they did it, and when I did it it was ludicrous. Establishing a tacit understanding with the audience that I *wasn't* going to perform, however, generated an air of complicity which I dimly saw might be a way ahead. A ski resort in Austria was an odd spot to be struck with such a formative notion, but that's often how these things happen. Developing a personal style is largely a matter of recognizing one's limitations, and the best place to recognize them is somewhere off the beaten track. At the end of the concert I felt pleased with myself. Next day there was a last morning of skiing before we packed up to go home. Pride the night before was duly followed by a bad fall.

I was having one of my customary rests at the side of the red piste on the Death's Head when Marenko appeared from above, heading straight down the mogul field through which I had just spent half an hour painfully picking my way. I was amongst a pack of other heavy-breathing rabbits so he didn't see me. He must have been skiing back the quickest way to the hotel after doing his usual half a dozen black runs in succession. Holding both poles in one hand, he had his dark glasses off and was breathing on the inside of them as his heavy metal skis kissed the crests of the moguls like a flat stone bouncing rapidly across a rippled pond. Below me, where the moguls eased into a smoother piste, he decided he wasn't going fast enough and started to skate. He hooked his dark glasses back on, redistributed his poles so that he had one in each hand, sank slightly at the knees, planted his right pole, and disappeared in a diving turn over the side of the piste. Half a minute later I saw him far below and far away. He had *schussed* across the face of an old avalanche covered with fresh powder. The rabbits around me sighed with admiration.

Deciding that I had not been daring enough, I tried to straight-line the rest of the mogul field. Miraculously I got through it, although my knees, which despite my fear I somehow managed to keep loose, must have looked ridiculous bouncing up around my ears. The predictable result didn't happen until I reached the smooth bit. I was going the fastest I had ever gone and perhaps it was a mistake to be yelling with exultation. 'WEE HAH!' I cried. 'WHOOEE!' The ensuing fall was the most embarrassing kind you can have. The skis went outwards to each side, spreading my legs so wide that they were practically in a straight line. Luckily the bindings snapped open almost straight away, otherwise my nose would have been broken. Like an arrowhead I flew on for some distance, still with a pole in each hand. Making a three-point contact – mouth, chest and seriously shrivelled genitalia – I kissed the piste and slid on at full speed, slowing down only very gradually. The main braking effect was provided by the snow accumulating inside my clothes. About fifty pounds of it was forced into my stretch pants. When I finally con-trived to stand up again my pants wobbled like bags full of water. I was so completely winded that I thought all my ribs were broken. Symbolically, my recently eloquent lower lip was badly bitten, the blood seeping through the caked snow around my mouth to give the effect, I was later told, of an Italian raspberry *gelato*. My lucky break was that my skis both missed me. Travelling very fast, they went past me on each side on their way down to the hotel, where I joined them an hour later, feeling chastened. The abyss between wanting to and being able to had once again made itself manifest. A man can fall into that gap and vanish. To him it will be small consolation that those who never aspire never appear in the first place.

13. FANTASY ISLAND

Thus my first year as a PhD student took shape. The academic year was short anyway, but there was no gainsaying the fact that I was working on my thesis for an average of one hour per month or perhaps less. No gainsaying it by anyone except me. As usual I told myself that everything would change tomorrow. Tomorrow never came, because it couldn't. I just had too many commitments. Alarmed by their number, I distracted myself from them by adding others. In Footlights my new styleless style of performing made enough progress to attract the attention of student producers in other branches of the theatre. It struck someone who shall remain nameless that I would make an ideal Jourdain in the Cambridge Opera Society's forth-coming presentation of the original version of *Ariadne auf Naxos*. I wouldn't have to sing: in the original version Jourdain is the leading role of a play which is eventually, although not soon enough, dis-placed by the opera. It should have been obvious that if I didn't have to sing I would have to act, but somehow I convinced myself that I wouldn't have to act either. At that time I was enslaved to the music of Richard Strauss. I knew *Der Rosenkavalier* note for note, could do a traffic-stopping imitation of Ljuba Welitsch in the final scene from *Salome*, and would contentedly croon both parts of the long two-girl duet from *Arabella* while sitting in the Whim writing a nit-picking review of *Accident*. Considering that I couldn't sing the National Anthem in a way that made it sound significantly different from 'Rock Around the Clock', this incantatory Strauss-worship must have sounded pretty strange from the outside, but inside my head it had the full, drenching beauty of that reprehensible old opportunist at his most sumptuous: the shimmering swirl of strings that drapes the soprano like a Fortuny gown, the passing phrase, the orgasmic crescendo, the sudden silence. Not too much, in my version, of the sudden silence. In particular I loved the last pages of *Ariadne auf*

Naxos where Bacchus got the lion's share of the duet with the epony-mous goddess. To all intents and purposes he had a grandstand aria, of which I knew every phrase. Yes, if destiny had denied me the wherewithal to sing Bacchus, at least I could play Jourdain. So what I said to the producer was yes, when what I should have said was no. And if he didn't understand it when I said it in English, I should have sung it in German. *Nein!*

It wasn't his fault. Always in the theatre, as in all the arts, it is dangerous to go against one's instincts, but this doesn't mean that it is always safe to go with them. You can take on a project from the depth of your heart and it will still end up stuck all over your face, like egg. I already knew that, but there aren't many operas with a starring role for a non-singer, and I wanted to be an opera star. So I ignored the law of probability, which declared that no student producer, unless he was Max Reinhardt reborn, would be able to hire the opera singers, organize the orchestra, supervise the designs, stage the main action, and also prevent the play-within-the-opera from sabotaging the opera in a manner less decisive than that which had persuaded Strauss and Hofmannstahl to abandon the original version in the first place. This particular student producer's utter innocence – although a brilliant scholar, he had never produced anything except a weekly essay – helped to persuade me for the first half-hour of rehearsal that he might get everything right by sheer purity, like Parsifal. When he turned out not to be completely certain about the difference between stage left and stage right I started to worry. I should have worried more. For years afterwards, to my shame, I vocally blamed him. The fault was mine for not taking drastic action. Either I should have demanded an experienced pro-ducer or else bailed out, if necessary without a parachute. The idea of a non-singing Australian Jourdain was a good one. The idea of a non-singing non-acting Australian Jourdain was a possible one, as long as he learned his lines, hit the marks, and kept his good humour when the set collapsed around him. But with everything else going wrong, I worried about that instead of about getting my bit right. Instead of providing a still centre, I was part of the chaos. The play-within-the-opera was a mess. *Ariadne auf Naxos* was scheduled to go on at the Arts Theatre for four nights running, come what might. Luckily the opera-without-the-play was going reasonably well. Pro-fessional opera singers are usually able to produce themselves. Alberto

Remedios, appearing in the role of Bacchus, was at that time still on his way up as one of the best Wagnerian tenors in Europe, but he had already had plenty of practice at getting on and off a strange stage at short notice. Despite his exotic name, Alberto was a Scouse plug-ugly with a delightfully foul tongue who knew a potential catastrophe when he saw one. It rapidly became clear that he was unimpressed by the visual aspect of the conditions in which he was being asked to work. 'Shit,' he said when he saw the set. 'Who shat?' And indeed Naxos did look very brown. For an island, it was remarkably short of greenery. The designer had sketched some rocks, which had been faithfully reproduced by the Arts Theatre paint shop. On a large scale the rocks looked like the petrified turds of a mastodon. Ariadne was to be sung by Margaret Roberts, a trouper. It was the other kind of trooper that she swore like when she saw the costume which had been provided for her. Diaphanous in all the wrong places, it looked like Eva Peron's negligée, an impression abetted by the platform mules with pink pom-poms and the sequined cloche flying helmet. A down-to-earth sort of girl, Margaret was prepared to act the temptress, but not in a comedy. Nor was she any more tolerant than Alberto of bright young people dabbling in the arts. She handed back the dress. 'You can burn that,' she said, 'and don't forget to bury the ashes. It might grow again.' From her travelling wardrobe she produced a complete Ariadne costume of her own. Previous experience of semi-professional productions had told her to be prepared.

Alas, not only was I part of the semi-professional production, I exemplified it. For me, *Ariadne auf Naxos* was a personal disaster. I could have called it wounding, but only if I had lived. I died, ten times a night for four nights on the trot. Though the general lousiness of my performance improved toward the merely inadequate as the short run went on, if the show had stayed in repertory for ever I still wouldn't have been able to haul my contribution out of the fire. Romaine Rand, writing a notice for the *Cambridge Review,* said that watching my performance was a strange exercise in compassion, like seeing a man who deserved punishment being beaten up more thoroughly than his crime warranted. She was uncharacteristically kind to the production as a whole, contenting herself with the suggestion that it be sealed in lead-lined containers and buried down a disused coal mine. Looking back on the catastrophe – and even today

I look back on it through a veil of tears – I like to think that if I was placed in the same circumstances now I would be able to look after myself, if only by the cheap method of making a virtue of everything going wrong around me. Because everything *did* go wrong, every night. In the play-within-the-opera, a banquet has to be served on stage. On the first night, the banquet was brought in by a single liveried flunkey. There were supposed to be two liveried flunkeys. One of them had gone missing. The remaining liveried flunkey, before he went off to get the banquet, had already entertained the audience by the way his buckled shoes were so obviously a pair of buckles loosely attached to a pair of down-at-heel Chelsea boots. While he was off, we all had a lot of lines about how lavish a banquet it was going to be. When the liveried flunkey reappeared, he was carrying a single tureen. He pretended to stagger under its weight. This merely encouraged the putatively silver cover of the tureen to bounce slightly, as if to prove what the dullest eye already suspected, that it was made of papier mâché thinly caked with silver paint. The audience was thus well prepared to absorb the possibility that the silver cover of the tureen might not conceal anything very wonderful. When the cover was lifted to reveal nothing but a heaped plate of pineapple chunks, however, there were people in the audience who could take no more.

Little could they know how much more they would have to take. When I shut an allegedly heavy ornamental door behind me, it drifted open again to reveal a crouching stage-hand in blue jeans. The audience saw him long before I did, so why was he still there when I turned around? It was because he was trying to stop the purportedly massive solid marble fireplace from falling over. He didn't and it did. It floated to the floor and lay there like an extra stage cloth while the cast assembled around it to discuss the unexampled luxury of Jourdain's surroundings. I got exactly one intended laugh. When Jourdain proclaimed his delight at having discovered that he had been speaking prose all his life, the line worked, but that was because it had worked for Molière. The *bourgeois gentilhomme*, however, must have more than one line. He must have character. To be a fool, he must first have his dignity, or he is just ridiculous. My only consolation was that the revival of the original version of *Ariadne auf Naxos*, though worse than a failure on every other level, was a triumph in the musical department – which was, after all, the only thing that mattered. On the last night, the last act sounded lovely beyond description. Conducted by David Atherton, then at the beginning of a glittering career, the orchestra played those marvellous climactic pages in a long, creamy legato line that held Jourdain – watching from a spotlit box but at last released from his terrible obligation to be amusing – spellbound even in the aftermath of his humiliation. Alone on stage among the mastodon droppings, Margaret sent out a languorous invitation to Bacchus that made Sieglinde's song of longing in *Die Walküre* sound like a jingle. The beauty of the music was a sacred rite, but the gremlins had not departed. Alberto's reputed opinion of the set had finally sensitized the student producer to the point where that helpless young man was ready to do anything to put things right. If Alberto couldn't stand the way the set looked, the producer had the solution. As Bacchus, draped in cloth of gold and carrying a priapic stave wreathed with laurels, sang his first heroic phrase and strode masterfully on to the stage, the lights went out. Almost invisible, Bacchus and Ariadne could both still see the conductor, so the sublime duet proceeded on schedule. Indeed it had never sounded better, because now it *looked* so much better. Alberto, however, was not pleased. He controlled his feelings until after the curtain fell. When the curtain went back up again for the first call, the applause for Ariadne and Bacchus was like thunder. You could see the god's mouth moving. It was assumed he was congratulating the goddess. The applause for Ariadne's first individual call was even more cataclysmic, but this time Bacchus, although he was invisible somewhere in the wings, was clearly audible to the whole audience. 'WHICH PRICK TURNED OUT THE FUCKING LIGHTS?' He got a laugh that I walked into, and I was hypocritical enough to bow as if it were mine.

After a cock-up on that scale, Cambridge wasn't big enough to hide in. For Easter I was back in Florence, where the extent and intensity of the destruction caused by the floods put my personal misery into perspective. Though the water had gone down again, the thick tide mark left by the thousands of gallons of spilled oil was still there on the walls, at an impossible height. Everything up to that sinister Plimsoll line had been either washed away or else ruined where it stood. In the *quartiere* between the back of the Palazzo Vecchio and Santa Croce, the fatal black stripe was half-way up the second storey of the buildings. Anita and her family had all survived, but the trattoria was gone, gutted as if by a flamethrower. You would have sworn that fire instead of water had done the work: the walls looked scorched. The whole low-lying little principality of the *popolo minuto* had been soaked with poisons. Sections of the historic centre which lay a few feet higher had suffered less, but more than enough. The cost to the art works and the books was devastating. The human cost was worse than that – it got into my dreams. The underground walkway at the railway station had been full of people when the first big wave had come boiling down the river. People trapped in the walkway had drowned against the roof. None of my friends had been killed, but Florence was my city, so I took the loss of strangers personally. The stricken commune had made it clear that only professionally qualified helpers were welcome. Otherwise, I tried to convince myself, I would have been in there with the first army of saviours. Being useless made the sense of loss more bitter. All over the world, people were horrified by the damage to the patrimony, which they correctly pointed out belonged to all mankind. Would-be realists among them said that the dead people could be replaced but that the works of art should never again be left to chance. They were right. Yet up close it was harder to separate the eternal patrimony from the evanescent human beings who lived and died amongst it. Like everyone else who has ever lived in Florence for however short a time, I had been marked by the city and wanted to feel that I had left my mark on it, even if the mark was only in my memory. In the bar near the Badia, though I hadn't carved my name on the table where I had read and written by the hour, I had been careful to print the table in my recollection. The bar was open again but all the furniture was new. The Biblioteca Nazionale was also, miraculously, open for business, but the desk where I had sat was different and the books I had read were all rebound and their pages were wrinkled from the drying rooms. Somehow the effacement of personal memories was even harder to take than the damage to the Cimabue crucifix in Santa Croce. There was a chance that the Cimabue might be saved. In the Trattoria Anita the decor would never be quite so self-confidently scruffy again. Tat needs to be time-honoured. The level of the Arno had sunk again to the status of a puddle, so we could look over the wall at where the Summer Firefly should have been. It was gone. It has never been put back. With prompt and generous help from America, every shop on the Ponte Vecchio was fully restored, but nobody would bet on the likelihood of people sitting there in the dry river bed to watch *Quel treno per Yuma*. Obviously it was assumed that they would always be listening for another noise in the distance: the roar of water rolling down the valley like a moving wall at the end of an episode of an adventure serial, except that this time, at the start of the next episode, there would be no escape.

At that time I was in one of my beardless periods, so I found it especially noticeable that some of the young male Florentines among our acquaintances had acquired intentional-looking outcrops of facial hair. Beppe and Sergio both looked like preliminary studies for Titian's portrait of Ariosto. These were the first beards seen on native Italians since the time of Verdi. The floods were the reason. Student life in Florence had been distracted, and had restarted at a broken rhythm, with a new seriousness. The *pappagalli* disappeared overnight, never to return. There had been one notorious occasion when a bus bearing a touring party of French schoolgirls had turned around in front of Santa Maria Novella and gone back to Paris: the teachers in charge had taken one look at the assembled young Italian male pests and decided not to let the girls get off. Now it was different. Foreign girls were no longer followed in the street. In such women's magazines as *Grazia*, which had previously been exclusively concerned with the mysteries of the trousseau, there was new talk of equality. By the following year, the whole of young Italy had become more serious, to the extent that everyone had forgotten where the mood started. But I was there, and I remember. It was in Florence after the flood. The tragedy had worked like a one-day war. Its sheer arbitrariness had concentrated the minds of those who had taken life as it came. They were still subject to intellectual fashion, just as they were still subject to every other kind of fashion. Suddenly all the young men had beards to trim and all the young ladies had blue jeans to bleach. Women in trousers! It was too daring to be true. Yet the surface froth had a deep and potentially violent undertow. There was a demand for justice which the university system was not best placed to supply. You didn't have to be a seer to sense trouble.

Flattering myself that I might do some good, I wrote an article about the aftermath of the Florence floods which I published in *Granta* when I got back. In my capacity as arts editor I allocated to myself three pages of the magazine, with another page for some impressive photographs taken by Françoise. The photographs were rather better judged than my prose, if the truth be told, but the impresario could scarcely be expected to give himself less than star billing. This time I saw the whole thing through the press myself. The viewpoint of the article was perhaps needlessly egocentric – even for myself, I would have done better to leave myself out of it – but there was no chance of muffing the evocation. I could still smell the mud and oil. This article is worth mentioning because it was to have long-term effects on what I have since had to get used to calling my career, so in fairness to an earlier self I should record here that I wrote it out of no great calculation beyond the usual urge to burst into print. At the *New Statesman*, Nicholas Tomalin had just taken over as literary editor, in circumstances which dictated that he find some new book reviewers, and find them in a tearing hurry, because most of the old ones were boycotting him. Tomalin was a feature writer of originality and courage, whose pieces from Vietnam had done a lot to convince Britain – and the Americans in Cambridge – that the United States was in a jungle over its head. The modern determination of the British intelligentsia to keep itself specialized being already far advanced, Tomalin's obvious qualifications as a journalist were held to be disqualifications in a literary editor. Those of the ambitious young who were lit on by his roving eye thought otherwise. Abramovitz, President of the Union in his final term, invited Tomalin to debate some such footling topic as 'This House Would Rather Be Amused'. Abramovitz invited me to be on Tomalin's team. It was billed as a Funny Debate. I had still not learned never to go near anything labelled as Funny. People who tell jokes don't make me laugh. My experience as a guest speaker in Funny Debates at both Cambridge and Oxford eventually helped to convince me that the only place to be amusing is in a serious context. But at that stage I had not yet formulated this important principle, so I agreed to appear in the debate. After the usual interminably facetious opening diatribes by the student politicians, Tomalin rose to speak sensibly about the necessity of writing in an entertaining manner if one wished to convey a serious message. The United States, by bombing Haiphong, had started something which the North Vietnamese army would probably finish. Getting this likelihood across to young Americans before they themselves were drawn into the mud and flames would require all those whose job was to tell the truth to tell it in an arresting manner. There was no use pretending that the story would be a million laughs. Finally what counted was to be serious, a different thing from sentimentality. The Strauss waltzes that had been played in the concentration camps were not only a glaring instance of inappropriate gaiety, they were noxious in themselves. *Der Leichtsinn* was dangerous. Like the official language meant to conceal evil, it really embodied it. Flummery was lethal. Thank you and good night.

Abramovitz understood Tomalin's speech and I could tell from the appreciative laughter that there were some American graduate students in the audience who got it too. For the student politicians it might as well have been a lecture on quantum theory. Why the Oxford and Cambridge Unions should attract recruits of such fatuity is a question that I have never been able to answer. Then as now, they bounced to their feet to make foolish interruptions, gave way, refused to give way, were ruled out of order, and begged the indulgence of the house. Peregrine Sourbutts-Protheroe was there, as usual wearing plimsolls with his evening dress. You could tell he was wearing plimsolls because he was sitting backwards with his legs over the back of a bench. There was a character calling himself Abelard Lakenheath-Bagpuize who shouted at random while eating a raw egg out of his bare hands. It was a madhouse. The libretto was by Tristan Tzara, the choreography by Hieronymus Bosch. When my turn came to speak I let anger rob me of whatever mirth I might have been able to summon. No doubt I deserved to be interrupted by Sourbutts-Protheroe but I refused to give way to him. Nevertheless he unleashed a stream of rip-snorting jokes about the Antipodes, kangaroos, aborigines, and the necessity of walking around upside down in the outback. The audience thought he was hilarious. Even Abramovitz, who was no fool, had been so caught up in the Union's idea of badinage that he felt compelled to laugh. You could tell he felt *compelled* to laugh because he shook his shoulders in a way currently made famous by Edward Heath. Real laughter never looks like that. I was desolate. Tomalin, sensibly, had gone to sleep. Hours afterwards, when the thing was finally over – there were more student speeches to end with that made the opening ones sound like Plato's *Symposium* – Tomalin took me aside before he climbed into his car to go back to London. 'I liked that thing you wrote about the floods,' he said, looking past me. 'You could do some pieces for me if you've got the time.' With an effortful affectation of off-handedness, I told him that I was busy until May Week but after that I would have some time in hand. Later on I learned he always looked past people. He had a stiff neck. Luckily for me it was only real, and not metaphorical.

My piece about the floods had counted in my own mind as serious writing. It was encouraging to hear that a professional literary journalist concurred in the opinion. Suddenly all my other work in student journalism counted, in my own mind, as serious writing too. I was a serious writer. Whoopee! This was something to set against the nagging fact that I was not doing much serious writing on my thesis. The further fact that I was not doing much serious reading for it either was harder to gainsay. Somehow, along with everything else, I had managed to read a lot, but as usual none of it was immediately relevant to the task in hand. Not having yet accepted that my whole life would be like that, I convicted myself of dereliction. Guilt drove me between the pages of a book – always, since my earliest childhood, my favourite place to hide. In English I read anything at all unless it stemmed from the early part of the nineteenth century, in which case it might have been germane to my subject and thus felt like work. For the only time in my adult life, I became incapable of reading Keats. On the other hand, I could not put Yeats down. The majestic later poems committed themselves to my memory. Where previously I had admired but kept my distance, now I submitted. The long process of growing old enough to appreciate his late achievement was well begun. I tried not to become a Yeats bore. The indomitable Irishry remained an opaque sphere of interest, like the mysticism. But then, as indeed now, I could imagine nothing better than the way Yeats conducted a prose argument through a poetic stanza, compressing syntax as if it were imagery, dislocating rhythm locally so as to intensify it in the aggregate, raising plain statement to the level of the oracular. In my dusty room with the cardboard suitcase open on the curried floor, he was my luxury.

There was now the additional pleasure of being able to read with fair fluency in Italian. I reinforced this nascent ability by raiding the Modern Languages Faculty library, which occupied a floor of the unlovely Sidgwick Avenue site and had a room for each language. I found it hard to keep out of the other rooms as well. The sight of books in languages I couldn't read was a potent stimulus to set about repairing the deficiency. The means of repairing it were near to hand, in an air-conditioned basement under the site. The Language Laboratory looked like the NASA Mission Control Centre in Houston, although – since the space missions had not then yet attained their full glory and coverage – I have always thought of the mission control rooms, whether in Houston or Kaliningrad, as looking like the Sidgwick Avenue language laboratory. The bulky tape decks and discus-sized reels of ¼-inch tape would have looked, to any child of the cassette age who came back from the future, as if they were props from a silent movie about a training camp for mad scientists, but they worked. Picking my way through Proust was a slow way of improving my ability to read French. Studying French in the language laboratory was a faster way. The intention of the course was to teach the student to speak. Leaving that aside until later – decades later, as it turned out – I cashed in on the unintended effect of a language laboratory course, which was to teach the student to read. It was a painless way of absorbing grammar. Over the next year or two I used the laboratory to recapture and improve my primitive German. I also made a good start with Russian. If there had been a Latin course available I would have devoured it. As it was, I picked up a useful if scrappy knowledge of the Latin classics by using parallel texts as portable dictionaries, until finally I could get quite a long way by covering up the page in English and construing the page in Latin from context. But I missed hearing the voices. If Cicero had been on tape I would have memorized the speeches against Catiline and got my quantities right. For me, the language laboratory was the brightly lit basement shopping mall of the Tower of Babel. I couldn't stay out of it. It was a roundabout and belated way of getting an education. Perhaps it wasn't an education at all. People who knew what I was up to thought I was nuts. They might have been right. There was something pathological about my evasiveness. I hid from my thesis in the pages of books, hid from my native language in a sub-world of smatterings, and hid from myself in the theatre – the place where those who know themselves just well enough to want to get away go to be together.

14. FRISBEES FLY AT DUSK

Not that the cast members of the May Week revue were anything like as neurotic as their director – a post to which I had been unanimously elected by the Footlights committee. Since any member of the committee who voted against me would have felt himself obliged to resign on the spot, the unanimous vote was no surprise. I took it as a compliment. I also, I can safely say, took it as an obligation. Night and day, with the exception of the examination period, the whole of Easter term was devoted to rehearsals. Ruling by decree, I had stipulated that the cast would be large. Like many another despot in history, I had talked myself into believing that democracy could be imposed by ukase. I should have known better. I *did* know better, but was carried away by a personal conviction that the club had had its mind on London for too long. Small-cast revues with one eye on the West End had arrived there looking would-be professional and not much fun to be in even when they were funny. A large-cast revue would be a sign that we weren't out for ourselves as individuals. There would be no stars, just a happy ensemble. Though I loathed all of Brecht except the Weill operas, I had been mightily impressed by the Berliner Ensemble when it came to the Old Vic. As Macheath in *The Threepenny Opera*, Wolf Kaiser had writhed against the bars of his gaol in a suitably alienated manner, yet it was the inventiveness of the group movement that had stayed with me. It was like the circus. I liked circuses, too. Though sketches, as always, would be the basis of the show, what attracted me most was the prospect of getting that large cast into concerted action, of creating group effects, of – not yet a word made dreadful by pious use – *improvising*. In the cast there were tall men, small men, thin men, fat men. There were four girls, one of whom was Julie Covington. Normally she would have been the star of the show. In this show without stars I at first looked on her conspicuous ability as a limitation. She was pretty, she could act, she could sing and she could dance. All of that rather got in the road of my general plan to have big production numbers in which nobody would stand out. All day in the clubroom and far into the night, while the smell of fish rose from below like an oily miasma, I carried on like Kim Il Sung, motivating my huge company to perform as one. Possessing an overbearing personality anyway, and fired by the powerful ideals of social engineering, in my ideological determination I was hard for those youngsters to resist. Luckily for us all, they resisted, or there would have been a débâcle.

The show was called *Supernatural Gas* and sold out the Arts Theatre for the whole two-week season. Every Footlights May Week revue always did. At least this one didn't do less. There was oblique evidence that the show was not, in advance at any rate, judged an outright flop. Positive evidence that it was entertaining came from the audience's laughter, which was quite frequent. It might have been more frequent if I had placed due emphasis on the sketch writing. Some of the monologues had not been worked on sufficiently since they had done the usual round of the club and college smokers. Ideally a monologue should be the unique experience of the person who writes it, who, also ideally, should be the same person as the person who delivers it. In reality, scarcely anybody under the age of ninety is self-critical enough to do his own cutting and rewriting. Throughout the Footlights Dramatic Society's modern history (we had better forget about its ancient history, which was spent, almost exclusively, screaming around in high heels and beads) the best monologues had been worked on by so many hands that they amounted to group creations, like the pyramids or the atomic bomb. I would have done better to apply my group motivation approach to the sketches as well. Instead, I confined it to the production numbers and the mute movement routines. Actually these took so long to rehearse that there was no real prospect of keeping the cast together for further periods of group script editing, desirable though that might have been. Getting the cast together at all proved far more difficult than I had expected.

Russell Davies was in nearly every sketch and musical number. Though the aim was to distribute the plum parts equally, in cold fact he was the best man available for almost everything. No other performer was disgruntled if I replaced him with Davies. Even more gratifyingly, Davies was not disgruntled, or did not seem so. Rehearsing continuously all day and far into the evening, however, he began finding it harder to get up in the morning. We had to send a taxi for him, and it got to the point that if the taxi driver failed to wake him up he would sleep on. It was typical of Davies that he could not bring himself to point out the connection between overwork and narcolepsy. I had underestimated his modesty, and he my insensitivity. The mêlée of an urgent group activity is not as good a time as it is cracked up to be for people to find out about each other. I needed his abilities, so I treated him as if his energies were infinite. They almost were. As for his powers of invention, they seemed to have no limit at all. In a big production number called 'The Fantastograd Russian Dance Ensemble', he played the victim in the Dance of the KGB Interrogators. I was very proud of the whole number and had a satisfactorily dictatorial time making everyone bounce around shouting '*Da!*' with their arms folded, but there could be no doubt that the way Davies looked suitably grateful while being straightened out by the heavies – the way he made an actual *dance* of it – was a work of art which brought a lump to the throat. All that inventiveness being lavished on a single moment which would live, at best, in a few thousand memories! Having him to hand was so gratifying that I forgave him his strange habit of falling asleep in his chair and needing to be shaken awake every time the next number to be rehearsed required his presence – which was, in effect, every time.

Robert Buckman, later to be famous as the Pink Medicine Man on television, was the youngest member of the cast and presented the opposite kind of trouble. He was so energetic that you had to hold a cushion over his face to slow him down. I could cope with him, however, by shouting at him loudly. This did not work with a strange young man calling himself Rusty Gates, who had done some very droll, off-trail sketches in club smokers but who now, having been cast for May Week, revealed an enhanced capacity for obliquity that made him hard to comprehend. He grew his hair in a page-boy cut. He addressed me as 'man'. When he arrived, always progressively later, he crossed one brothel creeper randomly over the other so that there was no telling which wall he would walk into. Either he would stop just short of the wall and address it as 'man' or he would make actual contact with it, but never at sufficient velocity to cause pain. Finally, when he was arriving so late that his eventual appearance was the same as not having turned up at all, he would walk in so slowly that each foot was in the air long enough to make you wonder if paralysis had struck. Even though he is now a highly respected theatre director, he won't mind my saying all this, because his abstracted manner of that time was part of the political position which he has since pursued undeviatingly and with great success. He was the first home-grown English hippy I had met. He regarded me, correctly, as hopelessly square. Certainly I was too square to realize the significance of the hand-rolled cigarettes he smoked in such quantities. In Strad's company I had had the odd puff myself without realizing that there was a new religion on the way which would have devotees and would scorn dabblers. Rusty Gates was a hard man to rehearse. He had a manifest contempt for the material. In retrospect I was to decide that he was three-quarters of the way to being right. At the time I regarded him as a disciplinary problem. I condemned him to the worst role, that of the perambulating HP sauce bottle in a clever number called 'Cinquante Sept', written by two exceptionally tasteful young men called Ian Taylor and David Turner, who later on were to do show business a serious disservice by staying out of it. The song had everything. In later days, when I knew more about pacing a show, I would have made it the finale and poured on the effects. As it was, the song had almost the entire cast in it. Even Jonathan James-Moore, who couldn't sing at all, delivered a spoken announcement in the middle of the number. He just read out the label of an HP sauce bottle in a sepulchral voice. He would have brought the house down if it hadn't already been down. The house was already down because of Rusty Gates. His arms imprisoned inside the giant HP sauce bottle, from which only his feet and his closely framed face protruded, he was supposed to toddle out to centre stage and stay still. But a man who, under the influence of the dreaded weed, had an ideological objection to walking straight even in daylight, was unlikely to toe any given line while clad in a papier mâché HP sauce bottle. He wandered around the stage arbitrarily, leaning over at angles from which recovery should have been impossible. The rest of the cast moved smoothly aside to avoid him. It all looked quite meant if you were not the choreographer. I was, and got foolishly annoyed.

Looking back, I am annoyed in a different way, for having become obsessed with technical effects at the very moment when a new maturity of content, made possible by the waning influence of the Lord Chamberlain, was not only possible but called for. The truth was that the theatre, which I had approached, correctly, as a temple, had turned out to be, in the first instance, a box of tricks. Immediately I had become fascinated with the tricks, to the detriment of my sense of proportion. The things that could be done! Normally inhibited young people could be organized into kick-lines wearing funny hats. They could be slung on wires and flown around. They could be made to disappear through trapdoors. Things could be done with lights. Julie Covington looked so elegant singing in a spotlight that I spent hours arranging a slow fade to silhouette and forgot about the songs she was supposed to be singing. Luckily they held the audience, but she deserved better. The whole cast deserved better. I could do it now, but you can't go back into time except through memory, and even that form of transport is dangerous when the question turns on what might have been. At the time it seemed that I had nothing to reproach myself with. Quite the reverse. The show was greeted, if not hailed, as a success. Well, a half-success. It seemed to me that the Six Day War, which broke out at the same time, was a secondary occurrence. I was very pleased with myself and might have modelled my swagger on that of Moshe Dayan. Every night of the run I saw the show and gave notes, but spent little time in the day cutting or re-rehearsing. (In later years I would have rebuilt the show every afternoon until there was not a flat spot left in it.) The mysterious May Week that lasted a fortnight and took place in June was a mystery no longer. It was a time for youth to celebrate itself. I was a tiny bit past being a legitimate celebrant. That just made the feeling sweeter. While the exhausted cast slept the sleep of the just through the long morning, I would walk the gravelled paths of the backs, clutching the jewel of Pembroke's library, Aubrey Attwater's copy of the Leopardi edition of Petrarch. At ease on a bench, with Trinity's Wren Library in clear view and the river dotted with drifting clumps of girls, I would part the gilt-edged pages and imagine myself *Rotto dagli anni e dal cammino stanco.* Broken by the years and by the tired road. God help me, I fancied that what I had faced and conquered had been adversity, instead of just another self-set challenge, easily encompassed.

Marenko and the Americans should have been a healthy antidote. Accompanied by Girton girls who had been carefully chosen and gallantly presented with a bunch of carnations each, they loyally attended the revue but didn't pretend to be impressed by anything except the logistics of mounting such a huge venture when everyone involved was supposed to be studying. They, the Americans, were still studying every day, even though, for some of them, the last examinations were over. A sound mind needed a sound body, however, so in the afternoons they were to be found down in the meadow behind the Mill, benefitting immodestly from the sunlight. Marenko looked so magnificent with his shirt off that a Newnham girl, nowadays world famous as a romantic novelist, rode her bicycle straight into the Cam. For Marenko, exposing his torso to the sunlight was a quasi-sacred act which he called 'baking bod'. At lunch in Hall he would propose this Aztec-like ritual to the assembled company. 'Why don't we all saunter down to the Mill and bake bod?' Delmer Dynamo having copped out on the excuse that his new set of the Nonesuch Dickens needed its pages cut, we would trail down to the meadow and lie around. At one of those meetings – which would have been a bit *Kraft durch Freude* if not for the high quality of the laughter – the first Frisbee I had ever seen was produced. A large black plastic dish with its name, WHAM-O FRISBEE, applied in gold, inevitably it had been imported by Strad. It turned out, however, that all the Americans could make the thing perform. Strad could make it go about fifty yards and then hover like a black and gold halo over Marenko's head. Marenko favoured an underarm flick of the wrist which sent the enchanted disc zipping along about three inches above the ground for an improbable distance until, instead of crashing, it rose remarkably into the air, tipped to one side, and slotted into Strad's upstretched hand as if drawn there by a string. To my shame I went crazy with frustration at being unable to make the bloody thing fly straight. Moving my wrist forward as instructed, I merely delayed the disc's inexorable swing to the right. The accursed object moved to the right like Sir Oswald Mosley. It headed for the Cam like Hitler for the Rhine. Observant young ladies laughed from beneath the willows. When Marenko, like a languishing Discobolus, airily unleashed a fizzer, there were long sighs from the dappled shade. 'Blow it out your ass!' cried Delmer in the distance, appearing in slow stages from the direction of the Mill as he grappled intermittently with a prematurely opened deck-chair. Boatered, blazered and monocled, he sat in full Wodehousian splendour, sending up puffs of smoke from his cigar while his pipe-clayed white shoes acquired grass stains that looked as if they had been brushed on by Monet. When I fluked a straight throw he applauded like a member of the MCC. 'Oh, well propelled, old fruit! Well *chucked*!' The ten-day idyll seemed to last a year. There was the Footlights tour to prepare for. The details must have taken at least a week. Probably it was less than a week, then, that I basked in that perfect light. My whole soul baked bod. At the lawn parties I basked in glory while adroitly dodging Consuela. For someone of my temperament, going over the top is a necessary step towards coming to terms. Those were the days when I gave way to the dementia of celebrity. Critics who think I am out of control now should have seen me then.

And then it was over. Though the tour was no disaster, it was no triumph either. The small-cast show with one eye on London, the kind of show I hadn't wanted, was the kind of show the provincial audiences *had* wanted. It meant nothing to them that the large-cast revue gave the less talented an equal opportunity to share the stage with the more talented. The audience wanted an unequal opportunity to laugh and admire. Sketches which had held the stage in Cambridge ran to comparative silence in Nottingham. They didn't exactly die the death, but they contributed nothing except running time. Standing in the back of the auditorium and wondering how to patch things up sufficiently well to keep the show on the road and some of the cast from suicide, I became a worried man again. At the end of the long vacation I was due to take an abridged version of the show to the Edinburgh Fringe. At that juncture I would have a chance to re-cast along less egalitarian lines. It would be an act of mercy. Performers out of their depth drown. Though they do it in air instead of water, you can see them struggle. Beginning at last to take in, at the level of experience, the lesson which I should have been able to learn at the level of theory, I packed my carry-all and headed for Venice. Françoise was studying there again and as usual she would make all the arrangements, but this time I was not entirely a free loader. In Venice there was to be a major exhibition of Canaletto, Guardi and the rest of the view painters – the *Vedutisti*. To Nicholas Tomalin I had proposed that I should cover this event in a piece for the *New Statesman*. He had agreed. It was a commission. The piece would be paid for. All I had to do was write it.

I wrote it with suspicious ease. Françoise and Venice were at their most beautiful. The wine at Trattoria al Vagon was cheap and plentiful. When I arrived at the exhibition I felt happy and confident. The paintings of Canaletto looked happy and confident. The paintings of his nephew, Bellotto, looked less happy and less confident. Canaletto was light blue but Bellotto was dark green. Guardi was dark blue with too much pink. He was neither happy nor confident, Guardi. You could tell just by looking. I am afraid that my analysis of this entire, quite important movement in Italian painting was all on an elementary, not to say infantile, level. With a set length of only fifteen hundred words in which to express my opinions, a paucity of information was an advantage. As far as I can remember – it wasn't far even at the time – I wrote the piece in a matter of hours. Looked at again today, it has a speciously authoritative bravura which I can only envy. Nowadays a piece the same length, on any subject, would take me at least a week. My brain has grown sclerotic, my wind short, and with experience I have become more fearful instead of less, but the main reason for being slower to get things done now is that I know more about them. Possessing more information than will fit easily into the space, I must sweat at the task of choosing what to leave out, and of making what I put in imply the rest. Though often accused of putting everything I have in the shop window, it is no longer among my vices. In the days when I did, I wrote like lightning. At the bar at the foot of the Rialto, Françoise read the finished piece through, suggested a few corrections, and looked, I thought, slightly ashamed, as if she had taken up with a confidence man – which, at that time, was exactly what I was. Not only was I out of my depth, I was staging an aquacade instead of calling for help. She particularly deplored, I suspect, my knack of suggesting that what I was saying was only the tenth of the iceberg that showed above the water. She was well aware that what showed was all there was: the tip of an iceberg floating on a raft. Dead on cue, seven gondolas lashed side by side emerged from under the bridge. Full of Americans, they rode low in the water while the massed gondoliers provided choral accompaniment to a plump middle-aged tenor who stood in the prow of the central gondola facing backwards. His mouth opening wide enough to swallow a melon, he uncoiled the high wailing melodic line of a love song. He was a professional and so was I. You have to start somewhere, and you can't do so without taking the risk that you might one day end up somewhere else than the place you hoped to reach. A scholar takes a job. A writer takes a chance. Carefully I explained this to Françoise over several carafes of wine paid for by her. Arriving at the post office, where with her help I planned to send the piece off to London by registered mail, I was feeling pretty dauntless. During the long process of acquiring the right stamps, stickers, sealing wax and bits of string I gradually sobered up, until by the time the parcel was ready for acceptance I had qualms. What if it got rejected? Why, indeed, should it be accepted? Three days ago I had scarcely known the *Vedutisti* from the Watusi, Canaletto from a can-opener, Guardi from a mudguard. All I had ever done was look at the pictures. That, basically, Françoise assured me, was all that anyone had ever done. She was a model of strength as I sat there sobbing. The Italian post offices were temples of bureaucracy in those days, sufficient all by themselves to cause a breakdown in civil order. Constantly mutating meaningless regulations ensured that your parcel, when you finally got to the head of the queue, would never be accepted the first, second or third time. Even when you had the right gauge of brown paper, thickness of string and redness of sealing wax, unless you timed your run for the end of the day they would have introduced some new rule about writing the address four times or tying the thing up with a pink ribbon. Coping, Françoise grew cooler as I grew angrier. Finally, when I was down on the floor on my knees, pounding my fist into the tiles, she was smiling seraphically at some official in a cap. He was the one who said there was no problem; of course we shall accept your parcel; he couldn't understand how the difficulty had arisen; was the *signorina*'s friend perhaps the victim of some unfortunate mental disease?

In debt to my college and with a long, long vacation ahead before the next grant cheque came through, I was dependent on Françoise for the necessities of life. This drain on her resources left nothing over for travel, so we were obliged to hitch-hike. In her two-piece raw silk suit and high heeled sandals, Françoise must have been the best dressed hitch-hiker since Lola Montes. On the approach roads to the autostrada, Italian male drivers of expensive sports cars were eager to break the law and stop, especially if they thought she was alone. I encouraged this misapprehension by hiding myself behind a bush. If there was no bush available I would conceal myself in the nearest depression, feeling pretty depressed myself. In shallow holes lined with dried mud I would cower cursing. When I heard the shriek of brakes I would dustily emerge and shamble forward. Some of the drivers looked a bit pissed off but very few of them tried to cancel the deal. A guy with an Alfa Romeo Giulia *ti* got us to Bologna in no time. The next bit was the hard part. The recently completed stretch of autostrada down from Bologna through the mountains towards Florence had instantly established itself as one of the most frightening experiences in modern Europe. There were three lanes each way. None of them was a slow lane. Articulated trucks with two trailers in tandem swung out from lane to lane without warning just as you were trying to overtake them. The chance of getting cut in half was very high, even if you had a great big car with plenty of hot lights to flash in the mirrors of the trucks. The car that picked us up was a little Fiat Berlinetta whose driver thought he was Eugenio Castellotti, the late lamented Mille Miglia ace revered in Italy for the flair he had shown in driving at 150 miles per hour on the footpath when the road was full of spectators. When a truck pulled out, our boy would try to duck inside, ignoring the possibility that the truck might try to go back to where it had come from, thereby crushing us against the wall of a tunnel or propelling us a thousand feet down into a rocky gorge. All this was happening at about ninety. The hard shoulders of the road were littered with wrecks. Particularly affecting was a Lancia saloon divided into two widely separated pieces. Françoise had insisted on climbing into the back seat with me. Our driver kept turning around to compliment her on the perfection of her Italian and insert his nose into her cleavage. Meanwhile I attempted to draw his attention to the imminent death looming in front. It was a nice exercise in relative time. We got to Florence in a few hours, having aged ten years.

This time Florence was only a staging post. After a night at the Antica Cervia I humped our two bags out to the autostrada and we hitched south to Rome. The driver was a gentleman who had a kind word for my Italian as well as Françoise's. That did me the world of good. I forget what make the car was, but in a quiet way of business it was a road-eater. It wasn't an Alfa or I would have remembered. Though the Alfas were fast, they floated sideways on their suspension and had to be steered all the time. This car ran like a train. Probably it was the big Fiat, the one with four headlights. The driver was stopping in Arezzo for a couple of hours. He offered to take us on if we cared to wait. We visited the Piero della Francesca frescoes. I'm glad I saw them then. Later on they were overcleaned and almost ruined. At that time they were as much as I could take in at one sitting – or, rather, standing. I just stood there, with that unmistakable feeling of being returned to the source, of starting again. A clear outline filled in with colour will always be my ideal. Admiring the cinquecento for its intellectual daring, nevertheless I am a quattro-cento man at heart. I like that odour of the workshop; of wood shavings and glue. Behind it, of course, is the odour of the classroom; of paint on the finger. I remembered how I had once decorated the margins of my schoolbooks, and wondered if, had I been born four hundred years earlier, I would have decorated churches. It would have been a perfectly satisfactory occupation, apart from the occasional heresy hunt and visitation of plague.

Rome hove into view and there was a whole new Renaissance to contend with. This was where even the Florentines came to make it big. The Vatican was their Hollywood. All the paintings were in wide-screen processes. There was nothing smaller than Cinemascope. The candle smoke of centuries having not yet been expunged from the Sistine ceiling, it was up there like a brown cloud, but what you saw stirring in the murk was enough to keep you going, and Christ came hulking out of the Last Judgment like a line-backer unexpectedly carrying the ball. With Françoise's help I was picking my way through Michelangelo's sonnets. I had all the makings of a Michelangelo bore. It was Raphael, however, who did the permanent damage. By being so much more transparent than his paintings in oils, the wide-screen frescoes in the 'Stanze' convinced me that there is a desirable lightness in art which must be planned for so that it is not perfected away: refinement, beyond a certain point, kills itself. That, or something like that, I wrote in my ever-ready journal. Somewhere off the Via del Corso, Françoise had found a room which had once been the bottom half of another room twice as high. Using that as a base, we went out on art orgies. We had a Bernini binge. I fell for him where Daphne flees from Apollo, in the Galleria Borghese. Until then I had been under the impression that I hated the Baroque. By the time we were relaxing over an iced coffee at an open-air café in the Piazza Navona, I was Baroque-berserk. The horse's head in the central fountain I thought the wittiest thing I had ever seen: light, fluent, poised, graceful, alert with the accepted tragedy of passing things. Anticipating the rejection of my piece about the Venetians, I was

planning a second assault on the *New Statesman* by way of an uncom-
missioned Italian diary. I had already done a short piece about the
autostrada down from Bologna. Now I added a thing or two about
Bernini. This time I made strategic use of a semblance of honesty,
admitting that I hadn't thought much of him before. (The admission
that I hadn't known much of him before might have unsettled the
reader.) This affectation of candour struck me as quite touching. It
reminded me of a poignant moment, much earlier in my career,
when I had shyly put my hand up to confess that it was I who had
broken wind. At that stage in Italy's continuing history of inflation,
coins of small denomination were made of an alloy so light that they
almost floated. When we threw our coins into the Trevi fountain
they took a long time to flutter to the bottom. I wrote a poem
about it. Françoise couldn't complain that I wasn't responding to the
country she loved. I responded to everything about it, with an intensity that left Shelley himself sounding as if he had gone to Disneyland
instead. What she *might* legitimately have complained about was that
the huge two-volume American biography of Shelley which I had
humped all the way down there with me remained unopened. I
had my answer ready. To know how Shelley had been overwhelmed,
I had to be overwhelmed. Why don't we ask the waiter to just leave
the whole bottle of Cinzano here?

After Rome it was Naples, where we set a new all-comers record
for not getting robbed. We had nothing to steal so it was easy. Had
we possessed anything more valuable than my two-volume biography
of Shelley it would undoubtedly have been whipped. This was the
town in which, after the Italian surrender but before the end of
the war, a fully laden Liberty ship had been stolen, and the skills
learned then had been inherited as an art. In a sensationally hot late
morning we were sitting at an open air table in front of a café. The
open air tables were divided from the street by a line of bushes in
concrete tubs. Françoise, whose task in Naples was to visit the
museum that had been made of Croce's house, was mugging up on
the catalogue. I was busy trying to unknot the syntax of a Michelangelo sonnet. Neither of us was especially delighted when we were
joined unasked by Brian C. Adams and his newly acquired wife. They
had driven down all the way from Cambridge in order to break into
our idyll. What they didn't realize, as they sat there, was that the
Neapolitans were breaking into their car. It was parked in plain sight

of us all, about ten yards away on the other side of the bushes. All we could see, though, was the top half of the car, which proved not to be enough. Our visitors having turned out to be unexpectedly charming in this alien context, they left us with a cheery wave which was shortly succeeded by a squeal from her and a low, unbelieving moan from him. It could be deduced that the thieves must have crawled along the side of the car, forced the lock, and hooked out the cameras, wallets and passports. Harder to figure out was how they had removed all four of the car's wheels without making any noise. The car was supported on neat piles of bricks, like an art exhibit. Françoise was at her most diplomatic talking to the *Polizia Stradale*. Gallant in their blue jodhpur suits and white Sam Browne belts, they were clearly prepared to give our friends a motorcycle escort in any direction, as long as Françoise came too. Alas, there could be no question of restitution for lost property. Yes, they realized that to the outside observer it might seem remarkable how such a thing could occur in full view of everyone in the street, including the traffic policeman. That sort of thing happened. They forgot to add that in Naples it happened every ten minutes, and had been happening since the famous day in 1943 when the American ship went missing from the harbour. Having returned to our table while these fruitless negotiations went on, I was writing in my notebook. My *New Statesman* Italian diary had acquired another episode.

Relishing the freedom of the unencumbered, after a ritual visit to Pompeii – the heat was so great that I felt I had once shared in its demise – we hitched all the way back up the boot to Florence, where we paused to count our money and lick our wounds. All of the former had belonged to Françoise and was now gone. All of the latter belonged to me. She still looked like a *haute couture* mannequin. I was showing the effects of several weeks of diving into ditches every time we heard a powerful car in the distance. When we checked into the Antica Cervia I was ready to quit.

The staff of life was waiting for me. Tightly rolled up in plain brown paper, like the baton of a Field Marshal in a people's army, were two copies of the *New Statesman* featuring my article on the Venetian view painters. It was the leading piece in the arts section at the back of the magazine. It covered one and a half pages. My name was in the contributors' list on the front cover. I drew Françoise's attention to these points before settling down to read the piece several hundred times. Even then, in the middle of being carried away, I reminded myself of myself: of how, when my first short book review had come out in the *Sydney Morning Herald*, I had bought ten copies of the paper so that there would be one left over for posterity if I were to suffer nine fatal accidents. Before that, there had been my first poem in *honi soit*; and before that, the first thing I ever published – a contribution to the Sydney Technical High School *Journal* which I had based loosely on a piece in an old war-time issue of *Lilliput*, borrowing only the plot, the names of the characters, the descriptive prose and the dialogue. If, in later years, I had become more capable of making up my own words, I had become no more capable of staying calm when I saw them in print. Debarred by nature from becoming blasé, the best I could manage was an affected air of detachment, and even that fell apart at a moment like this, when an important new step had been taken. I saw, stretching ahead, the dazzling prospect of a professional career as a freelance journalist. After telling Françoise all about it until she fell asleep, I sat up all night completing my Italian diary piece in long-hand. Next morning I mailed it to the *New Statesman*. A whole issue would have to go by without me in it, but there was just a chance that I might catch the one after that.

The article safely on its way to London by plane, I followed it by road. Françoise was due to live in Cambridge during the next academic year, as a don in New Hall. This was a major development which would entail, on my part, some large-scale personal stock-taking. For now, until term started, she would be staying in Florence. I, on the other hand, had to get back to London to earn a much-needed week's wages on *Expresso Drongo* before I went back up to Cambridge to begin rehearsing the Footlights late-night revue for the Edinburgh Fringe. Richard Harris, known as the other Richard Harris to distinguish him from the then up-and-coming film star, was an architecture student and Footlights actor-singer who was heading home from Florence at that very time so as to submit himself to my dictatorial discipline. He had a large heart to go with his small car – a glorified Mini that had a vertical radiator grille effect stuck on the front so it could be called a Wolseley. With him and his stuff in the car there wasn't really any room for me and mine, but I soon talked him out of any qualms. After two solid days of filling in forms at the bank, the *New Statesman* cheque had been turned into Italian money. All of this I gave to Françoise as part payment of my debt, before borrowing it all back again to pay for my share of the petrol. I also generously offered to navigate. What I couldn't do was share the driving, because I had never learned to drive. This fact became especially regrettable by the time we were winding up towards Bologna through the same hideous stretch of autostrada on which Françoise and I had already faced death coming down the other way. It was getting dark and Richard was tired. When it became evident that we would soon be cut in half by a road train if we kept on, he pulled into a lay-by and we sacked out in the open. If this sounds only mildly adventurous, it is because I have not sufficiently evoked the scene. There was only just enough flat ground to sleep on. A cliff led down to a tumbling river far below. The edge of the cliff had been inaccurately used as a latrine by many a desperate driver. Avoiding all that, we were obliged to lay down our heads within a few feet of the hard shoulder. The wheels of the passing trucks were near enough for us to hear them fizz angrily over the roar of the diesels. On the crappy edge of the precipice, with our naked heads presented towards the sizzling wheels of the juggernauts, we stared straight up and pretended to sleep under the stars, or under where the stars had been before the clouds had covered them. When rain started falling out of the clouds, we retired to the car and tried to sleep sitting up. The result next morning was that we couldn't stand.

Things got better during the day. We stopped in Geneva and I took a dip in the lake, defying a sign that said it was forbidden. I drew a small crowd of curious people. Richard was curious about their curiosity and asked them why they found me so fascinating. A small girl with pigtails and steel-rimmed glasses said that the last man who had gone swimming in the lake was already dying when he climbed out. His skin had turned bright pink, she said, with blisters that dripped pus. Apparently the lake was so polluted that there were no bacteria left in it. Nothing was alive in there. Apart from the fact that she said all this in French, she looked and sounded exactly like one of those terrible girls in Hitchcock movies who point out unpleasant truths. Until we lunched next day in Besançon, I spent the whole time taking my pulse and checking the colour of my tongue in the rear-view mirror. The restaurant wouldn't serve us a half carafe of wine, so I had to drink a whole carafe, because my companion was driving. I felt better after that, and slept most of the way to the Channel ferry. On the ferry I once again had two shares of drinking to cope with. The next thing I saw was London. Either we had got there in twenty minutes at an average speed of 600mph, or else I had slept the hard-earned sleep of the navigator. Young Richard showed scarcely a sign of his ordeal. Already a gap was showing up between me and those only a few years younger. There were physical things they could do that I couldn't. For instance, some of them, after having had a certain amount to drink, could walk quite a long way before bumping into a wall. I couldn't. Something would have to be done about that sooner or later. Perhaps I could get the walls moved further away.

15. HIT OF THE FRINGE

In the week before rehearsals for the Edinburgh Fringe began, I was scheduled to work, for the usual small but significant financial reward, as Dave Dalziel's assistant in the Sisyphean task of keeping Keith Visconti's film from being cancelled. I needed the cash. The *New Statesman* printed my Italian diary, but the cheque vanished into a party. *Expresso Drongo* was now well into its second year of shooting. On behalf of its director, Dalziel had applied for yet another extension to the original grant so that the film's budget could be expanded to meet its burgeoning projected costs. In Hollywood terms, the overruns had taken off. As head of the production board's operational unit, Dalziel had a persuasive voice in the allocation of funds, but finally it was the board that decided. As chairman of the board, Sir Michael Balcon told Dalziel, in the friendliest possible way, that the film had better enter its post-production phase fairly soon, or else it would have to be shut down – and, by implication, Dave's office along with it. Dalziel, in his capacity as Balcon's protégé, felt a crushing sense of obligation on top of his already burdensome professional commitment to finishing what he had started. He was a worried man. At work he maintained his usual cool air. At home he would stare into space. This was made hard to do by the continuing presence of half a dozen Nigerian ex-government officials in exile, but he managed it. In these worrying times for him and Cathleen, I think I helped by eating any scraps of food that might otherwise have been left lying around. My old friend Robin having unaccountably declined to take me in, I was sleeping in the Dalziels' loft. It wasn't a very big loft but my needs were simple. Cathleen was probably more pleased than she looked when I sat up drinking with her husband late at night. It could have made all the difference to his morale. He was a man under threat. He needed someone to confide in. The main thing he had to confide was his dawning suspicion that Keith Visconti was insane. 'He's a few bricks short of a load,' said Dalziel abstractedly. It was the first time I had heard this expression, which now appears in dictionaries of Australian slang. Either Dalziel made it up, or he got it from Bruce Jennings, and he made it up. From his suite at Claridge's, Jennings would arrive by Rolls-Royce to help soothe Dalziel's anguish with a jeroboam of Krug. They would spark each other off. I was content to be an auditor. 'Of course you could always have Keith *killed*,' Jennings would suggest. 'The problem would be disposing of the body. Physical contact *not* advisable.'

In consequence of all the dire warnings, a new urgency could be felt on the set of *Expresso Drongo*. A tricky scene was being shot in which Nelia, in the role of the woman seated at the table in the coffee shop, rises from the table and crosses to the window in order to check up on whether another woman, perceived in the distance, is the Other Woman. In the finished film Nelia would be playing the role of the Other Woman as well. For now, she was still the woman at the table. So that Nelia might adopt the right eyeline when she reached the window, I filled in for the Other Woman. Keith Visconti made me stand the right distance away and then rehearsed Nelia in the tricky transition from the table to the window. The camera would be tracking with her, which involved all sorts of problems in focusing and lighting. Just solving these would have been finicky enough. Keith made things more complicated by deciding that Nelia's eyeline was not at the right height. I was a touch too tall. After Keith called 'Action!' I would have to crouch slowly so that Nelia would be looking at the right place. The first time I crouched too late, so that Nelia's eyes slipped downward. The second time I crouched too far, so that it seemed as if she were looking, Keith said, at a dog. The twelfth time Nelia and I both got it right but a lamp blew out. It went on like that for days, with Keith always finding another reason for calling 'cut'. Dalziel spent a lot of time with one hand over his eyes. Nelia wasn't bothered. Her capacity for not being bothered, I had by now decided, had less to do with inner serenity than I had once thought. Nor could it be put down to avarice. Although it was true that as long as filming lasted she had employment, what really enabled Nelia to retain her equanimity in conditions of stress was her almost complete lack of a brain. Either that organ had been surgically removed, or it had been cut off from all information. She was a monster. By the third day – the big day when I, doubling for the Other Woman, had to turn and walk away – I could feel Nelia's eyes on my spine as if they belonged to Catherine Deneuve in Polanski's *Repulsion*, currently packing them in at the Academy. Dalziel still strove to convince himself that *Expresso Drongo*, if it ever got finished, would have the same effect. He was whistling in the dark. You could tell he knew it. Deep down, where it counted, he was on the rack.

Dalziel would take Keith aside for urgent talks but found it hard to shout into his face. Keith had still not taken a bath. He was even less nice to be near than he had been a year before. 'You can't stand over that guy without a ladder,' said Dalziel. 'And his breath! It smells like a dead bear's bum.' We were sitting in the Jaguar, which had been taking us back to Brixton until something went wrong again in the transmission. Waiting for the RAC man in the middle of Knightsbridge, we watched the girls go by, or rather I did. Dalziel, the married man, had either lost something of his former keen interest or thought fit to conceal it. Perhaps already feeling the weight of gravity myself, I found a certain melancholy invading my fond regard, like smoke drifting into a beam of light. The female figure was at its slightest since the 1920s. Some of the girls had white lips to match their high lacquered boots. Hairstyles were like tight black helmets. A challenging length of leg still showed between boot-tops and mini hemlines, but otherwise the feminine element had become hard to find. On the most obviously fashionable women, creations carried out in Piet Mondriaan plastic had been imposed, drawing their bodies up into an unyielding grid. The sense of confinement was palpable, or would have been if you were allowed to touch it. These flattenings and polishings, this kit of structures, made beauty less unbearable to look at, but to be thus rescued from the desperation of longing was to be made lingeringly sad.

Girls in uniform. There was a regimentation to this vaunted spontaneity which made 'trend' a more descriptive word than it was meant to be: a viscous, inexorable flow in one direction. The generic word 'pop' made me feel old before my time. It sounded like the unavoidable fate of a bubble. But still there, at the centre of the largely manufactured pop era, was popular music, and that was too abundant to stifle, too witty to ignore. With doom staring him in the face, Dalziel threw a tumultuous Thursday night party at the house in Brixton. The Animals shouted from the loudspeakers. The Nigerians danced. All the Australian expatriates were there. Johnny Pitts, the rebel guitarist of the Downtown Push, for a moment resurrected Leadbelly from the distant past, before forgetting the words and falling sideways. Dibbs Buckley drew a mural in the loft. Bruce Jennings arrived with his next wife. He hadn't married her yet, but he was already calling her by his last wife's first name: a sure sign, with him, of impending nuptials. Dandyishly clad, in show-stopping form, he spoke as if he were still on his first drink. 'I did *indeed* peruse your *obiter dicta* on the subject of the Venetian painters, young Clive,' he pronounced with a vulpine leer, 'and I rather got the impression that you had known them *personally*. One of the two of Canaletto's working drawings are in my possession. There is a drawing of a virile head which at one time led me to suspect that the great man had spent some time in Australia. *Now*, of course, I *realize*. He caught your eyes exactly. *Not an easy task*.' In fact he was on his last legs, but there was no guessing until he fell, and the only way you could tell that he was falling was if you knew he didn't dance. He went down with arms flailing, taking his next wife with him. Since everyone else was dancing in roughly the same manner, nobody realized Jennings had fainted. His next wife, pinned under him, cried for help but was not heard. In the clear space around Keith Visconti, I danced with Nelia. I had gone off her, yet there was no denying her gentle beauty, so spiritual-looking if you did not know her. She smiled at me fixedly, no doubt thinking of John Newcombe.

Next afternoon at the NFT there was a BFI production board screening for the board members and journalists. This was an important day in the career of Dave Dalziel. All the short films on which he had given technical advice, and for which the BFI had provided the facilities, were to be screened one after the other in a programme which he had carefully planned so that a finished fifteen minutes of the Keith Visconti film would be next to last, as a quiet interlude before the final, powerfully rhythmic *San Francisco*, a ten-minute documentary montage to the music of an unknown pop group strangely calling itself Pink Floyd. In the crucial spot just before *Expresso Drongo*, Dalziel had carefully placed a short puzzle picture which would ensure that a simple story of a waiter bringing a woman a cup of coffee would come as a welcome relief. The puzzle picture had been directed by the well-known experimental writer J. D. Sullivan, who committed suicide a few years later, some said because of too much competition from other experimental writers. At the time we are talking about, J. D. Sullivan still had the only game in town. His Arts Council grant for experimental writing had been renewed year after year while he turned out a succession of defiantly unreadable experimental books. Years before John Fowles ever thought of it, J. D. Sullivan had written a novel with alternative endings. He had also written a novel whose chapters came loosely arranged in a box, so that you could rearrange them in any order you pleased, or, some cynics had suggested, so that you could throw away the ones you didn't like. He had published a novel with a hole through the middle so that you could read the last page while you were reading the first. There was nothing experimental that J. D. Sullivan had not done as a writer. Now he wanted to be an experimental film-maker. I had been in on the meeting at which he had first expounded the idea of his film to Dalziel. It had taken place in a Japanese restaurant in Soho. Sullivan, a big man with a bull neck, had explained why Shakespeare was really no good as a playwright. 'People don't talk like that, do they?' he had asked, stabbing a piece of raw fish with his chopstick. '*Do* they?' he had asked again, looking at me. I had had to admit that they didn't. J. D. Sullivan was well organized. Everything Dave taught him, he learned immediately. The film got made. A heavily compact assemblage of cross-cut imagery, so intricately elliptical that it made your brain ache like a sore foot, it had authority: it looked *meant* in its meaninglessness. You could tell, when the screen filled with rotting flesh, that bourgeois society was being somehow criticized. When a building collapsed, it was a fair inference that a rotten social system had been rumbled. J. D. Sullivan's film was a testament. It was dissatisfied. It made *you* dissatisfied. Above all, it made you dissatisfied that it went on so long. Though short, it lasted for ever. Even *Expresso Drongo* would seem sprightly by comparison. A nice sweet dose of Nelia's impassive face would be just what the doctor ordered.

At the screening, J. D. Sullivan's film was barely half over before it became obvious that the packed audience was inwardly begging for relief. They were squirming under the impact of J. D. Sullivan's pitiless symbolism. 'We'll be starting with the shot where Nelia's sitting there with her legs crossed and her mouth slightly open in anticipation,' whispered Dalziel loudly. 'She looks like she's thinking about the pork sword. Ought to go down well.' A female journalist seated in front of us turned round in what I guessed was outrage. Dalziel didn't notice. He was a tense man. A lot depended on the extract from *Expresso Drongo* being well enough received to warrant further financing. Otherwise the single most expensive project the BFI had ever backed would be remembered only as a dead albatross slung around Dalziel's neck. There was cause for hope, however, as the end titles of J. D. Sullivan's film came up, superimposed over a close-up of a calf being born. Polite applause from the audience was punctuated by the occasional muffled cry of 'Thank God'.

For the lovely face of Nelia, that mystery so haunting until solved, a place had thus been prepared, in the audience's collective mind, as yearningly welcoming as the wall of a monk's cell primed with fresh plaster so that Fra Angelico might draw an angel. What we saw next, however, were the words A MAN ALONE, *un film de* Alain le Sands. Dalziel's seat snapped back. He would have been off and running to the projection box if I hadn't stopped him. Caution was the right reaction. If Dalziel had reached the projection box he would have strangled Alain le Sands and thus attained the wrong kind of fame, as a murderer, although it would have been the right thing to do. Alain le Sands was in there, of course. Craning back awkwardly over our shoulders, we could see his wildly grinning face looking out through one of the observation ports. What we suspected at the time later proved to be untrue: le Sands had not held a gun to the projectionist's head. Le Sands had merely turned up during the screening with his can of film under his arm and convinced the projectionist that there had been a last minute addition to the schedule. The projectionist, like many in his trade, had been too blind to notice that le Sands had the eyes and teeth of a fanatic. *A Man Alone* unspooled its familiar, incompetently captured obsessions. It turned out, though, that le Sands had acquired a hitherto unprecedented sense of proportion. His film was no longer a fragment of a feature. It was now a complete short film, with an ending to go after its beginning. There was a last scene. It was set in Soho. There was a doorway. From it emerged Dave Dalziel and myself. A rear view of Alain le Sands lurched towards us. His dialogue was roughly as it had been on the day, but new words had been dubbed over Dalziel's moving mouth. 'Your film is too challenging, Mr le Sands,' Dalziel seemed to say, 'too dangerous to our establishment values. It must be suppressed.' We got into the car and sat there while Alain le

Sands lectured us through the windshield. A shot from another angle, obviously secured at another time and with a different car, enabled the lecture to last longer. 'The true creator thrives on frustration,' orated le Sands. 'You and your cohorts can no more stop this new upsurge of . . . than . . . thus . . .'

Surprisingly few among the audience laughed aloud while *A Man Alone* was on the screen, but everyone was well prepared to pick nits by the time the extract from *Expresso Drongo* came on. The effect was not as planned. Though Nelia looked suitably serene, gratitude for tranquillity was not the prevailing emotion. There was widespread, vocal disbelief at how long it took to be served a cup of coffee. The exquisite touch of the shooting and editing provoked no applause. *San Francisco* saved the day for the screening as a whole, but *Expresso Drongo*, one felt, had run out of its borrowed time. As the crowd dispersed, Dalziel received many congratulations from board members and critics. There was no word of praise for Keith Visconti. Even Alain le Sands was held to have more talent. 'You're on to something with le Sands,' said one film critic from behind the dark glasses he was famous for never taking off. 'I like the way his camera work always *declares* itself. Like to do a piece on him. Give you a bell.' Dalziel nodded glumly. 'That coffee commercial,' said Sir Michael Balcon, 'is the only really big mistake you've made, David.' Dalziel was downcast. As always there was his lovely car to distract him. This time the Jaguar started at the first turn of the key. We had almost reached home before the engine fell out on to the road. Not even the sudden, total loss of power and the shriek of scraping metal from under the car made it easy to believe, so we got out to check up. This was lucky, because the fire started with a thump. A puff-ball of flame filled the front seats where we would have been sitting. 'The guy who sold it to me had great timing,' said Dalziel thoughtfully. 'I only just finished paying for it.' A woman in a nearby house had already rung the police. She came running out with a bucket of water. Dalziel waved her back, telling her it would only help the burning oil to spread. Watching his strength in adversity, I wondered if I had what it took to succeed in the theatre. For a writer to stay true to his gift, provided he has one, is not as hard as writers are fond of making out. To keep going in any of the collaborating arts requires steadfastness. Misfortunes sooner or later must occur. I caught the train back to Cambridge in a pensive mood.

Luckily, when I got there, the task of putting the Edinburgh Fringe Footlights revue together was so pressing that there was not time to brood. Compressing the two-hour May Week spectacular into a one-hour intimate late-night revue, I had every excuse to trim the cast. I might have done this more gracefully, but to lighten the ship was certainly the right approach. As I remember it, the number of on-stage participants went down from about sixty to about six. New opening and closing numbers were written. The Fantastograd Russian Dance Ensemble number was cut in half, making it twice as funny. Julie Covington was unavailable for Edinburgh that year, but Homerton had produced yet another lovely singer called Maggie Henderson, and she was enrolled to sing the two best of the spotlight songs which Pete Atkin and I were continuing to turn out with a great show of dedication on my part, and real dedication on his. Actually, when I look back on it, I realize that I was then understating, rather than overstating, the amount of work we were all putting into every number. I got very little sleep. There was no need, although I behaved as if there were, to purse my lips and make tired noises. My tired eyes must have conveyed the message. My wisdom teeth were the only part of my body that physically collapsed. They started to ache and there was no time to fix them. Finally, in the Footlights clubroom, with the whole cast singing and dancing its way through the intricacies of the closing number, the moment came when I had to go to hospital or pass out with pain. The orthodontist at Addenbrooke's hospital looked into my mouth and said, 'How long is it since you've seen a dentist?' I told him. He nodded. 'We'll get the wisdom teeth out straight away. They're all impacted. But you've got plenty of other things wrong that you'd better have seen to fairly soon. Fact is, it's a while since I've seen anything like this. I'd like to get some photographs of your mouth for a paper I'm doing. With your permission of course.' I signalled my compliance, unable to speak because by that time he had my mouth propped open with a metal jack. The wisdom teeth were cut out under general anaesthetic and I was back at work next day with enough stitches in my rear gums to make it feel as if I were halfway through swallowing a rattan mat. On a diet of antibiotics, Dexedrine and creamed potatoes, I finished rehearsals and we headed north in a fleet of cars. Once again I was Richard Harris's passenger. While he drove all the way to Edinburgh I sat hanging in my seat belt, delirious. In a day made dark by rain, huge illuminated signs said THE NORTH. I dreamed my primal dream of inadequacy, the one in which I am trapped with no pants on up a tree in a playground of the girls' high school. They pretend not to notice me. Many hundreds of times I have woken up sweating from this dream, without ever being able to decide which kind of fear it is meant to embody, the fear of being humiliated or the fear of being ignored.

In Edinburgh the latter fear receded, temporarily if not permanently. The Footlights late night revue was the hit show of the Fringe. This was not as remarkable an occurrence as I was later able to make it sound. There were hundreds of events on the Fringe. Most of them were starting from zero and not likely to get even as far as square one. The universities were able to mount a concerted effort, and of the universities Cambridge was the one with the glowing theatrical tradition, so the audience came anyway. And of the various plays and shows put on by Cambridge, the Footlights was the one with the internationally resonant name. The theatrical correspondent of *Die Zeit* had us on his must-see list. In Lauriston Hall, the best venue on the Fringe, we were the last show of the night for an audience that had spent the early evening being less than thrilled by the official production of *The Rake's Progress* in the Assembly Hall. Sold out for every night of the run before we even opened, we couldn't lose. It is nice to be able to report in all objectivity, however, that the show was pretty good. If it was running tonight and had my name in the programme, I would still be proud of its precision, energy and sheer glamour, although some of the material would look more out of date than the flared trousers, zipped boots and velvet jackets that adorned the male members of the cast. Most of these items of clothing have since come back into fashion, if only as parody. Much of the apolitical, would-be surrealist verbal humour, however, would now seem irredeemably passé. Striving to separate itself from previously successful styles, it sounded like all of them without attaining any lasting originality. In the technical sense, it was reactionary. The writing was attempting *not* to do things – always a choking brief. It was trying not to sound like the Goons, like *Beyond the Fringe*, like *Cambridge Circus*, like ten other things. Almost the only area left open was television parody.

My own best monologue, delivered by Jonathan James-Moore far more funnily than I could have done, was a lampoon of one of

those BBC winter sports commentators who wore white sweaters
and beanies and told you nothing useful. (Nowadays they wear
parti-coloured Goretex anoraks and tell you nothing useful: they
have gone down-market without uprating the info.) This was my
first fully effective monologue from end to end. I had kept cutting it
and sharpening it up until there wasn't a line in it that didn't work.
Having a thousand people a night laughing as one at every gag was
a great pleasure, and the editorial rigour I developed in this way
was to stand me in good stead in future years. If I hadn't written
those monologues, and especially that one, I would never have known
how to write a thousand-word column with a cumulative effect. But
when you took the thing apart, it was standard stuff. I was merely
doing a more refined version of what I had been doing since I was
in high school – raising a laugh by guying some recognizable, self-
revealing speech mannerisms on the part of the prominent. My winter
sports commentator, Alexander Palace, patronized foreign competi-
tors while confidently predicting success for the British ones. Everyone
knew that this was what BBC sports commentators did, so there was
a yelp of recognition when a fictitious BBC sports commentator
stood there doing nothing else. To this day, the laugh of recognition
remains the one I seek. It comes from values communally shared. At
its best, that kind of humour can push back a barrier, by articulating
what is already suspected but nobody has yet dared to say. At its
worst, it is complacent. At the time we are talking about, I was more
comfortable than courageous.

In retrospect the discrepancy between what was going on in the
world, and what I was prepared to say about it, seems glaring – at
least to me, the only person really interested. Then, however, I struck
myself as adventurous enough in what I wrote, and for stagecraft
I was ready to take any kudos going. After the evening performance
of *Love's Labour's Lost* there was only thirty minutes to erect the
Footlights set, so it had to be simple. I made a virtue of this, personally designing a three-piece hardboard screen like a triptych,
with a doorway in each of the side panels. The screen was painted
white and covered in learned graffiti done by me and Atkin with
black and red felt-tip pens. Slogans like IT DON'T MEAN A THING IF
IT AIN'T GOT THAT SWING (Duke Ellington) and MEREDITH IS A SORT
OF PROSE BROWNING, AND SO IS BROWNING (Oscar Wilde) proclaimed
our ideals of catholicity without eclecticism, a universal intensity of

effect, etc. Lit brilliantly by the Fresnel spotlights on the gantries, the screen looked like the wall of a loft that had been inhabited by all the students in history. In its disfavour it could be said that it was exactly the appropriate setting for a clever-dick undergraduate revue, but it had a conspicuous virtue. The next act could be prepared behind it and come on in the dark through one door before the previous act had finished going off through the other door, so there was no gap between numbers. This gave an exhilarating effect of speed. The jazz band led by Robert Orledge could be positioned conspicuously in front of the screen and still leave plenty of acting area down-stage. To isolate a monologuist or singer, all we had to do was switch off the spots and floods of the general lighting and switch on one of the two limes positioned high in the gallery at the back of the hall. Picked out in the soft circle of a lime, Maggie Henderson sang a song by Atkin and myself called 'If I Had My Time Again' to such effect that Harold Hobson, the *Sunday Times* critic, made public love to her in his column. I was proud, no doubt too proud, of the precision of all these effects. Nothing was allowed to go wrong. It turned out that Jonathan James-Moore, after he had finished his winter sports monologue, had trouble getting off the stage in the dark. His spectacles didn't work without a modicum of light. On the first night, he groped his way into the drum-kit, turned around, and groped his way off the front edge of the stage, which was about four feet from the floor. He fell into the front row and sat there between two members of the audience for the whole of the next number. They were stunned, but not as stunned as he was. The risk was eliminated from the second night onwards. Someone was detailed to go out and get him and lead him off. Every move, including this, was plotted on the stage manager's chart. I monitored the show every night, ran drills each day to eliminate faults, and one way and another indulged myself in the role of overseer.

Actually all these refinements, once the aim of slick, high-speed, value-for-money, stop-for-nothing efficiency had been decided on, were matters of simple mechanical deduction. I had more right to be proud of the production numbers, in which cutting and long rehearsal had improved already successful pieces into gosh, how-did-they-do-*that*? *coups de théâtre*. Squeezed to half its original length and re-rehearsed so that every move was a gag, the Fantastograd Russian Dance Ensemble made the ideal pre-closer. Russell Davies did one of those Cossack dances performed in the sitting position, with the cocked feet kicking sideways as if at two soccer balls placed a couple of yards apart. He had never had any dance training but once he had seen or heard anything, he could copy it. When he folded his arms, squatted and kicked, the audience rose to its feet in a panic. After about a week of bringing the house down, Davies mildly complained that his feet were hurting a bit. I slapped his back with comradely understanding and discovered only several nights later, when he held up one of his boots in the dressing room and blood ran out of it, that he had been kicking his way towards hospital. His dedication to the show went beyond the heroic. Suicidal was a better word. The whole cast was motivated like fanatics.

It was my misfortune, however, not to be in the show. Having my name on it wasn't enough. Even after running drills and re-rehearsing for a couple of hours a day, I still had too much time on my hands. The Scottish National Gallery had some useful Poussins but I couldn't look at them for ever. At the Traverse I joined in discussions, usually unasked, but the Americans from the La Mama company liked their own voices too, and they had a social revolution to proclaim. I saw matinée performances by other revue groups. Some of them were rather better than I was prepared to allow: the Scaffold, for example, were on at the Traverse and performing material which must have made our stuff look class-ridden to anyone with an objective eye. But most of the revue groups, especially the ones from other universities, were just less disciplined and more thinly cast versions of ours. There was no point going on with the search. Anyone who saw everything on the Fringe would end up in a basket. So with Daryl Runswick and his band I organized a poetry-and-jazz programme for the afternoons, featuring my poetry and his jazz. It is a matter of regret among poets, however, that poetry lovers, or at any rate poetry lovers who turn up to poetry readings, are not a glamorous bunch. Everything E. M. Forster says about his fellow music lovers applies with bells on to poetry lovers. They wear person-ally-knitted beanies. They bring their own sandwiches. Intoning my translation of Montale's *The Sunflower* while the Daryl Runswick trio backed me up with dulcet riffs, I gazed out over the thinly populated hall – they all sat a long way apart, so as to facilitate concentration – and resolved to try something more ambitious next year. That I would be back next year I didn't doubt. It felt like home. Like all those who have left home, I know exactly how home feels when I find it again, wherever that might happen to be. Haunting the second-hand bookshops, swaggering along the Royal Mile, taking an ill-advised short-cut through the Grass Market late at night in the sad hour before the alcoholics so far gone that they were eating boot polish had crawled away to sleep, I treated Edinburgh as if it were at my feet. Actually I was at its. The strict romance of the city had found a suitably compliant devotee.

16. BLACK TIE, WHITE KNUCKLES

Back in Cambridge, I should have settled to my studies. It hardly needs saying that I was unable to. Instead of disappearing into the University Library I disappeared into the language laboratory. If I could have my way, I would still be down there, learning Persian by now, or perhaps Basque. The language laboratory was my bunker. In it, like Hitler in his last days, I could plot the manoeuvres of phantom armies and hide from the implications of the flashes in the distance, the trembling of the earth, the drone from overhead. Another bunker was the Copper Kettle, which at that time began rivalling the Whim as a hangout for the aesthetes. Internally, the difference between the two places was no more striking than that between, say, the Deux Magots and the Flore. Through the big front windows of the Copper Kettle, though, a diarist could look across at King's while he sucked his pen. Establishing rights to a small table by the simple expedient of piling my books on it, I sat for hours bringing my journal up to date and pursuing my brilliantly successful strategy of adding depth to my view of Shelley by reading anyone except him. Wittgenstein induced the same passion as Croce but at a different temperature. Wittgenstein was liquid helium. Saturated arguments crystallized out as aphorisms. I read him as literature: an approach which, I much later realized, is probably the correct one for anyone except the professional logician. Nowadays I can see his sentences, each resonating like a leaf of a xylophone made of ice, as part of an Austro-Hungarian imperial tradition which he fits as surely as Schnitzler or Klimt, as well as part of the larger German aphoristic treasure-house that includes Lichtenberg, Schopenhauer and Goethe himself. But if that whole expressive effort is now one of my touchstones – one of the things I would like my work to be *like* – then Wittgenstein was the way in, and still rules that long corridor by a tall, uncompromising head. It is so hard to register the thrill of discovery. You have to think yourself back to a time when part of what built you was not there. You have to unbecome yourself. This much I can say for sure, however: Wittgenstein's demonstration that the multiplicity of the self could not only be lived with, but could actually be an instrument of perception, was a revelation to me, and partly because I already knew it. The things that influence our lives don't necessarily just give us the courage of our convictions – they usually help to alter those, or at least refine them – but they do usually make us feel better about our propensities. Croce had made me feel better about being unable, or unwilling, to distinguish between high art and popular art. Wittgenstein made me feel better about being unable, or unwilling, to construct a coherent self. Intelligence had pulled him apart. In Sydney, when I was first a student, Camus had helped console me for the feeling that my life was in pieces. Everybody's life, he said in *The Rebel*, feels like that from the inside. I had acknowledged his assistance by cultivating an existentialist air of amused resignation: a set of the eyebrows which incorporated, no doubt too successfully, the concept of the Absurd. But a wish that the pieces might one day be reintegrated was hard to quell. Now here was Wittgenstein, whose personality was in a million fragments. They shone. I got his aphorisms by heart. They were a star catalogue. Croce had carried me away. Wittgenstein carried me back to myself. There must have been a self there of some kind, or I wouldn't have been able to register these comings and goings. I luxuriated, however, in the awareness of an undiscovered country in the mind. Every man his own *terra incognita*. With the slim volumes of Wittgenstein's output piled up like poetry, I sipped coffee, scattered ash, and soaked up the *Philosophische Bemerkungen* like a parallel text of the *Duino Elegies*. It was a cool love and that could be why it has lasted. Even today, in moments of depression, I still visit Trinity College Chapel and commune with his brass plaque. Now he *was* depressed, and look what *he* got done. How? Because he knew that his unhappiness was only personal.

Other bunkers were the various cinemas, at which my attendance increased, as if that were possible. The *Cambridge Review* appointed me film critic. In London, recent *cinéaste* publications such as *Movie* magazine had already imported the *Cahiers du cinéma* approach into English. In Cambridge, it was still unheard-of for anyone to take Hollywood movies as seriously as continental art films. Treating

movies and films as if they were part of the same continuity was a
kind of heresy. As always, heresy made for more sparkling copy than
orthodoxy. There was no particular posturing involved on my part.
The propensity to take popular art seriously was in me by nature.
eek by week in the *Cambridge Review* I would talk about Fellini
or W. C. Fields, Kurosawa or Don Siegel, as if they were in the
same business, which I believed they were. I explained, perhaps too
confidently, why Fritz Lang's best film was not *Metropolis* but *The
Big Heat*. I was tireless. I was tiresome. I was omniscient. I was a
pain in the arse. But my *Cambridge Review* film critic's job, though
unpaid, was invaluable practice at writing a thousand-word column
each week. Employing my Footlights monologue training, I shaped
each column as a performance, with a set up, an early pay-off, a
development section, a late pay-off and a closing number. I learned
that it wasn't necessary to cram one's whole *Weltanschauung* into this
week's piece: save some of it for next week. Above all, I learned how
to make the writing not sound like writing. If a parenthesis grew to
such a length that it would have sounded unnatural read out, I recast
it as another sentence. I tried to make every sentence linear, so that
the reader never had to look back This trick, the essence of writing
for the theatre or television, is not so necessary when writing for the
page, but readability depends on it. Well before my year as a film
critic was up, I had evidence that I was getting somewhere. Since
everyone, even the dons, went to the cinema, everyone had his own
opinion. Since everyone, even the dons, saw the *Cambridge Review*,
he wanted to discuss his opinion with me, especially if his differed.
The *Cambridge Review* had an illustrious heritage. It had prestige.
But that wasn't why I enjoyed writing for it. What I enjoyed was the
communal aspect. It was like preaching a weekly sermon and then
having to justify it to a rebellious congregation filing out of church.
There was an aspect of showmanship that suited my temperament,
and an aspect of obligation to the complexity of events which suited
the only sense of responsibility I had. Already the evidence was
accumulating that whatever I eventually wrote, I wouldn't be writing
it in an ivory tower. A circus tent would be more my pitch. So even
when I was lounging in the dark I was thinking about the hot lights.
The only reason I was hiding, I told myself, was that I was in a false
position. My ditherings were nothing to those of my nominal thesis
subject Shelley, whose two-volume biography I finally got around to

finishing, with some alarm at the erratic nature of the hero I had
chosen. Here was another lesson. Since then I have selected my role
models with more care.

In the underground maze which I mentally, and to a great extent
physically, inhabited, the connecting tunnels that led from the language laboratory to the coffee bars to the circuit of cinemas led on,
I need hardly add, to Footlights, where I would finish the day by
adding to my already monumental bar bill. With Barry Brown now
safely installed as President, I had no duties except to fill my self-
elected office as elder statesman and wise counsellor. After a special
screening of *The Bank Dick* in the clubroom I gave a detailed lecture
on the art of W. C. Fields. 'He never *led*,' I announced, as if I had
learned the lesson myself. 'He just let himself be overheard.' Ruthlessly
exploiting my friendship with Joyce Grenfell, I arranged for her to
be guest of honour at the Footlights annual dinner. The first great
lady most of the club members had ever seen in action close up, she
wowed them with her perfect manners. I was pretty proprietorial
about her afterwards. Far into the night I laid down the law about
Ealing comedy. Why had it gone so far and no further? Because
the social forces that gave it shape held it reined in. Why were the
Americans so much more penetrating? I had my theories. I
expounded them. Another round? Put it on my card.

Looking back, I can now see that I must have been a bit of an
Ancient Mariner, telling tales of old that held people riveted only
because I had them pinned against the wall. Yet some of the time I
spent haunting the place was spent well. Atkin and I seemed always
to be writing at least four songs at a time. One of the best things
about our collaboration was that I received more instruction than
I gave. Atkin's justified enthusiasm for the Beach Boys and the
Lovin' Spoonful he passed on to me. An instigator, he organized
the recording of a limited-edition disc of what we fancied to be our
best songs. The edition was limited to whoever could be persuaded
to fork out for a heavy shellac pressing in a cardboard cover. A
surprising number of people did. Atkin and Julie Covington did the
singing. I forget where the recording sessions took place, but
remember well that they didn't happen in a proper studio. The venue
must have been somebody's college rooms. I recall that a grey blanket
was hung up to make a sound booth. The sound quality was frightful.
Julie's voice came purely through the static as it would have come

purely through a war, but in all other respects the disc caused us misgivings even in our moment of creative euphoria. We distributed it with solemn warnings to ignore its limitations. This was a grave mistake. Nothing except a finished product should ever be put up for judgment. Art is a matter of deeds, not intentions. That art was what we were involved in we had no doubt, and might even have been right. The title of the disc was taken, in all solemnity, from Eliot: *While the Music Lasts*. Later there was a sequel called *The Party's Moving On*. Today, copies of both change hands at too high a price for either me or Atkin to buy them up and melt them down. Our songs always had fans. Just why the fans, over the next six or seven years of hard work, never accumulated into a listening public big enough to keep us alive, had better be the subject of another, and different kind of, book. This is a book about becoming, not being, and it is getting near the end, because by this time my extended apprenticeship was clearly in its terminal phase. If I wasn't quite ready to ply my trade, whatever that was, I certainly couldn't go on preparing for it much longer. There was a credibility problem. In London, among Nick Tomalin's hard-bitten Fleet Street friends, I was known as the world's oldest student. In Cambridge I was known as an aspiring Grub Street scrivener living cheap on college food, or a would-be theatrical assiduously preparing for his advent into the West End. These contradictory views both had something to them. I was caught in the middle.

As a Footlights sketch writer and performer I might have, and perhaps should have, gently faded away at this stage. To inspire an Indian summer of activity in this area, Tony Buffery returned from post-graduate studies in psychology at Toronto. When an under-graduate in Cambridge he had been the member of the original *Cambridge Circus* cast who had pulled out because he wanted an academic career. In his absence, many Footlights cognoscenti, Eric Idle included, had assured me that Buffery was the most inventive cabaret talent ever: not as aggressive as John Cleese, perhaps, or as intellectually wide-ranging as Jonathan Miller, but with an ear like Peter Cook and a mind from outer space. Though some of this sounded like legend-building, it is always interesting when people adverse to that activity make a common exception. When Buffery returned to Corpus Christi as a don, I was ready to find him remark-able, although I didn't expect to see much of him. After a week of the port and walnuts, however, he was up the wall, over it, and into Footlights as if he had never been away. Very tall with thick glasses and curly hair like Harold Lloyd, he was so lacking in arrogance that the young made him nervous. He couldn't have been more approachable, so I approached him. Partaking of the strong Footlights oral tradition by which fragments of sketches are passed down from one intake to the next, Idle had once told me a killing line from a Buffery sketch in which the Queen Mother, played by Buffery in a floral hat, made a speech to open a redbrick university, which was gradually revealed, as the speech proceeded, to have very little going for it. 'Plans have already been drawn up to equip the seventeen-storey science block with a lift. Or a staircase.'

'He used to take the laugh after the bit about the lift,' Idle had explained, 'and then hit them with the staircase. They were helpless.' Remembering this vivid fragment, I now asked Buffery what had come next. 'I can't remember,' he said, with a slight stutter. 'I kept changing it all the time and never wrote it down. I remember she said: "I name this library, Library." They liked that. But I never finished anything. Lacked discipline. Still do, really. Why don't we write something together?'

I had some notes for a sketch about the Olympic games in my pocket. After my tried and tested winter sports number I wasn't too keen on the idea of another monologue. Maybe it would work better as a two-hander. I read out some bits of it to Buffery, suggesting that we could share it out for two voices. 'No, you do the words,' said Buffery, with a light switching on behind his spectacles, 'and I'll be the athletes.' After a grand total of about two hours' rehearsal we tried the number out at the next Footlights smoker. From off-stage I supplied a BBC-type commentary full of the usual wretched optimism about British athletes who had no chance. Buffery kept crossing the stage in various *personae*. He was the German superman Hans-Heinz Reichstagger. He was the Russian female javelin thrower Olga Stickintinskaya. He was Tomkins, the perennial British loser with the pulled hamstring who might have done so much better. Hidden in the wings, I sometimes lost my place in the script, so entranced was I by the way Buffery became these people. Without leaving the ground, or not by much, he could mime Reichstagger doing a sixteen-foot pole vault, clicking his heels in mid-air as if he had suddenly met a superior officer. Russell Davies was still the most protean performer I had ever met, but in his case there was one dour and reticent personality holding it all together. Buffery had multiple selves. By day he was a scientist, probing the human brain to find out which sections of it did what. By night, as a performer, he was a dozen other people. He was also a married man with children. Dr Jekyll and Mr Hyde weren't in the running. Neither of them ever made anyone laugh. Buffery made people laugh until they ached. If he wanted to work with me, I would be crazy to turn the chance down.

I was also, considering my other obligations, crazy to take it up. My best excuse was that the collaboration provided a modicum of extra income. The Footlights fielded a cabaret team which would perform anywhere in Britain for a suitable fee. When half the fee was given to the club and the rest was divided amongst the participants, it was an unsuitable fee, but it helped me believe that I could earn my own living. It was more fun than supervising undergraduates in Sidney Sussex and easier on the nerves than trying to sweat a thousand words for the *New Statesman* into a gleaming block of lapidary prose – both of which things I was doing as often as I could, although without showing any signs of digging my fingers into the slipping side of the pit of debt in which I helplessly trod slime. I was still in hock to Footlights and now that I was an ex-President the Senior Treasurer tended to clear his throat significantly when we met. A don from Selwyn called Harry Porter, he was a sweet man and a great friend, but neither the university bye-laws nor his own impeccable probity allowed him to encourage the notion that a club could be a bank. My levels of expenditure effortlessly outsoared my levels of income. Even the train journey to Oxford cost money. When Françoise moved to Cambridge in order to become a don at New Hall, domesticity loomed, with all its requirements of financial equilibrium. Also there was the challenge of performing away from the home patch, where the audience would not be so indulgent.

I was right about that. At Goldsmith's College Ball in London, John Cleese, by then an ex-Cambridge professional and already well known, was the first act on. His monologue was brilliant. The huge audience, pissed and impatient to dance, barely heard him out. I watched one purple-faced student at the back of the crowd shout 'Harold Wilson!' over and over while Cleese was performing. Cleese was pretending to be a wartime air force officer in a hurry to recruit new pilots. 'Can anyone fly a B-17 [Pause] All right, can anyone fly

a B-16? [Longer pause] A B-3? [Very long pause] Can anyone *drive*?'
I was wide-eyed at the perfection of his delivery, and at his courage,
because during all the time he was at work, this florid dick-head at
the back was shouting out, 'Harold Wilson! HAROLD WILSON!' Then
a newly-formed band weirdly known as Cream came on to play a
set. I had never heard such a noise. Until then, my idea of an
electric band had been the Dave Clark Five. Cream were more like
an earthquake. Loudspeakers the size of coffins emitted sound that
compressed the air. It was a beat that hurt. Buffery and Atkin and I,
our throats dry from the impact of the tumult, retreated to our
dressing room to consult. Our dressing room was, literally, a toilet.
'We can't go on,' I shouted thinly. 'We have to,' croaked Buffery. He
was right, as usual. When we were announced, the hissing was not
universal: it came only from those who had heard the announcement.
Luckily the ginger groups in the audience found it easier to attack
each other than us. High up on the stage, we were hard to reach
except with bottles more accurately thrown than the vast majority of
those that flew towards us. Buffery's song about Richard III made a
few nice girls laugh. Riding on the shoulders of their partners, they
were within earshot. Our Olympics number, however, went for
nothing. Working on a bare stage, Buffery had no wings to disappear
into and reappear from, while I found it impossible to raise my voice
above the growing brouhaha, in which the only words that could be
heard clearly were the first and last names of the Prime Minister,
piercingly repeated like a horn motif in a Mahler symphony. We
managed to make our act look meant, though. An objective observer
would have found it impossible to tell if we were failing. Perhaps we
were succeeding at some mimed ritual.

The Footlights cabaret team was well rehearsed and usually got
away with it. Often we did better than that. Natty in our dinner
jackets, we felt pretty pleased with ourselves as we sang a planned
encore after slaying them for a solid thirty minutes. Audiences who
had once been undergraduates themselves liked us best. There could
be an awkward amount of chippy social edge if they thought we
needed reminding of our advantages in life. Facing some revelling
groups, we wondered why we had been booked. Apart from the
Goldsmith's inaudible non-event, which could largely be put down
to bad acoustics, we had but one unarguable disaster, explicable only
in terms of a mistake on somebody's part. Coming after a string of

successes, it was a failure on a scale that builds character, but while the fiasco was in progress we would have given a lot for a hole to open in the floor so that we could have disappeared into it, still waving and singing. The audience was composed of the farmers of Needham Market, a town within easy driving distance of Cambridge. We imagined the kind of prosperous farmers who drove Aston Martins and in January took their elegant wives to ski at Davos. When we came dancing into the dining room, the farmers were all sitting there as if a giftless artist had drawn them. They didn't have the word 'Farmer' written on their hats, but there was something on their shoes that looked like loam. Perhaps loam was what they had been eating. They looked glum and we did nothing to cheer them up. Buffery and I did our Olympics number to less reaction than we would have earned by slowly deflating a large rubber raft. The farmers looked resigned, as if waiting for the death of a sick cow which had never been very valuable when well. It wasn't just that they didn't laugh. They didn't smile. They hardly breathed. A carefully planned half-hour of entertainment was all over in seventeen minutes. When we went dancing off, there was a perceptible difference in the quality of the silence. Throats were being cleared in relief. As we stood white-faced outside in the foyer discussing the details of our escape, a representative of the farmers' committee joined us. 'Do you get *paid* for this sort of thing?' he asked with open scorn. 'We certainly do,' said Buffery. 'The agreed fee. And we might as well take it in cash, if you can arrange it.' I was very impressed with that. It was a good lesson all round. Jokes aren't necessarily pearls just because they fall before swine, but a deal's a deal. A performer always feels guilty when he fails. If his guilt overcomes his business sense he will quickly starve. To flop is already penalty enough. Don't punish yourself. The audience will do it for you.

17. WITH A HUMAN FACE

Winter wore on and the very idea of my PhD thesis slipped further back into the past. Spring was in the air again but my heart was heavy with undeclared anguish. Fooled by an early mild spell, the crocuses came up along the barbered edges of the backs, were duly filled with snow, survived for a few hours like candy baskets of sorbet, and so died. Reality had intruded. A similar crisis was being played out in my soul. My nagging conscience was partly stilled by Stakhanovite devotion to whatever work I was doing instead of the work I was being given a grant for. Everything the *New Statesman* asked me to do, I did, even if it was beyond me. In Prague, Dubček's life was on the line. Now was the time to come to the aid of Socialism with a Human Face. Socialism with an inhuman face had already impressed me as the salient moral fact of the twentieth century, a disaster outstripping even Nazism, which has at least worn its true colours on its sleeve. Weighed down by the evidence of history, my erstwhile radicalism had modulated into a version of social democracy which, while still hospitable to the idea of universal popular enfranchisement, was concerned about the milk being delivered on time to the doorstep. In short, I was no longer a revolutionary. No doubt the *Zeitgeist* would have been relieved to hear this news. I did my best to let it know. Nicholas Tomalin sent me books to review that were hard to make relevant to the temper of the times. I developed a technique for turning any subject into an occasion for an anti-totalitarian essay. I tried to write as if George Orwell were looking over my shoulder. When Eric Bentley's excellent short biography of George Bernard Shaw was reissued, I identified, surely correctly, Shaw's failure of imagination with regard to Stalin as clear evidence that the creative mentality should guard itself against its own inevitable pretensions to omniscience. Less correctly, and ignoring my own homily, I signed off by lamenting that Bentley, presumably through ignorance, had paid so little attention to Shaw's music criticism – a body of work with which, I made it plain, I was intimately familiar. When the piece appeared in the magazine it struck me as having the effortless *auctoritas* of holy writ. This mood was punctured when the *New Statesman* forwarded me another book by Eric Bentley, sent, not for review but for my information, by Bentley himself. It was a reprint of *Shaw on Music*, edited, with a long introduction, by Eric Bentley. He could have humiliated me much more thoroughly by writing a letter of protest to the magazine. Thankful that he had taken such a generous course, I resolved never to fudge again. The intellectual community is self-policing. Nobody who tries to pull a fast one will get away with it for long. Also the memory plays such cruel tricks that you will make enough embarrassing mistakes just writing about what you are sure of.

Shamed into flight by the unremitting uproar of Romaine Rand's supercharged typewriter, I had left the Friar's House and gone into exile in digs across the river. My new nest was a front room with a bow window on Alpha Road. The light bulb had a shade. There were shelves for some of my books. I was halfway to respectability already. New Hall was only a few hundred yards up the hill. Françoise lived there in a set of rooms whose austere white walls and plain wooden appointments did not preclude an air of luxury verging on decadence. There was so much shelving that even after all her books had been installed there was room for the rest of mine. I also installed my ashtray: a hubcap off a Bedford van, it could hold the stubs of eighty cigarettes, so I only had to empty it once a day. Life was beginning to seem settled, apart from the nagging disjunction between my nominal role and my actual practice. Even the saintly Professor Hough was showing disturbing signs of having at last remembered that I was supposed to be writing a thesis. I promised to show him the finished article soon. It was easier than telling him I hadn't started. The only finished articles I was turning out were for the *Cambridge Review* and the *New Statesman*. Then *The Times Literary Supplement* – in the person of its assistant literary editor, Ian Hamilton – asked me to review some poetry books. Contributions to the *TLS* were still anonymous in those days. This policy didn't suit my lust for glory but it had the merit of not tipping off the dons that my whole attention had turned towards London. It would have been a false conclusion anyway. The university remained, in my mind and feelings, the one place where I could be everything I wanted to be all at once. To a certain extent I feel that even today. Certain kinds of people belong *only* in universities. Later on they make more or less, usually less, successful attempts to convert the rest of their lives into yet another university. Although nowadays I have to get up early in the morning, on the whole I have been lucky enough to arrange my working life along university lines. Mentally I am still *in statu pupillari*, still pursuing extracurricular activities, still torn between all the attractions of the stalls at the Societies Fair.

The difference is that nowadays I am not so worried about living out an anomaly: let the public judge. In the spring of 1968 I was less confident, and being that, more strident. If Cambridge thought of itself as the centre of the world, I was determined to take it at its own estimation. With the universities in turmoil throughout the free world, the Cambridge undergraduates regarded their own activities as being of planetary importance. Apart from Delmer Dynamo, who was engaged in an extensive tour of Britain at the wheel of the Bentley which he had at last coaxed out of the car park, most of my Americans were gone. It didn't need the debacle of Tet to tell them that the war in Vietnam was a national catastrophe. They had a real moral decision to make. Some of them went into the Peace Corps to do good in Africa, some into the American universities to avoid the draft, some into battle against Mayor Daley's police, some into a long, cold exile. As fast as they left Cambridge, however, more Americans arrived: a new, more vocal bunch who preached direct action. Rome university closed in March. Danny Cohn-Bendit became famous at Nanterre. The new Cambridge Americans wanted to be noticed too. King's College, with a typically canny diplomatic stroke, provided facilities for a Free University. Essentially the facilities were a large room with unlimited supplies of instant coffee, but they were sufficient to supply what the student revolution really wanted – the opportunity for a perpetual meeting. Elsewhere, the world shook. LBJ called it quits on a new term. Bobby Kennedy ran for President and died in the attempt. Martin Luther King was murdered. In the Free University at King's, the rhetoric reached a pitch of ecstasy. A list of Demands was drawn up. A Demand for the complete restructuring of Western civilization was high on the list. Imported simulacra of Abbie Hoffman and Jerry Rubin called for an assault on the university's property, whereupon, it was promised, the repressive nature of the institution would reveal itself. Called upon to speak by a chairman who was later universally upbraided for truckling to bourgeois elements, I argued against the notion of making demands that could not be met, and thereby provoking a confrontation. There were legitimate demands that *could* be met. The whole apparatus of *in loco parentis*, for example, could be dismantled, with no loss of jobs among the townspeople employed in the colleges and a clear gain in freedom for the undergraduates. This part of my address was listened to in a silence which I construed to be respectful, but when I got to the point of casting doubts on the efficacy, or even the feasibility, of direct action there were snorts of derision from the radical young academics standing at the back, which were soon accompanied by pitying smiles from the undergraduates sitting at the front. I argued against the proposed defacement of King's College Chapel, on the grounds that it would dramatize nothing except propensities towards vandalism; that it would alienate the proletariat, who, if they didn't care for great architecture, cared for militant undergraduates still less; and that there were students in Prague ready to die for the freedoms which in Cambridge were being condemned as illusory.

I was more proud of this impromptu speech than the occasion warranted, since it changed nothing. Speeches rarely do. What changed things in Cambridge was the demonstration outside the Garden House Hotel, staged for a reason now lost in history. Either the hotel had been too hospitable to some representative of the US government, or it had not been hospitable enough to Rudi Dutschke, or perhaps both. Anyway, the students besieged the place. During the siege, a few of them picked up stones and threw them at the windows. All the rest suddenly realized that they liked the talking and shouting part of the revolution but didn't like the part where things got broken and people got hurt. The student revolution in general, not just in Cambridge but in Britain as a whole, was over as from that moment. Effectively the same thing happened in Paris, where, although many more and much bigger stones were thrown, the rhythm of events was dictated by the clubs of the CRS, which descended with a precisely calculated force so as to induce headaches that felt like death but were not it. May of 1968 was theatre. I was glad to be in the cast, if only in a bit part, but like almost everyone else involved I had no intention of relying for long on the unrestrained instincts of my fellow man. The perpetual meeting of the Free University should

have proved conclusively to all those in regular attendance that they
didn't even know how to conduct a meeting, let alone run a society.
In Cambridge the real May, as always, was in June. Well before exam
time, indeed well before the time for final revision, the Free University
had dissolved, leaving nothing but a rump of misfits who had declared
their intention of existing on a single bowl of rice a day so as to
dramatize their solidarity with the great, continuing social experiment
of the Chinese People's Republic. China was their dreamland. Critical,
with some justification, of institutionalized power in the democ-
racies, they managed to believe, because they wanted to, that the
centralized, perpetuated and unlimited power of a totalitarian nation
was somehow more open to argument, more compassionate, more
democratic. Impatient for the millennium but oddly prepared to
remain stationary until it arrived, they sat on crossed legs and regaled
each other with the prospect of what Cambridge would be like when
Mao's vision finally prevailed. Whether King's supplied them with
their daily bowl of rice I can't be sure, because by then I had gone
too, back to Footlights with a new faith in the validity of the purely
frivolous. The impurely frivolous had been on display for a month,
and I hadn't liked its inhuman face. The undergraduates could be
forgiven their ideals. Experience and knowledge are required before
one can accept that an ideal can be murderous, and perhaps they
should not come too early. The young dons who had urged the
students on, however, were in a different case. Preaching cold-eyed
against Repressive Tolerance, safe in their own jobs while urging their
pupils to opt out, they were hypocrites and pleased about it: with
the taste of cynicism in their tight-lipped mouths they reminded
themselves of Lenin, a name they often invoked. Still working out
where I stood, I knew where I didn't stand – with men like them. Not
just as a displacement activity, but in a kind of wordless affirmation, I
directed, for the last Footlights smoker of the year, a sketch baldly
entitled 'Slow Motion Wrestling'. Russell Davies was the referee.
Robert Buckman, who was very agile, and Alan Sizer, who was large
and very strong, very slowly wrestled each other. Russell Davies very
slowly tried to stop them cheating. The whole thing happened
very slowly indeed. At one point Sizer very slowly punched Buckman
in the stomach while equally slowly lifting him bodily into the air
with his other hand. Buckman was airborne for an age, mouthing
his agony with agonizing slowness, while Davies moved like a glacier

to intervene. The audience rioted. I felt cleansed. This was worthwhile. Sartre hailing the Chinese Cultural Revolution as an act of liberation: *that* was a waste of time.

A far bigger success than *Supernatural Gas*, the May Week revue that year was directed by Kerry Crabbe, who generously included 'Slow Motion Wrestling' unmodified as the second-half pre-closer. The audience rioted again. I had other material in the show, including several songs written with Atkin and sung by Maggie and Julie, but 'Slow Motion Wrestling' was my apotheosis in the Footlights. Though all three participants in the sketch contributed to its inventiveness, I was its editor. I took out what didn't work and packed the rest up tight. For hours we shaped the piece until nothing was superfluous and everything flowed. It was a piece of sculpture extended into time, an elastic Laocoön, a brawl by Balanchine. Nothing could justify so much effort and that was its justification. Some of the upcoming Footlights disapproved of us who were now the *ancien régime*. David Hare, a brilliant talent with a capacity for organization almost unheard-of among undergraduates, had a look on his handsome face that plainly suggested one or two of us, and especially one of us, had been around too long. He had a case. From the viewpoint of a politically committed young dramatist with big plans for a new British theatre of Brechtian social analysis, there *was* something irredeemably insignificant about Footlights. But when I stood at the back of the Arts Theatre and watched hundreds of ordinary members of the public rocking with laughter at the antics of my three inspired clowns, I couldn't persuade myself that such a moment of communal joy was reprehensible, even if it was socially irrelevant. No society worth living in is without the irrelevant.

I wasn't at the back door of the Arts Theatre every night. Only every second night. Twice with Buffery and once as a solo act I went through the gruelling experience of a May Ball cabaret. There was applause to be garnered but you had not to mind that it was mixed with the popping of champagne corks, the braying of imported Hooray Henriettas, and the splintering sound of furniture being reduced to toothpicks by a scrum of Hearties. The Pembroke May Ball was the occasion of my solo appearance. Somewhere at the back, the Hearties were duelling with empty bottles of Bollinger. Broken glass fell like rain. On the river that year, Pembroke won the Bumps, or the Lumps, or whatever it was called. The runners-up consoled themselves by burning their boat and throwing the college cat on the fire. David Hare and his admirers would have plenty to react against. They would never forgive themselves for having been at Cambridge. I, on the other hand, had always known that I was just passing through. I took the place for what it had to give, gave back what I had in me, and kept the soul-searching to a minimum, protected by a natural capacity for putting off the moment of reckoning. Everything was a prelude.

18. THE KID'S LAST FIGHT

May week was not only in June, it was two weeks long. Did I remember to say that? In the second week Françoise and I got married. My sole but sensational contribution to the organizing of the event was to schedule the reception so that it took place before the ceremony. In the garden of New Hall's Storey's Way annexe the Footlights gathered, along with all the editors and leading contributors from the university magazines I had burdened with my contributions. Françoise's friends, some of them from Italy, looked on with apprehension as the theatricals and the *literati* tanked up on white wine. It was a bright day and the heat helped. Just in time, the whole party headed off down Castle Hill towards the register office. Françoise and I were in the lead, she looking stunning in a white silk two-piece ensemble, I looking stunned in a grey Carnaby Street suit which had already started to fall apart. Stomping along at the rear came a jazz band featuring Atkin, Sizer, Buckman and Davies. They had played better in their lives, but not when as drunk as that. When the registrar recited my full name there was spluttering in the congregation. Clive Vivian Leopold James wasn't feeling very solemn either. Or perhaps he was, and was covering up. It would have been characteristic. I always was the kind of bohemian who had to work hard to keep the bourgeois within himself from breaking out. *For how but in custom and in ceremony / Are innocence and beauty born?* I wasn't innocent and I wasn't beautiful, but she was both. I swayed while she stood still. Then we all went up the hill again to continue the party. The lawn was so crowded that the jazz band had to stand in the flower bed. Strad Blantyre had flown in, on the way through to Germany for one last grand tour before he left for Africa. He had news of Marenko. After long thought, Marenko had burned his draft card. This should have given me pause, but there was no pause to be had. Delmer Dynamo arrived. His tour of Britain had ended in

Scotland, when the Bentley got stuck on a narrow stone bridge high
over a little river. 'I was actually in a phone booth calling the AA,'
shouted Delmer happily, 'when I saw the motherfucker start to roll.
She swerved off the end of the bridge, she nosed through this *ridiculous* little wall, she bounced down into the river and she ended up
on her back in about three inches of water. I sold her to the guy who
owned the pub for a hundred quid and came down by train. Let 'em
have it. You can blow it out your ass.'

As happens with all empires, the moment of fruition marked the
beginning of decline. My academic career was to linger for another
six months before I packed it in, but effectively it was all over.
My time at the university was almost up. Later that year I directed
the Footlights for the Edinburgh Fringe and had the biggest success
I was ever to experience in the theatre. If the show had come to
London it would have run for a year and my life might have taken
a different course. Equity wouldn't let the show transfer. At the time
I thought it was a personal tragedy on a Sophoclean scale. I fought
a long delaying action in a doomed attempt to regain the lost
momentum. Probably it would have made no difference in the long
run. Theatre didn't really suit me. It didn't occur to me that this was
because the audience was too small. I thought it was because the
audience was too large. My picture of myself was as a lonely writer.
On a trip to London I met Ian Hamilton at a pub called The Pillars
of Hercules in Soho. He had asked me, by post, to write for his
influential little magazine *The Review*. I was already working on my
first article, a long piece about e. e. cummings. Other poets and
critics from whom Hamilton had commissioned or was about to
commission articles dropped into the pub on the strict understanding
that they were staying for only one drink or perhaps two. Ten rounds
later they were all still there. Almost instantly I felt about Soho the
way I had once felt about Cambridge. Over the umpteenth combination of a pint of bitter with a straight scotch for a chaser, I
explained to Hamilton that I had reached another decisive point in
my life. 'You're a very complicated character,' Hamilton observed
sardonically. I wasn't, but I resolved to become one as soon as
possible. Literary London! I could already see myself in that setting:
shy, self-effacing, trembling on the edge, but *there*. The metropolitan
critic.

That story, if I tell it at all, belongs in another book, which will have to be a collection of fragments. It might be a more reliable account than the one I have written up to now, but of necessity it will be less complete. My unreliable memoirs, in which I have tried to tell the full story even if only in edited form, must now come to an end. I could give up my own privacy as I chose. Where other people are concerned there is no choice. Nor should there be. Beyond the point when it ceased to be my own, my life gets harder to write about, and not just because I must tread carefully. There is so much more to say. In a multiplicity of nuance, only fiction can catch the essence. To rearrange the facts is no longer enough. A young man on the make is a comparatively simple mechanism.

Let us take a last look at him, in Cambridge, in that lovely late spring of 1968. The poetry magazine *Carcanet* has brought out a special issue with a lot of his poetry in it and not much of anybody else's, which is not *necessarily* the way he likes things, but if that's the way they feel, well, let them be happy. A finely burnished piece called 'Cambridge Diary' has just appeared in the *New Statesman*. In the Arts Theatre, actors are saying his words. His songs are being sung. He has married a don. He is on top of his little world. Against a willow tree across the river from the Wren Library, he sits writing in his journal. He has just told it that he is reasonably satisfied. The insistent suspicion that he has not yet begun, and has nothing to show, is too frightening to record. For someone who has good reason to believe that he doesn't exist apart from what he does, to doubt that he has done anything worthwhile is to gaze into the abyss. On the surface of the water, a midge vanishes into a hungry ripple. *I'm not ready yet.* He wonders why, at his age and having come so far, he still feels that. The culmination of his luck is that he doesn't yet realize he will never feel any other way.

Epilogue

All I can do is turn a phrase until it catches the light. There was a time when I got hot under the collar if the critics said I had nothing new to say. Now I realize that they had a point. My field is the self-evident. Everything I say is obvious, although I like to think that some of the obvious things I have said were not quite so obvious until I said them. In my younger and more nervous years, I sustained myself by thinking myself remarkable. It took time to accept the fact that I was ordinary, and more time to be thankful. Born without a sense of proportion, I had it imposed on me by the weight of evidence. My solipsism was already crumbling when I played my World Record Club 12-inch LP of Beethoven's 7th Symphony over and over at top volume until it drove my mother mad. It was in the glazed-in back veranda of our house in Kogarah, the year I turned eighteen. My Pye carry-gram, with the lid that split into two stereo speakers, had been hefted into position on a chair, with a book underneath to bring it level. Willem van Otterloo conducted the Concertgebouw of Amsterdam. I danced to the scherzo. During the adagio I sat on another of the wooden chairs, closed my eyes, and rocked slowly back and forth so that the front legs of the chair lifted an inch off the linoleum. That must have been how Blinky bought the farm. Blinky was my mother's budgerigar. When the day was cool enough to permit the closing of the Cooper louvres, Blinky was allowed out of his cage to roam the floor. On that day he must have roamed under one of the front legs of the chair and been crushed just enough to limp away and die under the crockery cupboard. Though I declined to admit culpability, the thought was never to leave my mind that I might be someone who loved art so much he could kill while in its thrall.

My mother survived the shock of Blinky's death, and of all the other outrages I have since perpetrated. Readers of the first two volumes of this autobiography often ask me whether she lives and thrives. The answer is that she does both, although she is a different person from the one I have portrayed – no less kind and brave but much more sophisticated, a natural psychologist whose prose, in her letters, has a rhythm and an easy-seeming perspicuity of detail which I would be pleased to hear it said that I had inherited. The point is that I didn't realize any of that until later. Not realizing things until later is the story of my life. This applied, still applies, to the awkward philosophical problem generated by the existence of other people. Even the people I knew best I seldom paused to appreciate. There have been those I loved who had to disappear before I saw their outlines. Usually it was only my story that they dropped out of, so as to continue theirs. Perhaps, in order to forestall enquiries, I should close by giving a quick account of those personages in these three volumes who, having played a formative part in my own dazzling course, influenced it still further by their daunting ability to have destinies of their own. The Australians, in particular, showed a disconcerting tendency to forget that I was meant to be the captain of the ship they filed aboard, laughing and waving, on that summer night, almost thirty years ago, when the band played and the cicadas sang and we all went sailing to adventure.

As I recounted in *Falling Towards England*, Lilith Talbot went home to marry Emu Coogan. She thought better of it when she got there, perhaps because as a husband he would have been out of his role, which was to be a radical, a gambler, a battler and a legend. A woman can marry a man like that and still stay sane, but she can't teach school, which was Lilith's vocation. The year after she went home, Lilith was taken ill with meningitis, and for a further year was on the point of death. Her great beauty melted into the pain. But she was saved, and her marvellous looks returned, and now, at a huge school in the Western Suburbs of Sydney, she has taught a whole generation of young Australians from different ethnic backgrounds how to construct an English sentence – the lesson at the foundation of our democracy, and one which the old country needs to learn again. Much loved by the thousands of pupils who are the children she never had, Lilith lives alone in an apartment at the edge of the harbour. From her window in the evening can be heard the tinkle of the moored yachts, like windchimes in a water garden. After twenty years I found her again, and although I do nothing for her except invite myself to tea, I am a better suitor to her now than I ever was when we were lovers. My past, of which she was a crucial part, served to civilize my future, and now, in the present, and despite the handicap of my frozen heart, our friendship, restored through good fortune after being broken by neglect, will last until one of us dies, to be mourned by the other.

Robin was three different women, all Catholics: a Holy Trinity. With an overwhelming two-thirds of this group I failed to establish the intimacy here recorded. One by one they went home to Australia, where they now think of London as a part of their upbringing, in which – so one of them secretly assures me – I featured as a marginal, affectionately tolerated part of the geography, like Soane's Museum or Madame Tussaud's. At the time I preened myself as no end of a rogue. Now I see that my love life was a cliché outclassed by that of any tomcat. The tremendous, condemnatory last act of *Don Giovanni* was written for Don Juan, not for a feckless young opportunist whose beard had grown because he was too lazy to shave. From the women I did not marry I took what I could get away with, including – a gluttony which can look like generosity in the right light – pride at having given pleasure. More often I gave pain, and probably more often than I thought. It would be hypocrisy, however, to say that I didn't enjoy being a free agent. It would also be ill-advised to say that I did. Marriage is supposed to put a stop to all that. Françoise is not the woman I married, who certainly has the quality of innocence, but only in the sense of being incorruptible by the knowledge to which her high intelligence gives her access. She knew all about me. She knows all about me now, and knows above all that the real blank in this book is not where she should be, but where I should be. In our prurient time, this true age of revelations, even the most sensitive sometimes find it hard to accept that the lasting involvement of two human beings must remain a mystery. The reader has the right to know, however, that something like the wedding in the last chapter happened something like that, and that something like the same marriage is still in existence twenty years later. The long storm of divorce that has blown away the marriage contracts of our generation continues to leave my hair unruffled – what there is of it, and for what such an exemption is worth. Perhaps my house is being saved up for last. Anything more specific I will have to say in a novel, where one can pile on all the right facts, as long as they lead in the wrong direction.

Some of the Australians went home, some stayed away, and much has since been made of who fulfilled his duty and who betrayed it; but the truth is that it all came down to personality in the end. Brian C. Adams, who had struck me as the prototype of the prematurely middle-aged academic, just as I had struck him as the extreme case of the delayed adolescent, went back to Adelaide to begin a university career which I loudly condemned in advance as a caricature. As things have turned out, he has played an important part in furthering the movement to give the study of Australian literature its due dignity without succumbing to provincialism. Particularly impressive, in every article he writes, is his mature, humane judgment, which I would once have said – did often say – that he could never possess. Some people develop, and sometimes they have to do that by throwing off the limiting estimation of those who know them. The privilege I always claimed for myself, of putting off until later the onus of knowing better, I should have more readily extended to others. It might even have been preferable, in the matter of success and failure, never to have judged people at all. Though the Australians who stayed abroad have made their mark, some of those who returned home have changed the history of their country. A few years back, Romaine Rand and I were in Sydney to appear on a television programme together. Romaine's first book, whose early drafts kept me awake while she typed, had long since made her one of the most famous women in the world. We went to see *Il Trovatore* at the Opera House. Romaine, not liking the production, talked to me animatedly throughout the first act. (Proust, when gladly accepting an invitation to the opera from the Baroness de Pourtalès, said: 'I've never heard you in *Faust*.') During the first interval we looked out through the screen of glass at the harbour and the city lights. 'It's beautiful,' I said. 'It's pretty,' said Romaine. 'Venice is beautiful.' She was right, but there was no denying that the city we had left behind had come a long way. The expatriates who had repatriated themselves had realized their dreams at least as well as we had. Australia had done very well without us. We could count ourselves part of it only to the extent that our books were on the racks in the shop at the airport. After the performance we walked, middle-aged and arm-in-arm, up Macquarie Street past the Mitchell Library. In the branches of the

Moreton Bay fig trees arching overhead, the possums, driven mad by
the spring, were behaving shamelessly. It was a sweet moment, but
we didn't even reminisce. We hardly ever meet except in television
studios, and even then, for preference, one of us is there only as a
satellite image. The stayaways are all like that, more or less. Lost in
space, they have only so much time for one another. Huggins, who
left us behind in volume one of these memoirs, wrote a book about
the early days of Australia that is now being translated into every
language on earth. New York, though, is his home. He needs something that tall at his feet. As for Spencer, he is beyond achievement,
far gone in a version of our search from which no messages come
back. The last I heard of him, he was in Brazil, teaching linguistics.
It is less than certain that he will ever go home, and more certain
than it should be that he will never publish a thing. He, however,
was the man with the gift. Given a brilliance of phrase the way
Mahler was given melody, Spencer, if he leaves behind nothing more
than a thin exercise book with his ten best poems in it, will be
the writer in whose work our wandering generation of Australians
finds its purest voice. Why did the children of paradise go out
into the world? Why did they give themselves up for lost? We will
hear the answer in a cadence.

The same way they had come, on expensive silver wings, the
Americans all went home again, because to an American there is so
little to be gained by staying away. Sometimes the route home was
circuitous, but it always led there. Strad Blantyre was with the Peace
Corps in Africa. In his letters he insisted that he could have done the
same work in Harlem to better effect. Milos Forman was right when
he said that there are only two places where we feel at home: home,
and in America. My American friends were fighting for their country,
but the war to be won was within its borders: in a cruel dilemma,
they grew through the seeking of its cure. Chuck Beaurepaire, who
knew everything, put his egregious self-confidence to good use as a
lawyer in defence of civil liberties. Even Delmer Dynamo, exempted
from the draft on about seventeen different counts of physical inadequacy, lent himself to the struggle. At Berkeley, in the bad days
when Ed Meese sent in the cops, Delmer, according to other accounts
beside his own, saved the life of the most luscious girl student on
the campus by throwing himself on top of her. In his version of the
story, he did this several hours before the riot even started. He is

probably understating the case in order to sidetrack nemesis, a trick I know well. Delmer is a funny man who makes his friends funny too. I should see him more often, but I am seldom in New York long enough, and the passing of time becomes hurtful between friends if they don't see each other regularly. Strad Blantyre I see often, but that is partly because he is one of my American publishers. It comforts me that he has lost almost as much hair as I have. In New York he takes me to lunch at the Princeton Club; in London I take him to dinner at the Garrick; and it pleases us both to impersonate pillars of the Establishment. What we really share is an unspoken dread of how the dice roll. Stability, for both of us, is a nostrum against caprice.

Marenko is dead. Having decided that the war in Vietnam was a criminal enterprise, he opposed it with a determination and bravery that could have cost him his life, and would certainly have cost him his career if he had not been so – the, military word somehow seems apt – outstanding. When the tear-gas cleared, the campuses that he had helped turn into battlefields vied to appoint him. His first book of literary criticism carried a charge of abstraction that I was glad to see being partly unloaded in the second, by which time he had become the youngest associate professor in the United States. He married a fellow teacher called Rosalind. They gave their baby another Shakespearian name, Miranda. When they were doing well enough to have a vacation cabin in Maine, Marenko typically built the cabin. I still have a photograph of him, naked from the waist up, hefting an axe and looking like Li'l Abner filtered through a pipe-dream by Thoreau. Miranda, about five years old, looks up at him in adoring awe as he stands there, baking bod, in confident possession of the summer. In the winter of the following year, when he was out with Miranda on the frozen lake teaching her to skate, the ice gave way under her. Trusting his strength, he jumped in with his skates still on. It took him too long to find her and bring her up. They were both already gone when Rosalind got back from the store. My guess is that the little girl died first, and that when he realized this he gave up the struggle, and let the terrible weight of what he had allowed to happen take him down. I knew him, you see. He felt responsible for everything.

Was he wrong about that? I find it hard to be sure. A sense of guilt, it seems to me, is inseparable from having grown up in our share of the twentieth century, when to die young, and for no reason, has been, if not the typical childhood, then certainly the representative one. When I was first old enough to look back on my infancy, I thought it the epitome of dislocation. My mother's fears while my father was a prisoner of war; her grief when he failed to return; her lonely struggle to bring me up – all this struck me as dramatic, and it was a mystery to me why my mother seemed more inclined to count our blessings than to curse fate. I was a long time, by now stretching to a lifetime, in grasping how reality has a texture to which histrionics are an inadequate response. Those millions of young lives apparently rendered meaningless by arbitrary death were taken from us too: a deprivation for which we can compensate only by making ours meaningful. When I was five years old and sobbing in my mother's arms because the bull ants had stung my foot, children my age were being rounded up all over Europe, to be crammed into boxcars and dispatched into oblivion. There were mothers who were obliged to kill their children so as to save them from the protracted agony of medical experiments. Compared with that, the story of my mother and her little boy, and of her husband who did not come home, was something old under the sun, and possible to understand if hard to bear. One day, if I am granted life, I will write a book about what happened in the Pacific when two nations, Australia and Japan, strange to each other in every conceivable way, met and fought, and about what has happened since, in the long, blessed peace which by some extraordinary stroke of good fortune has coincided with my own life. If I have an important book in me, that will be the one, but I will have no warrant to take pride in it, because it will be the book into which I finally disappear, having overcome an inordinate need for attention the only way I could, by reducing it to absurdity. For such a book I will need a decade to prepare before I even begin to write, which is asking a lot. Ten years ago, the joke behind the first volume of these memoirs was meant to be that I was too young to be writing it. Now I can hear the clock. As I bring this slight manuscript to an end, in the fiftieth year of my life, and the first year of the Heisei Era, the swags of blossoms on the cherry trees in the many cemeteries of Tokyo are falling softly apart under their own weight, covering the asphalt walkways with faded pink petals. The year before last, at the cemetery in Aoyama, when there was no hint of a breeze, and I saw the strewn petals change their pattern as if driven by the sad cry of the chestnut vendor, I could already feel the texture of what I will one day write. It will be frail, but as the surface of the sea is frail. The transparency which is all I have ever been capable of will have at last justified itself, by joining up. Inside that opalescent bubble, I will be invisible at last. There is not much time left, though. Already I have lived half as long again as my father did, whose fading daguerreotype, as Rilke once said, I hold in hands that are fading too.

Merely to be clear would have seemed an aim too trivial to be considered by the eternal student commemorated in these memoirs, which have that much truth, if no more: they are faithful to my ignorance. Through hindsight, I could have given myself foresight. It would have been a bigger lie than any I have told here. I thought I was Jason the Argonaut, Odysseus the long voyager, or one of the children in the radio serial I listened to every week when I was still too young to read – children who never had to go to school, and who were always free to continue their quest, the Search for the Golden Boomerang. It just never occurred to me that the real distance I would cross would be in my own mind. In that respect, I had flown half a million miles before I moved an inch, and these three volumes are just the rattling the side of my cot made when I climbed over, on the first stage of that long, momentous journey across the carpet, towards the light of the open door.

picador.com

blog
videos
interviews
extracts